The United States Supreme Court: From the Inside Out

Phillip Cooper
University of Vermont

Howard Ball
University of Vermont

PRENTICE HALL, Upper Saddle River, New Jersey 07458

Library of Congress Cataloging-in-Publication Data

Cooper, Phillip J.
    The United States Supreme Court : from the inside out/Phillip
Cooper and Howard Ball.

Includes bibliographical references and index.
    1. United States.   Supreme Court.   I. Ball, Howard.
II. Title.
KF8742.C66   1996
347.73'26—dc20
[347.30735]
ISBN 0-13-063850-1   95-7018
                                                        CIP

Acquisitions editor: Michael Bickerstaff
Editorial/production supervision and
    interior design: Barbara Reilly
Buyer: Robert Anderson
Copy editor: Carole Brown
Editorial assistant: Nicole Signoretti
Cover design: Bruce Kenselaar
Cover photo: Howard Ball

Printed in the United States of America
10 9 8 7 6 5 4 3 2 1

ISBN 0-13-063850-1

Prentice-Hall International (UK) Limited, *London*
Prentice-Hall of Australia Pty. Limited, *Sydney*
Prentice-Hall Canada Inc., *Toronto*
Prentice-Hall Hispanoamericana, S.A., *Mexico*
Prentice-Hall of India Private Limited, *New Delhi*
Prentice-Hall of Japan, Inc., *Tokyo*
Simon & Schuster Asia Pte. Ltd., *Singapore*
Editora Prentice-Hall do Brasil, Ltda., *Rio de Janeiro*

To Professors Dwight Waldo and Gene Meehan,
teachers who taught more than they realize,
and to the memory of a wonderful student-teacher,
Jeffrey Hausmann

Contents

Getting There: Appointment to the Court   31

3

Taking Office: Welcome to the Institution   75

4

What's on the Desk and How Did It Get There? Docket Control   100

The Office of Chief Justice: *Primus Inter Pares*   132

Getting to Know the Customers: Litigants Before the Court   159

The Business of the Court: The Organization in Action   194   8

Supreme Court Decision Making:
The Heart of the Job   224   9

To Judge a Justice: Statesmanship and Craftsmanship   245

10

After Hours: The Justices off the Bench   288

11

The Supreme Court and the Coordinate Branches   312

12

Supreme Court Impact and Change   334

Leaving the Court   354

Bibliography   369

Opinions Cited   377

Index   383

Preface

This book has been written for use at the undergraduate and graduate levels for classes on judicial process and behavior as well as for courses on the U.S. Supreme Court. *The United States Supreme Court: From the Inside Out* is unique because of its perspective on the Court and because of the research data and Court documents that sustain this perspective.

This perspective is conveyed by the title of the book. The reader will be "sworn in" at the outset and will see the Supreme Court as much as possible from the vantage point of a sitting justice on the Court. She will be taken into the Court as though actually preparing to undertake the work of the justices, and in the course of doing so she will develop a thorough understanding of the character and history of the institution. To further enhance this "inside-out" perspective, there appear throughout the book copies of actual documents circulated by justices to their colleagues.

This approach is unique among existing works on the Court. Unlike texts that attempt to illuminate the president's or legislator's problems, options, and constraints, most of the materials on the Supreme Court tend to consider the Court's position as a unit of government from the outside in, from a more-or-less retrospective vantage point. These books don't ask what a justice sees and what options are available to her as she interacts with her colleagues on the Court. They all tend to present a general description of the Court but without the coherence offered by this inside-out approach to understanding the Supreme Court.

Also setting the *United States Supreme Court: From the Inside Out* apart is its research into the collections of Supreme Court justices' papers (including those of Justices William J. Brennan and Thurgood Marshall) as well as some materials not yet available to the public. Interviews with family, friends, clerks, and a number of justices themselves add to the rich data sources that have been incorporated into this book. This fertile lode of information about the Court forms the basis for examples and fully developed case studies that provide a better understanding of the inner workings of the U.S. Supreme Court.

The first nine chapters concentrate primarily on the Court as a decision-making institution of the national government, covering its history, tasks, general goals, and the environment in which the justices function, both within the Court and beyond the Marble Temple. The remaining chapters focus on the role of the justice as policymaker in the dynamic, complex world of political jurisprudence. All fourteen chapters use actual Court documents to illuminate the many issues discussed in the book. Case studies, too, are presented to the reader to provide him with an additional perspective on the issue discussed.

The Court has a very unique position in American politics. By the time the reader reaches the last chapter, "Leaving the Court," he will have come to understand and appreciate this uniqueness. As the book documents, the U.S. Supreme Court is a very different kind of political institution in America. Viewing its actions from the inside out will provide the reader with an exciting, novel way of learning about and coming to fully understand the important place of the Supreme Court.

ACKNOWLEDGMENTS

This book grew from two observations. The first, a product of years of experience in judicial biography, is that, because of their strong interest in particular issues or rulings that emerge from the Court, court watchers, both citizens and scholars, sometimes ignore the realities of the task of the justices and the nature of the institution in which the justices work. Second, anyone who tries to see the job from the perspective of a justice cannot help but be impressed with the complexity of the office and the uniqueness of the institution.

It is difficult to acknowledge all of those—the Justices, their families, friends, and their law clerks, as well as the legal professionals and academics—who have assisted us in one way or another over the years. Some of them never even knew that their comments and questions would eventually contribute to this project. Even so, it is important to recognize some of them.

Several members of the Supreme Court have been extremely helpful, especially Justices William J. Brennan, Jr., Lewis Powell, Byron White, and Harry Blackmun, and the late Justices Arthur Goldberg, William O. Douglas, and Hugo L. Black. Justice David Souter and Toni House, the Supreme Court's public information officer, have also generously given us information and insights about the Court.

Many of our colleagues have suffered through conversations about portions of the volume and have contributed a great deal whether they knew it or not. They include Professors William Richardson (Georgia State University); Tom Lauth (University of Georgia); Dalmas Nelson (University of Utah); David O'Brien (University of Virginia); and Jim Tubbs (University of Vermont). Reviewers Nancy Maveety, Barbara Perry, and John Vile also offered many helpful suggestions and valuable insights.

We are grateful to our wonderful students of the State University of New York at Albany, the University of Utah, the University of Kansas, and the University of Vermont. Their contributions have been more valuable than any of them would ever have imagined.

Finally, no author can fail to appreciate the importance of the support that comes from home, and every author knows how inadequate mere reference in an acknowledgment is to express one's gratitude. With that in mind we nevertheless include such reference: to our wives, Claudia and Carol, and our families, we express our love and appreciation.

Looking at the Supreme Court from the Inside Out

It is a strange and fascinating day in your life. You are about to take the oath of office as an associate justice of the U.S. Supreme Court, the second of two swearing-in ceremonies you will experience this morning. The first took place before you came to the bench, in the presence of the other justices. As you stand before the Court and the assembled public for the open ceremony, you repeat the words

> I, . . . , do solemnly swear that I will administer justice without respect to persons, and do equal right to the poor and the rich, and that I will faithfully and impartially discharge and perform all the duties incumbent upon me as Associate Justice of the United States according to the best of my abilities and understanding, agreeably to the Constitution and Laws of the United States.
>
> So help me God.

With that said, you take your seat at the end of the long bench, and the Court's workday begins.

As you take your place, you look around at the trappings of the ornate courtroom. These are all an important set of political symbols, the elements of what some call the "cult of the robe,"[1] but that most Americans think of as the indicators of the majesty and fierce independence of the Supreme Court. But you have come to more than a symbolic body. The Supreme Court is a well-developed institution with a complex set of workways and a heavy burden of cases drawn from around the nation. You are now expected to interpret the Constitution and other laws of the United States so as to deal with some of the most difficult questions presently plaguing American society. As one foreign observer of the American scene in the early eighteenth century put it, sooner or later every significant social and political problem in America seems to find its way to the courts.[2] You and your colleagues on the bench are expected simultaneously to maintain the stability and predictability of the constitutional order and to ensure sufficient flexibility so that the Constitution can endure in a rapidly changing society.

Beyond all that, though, you are a political person, in the best sense of the word. Public policy matters to you. How will you address the complex policy issues that are at the core of the cases before you? What can you do to advance what you perceive to be the correct positions? To this end, what can you do to convince the other justices of the correctness of your conclusion? And if they agree, how can you influence the society to accept and comply with your decision?

In making these judgments about your own behavior as a member of the Court, you are obliged to remember three critical facts of Supreme Court life. First, for most of the things you would like to achieve, you will need to acquire the support of a majority of the justices, four additional votes beyond your own. Second, you cannot force any of the members of the Court to do anything. Like you, each of them was appointed by a president and confirmed by the Senate, and like you, their appointments are, for all intents and purposes, for life, unless and until they choose to retire. That leads to the third critical reality: You will have to work with these people for a long time, sometimes decades, since on average only one member is replaced every two years. Therefore, what you do and the positions you take today will affect your ability to work with these men and women in the future.

Regarding the Court's influence outside the walls of the Marble Temple (so named because the Court building is a magnificent marble edifice), there are critical first principles. To begin with, the Court is basically an antidemocratic body, in the sense that it is a small, elite group of generally nonrepresentative, unelected Americans who make critically important decisions that occasionally overturn the wishes of the populace as expressed through their elected legislators and executives. This happens within a nation that constantly celebrates the fact that it is a constitutional republic based on democratic principles. Therefore, the task of the Court is difficult, and its political legitimacy is always, to one degree or another, precarious. Beyond that, the Court needs help to accomplish virtually everything it wishes to have done. While Alexander Hamilton's famous description of the judiciary as "the least dangerous" branch may have been an overstatement, it is true that the Court possesses neither the "power of the purse nor the sword;"[3] it has no means to compel obedience to its rulings. Therefore, you and your colleagues must always be mindful of the need to elicit compliance from members of the other branches of the federal government and from state and local officials.

BUT WHAT IS IT REALLY ABOUT?

So much for the high-sounding challenges; what is the job really like? How does the institution operate? What difference does the Court's decision-making process make? The rest of this volume explores these questions. The answers to many of these questions are mixtures of fact and judgment. Not even all members of the Court agree on what the institution of the Court is "really" like. There is considerable disagreement about appropriate styles of interaction among members of the Court and the Court's relationship to other branches and levels of government. Many justices differ with each other rather sharply regarding priorities within the Court's workload. Yet for all of those differences, there are more-or-less common understandings in a variety of areas.

The approach this book takes in its study of the Court as an American political institution is that of judicial biography, understanding the Court from the inside out. Using the papers of the justices, interviews with members of the Court, and other sources, this text asks the reader to think of himself as a person approaching the Court as a justice.

Interior view of the Supreme Court's courtroom.

REALPOLITIK AND THE VALIDITY OF IDEALS

There is a certain danger that comes with an effort to understand the Supreme Court as a critically important political institution. Whether one defines politics as "who gets what, when and how,"[4] "the authoritative allocation of values,"[5] or any other reasonable way, the Supreme Court is heavily involved in politics and cannot be otherwise. At the same time, its politics are not quite the same as those of the Congress or the executive.

Yet it runs against the grain of American society to think of the Supreme Court as a political body. After all, the Court is supposed to be an institution above politics, isn't it? Only if we think of politics in the popular sense, that of a low art of pleasing the populace in the short term as a means of getting votes to obtain or retain an elective office, or that of representing a relatively narrow constituency on whose behalf the political figure makes deals with little consideration of the public interest can it be said that the Court is "above politics."

A common reaction to this problem is to begin with the myth that it is possible for the Court to be totally unaffected by political forces, either internal or external. It is a rather comfortable myth, but it is a myth nonetheless. One can retain it only until study reveals sufficient evidence that the Court is necessarily political. That sometimes produces a cynicism, a sense that the Court is somehow impure and that the law really matters little. But there is a third view—one that we hope this book will help the reader reach—that comes with an appreciation of the fact that the Court is so central to the American polity in large part because its members have understood its critically important political character. Indeed, a scholar of the Court comes to appreciate the fact that many of those justices most often considered the greatest occupants of the high bench are precisely those who held a simultaneous respect for the law and for the American political community.

One other problem often arises for students who seek to study the Court. As Walter Murphy, a distinguished Supreme Court scholar, has observed, those who are new to the study of the institution sometimes find efforts to understand the Court politically a kind of blasphemy.[6] However, as will be presented in subsequent chapters, the only way to truly understand the Court is as a political agency of government.

HUGO BLACK: MODEL OF A MODERN SUPREME COURT JUSTICE

Few members of the Court have typified this combined sense of realpolitik on the bench and a devotion to the institution better than Justice Hugo Black. A battle-hardened veteran of local politics in Alabama with skills polished in the U.S. Senate, Black was President Franklin D. Roosevelt's first appointment to the high court. He was appointed in large part precisely because he had championed FDR's Court-packing plan in the Senate.

Though it was presented as an effort to increase the Court's size and effectiveness by providing an increased number of younger justices, to assist aging justices who refused to retire, the Roosevelt proposal was in fact a backlash against a Court that had repeatedly struck down New Deal programs designed to deal with the ravages of the Great Depression. These new men would come to the Court with a commitment to Roosevelt's New Deal economic policies. Black had arrived at the conclusion that the Court was abusing its power, subordinating democracy and the role of the Congress to the personal economic and political philosophies of the justices. He had come to that position before FDR announced his Court plan.

Black came from Clay County, Alabama, where he had seen firsthand the effects of the economic turmoil of the early twentieth century. And he was a U.S. senator from that state when the Great Depression hit in 1929. He saw the devastation of the rural South while he simultaneously uncovered financial skulduggery in utility companies and government contractors. While these wealthy corporate moguls were reaping financial gains, the poor in America were being devastated by the depression. Black's role as the chair of Senate investigations into these industrial and corporate abuses brought him into the national limelight and earned him the everlasting enmity of very important conservative economic and political interests.

The juxtaposition of poverty for millions of Americans who had done nothing to deserve their fate and ill-gotten wealth for the privileged few demanded legislative action. Yet the Court was using a narrow interpretation of Congress's power to regulate interstate commerce and using the Fourteenth Amendment's due process clause to rigorously protect businesses against state and local regulatory efforts. The Court struck down more legislation in a decade than it had in its entire history. Black simply could not abide such a situation.

According to Black, the Court has a limited role. Its task is to apply the Constitution as written, not as the justices would like it to have been written. In most areas, the task of lawmaking belongs to the legislature, not the judiciary. At the same time, during the turmoil of the depression the judiciary seemed unwilling, in Black's eyes, to apply with sufficient vigor the protections specified in the Bill of Rights. The Court has a countermajoritarian role to play, but only in those areas where the Constitution specifies limitations as in the Bill of Rights, not wherever the judges decide that limits should be drawn.

Once on the Court, Black pursued both his appreciation of the democratic process and his commitment to individual liberty, defending against the political winds that frequently blew in the face of those whose political views were not in vogue. Of course, conflicts between majority rule and individual rights brought disagreements within the Court and outside it as well. Whether dealing with cases concerned with religion or the criminal justice process, all sides claimed to defend liberty and democracy while arriving at diametrically opposed positions on the meaning of government power and individual freedom.

Every inch the politician, Black possessed the grace and charm for which the South was so well known. Yet beneath that personable exterior was cold intellectual steel. In a now-famous characterization, Justice Robert H. Jackson declared that one could not disagree with Black, one had to go to war with him.[7] Black sometimes took time to develop his position on a particular issue, but once he had made his decision, Black was often unmovable. As one of his colleagues recalled, one of the indicators of Black's persistence was his unwillingness to join an opinion of the Court if it cited a precedent case in which he had dissented.[8]

Black served with nearly a third of all the justices ever to sit on the Court, and with five of its twelve chief justices. Among that group were men whose personalities and intellect were every bit as strong as his own and who were perfectly

Justice Hugo L. Black in his chambers.

content to cross intellectual swords when the need, or even the opportunity, presented itself. Black's widow recalled the time when Black returned to his chambers (she was his secretary at the time) and proclaimed that he thought that Felix Frankfurter was about ready to hit him at one point during the conference session that day.[9]

Whatever their positions on the cases before them, members of the Court thought of Black as a man committed to the Court as an institution. As Justice Arthur Goldberg put it, "Justice Black loved the Court."[10] He cared deeply about its decisions, its internal operation, and its external image. To the end of his long tenure on the bench, Black fought every action he believed threatened the Court's prestige.

Yet there was considerable disagreement among the justices about how best to protect the Court. For his nemesis, Frankfurter, the problem was to keep the Court out of the "political thicket" by using the Court's jurisdictional rules and discretion over its docket to avoid cases that should be resolved in Congress or by the chief executive. Black on the other hand felt the Court should not refuse to address properly presented cases, particularly those calling on the Court to play its critical role as defender of constitutional rights and liberties. Nevertheless, it should resolve those cases according to the Constitution and not as though the justices were legislators voting on the floor of the Congress. For him, what mattered most was that cases be decided in accordance with the written Constitution.[11]

Ironically, his commitment to the words of the Constitution and his unwillingness to have those words superseded by the personal predilections of the judges led others, on the Court and off, to hang the dreaded label of "activist" on Black, the man who had fought so hard against judicial self-aggrandizement. His literalism meant that he was an absolutist about controversial topics like freedom of speech. When the First Amendment said that "Congress shall make no law . . . abridging the freedom of the press," Black took that to mean no law at all; not a good law, a useful law, or any other kind of law. His position on this and other issues caused colleagues to label him a liberal intent on expanding constitutional rights and liberties. Additionally, the fact that he was not willing to follow precedents if they were based on an incorrect reading of the Constitution led to charges that he was an activist who failed to honor the need for stability in the legal system. And Black's view was that his deference to the elected branches ended when he saw a clearly defined constitutional issue that challenged an action of Congress or the president. Black's willingness to have the Court hear these cases, such as reapportionment of state legislatures and congressional districts, even if previous Courts had refused to take on the challenge, caused his adversaries to label him an interventionist activist who was behaving more like Senator Black than Justice Black.

Black rejected these charges out of hand. His view was that just as there were outer limits to the proper performance of the judicial function, so were there obligations to respond to properly presented cases with adequate answers. What is properly presented and what answers are adequate are decisions that come from the Constitution, not the judge's own ideas regarding the politically appropriate thing to do. Neither, he thought, should procedural devices and decision avoidance be used to disguise political positions. Hence, later students of the Court have come to the conclusion that Frankfurter used his philosophy of judicial deference to disguise the fact that he wanted to support conservative government actions to which he was favorably disposed while maintaining his liberal credentials in public.

But the constitutional debates change because the people, the cases, and even the Court itself change over time, just as all other aspects of American political life do. On the other hand, the Court retains critical elements of its unique institutional nature. The challenge is to understand both what makes the Court unique as an institution, with important characteristics developed over its history, and how its justices meet the changing demands that come to it on an almost daily basis.

ORGANIZATION OF THE TEXT

Our exploration of the Court begins with your appointment to the bench. It first considers the system of which the Court is a part, the character and workways of the Court itself, the work on your desk, and the process by which you accomplish it. It goes on to deal with your efforts to make the actual decisions and to influence your colleagues to join your judgments. It is concerned as well with how you deal with the other participants in the American political community to make certain that your opinions are more than words on paper in dusty law books. In that regard, we consider some of the limits placed on your behavior by virtue of the nature of the Court and its place in American political life. Finally, we contemplate your decision to retire from the bench to be replaced by another justice who, like you, will face the challenge of a professional life in this amazing institution.

NOTES

[1] John Brigham, *The Cult of the Robe* (Philadelphia, PA: Temple University Press, 1987).

[2] Alexis de Tocqueville, *Democracy in America* (Garden City, NY: Doubleday, 1969), p. 270.

[3] Alexander Hamilton, James Madison, and John Jay, *The Federalist Papers* (New York: Mentor, 1961), no. 78, p. 465.

[4] Harold Laswell, *Who Gets What, When, How* (New York: Meridian Books, 1958).

[5] David Easton, *The Political System* (New York: Knopf, 1953), p. 129.

[6] Walter Murphy, *Elements of Judicial Strategy* (Chicago: University of Chicago, 1964), p. 2.

[7] Howard Ball and Phillip J. Cooper, *Of Power and Right* (New York: Oxford University Press, 1992), pp. 93–98.

[8] Justice Harry Blackmun, interview with authors, Washington, DC, Nov. 19, 1986.

[9] Elizabeth Black, interview with authors, Arlington, VA, Aug. 28, 1987.

[10] Justice Arthur Goldberg (retired), interview with authors, Southwind, VA, Aug. 27, 1987.

[11] Hugo Black, *A Constitutional Faith* (New York: Knopf, 1968).

Benchmarks: The Supreme Court in the Political and Judicial Systems

2

You have left your seat in the courtroom and step behind the velvet curtains into the robing room. As you step through the velvet curtains that form the backdrop to the courtroom, it strikes you that only little more than one hundred men and two women have sat on the Court in its over-two-hundred-year history. You turn and, peering through the curtains, take another quick look at the ornate setting of the "public" Court, the courtroom with its Gothic columns, gleaming mahogany benches, high-backed chairs, glistening brass trimmings, including decorative spittoons. Then you stride into the room beyond the curtains. You disrobe and walk toward your new chambers. But you decide to drop into the justices' conference room, a room that you will soon be entering regularly to discuss petitions coming to the Court as well as the cases you and your brethren hear in open Court every two weeks.

Directly over the fireplace is the portrait of John Marshall, third chief justice of the United States, 1801–35. You pause and stare into the eyes of the man who, by force of will and personality, molded the Supreme Court and the federal judiciary in the critical early days of the republic. Marshall's actions as chief justice established the Court as a coequal partner in the national government and, through a number of important cases that gave formal recognition to the concept of judicial review of the actions of government officials, established the Court as the overseer of national and state action[s] in light of the basic governing principles of the U.S. Constitution.

Given your natural urge to get started, you have a desire quickly grasp the impact of the federal system on the dispensation's federal justice in America. Clearly, you know that dispensing justice in A

tem is unlike most other countries' judicial systems, even those that operate as part of what is termed a federal system.

JUDICIAL FEDERALISM: THE JUDICIAL SYSTEM IN AMERICA

To understand the concept of judicial review, the power of courts in America to overturn legislation because it is judged to be unconstitutional, the context of the legal
system in America must be understood. The nation is structured in light of the
Constitution's federal character. There is a dual federalism in America. There are
sovereign state governments and a central, or national, government. There is also a
dual court system in our society. There are, in America, fifty states, each with its own
legal structures, and one national government, with its own separate legal structure.

Given the federal character of the American system, the notion of a
responsible sharing of powers by both levels of government has developed, especially in the past fifty years. Nevertheless, operating as well is the eighteenth-
century reality of exclusive responsibility of the national government in the areas
of national defense, international diplomacy, interstate commerce, and other
areas that have recently, through the "preemption" doctrine, become the exclusive responsibility of the national government.[1]

Each of the states has its own judicial system; over one dozen antedate the
federal judicial system's creation by one hundred or more years. Each state judicial system is complete, with statutes defining civil and criminal law and a judicial
bureaucracy consisting of judges, clerks, marshals, and court reporters, and some
operate with almost three centuries of judge-made precedents to draw on when
deciding cases and controversies.

The state judicial systems generally have a four-tiered structure with the trial
court at its base (see Figure 2.1). These courts, often called justice of the peace
courts, or district courts, hear and dispose of minor civil and criminal (misdemeanor) cases. The next tier of state courts is the superior court system, where
all criminal and civil cases are tried. Most states have some form of intermediate
appellate court system, which hears appeals from the trial courts. Finally, all state
judicial systems have at their apex a state court of last resort, generally called the
supreme court, or the state court of appeals. (If a federal question has been raised
during the trial proceedings, state supreme court opinions can be appealed—to
the U.S. Supreme Court.) The state courts, in the 1980s, annually heard and disposed of over thirty million civil and criminal cases annually.

The federal Constitution, constructed at the constitutional convention held
in the summer of 1787 in Philadelphia, also provided for a national, or federal,
judicial system. Interestingly, the "monstrous appearance"[2] of a federal judiciary
in the new federalist political system was the subject of "more severe criticism and
greater apprehension than any other portion of the Constitution."[3] Clearly, this
new federal judiciary was perceived as a threat to the power of the state courts,
which had been reasoning for over a century in colonial America.

The "states'-rights" power of the constitutional era argued that a federal judiciary
would weaken the power state courts. They urged the convention to reject

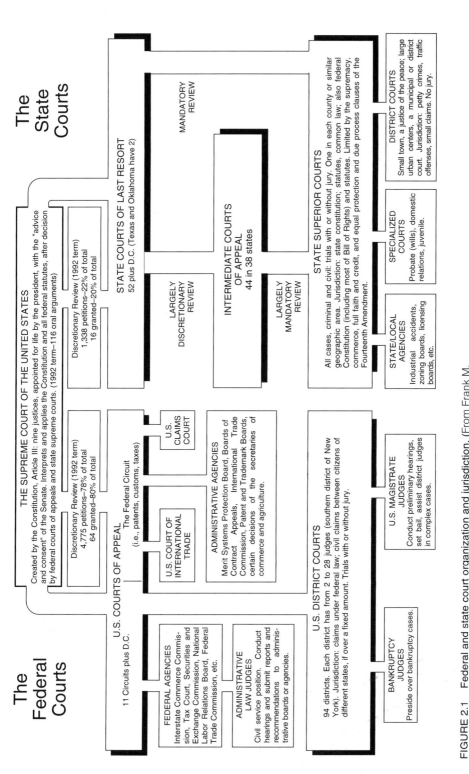

FIGURE 2.1 Federal and state court organization and jurisdiction. (From Frank M. Coffin, *On Appeal*, W.W. Norton, New York, 1994, pp. 48–49.)

the creation of the federal judicial system. However, the federalists at the convention, convinced that a federal judiciary was necessary for the new political system to survive, urged the ratification of the Constitution with the federal judiciary's powers (in Article III) included. For the federalists at the convention, the new political system "depended on the existence of a supreme national tribunal, free from local bias or prejudice, vested with power to give an interpretation to Federal laws and treaties which would be uniform throughout the land . . . and to control State aggression on the Federal domain."[4]

It took more than a century for the new federal judiciary to find an integral place in the American legal system. Article III enabled the national legislators to create "such inferior [federal] courts as the Congress may from time to time ordain and establish." Due to the intense political and legal opposition to the very idea of a federal judiciary, and realizing that this was "a task of the most delicate nature,"[5] however, the national legislators moved very cautiously. In the first Congress, which met in 1789, a federal judicial system was created, but for almost a century its jurisdiction was limited to diversity of jurisdiction, that is, suits brought into federal court involving citizens from two or more states, and maritime cases. U.S. district courts, the federal trial courts, were created in 1789, but their jurisdiction respected state lines and, for the most part, state judicial authority.[6] It was not until the 1875 Judiciary Act that Congress gave the federal judges broad federal "question" jurisdiction; that is, federal judges could hear all suits "arising under the Constitution, or laws of the United States, or treaties made."

In 1891, with the passage of the Circuit Court of Appeals Act, Congress finally accepted the validity of the federal judiciary by providing for an intermediate appeals court system with substantive jurisdictional power.[7] The 1891 legislation created nine intermediate courts of appeal, each with three federal judges, with the authority to hear appeals from the district courts, thereby alleviating the Supreme Court's burden of having to review all appeals from the federal trial courts.

As presently constituted, the federal judicial system consists of almost one hundred trial courts, the U.S. district courts, with at least one in every state in the Union (Figure 2.2). The thirteen U.S. courts of appeals, the regional federal appellate courts, now form the federal system's very active intermediate appeals level. The U.S. Supreme Court is the highest court in the federal system, hearing, at the justices' discretion, cases from the federal courts of appeals as well as from the state supreme courts. Much like the state judiciary, the federal judges and the justices of the U.S. Supreme Court receive their authority, their legitimate power, to hear cases, from the Constitution's language in Article III and from the statutes passed by Congress that provide for the appellate jurisdiction of the federal judiciary.

To understand the power of judges, one must be familiar with the sources of law that judges and justices of the U.S. Supreme Court draw on regularly when deciding cases or controversies. There is the black-letter law, the law documented in books that every law school student comes to know perhaps too intimately during law school—and beyond. Then, too, there are the precedents, that is, the past decisions of the state courts and of the federal courts, including the Supreme Court, that are the lodestars for all attorneys. Statutes and administrative regulations, whether state or national, are other important sources of law. Additionally,

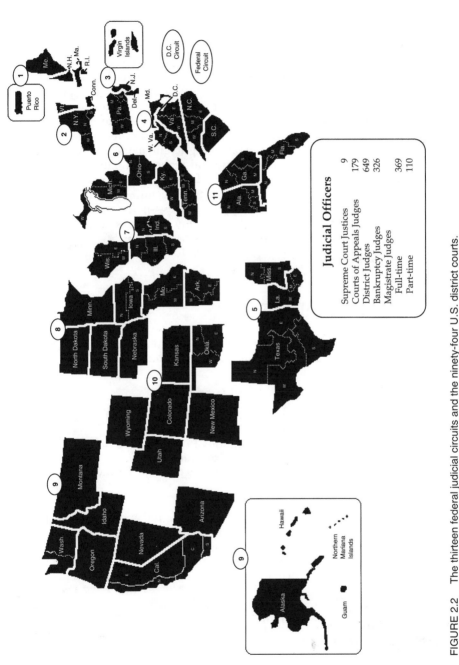

Judicial Officers

Supreme Court Justices	9
Courts of Appeals Judges	179
District Judges	649
Bankruptcy Judges	326
Magistrate Judges	
Full-time	369
Part-time	110

FIGURE 2.2 The thirteen federal judicial circuits and the ninety-four U.S. district courts. (From *Understanding the Federal Courts, 2nd Edition*, Administrative Office of the Courts, Washington, D.C., 1994, p. 8.)

treaties and compacts entered into by the United States with other sovereign nations or, in the case of compacts, by a number of states (with the approval of the Congress), constitute another source of law for the society. Finally, there is the highest form of law in civil society, the law of the Constitution.

There is an association between the black-letter law and the responsibility of judges to make decisions in light of the law and, most especially, in light of the constraints existing in the law and in the Constitution on the use of power. All judges, federal or state, are committed to the value of constitutionalism; that is, that there are constitutional limits to the uses of power by legislators, executives, and government employees. Constitutionalism, consisting of checks and balances, separation of powers, the liberties in the Bill of Rights and in the Civil War amendments, the many statutes that protect liberty and make criminal the taking of a person's constitutional and statutory rights and liberties, is maintained initially by the people's representatives—the legislators and executives. But if liberties and rights are threatened or allegedly deprived, the judges—in the states as well as in the federal judicial system—have the responsibility, if the case is properly presented before them, to respond to these actions or inactions. This critically important responsibility of judges brings into sharp focus that uniquely American contribution to politics: judicial review.

JUDICIAL REVIEW AND INTERPRETATION

To understand the power of judges to invalidate an action of a legislature or an executive, one must understand the concept of constitutionalism. That concept suggests

> a complex of ideas, attitudes and patterns of behavior elaborating the principle that the authority of government derives from and is limited by a body of fundamental law. For Americans, distinctively, the word "constitution" had come to mean a single document embodying the sovereign will of the people—a document that established or reorganized a government, prescribing its structure and endowing it with power, while at the same time restricting that power in the interest of personal liberty.[8]

If a constitution, embodying the will of the people and enumerating the powers and restraints on those powers by government, is to be the foundation of political and social action, there has to be some mechanism for resolving conflicts that emerge when policymakers act in light of their interpretation of the constitution—and others disagree with that interpretation. Both federal and state courts have, for centuries, been called on to clarify the ambiguities in the black-letter law and when confronting concrete cases and controversies to give meaning to the general language of the Constitution, the fundamental law for both the nation and the states. In both judicial systems, judges have used the power of judicial review to resolve such conflicts.

Yet judicial review is an extraconstitutional power; it is not mentioned at all in the most significant grantor of legitimate, authoritative power: the 1787 Constitution. When James Madison spoke of "auxiliary precautions" in the American political and legal systems that would maintain America's republican, representative form of government, that is, those mechanisms in the new system of government that would prevent tyranny from emerging, he was alluding to judicial review. What is judicial review and why is it so central in the American system, even though it was not made a formal part of the Article III powers of the federal judiciary?

The Concept of Judicial Review

One of the most important and most often used mechanisms of constitutional change is judicial review, the process of judicial interpretation of the Constitution in cases that challenge government actions or legislative enactments. Judicial review is the power of a court, either state or federal, to review an action of a policymaker to determine whether it is consistent with the language of the Constitution or whether it is beyond the constitutionally derived power of the policymaker.

The more obvious political agencies have the first crack at constitutional interpretation. The Congress or the president takes actions in accordance with an interpretation based on powers designated in the Constitution. For example, when constructing legislation affecting commerce, Congress interprets the "commerce" clause enumerated in Article I, Section 8 of the Constitution. Someone or something (corporations are "persons" and can sue in court) adversely affected by the legislation can go into federal court and challenge the legislation's constitutionality, that is, its legitimacy, by arguing that Congress legislated in a manner that exceeded its constitutionally derived power.

The president, too, must act in a manner consistent with the language of the Constitution. Its fundamental law frames the parameters for the legitimate use of presidential power. The president will, for example, interpret his powers as commander in chief and take military action in the Middle East. Such action may be challenged in a federal court. The argument for the federal judge to review is this: The president has exceeded his constitutional authority by sending troops, and the action must end because it has no constitutional validity.

If the judge determines that the action of the policymaker goes beyond the legitimate power granted by the Constitution, then the judge has the power to declare such action unconstitutional, that is, without any authoritative foundation, and therefore null and void. So the federal judge is a second or even third reviewer of an action premised on an interpretation of a power in the Constitution. If the judge believes that the court has the power and authority to hear the case and, in addition, there is a belief that the controversy is resolvable by the judiciary, then the judge will hear the case and arrive at a substantive decision regarding constitutionality.

The Origin of Judicial Review in the United States

The concept of judicial review first emerged in the 1610 opinion of Great Britain's Chief Justice Coke in *Dr. Bonham's Case*. But there is irony in the way Coke's opinion was received. While he spoke of the power of the judiciary to nullify an action of Parliament, his views were never accepted in England, and even to this day there is a fundamental commitment to parliamentary supremacy. But his words struck a chord in the colonies, especially in the era of rebellion followed by revolution. He said that when an action of the legislature "is against common right and reason, or repugnant, or impossible to be performed, the common law will control it, and adjudge such Act to be void."[9]

The colonists and the men of the 1787 constitutional convention in Philadelphia also knew the principle of parliamentary supremacy. William Blackstone was very clear about parliamentary supremacy: "If the Parliament will positively enact a thing to be done which is unreasonable, I know of no power that can control it. . . . Judicial review would set the judicial power above that of the legislature, which would be subversive of all government."[10] The delegates to the 1787 constitutional convention were extremely concerned about legislative supremacy. As Madison noted in *The Federalist Papers*, such absolute power can only lead to tyranny in a political system. Thus, while judicial review was not formally incorporated into the final version of the document that emerged from the Philadelphia constitutional convention in September 1787, the fear of legislative supremacy led the delegates to create a federal system with a complex pattern of checks and balances, separation of powers, and other precautions against the formation of tyranny. Judicial review, Coke's idea, was viewed as one important kind of precaution, and there were many indirect references to the concept during the convention, as well as in the document that was created, and in the ratification and postratification days.

Article III of the Constitution states that the "judicial power of the United States shall be vested in one Supreme Court and in such inferior courts as Congress may from time to time ordain and establish." Regarding the powers of the federal judiciary, Article III states that the "judicial power shall extend to all Cases, in law and equity, arising under this Constitution, the Laws of the United States, and Treaties made, under their authority [and] to Controversies to which the United States shall be a party." Furthermore, the sixth article's supremacy clause provides "that the Constitution, federal laws 'made in Pursuance thereof,' and all treaties shall be the supreme law of the land, and 'the Judges in every state shall be bound thereby, anything in the Constitution or laws of any State to the Contrary notwithstanding.' At a minimum, the supremacy clause requires federal courts to review the actions of state governments."[11]

From an examination of America's constitutional-era history, we know that the framers had a much clearer understanding and appreciation of the concept of judicial review than is generally acknowledged. Any number of precedents had supported and validated the use of judicial review by judges at both the state and federal levels, before and after the adoption of the Constitution.

Although the great chief justice John Marshall has been credited with— or blamed for—establishing judicial review in *Marbury v. Madison* (1803), he clearly did not create the concept. His decision, in which he crafted a justification and defense of *national* judicial review, that is, Supreme Court review of actions of the coordinate branches of the national government, was essentially a summarization and reflection of American thought and practice from the colonial period, from earlier Supreme Court judgments regarding *federal* judicial review, that is, Supreme Court review of actions of state legislators or executives, and from the 1787–88 constitutional convention and ratification debates.[12]

Colonial Precedents

Colonists used the judicial-review argument to contest the hated Stamp Act,[13] the Writs of Assistance, and the enforcement of the Navigation Acts. In the Writs of Assistance case, argued in February 1761, James Otis maintained that "such act of Parliament was against the Constitution and 'against natural equity'" and was therefore void. Although in England the concept of legislative supremacy held sway, and still does, Otis relied on the 1610 decision in *Dr. Bonham's Case*, hearkening back to Lord Coke's words that "when an Act of Parliament is against common right and reason, or repugnant, or impossible to be performed, the common law will control it, and adjudge such Act to be void."[14]

The creation of the U.S. Constitution in 1787 followed constitution making in a number of the states during the Articles of Confederation period (1781–89). "By 1787, [in the states] it was . . . accepted doctrine that a constitution ought to be framed by a convention elected solely for that purpose. By 1787 it had also been demonstrated in several state court decisions that a constitution as fundamental law was not merely hortatory but could be enforced by judicial invalidation of legislative action."[15] A number of state courts, New York, New Jersey, New Hampshire, Rhode Island, and North Carolina,[16] employed judicial review prior to U.S. Supreme Court rulings in the early years of the American republic. Clearly, precedent "supporting judicial review existed at the state level."[17]

The 1787 Constitutional Convention

There is no doubt that by 1787, there was "near-unanimous agreement" that the legislative powers of the new national congress had to be restrained by external forces.[18] "At the onset of the Federal Convention in Philadelphia, the idea of limiting legislative power by judicial nonapplication of statutes in certain cases was clearly understood."[19] While the men of the convention did not in the Constitution specify the power of judicial review, they assuredly knew what it was, and many expected it to be a fundamental part of the newly created federal judicial powers, inherent in the contours of Article III.

The evidence appears in the premises of the new Constitution, especially the description of the judicial power, as well as in statements made during the convention and afterward. A major concern for the founders was the existence of thirteen separate sets of legal interpretation. For Hamilton, "Thirteen independent courts of final jurisdiction over the same causes, arising upon the same laws, is a hydra in government from which nothing but contradiction and confusion can proceed."[20]

Concerns about legislative abuse led to a search for checks on legislative powers. One possibility, on which there was discussion and a vote, was the Council of Revision. Had it been incorporated into the Constitution, the council, consisting of the president and the Supreme Court, would have been empowered to review the actions of the Congress and invalidate legislation thought to contravene the parameters of constitutional power. It failed muster because the members of the convention believed that the court would, in the ordinary course of legal business, hear cases involving the constitutionality of acts of Congress.

Rufus King, one of those participating in the 1787 Convention in Philadelphia, observed that the council was not a good idea because the Supreme

Court "ought to be able to expound the law as it should have come before them, free from the bias of having participated in its formation." Likewise, Elbridge Gerry was critical of the Court's participation in a council of revision because the judges "will have a sufficient check against encroachments on their own department by their exposition of the laws, which involved a power of deciding on their Constitutionality."[21]

Luther Martin, a convention delegate from Maryland who favored the creation of a national government, also argued against the Council of Revision. "As to the constitutionality of laws," he said, "that point will come before the judges in their official character. In this character, they have a negative on the laws. Join them with the executive on the [council], and they will have a double negative."[22] A colleague of his also spoke out against the new federal Supreme Court being involved with the executive in the council. John Rutledge, later to serve briefly as the nation's chief justice, argued that there was no need for the court to be involved because "the judges of all men [are] the most unfit to be concerned in the revisionary council. The judges ought never to give their opinion on a law until it comes before them."[23]

James Madison's records note that "Mr. Gerry doubts whether the judiciary ought to form a part of [the Council of Revision] as [the judges] will have a sufficient check against encroachment of their own department by their exposition of the laws, which involved a power of deciding on their constitutionality. In some states the judges actually set aside laws as being against the constitution. This was done with general approbation."[24] Madison reflected the views of the majority at the convention when he wrote in his diary that "the judges ought to be able to expound the law as it should come before them" and that "a law violating the Constitution established by the people themselves would be considered by the judges as null and void."[25] The council idea was defeated, on July 21, 1787, by a vote of four to three.

Almost all of the delegates thought that Congress should have veto power over state laws. For them, the veto, judicial review, and the legislative protection provided by the supremacy clause (Article VI) were sufficient protection against weakening of the new central government by the state governments. Roger Sherman, however, and others, including Gouverneur Morris, felt that the legislative veto of state actions was unnecessary and politically less than astute because the courts of the states would not consider valid any state law that contravened the authority of the Union and also because the congressional veto was a measure that would disgust all the states.[26]

Opposition to the Constitution and to judicial review came from persons who were concerned about the centralizing powers of the newly created judiciary. Brutus, one of the *Anti-Federalist Papers* authors, bitterly attacked the proposed powers of the Supreme Court. Judges, Brutus wrote, would be "superior" to the elected representatives of the people:

> The judges in England are under the control of the legislature, for they are bound to determine according to the laws passed by them. But the judges under this Constitution will control the legislature, for the supreme court are authorized in the last resort, to determine what is the extent of the powers of the Congress. They are to give the Constitution an explanation, and there is no power above them to set aside their judgment.[27]

There are still judicial scholars who maintain that judicial review by the federal courts should be limited primarily to review of state actions. Louis Fisher, for example, quotes James Madison during the Virginia ratifying convention, in June 1788, arguing that the Supreme Court "was given jurisdiction over cases that may arise under the Constitution in order to protect federal power from state encroachments."[28] Over the years, however, the Court has moved to extend its jurisdiction to cases and controversies involving the coordinate branches of the national government.

These arguments did not weaken the federalists' commitment to curb the powers of the states in a new federal system. At the convention, they were able to draft and obtain approval from a majority of the delegates on procedures and protocols that placed checks on state power, including state judicial power. Their views on the relationship between the new central government and the preexisting colonies were presented in the American classic *The Federalist Papers*, authored by James Madison, Alexander Hamilton, and John Jay.

The Federalist Nos. 78 and 81

Specifically regarding judicial power, Hamilton set forth, in *The Federalist Papers* 78 and 81, the federalists' justification for and the parameters of judicial review. The argument developed by Hamilton was a demonstration for judicial review, that it was "essential to prevent the deputy [the legislature] from being greater than the deputy's principal [the Constitution]. Judges had to restrain the legislature from exceeding its powers."[29] In the effort to "defuse the virulent Anti-Federalists in the fight over ratification,"[30] Hamilton wrote:

> The judiciary . . . will always be the least dangerous to the political rights of the Constitution. . . . The Courts were designed to be an intermediate body between the people and the legislature, in order, among other things, to keep the latter within the limits assigned to their authority. The interpretation of the laws is the proper and peculiar province of the courts. A constitution is, in fact, and must be regarded by the judges as, a fundamental law. It therefore belongs to them to ascertain its meaning, as well as the meaning of any particular act proceeding from the legislative body. If there should happen to be an irreconcilable variance between the two, that which has the superior obligation and validity ought, of course, to be preferred, or, in other words, the Constitution ought to be preferred to the statute, the intention of the people to the intention of their agents.[31]

Hamilton, Madison and the federalists were, ultimately, successful in their effort to defend and justify the necessity of a federal, national judiciary, but a hard, closely decided ratification campaign had to succeed.

The Ratification Campaign

During the ratification campaign of 1787–88, Madison argued that "a law violating a Constitution established by the people themselves, would be considered by the Judges as null and void."[32] James Wilson, a delegate to the 1787 Convention from Pennsylvania, wrote:

Under the Constitution, the legislature may be restrained, and kept within its pre-scribed bounds, by the interposition of the judicial department. . . . The legislature may transgress the bounds assigned to it, and an act may pass notwithstanding that transgression; but when it comes to be discussed before the judges—when they con-sider its principles, and find it to be incompatible with the superior power of the Constitution, it is their duty to pronounce it void.[33]

Oliver Ellsworth, another delegate to the 1787 constitutional convention, argued, in a debate in Connecticut over the merits of the Constitution, that "this Constitution defines the extent of the powers of the general government. If the legislature should at any time overleap their limits, the judicial power is a consti-tutional check. . . . If the United States . . . make a law which the Constitution does not authorize, it is void; and the national judges . . . will declare it to be void."[34]

During the ratification debates in Massachusetts, Samuel Adams stated, "If any law made by the federal government shall be extended beyond the power granted by the proposed Constitution, and inconsistent with the constitution of this state, it will be an error, and adjudged by the courts of law to be void."[35]

In Virginia, both the supporters and the opponents of the new constitutional system spoke about judicial review during the ratification period. Patrick Henry, who "smelled a rat" and did not attend the convention, said that the constitutional supporters

did our judiciary honor in saying that they had firmness to counteract the legislature in some cases. Yes, sir, our judges opposed the acts of the legislature. We have this landmark to guide us. They had the fortitude to declare that they were the judiciary and would oppose unconstitutional acts. Are you sure that your federal judiciary will act thus? Is that judiciary as well constructed and as independent of the other branches, as our state judiciary? . . . I take it as the highest encomium on this country that the acts of the legislature, if unconstitutional, are liable to be opposed by the judiciary.[36]

John Marshall, also of Virginia, and, little more than a decade later, the chief justice of the United States, countered, writing that "if they were to make a law not warranted by any of the powers enumerated, it would be considered by the judges as an infringement of the Constitution which they are to guard. They would con-sider such a law as coming under their jurisdiction. They would declare it void."[37]

During the ratification campaign in Pennsylvania, Wilson defended the no-tion of judicial review, saying that "if a law should be made inconsistent with those powers vested by this instrument in Congress, the judges, as a consequence of their independence, and the particular powers of government being defined, will declare such law to be null and void; for the power of the Constitution predomi-nates. Anything, therefore, that shall be enacted by Congress contrary thereto, will not have the force of law."[38]

The First Congress, 1789

It seems clear that when the First Congress met in 1789, the legislators be-lieved that the Supreme Court had the power to review all actions of state politi-cal actors. Congressman Elbridge Gerry said that "the judges of the United States, who are bound to support the Constitution, may, in all cases within their jurisdiction, annul the official acts of State officers, and even the acts of the members of the State Legislatures, if such members and officers were disqualified to do or pass such acts."[39]

Some scholars argue that definite limits on the use of judicial review were discussed during the constitutional era and into the early days of the Congress. For them, the parameters for the use of the power are limited to *federal* judicial review, that is, review by federal judges of the constitutionality of a state constitution or state laws. Judicial review is seen "as a weapon of self-defense, [that is,] to strike down federal statutes that invaded the judiciary and threatened its independence. Beyond [these uses], the picture is decidedly murky."[40] Some, like Fisher, approvingly quote Thomas Jefferson, who said in a letter to Mrs. John Adams on July 22, 1804, that to give the federal judges the power of *national* judicial review, that is, the power to review the constitutionality of the actions of a coordinate branch of the national government, "would make the judiciary a despotic branch."[41]

However, Congressman James Madison presents a much different picture of the attitudes of the First Congress. Introducing the Bill of Rights to the Congress, Madison said, borrowing liberally from Jefferson: "If they are incorporated into the Constitution, independent tribunals of justice will consider themselves in a peculiar manner the guardians of those rights [and] they will be an impenetrable bulwark against every assumption of power in the Legislative or Executive."[42] As the Bill of Rights were intended as protection against intrusions on liberty and freedom by the national government ("Congress shall not . . ."), surely Madison's words were a strong defense of the federal judiciary's power, especially the Supreme Court's, of *national* judicial review.

Early Federal Cases Involving Judicial Review

In *Hayburn's Case,*[43] decided in 1792, the justices, riding circuit, held that the Pension Act of 1792, a statute passed by Congress authorizing federal courts to decide pension claims against the government, subject to revision by the secretary of war, was a violation of the separation of powers. The judicial power in Article III did not allow for such a relationship. Said the Court, "By the Constitution, neither the Secretary of War, nor any other executive officer, nor even the legislature, are authorized to sit as a court of errors on the judicial acts or opinions of this court."

In *Hylton v. United States,* a 1796 case, the Supreme Court upheld a carriage tax passed by Congress. As Louis Fisher noted, "If the Court had the power to uphold a congressional statute, presumably it had the power to strike one down."[44] The court, through Justice Salmon Chase, did say on this matter that it was not appropriate "at this time, for me to determine, whether this Court constitutionally possesses the power to declare an act of Congress void, . . . but if the courts have such power, I am free to declare, that I will never exercise it, but in a very clear case."[45]

As late as 1800, the judges of the Supreme Court were still privately and publicly, through their written opinions, discussing the concept and scope of judicial review. In that year, Chase wrote that if the Constitution was supreme law, and a congressional statute was obviously in conflict with the fundamental law, "it still remains a question, where the power resides to declare it void."[46] This question was soon to be answered by the Court led by the new chief justice, John Marshall.

At the Virginia ratifying convention, Marshall clearly stated his answer to that question. The Supreme Court, he argued in the confrontation with Patrick Henry, is the guardian of the Constitution, and the tribunal would have to declare an action contrary to the Constitution's parameters void.

Marbury v. Madison, 1803

When Marshall, as chief justice in the 1803 case of *Marbury v. Madison,* gave full voice to the powerful doctrine of judicial review, it was "but a formalization of a concept that had been generally accepted by Americans for generations."[47] In the 1800 case of *Cooper v. Telfair,* for example, the Supreme Court stated that "it is, indeed, a general opinion expressly admitted by all at this bar, and some of the judges have, individually, in the circuits decided, that the Supreme Court can declare an Act of Congress to be unconstitutional, and therefore, invalid; but there is no adjudication of the Supreme Court itself of this point."[48] *Marbury* gave the justices of the Supreme Court the opportunity to "adjudicate" this matter. *Marbury* revealed both colonial era and constitutional convention practices and beliefs.

William Marbury "filed the most significant lawsuit in American history."[49] Marbury was one of forty-two Federalist partisans appointed to judicial positions by President John Adams (Federalist) days before the president turned over, in March 1801, the power of the executive to his arch political rival, Thomas Jefferson (Democratic-Republican). Nominated to serve as justice of the peace in Washington, D.C., Marbury's nomination had passed Senate review, his commission of office had been signed by Adams, and the great seal of the United States had been fixed on the commission itself. The commission, however, was one of four still in the office of the secretary of state (an office occupied by John Marshall while he was also serving as chief justice of the United States) when Jefferson and his administration took office.

Jefferson refused to deliver the commissions still left in the secretary of state's office and so instructed his secretary of state, James Madison. Marbury, with the three other men who had not received their commissions,[50] then went to the Supreme Court to ask the justices, led by Marshall, Madison's predecessor in the Department of State, to issue a writ of mandamus that would, if granted, command Madison to deliver the commission to Marbury and others. A writ of mandamus is, when granted, an order directed to an administrative officer that requires that a duty prescribed by law, not subject to administrative discretion, be performed.

Marbury went to the Supreme Court because of Section 13 of the 1789 Judiciary Act passed by the First Congress.[51] The Act was an omnibus bill that contained many sections that addressed structure and jurisdiction of the brand new federal judiciary. Section 13 authorized the Supreme Court to issue writs of mandamus "in cases warranted by the principles and usages of law, to any courts appointed, or persons holding office, under the authority of the United States." Marbury asked the Court, using its powers of original jurisdiction, to order the new secretary of state to come into federal court and show cause why the Marbury commission should not be issued and to have the federal court issue a ruling that would force Madison to issue the commissions.

"Politics was not far from Marshall's mind as he composed the *Marbury v. Madison* decision."[52] Clearly, *Marbury v. Madison* was a classic political struggle between the Democratic-Republican Jefferson administration and the Federalists on the federal judiciary. "If Marshall had upheld the constitutionality of section 13 of the Judiciary Act of 1789, he could not have forced the Secretary of State to deliver the commissions. Marshall would have been ignored [by Jefferson]. . . . The Court could [not] stand ridicule, and the ale house would [have] rock[ed] with laughter"[53] had Marshall granted the Marbury request to grant the writ of mandamus. Another scholar notes that "Marshall adroitly teetered between the political sin of bowing to Jefferson Republicanism and the personal catastrophe of giving Jefferson grounds for impeaching or, perhaps worse, ignoring him and the Supreme Court."[54]

Three questions were raised in the Marbury suit: Did Marbury have the right to the commission? If he had the right to the commission, was there an available remedy to relieve him from a wrong? And if there was such a remedy, could the Supreme Court provide it? Marshall saved the critical question, the jurisdictional one, for last. He used the opinion to morally indict Jefferson for failing to give Marbury his deserved commission as well as to tell Marbury that he was entitled to his commission and that mandamus was an appropriate remedy. When Marshall finally arrived at the jurisdictional question, he concluded that Marbury "had come to the wrong place to seek redress."[55]

In answering the jurisdictional question, Marshall came to the concept of judicial review of the actions of coordinate branches of the national government. Employing judicial review, Marshall concluded that the Court had no jurisdiction to act in the case because Section 13 of the 1789 Judiciary Act, which, to Marshall's eye, gave the Court original jurisdiction was void.[56] Original jurisdiction was enumerated in Article III of the Constitution. Nowhere in that article's description of original jurisdiction was there the judicial power to issue writs of mandamus. Can the Congress, without going through the formal, elaborate process of amending the Constitution, as described in Article VI, amend the fundamental law through the mere passage of legislation (Section 13 of the 1789 Judiciary Act)?

Answered Marshall: "The question whether an Act repugnant to the Constitution can become the law of the land, is a question deeply interesting to the United States. . . . It is emphatically the province and duty of the judicial department to say what the law is. Those who apply the rule to particular cases, must of necessity expound and interpret that rule. If two laws conflict with each other, the courts must decide on the operation of each."

For the chief justice and his associates,[57] "the very essence of judicial duty" is to determine whether an ordinary action of a legislature is in conflict with the Constitution. For the Court, the Constitution was "superior to any ordinary act of the legislature . . . [and the judiciary is guided by] the principle, supposed to be essential to all written constitutions, that a law repugnant to the constitution is void; and that courts, as well as other departments, are bound by that instrument." Therefore, the case had to be discharged by the Court, for the federal tribunal did not have jurisdiction to hear it. (The Court did not declare an act of Congress unconstitutional until the 1857 case of *Dred Scott v. Sandford*.)[58]

Jefferson was surprised and none too pleased with the decision in *Marbury*. He bristled at the "impropriety of this gratuitous interference" by the Court when it did not have the legitimate authority to hear the case. "This practice of Judge Marshall," wrote Jefferson in 1823, "of traveling out of his case to prescribe what the law would be in a moot case not before the court, is very irregular and very censurable. . . . *Marbury v. Madison* [is] merely an *obiter* dissertation of the Chief Justice."[59]

Clearly, the matter before the Marshall Court was very political; equally clear was the political response of the Federalist Supreme Court justices. As Jefferson noted, normally where there is settled law, courts will dismiss a claim for want of jurisdiction without taking any time in the opinion to discuss the merits of the dispute.[60] Marshall did dismiss the *Marbury* petition for lack of jurisdiction, but he took almost twenty pages to chastise Jefferson and Madison *before* reaching the crucial question of jurisdiction. Whatever else may be said about the Marshall opinion and the formalization in it of the doctrine of judicial review, the political sagacity of the nation's outstanding chief justice must be admired.

Changes Brought About Through Judicial Review

Since the 1803 Marbury opinion was announced, judges—both federal and state—have employed the power to examine the constitutionality of legislative and executive actions that have properly, that is, falling under the authority of the court to hear the case, come before the courts. Assuming that the judge has the authority, that is, the jurisdiction, to hear the case or controversy, she will examine the law to determine whether the actions taken by an agency of the government are consistent with the constitutional grant of power to that agency.

These judgments by the courts and judges reflect different views of constitutional interpretation. Who sits on the court and what interpretation of the Constitution that person brings to the bench determines, in significant ways, the outcome of the litigation before the court. Employing the power of judicial review, judges can and do affect public policy, and they are nominated because of their views on a number of significant policy issues as well as for their judicial temperament and legal scholarship. "If federal judges [were] appointed solely on the basis of merit, that would be the millennium," said Chief Judge Edward Devitt of the U.S. District Court for Minnesota.[61]

Clearly, an examination of examples of judicial review in recent decades reveals a mix of public policy, politics, and legal dynamics. The federal judiciary, essentially the U.S. Supreme Court, has become, because of the nature of the federal system, the balance wheel of the constitutional system. Using judicial review, the Court has a "unique role to play in sorting out the balance required by federalism."[62] But the Court is really not a neutral, objective umpire of the federal system. Using judicial review, the Court has acted to reinforce the powers of the national government and to maintain federalism. An example is the Court's role in reviewing actions of the national legislature in the area of voting rights.

Voting Rights   The 1965 Voting Rights Act was a radical piece of legislation that attempted to stop discrimination against minorities by segregationists who denied them the right to vote. Led by a powerful president, Lyndon B. Johnson, who was committed to ending voting discrimination in the nation, Congress passed the legislation based on its interpretation of the Fifteenth Amendment. The Civil War Amendment's first section prohibited voting discrimination; Section 2 gave Congress "the power to enforce this Amendment by appropriate legislation."

The legislation, prepared by two Johnson staffers in the Department of Justice after the November 1964 election,[63] as finally passed by Congress and signed by Johnson, contained a number of significant protections against racial discrimination in voting. Based on Section 4 of the act, all tests and devices, such as literacy tests, were prohibited in the seven covered states (Alabama, Georgia, Louisiana, Mississippi, South Carolina, Virginia, and portions of North Carolina). Federal employees in the region were assigned the task of monitoring the voter registration process to ensure that discrimination would not occur.

And there was the very controversial Section 5 of the Voting Rights Act, put into the legislation to "guard against ingenious actions by those bent on preventing negroes from voting."[64] This section prohibited the introduction of any voting change until it was cleared by the U.S. district court judges in Washington, DC, or by the staff of the Voting Section in the Department of Justice's Civil Rights Division.

South Carolina and five of the other affected states immediately challenged the constitutionality of the Voting Rights Act. In effect, their suit asked the Supreme Court to use the power of judicial review to determine whether the Voting Rights Act was an unconstitutional, illegitimate use of congressional power. The southern states were asking that the justices use their power of judicial review to determine whether the congressional action "encroached on an area reserved to the states."[65]

The Court took the case under its original-jurisdiction powers, although it was unusual for the Court to hear cases under original jurisdiction because the justices prefer to work with a developed lower-court file. Original jurisdiction cases are those that come directly to the Court, in light of the contours of Article III. Arguments were made in the Court before the nine men, and shortly thereafter a near-unanimous Court announced its decision.

Chief Justice Earl Warren, for the Court, answered the question put to the justices by South Carolina by legitimizing Congress's use of Section 2 of the Fifteenth Amendment: "As against the reserved powers of the states, Congress may use any rational means to effectuate the constitutional prohibition of racial discrimination in voting." Congress, the Court concluded, could create "inventive" methods to implement the Fifteenth Amendment, for the national legislature had the power to "banish the blight of racial discrimination."[66] Congress, with the active help of the president and the Justice Department, was considered by the Court to be the initial interpreter of the Fifteenth Amendment. Using judicial review, the Supreme Court validated the national legislation, and the justices put their imprimatur on the actions of the coordinate branches of the national government.

New Rights   The Court has, on a number of occasions in American history, used its power of judicial review to articulate new rights. This "new-rights" notion was present in the recent controversy, during the Reagan administration, between Attorney General Edwin Meese and Justice William J. Brennan, Jr. Meese, a critic of the goal-oriented, liberal Warren Court, charged that the justices' use of judicial review was improper because they were substituting their own ideas and values for those of the Founding Fathers when interpreting the words of the Constitution. "Far too many of the [Court's] opinions are, on the whole, more policy choices than articulations of constitutional principle." Instead, Meese held, the justices ought to adopt a jurisprudence seriously aimed at the explication of original intention, [which] would produce defensible principles of government that would not be tainted by ideological predilection. . . . The Constitution represents the consent of the governed to the structures and powers of the government. To allow a Court to govern simply by what it views at the time as fair and decent, is a scheme of government no longer popular.[67] For the attorney general, judges should "judge policies in light of principles, rather than remold principles in light of policies."[68]

Critics of Meese's position, including federal judges and Supreme Court justices,[69] charged that his view was, in the words of Justice Brennan, "arrogance cloaked as humility." For Brennan, "Those who would restrict claims of right to the values of 1787 specifically articulated in the Constitution turn a blind eye to social progress. . . . The genius of the Constitution rests not in any static meaning it might have had in a world that is dead and gone, but in the adaptability of its great principles to cope with current problems and current needs."[70] Brennan believed that "federal judges use the power of judicial review, when necessary, to invalidate the expressed desires of representative bodies on the ground of inconsistency with higher law."[71]

Nowhere is this conflict between originalists and evolutionists more clearly seen than in the Court's use of judicial review to examine the right-to-privacy controversy. For a number of justices, especially Hugo L. Black, there was no constitutional right to privacy, for that language did not appear in the Constitution. On the other hand, for justices such as William O. Douglas, the Constitution was an open-ended document to be read and interpreted anew by the Supreme Court. He believed that "it is the Constitution which we have sworn to defend, not some predecessor's interpretation of it."[72]

The "Right to Privacy"   The "right to privacy" is a concept that has been discussed for over a century. Civil libertarians have claimed that all persons have a constitutional right to be left alone. Cases raising the issue of the purported constitutional right of sexual/marital privacy had come to the Court for decades prior to 1965, but Court majorities had sidestepped the issue by not using the power of judicial review to examine the issue.[73] In 1965, however, the Court took a case, *Griswold v. Connecticut*, and used judicial review to determine whether a state statute that prohibited the distribution of birth control information was constitutionally valid, that is, consistent with higher law.[74]

For the majority of the men on the Court, the Connecticut statute was unconstitutional because it ran afoul of the constitutional right to privacy. However, the justices had to find that premise in the Constitution's principles so they could justify overturning the state law. Douglas was the advocate for privacy as a constitutional right beyond the criminal-law (Fourth Amendment) context. But it was Brennan who suggested that Douglas base the Court's judgment on a number of specific amendments that had, in the past, been read by the Court to protect a wide variety of unstated but implied freedoms.[75] "The specific guarantees in the Bill of Rights have penumbras formed by emanations from those guarantees that help give them life and substance [and] various guarantee zones of privacy."[76] Brennan and Douglas noted that the First, Third, Fourth, Fifth, and Ninth amendments in the Bill of Rights contained these zones that, together, reflected the right to privacy, the right to be left alone. In the Connecticut case, they wrote, "we deal with a right of privacy older than the Bill of Rights—older than our political parties, older than our school system. Marriage is a coming together for better or worse, hopefully enduring, and intimate to the degree of being sacred."[77]

Needless to say, Justice Black, who believed in the value of the original words of the Bill of Rights and opposed substantive interpretations of the original language by evolutionists such as Douglas and Brennan, dissented in the *Griswold* case. Black felt, along with Potter Stewart, who joined Black's dissent, that the law was stupid but nevertheless was not unconstitutional. "I like my privacy as well as the next one," he wrote, "but I am nevertheless compelled to admit that government has a right to invade it unless prohibited by some specific constitutional provision."[78]

The marital-privacy case places the uses of judicial review in stark perspective. For the dissenter Black, and for other originalists like Meese, the majority "had no business departing from the clear language of the Constitution."[79] Judicial review did not empower judges to strike down legislation they believed violated some abstract standard of civilized decency. For the seven-person Court majority, however, judicial review enabled the Court to properly invalidate state legislation that, in their view, interfered with the personal and protected marital and sexual liberties of men and women.

SUMMARY

By the midnineties, as you have learned when preparing for your appearance as a Supreme Court nominee before the Senate Judiciary Committee, the U.S. Supreme Court, implementing its power of judicial review, had invalidated more than 100 congressional statutes and over 1,000 state laws or municipal ordinances such as the Connecticut contraceptive statute, and had also directly overturned more than 175 earlier Supreme Court decisions.[80] Some scholars, such as Edwin Corwin, have thrown up their hands in the futile effort to come to closure on the question of the scope of judicial review: "These people who say the Framers intended judicial review are talking nonsense; and the people who say that [they] did not intend it are talking nonsense. There is evidence on both sides."[81]

Some critics of the Court argue, still, that there is no evading, as the late justice Robert Jackson noted, "the basic inconsistency between popular government and judicial supremacy."[82] But, you cautiously observe, perhaps your late brethren misspoke. Perhaps, "like other powers in the Constitution, the issue is not the existence of judicial review but the degree to which it is exercised."[83]

The Court, as you know, certainly does not have a monopoly on interpreting the Constitution. Employing judicial review, the Court examines how other policymakers have already interpreted the words of the Constitution. It is a secondary reviewer, determining whether congressional, executive, or state policymakers used the power and authority granted to that unit in an appropriate manner, that is, in a manner consistent with constitutional guidelines. From your perspective, and at this time in your career as a justice of the Court, you have an understanding of judicial review that suggests judicial *authority* but not *supremacy* in interpreting the Constitution in cases before your Court.[84] You dwell on that last thought, for, indeed, after your confirmation by the Senate, you are now an integral part of the Court.

NOTES

[1]The preemption doctrine acknowledges the absolute superiority of the national government over the state governments in certain areas of public policy that clearly fall under the responsibility of the national government. Because the national government is heavily involved in regulating or controlling action in certain areas, state laws in those fields could undercut the effectiveness of the national effort. For example, the Supreme Court, in *Pennsylvania v. Nelson*, 350 U.S. 497 (1956), said that federal legislation had "occupied the field," that is, prevented the forceful overthrowal of the U.S. government by subversive organizations and that state sedition laws that addressed this same issue were ruled unconstitutional.

[2]Charles Warren, *The Supreme Court in United States History* (Boston: Little, Brown, 1926), p. 8.

[3]S. Kelly Wright, "Commentary: In Praise of State Courts—Confessions of a Federal Judge," *Hastings Constitutional Law Quarterly* 11 (1984): 11.

[4]Warren, *Supreme Court*, p. 8.

[5]Ibid., p. 7.

[6]1 Stat 73. The Judiciary Act of 1789 established the district courts and three courts of appeals, staffed by district court judges and justices of the U.S. Supreme Court.

[7]Unsuccessful congressional efforts to create a court of appeals took place in 1802, 1848, 1854, and 1865.

[8]Don E. Fehrenbacher, *Constitutions and Constitutionalism in the Slaveholding South* (Athens: University of Georgia Press, 1988), p. 1.

[9]77 *Eng Reports* 646 (1610), at 652.

[10]Quoted in Louis Fisher, "The Curious Belief in Judicial Supremacy," *Suffolk University Law Review* 25, nr. 1, (Spring 1991): 88.

[11]Ibid., 88.

[12]See *Marbury v. Madison*, 1 *Cranch* 137 (1803). Federal judicial review occurs when the Supreme Court reviews an action of a state, and national judicial review occurs when the Court reviews an action of a coordinate branch of the national government.

[13]A Virginia court declared the Stamp Act void when the court applied the power of judicial review. Of course, as a colonial court in a political environment that had legislative supremacy as its hallmark, such judgments were not valid.

[14]See also *Day v. Savage* (1614); and *City of London v. Wood* (1702).

[15]Fehrenbacher, *Constitutions and Constitutionalism*, p. 2.

[16]See, for example, *Bayard v. Singleton* (1787–NC); *Trevitt v. Weeden* (1786–RI); and *Holmes v. Walton* (1780–NJ).

[17]Fisher, "Curious Belief," 88.

[18]Robert L. Clinton, *Marbury v. Madison and Judicial Review* (Lawrence: University Press of Kansas, 1989), p. 60.

[19]Ibid., p. 56.

[20]Isaac Kramnick, ed., *The Federalist Papers* (New York: Penguin, 1987), no. 78, p. 281.

[21]Both quoted in Fisher, "Curious Belief," 91.

[22]Quoted in Winton U. Solberg, ed., *The Federal Convention and the Formation of the Union of the American States* (Indianapolis, IN: Bobbs-Merrill, 1958), pp. 238–39.

[23]Quoted in Saul K. Padover, *To Secure These Blessings: The Great Debates of the Constitutional Convention of 1787* (New York: Ridge Press, 1962), p. 411.

[24]Ibid., p. 418.

[25]Solberg, *Federal Convention*, p. 98.

[26]Padover, *To Secure These Blessings*, pp. 416ff.

[27]Quoted in Ralph Ketchum, ed., *The Anti-Federalist Papers of the Constitutional Convention Debate* (New York: New American Library, 1986), pp. 304–5.

[28]Fisher, "Curious Belief," 89.

[29]Ibid., 92.

[30]Frank M. Coffin, *On Appeal: Courts, Lawyering, and Judging* (New York: Norton, 1993), p. 45.

[31]Kramnick, *Federalist Papers*, pp. 436–41, 450–58, passim.

[32]Quoted in Padover, *To Secure These Blessings*, p. 414.

[33]Quoted in Clinton, *Marbury v. Madison*, p. 59.

[34]Quoted in Fisher, "Curious Belief," 93.

[35]Ibid., 91.

[36]Quoted in Clinton, *Marbury v. Madison*, p. 67.

[37]Quoted in Fisher, "Curious Belief," 89.

[38]Quoted in Solberg, *Federal Convention*, p. 178.

[39]Quoted in Fisher, "Curious Belief," 92.

[40]Ibid.

[41]Ibid., 94.

[42]Quoted in Clinton, *Marbury v. Madison*, p. 27.

[43]2 *Dallas* 409 (1792).

[44]Fisher, "Curious Belief," 95.

[45]*Hylton v. U.S.*, 3 U.S. 171 (1796), at 175.

[46]*Cooper v. Telfair*, 4 U.S. 14 (1800), at 19.

[47]Howard Ball, *We Have a Duty: The Supreme Court and the Watergate Litigation* (Westport, CT: Greenwood Press, 1992), p. 6.

[48]4 *Dallas* 14 (1800).

[49]Jethro K. Lieberman, *Milestones* (St. Paul, MN: West, 1976), p. 73.

[50]The other three were Robert T. Hooe, Dennis Ramsey, and William Harper, all Federalists who, like Marbury, did not receive their commissions in a timely manner and thus became a footnote to a major Court case. See, generally, Donald O. Dewey, *Marshall Versus Jefferson: The Political Background of Marbury v. Madison* (New York: Knopf, 1970).

[51]1 Stat 73 (1789).

[52]Dewey, *Marshall Versus Jefferson*, p. 117.

[53]Fisher, "Curious Belief," 96.

[54]Dewey, *Marshall Versus Jefferson*, p. 109.

[55]Ibid., p. 110.

[56]One scholar argues that "textually, the provision regarding mandamus says nothing expressly as to whether it is part of original or appellate jurisdiction or both, and the clause does not speak at all of 'conferring jurisdiction' on the Court" (Van Alstyne, "A Critical Guide to *Marbury v. Madison*," *Duke Law Journal*, no. 1 [1969]: 15).

[57]A few of his associates were either in Congress and took part in the creation of the Judiciary Act or had been major participants at the 1787 constitutional convention (Dewey, *Marshall Versus Jefferson*, p. 130).

[58]60 U.S. 393 (1857).

[59]Jefferson to William Johnson, June 12, 1823 (in Albert Ellery Bergh, ed., *The Writings of Thomas Jefferson*, vol. 15 [Washington, DC: Thomas Jefferson Memorial Association, 1907], pp. 447–48).

[60]Clinton, *Marbury v. Madison*, p. 88.

[61]Quoted in Howard Ball, *Judges and Politics: The Federal Judicial System*, 2d ed. (Englewood Cliffs, NJ: Prentice Hall, 1987), p. 174.

[62]Douglas Ross, "Safeguarding Our Federalism: Lessons for the States from the Supreme Court," *Public Administration Review* 45 (Nov. 1985): 724.

[63]See, generally, Howard Ball, Dale Krane, and Thomas Lauth, *Compromised Compliance* (Westport, CT: Greenwood Press, 1982), p. 47.

[64]*Allen v. Board of Education*, 393 U.S. 544 (1968).

[65]*South Carolina v. Katzenbach*, 383 U.S. 301 (1966).

[66]Ibid.

[67]Edwin Meese, "The Attorney General's View of the Supreme Court: Toward a Jurisprudence of Original Intention," *Public Administration Review* 45 (1985).

[68]Ibid., 704.

[69]See Howard Ball, "The Convergence of Constitutional Law and Politics in the Reagan Administration: The Exhumation of the 'Jurisprudence of Original Intention' Doctrine," *Cumberland Law Review* 17, no. 3 (1986–87): 881ff.

[70]William J. Brennan, Jr., Address given at Georgetown University, Washington, DC, Oct. 12, 1985 (reprinted in *The New York Times*, Oct. 13, 1985, sec. A).

[71]Quoted in Ball, "Convergence of Constitutional Law," 881.

[72]William O. Douglas, "In Defense of Dissent," in Alan Westin, ed., *The Supreme Court: Views from the Inside* (Westport, CT: Greenwood Press, 1983), p. 83.

[73]The Supreme Court, however, had been examining the concept of privacy as it related to criminal justice matters such as Fourth Amendment "search-and-seizure" cases that addressed the issue of invasion of privacy by law enforcement officials.

[74]381 U.S. 479 (1965).

[75]See Ball and Cooper, *Of Power and Right*, pp. 284ff.

[76]*Griswold*, at 484.

[77]Ibid., at 486.

[78]Ibid., Black dissent, at 510.

[79]Ball and Cooper, *Of Power and Right*, p. 288.

[80]Mark W. Cannon and David M. O'Brien, *The Judiciary and Constitutional Politics: Views from the Bench* (Chatham, NJ: Chatham House, 1985), p. 3.

[81]U.S. Congress, Senate Committee on the Judiciary, Testimony, *Reorganization of the Federal Judiciary, Part 2: Hearings Before the Senate Committee on the Judiciary*, 75th Cong., 1st sess., 1937, p. 176.

[82]Robert H. Jackson, *The Struggle for Judicial Supremacy* (New York: Knopf, 1941), p. 311.

[83]Fisher, "Curious Belief," 115.

[84]Ibid., 97.

Getting There: Appointment to the Supreme Court

3

It is now your second day at the Court, and the celebrations are over. Before plunging into the pile of bench memos (case summaries prepared by clerks) and briefs on your desk, you pause over a cup of coffee to think about just how you got here. Being politically savvy (it is unlikely that you would have made it to the high bench if you weren't), you know that the process of selection and confirmation has many elements.

The issue is an important one for members of the Court as well as for political pundits and professors who occupy themselves by speculating about who will be elevated to the Court and what difference it will make. In October 1993, for example, the question was how important the "Ginsburg factor" would be, referring to the impending arrival on the Court of Justice Ruth Bader Ginsburg. The process by which justices are selected and confirmed helps explain why the institution tends to be staffed by the kinds of justices who have served there over time. In some sense, one gets to know one's colleagues in part by understanding their careers and how they came to be on the Court. Indeed, the public and your colleagues have formed impressions of you based in some measure at least on the picture that emerged during the nomination and confirmation process. Some justices have even gone so far as to try to shape the process themselves by prevailing on a president to make the "right" selection for a given opening.[1]

For members of the Court, the appointment process is also important because it can pose dangers, risks that the Court will be perceived as a body that is political in the worst sense of the term. Partisan and ideological debate may suggest that justices prejudge important issues merely because of their backgrounds. It may convey a picture of partisan loyalty or debts to the president who chose the new justice, another threat to the perceived legitimacy of the Court and its justices. Institutional independence is one of the Court's most prized possessions.

Finally, the process matters because lengthy delays in replacing a justice can place the Court in the difficult position of adding extra work to already heavy burdens. Dividing the opinion-writing load among eight justices rather than nine means more work for the justices. Circuit duties (each justice is assigned special responsibilities for one of the federal judicial circuits) also need to be shared by a "short court." An even number of justices can also produce unusual numbers of tied votes on important cases, effectively leaving important questions unresolved and complicating decisions over which cases to accept for review.

One of the most controversial cases of appointment to the Court in modern history was President Ronald Reagan's unsuccessful nomination of Judge Robert Bork to replace the retiring justice Lewis Powell. It casts many of the critical dynamics of the appointment process in high relief.

THE BORK BATTLE: AN INTRODUCTION TO THE APPOINTMENT PROCESS

A variety of factors faced the Reagan administration when Justice Lewis Powell retired from the Court in 1987. At the heart of the issue of who would be appointed to the vacant seat was the legacy of "Justice Wrong."

Ronald Reagan and the "Justice Wrong" Syndrome

As governor, Ronald Reagan, like other chief executives before and since, found that his choice for chief justice of the California Supreme Court behaved far differently on the bench than the governor had anticipated. As his misjudgment became more apparent, the conservative Reagan began to refer to his nominee as "Justice Wrong." He vowed to be more careful, and the appointments he made during his presidential administration indicate that he was taking no chances, if he could help it, in selecting committed conservatives for the vacant seats in the federal courts.

Ideological Politics: Perception and Reality

There was also a need to deal with the right wing of the Republican party, so important to Reagan victories in 1980 and 1984. While the president had been tough with the Russians, had fought regulation, and had used the budget to pare down a variety of domestic social programs, he had not accomplished many of the goals of the conservative social agenda. Abortion remained legal, teacher-led prayer in public school was not, the Departments of Energy and Education remained in place despite his campaign promise to kill them, and affirmative action, though modified, was still in use.[2] It was time, from the perspective of stalwart

Republican conservatives, to put someone on the Court who would carry unimpeachable conservative credentials and pursue these issues on the bench when the opportunity presented itself. More than that, it was important that the nominee be seen to be such a person, for the impression was as important as the reality.

Thus was raised the question of how to handle the Powell replacement in light of Reagan's previous selections. His first opportunity for a nomination to the Court came when Justice Potter Stewart retired in 1981. The president's campaign commitment to appoint the first woman to the Supreme Court had to be honored, and it was. From Arizona, where she had served in the state legislature and later sat on a middle-level state appeals court, Justice Sandra Day O'Connor came to the bench with impeccable Republican political credentials. Still, many conservatives blanched when she refused to give clear signs during confirmation hearings that she would oppose abortion and take other positions crucial to the domestic agenda of the Right.[3]

Once on the Court, O'Connor proved to be a tough-minded conservative, but not conservative enough for many of the faithful. As the administration considered its replacement for Justice Powell, O'Connor's concurrence in *Wallace v. Jaffree*,[4] striking down an Alabama school's "moment of silence" and another concurrence in a decision overturning a Louisiana "creation science" statute[5] were fresh in their minds. The moment of silence case in particular brought sharp criticism from the Right and considerable disappointment to the administration.

The departure of Chief Justice Warren Burger at the end of the 1985 term gave Reagan the opportunity to select the next occupant of the center chair, a person whose name would thenceforth be used to speak of the upcoming era in the Court's history. It was an important selection, for it was clear that Democrats had a strong chance to take back control of the Senate in 1986, and with it the leadership of the Senate Judiciary Committee, which plays a crucial role in confirming judicial appointments. Were the nomination to be unsuccessful and delayed until the next year, there would even be the danger that President Reagan would be a lame duck, facing a situation in which Senate Democrats could stall a nomination in the Senate until the 1988 campaign got underway and, ultimately perhaps, deprive this president, and possibly the Republican party, of the selection of a new chief. The Republicans, with the assistance of Southern Democrats, had done precisely that when Lyndon Johnson attempted to elevate Abe Fortas to the center chair in 1968.[6]

The need for dispatch and the desire for a surefire, absolutely predictable choice (as much as any appointment can be) favored the Court's most conservative member, William Rehnquist. There were indeed signals that that hard-line conservative nomination might fail, as adversaries challenged Rehnquist's nomination as chief justice far more than many had in 1971 when he was first named to the Court. His original appointment came in the wake of the unsuccessful nominations by President Richard Nixon of Clement Haynsworth and G. Harrold Carswell. There was little stomach for further close examination of nominees in the Senate at that time, and issues in Rehnquist's background were overlooked. Allegations that he had worked to discourage minority voters and that he had purchased property with a racially restrictive deed covenant (one that precludes sale or purchase of the property by non-Caucasians) surfaced during later hearings on the chief justice appointment. His record on the Court brought criticism as well, particularly his pivotal participation in a case concerning domestic surveillance activities by the military, even though he had been involved with the case while at the Department of Justice.[7] Still, there was little likelihood that his nomination would be defeated, and later that year, America was introduced to the Rehnquist Court. That process left an associate justice seat to be filled.

Judge Antonin Scalia, a very conservative appointment, was not well known outside the Washington beltway by the public, though he had developed a growing reputation in the legal community as a scholar of administrative law while at the University of Chicago Law School. His nomination to the D.C. circuit in 1981 came as no surprise to those watching the Reagan administration's appointments. Around the Capitol, Scalia was viewed as riding the fast track to the High Court. He had been appointed to the D.C. circuit only two years earlier. Popular on the Washington social circuit, he was nevertheless clearly a strong conservative choice. His performance on the lower court indicated that he would bring his skills to bear to implement his conservative reading of the law. The president named him to succeed Rehnquist. It was a popular appointment, and Scalia was promptly confirmed by the Senate, though some on the Hill were angry at what they regarded as an uncooperative attitude during the confirmation process. Still, Scalia was not well known nationally, not the symbolic conservative that many in the administration and its supporters on the outside truly desired. Enter Robert Bork.

The Bork Battle Begins

When the news of the Powell retirement broke in late June 1987, speculation mounted regarding Reagan's fourth Supreme Court choice. A number of names surfaced immediately; indeed, they had been prominent a year earlier when Scalia was chosen. At the top of most lists were Robert Bork, then a Reagan appointee to the U.S. Court of Appeals for the D.C. Circuit (the same court from which Scalia had been elevated), and Judge Richard Posner of the U.S. Court of Appeals for the Seventh Circuit, based in Chicago. Would it be one of these or someone else?

This time confirmation politics was an issue. The Democrats now controlled the Senate, and some nasty fights had broken out over lower-court nominees who were opposed by a number of Republicans because they were not sufficiently pure ideologically and by Democrats who challenged them on grounds of competence but also because a few nominees were considered to be simply too ideologically extreme.[8] Within broad boundaries, presidents are usually allowed just about any choice they make, but at some point there is a limit. While Bork's name circulated at once as a potential Supreme Court candidate, it was clear for several reasons that his nomination would pose a severe test in the Senate.

The first issue sure to develop in a Bork confirmation investigation would be the role he played in the so-called Saturday Night Massacre in 1973. In a showdown over whether he would turn over White House tapes, President Nixon ordered Special Prosecutor Archibald Cox fired, but then Attorney General Elliot Richardson and Deputy Attorney General William Ruckelshaus both resigned rather than carry out that order. Solicitor General Bork remained and terminated Cox.

While other issues included Bork's comments and writings as a scholar, particularly on constitutional rights and liberties questions, and his opinions as a

President Ronald Reagan with his nominee to the Supreme Court, Robert Bork, July 1987.

judge, the conflict expanded significantly beyond those boundaries. The confirmation process itself became a significant issue, with debates raging over the kinds of questions that could be asked by senators, the kinds of testimony and evidence to be taken from others, and the proper conduct of a nominee. It was also a symbolic battle for both liberals and conservatives.[9] At times, in fact, the drawing of the line in the sand between opposing political forces seemed to overshadow the other questions presented by the nomination. So vitriolic were these clashes that the Bork battle was to be a factor in Senate relationships long after the vote was taken, most notably in the conflict surrounding the unsuccessful nomination of former senator John Tower for Secretary of Defense in 1989.

The Watergate Legacy: Ghosts of the Saturday Night Massacre

The Saturday Night Massacre issue might have been a more critical factor in the confirmation fight had it not been for testimony by Elliot Richardson and Philip Lacovara, both men with a reputation for integrity and independence. Richardson acknowledged the importance, in 1973, of continuity in the Department of Justice and that, by remaining at his post, Bork was able to povide it. Lacovara, formerly the number-two official in the special prosecution force, did not agree with Bork but concluded: "He made a choice that was within the range of reason, even though in my view it was not the correct choice. . . . But it was not one that reflected evil motives or a fundamental misunderstanding of constitutional law."[10]

As Bork explained it, Richardson and Ruckelshaus had suggested that he not resign, and thus he would be able to provide continuity in the Justice Department and make sure that the special prosecutor's staff continued its work.[11] The other argument made in his defense was that Professor Alexander Bickel, a close friend from Yale Law School days and noted public-law authority, had written an article just before the incident, supporting the authority of the president to fire the special prosecutor.[12] Bork later left the Justice Department to take up the Bickel Chair of Public Law at Yale. President Ford; his attorney general, Leonard Levy; and former chief justice Burger, author of the opinion in the Nixon tapes case,[13] all appeared on Bork's behalf before the Senate Judiciary Committee.[14] The final factor in his favor was time. It had been nearly fourteen years since Watergate, and the memory of it had faded significantly.

Still, not everyone was satisfied.[15] Two members of the special prosecution force, Henry Ruth and George Frampton, disagreed with the picture that was presented of a beleaguered Bork defending the integrity of the special prosecutor's effort. Ruth cautioned: "I don't want to see history rewritten just to confirm a Supreme Court justice."[16] In particular, Ruth indicated that there was no sense of support within the special prosecution force when Bork took over. Within a week that fear evaporated. Most of the attorneys remained because "we thought the Republican congressional reaction was going to force Mr. Nixon to appoint a new special prosecutor."[17] Bork testified at the hearings that

> initially, we intended to leave the Special Prosecution Force intact but not to appoint a new special prosecutor, and they would go on under Mr. Ruth and Mr. Lacovara as before. But we did not initially contemplate a new special prosecutor until we saw that it was necessary because the American people would not be mollified without one.[18]

Beyond that, Senator Edward Kennedy (D–Mass.) pressed the fact that Judge Gerhard Gesell had ruled the Cox firing illegal.[19] In any case, it seemed difficult to accept testimony that there was no problem in a situation in which the top two figures at the Justice Department had resigned rather than follow the president's directive.

In the end, Watergate was more of a problem than Bork supporters had hoped but less of an obstacle than many opponents had wanted it to be. The success of the nomination would not turn on the Saturday Night Massacre.

Bork Center Stage: The Confirmation Hearings

The main event was the testimony presented by the nominee himself. For it was during the hearings in September that the national television audience saw Judge Bork explain his academic writings, his record as a jurist, and his thoughts as a potential Supreme Court justice. In addition to probing his role in the Saturday Night Massacre, committee members asked him a wide range of questions about his positions on antitrust policy, a specialty and a field in which he had written a book.[20] But the more spirited discussion arose from an *Indiana Law Journal* article that Bork had authored on the First Amendment and from judicial decisions he had rendered on the circuit court of appeals dealing with civil rights issues.[21]

Bork had previously taken the position that the courts, particularly the Supreme Court, had interpreted rights too expansively and created rights where none existed in the Constitution or in the minds of its framers. Defending the approach to constitutional interpretation popularized by Attorney General Meese in his controversial 1985 speech to the American Bar Association,[22] Bork insisted that the intent of the framers was the primary storehouse of knowledge about the boundaries of constitutional freedoms. Bork had earlier criticized Supreme Court rulings accepting wide-ranging conceptions of freedom of speech, including speech challenging the very foundations of the constitutional order.[23] Beyond that, he had rejected the idea that the First Amendment protected anything except political speech, thus exempting literature, art, and academic expression. He had criticized the announcement by the Court of a right to privacy in the 1965 *Griswold v. Connecticut* case[24] and rulings like those in the abortion cases that followed from it.

However, Bork announced during his testimony that he was no longer committed to those positions as adamantly as before. He accepted the right to privacy, agreed that the First Amendment protected more than just purely political speech, and acknowledged that the equal protection clause protected against discrimination on the basis of gender as well as race. While he still disagreed with many of the decisions he had criticized earlier, he was committed as a judge to applying those precedents, not because they were right but because they represented "settled law."[25]

That placed the nominee on the horns of a very difficult political dilemma. Bork's support came from the right wing of the Republican party, people who would be mightily offended if their champion equivocated on the mission to change the Supreme Court and reverse its earlier errors. If, on the other hand, the would-be justice held firm to his previous criticisms of landmark rulings announcing constitutional rights and liberties now taken for granted by most Americans, his chances for confirmation would be substantially diminished.

Opinions regarding the quality of Judge Bork's performance varied widely and followed expected divisions. His supporters found his presentation powerful and enjoyed what they saw as Bork besting his Senate adversaries. Opponents found him evasive and contradictory; willing to say anything that seemed likely to secure Senate approval. This behavior came to be known as the "confirmation conversion."

The Judiciary Committee's Debates

There was never any doubt that the Bork nomination would be controversial. To many Bork advocates, that was all to the good. It was time for a political showdown in the Senate and in the court of public opinion. In fact, some senators looked forward to taking on adversaries they considered emotional, unpopular with the mass of Americans, and politically unskilled. Senator Alan K. Simpson (R–Wyo.) was heard to say:

> We were hoping to have Ellie Smeal [former head of the National Organization for Women] up here screaming about abortion rights. We would have liked to have Ralph

[Neas], too, so we could ask him how many dying organizations have been refueled and larded up their treasuries on this issue. But they didn't come.[26]

Instead, Bork opponents did a superb job of organizing their campaign, while the usually savvy Republicans, lacking White House leadership, did not.

Opponents began working together under the leadership of Ralph Neas, executive director of the Leadership Conference on Civil Rights. The individual organizations, more than three hundred according to some estimates, agreed to work together through a steering committee that met regularly to plan strategy and manage the fight. Three decisions made by the group were critical.[27] The first was that member groups would decline invitations from Judiciary Chairman Joseph Biden to testify. This was to avoid having the focus shift from Bork to his opponents. Instead, the group chose three leading African American figures, former transportation secretary William Coleman, former member of Congress and Judiciary Committee member Barbara Jordan, and Atlanta mayor Andrew Young to be the primary spokespersons. These witnesses, along with judges and law professors, would be the primary challengers. The second decision was to shift the terms of the debate to the right to privacy rather than abortion, and to civil rights broadly defined. The third decision was to concentrate on Southern Democrats, who needed the votes of African Americans to stay in office, and who would find it difficult to oppose protection of privacy.

The organized opposition had help from independent professional reactions against the nominee. Bork had a substantial record of writings and opinions, and the legal community scrutinized that record carefully. The American Bar Association Standing Committee on the Federal Judiciary report on Bork's qualifications termed him "well qualified," but its chair, Harold R. Tyler, Jr., reported that one member had voted "not opposed," and four members had voted "not qualified."[28] The Judiciary Committee later observed that "no Supreme Court nominee who has received even a single 'Not Qualified' vote from the Standing Committee has ever been confirmed by the Senate."[29] The Senate Committee received two thousand letters in opposition to the appointment from individual academics, a letter signed by seventy-one constitutional law professors, and a letter signed by thirty-two law school deans warning against confirmation. There were letters from lawyers around the country and allegations by a judge who had served with Bork, suggesting a lack of effective collegial working relationships. Judge James F. Gordon wrote the committee that this was "a story of actions taken by Judge Bork which I believe reflect serious flaws in his character. So serious, in my judgment, that they go to his basic honesty."[30] Gordon complained that Bork had deliberately manipulated a court of appeals opinion to take a position that the three judges had agreed was not to be the foundation of the opinion without consultation. Gordon was then forced in the eleventh hour to write a new majority ruling for himself and Judge Roger Robb, who was then terminally ill in the hospital.

The administration's supporters were taken by surprise at the effectiveness of their opponents' campaign. The White House had not worked systematically to manage the confirmation as it had so many congressional battles over the previous six years. It waited until very late in the contest, really after Bork's testimony in September, to wade into the fray in earnest. By then, the nomination was already in trouble.

Even Republicans on the Senate Judiciary Committee had trouble attacking the opposition. As one commentator pointed out, the effort to challenge witnesses against Bork backfired. The opposing witnesses appeared early in the proceedings while the public was watching the televised hearings. Prolonged efforts to cross-examine the witnesses meant more media time for Bork opponents.[31]

The Hearings and the Battle for Public Opinion

The battle was raging outside the Senate as well as within it, and the evidence was growing that the nomination was losing. Several polls done after the hearings agreed.

> Among 1,249 people questioned by Louis Harris Associates, 57 percent said the Senate should rejected [*sic*] President Reagan's nominee to the high court, while 29 percent said they favored his confirmation. Those who said they watched Bork's testimony on television or followed it closely in the newspapers opposed his confirmation by a 61–32 margin.
>
> An NBC–*Wall Street Journal* poll of 1,544 adults taken Sept. 21–22 found 42 percent opposed to Bork, 34 percent in favor and 24 percent undecided.
>
> A CBS–*New York Times* poll of 836 persons taken Sept. 21–22 found 26 percent against, 16 percent for and 57 percent undecided.
>
> An ABC–*Washington Post* poll of 2,116 persons Sept. 17–23 found 48 percent opposed and 44 percent in favor. In early August, the same polling group found Bork had a 45–40 percent margin of support.[32]

It seemed that the administration that had so often appealed to public opinion to force a reluctant Congress into cooperating with the president was in trouble. There was a real danger that the more the administration used its political capital in what appeared to be a losing cause, the greater the loss would be for it if the attempt to salvage the nomination should ultimately fail.

Dynamics at work within the Senate made defeat even more likely. Bork supporters' assertions that the president had a right to his own selection challenged Senate legislative prerogatives. Whatever their positions on this particular nomination, a number of senators felt it necessary to defend their institutional powers. The requirement that the president have the "advice and consent of the Senate" did not after all mean automatic approval.

Important factors were also shaping the conduct of the Judiciary Committee proceedings as well. For one, Chairman Biden was a Democratic candidate for the 1988 presidential nomination and was therefore constrained by close scrutiny of his conduct of the process. Charges of partisanship or unfairness would be laid at his feet. There were also several undecided Republicans and Southern Democrats in the Judiciary Committee whose votes either way could hurt them in the next election. Majority leader Robert Byrd (D–WVa.) suggested moving the matter to the full Senate without a recommendation, thus avoiding the need for an up-or-down committee vote.[33] But Bork advocates would have none of it. They wanted a vote and made it very clear that they intended to use members' negative votes against them in the next election. Even Bork opponents, by this point, wanted a showdown.[34]

There was also a nascent bandwagon effect. On September 29, with a committee vote likely in less than two weeks, Senate Democratic party whip Alan Cranston (D–Calif.) announced that there were already forty-nine firm votes against Bork in the full Senate. He proclaimed: "I think he's licked."[35] Supporters charged that it was an effort to stampede undecided senators into joining the opposition. There were, at that point, four critical undecided votes in the committee, Senators Byrd, Howell Heflin (D–Ala.), Dennis DeConcini (D–Ariz.), and Arlen Specter (R–Pa.), with five sure negative and five strong positive votes among the remaining members.

The Southern Democrats' Dilemma

Howell Heflin of Alabama was a vote that the pro-Bork forces had hoped to win, notwithstanding his opposition to a previous nomination for the federal district court from Alabama, Jefferson B. Sessions III.[36] They wanted his individual vote, of course, but more important was the fact that Heflin was a potential bellwether for other uncommitted Southern Democrats whose votes were desperately needed if the administration was going to save the Bork nomination. In fact, the day before the scheduled committee vote, newspaper stories reported that nine of an estimated fourteen uncommitted votes were in the hands of Southern Democrats who would watch Heflin carefully.[37]

The pressure on Heflin was tremendous. He reported during the hearings that "my arms have been twisted so much on the right and on the left that both of them are ready for transplants."[38] A Heflin staffer complained that they had too few people in the office to open the thousands of letters that were pouring in.[39] Heflin was still agonizing over the decision on the weekend before the vote. He characterized the decision as "a plank-walker. . . . You walk to the end of the plank to take off your blindfold, and you see a bunch of barracudas on one side and swarming sharks on the other."[40]

Among the pressures on these generally conservative southern senators was their heavy dependence on minority voters to retain their office. It was a fact that had been made very clear during the 1986 senatorial elections: "Senators Terry Sanford of North Carolina, Richard C. Shelby and Howell Heflin of Alabama, and John B. Breaux of Louisiana, all crucial swing votes, were all elected with more than 75 percent of the black vote. . . . At the same time, none of them carried a majority of the white votes in those elections."[41] Both Shelby and Breaux, it was reported, had received over 90 percent of the black and less than 40 percent of the white votes in their respective states.[42] Thinking out loud about the implications of that fact and the united minority opposition to Bork, Breaux said: "If you vote against Bork, those in favor of him will be mad at you for a week, . . . but if you vote for him, those who don't like him will be mad at you for the rest of their lives."[43]

It was not just the threat of adverse votes that weighed on the minds of the southerners, though. The thought that the Court, with Bork encouraging it, might retreat from the great strides made in civil rights over the last three decades threatened to open old wounds. Heflin and the others could not decide whether Bork was simply a conservative or a reactionary likely to lead such a move.

The End Game

The committee vote was rapidly approaching by the time the administration made its all-out push to save the nomination. The president tried to counter the momentum that was building by painting the opposition as "liberal special interests," but it was one time too many for that tactic.

When on Monday, October 5, Republican Arlen Specter and Democrats Dennis DeConcini and Robert Byrd announced their intention to oppose the nomination, the committee vote against the nomination was guaranteed. In announcing his position, Senator DeConcini observed: "Judge Bork views the Constitution as a bloodless and sterile contract. . . . I do not believe the U.S. Senate can take the risk that putting Judge Bork on the Supreme Court entails."[44] That risk, that they still did not know what Bork really thought about the critical issues of the confirmation discussion, was important to several of those announcing decisions as the committee vote scheduled for Tuesday approached.

The only remaining question on Tuesday was what Heflin would do, more important for what it might say about the Southern Democratic vote in the full Senate than for purposes of the committee vote. Rumors had been circulating that there was a last-minute effort to win the Alabama senator by considering his friend and successor on the Alabama Supreme Court, Clement Torbert, Jr., for a seat on the U.S. Court of Appeals for the Eleventh Circuit. The Justice Department admitted that the administration had been evaluating Torbert for the position since July and that he had been interviewed about the post.[45] The administration denied that the consideration of Torbert was an attempt to influence Heflin, but the fact that Torbert would have been the first Democrat appointed to an appellate court judgeship in the more than seventy appointments during the Reagan administration caused considerable doubt about that claim.

When Heflin announced his decision to oppose Bork, that made the committee vote against the nomination nine to five and virtually guaranteed that the votes were already in place to defeat the nomination in a vote in the full Senate. But Bork had insisted on a final vote, and the White House had vowed to continue the fight.

Debate over the Politics of the Confirmation Process

After the Senate committee vote, the issue became the confirmation process itself, with Bork supporters charging that the process was unfair and inappropriate. They attacked it on two primary points. Their first point was that mere ideological disagreement with a nominee or the president who chose him or her was not a ground for rejecting the nomination. The second was that the confirmation process had involved campaigns for and against the nominee, including the use of television advertising. And one long-term concern remained after the Senate committee vote. This was whether the confirmation process itself had been so fundamentally altered that all future selections for the Court would face some of the same problems encountered during the Bork battle.

Senator Orrin Hatch (R–Utah) argued vigorously from the moment the first opposition arose that the problem was simply liberals who objected to a conservative choice—it was all ideological. The opponents, he and other Bork supporters charged, were bent on politicizing the process of confirmation because of that ideological disagreement. The president was entitled under the Constitution to choose a person whose philosophy was compatible with that of the administration.

As the confirmation fight raged through the summer and into the fall of 1987, others became increasingly critical as well. Lloyd Cutler, former counsel to President Jimmy Carter but a Bork supporter, complained: "We're getting perilously close to electing a Supreme Court Justice."[46] Former Carter administration attorney general Griffin Bell concurred: "We have abandoned the constitutional process for confirming judges and we go on now into the Gallup Poll business."[47] Even Senate majority leader Byrd agreed that the process was "taking on the character of an election."[48] Senator Charles E. Grassley (R–Iowa) took the challenge even further. "I've been in public office 28 years of my lifetime," he said, "and never have I seen such an unjustified and untrammeled assault on a distinguished American citizen as I have witnessed these last few days."[49] Senator Jake Garn (R–Utah) exclaimed: "I've never been so mad in my life. . . . If Bork loses in the full Senate, there will never be a liberal judge confirmed by the Senate as long as I am here. The whole damn Senate will be tied up."[50]

Bork opponents shot back that it was clear that the Republicans did not like getting a dose of their own medicine. The Republicans seemed to forget that it had been the Republican White House under Ronald Reagan that had politicized judicial nominations as never before and that Senate Democrats had choked down dozens of politically extreme nominees out of deference to the president. Now, when others challenged them on precisely the same grounds they had employed for years, the administration's allies found it hard to swallow. Yale law professor Paul Gewitz observed: "I would prefer less ideologically charged nominations and am confident that that would produce less charged confirmation hearings."[51] And Senator Biden argued:

> As we approach the Senate's moment of action on this nomination . . . we have been told that the judiciary is being dangerously politicized and that as a result the independence of the judiciary, and the Supreme Court in particular, is in great jeopardy. Well, I'll acknowledge there has been politicization, but any politicizing has been driven by President Reagan's single-minded pursuit of a judiciary packed with those who are his ideological allies.[52]

Appeals to public opinion were also politicized. The need for calm deliberation had never stopped the administration and its supporters from using the media to achieve its goals, Bork opponents said. Why was it wrong now? And if there had been a campaign involved, surely no one involved was campaigning any harder for the post than the candidate himself. No other candidate for the office had been willing to answer so many detailed questions about his views on the law to gain confirmation, and the confirmation conversion phenomenon had caused many observers to question where the nominee would draw a line.

Finally, Bork opponents found it fascinating that some of the same people who were willing to make ideologically based assessments of Justice Abe Fortas when he was nominated to replace Chief Justice Earl Warren in the center chair now found ideology to be beyond the bounds of propriety. Senator Strom Thurmond (R–S.C.), who voted for Bork, had lambasted Fortas for liberal rulings that had been rendered by the Warren Court before Fortas had even been appointed to the bench.

President Reagan's Belated Response

There was an interesting counterpoint as the president seemed to work harder for the nomination after it appeared to everyone that the battle was lost than he had before the vote in committee. There was concern within the White House about Reagan's belated energy, and staff members toned down one speech in which the president planned to attack his critics. Reagan accepted the modified version, but in later comments following his prepared remarks, he said that if the Bork nomination failed he intended to name another person "that they'll object to as much as they did to this one."[53] Reagan suggested that senators voting against Bork were manipulated or were engaging in a liberal attempt to protect criminals from rigorous judges. He even went so far as to indicate that no person of intelligence could oppose Bork. Reporters asked if the president meant to include former Duke University president and then senator Terry Sanford (D–N.C.), to which the president replied: "Make your own judgment."[54]

Sanford and other Bork opponents were not amused. "We are tired of having our integrity impugned. We are tired of having our sincerity questioned. We are tired of having our intelligence insulted."[55] Democrats and nonconformist Republicans like Connecticut senator Lowell Weicker were not the only ones angered by the White House handling of the late-breaking Bork campaign. Uncommitted Republicans were angry that they were going to be forced to take difficult public positions in what was guaranteed to be a losing cause. Even committed conservatives were upset, but for different reasons. They were convinced that the president could have saved the nomination if he had put the full force of his administration behind Bork from the beginning and if he had made it the kind of straightforward confrontation with liberals that conservatives had wanted all along. Senator Grassley complained that the White House had been "asleep at the switch." He said, "While Ron and Nancy were riding horses in August, . . . the opposition was organizing."[56] The Far Right, represented by spokesmen such as the Heritage Foundation's Bruce Fein, remained convinced the battle could have been won if the administration had not tried to soft-pedal the nomination. But White House lobbyists were convinced that such a strategy would have been doomed from the start. As one advocate put it, "I'd rather argue that argument [confirmation conversion] than right-wing zealotry and ideology."[57]

The Bork battle ended on Friday, October 23, 1987, when the Senate voted fifty-eight to forty-two against confirmation. It had been seventeen years since the last unsuccessful nomination to the Court. And it was not the end of conflict over Reagan Supreme Court nominations.

The Ginsburg Nomination: A False Start at a Bad Time

Names of possible second choices had been circulated since early October. The pressure to move quickly was intensified by two quite different factors. The 1987 term had begun at the Court, and every month that a new justice was not in place meant difficulties for the Court, since the likelihood of an evenly divided Court increased the possibility of ambiguous outcomes in important cases. Then there was the problem of circuit justice duties. Justice Powell had been circuit justice for the fourth circuit and as such had been available to hear last-minute appeals in critical cases like death penalty stay petitions.

The second issue was timing. The longer it took to get a nomination to the Senate, the longer it would take to complete committee action and confirmation. It was already November, and the battle for the presidential nominations had been underway for some time. The later the process stretched into the election year, the more danger there would be of a stalled nomination.

Reagan staffers prepared a list of names for the president to review. First a list of thirteen, it was narrowed to nine after meetings with Senate Republicans. Most of the potential nominees came from among Reagan appointees to the U.S. Court of Appeals. The critical debate over who would be chosen came between two White House insiders, Chief of Staff and former Senate minority leader Howard Baker and Attorney General Edwin Meese. Baker represented the pragmatists who saw in the Bork debacle a clear message that it would be fruitless to press an ideologically extreme nominee. While some believed the Senate would not have the stomach for another fight so soon after the Bork battle, Senator Allan Cranston warned the administration that the Senate would be on guard against efforts to push through another Bork.[58]

At the same time, to many archconservatives like Richard Vigurie, who were convinced that this was the last chance for Reagan to implement the Reagan revolution in the judiciary, Baker's plan symbolized a Faustian bargain with moderation. Meese pressed that theme inside the White House, and, as a Reaganite of longstanding, was able to carry the day.[59] Efforts by some regarded as moderates to push for a southerner were rebuffed. Southern senators had not appreciated the loss of a southern seat on the Court with the retirement of Justice Powell, a Virginian. But the administration was in no mood to deal with the Southern Democrats and moderates who had deserted it on the Bork nomination.[60]

On the other hand, Meese had an interesting candidate in Judge Douglas Ginsburg of the U.S. Court of Appeals for the D.C. Circuit. First, Ginsburg was considered by the key players to be a bona fide conservative and not a moderate, though just how he gained a reputation for those credentials was a mystery. He had been named to the appellate court only a year earlier and had written relatively little before that, which had been a problem when he was up for tenure as a Harvard Law School professor. Though he was successful in that effort, he left the university to join the Justice Department. He later moved from there to the Office of Management and Budget, where he was an important actor in the administration's regulatory review program. He returned to the Justice Department, and was later named to the court of appeals.

He was an interesting candidate in part because, although he was considered a genuine conservative, unlike Bork before him he had a limited public record that could be a target.[61] He had two other characteristics to commend him. He was young, only forty-one. He would be the youngest person to join the Supreme Court since William O. Douglas in 1939. He was also Jewish, and that, said some administration officials, would make him harder for some Democrats to oppose.[62]

Baker had advocated a seemingly more moderate choice, Judge Anthony Kennedy of the U.S. Circuit Court of Appeals for the Ninth Circuit, but Meese prevailed. President Reagan announced his appointment of Ginsburg on October 29, 1987, less than a week after the Bork defeat. Yet within ten days this nomination, too, would fall.

The first problem that emerged was Ginsburg's lack of experience. When reporters and others checked the forms filed when Ginsburg became an appellate court judge, they discovered that he had claimed litigation experience for the cases that were handled by attorneys he supervised at the Department of Justice even though he had appeared only technically by virtue of having signed Justice Department briefs. Then there were allegations of conflict of interest. The first of these came on charges that Ginsburg had participated in cable television litigation decisions at the Department of Justice even though he owned a substantial amount of stock in a cable company.[63] The second concerned Ginsburg's participation in a case on the D.C. circuit in which he was said to have participated while he was with the Justice Department.[64]

The final blow came, however, on Friday, November 5, when the judge admitted that he had smoked marijuana as a youth and later while a member of the Harvard Law faculty, even though he had previously strictly enforced Justice Department policy against hiring anyone who admitted to the use of illegal drugs.[65] The story developed when National Public Radio judicial correspondent Nina Totenburg interviewed some of Ginsburg's former Harvard colleagues, one of whom revealed that he had smoked marijuana with Ginsburg at parties.[66]

The embarrassment to an administration that had declared a war on drugs was obvious and immediate. First Lady Nancy Reagan's "just say no" campaign seemed to be a laughingstock in light of the Ginsburg revelation. While the administration maintained a public position in defense of its nominee, clearly his days were numbered. Attorney General Meese, Ginsburg's original advocate in the administration, began to distance himself almost immediately.[67] Education Secretary William Bennett reportedly phoned the president, offering to call Ginsburg and seek his withdrawal from the nomination. News reports indicated that Reagan told Bennett to "do what you think is right."[68] On Saturday, November 7, Ginsburg removed himself from consideration.[69]

Anthony Kennedy and Success at Last

Once again the White House was embarrassed, and once again there was turmoil within administration circles as conservatives lambasted their champion, Meese, for poor groundwork. This time they could not blame the Democrats or the "liberal special interests" who had made such a useful target during the Bork fight. For their part, Democrats were able to sit back and enjoy the Republicans' plight. They were even magnanimous in victory, with Judiciary Committee chairman Biden promising to move promptly on the next nomination.

This time, Judge Anthony Kennedy quickly emerged as the new nominee. The fifty-one-year-old Sacramento, California, native had been educated at Stanford and the Harvard Law School. He had been in private practice before President Ford named him to the ninth circuit in 1975. Kennedy was regarded as a moderate conservative, though with a few exceptions, he had not been forced to take positions on some of the more controversial issues with which nomination watchers were most concerned.

In fact, one of the only problems that Kennedy faced was anxiety over whether there might be anything in his past that would once again leave the administration with egg on its face. The FBI, which had not found the facts in Ginsburg's background that led to his downfall, was particularly committed to assuring that there would be no untoward surprises. One news report quoted an FBI source who "said the FBI background check was so exhaustive that 'we know when he stopped sucking his thumb.'"[70] For the same reason, few Republicans were ready to take immediate and firm positions in support of this new nominee until they had time to study all of the available information.[71]

While only one major group, the National Organization for Women, took a strong position against Kennedy, considerable concern was expressed by conservatives about the kind of grilling the nominee was likely to face before the Judiciary Committee. The warning was sounded by none other than Robert Bork. In a December 3, 1987, speech in Chicago, Bork said he had made a mistake in answering too many detailed questions during the hearings and that his willingness to answer questions would be expected of future selections. He warned, "What I did is now being taken as a precedent for future nominees, and I feel that it should not be taken as a precedent."[72] But senators warned Kennedy that he had better be prepared for tough questions and that he would not be permitted to avoid answering them. Senator Patrick Leahy (D–Vt.) warned him that "there would never be another Scalia confirmed by the Senate" (a reference to the refusal by Justice Scalia to respond to a variety of questions during his confirmation hearings).[73]

Despite some ominous warnings, however, the Kennedy hearings, which got underway on December 13, 1987, were far different from the Bork confrontation. While Kennedy did face two days of questioning, the committee members maintained a positive, even congenial atmosphere. Though he was questioned about his opinion for the ninth circuit, in which he rejected "comparable worth" in public-employee pay programs, the primary focus of NOW opposition, there appeared little chance that that alone would pose a serious impediment to confirmation.[74] Kennedy emerged with a unanimous favorable committee recommendation and was promptly confirmed by a relieved Senate.

MAKING THE CHOICE: THE SELECTION PROCESS

The story of the Bork nomination highlights a variety of issues that arise during the process of selecting and confirming justices of the Supreme Court. In some respects the Bork case is extremely unusual, but it also demonstrates a variety of common issues that affect, to one degree or another, virtually all modern nominations. These facets of judicial nomination include the dynamics of the process itself, the factors most often considered in selection of the nominee, the challenge of packing the Court, and the question of obtaining the nominee's agreement to be a candidate for the position in the first place.

Choosing a Nominee

From the moment a justice resigns (and sometimes even before), a complex process is set in motion that results in the elevation to the Court of a new justice. A number of key players line up to participate, hoping to influence the nomination and even to shape the process itself.

Usually, one of the first on the scene is the attorney general, whose job has been to assemble a list of possible nominees as discreetly as possible. That is no mean feat given that every news organization around the nation will begin to speculate about likely nominees as soon as word of the resignation gets out. The job must be done carefully to ensure that sufficient information can be collected to fully inform the president of the qualifications, political and otherwise, of the potential nominees. This information is also critical to ensure that anyone who is eventually selected is confirmable in the Senate. One part of the assessment rests on as full an understanding of the candidate's background as possible. The fear of a Ginsburg-type disaster haunts those seeking to avoid a candidate with skeletons in the closet, skeletons that when exposed—as they surely will be under the glare of confirmation publicity—will damage not only the personal life and career of the nominee but the credibility of the president who made the appointment.

Over the years, the FBI has come to play an important role in these investigative efforts. Agents thoroughly examine the nominee's life and check with his or her acquaintances. As the FBI put it after the Ginsburg problem, they are out to find out everything, including "when he stopped sucking his thumb." That was not always the case, however. While there is, for example, dispute over how much President Franklin D. Roosevelt knew about Hugo Black's former membership in the Ku Klux Klan when he named Black to the Court, that fact did not become widely known until after Black was already confirmed. The revelation led to charges of laxity by the bureau. The charges outraged FBI director J. Edgar Hoover, who was "indeed grateful to [the few broadcasters and newspapers who supported the Bureau] for taking this opportunity to squelch some of that criticism."[75] Fifty years later, the newspapers were no kinder to the bureau when the revelation of Ginsburg's marijuana use broke.

The preparation of the list of nominees is important to players outside the administration as well. In recent years, the challenge for interest groups who care about the process is to get their candidates onto the list before the range of potential candidates begins to be narrowed. During the Bork nomination saga, critics charged conservative Bruce Fein with deliberately seeking to get names of potential nominees into newspaper stories with the hope that doing so would influence the administration. Similarly, the presence of a foe on the list can trigger action by likely opponents as well. It is difficult to defeat a nominee in the confirmation process, and a preemptive challenge to potential nominees may stop a name from getting that far.

Knowledge of the roster of possibles can trigger action within the Senate, the body that will ultimately have to confirm the nominee chosen by the president. In the Bork case, Senator Edward Kennedy began mobilizing to oppose the nominee even before the announcement, despite efforts by the administration to keep the selection a secret. Within minutes of the nomination, Kennedy was on the floor of the Senate, delivering a sizzling attack on Bork.[76] And, long before the final votes on Bork were taken, players on both sides were watching for the names that would emerge on the new list.

Senatorial involvement in the confirmation process for Supreme Court justices is different from that in lower-court appointments. There, senators from the nominee's home state may exercise "senatorial courtesy," a tradition that allows a veto by the senator of a candidate whom the senator finds personally repugnant. The prerogative has been exercised on rare occasions in the past with regard to Supreme Court selections,[77] but senatorial courtesy is generally not a factor in contemporary Supreme Court nominations. These are truly national selections, and a president is unlikely to get more than two such opportunities during a term of office. Under those circumstances, it is unlikely that a single senator will be able to assert anything like a veto in the modern political environment. Nevertheless, the new nominee will have to face the Senate confirmation process, and lobbying efforts with senators begin almost immediately on nomination of a candidate.

Meanwhile, the American Bar Association (ABA) undertakes its traditional role as commentator on the qualifications and fitness of the nominee. While the ABA committee rarely finds a nominee unqualified, its recommendations are often viewed with considerable care, and the subtleties of its ratings are not lost on senators. The ABA Standing Committee on the Judiciary rates Supreme Court candidates as "well qualified," "qualified," "not opposed," or "not qualified."

The amount and character of the ABA committee's influence has varied over time.[78] Departing from the common pattern, the Reagan administration did not work with the ABA before naming its nominees. Indeed, the ABA began its study of Bork on July 2, 1987, the day after the announcement of his nomination, and only completed its work on September 8, just in time for the Senate confirmation hearings. Although the committee had no influence on the selection of the candidate, it played an important role in the confirmation process when it rendered a report in which the members were split. Ten indicated that Bork was well qualified, one voted "not opposed," and four voted "not qualified." The Senate Judiciary Committee report on Bork found that disagreement and substantial criticism important.[79]

The role of the ABA has come under criticism by both the political Right and Left. The general criticism is that because it is often consulted by the Justice Department on behalf of the White House before nominations are made, the ABA has effectively become a part of the nomination process, but it is not required to operate in public or to disclose the information on which its advice to the president is based. Indeed, the Washington Legal Foundation (on the political Right) and Public Citizen (a Ralph Nader–affiliated group on the political Left) challenged the Justice Department relationship with the ABA committee, claiming that the committee was an advisory committee within the meaning of the Federal Advisory Committee Act. If that statute did apply, then the committee should be treated as a public entity subject to a variety of controls and restrictions. And if the committee did have that status, its challengers thought, it might be vulnerable to attack on wider constitutional grounds. The Supreme Court ultimately rejected the challenges.[80]

By the time a candidate gets to the confirmation process, the ABA committee has already talked to his associates, judges, members of the Supreme Court, law clerks, and academics about his qualifications. Members of the committee also have interviewed the nominee and have read a large portion of his writings and opinions. In the Bork case, the committee spoke with over 400 people, including over 150 attorneys, 11 of Bork's former law clerks, most of the sitting members of the Supreme Court, 142 state and federal judges, and 79 law professors and law school deans.[81] It met twice with the nominee.

Before turning to the dynamics of the confirmation process, though, the question arises regarding just why the president selected any particular nominee. What are the factors that seem to influence the selection of nominees?

What Counts? The Selection Criteria

The debates over what characteristics presidents have used in selecting members of the Court have continued for a host of reasons. To some, the question is about whether we can explain the Court's behavior by virtue of the criteria used to staff it. To others, the task is to try to determine indicators that let a president know whether a nominee's behavior as a justice will be predictable, since most presidents would like to name members to the Court who will represent their general perspectives. For many, the discussion is really normative and seeks to define qualities that a president ought to consider both for the good of the Court and to better serve the nation. How do we pick a good justice? Are there qualities beyond technical competence that should count? If so, what are they?

Merit, Politics, or Something Else?　One way the debate over selection is phrased is represented by the exchange between Henry Abraham[82] and David O'Brien.[83] Abraham argues that what should and often does matter most is merit. He begins from the proposition that "there is indeed a rather wide, general index of agreement on what constitutes 'greatness' on the Court" and that we evaluate justices not only according to their standing on that index but also properly hold presidents accountable for the quality of their appointments as measured against the "greatness" criteria.[84] Abraham contends that presidents understand that fact and generally avoid "nominating patently unqualified individuals."[85] He is not bothered by the fact that there are differences of opinion regarding the importance and measurement of particular qualities. "Simply to brush off clarion calls for merit-based appointments on the grounds of eye of the beholder is at best a crude oversimplification and at worst intellectually dishonest."[86] His study of the history of appointments convinced him that, with rare "exceptions, the caliber of the Supreme Court has been universally high."[87]

For O'Brien, selections are and will be based on politics rather than merit. Indeed, he concludes that the idea that the Supreme Court is a meritocracy is a myth that has been perpetuated by academics and judges.[88] "The reality is that every appointment is political."[89] In the first place, he argues, "any definition of 'judicial merit' is artificial."[90] Beyond that, the politics of the selection process are far more powerful than any concern with meritocracy.

As with most dichotomies, however, arguments that press too far toward either pole can be troublesome. On the one hand, it is plainly true that any number of nominations that were anticipated by legal scholars and practitioners because of the presumed merit of the candidates were never made because of political factors in the particular setting. The two most commonly cited examples are those of U.S. Court of Appeals judge Learned Hand and Professor Paul Freund. Both were widely regarded as eminently qualified for the post and yet were passed over. It is also true, however, that presidents have occasionally passed over members of their own party and close political allies to name well-qualified nominees. The appointment of Justice Benjamin Cardozo is a case in point. O'Brien points out that Cardozo was appointed because an embarrassed president had just suffered an important defeat and countered with the Cardozo appointment, because the nomination of someone almost universally regarded as the best-qualified candidate would allow him to recover. Of course, the point is that it was possible, and in this case good politics, to name someone widely thought to be the best-qualified candidate available. There is no necessary conflict between quality or other criteria and good politics. Taken too far, the argument that "it's all political and nothing else really matters" can lead to cynicism and provide no guidance for making good choices. And there is evidence that a number of appointments were influenced by the candidate's religion, geographical origins, and experience. However, the merit argument risks naive explanations of the appointment process if it is pressed too far. Doing so plays down the political forces at work in selection of nominees and encourages the notion that there is consensus about the qualities that make up what we term merit.

Why Do So-called Selection Factors Matter?   The factors that go into the consideration and selection of nominees are important for several reasons.[91] First, presidents have long been in search of the right set of background experiences along with personal and professional characteristics that would provide maximum predictability of performance on the bench. In truth, of course, no guarantees exist, and a number of presidents have been sorely disappointed because their nominees turned out to be very different people once appointed to the Supreme Court than their credentials suggested they would be. Quite apart from their political agreement with the president, the question is whether some qualifications are more likely than others to predict who will be an effective justice. In this sense, presidents want to select not merely the right judge in a political sense but also a jurist who will be judged great or near-great when the history of the Court is written.

Conversely, are there cues that warn the president that a particular nominee may perform badly? President Woodrow Wilson was chagrined not merely because Justice James C. McReynolds's political views on the bench were contrary to his own but also because his appointee turned out to be, by all accounts, one of the most obnoxious people ever to sit on the Supreme Court. Chief Justice William Howard Taft described McReynolds as "selfish to the last degree, . . . fuller of prejudice than any man I have ever known, . . . one who delights in making others uncomfortable. He has no sense of duty. He is a continual grouch; and . . . really seems to have less of a loyal spirit to the Court than anybody."[92] Chief Justice Fred Vinson, who was appointed by Harry S. Truman to the center chair because of his reputation in the House of Representatives and the executive branch as an effective political player who might bring peace to the sometimes harsh conflict within the Stone Court, turned out to be an extremely divisive force.

Second is the issue of what judicial scholars call "representativeness." Will the Court have sufficient diversity to reflect, at least in some limited measure, the diversity of the nation it serves? Perhaps of equal importance for a body that is by design antidemocratic, or at least undemocratic, is the question of whether the citizenry will perceive the Court to be at least minimally representative and therefore accord it greater legitimacy than if it were dominated by a few rich, old, white Protestant males from the Northeast educated at the Ivy League schools and still effectively wearing the old school tie. If the purposes for the use of selection criteria are to determine ability, predictability, representativeness, and perceived representativeness, what specific criteria have been most often used in pursuit of those goals? Political scientist Robert Scigliano classified them as "representational qualifications," "professional qualifications," and "doctrinal qualifications."[93]

Representational Qualifications The representational category often includes a wide variety of characteristics not strictly professional or legal but instead personal and political. In evaluating the backgrounds of various candidates over time, presidents have considered political party, socioeconomic status, age, home geographic region, religion, race, and gender.

One of the interesting dynamics of the Bork and Ginsburg nominations was the battle that raged within the administration to ensure that nominees would not only be Republicans but that they would be particularly orthodox, even relatively extreme, in their commitments to the dominant wing of the party. Of course, it is no surprise that presidents who are likely to have few opportunities to select potential justices will confer justiceship on those whose political backgrounds are consistent with their own. And when a party has, like the Republican party, made change in the composition of the High Court a key element of its political agenda, the selection of a committed partisan comes as no surprise.

While it is true, however, that presidents have overwhelmingly nominated members of their own party, there have been exceptions. Indeed, eleven presidents have named a total of thirteen nominees from other parties (see Table 3.1).

Occasionally, the appointment of a member of an opposing party can be a useful and significant aspect of nomination and confirmation. Justice Robert Jackson very badly wanted to be named chief justice and thought he had an understanding with President Franklin D. Roosevelt along those lines. But the man who was closer to Jackson on the Court than anyone else urged FDR to take another course. When the president asked Justice Felix Frankfurter whether he would select Jackson or Harlan Fiske Stone, Frankfurter chose Stone and said:

> For me the decisive consideration, considering the fact that Stone is qualified, is that Bob is of your political personal family, as it were, while Stone is a Republican.
>
> Now it doesn't require prophetic powers to be sure that we shall, sooner or later, be in war—I think sooner. It is most important that when war does come, the country should feel that you are the Nation's, President, and not a partisan president. Few

TABLE 3-1 **Cross-party Nominations to the Supreme Court**

President	President's Party	Nominee	Nominee's Party
Tyler	Whig	Samuel Nelson	Democrat
Lincoln	Republican	Stephen Field	Democrat
Harrison	Republican	Howell Jackson	Democrat
Taft	Republican	Horace Lurton	Democrat
		Edward White	Democrat
		Joseph Lamar	Democrat
Wilson	Democrat	Louis Brandeis	Republican
Harding	Republican	Pierce Butler	Democrat
Hoover	Republican	Benjamin Cardozo	Democrat
F. D. Roosevelt	Democrat	Harlan Stone	Republican
Truman	Democrat	Harold Burton	Republican
Eisenhower	Republican	William Brennan	Democrat
Nixon	Republican	Lewis Powell	Democrat

things would contribute as much to confidence in you as a national and not a partisan President than for you to name a Republican, who has the profession's confidence, as Chief Justice.[94]

The selection of Justice Benjamin N. Cardozo by President Herbert Hoover is another well-known example, but it occurred for different reasons. The president's nomination of U.S. Court of Appeals judge John J. Parker was resoundingly rejected by the Senate after a forceful campaign by labor unions and the National Association for the Advancement of Colored People. The seat was eventually filled by Justice Owen Roberts. When Hoover faced his next chance for an appointment, he remembered the defeat and was willing to listen to Senator William Borah of Idaho, who, although a Republican, joined the chorus of politicians and professionals calling for the appointment of the person virtually everyone thought to be the most qualified choice, Cardozo, a Democrat. The story is often told of Borah's visit to the White House, where Hoover showed him a list of choices, the last of which was Cardozo. To this Borah replied, "Your list is all right, but you handed it to me upside down."[95]

When looking for characteristics in one considered for elevation to high office, Americans are wont to recall the Horatio Alger legend in which a virtuous person rose from humble beginnings to achieve greatness by dint of character and diligence. It is also one of the more salable political profiles. The fact that Pierce Butler was born in a log cabin in the Minnesota woods was one of the factors that figured in his appointment to the Court.[96] William O. Douglas's rise from meager beginnings to champion the cause of the weak and powerless has become nearly legendary. More recently, Clarence Thomas's rise from poverty in Pinpoint, Georgia, in the days of legal segregation was a central feature in the praise provided by Bush administration officials. Thomas expressed the strong personal conviction that his humble beginnings in the segregated South, together with the educational influence of the nuns in his Savannah school, were central attributes in his success.[97]

However, as a leading student of judicial backgrounds, John Schmidhauser, has observed, "Only a handful of the members of the Supreme Court were of essentially humble origins."[98] He found that the members of the Court "were chosen overwhelmingly from the socially prestigious and politically influential gentry class in the late 18th and early 19th century, or the professional upper middle class thereafter."[99]

There is little doubt that age has been a factor in selection. To a president who hopes to shape the Court, selection of a person old enough to be seen as sufficiently experienced but young enough to have a long career on the bench after appointment is a significant consideration. Most modern appointments have been of people in their fifties. Justice Douglas was an exception, a particularly youthful forty-one at the time of his nomination. Clarence Thomas was another exceptionally young choice who enjoys reminding his critics and his colleagues, for example, in his speech to the Second Circuit Judicial Conference in 1994, that he hopes to sit on the Court for another four decades.

Commentators on Reagan administration nominations to the federal courts generally observed that youth was a particularly valuable characteristic for Reagan's potential judicial choices. In his first term, more than 10 percent of his nominees were under forty, and in his second term, more than a third of his choices were under forty-five.[100] Judge Douglas Ginsburg's candidacy was attractive to some Reagan insiders precisely because, at forty-one, he would have been the youngest justice since Douglas. The fact that Solicitor General Kenneth Starr was only forty-four made him an even more interesting possibility to replace William Brennan than he might otherwise have been.

While nominees have not been selected to be particularly representative on the basis of party or socioeconomic status, region may play a role. Geography was important in the early days because the justices rode circuit (that is, traveled in one of the federal circuits to hear cases) when they were not in session in Washington. It made sense to contemplate a nominee's home area and familiarity with a region with circuit duties in mind. At the same time, there were state and regional sensitivities to be considered. Over the history of the Court, scholars have identified what they have termed the New York seat,[101] the Virginia–Maryland seat,[102] and the New England seat[103] because they were consistently held by nominees from those areas over long periods of the Court's history. Justices have been named to the Court from thirty one states.[104]

While there has been considerable debate over whether geography matters in the modern era, it is generally agreed that while one's state or region will not guarantee appointment, it may be a factor that discourages selection. For example, when President Franklin D. Roosevelt was considering William O. Douglas to succeed Justice Louis Brandeis, there was considerable expectation that it was time for an appointment from the West. While Douglas had spent most of his formative years in Yakima, Washington, and his mother still lived there, he had lived in the East since entering Columbia Law School. The president came down to a choice between Douglas, then chairman of the Securities and Exchange Commission and an FDR insider, and Senator Lewis Schwellenbach of Washington State. Jerome Frank worked behind the scenes to rally support from prominent western senators for Douglas. When Senators Borah of Idaho and Hugh Bone of Washington came out for Douglas on grounds that he was, by any reasonable assessment, a westerner, the way was clear for the nomination.[105]

More recently, there was controversy over Bork, Ginsburg, Powell, and the southern seat. When the time came to replace Justice Powell, a Virginian, there was consternation over the decision by the president not to appoint a southerner. And when Bork was rejected in part because of the influence of southern senators, the administration rejected the suggestion that the next nominee be from the South or Southwest. The lack of a person in Powell's seat during the prolonged battle that ultimately brought Anthony Kennedy to the bench meant that the other justices had to share Powell's former duties as circuit justice, the most significant of which at the time was responding to stay-of-execution requests from prisoners awaiting the death penalty in prisons in the states that make up the fourth judicial circuit. One of the factors fueling speculation over Bush's replacement for Justice Brennan was the fact that he could name an Hispanic nominee from the Southwest and respond to two concerns simultaneously.

Another factor that has played a role in the selection process is religion, though the Court, like the country generally, has been predominantly populated by Protestants. The confirmation battle, in the winter of 1916, over the appointment of Louis Brandeis was one of the longest and most difficult such fights in the history of the Court. Debate remains over just how much of that conflict could be attributed to his record as a legal reformer who challenged the establishment during what has come to be called the Gilded Age and how much really stemmed from the fact that he was the first Jewish justice appointed to the Court.[106] From the point of his service on, however, there have been claims that the Court has had a Jewish seat, later occupied by Justices Cardozo, Frankfurter, Goldberg, and Fortas. The alternative explanation is, however, that once the barrier had been broken, the fact that one was Jewish was of no major consequence and the appointments had to do with factors other than religion. Still, the Jewish seat discussion reemerged, along with gender, during the period leading up to the confirmation of Justice Ruth Bader Ginsburg.

It has been argued that the Court also had a "Catholic seat," recently occupied by Justice William Brennan. The first Catholic named to the Court was Chief Justice Roger B. Taney in 1835, but the so-called Catholic seat is usually traced to the late nineteenth century, from which point the Court has seen at least one Catholic on the bench with the exception of the period from 1949 to 1956.[107] One of Justice Frank Murphy's leading biographers, for example, concluded that Murphy was "appointed from explicitly religious criteria."[108] Justice Robert Jackson confirmed that claim in his unpublished autobiography, though he added that he had tried to get FDR to choose some other Catholic.[109] Still, there is considerable dispute about just how important religion was in the selection of these jurists.

Rejecting the oft-repeated assertion that religion plays no central role in appointments, Barbara Perry found:

> A thorough examination of the Court's seven Catholics reveals that their religious affiliation was a factor, to varying degrees, in all but one of the appointments [Taney]. Moreover, evidence exists to indicate that all appointing presidents made deliberate efforts to nominate particular justices to "represent" (in the "descriptive" sense) Catholics in the population.[110]

Still, she did not argue that these men were named to the Court solely or primarily because of their religion. Rather, she suggested that in these cases, religion had moved from something that was not a factor to an "over-the-top factor," a characteristic that was not in itself sufficient to assure appointment but that could, all other things being equal, add weight to the scales in favor of a potential nominee.[111] She speculated, however, that the election of the Catholic president John F. Kennedy signaled an opening of the political arena to full participation by the nation's Catholics and a reduction in the need for special representation on the Court.[112]

On the other hand, religion had played a number of roles other than simple representation. The fact that Pierce Butler was Catholic was exploited by his advocates, who rallied support from his home diocese for the appointment. It is clear that one of the considerations that made Douglas Ginsburg a desirable choice to some Reagan insiders was that they thought a Jewish nominee might fragment potential opposition.[113] However, American Jewish leaders promptly informed the administration that any such assumption was misinformed.

Religion has occasionally mattered in the lives of some of the justices once they came to the Court. Justice Brandeis was continually the victim of Justice McReynolds's anti-Semitism. Justice Frankfurter appealed to Justice Murphy's Catholicism in attempting to win his vote in a close church/state case. Justice

Clarence Thomas testifying at his confirmation hearings, October 1991.

Harry Blackmun called on Justice Brennan for help in reviewing the language of the *Roe v. Wade* opinion so that language that Catholics might find offensive could be removed. On the other hand, as Justice Brennan's consistent support for *Roe* indicates, religion is no guarantee of one's likely voting pattern.

At least since the 1960s, one of the more controversial issues of the representative character of appointments has been race and ethnicity. President Lyndon Johnson made no secret of the fact that he was appointing Thurgood Marshall because Marshall was an African American. Marshall had enjoyed a distinguished career as an attorney, leading the National Association for Advancement of Colored People, Legal Defense and Education Fund; he was appointed to the U.S. Court of Appeals and was named solicitor general before he was elevated to the Supreme Court in 1967.

At the beginning of the 1990s, speculation ran, as it periodically does, to the opportunities that President Bush would have to shape the Supreme Court through the appointment process. Given Marshall's advancing age, Court watchers contemplating his retirement began to ask whether Bush would honor a claim by African Americans to continued "representation" on the Court, or whether he would respond to the Hispanic community's increasing expectations for inclusion. When Justice Brennan retired in July 1990, speculation about possible successors immediately raised the question of whether President Bush would nominate someone within his administration, such as Solicitor General Kenneth Starr, or a close White House insider like Chief of Staff John Sununu, White House Counsel C. Boyden Grey, or Attorney General Richard Thornburgh. Would Bush surprise many and turn to one of the potential Hispanic nominees?

Anita Hill testifying before the Senate Judiciary Committee hearings on the nomination of Clarence Thomas to become a justice of the Supreme Court, October 1991.

Still, some ask whether the fact that the race, ethnicity, and religion barriers have each been broken means that those issues will no longer be as important as they once were.

Bush's choice of conservative African American Clarence Thomas, after Marshall's retirement, suggests that concern over representation continues, though there is considerable debate over whether that concern stems from primarily political motivations or because of a genuine interest in diversity on the Court. Thus, many African American opponents of the Thomas nomination argued before the Senate Judiciary Committee that the president named him with the idea that his race and rise from humble beginnings in the segregated South would overcome opposition to the very conservative positions he had previously taken in print and from the rostrum. But African American conservatives countered that opposition stemmed from the fact that Thomas was not a liberal. These more prosaic issues were quickly set aside when the Senators had to confront the charge, made by Anita Hill, that the Supreme Court nominee, Thomas, had sexually harassed Hill a decade earlier.

It was clear during the 1970s that pressure for gender representation was building. As the numbers of women in law school, legal practice, and, particularly in the late 1970s and into the 1980s, in lower courts both state and federal grew, the argument of lack of qualified and experienced candidates was plainly unacceptable. President Reagan fulfilled his campaign promise to nominate a woman to the Court with the appointment of Sandra Day O'Connor (though he was not one to appoint women to the many open lower-court seats available). Again, however, with the gender barrier broken, there was some question whether other presidents would consider gender representation to be a critical variable in future appointments. On the other hand, with the increasing role of women in all facets of American political life and the increasing number of women with undoubted qualifications and experience in the legal community, gender would very likely be an important issue in years to come. Indeed, it became clear that the Clinton administration wanted a woman to replace Justice Byron White and appointed Judge Ruth Bader Ginsburg.

Even though there is no evidence that his ethnic background had any relationship to his appointment, Justice Antonin Scalia was celebrated as the first Italian American appointment to the Supreme Court. Whether representational factors are crucial variables or over-the-top factors, they seem destined to play some kind of role in appointments. In the end, they seem less a result of any naive perception that race, gender, or religion will predict performance on the bench and more a response to the force of public perceptions of and expectations about the openness of the Court as an institution.

Professional Qualifications   While the debate continues over whether representational factors should or do matter, nearly everyone insists that professional qualifications are what should matter most. Senator Roman Hruska's argument in defense of Nixon nominee G. Harrold Carswell, that mediocre people deserve

President Bill Clinton with his nominee to the U.S. Supreme Court, Ruth Bader Ginsburg, in the White House Rose Garden, June 1993.

representation on the Court too, did not meet with a receptive Senate or popular approval. The nomination was defeated largely on professional grounds. The split decision by the ABA on Judge Robert Bork's qualifications did not help his effort at confirmation; neither was Clarence Thomas aided by the lukewarm ABA response to his selection.

Notwithstanding all the agreement about the need for unquestionable professional competence, there is still considerable disagreement about precisely what constitutes the proper professional background and experience for a justice of the Supreme Court. The answer to that question, of course, requires that we know the kinds of characteristics that we think make a good, or even great, justice. Henry Abraham asserts that they include:

> One, demonstrated judicial temperament. Two, professional expertise and competence. Three, absolute personal as well as professional integrity. Four, an able, agile, lucid mind. Five, appropriate professional educational background or training. Six, the ability to communicate clearly, both orally and in writing, especially the latter.[114]

Sheldon Goldman, another noted Supreme Court watcher, has a slightly different list:

> 1. Neutrality as to the Parties in Litigation. 2. Fair-mindedness. 3. Being Well Versed in the Law. 4. Ability to Think and Write Logically and Lucidly. 5. Personal Integrity. 6. Good Physical and Mental Health. 7. Judicial Temperament. 8. Ability to Handle Judicial Power Sensibly.[115]

Still others who have studied the "great justices" have determined that the members of the Court widely regarded as great possess

> . . . scholarship; legal learning and analytical powers; craftsmanship and technique; wide general knowledge and learning; character, moral integrity and impartiality; diligence and industry; the ability to express oneself orally with clarity, logic, and compelling force; openness to change, courage to take unpopular decisions; dedication to the Court as an institution and to the office of Supreme Court justice; ability to carry a proportionate share of the court's responsibility in opinion writing; and finally, the quality of statesmanship.[116]

The fact that some of these qualities are difficult to define does not stop the search for the well-qualified nominee.

Whatever else may have figured in the evaluation of a candidate's qualifications, the White House certainly examines education and prior professional experience. Of course, nothing in the Constitution requires that nominees to the Court be lawyers or have a law degree. And a number of justices never graduated from a law school. However, they have been lawyers, and there is no likelihood that a nonlawyer would be appointed or could be confirmed. It was possible for attorneys as late as the early 1950s to qualify for practice without a law degree because they were permitted to read law, rather than go to law school, and stand for examination for entrance to the bar. That is no longer true. The question often is, where did a candidate attend law school and what was his or her record as a student and thereafter? A number of Ivy League schools have been disproportionately represented on the lists of appointees, but that is not uniformly the case. It is, however, accurate to say that one named to the Court probably graduated from a prestigious law school.

While there is no specific tradition of appointing persons who clerked in the Supreme Court following law school, a number of modern appointees have done so, including Chief Justice William Rehnquist (for Robert Jackson) and Justice Byron White (for Fred Vinson). President Clinton's second nominee, Judge Stephen Breyer, clerked for Justice Arthur Goldberg. Normally, the clerkships go to the top graduates of major law schools and frequently to those who have already clerked for a lower-court judge. More will be said of the clerks in a later chapter.

Whatever else a nominee did after law school, it is likely that it included a stint on the bench, and probably, as is true in most recent cases, as a member of the U.S. Court of Appeals. Apart from the fact that many evaluators consider prior judicial experience to be an important requirement for a would-be justice, it is also viewed as the experience most like working on the Supreme Court. Therefore, selection of a court of appeals judge is said to give presidents the best chance of predicting a nominee's behavior and legal positions on the High Court. Indeed, during the Reagan administration, it was often observed by those hoping for a reshaping of the Supreme Court that Bork, Posner, Scalia, Starr, and others were appointed to the court of appeals so they could "punch their tickets" prior to possible elevation to the Supreme Court. Among those nominated from the Nixon years on, Justices Kennedy, Scalia, John Stevens, Harry Blackmun, and Warren Burger all had circuit court experience. Judges Bork, Douglas Ginsburg, Thomas, and Ruth Bader Ginsburg were all nominated while sitting on the D.C. circuit, and Breyer was named from the first circuit. During the Eisenhower, Kennedy, and Johnson administrations, Marshall, Potter Stewart, Charles E. Whittaker, and John M. Harlan II, all came to the Court with similar credentials.

Among recent appointments, both Sandra Day O'Connor and David Souter came from state courts. (Although Souter technically came from the U.S. Court of Appeals for the First Circuit, he had not served long enough by the time of his elevation to have written opinions or develop a voting record on cases.) While they both had been appellate judges, the dockets of the state courts on which they served were very unlike what one finds in a federal court, particularly the circuit courts or the U.S. Supreme Court. That difference, however, did not seem to bother Justice Oliver Wendell Holmes, who had come to the Court from an illustrious career on the Supreme Judicial Court of Massachusetts, or Justice Brennan, who came from the New Jersey Supreme Court. On the other hand, Justice Cardozo, whose performance on the New York State Court of Appeals (that state's highest court) brought demands for his elevation to the Supreme Court, did not relish his move from one of the nation's premier common-law courts to face the Supreme Court's very different docket.

Not everyone has been pleased by the emphasis on U.S. circuit courts as the place to look for future Supreme Court justices. Retired justice Arthur Goldberg watched the growing trend toward circuit court appointments with concern. His view was that "Court of Appeals Judges are largely parochial. What you really need in the Supreme Court are really worldly people."[117] Comparing the changing Court with what he had known, Goldberg said, "The virtue of the Warren Court was its composition. Warren had been a governor. White had been a corporate lawyer. Goldberg was a labor lawyer. Bill Brennan had been a state court judge. Tom Clark had been an attorney general."[118] Of the justices after Goldberg's departure from the Court, only Powell came from private practice, and only Rehnquist came from a federal government legal post.

There is some irony in the fact that, in contemporary debates over appointments, so much emphasis is placed on prior judicial experience, given the fact that only a handful of justices (seven) in the nineteenth century had had experience on the federal bench. Abraham noted that of justices appointed by mid 1984, "Only 22 had ten or more years of experience on any tribunal—federal or state—and 42 had no judicial experience at all."[119] Indeed, many of the most famous members of the Court had no such experience, including John Marshall, Joseph Story, Louis Brandeis, Charles Evans Hughes, Felix Frankfurter, Robert Jackson, Earl Warren, William O. Douglas, and, if one does not count a brief stint as a police court judge, Hugo Black. Still, times change, and so do expectations.

Doctrinal Qualifications   The most common explanation for the increasing popularity of circuit court of appeals nominees is not experience but predictability. Those with experience on such a court, whose docket is reasonably close to that faced by the Supreme Court, have a record that can be evaluated. If a candidate was selected from a court in which he or she overwhelmingly voted for the government's position in criminal justice cases, as in the case of Warren Burger, there is reason to believe the nominee will retain that view of the law once elevated to the Supreme Court.

Presidents who, like Ronald Reagan, have a "Justice Wrong" in their past want all the indicators they can get that their nominee is the right person in terms of his or her views of the law, the role of the Court, and the issues that matter most to the president. In the absence of that kind of record, it can be difficult to guess what a nominee's position on these matters might be, since it is not generally acceptable to ask nominees to disclose their positions on issues that are likely to come before them on the Court. At some point, however, the express or implied desire of the president to appoint justices whose views are compatible with those of the administration on important issues and legal questions becomes what is known as "Court packing."

The President's Justice? Attempts at Court Packing

The Bork battle, as well as the Kennedy, Souter, and Thomas (though not the Ruth Bader Ginsburg) appointments that followed, raised the volume and intensity of the debate over the degree to which a president ought to be able to shape the Court in his or her own political image. Chief Justice Rehnquist was among the chorus of voices demanding deference to the constitutional prerogative of the president to appoint any qualified candidate to the Court.[120] However, noted Harvard Law School Professor Laurence Tribe and others insisted that the Senate has an obligation to block nominees whose political philosophies are well outside the political mainstream. Ironically, Ruth Bader Ginsburg addressed this subject in a 1988 law review article. She recalled having previously challenged the scope of the questions that were appropriate for senators to pose but later changed her mind, recognizing as appropriate a relatively broad spectrum of questions, including matters of philosophy and values.[121]

Regardless of one's position in that debate, it is clear that many presidents have tried diligently to pack the Court, and there is every reason to assume that future presidents will continue that time-honored tradition. What has been the historic fate of Court-packing attempts? What are the problems would-be Court packers encounter? And what can be said about the success of Court-packing efforts?

Historical Efforts   While most discussions of Court packing emphasize twentieth-century presidents, the tradition, in fact, dates back to the beginning of serious competition for political power. As the Jeffersonians, also known as Jeffersonian Republicans, emerged as political challengers to the Federalists, led by President John Adams, the importance of the bench became clear. The same Thomas Jefferson who later complained of the arrogation of power by the Marshall Court in claiming authority to conduct judicial review of the constitutionality of legislation had, during the Adams administration, criticized the Court for its failure to strike down the Alien Law and the Sedition acts used to punish pro-Jefferson newspapers and to thwart presumed French support for the rising Republican party.[122] When the Jeffersonians swept the election of 1800, it triggered the now-famous effort to pack the federal courts of every description with Federalists before Adams's term expired.

Ever since then, presidents have tried to get nominees to the bench who would presumably be dispensing justice agreeable to that chief executive's philosophy long after he had departed from office. Of course, the ability to pack the Court depends on the opportunity to appoint justices and the willingness of the Senate to confirm them. Some presidents, like Franklin Roosevelt, had both the will and the opportunity to pack the Court because they were in office as vacancies became available. Roosevelt was able to appoint nine members of the Court. Others, like Jimmy Carter, had no appointments at all. Some, like Richard Nixon, who made shaping the Court a priority, were able to have a major impact on the Court, even though some of their nominees went down to defeat.[123] Like Nixon, Ronald Reagan made the goal of packing the Court an announced policy, and George Bush sought to finish the Republican party's goal of reshaping the Court.

Problems of Court Packing   It is one thing to attempt to pack the Court and quite another to do so successfully. The cases of presidents who felt betrayed by their appointees are legion. Since James Madison's effort to counter the force of Chief Justice John Marshall by appointing Joseph Story, who then out-Marshalled Marshall, there have been numerous frustrations. Dwight Eisenhower was once asked what major mistakes he had made in office that were a source of regret. He answered, "Two and they're both on the Supreme Court." It was a reference to Chief Justice Earl Warren and Associate Justice William Brennan, who became cornerstones of what is now often known as the Warren Court. Justice Sandra Day O'Connor's failure to support the state in the moment of silence case sent Reagan supporters into fits of rage. Justice Harry Blackmun's announcement in 1994 that he had rethought the death penalty issue and could no longer support it was seen by supporters of the Nixon administration that nominated him as a complete rejection of the political premises he had been chosen to uphold.

The general frustration often has to do with the long-term voting record of appointees, but presidents have also been disappointed by the outcome of particular cases. For those convinced of the futility of Court packing, the Watergate tapes case is a benchmark. Few modern presidents have worked harder to shape the Court by appointments than Richard Nixon did. Yet, when the case that triggered his departure from office came before the bench, none of his appointees supported him. Harry Truman was beside himself with anger over the rejection by the Court of his decision to seize the steel mills during the Korean War, after labor turmoil brought strikes. He wrote a letter to Justice William O. Douglas, which he ultimately decided not to send, exclaiming:

> I appreciated very much your letter of July third and I am sorry that I didn't have a chance to talk with you before you left. In fact, I am sorry that I didn't have an opportunity to discuss precedents with you before you came to the conclusion you did on that crazy decision that has tied up this country. I am writing a monograph on just what makes justices of the Supreme Court tick. There was no decision by the majority although there were seven opinions against what was best for the country.
>
> I don't see how a Court made up of so-called "liberals" could do what that Court did to me. I am going to find out just why before I quit this office.[124]

Can It Be Done?   Despite the individual horror stories, however, the answer to the question whether presidents can pack the Court is a qualified yes. Speaking of FDR's nominations to the Court, Chief Justice Rehnquist observed: "These men were most assuredly not peas in a pod, but on the major constitutional question which concerned Franklin Roosevelt—the constitutionality of New Deal economic legislation—they were pretty much of one mind. Only four years after the President was defeated in his effort to pack the Court, he had appointed six out of the nine Justices of the Court. The doctrine of the 'Old Court' that had been used to invalidate New Deal legislation before 1937 was sunk without a trace."[125] Nixon's four appointees moved generally and over time in the direction of Nixon administration positions in several areas, including civil rights, criminal justice, and access to the federal courts. And while there have been highly publicized exceptions, such as the Court's refusal to permit the moment of silence in public schools in order to circumvent earlier rulings based on the establishment of religion clause of the First Amendment, and the unwillingness of a majority to reverse the *Roe v. Wade* decision legalizing abortion, the Reagan and Bush nominees have moved in the direction most observers would have anticipated in a number of fields. Like the Nixon justices, their overall voting patterns tend to show considerable agreement with each other, even if their opinions on individual cases differ widely.

What the president cannot do is be certain of the actions of any particular justice over time or of the Court as a whole on any given issue or case. Neither can a president expect large-scale overt change in any short term. While it happens occasionally, the Court is not normally in the business of engaging in wholesale rejection of its precedents. Thus, if success in Court packing is defined in terms of the ability of the president to have a significant impact on the law over time through the appointment of Supreme Court justices, then presidents can and have succeeded. If, however, one means that a few appointments can make dramatic and completely predictable change, then plainly, Court packing is little more than a president's fond dream.

Of course, presidents are sophisticated in these matters and are happy enough to settle for the impact they can have. The fact that others understand the potential as well means that battles over nominees can be very difficult. It also means that someone nominated for the Court must make the very important decision to accept.

Getting the Nominee to Serve

The story is told of the day Lewis Powell got the call informing him that he was to be the nominee for the Supreme Court. He drew back like someone who had just touched a hot stove. Indeed, he said no on at least three occasions, including to the president himself. Ultimately, he agreed only when the nomination was pressed on him as a matter of duty and patriotism. Even so, after a sleepless night and a long conversation with his wife, Powell called Attorney General John Mitchell and tried unsuccessfully to change Mitchell's mind.[126]

What kinds of questions come to a nominee's mind? On the one hand, can any contemporary American seriously entertain the idea of refusing appointment? Perhaps that is not too far-fetched a notion in our contemporary environment. At least it has historically been the case that some prospective nominees either refused outright or had to be talked into the idea. In any case, it would go too far to assume that the president can have any nominee that she might wish.

In the Court's early years, the job of Supreme Court justice was not terribly attractive. The best-known story, of course, is the resignation of John Jay so that he could run for the governorship of New York. After all, the Court had no significant prestige and no clearly defined institutional role, and it carried with it the arduous burden of circuit riding. President Washington had difficulty filling the job. Hamilton refused the position. John Rutledge suggested himself and was nominated, but the nomination was rejected because of Rutledge's criticism of the Jay Treaty, which was, by implication at least, criticism of the administration. Patrick Henry refused, and so did William Cushing. Eventually, Oliver Ellsworth was appointed.

Probably the most interesting case of the reluctant justice was President Lyndon Johnson's appointment of Abe Fortas.[127] Fortas's longtime friend and former mentor William O. Douglas joined with Hugo Black and Earl Warren in an effort to convince Fortas and his wife, attorney Carolyn Agger, that he should take the appointment. It was a difficult prospect to consider leaving one of the nation's most prestigious law firms, Arnold and Porter, for the cloistered life and much lower pay of the Supreme Court. Douglas wrote Black that "Abe Fortas' wife is very upset over Abe's appointment. It is apparently a very serious crisis. I thought maybe you and Elizabeth [Black] could think of something to do."[128] Black acknowledged the problem and wrote to Warren: "Immediately after our telephone conversation of a few days ago I called and talked to Abe Fortas, telling him that both of us hoped he would agree to come to the Court. He seemed much gratified, and I was glad we gave him the message."[129] In the end, of course, LBJ would not take no for an answer, a quality for which he was well known, if not always appreciated.

Historically, the two most common reasons that nominees have been reticent to accept nomination are money and political constraints. To the degree that presidents seek prominent private-practice attorneys like Fortas or Powell, they are asking the nominee to take a significant decrease in pay. With the increasing tendency to select lower-court judges for elevation, that problem is reduced. Some nominees, like Frank Murphy, hesitated to accept appointment because it seemed to mark a certain end to what might have been, at least in the candidate's own mind, a promising political career.[130]

A contemporary reason for reticence, especially since the Bork debacle, is the nominee's fear of the "fishbowl" phenomenon. The glare of publicity surrounding Supreme Court nominations may cause some potential nominees to think twice before accepting. Some may even go so far as to attempt to block consideration of their appointment. Even the most noncontroversial appointments will, in the contemporary environment, face intensive scrutiny in all areas of their lives. The Douglas Ginsburg nomination demonstrated the point graphically as a radio interviewer conducted an interview with a former Ginsburg faculty colleague who revealed the allegations of drug use that played a central role in the demise of the nomination. David Souter, hardly a controversial figure at the time of his appointment to the Court, experienced the phenomenon of having the book of one's life opened page by page, with literally dozens of probing eyes seeking skeletons, relevant or not, in one's past. The president was charged with seeking a "stealth candidate" (named after the military aircraft intended to leave few identifiable traces on radar screens) in selecting Souter. During his confirmation hearings, Clarence Thomas recalled his wife's comment that if Souter was the stealth candidate, then Thomas was "Big Foot" because of his substantial and visible record on controversial issues, each of which was probed in depth during the Senate process. Of course, just as the debate over Thomas's background and views was nearing an end in the Judiciary Committee, Professor Anita Hill's allegations of sexual harassment effectively reopened the nomination and radically altered the discussion.

THE CONFIRMATION PROCESS: RUNNING THE GAUNTLET, OR A SIMPLE QUESTION OF ADVICE AND CONSENT?

As the preceding discussion suggests, and recent experiences with the confirmation process doubtless demonstrate, the role of the Senate is to provide "advice and consent" on appointments. However, the apparent changes in tenor and emphasis of that phenomenon do not alter the fact that some elements of the process are appropriate to virtually all nominees in recent memory.

Advice and Consent of the Senate

With few exceptions, the Senate has largely had the opportunity to provide or withhold "consent" but little or no significant opportunity to provide "advice" on Supreme Court appointments. (Fig 3.1 is the letter sent to the President after a candidate is confirmed by the Senate.) Two historical examples, however, stand as notable exceptions to this more common pattern. President Lincoln was asked by all but a few members of the House and Senate to name Samuel Miller to the seat formerly held by Justice Peter V. Daniel. When the president sent Miller's name to the Hill, it was confirmed "within half an hour of receiving it."[131] The

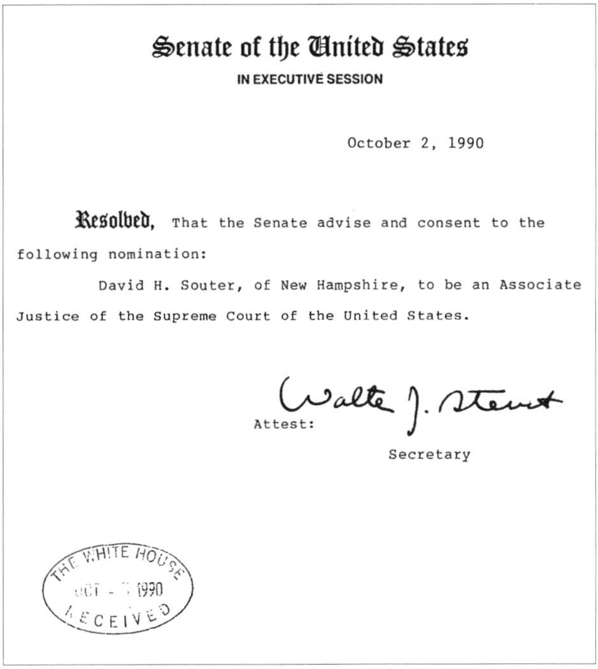

Senate of the United States

IN EXECUTIVE SESSION

October 2, 1990

Resolved, That the Senate advise and consent to the following nomination:

David H. Souter, of New Hampshire, to be an Associate Justice of the Supreme Court of the United States.

Attest: *Walter J. Stewart*

Secretary

THE WHITE HOUSE
OCT - 1990
RECEIVED

FIGURE 3.1   The advice and consent of the U.S. Senate.

second example involved President Ulysses S. Grant, who was pressed by the Congress to name Edwin Stanton to replace Justice Grier. The Congress had leverage in this instance because there was a pending nomination of Ebenezer Hoar before the Senate at the time. Grant named Stanton to clear the Hoar nomination but lost in the end when Stanton died shortly after the nomination. Hoar was not confirmed.[132]

Of course, although there has rarely been concerted action by an individual house of the Congress to pressure the president with respect to a particular choice, there have often been efforts by advocates, in the Congress and elsewhere, on behalf of various candidates. The Meese/Baker battle over the Ginsburg nomination is one example. The continuing campaign by Felix Frankfurter to get Learned Hand elevated is a classic case in point, and Frankfurter was not by any stretch the only justice to lobby the White House for a particular candidate. Chief Justice William Howard Taft probably was the most active in efforts to support or block specific nominations, including his own. Justices Black and Douglas reminded FDR of his promises to Jerome Frank to name him to a judgeship in return for his service on the Securities and Exchange Commission (SEC). There appeared some likelihood that the president was not going to make good on the promise he made to Frank on Frank's appointment to the SEC. On January 12, 1939, Frank dropped a quick note to Hugo Black: "My Dear Mr. Justice: I learned this morning that there is some reason to believe that, because of Frankfurter's appointment, the President feels hesitant about appointing me. Perhaps you would be willing to say something to Tom which he could report."[133] On January 31, 1941, Frank wrote to thank Black for a letter of January 25. The file contains a letter from Black to the president dated January 31, 1941, recommending Frank for the position on the second circuit. Black's note of the 25th said, "Dear Jerome, The day before I received your note I had talked with the party you mentioned and along the lines suggested by you."

While there are those in Congress who suggest that they should play a more central role in the nomination process, as well as in confirmation, the best that most seem to expect is that during the confirmation process presidents will read the signs indicating the outer boundaries of congressional acquiescence. During the hearings on the Thomas nomination, witnesses urged the Judiciary Committee to respond to the nomination with the idea of sending a message to the White House. Chairman Joseph Biden repeatedly responded that he seriously doubted that any message the Senate might send would significantly alter the determination of the president to name justices in his own image.

Despite the fact that many critics want a more active and challenging role for the Senate, confirmation of a nomination is the norm and defeat, the exception. The Senate has defeated only twenty-seven nominations altogether, and only six in the twentieth century.[134] Beyond outright defeats, of course, a number of nominees have withdrawn from candidacy, including Abe Fortas, who stepped

Newly appointed Justice David Souter signing his judicial oath, while Chief Justice William Rehnquist waits to sign it as witness. Looking on are Associate Justices Antonin Scalia, Sandra Day O'Connor, Thurgood Marshall, Anthony Kennedy, Harry Blackmun, and John P. Stevens, October 1990.

back from Johnson's nomination of him for the center chair, and Douglas Ginsburg, who withdrew shortly after his selection by President Reagan.

Defeats in the Senate, regardless of the form they might take, have occasionally encouraged presidents to engage in what scholar Peter Fish has termed "spite appointments."[135] Reagan's threat to name a candidate who would be as frustrating to Senate critics as Robert Bork was exemplifies the idea. Of course, spite appointments have been made quite apart from prior Senate confirmation actions, as when FDR named Hugo Black, a Senate supporter of his failed Court-packing plan.

The Confirmation Process

Whatever the outcome, there are some well-established procedures that any nominee faces during the confirmation effort. Long before TV lights focus the nation's attention on the Senate Judiciary Committee hearings, the nominee is actively at work on the Hill. First, she becomes involved in a major information-gathering effort. Collections of her personal and professional files, compilations of her opinions, and evidence of her performance in other offices are requested by a variety of interested parties, including Senate staff. Personal visits with Judiciary Committee members and legislative leaders are undertaken.

The effort to lay political groundwork on the Hill, however, must be done delicately. First, the White House is concerned that the president's prerogatives

Justice David Souter in front of the U.S. Supreme Court building, October 1990.

Supreme Court of the United States

No. ------ October Term, 1990

I, DAVID HACKETT SOUTER, do solemnly swear that I
will administer justice without respect to persons, and do
equal right to the poor and to the rich, and that I will
faithfully and impartially discharge and perform all the
duties incumbent upon me as Associate Justice of the Supreme
Court of the United States, according to the best of my
abilities and understanding, agreeably to the Constitution
and laws of the United States.

    So help me God.

_____

Subscribed and sworn to before me
this ninth day of October, 1990

Chief Justice of the United States

FIGURE 3.2
Judicial oath of office taken by Supreme Court justices.

with respect to appointments cannot appear to be surrendered to Congress. Second, and in a number of respects more complex and significant, is the difficult position in which nominees find themselves with respect to the concept of separation of powers. When selected, a nominee is regarded as the president's person. As soon as the confirmation effort begins, however, nominees must establish their independence before the legislature and yet be responsive to Senate inquiries. At the same time, the candidate faces the need to behave as a future justice of the Supreme Court, and, as such, to protect the independence of that institution from both the White House and the Hill. The related task before the nominee is to preserve an image of openness in answering Senate questioners by avoiding commitments that might compromise her ability to sit in upcoming cases. At an earlier time, Chief Justice Warren openly cautioned then Associate Justice–Designate John Harlan II to guard against extensive responses during the confirmation process.[136]

    There is no likelihood that a candidate will be confirmed these days without a lengthy appearance before the Senate Judiciary Committee. The problem has been reduced to the decision about which questions to answer, which to re-

𝕾upreme 𝕮ourt of t𝔥e 𝖀nite𝖉 𝕾tate𝖘

No. ----- October Term, 1990

I, DAVID HACKETT SOUTER, do solemnly swear that I
will support and defend the Constitution of the United
States against all enemies, foreign and domestic; that I
will bear true faith and allegiance to the same; that I
take this obligation freely, without any mental reservation
or purpose of evasion; and that I will well and faithfully
discharge the duties of the office on which I am about to
enter.

     So help me God.

[signature]

Subscribed and sworn to before me
this ninth day of October, 1990

[signature]

Chief Justice of the United States

FIGURE 3.3
Constitutional oath of office
taken by Supreme Court justices.

ject outright, and which to evade by vague replies. In the Thomas nomination, most observers agreed that the strategy was to risk making some senators unhappy because of a refusal to respond in detail to many questions as a way of avoiding a few potentially disastrous answers that could trigger large-scale opposition to the nomination. Unless the Senate rejects nominations because of that strategy, the White House is likely to continue to employ it whenever a potentially controversial name goes to the Hill.

    Of course, the tenor of the confirmation process can be affected by the nature of the organized opposition. The Bork nomination was certainly not the first time that organized interest group efforts were made to defeat a nomination. President Herbert Hoover's nomination of Judge John J. Parker was stopped with the help of NAACP opposition. The Bork case was unusual in the strategic character and degree of cooperation among the groups. The Thomas nomination met with opposition from many of the same groups that successfully fought Bork but without the kind of carefully tailored and controlled presentation. Many of the groups chose to appear individually before the committee and faced some of the kinds of criticism that Bork supporters had hoped for during Bork's confirmation hearing. Thus, abortion advocates were pinned down even by generally sympathetic senators who asked them if they were not presenting a number of so-called litmus tests that a nominee must pass to be acceptable. It remains to be seen just how organized interest groups will approach future nominations. David Souter, President Bush's "stealth" candidate to fill the seat vacated when Justice William

Brennan retired, sailed through the process without any difficulty. Souter took his two oaths (constitutional and judicial) after Senate confirmation on October 2, 1990. (See Figures 3.2 and 3.3 on pages 68–69.)

Most scholars agree that, assuming candidates navigate the rocky shoals of the nomination process, there are questions that are of critical significance. The first is an accident of timing. Nominees selected by presidents nearing the election or the end of their service are more vulnerable than others. Of perhaps greater significance is the fact that nominees with substantial records of prior political controversy are more vulnerable than relatively low-visibility candidates.

SUMMARY

The degree to which all of these factors will constrain future choices is unclear, but, as a member of the Court, you know that the colleagues with whom you work each day came to the Court amidst these political realities. There is no question that they were selected with a combination of concerns for merit and attention to political agendas. The combination of representative, professional, and doctrinal factors may not specify precisely who will be chosen in any given case, but under those categories are listed many of the characteristics that have been considered in the choice of the justices who have served on the Court in the past two centuries, and they will likely guide choices in the future.

The fact that efforts are made by presidents, with varying degrees of success, to pack the Court and by the Senate, with varying degrees of intensity, to block nominees only underscores the importance of the Court as a political institution. But before a new justice can have the kind of impact the president anticipates and the Senate fears, he or she must learn how to operate effectively within the Court. It is to that task that we turn in the next chapter.

NOTES

[1]Chief Justice Taft was one of the most active campaigners (see David Danelski, *A Supreme Court Justice Is Appointed* [New York: Random House, 1964]).

[2]See, for example, Herman Schwartz, *Packing the Courts* (New York: Scribner's, 1988), chap. 2; and Vincent Blasi, *The Burger Court: The Counter-Revolution That Wasn't* (New Haven, CT: Yale University Press, 1983).

[3]Elder Witt, *A Different Justice* (Washington, DC: Congressional Quarterly, 1986), p. 39.

[4]472 U.S. 38 (1985).

[5]*Edwards v. Aguillard*, 482 U.S. 578 (1987).

[6]See Laura Kalman, *Abe Fortas* (New Haven, CT: Yale University Press, 1990); and Bruce Allen Murphy, *Fortas* (New York: Morrow, 1988).

[7]U.S. Congress, Senate Committee on the Judiciary, *Report from the Committee on the Judiciary: Nomination of William H. Rehnquist to be Chief Justice of the United States*, 99th Cong., 2d sess., 1986, p. 13.

[8]See, for example, Schwartz, *Packing the Courts*, p. 64.

[9]See Ethan Bronner, *Battle for Justice* (New York: Norton, 1989).

[10]Kenneth B. Noble, "Law vs. Principle: Out of Watergate Comes New View of Bork," *New York Times,* July 26, 1987, p. 23.

[11]U.S. Congress, Senate Committee on the Judiciary, *Report of the Committee on the Judiciary: Nomination of Robert H. Bork to be an Associate Justice of the United States Supreme Court,* 100th Cong., 1st sess., 1987, p. 295 (hereafter cited as *Bork Report*).

[12]See Noble, "Law vs. Principle," p. 24.

[13]*United States v. Nixon,* 418 U.S. 683 (1974).

[14]See U.S. Congress, Senate Committee on the Judiciary, *Hearings Before the Committee on the Judiciary: Nomination of Robert H. Bork to Be Associate Justice of the Supreme Court of the United States,* 100th Cong., 1st sess., 1987 (hereafter cited as *Bork Hearings*).

[15]Kenneth B. Noble, "Bork Is Disputed About Watergate," *New York Times,* Sept. 30, 1987, p. A-1.

[16]"Bork Watergate Role Rapped, Lauded," *Albany Times Union,* Sept. 30, 1987, p. A-3.

[17]*Bork Report,* p. 70.

[18]Ibid.

[19]*Nader v. Bork,* 366 F.Supp. 104 (D.D.C. 1973), vacated, no. 74-1620 (D.C. Cir. Aug. 20 and Oct. 22, 1975).

[20]Robert Bork, *The Antitrust Paradox: A Policy at War with Itself* (New York: Basic Books, 1978).

[21]"Neutral Principles and Some First Amendment Problems," *Indiana Law Journal* 47, no. 1 (1971).

[22]Edwin Meese III, Address before the American Bar Association, Washington, DC, July 9, 1985 (reprinted in *The Federalist Society, the Great Debate: Interpreting Our Written Constitution* [Washington, DC: Federalist Society, 1986]).

[23]"Bork Watergate Role Rapped, Lauded," p. A-3.

[24]381 U.S. 479 (1965).

[25]*Bork Report,* p. 94.

[26]Mary McGrory, "The Supreme Sacrifice," *Washington Post,* Oct. 6, 1987, sec. A.

[27]Ibid.

[28]*Bork Report,* p. 4.

[29]Ibid.

[30]James F. Gordon to Joseph Biden, Aug. 24, 1987 (in *Bork Report,* p. 369).

[31]Stuart Taylor, Jr., "Politics in the Bork Battle: Opinion Polls and Campaign-style Pressure May Change Supreme Court Confirmations," *New York Times,* Sept. 28, 1987, sec. A.

[32]"New Poll Anti-Bork by 2-to-1," *Albany Times Union,* Sept. 28, 1987, p. A3.

[33]Linda Greenhouse, "Byrd Asks Panel to Avert a Vote in Debate on Bork: Wants It Sent to Full Senate, Letting the Uncommitted Avoid a Public Stand," *New York Times,* Sept. 29, 1987, sec. A.

[34]Linda Greenhouse, "Senate Democrats Split over Strategy on Bork," *New York Times,* Sept. 30, 1987, sec. A.

[35]"Bork Watergate Role Rapped, Lauded," p. A3.

[36]Schwartz, *Packing the Courts,* p. 96.

[37]Edward Walsh and Lou Cannon, "Reagan Spurns Call to Drop Back as Likelihood of Defeat Grows," *Washington Post,* Oct. 6, 1987, sec. A.

[38]Greenhouse, "Byrd Asks Panel to Avert Vote."

[39]Kenneth B. Noble, "Heflin, at Last Voting No, Weathers the Intense Heat on the Uncommitted," *New York Times,* Oct. 7, 1987, sec. B.

[40]Donna Cassata, "Reagan Reasserts Support for Bork," *Washington Post,* Oct. 5, 1987, sec. A.

[41]Robin Toner, "Saying No to Bork, Southern Democrats Echo Black Voters," *New York Times,* Oct. 6, 1987, sec. A.

[42]Nathaniel C. Nash "Bork Is Losing Southern Democrats While Picking Up G.O.P. Moderates," *New York Times,* Sept. 27, 1987, p. 26.

[43]Ibid.

[44]Linda Greenhouse, "Foes of Bork Gain Majority in Panel; Urge Withdrawal," *New York Times,* Oct. 6, 1987, sec. B.

[45]Kenneth B. Noble, "Bid to Influence Bork Vote Is Denied," *New York Times,* Oct. 1, 1987, sec. B.

[46]Taylor, "Politics in the Bork Battle."

[47]Greenhouse "Byrd Asks Panel to Avert Vote."

[48]Ibid.

[49]Steven Roberts, "9–5 Panel Vote Against Bork Sends Nomination to Senate Amid Predictions of Defeat," *New York Times,* Oct. 7, 1987, sec. B.

[50]Steven V. Roberts, "Bork Weighs Withdrawing Name as Reagan Aides Say Cause Is Lost," *New York Times,* Oct. 8, 1987, sec. A.

[51]Taylor, "Politics in the Bork Battle." p. B7.

[52]"Excerpts from Senate Debate on Bork Confirmation to Court," *New York Times,* Oct. 22, 1987, sec. A.

[53]Lou Cannon, "President Defiant on Court Pick," *Albany Times Union,* Oct. 14, 1987, p. A1.

[54]Steven V. Roberts, "Hostility Intensifies on Bork Nomination," *New York Times,* Oct. 16, 1987, sec. A.

[55]"Reagan Lobbies for Bork," *Albany Times Union,* Oct. 15, 1987, p. A10.

[56]Roberts, "Bork Weighs Withdrawing Name."

[57]Ruth Marcus, "Foes, Backers Agree: Bork Testimony Helped," *Washington Post,* Oct. 5, 1987, sec. A.

[58]Philip Shenon, "Leaders Predict Early Bork Vote on Senate Floor," *New York Times,* Oct. 12, 1987, sec. B.

[59]Steven V. Roberts, "Court Choice Renews Split in White House," *Albany Times Union,* Oct. 31, 1987, p. A1.

[60]Stuart Taylor, Jr. "More Names Are Quietly Studied for Nomination to Supreme Court," *New York Times,* Oct. 9, 1987, sec. A.

[61]"Court Pick in Bork Mold," *Albany Times Union,* Oct. 30, 1987, p. A1.

[62]Roberts, "Court Choice Renews Split," p. A1.

[63]Michael J. Sniffen and Joan Mower, "Ginsburg Investment, Cable TV Opinion Tied," *Albany Times Union,* Nov. 2, 1987, p. A1

[64]Jeff Gerth, "Ginsburg Had Two Roles in a Court Case," *New York Times,* Nov. 8, 1987, p. 36.

[65]Al Kamen, "Ginsburg Acknowledges He Smoked Marijuana," *Washington Post,* Nov. 6, 1987, p. 1.

[66]Dennis McDougal, "Reporter Says Pundits Miss Point on Ginsburg's Past," *Albany Times Union,* Nov. 15, 1987, p. C2.

[67]Ruth Marcus and Lou Cannon, "Ginsburg Urged to Withdraw in Call Cleared with Reagan," *Washington Post,* Nov. 7, 1987, sec. A.

[68]Ibid.

[69]Steven V. Roberts, "Ginsburg Withdraws Name as Supreme Court Nominee, Citing Marijuana 'Clamor,'" *New York Times,* Nov. 8, 1987, sec. A.

[70]Sara Fritz and David Lauter, "GOP Divided on Blame for Failed Nominations," *Albany Times Union,* Nov. 11, 1987, sec. A.

[71]Lou Cannon and Ruth Marcus, "Kennedy Said Likely Court Pick," *Albany Times Union,* Nov. 9, 1987, p. A2.

[72]F. N. D'Alessio, "Bork Breaks Public Silence, Blames Critics," *Washington Post,* Dec. 5, 1987, sec. A.

[73]Ibid.

[74]U.S. Congress, Senate Committee on the Judiciary, *Report of the Committee on the Judiciary: Nomination of Anthony M. Kennedy to Be an Associate Justice of the United States Supreme Court,* 100th Cong., 2d sess., 1988.

[75]J. Edgar Hoover to Boake Carter, Sept. 24, 1937 (in FBI Supreme Court File, FBI Headquarters, Washington, DC; hereafter, FBI Files).

[76]Ethan Bronner, *Battle for Justice: How the Bork Nomination Shook America* (New York: Norton, 1989), pp. 98–99.

[77]Henry J. Abraham, *Justices and Presidents*, 2d ed. (New York: Oxford University Press, 1985), pp. 27–28.

[78]Stephen L. Wasby, *The Supreme Court in the Federal Judicial System*, 3d ed. (Chicago: Nelson-Hall, 1988), pp. 107–9.

[79]*Bork Report*, p. 4.

[80]*Public Citizen v. Department of Justice*, 491 U.S. 440 (1989).

[81]Harold R. Tyler, Jr., to Joseph R. Biden, Jr., Sept. 21, 1987 (in *Bork Hearings*, vol. I, pp. 1228–31).

[82]Abraham, *Justices and Presidents*, pp. 27–28.

[83]David M. O'Brien, *Storm Center* (New York: Norton, 1986).

[84]Abraham, *Justices and Presidents*, p. 11.

[85]Ibid., p. 46

[86]Ibid., p. 11.

[87]Ibid., p. 61.

[88]O'Brien, *Storm Center*, p. 45.

[89]Ibid.

[90]Ibid., p. 46.

[91]See Danelski, *Supreme Court Justice*, chaps. 3–6; Abraham, *Justice and Presidents*, pp. 27–28; and Laurence H. Tribe, *God Save This Honorable Court* (New York: Random House, 1985).

[92]Alpheus T. Mason, *William Howard Taft: Chief Justice* (New York: Simon and Schuster, 1965), pp. 215–16.

[93]Robert Scigliano, *The Supreme Court and the Presidency* (New York: Free Press, 1971), p. 105.

[94]Joseph P. Lash, ed., *From the Diaries of Felix Frankfurter* (New York: Norton, 1975), p. 75.

[95]Abraham, *Justices and Presidents*, p. 203.

[96]Danelski, *Supreme Court Justice*, p. 4.

[97]Neil Lewis, "From Poverty to U.S. Bench," *New York Times*, July 1, 1991, p. 1.

[98]John R. Schmidhauser, *Judges and Justices* (Boston: Little, Brown, 1979), p. 49.

[99]Ibid.

[100]Schwartz, *Packing the Courts*, pp. 59–60.

[101]It was held by Henry Brockholst Livingston, Smith Thompson, Samuel Nelson, Ward Hunt, and Samuel Blatchford (Elder Witt, ed., *Guide to the U.S. Supreme Court*, 2d ed. [Washington, DC: Congressional Quarterly, 1990], p. 792).

[102]There was a Virginia–Maryland seat for years held by John Blair, Samuel Chase, Gabriel Duvall, Philip Barbour, and Peter Daniel.

[103]It was held by Caleb Cushing, Joseph Story, Levi Woodbury, Benjamin Curtis, Nathaniel Clifford, Horace Gray, and Oliver Wendell Holmes.

[104]Witt, *U.S. Supreme Court*, p. 793.

[105]Jerome N. Frank to Frank Murphy, Feb. 21, 1939, box 13, Robert H. Jackson Papers, Library of Congress (hereafter cited as RHJP).

[106]Philippa Strum, *Louis D. Brandeis: Justice for the People* (Cambridge, MA: Harvard University Press, 1984), chap. 15.

[107]Witt, *U.S. Supreme Court*, p. 794.

[108]J. Woodford Howard, *Mr. Justice Murphy* (Princeton, NJ: Princeton University Press, 1968), p. 444.

[109]Jackson autobiography manuscript, box 188, RHJP, pp. 223–25.

[110]Barbara A. Perry, "The Religion Factor in Appointments to the United States Supreme Court: The 'Catholic Seat'" (Paper presented at the annual meeting of the American Political Science Association, Aug. 30, 1987), p. 1.

[111]Ibid., p. 15.

[112]Ibid., p. 32.

[113]See Roberts, "Court Choice Renews Split," p. A1.

[114]Abraham, *Justices and Presidents*, p. 4.

[115]Sheldon Goldman, "Judicial Selection and the Qualities That Make a 'Good Judge,'" *Annals of the American Academy of Political and Social Science* 462 (July 1982): 114.

[116]Albert P. Blaustein and Roy M. Mersky, *The First One Hundred Justices: Statistical Studies on the Supreme Court of the United States* (Hamden, CT: Shoe String Press, 1978), pp. 50–51.

[117]Justice Arthur Goldberg (retired), interview with authors, Southwind, VA, Aug. 27, 1986.

[118]Ibid.

[119]Abraham, *Justices and Presidents*, p. 52.

[120]William H. Rehnquist, *The Supreme Court* (New York: Morrow, 1987), p. 235.

[121]Ruth Bader Ginsburg, "Confirming Supreme Court Justices: Thoughts on the Second Opinion Rendered by the Senate," *University of Illinois Law Review* 101 (1988).

[122]Charles Warren, *The Supreme Court in United States History*, vol. 1 (Boston: Little, Brown, 1926), p. 215.

[123]See James Simon, *In His Own Image* (New York: David McKay, 1973).

[124]Harry S Truman to William O. Douglas, July 9, 1952, Harry S Truman Papers (hereinafter cited as HSTP), Truman Library, Independence, Missouri.

[125]William H. Rehnquist, Address given at the University of Wyoming, Oct. 25, 1985 photocopy, p. 32.

[126]See John C. Jeffries, Jr., *Justice Lewis F. Powell, Jr.* (New York: Scribner's, 1994), pp. 1–9.

[127]On Fortas in the Supreme Court, see Kalman, *Abe Fortas*; and Murphy, *Fortas*.

[128]William O. Douglas to Hugo Black, Aug. 1, 1965, box 59, Hugo L. Black Papers, Library of Congress (hereafter cited as HLBP).

[129]Hugo Black to Earl Warren, August 3, 1965, Box 347, Earl Warren Papers, Library of Congress (hereafter cited as EWP).

[130]Howard, *Mr. Justice Murphy*, pp. 214–17.

[131]Witt, *U.S. Supreme Court*, p. 655.

[132]Ibid.

[133]Box 28, HLBP.

[134]Witt, *U.S. Supreme Court*, p. 653.

[135]Peter Fish, "Spite Nominations to the United States Supreme Court," *Kentucky Law Journal* 77 (1988–89).

[136]Earl Warren to John Marshall Harlan II, Dec. 14, 1954, Box 355, EWP.

Taking Office: Welcome to the Institution

4

Well, so much for that first contemplative cup of coffee, during which you pondered what brought you to the Court. Now the question is, just what is the workplace like and how do you settle into the work before you? These concerns may seem far from the lofty philosophical debates and political battles surrounding appointment and confirmation, and certainly a far cry from the rending constitutional discussions over the range of issues from abortion to presidential power that are commonly held to be what justices do each day, but they do matter. If there is one area in which there is agreement among most of those who have sat on the Supreme Court, it is that the Court is a very special working environment, and anyone who seeks to be effective as a justice must come to understand it thoroughly. That understanding requires knowledge of the work itself, the office setting, and the colleagues, justices, and staff members with whom you will work.

One of the first things that you discover on entering the Court is that, in one sense, Justice Felix Frankfurter was correct when he said that when a person enters the Court, he or she becomes a monk. He was wrong, and not a little disingenuous, when he defined that to mean that one ceases to be an active and significant political player.[1] It is true, however, that as justices settle in at the Court, they begin to lose their past and are instead viewed through the lens of the Court. It is ironic that all of the personal, professional, and political facts of your life that so captivated everyone during the appointment and confirmation process begin relatively quickly to fade. To be sure, that does not happen overnight. During your first few terms reporters watch closely to see if the president and the pundits were right when they predicted, implicitly or explicitly, how you were likely to vote on the Court. But soon your past fades. You take on the persona that comes with the job, losing your identity and becoming someone new, at least politically. Yet within the Court, you bring all of that background, all of those experiences to your everyday work. That was certainly true of Chief Justice Earl Warren, dubbed "Super Chief" by some of his colleagues.

EARL WARREN: FROM THE CITY OF THE BLESSED SACRAMENT TO THE MARBLE TEMPLE

In 1968, Richard Nixon rode a reaction against the rulings of the Warren Court and negative sentiment toward the social revolution of the 1960s to the White House. There is no doubt that Nixon ran against Earl Warren at least as hard as he campaigned against Hubert Humphrey, the Democratic nominee. There were any number of ironies in that contest. For one thing, both Nixon and Warren were California Republicans. Warren had successfully campaigned under the GOP banner in the Golden State for many years. They were both lawyers, well aware of each other's experience. Yet Nixon pictured Warren as a Supreme Court justice aloof from the consequences of the rulings rendered by the Court, rulings that, according to Nixon campaign strategists, had been largely responsible for the rise in crime and disorder with which Americans were so frustrated and by which they were so frightened. If Warren understood what it was like to be the victim of a crime or to have a loved one struck down by a vicious attacker, the critics charged, he would not have supported some of the rulings ensuring defendants' rights, like Miranda v. Arizona[2] and Escobedo v. Illinois.[3] If he had had to prosecute criminal defendants, said police officers and prosecutors, he would have realized how tough a job it truly was.

The campaign against the Warren Court was not a Nixon invention. The Court's rulings on criminal due process matters during the 1950s and 1960s were bound to produce criticism, but two factors ensured that the reaction against those rulings would be particularly harsh. The first was the relationship between due process and the hunt for Communists that was so much a part of life in the America of the 1950s. The procedural requirements of due process stood in the way of the rush to judgment of those labeled subversive or worse. The second was the turbulence of the late 1960s. Bitterness about American military intervention in Vietnam and riots and civil unrest over civil rights were the prime reasons for society's volatility. The fact that more people seemed to be taking to the streets and there was less respect for law and order came during the years when the Court was delivering some of its most controversial rulings, leading many to accept the assertion that the Warren Court was to blame.

The Real Earl Warren

The truth of Chief Justice Warren was radically different from the political caricature. Warren was not an upper-middle-class kid from the suburbs. He grew up in Bakersfield, California, in the days when that town was regarded as about as close to the old Wild West as one was likely to find in that era. One of his jobs was rousting trainmen from seedy establishments to get to their trains on time. He saw a rich mixture of the social and economic problems afflicting the area, including the effects of alcohol and gambling on families.

Warren went on from Bakersfield to attend college and law school at the University of California at Berkeley. From there he became first an assistant district attorney and later, and for a long time, district attorney of Alameda County. After years of prosecutorial experience, Warren earned a reputation as one of the nation's toughest and fairest district attorneys.

It was during his years as a prosecutor that Warren's father was brutally murdered, beaten to death by an intruder. Police encouraged Warren to permit the use of an informant who would be wired for sound and placed in the cell with the prime suspect in the killing so that a confession could be extracted. Warren refused.

From there Warren moved down the road to take up duties as the state attorney general and, thereafter, as one of California's most successful governors, serving three terms in that office. His service in Sacramento was not without controversial moments, however. Warren cooperated with military authorities in the enforcement of Executive Order 9066, under which Japanese, and other Asian Americans who were presumed to be of Japanese extraction, were removed from their homes and sent to concentration camps, euphemistically known as "relocation centers." That was the one act of his public life that Warren came to regret.

The future Chief Justice of the United States, Earl Warren, campaigning as Republican Presidential candidate, 1952.

Although he was one of the GOP's most likely presidential candidates, it became clear that he was no match for Dwight Eisenhower, who carried with him the title "Supreme Commander of the Allied Forces in Europe" and other badges of success as a leader of a victorious World War II military force. An ambitious fellow by the name of Richard Nixon was seeking to shape the race by turning the votes of the California delegation to Eisenhower. Warren would have none of it. Neither would he accede to a credentials fight by which Eisenhower opponents sought to pack the convention to support Senator Robert Taft. Warren stood firm on grounds that the California delegation was committed, and that support helped Eisenhower prevail in 1952.

Getting to the Court: From Governor to Chief Justice

Eisenhower was grateful for Warren's actions, but he told the California governor that he was in no position to offer him a Cabinet post. However, he promised Warren the first seat that became available on the Supreme Court. In the interim, Herbert Brownell, Eisenhower's attorney general, approached Warren with the idea of becoming solicitor general, the attorney representing the United States in the Supreme Court, a position often viewed as a steppingstone to the Court. Warren agreed, but before he could take up his duties, Chief Justice Fred Vinson died, an event that Justice Felix Frankfurter observed proved beyond a shadow of a doubt that there is a God.

Brownell was dispatched to explain to Warren that although the president had offered him the first vacancy, he had not meant the chief justiceship. Warren, however, insisted that a promise was a promise. President Eisenhower acquiesced and announced Warren's appointment, called a recess appointment because it came at a time when the Congress was in recess and therefore not able to undertake confirmation proceedings. Warren was later confirmed.

A Very Different Life

For Warren, life on the Court was a radical departure from what he had known. The Court itself was a unique environment, but there was also the challenge of assuming the chief justiceship at a critical moment in history and during a difficult period on the Court.

The Moment in Time   The reason for Frankfurter's expression of gratitude to God for the demise of Chief Justice Vinson was that the Court was truly mired in the wrenching debate over the school desegregation cases collectively known as *Brown v. Board of Education of Topeka.*[4] The justices had been through a set of desegregation cases earlier, as well as a number of rending cases growing out of the Red Scare, like *Dennis v. United States,*[5] challenging the convictions of the leaders of the American Communist party. But the desegregation cases were even more wrenching. The Court needed leadership if the justices, who were sharply divided in the early discussions of the *Brown* case, were to be brought together into a strong or even a unanimous position on the issue. Warren was just the person to bring that leadership, but it was a difficult assignment, even for someone as politically sophisticated and experienced as he. Vinson had been appointed to the Court by Harry Truman in an attempt to bring peace to a conflict-laden bench. But the chief, because he was not a leader, did not bring peace. Indeed, his lack of control over the brethren led to a worsening of interpersonal behavior on the Court.

To Still the Troubled Waters   As one observer put it, "The closing days of Stone's chief justiceship ranked as one of the bitterest, most schismatic periods in judicial history."[6] Justice Frankfurter had been frustrated since the mid 1940s by his loss of influence on the Court. Justice Frank Murphy was angered by Frankfurter's constant snide comments, both personal and professional. Justice William O. Douglas was convinced that if something went wrong on the Court, Felix was probably behind it. In 1945, the Court found itself locked in conflict, with Hugo Black and Frankfurter as the chief protagonists over, of all things, the contents of a retirement letter to be presented on the occasion of Justice Owen Robert's departure from the Court. Douglas complained, "It's all a goddam tempest in a teapot. FF is looking for trouble—some opening so R[oberts] can let go a blast."[7] Justice Robert Jackson waged a very public battle against Black, accusing him of attempting to undermine Jackson's promised appointment to the chief justiceship and, in the process, charged the Alabamian with conflict of interest in a case before the Court.

And Vinson was not a peacemaker, notwithstanding his years of political experience in the House. Justice Douglas recalled one event in which Vinson came to the end of his rope with Frankfurter. "At last Vinson left his chair at the head of the Conference Table, raised his clenched fist and started around the room at Frankfurter shouting, 'No son of a bitch can ever say that to Fred Vinson!' "[8]

It was against this background of strife and amidst debate over the desegregation issue, one of the most divisive in the Court's history, that Earl Warren was expected to provide leadership and rebuild a sense of collegiality. All these factors notwithstanding, Warren accomplished what some regarded as the virtually impossible task of forging a unanimous opinion in the *Brown* case. To do it, he employed all of his political skills. He avoided confrontation by delaying a vote on the case, as would have been the Court's normal pattern. He recognized early on that the difficult task would be to help the southerners on the Court, who would doubtless feel particular pressure. He moved the desegregation case to a moral high ground, effectively but carefully challenging the opponents of desegregation to defend discrimination. He lobbied the individual justices over lunches while the formal conferences were in progress. Slowly but surely, Warren moved the Court, with the help of a number of the justices, to its unanimous conclusion.

Building the Team

Given the situation and times, Warren had to learn the institutional reality of the Court quickly. He relied on his colleagues for help. Black presided over some the first conferences after Warren came to the Court. Warren accepted advice and counsel during the early months from Frankfurter on a range of issues, a role the former Harvard law professor was always willing to play.

The setting was so different from what he had known that the transition was not easy. Although the critics who charged that Warren lacked legal experience were obviously completely ignorant of his three decades of full-time practice, it was true that he had been away from the active practice of law for some years. Moreover, he had been directing a large staff and presiding over one of the largest and most complex governments in the nation, that of the state of California. Now the stuff of his daily work was sophisticated legal practice, but the staff support for accomplishing his tasks, even the special duties of the chief justice, was tiny: two clerks and a secretary.

The administrative operation of the Court could be charitably described as primitive and tradition bound. Warren found that even the smallest changes, like the installation of microphones in the courtroom, met with surprising resistance. And though he was chief justice, he could not simply direct that changes be made. While he was "first among equals," he was only first, not superior. The other justices voted on issues concerned with the operation of the Court and not merely with respect to legal decisions. He could not force them to do anything.

Although he continued to have stressful periods on the Court, as when he found himself in shouting matches with Frankfurter during oral arguments and occasionally in conference, Warren was acknowledged by his colleagues to be a superior leader. He used the skills he developed in his political days in California, but he learned the Court and what makes it the unique institution that it is.

THE MATTER OF INSTITUTIONAL CHARACTER

Anyone who has ever entered a new organization, from a new school to high office, knows that each institution has its own special character. The more unique and complex the organization and its function, the more significant that character, sometimes called "organizational culture," becomes.[9] The people who have participated in the institution over time, the special requirements of its mission, and the environment in which it finds itself have all helped to shape the Supreme Court into its present form. Some of the unique characteristics are obvious to the most casual observer. The appearance of the Court is strikingly different from that of the White House or the Capitol. The conversations to be heard are different, as is the attire and general behavior of the people.

David O'Brien refers to the process of institutional development and differentiation as "institutionalization" and observes, "Institutionalization is a process by which the Court establishes and maintains its internal procedures and norms and defines and differentiates its role from that of other political branches."[10] As his definition suggests, this process occurs over time. Therefore, to understand the Court today, one must understand something of how it was shaped by its past members.

Building the Supreme Court

The corner of First and A Streets in Washington, D.C., has been the site of a host of interesting and unusual events since the nation's capital was established in 1791. It was the location of the temporary Capitol building after the British destroyed the permanent structure during the War of 1812, the Circuit Court of the District of Columbia, a boardinghouse that at one time housed John C. Calhoun, a jail, a set of townhouses (one of which was occupied by Justice Stephen J. Field), and the national headquarters of the National Woman's party.[11] But few events that took place at that particular spot on Capitol Hill were as significant as the day in 1939 when the first justice moved into what is now the home of the U.S. Supreme Court.

But even though the story of the building of what is now called the Marble Temple is fascinating and despite the fact that the surroundings of the Court influence its institutional character, the process of shaping the emerging Court had been under way for nearly a century and a half before Hugo Black became the first justice to have chambers there.

The First Decade of the Supreme Court

When John Jay opened the envelope, he found a letter from President George Washington that read:

> It is with singular pleasure that I address you as Chief Justice of the Supreme Court of the United States, for which office your commission is enclosed. In nominating you for the important station which you now fill, I not only acted in conformity to my best judgment, but I trust I did a grateful thing to the good citizens of these United States; and I have a full confidence that the love which you bear to our country, and a desire to promote the general happiness, will not suffer you to hesitate a moment to bring into action the talents, knowledge and integrity which are so necessary to be exercised at the head of that department which must be considered as the keystone of our political fabric.[12]

The Judiciary Act of 1789, which determined that the Supreme Court would have six justices, had been enacted only two weeks earlier.

When Jay arrived at the first session of the Court, convened, under the authority of Article III of the Constitution and the Judiciary Act, at New York City's Royal Exchange Building that Monday morning in February 1790, he joined William Cushing of Massachusetts and James Wilson of Pennsylvania. The other half of the Court, James Iredell of North Carolina, John Blair of Virginia, and John Rutledge of South Carolina, was missing. Blair arrived on Tuesday; Rutledge resigned from the Court without ever having attended. The youngest of the six appointees was thirty-eight-year-old Justice Blair, and the eldest, Iredell, age fifty-seven. Two had been at the Philadelphia Convention in 1787, and the others had played key roles in their states during ratification.[13]

The Court got down to business on Wednesday, hiring its clerk and admitting the first members of the Supreme Court bar to practice. It adjourned its session a week later, however, since there were no cases pending on the docket. Thus began the process of building one of the most unique political institutions in the modern world.

Though most observers view Chief Justice John Marshall as the Court's leading institutional architect, important developments during the decade before Marshall came to the Court affected both the institution and the nation. They concerned the Court's place in the separation of powers, the concept of federalism, and life on the Court.

Observers who watched the festivities at the first term of the Court did not miss the fact that most of those who came for admission to practice at the bar of the Supreme Court, eleven of nineteen, were members of Congress: two senators and nine members of the House of Representatives. The anti-Federalist newspaper *The Independent Chronicle* observed:

It is alarming to find so many Members of Congress sworn into the Federal Court at its first sitting in New York. The question then is whether it is proper that Congress should consist of so large a proportion of Members who are sworn attorneys in the Federal Court; or whether it is prudent to trust men to enact laws who are practicing on them in another department.[14]

The question of just how close the relationship with Congress should be would remain for some time.

Another more immediate issue about the relationship between the branches arose when the executive branch sought the Court's advice on a pending issue in advance of litigation presenting the question. In 1793, George Washington directed then secretary of state Thomas Jefferson to refer questions on American foreign policy to the Court for advisory opinions. The Court refused on the grounds of separation of powers to provide advice to the president on issues that did not come to the Court as a properly developed case.[15]

Although for some time there were no fully developed cases on the Court's docket, the justices had other duties. In those days, the justices rode circuit and, as members of circuit courts, rendered important decisions on issues that later came before the entire Supreme Court. Thus, sitting on circuit, justices participated in striking down statutes or official actions taken by the states, establishing the power of the federal judiciary to conduct judicial review of the constitutionality of state law.[16] In the famous *Chisholm v. Georgia* case, the Jay Court underscored the jurisdictional assertions rendered by the circuit courts when it permitted a suit by a plaintiff of one state against another state,[17] a ruling that came as a profound shock to many state officials.

Beyond its responses to state policy making, circuit action brought the first refusal by federal courts on constitutional grounds to enforce congressional legislation. The Pension Act of 1792 called on circuit courts to rule on appeals by pensioners. These decisions would then be reviewed and possibly overturned by the secretary of war and Congress. Justices Jay and Cushing refused to participate in that kind of case because they would be forced to act more like commissioners in an administrative capacity than as independent Article III judges. Justice Iredell flatly asserted that the statute was unconstitutional. Justices Blair and Wilson, as part of a circuit court sitting in Pennsylvania, found the statute invalid on the grounds of separation of powers, concluding that "it is a principle important to freedom that, in government, the Judicial should be distinct from, and independent of, the Legislative department."[18] Of perhaps equal importance was an assertion by the Court of its ability to declare the validity of a statute in the carriage tax case.[19]

It should very quickly be added that at the same time was launched what Louis Fisher has called "constitutional dialogues."[20] Neither the other branches of the federal government nor the states were prepared simply to accept the judges' actions without responding. The *Chisholm* ruling engendered the first amendment to the Constitution since adoption of the Bill of Rights, an amendment (the Eleventh) which overturned the Court's decision in the Georgia case. In response to the circuit ruling on the first Pension Act, the attorney general attempted to get the full Court to issue an opinion clarifying the interpretation of the statute, and the Congress amended the Act. Both the fact of judicial assertiveness and the onset of the continuing set of action and reaction among the courts and other governmental units were important products of the Court's early years.

From the justices' point of view, sitting on circuit courts was pure punishment. Some, like Justice Iredell, who termed himself a "travelling postboy,"[21] literally traveled thousands of miles a year. Quite apart from the burden of travel, the fact that justices sat in circuit panels presented the possibility of conflict among circuits on issues of law involving members of the Supreme Court, who might later be called on to sit in these cases if the cases reached the High Court. If the cases did not get to the Supreme Court, the conflicting interpretations would lie unresolved. Despite the obvious problems, riding circuit was to be a bitter fact of Supreme Court life for years to come.

The obligation to ride circuit was one of a number of conditions that made the Court a relatively unattractive post for many potential justices. Justice William Johnson found the practice so onerous that he simply resigned rather than continue with it. That was not the only issue, however. The Court was relatively weak and apparently unimportant to most of American political life at the time. Jay resigned to run for the governorship of New York. Rutledge left to take a position on his state's highest court.

As President John Adams contemplated replacements, he was well aware of the difficulties and not a little worried about finding worthy appointees before leaving office. It turned out to be a difficult task indeed. The problem was intensified by the election victories in 1800 by the Jeffersonian Republicans, archenemies of Adams's Federalists, who swept both the presidential and congressional contests. The federal judiciary was likely to be the last bastion of Federalist power. Nevertheless, Adams had considerable difficulty finding candidates who were both acceptable and willing to fill the most important position, that of chief justice. Fortunately for the Federalists, Adams ultimately settled on his secretary of state, John Marshall of Virginia.

The Marshall Court and the Rise of the Court as an American Political Institution

Adams could hardly have found anyone in America who would have been as well qualified by experience and understanding as John Marshall to lead the Court in its formative years. Reared in the Northern Neck of Virginia, Marshall went off to the Revolutionary War as a member of the Culpepper Militia. He was later Provost Marshall, in charge of maintaining order and discipline, during the Continental Army's terrible winter at Valley Forge. He saw the results of a nation incapable of exercising effective governing power over its most vital affairs, issues such as national defense and control of the economy. As a member of the Virginia House of Burgesses, ambassador to France, and, eventually, secretary of state, Marshall understood the complex task of governing at all levels of government and in both the foreign and domestic arenas.

Marshall's legal training was extremely limited. He had attended the College of William and Mary for only a brief period, and the evidence from those days is that he was as busy recording thoughts of Polly Ambler, his future bride, in his notebook as he was in learning the law. Nevertheless, Marshall proved himself an able practitioner after he was admitted to the bar. Ironically, Governor Thomas Jefferson ultimately signed Marshall's bar admission papers, an act that Jefferson would live to regret.

Marshall brought all of his experiences to the Court, but he brought one thing more. He entered the Court with a sophisticated understanding of how to nurture a young and vulnerable institution. Much in the Supreme Court today was initiated by Marshall nearly two hundred years ago. Within the Court, Marshall fostered a set of workways and a spirit of collegiality that has been central to the Court ever since. Externally, Marshall led the Court to a declaration of judicial independence, firmly establishing its coequality with the other branches, reaffirming the supremacy of the Constitution over contrary state laws, and interpreting key provisions of the Constitution in a way that established a foundation for federal government action in a wide variety of fields.

The filling of what is now referred to as the Court's center chair was, however, not the end of the Federalist/Jeffersonian Republican clash over the judiciary and the elections of 1800. The effort by the lame duck Federalists to establish new judgeships and pack them with partisans before the Democratic-Republicans came to power provided the foundation for what is sometimes regarded as the most important decision rendered by the Supreme Court, *Marbury v. Madison.*[22]

It is difficult to overstate the level of hostility between the Republicans and the Federalist-dominated Court. No effort was spared in the legislature or by the president in attempts to counter the one remaining Federalist redoubt. The Congress repealed the Judiciary Act of 1801, delayed the 1802 term of the Supreme Court, and brought impeachment action against Justice Samuel Chase. Although successful in the House, the impeachment effort failed in the trial in the Senate.

Still, no one knew what Marshall and his colleagues would do with the *Marbury* case. The beauty of the course Marshall ultimately charted was that the result was to tell Marbury that although his appointment was valid and he was entitled to some remedy in some forum, the Supreme Court was the wrong place to turn, at least as a first step in seeking action. The Court was therefore unable to provide the writ that Marbury sought. Because no writ was issued to the secretary of state, Jefferson was left with no real way to fight the Court.

The Court also ruled later in 1803 that an order issued by the president to naval commanders was a violation of a statute, and the captain who seized a ship under those orders was liable for a claim of damages. Poor Captain Little, who seized a ship departing from a French port as he had been specifically directed by the president, faced a judgment of several thousand dollars for his pains.[23] Even in matters of foreign policy then, the Court was prepared to define a limit to the power of another branch. But again, this suit stemmed from an action taken under Jefferson's predecessors, and there was nothing Jefferson could do to respond to the Court.

These and other critically important rulings issued from the Marshall Court generally in the form of unanimous opinions authored by the chief justice. The character, form, and quality of the opinions is generally thought to be related to some developing factors of institutional life encouraged, if not totally initiated, by Marshall. First, the Court moved from the practice of seriatim opinions, in which each judge rendered a judgment orally from the bench, to a unified opinion, in which the Court issued an opinion for the Court, either unanimously or as an opinion for the majority of the justices. There are differences of opinion regarding whether the Court moved to unified opinions most often written by Marshall because of the chief's dominance of the Court or because of his persuasiveness and effective leadership in synthesizing the views expressed in conference by the justices. Second, it was also during this period that the Court formalized the process of reporting its opinions. The names Cranch, Howard, and the rest that appear in Supreme Court citations from the early years refer to the volumes of Supreme Court reports published by particular private publishers under agreement with the Court. In any case, the process of decision and the ability to reach unanimous or strong majority opinions on critical cases seems to owe a great deal to the nature of the decision process in the Court.

In those days, the justices lived together in a boardinghouse. They took meals together and gathered after dinner over a glass of Marshall's beverage of choice, Madeira, to discuss cases. These private group discussions became known as "the conference," the title still used today. The fact that the justices had the time and the privacy to develop consensus positions appeared felicitous for the resolution of complex questions. Important too was the fact of collegiality, necessitated by the close living and working relationships on the Court as well as by its relative isolation from the other political activities of the day. These characteristics became essential elements of the lifestyle of the justices.

It was important for the Court to develop effective, collegial workways that allowed a very small group of energetic and politically astute justices to deal closely with one another over a long period. It was important for the Court to create norms of behavior because the court was, after *Marbury*, to hear an increasing number of important cases. In addition to its *Marbury* ruling, the Court also handed down *Fletcher v. Peck* in 1810, firmly establishing the authority of the Court to strike down on constitutional grounds an invalid piece of state legislation.[24] In its ruling upholding congressional chartering of a bank of the United States, the Court made it clear that the Constitution was a creation of the people and not a treaty ratified by the states. As such, the states were answerable to the Constitution and not authorized to nullify federal government action.[25]

The bank decision was critically important as well because it interpreted the necessary-and-proper clause, also known as the elastic clause, very broadly to give Congress sweeping authority in the area of finance. The necessary-and-proper clause, after the Marshall Court ruled, was no mere throwaway phrase in Article I, Section 8. Marshall's Court determined that the enumerated powers are not self-executing and require "laws necessary and proper for carrying into effect the foregoing powers, and all other powers vested by this Constitution in the Government of the United States, or in any Department or officer thereof." James Madison argued in *Federalist* no. 44 that "without the Substance of this power, the whole Constitution would be a dead letter."[26] He went on to observe that, absent the elastic clause, the government that is to administer the Constitution would have to choose between doing nothing, and thereby ignoring the public interest, and violating the terms of the Constitution itself. When Marshall concluded that although the Constitution did not mention creation of a bank in the enumerated powers delegated to the Congress in Article I, Section 8, it did mention the coining of money, the laying and collecting of taxes, the construction of infrastructure like "post roads," and the raising and maintaining of an army and navy and those powers requiring financial mechanisms for their implementation, he opened the way for a wide range of policies developed by the Congress in connection with its power of taxing and spending, as well as other devices, ever since. And when the Court added a number of important decisions broadly interpreting the congressional power to regulate commerce, it handed Congress one of the most important tools of policy making in the nation's history. The taxing-and-spending powers and the commerce clause authority underlay most of the major agencies created by the Congress and most of its major domestic-policy actions.

The Taney Court

The battle over the Second Bank of the United States was an important factor in the career of Marshall's successor, Chief Justice Roger Brooke Taney. An insider in the Andrew Jackson administration, Taney's first nomination to the Court went down to defeat because of reaction against the administration's position, led by Taney as secretary of the treasury, opposing the bank. But Taney was ultimately successful when nominated as chief justice in 1835 and was confirmed in 1836.

The sad fact is that Taney's career is often summarized with the one brief and disastrous fact that he authored the Court's opinion in the 1857 case of *Dred Scott v. Sandford*.[27] The rejection of the petition for freedom by a slave brought to free territory had a profound effect in many quarters of American life. Most scholars consider it important because it helped to assure the Civil War that followed not long thereafter and because it marked another example of the inability of American institutions to purge the society of slavery. But it also indicated something else; it was evidence that the Court was a central player in the drama of American political life and that, exercising its considerable power, the Court could do great harm as well as good.

Dred Scott generally obscures everything else that took place at the Court at the time, but two points are particularly worthy of consideration in terms of later developments. First, the Court grew during this period to nine members, which, notwithstanding a fluctuation or two after that time, remains its size today. Despite the effort by President Franklin D. Roosevelt to pass a bill that would have expanded the size of the Court when the justices reached retirement age, most commentators have been satisfied with the size of the Court as a good compromise between a body large enough to handle the work of the Court and yet small enough to remain an effective collegial body.

The second important fact is that, during this period, the Court moved from more than a quarter century of aiding the development of a strong national government to a position in favor of greater deference to action by the states. This factor became extremely important later in the century.

The Laissez-faire Era

The period from the end of the Civil War, particularly the 1870s to the 1930s is sometimes referred to as the era of laissez faire, the time of emerging reaction against government regulation of the marketplace. There were, however, contradictory trends.

In the post–Civil War period, many wondered if the states would cease to exist as important governmental units. The southern states had been under military rule and were ultimately readmitted to the union only after agreeing to ratify the Thirteenth, Fourteenth, and Fifteenth amendments, which placed very definite limits on state action. In an effort to implement the Civil War amendments, the national government passed civil rights legislation that not only prohibited official discrimination but also barred private segregation by operators of public accommodations. Yet the Tenth Amendment, preserving all "powers not delegated [by the Constitution] to the states respectively, or to the people," as interpreted by the justices, seemed to suggest that states had reserve powers that could not be infringed by the national government. Were there boundaries beyond which the national government could not reach? In a number of cases the Supreme Court answered yes.

The Court handed down a number of decisions that not only supported the states but weakened national authority. For one thing, it recognized that citizenship in the nation was distinct from citizenship in any given state and read the "privileges-and-immunities" clause of the Fourteenth Amendment narrowly.[28] The result was to say that Americans do not enjoy the same rights everywhere other than with respect to the national government. The Court also held that while the Fourteeth Amendment authorizes Congress to enact statutes prohibiting states from denying persons within their control the equal protection of laws, that authority does not extend to the prohibition of private acts of discrimination by individuals or businesses within the states.[29] With only Justice John Harlan dissenting, the Court went so far as to uphold a Louisiana statute permitting segregation of railroad passenger cars.[30]

Finally, the Court read the commerce power of the federal government much more narrowly than it had in the past, precluding federal policy making in such areas as mining, manufacturing, and agriculture despite their obvious impact on interstate commerce and the national economy in general.[31] The result was to cripple the national government's ability to regulate the burgeoning corporate giants who clearly were far too powerful to be controlled by the states. Indeed, although the Court had struck down only two federal statutes between 1800 and the Civil War, it struck down more than twenty between 1920 and 1932.[32]

However, the apparent victories by state governments against assertions of national government power were just that, apparent because the Court was developing a means for constraining the state governments as well. Using an interpretation of the Fourteenth Amendment, the Court employed the so-called substantive due process doctrine to protect what it called economic liberty from interference by the states. The idea was that when the Fourteenth Amendment insists that no state shall deny to any person life, liberty, or property without due process of law, it can be read to mean that the state may be prohibited from acting at all with respect to some facets of life. In particular, the Court included such liberties as freedom of contract. In the classic case of *Lochner v. New York*,[33] the Court struck down a limitation on hours and working conditions for bakery employees who worked very long hours in unhealthy conditions. The Court held that a bakery worker had every right when negotiating with his or her employer to sell as much labor under whatever conditions he or she chose.

On the other hand, the Court upheld a variety of other regulatory efforts by the state and federal governments in matters such as prostitution, gambling, narcotics, and other areas involving morality or lifestyle issues. Thus, the Court accepted the argument made by lawyer Louis Brandeis in *Muller v. Oregon* using what is now called a Brandeis brief (a brief relying primarily on scientific or social-scientific information rather than legal authorities), that an Oregon law setting special limitations on hours and working conditions for women because of their presumed more vulnerable physical condition was valid. The fact that the Court seemed quite arbitrary in its handling of such issues, along with its tendency to prohibit legislatures at both the national and state levels from addressing well-known social and economic problems, brought serious challenges to the Court from within the Court as well as from outside it. Justice Oliver Wendell Holmes, in one of the most quoted challenges to the Court's behavior, warned that "the Constitution did not enact Mr. Herbert Spencer's social statics," referring to the writings of the leading Social Darwinist of the time.

While much happened that was damaging to the Court during this period, it was also an important time in the Court's internal development. For one thing, the justices ended their circuit-riding chores with the adoption of legislation creating the U.S. Circuit Court of Appeals. Then came Chief Justice Taft.

Former president William Howard Taft wanted the chief justiceship for himself after he left the presidency, and he took the job with a commitment to strengthening the institution. Like Earl Warren some years later, Taft assumed the leadership of the Court during a period of internal strife. For example, Justice John H. Clarke resigned in part because of his dislike for the conflict in the Court generated by people like Justice McReynolds. Taft, too, had a terrible time with McReynolds.[34] His dissatisfaction on the Court and his fear of some of the potential nominees led Taft to be particularly active in efforts to lobby the president on future nominations.[35]

Taft was also not above lobbying the Congress. At the center of his reform effort was passage of legislation that ultimately became the Judiciary Act of 1925. At the core of the act was the opportunity for the Court to get control of its own docket by exercising certiorari jurisdiction, under which it would determine, as a matter of discretion, which cases were worthy of Supreme Court review. So zealous was Taft in this and other lobbying efforts that he was outraged that Brandeis seemed to be secretly opposing his congressional program. Ultimately, Taft got his bill, and the Court was transformed by it over the years.

The Court was also significantly shaped by another Taft victory, approval for construction of a building to house the Court. Though some justices criticized the opulence of the new home for the Court, constructed during a period of national economic disaster, and suggested that they would look like a bunch of beetles wandering around in the Temple of Karnak or that the only suitable way to move in was to ride in on the backs of elephants while the Grand March from Aïda was played, the Court building proved a huge hit over the years. Whatever else he did, Taft reestablished the strong chief justice role, in a manner not seen since the days of John Marshall.

The New Deal Clash and the FDR Court

Discussion of the Court's institutional development, however, gave way to criticism of the role it was defining for itself in American life as the nation moved into the Great Depression. The creation by the Court of a political no man's land in which neither the federal government nor the states were permitted to regulate economic activity would appear to be a popular position from a business perspective. But the Great Depression brought an immediate call from the business community for government action to buttress the economy, protect the banking and currency systems, stabilize the markets, and restore commerce.[36] When the

Court began striking down provisions of the programs designed to accomplish those ends, like the National Industrial Recovery Act and the Agricultural Adjustment Act, its decisions struck at conservative business interests as well as more liberal social concerns.

The Court was pictured as nine old men standing in the way of economic recovery and progress. In particular, the Court had a reactionary core of four justices popularly known as the four horsemen, Justices James C. McReynolds, Pierce Butler, Willis Van Devanter, and George Sutherland, who advocated the laissez-faire position to the end. If they had the votes of Justices Hughes and Roberts, as they often did until late 1936, there was a solid six-person majority for that view of constitutional restriction on political action.

President Roosevelt was not the only one frustrated by the Court's behavior. Future justice Hugo Black was then a senator from economically devastated Alabama, and he was outraged by the Court's seemingly single-minded commitment to prevent the Congress and the president from responding to the Great Depression. Nevertheless, it was the president who decided to take action in the form of a legislative proposal to add staff to the Court for each of the older members, purportedly to ease the burden of the elderly justices their demanding docket imposed. But the president had not laid groundwork in the Congress. For that matter, he did not even bother to consult with those he hoped would carry the primary burden of passing the legislation.

Roosevelt's efforts fell for three other reasons. First, Roberts and Hughes had switched their positions on key cases decided but not announced before the president revealed his plan. When the opinions were presented, there seemed to be little point to the president's plan except vindictiveness. Despite the fact that the change Roberts and Hughes made in their position is often referred to as "the switch in time that saved nine," the truth is that there is no evidence that the plan caused them to rethink their decision. Second, some of the four horsemen were as anxious to retire as the president was to be rid of them. Since the Congress had previously reneged on its promises regarding judicial-retirement provisions, however, some stayed on. The first of them retired as soon as Congress passed new retirement legislation in May 1937. Finally, Roosevelt did not count on the skill with which Chief Justice Hughes would counter the challenge. Hughes simply indicated to Congress that since the Court was fully abreast of its docket, there seemed little point in expanding its size. The larger case made by implication was that the president was attacking and attempting to politicize the Court as an institution. That tactic elicited considerable support for the Court and criticism of the president's position.

Still, Roosevelt ultimately won by the march of time what he could not win in Congress. He appointed Hugo Black, Stanley Reed, Felix Frankfurter, William O. Douglas, Frank Murphy, James Byrnes, Robert Jackson, and Rutledge, and for the most part his appointees did not disappoint the president. Before his death, the president saw what came to be called the Roosevelt Court dispose of most of the mischief of its predecessors.

However, the 1940s was a decade of tumult as the nation struggled with the end of the depression and the beginning of a world war. President Truman saw an increasingly conflict-ridden court, and his appointees did nothing to help that situation, including the chief justice he appointed precisely for the purpose of restoring harmony to the troubled Court. The fact that the Court was called on to play a key role in the anti-Communist witch hunt and in challenging racial segregation did nothing to ease the challenges facing the justices.

Warren and His Court

Enter Earl Warren. The restoration of national power that had begun in 1937 continued into the Warren years. The Court both recognized the authority of Congress to employ sweeping powers under the commerce and taxing-and-spending clauses of the Constitution and also to exercise wide authority over the states. So broad was this authority that Hugo Black was later moved to charge that, in some respects at least, the states had been reduced to the status of "conquered provinces."[37]

It is perhaps not surprising that Black's concern was expressed in the context of a debate over civil rights legislation. It was not that Black opposed the struggle for civil rights and racial equality—far from it. It was Black who insisted that at some point the time for permitting school districts to act "with all deliberate speed" had passed and the time for immediate action had arrived.[38] There had been far too much deliberation and too little speed in responding to the just claims of African American children for desegregation of the public schools.

On the other hand, Black, the great advocate of a literal interpretation of the Constitution and respecter of state autonomy, nevertheless led the effort on the Court to nationalize the Bill of Rights, or, put differently, to apply the protections of the Bill of Rights to the states through the due process clause of the Fourteenth Amendment. The Bill of Rights had, of course, been added to the Constitution to protect against abuses by the newly created strong central government. Over time, though, it became apparent that abuses were at least as likely to come from the states and that there seemed little reason to assume that state courts would protect the victims of that abuse, particularly if the victims were political, religious, or racial minorities. Hence, in a series of cases, the Court began applying the Bill of Rights protections to the states. Black called for a complete incorporation of all those protections but ultimately settled for a case-by-case incorporation of almost all of the safeguards. By the time he left the Court, Black could say that he had won his battle to incorporate the Bill of Rights into the Fourteenth Amendment's due process clause. On the other hand, the application of the rights and the availability of federal courts as places in which they could be vindicated clearly assured a greater involvement by those courts in the affairs of the states.

If the nation was in a state of change, so was the Court. Like Hughes, Taft, and Marshall before him, Warren asserted the importance of a strong chief justice, though in a very different way than his predecessors. His style was friendly, but no one doubted his stature. He made administrative changes in the Court, including opening Court at 10:00 A.M. instead of noon; moving the conference session from Saturday to Friday; ending the "opinion Monday" tradition under which the Court announced its opinions only on Mondays, instead releasing opinions as soon as the author had commenced presentation of the opinion in Court; and installing a sound system on the bench and in the courtroom.[39] This last change was opposed by Justice Frankfurter, who often disapproved of departures from tradition, however limited. In such matters, as a Warren biographer put it, Frankfurter was wont to call on his colleagues to "think twice and thrice before disobeying the injunction, 'Remove not the landmarks of thy Fathers.'"[40]

The Burger Court Years

Warren's successor, Warren Burger, was one of the most actively involved judicial administrators among the chief justices. Burger moved to modernize the administration of the Court, build its security and other institutional support staffs, improve relationships with Congress on budgeting and other administrative questions, and ensure adequate maintenance of the Supreme Court building itself. To aid in this process, Burger established the office of Administrative Assistant to the Chief Justice, the holder of which has served as the principal operating administrator under Burger and his successor, William Rehnquist.

There has been considerable debate about the degree to which the Burger Court represented the kind of "constitutional counterrevolution" many predicted when President Richard Nixon found himself with the opportunity to make four appointments.[41] Part of the problem with determining to what extent this "counterrevolution" occurred is the criterion used: Some observers would conclude that major change had been achieved only if massive numbers of direct reversals of Warren Court precedents had taken place, something that was hardly likely, at least put in quite those terms. Second, there were those who expected immediate action; but the Burger Court, as such, really did not come into its own until approximately 1974–75. Not until then did many of the Court's rulings in such areas as access to the Court, limitations on due process claims, and issues of federalism begin to demonstrate major trends contrary to those of the Warren years.

On the other hand, the Burger years saw recognition of the right to abortion and the creation of something called commercial free speech. Moreover, as O'Brien has noted, the Burger Court overturned more rulings than the Warren Court, striking down more congressional enactments (thirty-three as compared with twenty-five), and nullifying more state laws and almost as many ordinances.

The Rehnquist Court

What is clear from the Burger years is that there was considerable internal criticism of the chief justice, both regarding some of his opinions but even more with respect to some of his judgments about managing opinion assignments. William Rehnquist, a longtime member of the Burger Court, represented a major change from his predecessor. Said by some of his colleagues to "run a tight ship" in conferences as compared with Burger, Rehnquist is generally described as personally affable and pleasant. Some staff members have even gone so far as to characterize it as "the happy Court."[42] On the other hand, that characterization seems somewhat questionable in light of what Justice Sandra Day O'Connor has termed "the battle of the footnotes," a running conflict among some of the justices and the continued prevalence of sharply divided opinions.

While there are some respects in which the Rehnquist Court was not heralded as likely to be revolutionary, it has already rendered a wide variety of important rulings that would have been thought incomprehensible at the end of the Warren era. Justices William Brennan and Thurgood Marshall saw the changes coming and fought them, but to no avail. Of the Warren Court–era justices, only Byron White remained on the Court long enough to allow a Democratic president to name his replacement.

WORKING IN THE TEMPLE

As a new justice enters the Court, he sees the tourists milling around, and the security guards quietly but carefully keeping the visitors moving in one direction, the attorneys in another, and protecting the unseen operation of the Court taking place all around the public area. Like most people, justices can remember their first visit to the Court, for the Court is, as we have said, an enduring institution as well as a changing collection of men and women. The building (see Fig. 4.1) both houses the Court and symbolizes it as well. Yet the building is a shell; the organization that gives it life and makes it possible for the nine justices to perform their duty and the individual divisions of the organization headed by each of the justices is the Court's life force.

The walk up the steps in front of the Court brings the justice to the entrance to this impressive edifice. As one climbs toward the door, one's eyes move up to the words carved above the entrance, "Equal Justice Under Law," the great American ideal. The degree to which it is a reality has something to do with the decisions the new justice will make as a member of the Court. She takes an oath to do equal justice to the poor as well as to the rich.

When visitors enter the building for the first time, they gaze down the long high-ceilinged corridor, lined with marble columns and busts of the Court's chief

FIGURE 4.1   Layout of the U.S. Supreme Court building. (*From James MacGregor Burns et al., Government by the People 16/E, Prentice Hall, Englewood Cliffs, NJ, 1995, p. 417.*)

1. Courtyard
2. Solicitor General's Office
3. Lawyers' Lounge
4. Marshall's Office
5. Main Hall
6. Court Room
7. Conference and Reception Rooms

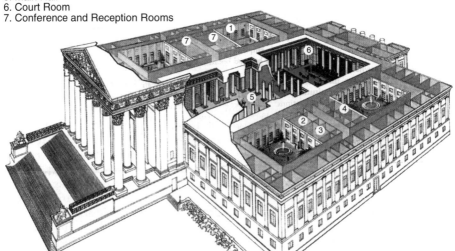

justices. At the other end of the hall is the small door to the courtroom itself. Most first-time visitors react to the courtroom with a mix of seriousness elicited by the design and decor of the room and a bit of surprise. The immediate comparison made by many is to a church. On either side of the room stand the double rows of marble columns, between them, sets of what look like church pews with an aisle in the middle and on either end. Before that stands the brass railing, the bar of the Court, through which the attorneys pass as they prepare to argue before the Court. Between the bar and the bench sit the counsel tables and, in the middle, the speakers' rostrum with two lights, one red and one white, obvious even to those in the visitors' seats. The small white light goes on to tell counsel that there are five minutes left for oral argument. The red light informs a lawyer that time has expired. On the right and left of the counsel tables are boxes for spectators. Those on the left are occupied by the press, and the seats on the right, on special occasions, by the families of the justices or other visiting dignitaries. Facing the room and, from its elevated position, dominating it is the high bench, with a rather odd-looking row of unmatched chairs behind. One of the perquisites of office is that a justice will have a chair made to his or her specifications. Above the bench is carved a picture of the great lawgivers of history, and behind it is the huge red velvet curtain through which the justices enter the room for the sitting of the Court.

If visitors come at the beginning of the day, they rise as the justices enter the room and stand beside their respective chairs. The marshal then intones the traditional call to business:

> Oyez, oyez, oyez. All those having business before the Honorable Supreme Court are admonished to draw near and give their attention for the Court is now sitting. God save the United States and this honorable Court.

It has not escaped the attention of some Court watchers that the marshal may sometimes unwittingly put the deity to a very serious challenge in asking for divine protection of the Court and the nation. Indeed, there is the story told by one well-wisher, Thurman Arnold, one of Justice William O. Douglas's colleagues on the Yale Law faculty, at an anniversary party for Douglas. Arnold recalled the first time that the daily formula was recited after Douglas had taken the oath of office:

> The Crier of the Supreme Court was obviously harassed and disturbed. I remember him saying immediately after Justice Douglas took his seat "God save the United States and this honorable Court."
>
> He had been saying the same thing long before the appointment of Justice Douglas but in those early days it was only part of a routine. When Justice Douglas took his seat, the Crier for the first time seemed to realize the tremendous difficulty of the task which he was imposing on divine Providence. There were anxiety and supplication in his voice when he petitioned that both the Court with Mr. Justice Douglas on it and the Nation be saved at the same time. He was conscious of the drastic character of the equitable relief contained in that prayer.
>
> But he was a man of courage. He did not amend his petition in the light of the newly discovered evidence that Bill had become a member of the Court. A lesser man would have modified his prayer to make the relief demanded appear more reasonable. He would have said "In the event that both of the following objectives seem

impossible of accomplishment in light of our new appointment, God save the United States or this honorable Court," thus giving Providence its choice.

But the Crier did not waiver. He did not compromise. He did not surrender to any policy of appeasement. He decided to go for broke asking Providence to save both the Court and the Nation simultaneously.[43]

Arnold added that Douglas knew his arrival at the Court might cause such consternation on the part of the Court crier and possibly even the deity, but "he crossed the Rubicon, he cut the Gordian Knot, he burned his dams behind him" and accepted the job nonetheless.[44]

Most visitors to the Court on their first trip leave the courtroom to tour the rest of the public portion of the building, which is principally the basement. There they find the Court's museum, cafeteria, and gift shop.

Those who come to the Court as attorneys see more of the Court and see it differently. They are often brought to the Court by the person sponsoring them for membership in the bar of the Supreme Court. The attorneys are introduced at the beginning of the Court's session and are welcomed to practice before the Court by the chief justice. Earl Warren thought that this small, brief ceremony was quite important to the attorneys before the Court and the institution itself. During Warren's tenure, he had the new members of the Supreme Court bar see the clerk's office where the cases are filed and processed for handling by the justices' chambers, the Court's elegant law library, and the marshal's office with its adjoining waiting room for attorneys preparing to present their cases.

When one comes to the Court as a justice, one sees the rest of the operation. Although the justice might enter the Court by elevator from the basement parking garage or one of the side or back doors, one might, like some other justices, make it a point to enter through the front door. If so, instead of proceeding down the large corridor toward the marshal's office and courtroom, he or she would turn off that corridor into another corridor and through a locked brass gate. This is the entrance to the hall, along which are found the chambers of the justices. The justice's chambers are positioned along both sides of the building and are joined behind the courtroom by a corridor and the Court's conference room. A similar set of offices is located on the basement level surrounding the museum area and public space; there the offices of the Court's support staff are located. Above the main level are the library, justices' dining room, and a gymnasium where some justices and their staffs have been known to play basketball or exercise. It is jokingly known as "the highest court in the land."

Most people react with a chuckle at the idea of basketball in the Supreme Court. That is not the only sports image that has engendered laughter with respect to the justices. During his early days on the Supreme Court, William O. Douglas came across a Herb Block cartoon lampooning the conflicts between the Court and the Roosevelt administration. The cartoon pictured the Court planning a baseball game with members of the cabinet.

Douglas wrote to his friend Franklin Roosevelt and said:

I have just received the original of a cartoon drawn by Herbert Block and published a month or so ago. It is entitled "Nine Young Men." It shows members of this Court in a huddle in the corridors of the Supreme Court building. One of the more spirited, whose identity is not disclosed is saying, "Let's phone the cabinet members and see if we can get up a ball game."

I did not want to take this matter up officially without first sounding you out informally on the proposition.

Of course, all "ringers" should be excluded. I refer especially to General Watson, Admiral McIntyre and Steve Early.[45]

FDR picked up the challenge and answered:

The thought behind the ball game between the Nine Young Men and the Cabinet is an excellent one, even though you may eliminate General Watson, Admiral McIntyre, and Colonel Early.

I come back with a counter proposal, however. The Cabinet insists that the Chief Justice pitch and Mr. Justice McReynolds catch. Our battery will be the Secretary of State, pitcher, and the Secretary of the Interior, catcher. Except for the Secretary of the Navy, who is away, these are our oldest members—and, incidentally, it gives some advantage to the Supreme Court because an experienced battery counts and yours will be about ten years older than ours.

We also suggest no substitutes be put in—and we suggest further that the Umpires be the President and the Speaker of the House. This seems fair. Finally, we insist that your "Nine" waive in advance any judicial authority over umpires' decisions, and that in publicity after the game no minority opinions will be filed. So far, so good![46]

There ensued a set of exchanges between the justice and the president about the conditions under which some kind of competition might take place. By this point the baseball season had ended, and they had to cast about for some alternative sport. The idea of a football game was out, owing to the age and physical condition of many of the likely competitors, but there was the possibility of poker! Since Douglas and FDR were participants in a more-or-less regular poker game at the White House, it seemed a natural. (Douglas would often get a call from the president's secretary announcing that there would be a command performance at the White House, the code word for a poker game.) Of course, there immediately arose a question of propriety. Would some of the justices' personal or religious convictions preclude such a contest? To answer this question, Douglas had prepared a legal memorandum on the question of "whether Baptists could play poker." Thus ended one of the more intense sporting negotiations in American political history.

As new justices enter their chambers, they find what is to many people accustomed to senior partnerships in large, prestigious law firms a very small set of offices and a limited staff. The office suite is elegant to be sure, but small. The oak walls and bookcases, the tall, thin windows with elegant draperies, and the fireplace give the room a feeling of warmth but not spaciousness. The computer terminal beside the desk is one of the only visible indications of the contemporary nature of the operation. Outside the justices' chambers is a place for two secretaries, and beyond that a smaller, and frankly rather Spartan, office for three law clerks. The number of clerks immediately available to an individual justice depends in part on whether he chooses to participate in the so-called cert pool, which is a collection of clerks on loan from most of the justices to prepare memoranda on the petitions.

For some functions, like the conferences at which the justices discuss cases, there is no staff presence at all except by virtue of the memoranda the clerks prepare that summarize facts and issues in the cases. In the conference room, like the courtroom, the seats are arranged around the conference table by seniority, which can produce interesting consequences. Thus, Justice Douglas was seated next to Justice Frankfurter, who entered the Court just before he did. Frankfurter spoke before Douglas in conference, and Douglas delighted in attempting to drive the former Harvard professor to the brink of distraction. The entire proceeding takes place seemingly under the gaze of former chief justice John Marshall, whose portrait hangs nearby.

The justices and their staffs have help from the Office of the Clerk, the marshal, the reporter of decisions, the librarian, the curator, the Public Affairs Office, the Legal Office, the administrative assistant to the chief justice, and Supreme Court fellows and interns. The clerk of the court is an office quite distinct from the clerks who work for the individual justices. With a staff of about fifty people, the Office of the Clerk essentially prepares cases from their initial arrival at the Court to the point where they are ready for decision by the justices. After the decision, the clerk's office handles any remaining interaction with the lower courts or the parties.

That seemingly simple set of responsibilities is far more complicated than it sounds. For one thing, thousands of the petitions that arrive at the Court each year are so-called *in forma pauperis* cases, filed by poor litigants who are attempting to represent themselves. These come from prisoners from around the nation.

The justices' conference room, where meetings, led by the chief justice, are conducted in secret, during which the justices reach preliminary judgments on cases to be heard by the Court in the future and hold substantive discussions on arguments heard in open court earlier in the week.

The clerk's office must ensure that all necessary documents and records are assembled for the Court's consideration.

While the justices decide which cases they will hear, the clerk's office manages the docket on a day-to-day basis. The office prepares the conference lists, schedules oral argument, and manages the scheduling of hearings. It also handles emergency petitions that come to the Court, such as petitions from condemned prisoners for stay of execution.

The actual conduct of the oral-argument phase of the decision process is also influenced by the marshal's office. While the simplest description of the marshal is head of Supreme Court security, the office also handles other duties. It serves, for example, as the protocol office, which is no small task for a body with as many visitors and as much contact with foreign leaders as the Court has on a regular basis. Justices receive numerous contacts from scholars and officials seeking to visit with them or have them address their groups or classes. The marshal's office tries to help them manage these activities without interfering with their own desires. During oral arguments, the marshal acts as Court crier and time-keeper.

The reporter of decisions is charged with publication of the Court's opinions, but on a day-to-day basis provides printing services for internal Court documents. The latter is a particularly important task because it involves preparation of draft opinions for circulation among the justices during the decision process. There can be many drafts, and they can change dramatically from the initial version before the members of the Court agree that the opinion is ready for delivery.

The reporter of decisions has the considerable task of providing rapid, accurate, and complete distribution of documents with complete secrecy. If a copy of a draft opinion were to leak or a copy of a pending case to be acquired prematurely, effects might be devastating. For the most part, the office has been amazingly successful in protecting the secrecy of the Court's deliberations.

The Office of the Curator is a small office charged with the management of the Court's memorabilia. It provides the justices with office items with historical value, such as Justice Black's desk to one justice who requested it. It collects items from current justices and provides photographic coverage of the Court's activities.

The staff of the library are an extremely important part of the justices' day-to-day business because they provide all of the legal research resources that the justices and their staffs will need.

The public-information staff is another very small office that provides communications between the Court and the media. In addition to handling calls from around the nation, the office works with the press corps assigned to the Court and manages the occasional high-visibility public-information activities associated with events like the retirement of a justice.

The Court maintains a legal office as an institutional advisory body. The task of that office is to assist in legal matters other than the decision of cases.

Finally, assisting the chief justice in the management of these staff offices is the Office of the Administrative Assistant to the Chief Justice. Created at the request of Chief Justice Burger, the administrative assistant has to date been a person with a background in public administration. In addition to her role in the internal operation of the Court, the administrative assistant helps the chief justice with external duties such as budgetary matters, interactions with Congress, and the chief's role as leader of the national judiciary.

SUMMARY

At bottom, life in the Marble Temple is shaped by some facts of life. First, despite its larger-than-life image, the Court is a small institution, less than three hundred people total. It has a meager budget. Second, because of its size, task, and character, the Court is a delicate institution that depends for its successful operation on a set of relationships among a small group of independent and coequal justices who are, as a practical matter, beyond any one justice's control. Therefore, issues like collegiality and ritual are very important to the maintenance of a working relationship. Just what the workload is that your colleagues and you find on your desks, how it got there, and what you do with it is the subject of Chapter 5.

NOTES

[1]See Bruce Allen Murphy, *The Brandeis/Frankfurter Connection* (New York: Oxford University Press, 1982).

[2]384 U.S. 436 (1966).

[3]378 U.S. 478 (1964).

[4]347 U.S. 483 (1954).

[5]341 U.S. 494 (1951).

[6]J. Woodford Howard, *Mr. Justice Murphy* (Princeton, NJ: Princeton University Press, 1968), p. 398.

[7]William O. Douglas to Hugo L. Black, Sept. 13, 1945, box 308, William O. Douglas Papers, Library of Congress (hereafter cited as WODP).

[8]William O. Douglas, *The Court Years* (New York: Random House, 1980), p. 226.

[9]See J. Steven Ott, *The Organizational Culture Perspective* (Chicago: Dorsey, 1989); and Edgar Schein, *Organizational Culture and Leadership*, 2d ed. (San Francisco: Jossey-Bass, 1992).

[10]David O'Brien, *Storm Center* (New York: Norton, 1986), p. 102.

[11]Harold R. Burton, "The Story of the Place: Where First and A Streets Formerly Met at What Is Now the Site of the Supreme Court Building." (Speech originally prepared for delivery at the dedication of a plaque presented by the Columbia Historical Society, May 1952, box 313, WODP).

[12]George Washington to John Jay, Oct. 5, 1789 (quoted in Charles Warren, *The Supreme Court in United States History*, vol. 1 [Boston, Little Brown, 1926], pp. 35–36).

[13]Ibid., p. 45.

[14]Ibid., p. 50.

[15]Warren, *Supreme Court*, vol. 1, pp. 110–11.

[16]Ibid., pp. 67–69.

[17]2 *Dall.* 419 (1793).

[18]*Hayburn's Case.* See Warren, *Supreme Court*, at vol. 1, pp. 69–71.

[19]*Hylton v. United States*, 3 *Dallas* 171 (1796).

[20]Louis Fisher, *Constitutional Dialogues* (Princeton, NJ: Princeton University Press, 1988).

[21]Warren, *Supreme Court*, vol. 1, p. 86.

[22]1 *Cranch* 137 (1803).

[23]*Little v. Barreme*, 6 U.S. 170 (1804)

[24]*Fletcher v. Peck*, 10 U.S. 87 (1810).

[25] *McCulloch v. Maryland*, 17 U.S. 316 (1819).

[26] Madison, James, Alexander Hamilton, and John Jay, *The Federalist Papers* (New York: Mentor, 1961), p. 284.

[27] 19 *Howard* 393 (1857).

[28] *Slaughter-House Cases*, 83 U.S. 36 (1873).

[29] *Civil Rights Cases*, 109 U.S. 3 (1883).

[30] *Plessy v. Ferguson*, 163 U.S. 537 (1896).

[31] *Hammer v. Dagenhart*, 247 U.S. 251 (1918); *E.C. Knight v. United States*, 156 U.S. 1 (1895); and *United States v. Butler*, 297 U.S. 1 (1936).

[32] Elder Witt, ed., *Guide to the U.S. Supreme Court*, 2d ed. (Washington, DC: Congressional Quarterly, 1990), p. 38.

[33] 198 U.S. 45 (1905).

[34] Alpheus T. Mason, *William Howard Taft: Chief Justice* (New York: Simon and Schuster, 1965), pp. 215–16.

[35] David Danelski, *A Supreme Court Justice Is Appointed* (New York: Random House, 1964).

[36] Howard Ball and Phillip J. Cooper, *Of Power and Right* (New York: Oxford University Press, 1992), chap. 4.

[37] See *Younger v. Harris*, 401 U.S. 37 (1971).

[38] *Alexander v. Holmes County, Mississippi*, 396 U.S. 1218 (1969).

[39] Robert J. Steamer, *Chief Justice* (Columbia: University of South Carolina, 1986), pp. 62–63.

[40] Bernard Schwartz, *Super Chief* (New York: New York University Press, 1983), p. 130.

[41] See Richard Funston, *Constitutional Counterrevolution?* (New York: Schenkman, 1977); Vincent Blasi, ed., *The Burger Court: The Counter-Revolution That Wasn't* (New Haven, CT: Yale University Press, 1982); and Charles Lamb and David Halperin, eds., *The Burger Court* (Urbana: University of Illinois, 1991).

[42] Peter Irons, *Brennan versus Rehnquist* (New York: Knopf, 1994).

[43] Thurman Arnold, twentieth-anniversary dinner, Washington, DC, Apr. 17, 1959, box 305, WODP, pp. 3–4.

[44] Ibid., p. 6.

[45] William O. Douglas to Franklin Delano Roosevelt, June 23, 1939, William O. Douglas, Franklin Delano Roosevelt Papers, New Hyde Park, N.Y. (hereafter cited as FDRP).

[46] FDR to William O. Douglas, June 27, 1939, PSF William O. Douglas, FDRP.

What's on the Desk
and How Did It Get There?
Docket Control

5

It's early, around seven in the morning, and it is the first Monday in October, the formal opening of the term of the United States Supreme Court. At 10:00 A.M. the new Term officially begins. You thought you would be the first to enter the building, yet you notice that at least five chambers are buzzing with action. Some justices, including recently retired justices Byron White and Harry Blackmun, used to arrive at their offices at the crack of dawn and were hard at work by 7:00 A.M.

You enter your oak-paneled office, lined with bookcases filled with the black-letter law that you must draw on when examining the cases that come before the Court and when writing your opinions for the Court. After hanging up your jacket, you slip into the comfortable leather chair, turn on the computer (a matter of habit at this point in your life), and look at your desk for the first time. It's the same desk you had while you sat on the court of appeals, and you asked the staff to have it restored and brought to this office. The first glance at the desk startles you, for piled up neatly are no less than four stacks of briefs, each over ten inches high. In the middle of the desk is a set of typed notes, the bench memos, evidently left for you by your clerks. And wheeled flush to the desk is a cart with additional briefs stacked on it.

You're surprised because you had just finished reviewing, in a three-day conference with the other eight justices of the Court, over one thousand petitions that had arrived at the Court during the break between terms. Because of the increase in the caseload of the Court, Chief Justice Warren Burger initiated during his tenure the special conference before the term actually began, so the petition backlog could be cleared. The preterm conference has continued under Chief Justice William Rehnquist. In this conference, you and your colleagues reviewed the accumulated certiorari petitions and discussed the more than two hundred cases that were placed on the discuss list by the chief.

Even though about one-sixth of the Court's workload for the term had been addressed in the preterm conference, at seven on Monday morning there were new stacks on your desk. When, you ask yourself, do the law clerks ever sleep? When you left your office on Friday at 5:00 P.M., the stacks of petitions were not there!

You quickly sense that the workday of a justice begins early and, judging by the size of the piles on the top of your desk, lasts long into the evening.[1] Looking at the piles of paper accumulated over just one week, you now understand the comment Attorney General Homer Cummings made when, in 1937, he said to a congressional committee that if a justice had to read all the material filed with the Court, "it would be like having to read *Gone with the Wind* every morning before breakfast."[2]

"A mountain of work . . . must be processed" annually by the Court.[3] The petitions accumulate in the Court at the rate of between eighty and a hundred per week throughout the year.[4] Supreme Court scholar David O'Brien has observed that by the end of the 1980s, the Court annually received and had to process 250,000 pages of appeals and petitions for certiorari review, 62,500 pages of responses opposing such review, and 25,000 pages of replies favoring review, as well as 37,500 pages of law clerks' memoranda on the cases. The total: "More than 375,000 pages of filings that must be reviewed, in addition to the briefs on the merits of the 150 to 180 cases that are granted review and oral argument each term."[5]

Before you even begin to review the materials and the notes prepared by your four law clerks (the chief justice has five clerks as well as an administrative assistant) and your secretarial staff, however, there's a sharp knock at the door. In bursts the chief justice, wearing a broad grin and carrying several sheaves of papers, one of which he hands to you. It is the revised agenda for the Friday afternoon "discuss list" conference session, he informs you. Two of the justices wanted a few cases added to the discuss list he circulated last week, he says. Only then does he warmly welcome you to the Court and remind you that the robing will take place at ten minutes before ten and that the first order of business in open court will be your taking the formal oath of office. Before you can say anything beyond hello, he turns and is gone. His brief visit, it will turn out, would be one of only a handful of informal visits you will have with him during the term of the Court. You return to the chair, plop into it, study the desk again, and glance at the papers he left you.

The discuss list contains a listing of case numbers. These are arranged, numerically, under two headings, the miscellaneous and appellate dockets. The former docket listing contains the indigent (unpaid), or *in forma pauperis* (IFP), petitions received by the Court, whereas the latter listing includes all paid petitions that will be discussed in the conference session on Friday afternoon. As you will shortly learn, for more than a decade, the IFP petitions have outnumbered the paid petitions received by the Court.

Glancing over the discuss list (which will be used by your clerks to prepare you for the Friday meeting), there seem to be over fifty cases on the conference agenda. There is also another list, the petitions thought not to be "certworthy" by the chief and his clerks. It contains hundreds of cases that will automatically be denied unless a justice wishes otherwise. Looking at your desk, you see that the documents on it are the ten- to twenty-page (not counting the lengthy appendixes attached to each of them) jurisdiction briefs filed, in accordance with the form detailed in Court Rule 33,[6] by the parties to the legal disputes being discussed in conference this Friday.

You know, however, that this staggering amount of written material has to be handled in a certain manner for the Supreme Court to do its job. There has to be an agenda-setting process that manages the paperwork received by the Court during its term. You'll find out that, while some of the brethren in the past, such as Justice Felix Frankfurter, wanted the Court to establish formal rules for the justices to follow when deliberating petitions, no such set of formal rules has ever been adopted.[7] There is, nevertheless, a process at work that leads to docket control by the Court. Indeed, with the dramatic increase in the number of petitions, the Court has been more selective in creating its agenda.

DOCKET CONTROL IN THE SUPREME COURT

Looking at the many hundreds of petitions for review, piled or strewn across the justice's desk, one realizes the importance of the justice's agenda-setting role. The Court cannot possibly hear all the petitions it receives in a year. By the early 1990s, the Court was receiving more than sixty-seven hundred petitions annually. More than 97 percent of them were not heard on the merits by the Court. All must be reviewed, however, to determine which ones will be set aside for plenary review by the Court, that is, fully examined on their merits. These determinations are made initially by the law clerks, then by justices in chambers after reading the case markups prepared by the clerks. The final judgment is made by the collected justices in the Friday afternoon conference sessions during the term of the Court.

The Supreme Court makes its own agenda based on what the justices decide should be heard and decided by them during the term of the Court. Ironically, it is in their own chambers that the justices make their decisions about the "certworthiness," that is, whether the case will be heard on its merits, of the petitions. Given the dramatic increase in the Court's caseload over the past half century, the collegiality norm has diminished significantly. In the early days of the republic, when there were very few cases for the justices of the Court to address,[8] collegiality was the usual mode of operation and led to the creation of "institutional" opinions, that is, opinions joined in by the entire Court. At present, isolation is more the norm.

Given the dramatic change in the case flow to the Court in modern times and the consequent time pressure on the brethren to get the work done, there is

Justice William O. Douglas sitting at his crowded desk in his chambers.

very little discussion between the chambers about the petitions prior to the conference session. Justice Lewis Powell once said:

> I had thought of the Court as a collegial body in which the most characteristic activities would be consultation and cooperative deliberation, aided by a strong, supportive staff. I was in for more than a little surprise. . . . The Court is perhaps one of the last citadels of jealously preserved individualism. . . . Indeed, a Justice may go through an entire term without being once in the chambers of all the eight other members of the Court.[9]

Indeed, the Supreme Court "acts much less strategically" in formulating its agenda than scholars and policymakers "might expect."[10]

Three Unique Characteristics of the Court's Agenda-setting Process

The Court's agenda-setting process, at bottom then, is unlike other political/legal processes: It takes place in a very unique setting. There are three general characteristics of this decisional context: (1) the justice functioning as the senior partner of his own small law firm, one of nine independent law firms; (2) the important role of the justice's law clerks in the law firm; and (3) the central importance of the memorandum to the conference (MTTC) as the vehicle used to communicate between these nine independent law firms.

Nine Individual Law Firms   The Supreme Court, as Justice Powell and others have said, is in reality nine small and independent law firms, doing business and, occasionally, battle with each other almost impersonally. As a law clerk said, underscoring the validity of the Powell observation: "Justices don't think that much about what the other justices are doing. They spend little time with them and rarely see each other. They often come in and sit by themselves day after day without really talking to any of the other justices."[11] The justice and company includes her four law clerks, her two secretaries, and her messenger. Although the clerks do socialize, over lunch and during and after their basketball games in the fourth-floor basketball court, and do occasionally pass tidbits of information to their justice, these are informal connections and do not form a strategic part of the business of each "firm."

The Law Clerks   The law clerk is of critical importance to the justices. By the early 1990s, each of the justices had four clerks, although Justice John P. Stevens continued to use only three clerks; he also did not participate in the cert pool process. This process involves the pooling of the law clerks of eight of the justices. These clerks are assigned petitions to read, and they prepare a memo that is then read by the eight justices.

In 1992, the thirty-four law clerks were each paid $38,861 for their year's service to their justices. All come from top law schools (one dozen of the thirty-four clerks in the 1992 term received their law degrees from Harvard Law School), and more than half of them had clerked for one or two years in lower federal courts prior to coming to the Supreme Court. After service as law clerk to a Supreme Court justice, almost half of them will go off to teach in a law school.[12]

Even though half of the clerks have had clerking experience in lower federal courts, most come to the Court with little knowledge of their important tasks. Many have not even met with their justice until the senior partner arrives in the capital prior to the start of the term of the Court. Interviews for the job were conducted by a panel of friends of the justice.

While they know so little when they arrive and are frightened to death about working on the certiorari petitions, they have to learn fast. One clerk confessed, for most of the clerks, that "when I got to the Supreme Court, I didn't know what I was doing."[13] As junior associates in the law firm, the clerks must do the important cert work, that is, screen the thousands of certiorari petitions, mark up the cert pool memos, prepare bench memos for the justice after the conference session and before the oral argument, and help the justice with the dozen or so majority-opinion writing assignments each Justice will receive once the term begins.[14] Typically, the brethren will come to rely on their clerks' judgments "as soon as [the justices are] confident that [their] new law clerks are reliable."[15]

Unlike other jobs, in which the junior associate is given some guidance by the senior lawyers in the firm, the Supreme Court's law clerks receive no guidance at all from the senior partner. They arrive in July and are greeted by one or two clerks from the previous term and by a stack of over one thousand certiorari petitions that have to be reviewed by the time the term begins in October. In these summer months, the clerks, with no cue from their bosses, screen about 25 percent of the cases, close to two thousand petitions, for the Court's upcoming term.[16]

The justice is not in chambers, and thus the new job begins in terror. As one of Justice Stevens's law clerks commented to two new clerks: "You never really get ahead of the work—you stay on top of it but that's all you can expect. It's a delicately balanced year and you're always on the edge of the precipice."[17] When the clerks have the cert petitions down to a science, they then learn to do markups, bench memos, oral-argument preparation, and help the justice in the opinion-writing stage.

The Memorandum to the Conference (MTTC)   Most Court decisions are "made in chambers, and with little discussion between the chambers."[18] There is very little personal communication between the justices during the term of the Court. Chatting on the telephone or visiting another colleague in her chambers is very rare. Instead, the written memorandum to the conference (MTTC) is the major vehicle used by the justices to communicate with each other. See Figure 5.1 for a view of a typical MTTC.

The MTTC is critical, for it puts the ideas of justices on paper and enables the other members to react to those ideas. The justices are much more comfortable when they can read the ideas of their colleagues in the MTTC. As Chief

FIGURE 5.1.   A typical memorandum to the conference (MTTC).

Supreme Court of the United States
Washington, D. C. 20543
March 14, 1972

CHAMBERS OF
THE CHIEF JUSTICE

MEMORANDUM TO THE CONFERENCE:

Re: No. 70-2 -- United States v. 12,200-Ft. Reels of
         Super 8 mm. Film, et al.

         Several of you have commented on my February 29
memo.

         I emphasize what I said at Conference before this memo
went out that it is in a sense merely a "trial balloon." For me,
this case is part of the whole fabric of the obscenity problem
and I have not abandoned the view shared in part with John Harlan and Harry Blackmun that this whole area ought to be primarily a state problem, with this Court reviewing only egregious
departures. .I do not now, and never have, accepted the idea
that every "chill" on expression or conduct is a threat to the
Republic. There is a lot of conduct passed off as speech that
ought to be put in deep freeze.

         I hope to have something on the Miller case before long
and then we can see how "alone" I am.

                                    Regards,

Justice Rehnquist said recently, he always asks his colleagues to put their thoughts in writing.[19] Justice Harry Blackmun recently commented on the value of the MTTC. He wrote that the MTTC does have "an impact on the decisional process . . . for it sets forth in specific language the concerns entertained by the author. In some respect, this is better than general observations made orally at conference. And they [the MTTC's] tend to fill in the gap occasioned by the lack of time for extended conferences or one-on-one conversations. By a MTTC, all nine are brought into the discussion."[20]

Threshold Norms and Access to the Court

To fully understand the agenda-setting activities of the Court, one must understand the value of the Supreme Court's general threshold standards. Certain technical requirements must be met for a petition to be considered for plenary review.[21] They are (1) Supreme Court jurisdiction, (2) standing to sue, and (3) justiciability. If the Court has no jurisdiction to hear the case, if the petitioner has no standing to bring suit in the Supreme Court, or if the case is a nonjusticiable one, then the petition will be denied certiorari.

Jurisdiction   The Supreme Court, while it now has almost absolute discretion over its docket, nevertheless is a court of limited jurisdiction, or authority (power), to hear a case or controversy: The justices cannot hear a petition that does not fall within the Court's constitutional and statutory authority. Supreme Court jurisdiction is spelled out in Article III[22] and in congressional statutes passed since the 1789 Judiciary Act, which have added significantly to the appellate jurisdiction of the Court.

Congress, since 1789, has passed various judicial statutes beginning with the Judiciary Act of 1789. In recent decades, Congress has passed environmental, health, crime control, worker safety, and civil and voting rights legislation statutes that have increased the caseload of the federal courts in America.

Additionally, since 1789, Congress has passed significant legislation that has enabled the Court to create its own agenda,[23] including the important Judges Act of 1925 and, in 1988, with intense lobbying on the part of Chief Justice Rehnquist,[24] the Act for the Improvement of the Administration of Justice.[25] Congress has the power to add to the Court's appellate jurisdiction, consistent with Article III. It has done so in earnest in the generations after the Civil War. Congressional statutes since the late nineteenth century have accounted, in great part, for the dramatic increase in the Court's caseload.

Consistent, too, with Article III is the other side of congressional power: Congress can reduce the appellate jurisdiction of the Court if it desires. While this has happened only once in Court history,[26] many scores of bills threatening to take away the power of the Court to hear cases and controversies in certain controversial areas have been introduced by angry legislators.[27] All petitioners must address the jurisdiction question in the petitions they present to the Court.

Standing to Sue   The second technical standard gets to the essential meaning of "case-or-controversy" language found in Article III. The Supreme Court is not authorized to provide advisory opinions to parties. Its jurisdiction extends to real cases and controversies. Justice Sandra Day O'Connor put it directly: "We have to have an actual, real live case or controversy"[28] to hear a case on the merits.

The question of standing to sue involves whether clear evidence is present in the record of a legally recognized personal adverseness or injury. Is the proper person, that is, the "injured" person, the party that has brought the petition to the Court? A third party, someone who has not been injured in some manner and who is not one of the parties to the alleged dispute, cannot properly file a petition in the Supreme Court. A related question is whether the petitioner who has been injured has exhausted all her remedies prior to petitioning the Court to hear her case. Has the petition been filed prematurely, or have the conflicts presented in the petition already been resolved between the parties? The party who files a petition in the Court must show actual adverseness for the petition to be reviewed for possible inclusion on the Court's docket.

Justiciability   Finally, and critically important, assuming some form of concrete injury, *can* or *should* the Court resolve or remedy the legal questions laid out in the petition brought to the Court? Over the generations, the justices have created a general guideline to assist them with justiciability questions. The "political-question" doctrine, created and modified over time by liberal and conservative Court majorities in specific cases and controversies,[29] is a framework to determine whether the petition should be rejected because the questions it raises are "political questions" better handled by Congress, the executive, or by state political agencies. Wishing to avoid entering "political thickets,"[30] the Court announces that the petition is a nonjusticiable political question and declines to rule on the merits. If a majority of the justices, in Bickel's words, "sense a lack of capacity" to resolve the questions raised in the petition, then the petition will be denied because it is nonjusticiable.[31]

Answering these general procedural and substantive access questions determines whether the Court will grant or deny certiorari in petitions brought before the Court. Petitioners filing with the Court must address these issues in the jurisdictional brief their attorney prepares for the Court. (Respondents, the other party to the dispute alleged in every petition, have thirty days to react to the petitioner's allegations.)

Obviously, the element of Court subjectivity enters into the application of these technical standards. Chief Justice Earl Warren summarized this essential reality when he wrote in a 1968 case, *Flast v. Cohen*, that each case before the Court has

> an iceberg quality, containing beneath the surface simplicity, submerged complexities [jurisdiction and justiciability] which go to the heart of our constitutional form of government. . . . Justiciability is a term of art. . . . It is not a legal concept with a fixed content or susceptible of scientific verification. Its utilization is the resultant of many subtle pressures.[32]

In large part, the Court's power is "the control it possesses over the amount and the character of its business."[33] The tension surrounding judicial appointments to the Court, including the grilling nominees receive from the president's opposition in the Senate, is due to the reality that the "decision as to who will make the decisions affects what decisions will be made."[34] The significance of the kind and amount of work done by the Court is clear. By creating its own agenda, the Court is telling the nation what it thinks is important as a matter of law and as a matter of public policy.

The Centrality of the Certiorari Petition

The agenda-setting process, the Court's "power to decide what to decide,"[35] begins initially with the receipt of a petition from a petitioner asking the Court to review a case from a lower court, either federal or state. Since 1988, almost all the requests for Court review are through petitions asking the Court to grant certiorari—"cert pets" as the clerks call these many thousands of requests.[36] These cert pets are filed in light of the Court's Article III appellate jurisdiction[37] and in accordance with the Court's own rules. While the Court does have original jurisdiction,[38] very few cases come to the Court under that grant of power.

The writ of certiorari, especially after the 1988 legislation, is central to the agenda-setting effort of the Court. Certiorari is a legal concept that had its origins in England and means, literally, "to be informed." If the Supreme Court grants the petition for certiorari, it means that the Court will be informed of the case by having the record sent up to the Court from the lower court. Since 1988, all (about 99 percent) but a handful of appellate petitions to the Court have been petitions for certiorari. (The special three-judge federal district court litigation, involving antitrust, presidential campaign funding, voting rights, apportionment, and civil rights cases, can still be "appealed as of right" to the Court. These appeals constitute a very small segment of the appellate petitions. It should be noted, by comparison, that prior to 1988, given the narrowness of the "appeal" category,[39] only about 10 percent of the appellate calendar consisted of appeals as of right.)

The writ of certiorari can be filed in any civil or criminal case in a U.S. Court of Appeals, before or after judgment or decree.[40] Requests for certiorari can also come from the state court system. If the petition comes to the Court from a final decision of a state's highest court, the petition must show either that a state statute's validity was drawn into question in light of its repugnancy to a federal statute, a federal treaty, a federal regulation, or to a clause in the U.S. Constitution or that a federal right—claimed in the state court proceedings—was violated and that the state court decision was not based on adequate nonfederal grounds.

Rule 10 of the Rules of the Supreme Court enumerates "considerations governing review on certiorari." Clearly, certiorari is a discretionary grant, for the rule begins by stating:

> A review on writ of certiorari is not a matter of right, but of judicial discretion, and will be granted only when there are special and important reasons therefor. The following, while neither controlling nor fully measuring the Court's discretion, indicate the character of the reasons that will be considered.
>
> (a) When a federal court of appeals has rendered a decision in conflict with the decision of another court of appeals on the same matter; or has decided a federal question in a way in conflict with a state court of last resort; or has so far departed from the accepted and usual course of judicial proceedings, or has so far sanctioned such a departure by a lower court, as to call for an exercise of this Court's power of supervision.

(b) When a state court of last resort has decided a federal question in a way in conflict with the decision of another state court of last resort or of a federal court of appeals.

(c) When a state court or a federal court of appeals has decided an important question of federal law which has not been, but should be, settled by this Court, or has decided a federal question in a way in conflict with applicable decisions of this Court.

In a 1949 address, Chief Justice Fred Vinson suggested some parameters for the proper application of the rule. For the chief justice, certiorari should not be granted for the "correction of errors" in lower-court decisions. For him, cert should be granted only for

> those cases which present questions whose resolution will have immediate importance far beyond the particular facts and parties involved. Those of you whose petitions for certiorari are granted by the Supreme Court will know, therefore, that you are, in a sense, prosecuting or defending class actions; that you represent not only your clients, but tremendously important principles, upon which are based the plans, hopes, and aspirations of a great many people throughout the country.[41]

Vinson's observations have been accepted by the justices of the Court both in practice and in rhetoric. For the Court, as Justice William Brennan observed, grants of certiorari are rendered because of the overall importance of the questions raised in the petition. He wrote that "only an exceptional case raising a significant federal question commands the review" of the Court.[42] Agenda setting by the justices, then, means ascertaining which of the almost seven thousand petitions for a writ of certiorari contains such "tremendously important" issues.

The Stages in the Court's Agenda-setting Process

The cert pet has been, since 1928, a jurisdictional statement that informs the justices and their clerks about the questions raised in the lower courts. Filed by thousands of petitioners annually, the petition, with the respondent's brief attached, starts the communications process within the Court that leads to the creation of the Court's docket of cases to be granted plenary review.

Petitioners are guided by Rule 15 of the Rules of the Supreme Court. Entitled "Jurisdictional Statement," it enumerates what is "required" in the petition:

15.1 (a) Statement of the questions presented by the appeal.

(b) List of all parties to the proceeding in the Court whose judgment is sought to be reviewed. . . .

(d) Reference to the official or unofficial reports of any opinions delivered in the courts below.

(e) Concise statement of grounds on which the jurisdiction of this Court is invoked.

(f) Constitutional provisions, treaties, statutes that the case involves.

(g) Concise statement of the case containing facts material to consideration of questions presented.

(h) Statement of reasons why the questions presented are so substantial as to require plenary consideration.[43]

Deciding to take a case in the Court is a process of "decisional steps or gates through which a case must successfully pass before it will be accepted. Failure to 'pass a gate' will usually mean that a case will be denied."[44] Every petition to the Court, over sixty-seven hundred in the 1991 term, goes through these gates. These gates in the Court's agenda-setting process include, in order of appearance: (1) the Office of the Clerk of the Court, (2) the cert pool, (3) the pool memo, (4) the nonpool process, (5) the markup process for pool memos, (6) the discuss list, (7) the Friday discuss conference, (8) the vote of four, (9) possible relisting, and (10) special situations such as the disposition of capital cases and the vote of four exception (rule of five).

Each of the certiorari petitions, no more than thirty pages in length (not counting the hundreds of pages of appendixes, including the written opinion of the lower court) and averaging about seventeen pages, contains basic information about the case. After noting Supreme Court jurisdiction, the central legal questions are listed along with the precise statement of facts as well as the final judgment from the lower court, the makeup of the panel that voted, as well as the author of the opinion (and who dissented), and counsel for the parties. Critically important for the reviewers of the petition is the statement by the petitioner of why the legal questions are so important that they require plenary consideration by the Court. The justices receive this information from the petition and then, recording the messages contained in each petition for certiorari by the clerks, they ultimately determine whether the petition is certworthy or not.[45]

This review process communicates important information, initially to the Office of the Clerk, then to the clerks, and finally to the justices, about the nature and character of each petition. Assuming the presence of threshold factors, these petitions are reviewed by all the justices—unless there is a reason for a justice to recuse herself from the proceedings.

Recusal   Recusal is when a justice, possibly because of personal bias or personal association with one of the parties in the case, declines to participate in a decision to grant certiorari and to decide cases brought up for plenary review. No guidelines defining the process are printed in the Supreme Court rules. Justice Rehnquist, for example, without reasons given (as is always the case), recused himself from participation in the *U.S. v. Nixon* discussion. (*Nixon*, heard and decided in July, 1974 by a unanimous, 8-0, Court, forced the president to turn over tapes to a federal judge.) He did not participate at all and was not present for any conversations, from the initial discuss conference that voted six to two to expedite the petition by taking it from the court of appeals, to the discussions and opinion-writing activities.[46] The speculation was that Rehnquist recused himself because he personally knew a number of the defendants in the *Nixon* litigation: He had worked with them in the Department of Justice prior to his elevation to the Court. This is not an uncommon practice; in the 1987–88 term of the Court, justices recused themselves in over two hundred cases.[47]

There have been occasions when one of the brethren believed that another should recuse himself because of some kind of association with one of the parties in the case being reviewed. A classic incident involved two powerful justices on the Stone Court in the 1940s: Justices Hugo Black and Robert Jackson. In a five-to-four labor relations case in 1945, *Jewell Ridge Coal Corporation v. Local 6167, UMW*,[48] Black was one of five who joined in the majority opinion written by Justice

Frank Murphy. Jackson believed that Black should recuse himself because a former law partner of his (two decades earlier) was one of the attorneys in the litigation. Black refused and voted with the majority on the merits and again when the Court majority denied the reconsideration petition. He thereafter received Jackson's scorn and contempt. Jackson's bitterness boiled over a little over a year later when, angered because he was not named chief after Harlan F. Stone died, he wrote public letters to Congress, the president, and the press denouncing Black and Douglas and pointing out Black's earlier judicial impropriety because he did not recuse himself in *Jewell Ridge.*[49]

The Role of the Office of the Clerk of the Court   Every petition sent to the Court is initially screened by the Court's central administrative agency, the fifty-person clerk's office. This office determines whether the petition follows the Court's technical guidelines for filing. Has it been filed within the sixty-day period that starts after the final judgment of the lower court has been formally recorded? Is it no more than fifty pages, excluding appendixes? Has the petition been printed on the proper size and weight paper? If all these technical questions are answered appropriately,[50] then the case, with the respondent's brief, is circulated to all the justices. If the petition has not followed the guidelines in the rules, especially Rules 15 and 33, the petition will be rejected and sent back to the petitioner.

The Cert Pool   These petitions for Court review, including all the *in forma pauperis* briefs (IFPs), are then examined by each justice's law clerks. Since 1972, there has existed a cert pool arrangement. In 1992, eight of the nine justices pooled their law clerks and divided the work between them. (Justice Stevens does not participate in the cert pool. He has his clerks go over the petitions and provide him with summaries of those they consider significant.) Each chamber, randomly, is given its one-eighth assignment, and all four clerks, again randomly, are given a number of certiorari assignments to summarize within a certain time.

The clerks are required to prepare summaries of the petitions for all eight justices. With little knowledge of the expectations of their justice, the law clerks must plow into the petitions, hoping that the advice they have received from outgoing law clerks as well as their sense of the task provides them with the appropriate guidance.

The Pool Memo   According to one clerk, the pool memo prepared by the clerks "reads much like a legal product from a law firm."[51] In about two to five pages, it summarizes the facts, the legal issues and questions, and the lower-court opinions, indicates the judge who wrote the opinion and who dissented or concurred, and briefly discusses the quality of the petition. All the pool writers must provide the readers with a determination of the correctness of the lower-court judgment and present them with a recommendation regarding the petition's importance and, consequently, its certworthiness by suggesting that the Court either grant or deny. The pool memos are all sent to the chief's office and are then copied and forwarded to the individual justices in the Court participating in the pool.

Justice John M. Harlan, II, who left the Court shortly before the establishment of the cert pool, would not have used the process because he felt that "frequently the question whether a case is 'certworthy' is more a matter of 'feel' than of precisely ascertainable rules."[52] This is a chronic problem that has essentially been set aside in the Court's effort to manage the caseload problem.

The Markup After the cert pool memos are received in each chamber, the justice's law clerks "mark up" the memo. Based on the interests of the individual justices, the values and the norms they eventually convey to their clerks,[53] the law clerks provide their senior partner with another analysis, somewhat more strategic, of each petititon. Each marked-up petition also ends with the clerk's recommendation to grant or to deny.

The Discuss List At this same time, the chief justice, working with his law clerks, prepares a discuss list, also called a conference list (see Figure 5.2), consisting of forty to fifty cases for circulation to the justices early in the week. There is also a second list, which contains the numbers of the petitions deemed not worthy of discussion that week. The former list he delivers to the justices prior to the conference session. This is the list of petitions , including IFPs and paid petitions, the chief believes should be discussed in the Friday morning con-

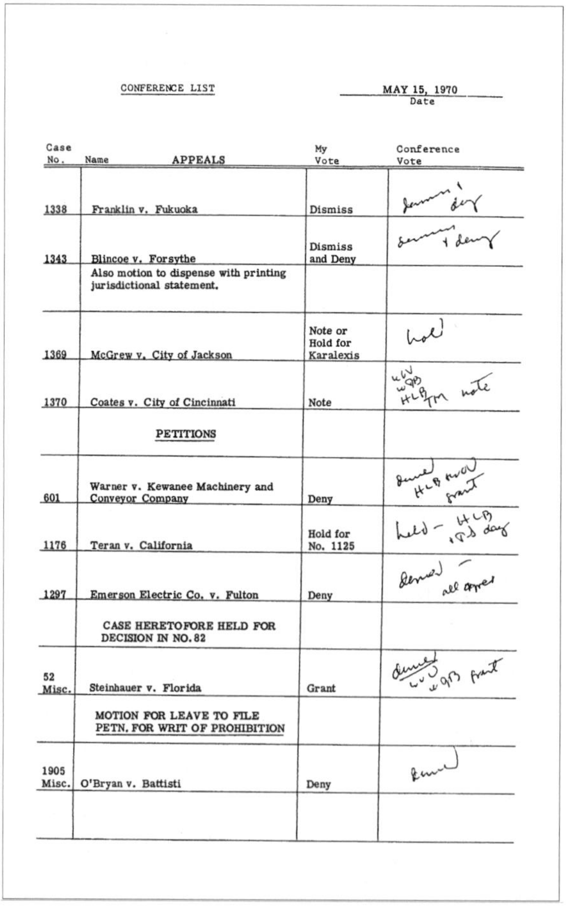

CONFERENCE LIST — MAY 15, 1970 (Date)

Case No.	Name	My Vote	Conference Vote
	APPEALS		
1338	Franklin v. Fukuoka	Dismiss	dismiss, deny
1343	Blincoe v. Forsythe Also motion to dispense with printing jurisdictional statement.	Dismiss and Deny	dismiss & deny
1369	McGrew v. City of Jackson	Note or Hold for Karalexis	hold
1370	Coates v. City of Cincinnati	Note	WOD WJB HLB TM note
	PETITIONS		
601	Warner v. Kewanee Machinery and Conveyor Company	Deny	denied HLB would grant
1176	Teran v. California	Hold for No. 1125	held — HLB IFP'd deny
1297	Emerson Electric Co. v. Fulton	Deny	denied — all agree
	CASE HERETOFORE HELD FOR DECISION IN NO. 82		
52 Misc.	Steinhauer v. Florida	Grant	denied WOD & WJB grant
	MOTION FOR LEAVE TO FILE PETN. FOR WRIT OF PROHIBITION		
1905 Misc.	O'Bryan v. Battisti	Deny	denied

FIGURE 5.2

A typical weekly conference list circulated among the justices. (*From the collections of the manuscript division, Library of Congress.*)

ference. Until the early 1970s, the chief circulated only the "dead list," that is, a list of petitions that were not deserving of discussion and would be denied certiorari.

Since the early 1970s, the chief has handed out the discuss list with the understanding that any of the brethren can add to the list by informing the chief's administrative clerk. Evidently, very few additions are made to the chief's discuss list, because the brethren see the role of the chief in creating the discuss list as "mostly administrative" and not political, ideological, or strategic.[54]

The Discuss Conference   On Friday afternoons when the Court is hearing oral arguments (scheduled in two-week cycles about fourteen times a term), the justices gather in conference to go over the discuss list. By this time, they have reviewed the cert pool memos, the clerks' markup notes and recommendations, and, on cases the justices think are important, the special case file, including the lower-court opinions. They come into the session ready to discuss and to vote on granting or denying certiorari.

Bringing the documents into the meeting, on a cart if need be, the brethren shake hands and then the conference begins. The chief commences the conference by leading the discussion for each of the petitions on the discuss list. He closes by giving his judgment whether to grant or to deny cert. Each of the justices, in order of seniority, then adds his or her thoughts to the discussion and announces whether the petition should be granted or denied.

Surprisingly, as Doris Provine and others have discovered, there has been a great deal of voting unanimity on the matter of "grant" or "deny" across the decades. Also, given the increase in the caseload, there is very little time for thorough discussion, a reality that has greatly concerned Justice David Souter and other justices. However, as Justice Antonin Scalia observed: "To call our discussion of a case a conference is really something of a misnomer. It's much more a statement of the views of each of the nine Justices."[55]

Conversations can be as brief as a justice stating that "I don't think this is a case that we need to hear; I deny." For cases in which a justice wishes to grant, she will "lay it out. I'll give my reasons and I'll say, 'therefore I would grant,' although there are some times I will put a case on and I will wind up suggesting to deny it because it is not ripe."[56] The most junior of the justices will talk and vote last; as Chief Justice Rehnquist noted, by this time, after eight have talked, there is not much the junior justice can add to the conversation.[57]

The conference generally concludes with denials for over 80 percent of the petitions on the lists. Even most of the cases on the discuss list are denied certiorari. At the conclusion of the conference, the junior justice reports the results of the discuss conference to the clerk of the court. (Until Burger's tenure, this reporting was done by the chief. However, because of his occasional errors in recording the results of the discussions, Burger turned the chore over to the junior justice. It has been the task of the junior since that time.)

The Vote of Four   If four justices agree that certiorari should be granted, an action known as the "vote of four," then the parties are so informed by the clerk's office. The petitioner then has forty-five days to file the brief (forty copies must be submitted to the clerk) on the merits, following the guidelines for filing found in the Court's Rule 33. The respondent, after receiving a copy of the petitioner's brief, then has thirty days to file a rejoinder. When this is done, the clerk's office schedules oral argument. If fewer than four vote to grant cert, the petition is denied and the clerk's office, in a Spartan, two-sentence note, so informs the parties.

There is some fluidity in conference,[58] but for the most part the justices just barely discuss the petitions and quickly vote as they had planned prior to entering the room. There are those occasions when, in the words of a justice, "I may get to conference intending to deny, yet later vote to grant because of something a colleague said on something I hadn't considered, and he might be right. But most times, though, I vote as I had planned to when I went in there. There are enough times that I change, though, to suggest that it happens."[59]

The "Freshman Effect"   There is a phenomenon, the "freshman effect," that one should be aware of, for it will, in all probability, be reported in the press that a junior justice is encountering this sensation. Albert Melone identifies three characteristics of this effect: (1) Freshmen are bewildered because of new duties and responsibilities; (2) freshmen are not assigned an equal share of the opinion-writing work for a number of years; and (3) freshmen do not immediately align with the Court's solid voting blocs.[60] The freshman justice, according to the concept, is "disoriented, uncertain, and vacillating" for a number of years. However, Melone doesn't believe that recent appointees have experienced the phenomenon, with the exception of a "paucity of majority opinion writing assignments" for new justices.[61]

Newcomers are brought into existing voting blocs in their first term. Also, given the reality of the nine-small-law-firms concept, "small group influences assumed to be important in explaining a freshman effect are not as salient today as they once were."[62] Yet, when one reads the words of freshman justice Souter about his arrival on the Court, one has to believe that new arrivals still tend to feel disoriented. He said:

> Coming in here is like walking through a tidal wave, and it is. . . . I don't have any sense about how I am going to solve the problems that every new Justice I know has coming on board in simply trying to handle both the flow of the work and keep a sense of balance despite the enormous effect of even the most trivial decisions that this Court makes.[63]

Unlike Justices Antonin Scalia and Arthur Kennedy, Souter, who came to the Court from service as a judge on the New Hampshire Supreme Court, and a very brief stint on the U.S. Circuit Court of Appeals, experienced the freshman effect. His observations are not surprising given his past experiences and practices as a state court judge. He recently commented on his frustration in having his clerks work with him on a very important activity: opinion writing. The justice took pride in the fact that he personally wrote every opinion while serving on the New Hampshire Supreme Court. He used his two clerks only to do basic research for him on the cases—and they did not even write drafts of opinions. Souter pointed out that Justice Brennan, the jurist he replaced, seeing Souter's anguish over this problem, told him sharply that he would have to use his clerks in opinion writing or else not be able to do the job.[64] Souter's junior colleague, Ruth Bader Ginsburg, has evidently not experienced the freshman effect at all. An experienced jurist who had served for thirteen years on the U.S. Court of Appeals, Ginsburg began fully participating as soon as she put on the robe of a justice of the Court.

Relisting   Infrequently, the justices will have a petition "relisted" or "put over" for discussion in an upcoming conference. Often this is because they are uncertain about the legal and political questions associated with a particular petition but are unwilling to deny cert at the time, or, alternatively, because the Court is short a justice.

For example, the eight-person Court, in 1971, relisted forty-five petitions while awaiting the outcome of the extended Court selection process. Harry Blackmun was finally selected, after Nixon's first two nominees, Clement Haynsworth and G. Harrold Carswell, were defeated in the Senate. After being confirmed, Blackmun took his seat on the Court as the ninth, junior, justice. At his initial discuss conference, these forty-five relisted petitions were discussed and resolved, although Blackmun was humbled by that experience because he found himself casting the decisive vote in these cases.[65]

Special Situations   A few special situations come to the Court's attention in the cert review process, and they are accorded special treatment by the brethren. For example, all death penalty cases that come to the Court are automatically discussed in conference by the brethren.[66] And there are occasions when a cert petition is denied even though there is a vote of four. The exception to the vote of four occurs because, while there is a four-person bloc that can grant cert, there is a five-person majority that is unswayable on the merits of the issue, in recent years, for example, obscenity and pornography cases. Under this condition, granting cert and having a plenary hearing on the question is a waste of the Court's precious time, and the four justices will accede to this reality.

The Certworthiness of the Petition

Almost 97 percent of the petitions reviewed by the Court are ultimately denied certiorari. The Court gives no reason for the denial when the clerk's office communicates to the unsuccessful petitioners. In determining certworthiness, the clerks look for certain qualities in the petitions. A Stevens clerk said that the clerks have to figure out "whether the petition raises an issue that is a matter of some controversy or is very specific to that litigation. The buzz-word [among the clerks] is 'fact bound,' where the case is of great concern to those particular litigants but Court resolution of it wouldn't help the other courts."[67]

Uncertworthiness   Any one of the following reasons or conditions when found in a petition will lead the Court, most of the time unanimously, to deny certiorari: (1) The case is frivolous; (2) the case is too fact bound; (3) insufficient evidence is presented in the briefs; (4) petition is a "clear deny" (because of the presence of a controversial issue that the justices want to avoid, such as tax, miscegenation, or ineffective assistance of counsel); (5) the legal issue, though important, has not percolated enough in the lower courts; (6) the briefs contain disputed facts; (7) a better case is in the pipeline; or (8) the petition will lead to intractableness (a fragmented court that does not know what to do with the issue).[68] There are, in addition, strategic, defensive denials of cert by justices. If the justice believes that the case is certworthy but she also knows that if there is a plenary review, she will not like the outcome on the merits, then the justice votes not to grant cert in that case. In 1972, one of the justices candidly remarked:

"[If] a decision [seemed] outrageously wrong to me but . . . I thought the Court would affirm it, then I'd vote to deny. I'd much prefer bad law to remain the law of the Eighth Circuit of the state of Michigan than to have it become the law of the land."[69]

The "Frivolous" Petition   In recent years, the justices have grown extremely impatient with the large number of what they call frivolous petitions. Justice John Harlan II thought that half of the petitions filed with the Court were frivolous. Justice William Brennan believed that fully 70 percent of the petitions were "obviously unworthy" of a grant of certiorari.[70] Chief Justice Warren Burger claimed that two-thirds of the new filings were not only unworthy of plenary review but "utterly frivolous."[71] Chief Justice Rehnquist believed that at least 50 percent of the certiorari petitions are "patently without merit; even with the wide philosophic differences among the various members of our Court, no one of the nine would have the least interest in granting them."[72] And Justice John P. Stevens confessed that "I do not even look at the papers in over 80 percent of the cases that are filed."[73]

Indeed, the Court majority's frustration level with unworthy petitions reached its peak during the 1989 term, when, for the first time ever, a five-person majority took the startling step of denying some petitioners the right to ever again file an IFP petition. One petitioner, Michael Sindram, was banned from *ever* filing a petition in the Court. He had filed forty-two separate certiorari petitions to the Court in the 1988, 1989, and 1990 terms, including the 1990 term petition that triggered the Court's rage. (He had tried to get the Court to expunge a thirty-five-dollar speeding ticket from his Maryland records).[74] The following term, the Court sent a similar message to a number of other petitioners.[75] And, during the 1991 term, the Court amended its rules governing IFP appeals to the Court: An IFP petition would be denied if the Court finds the petition "frivolous" or "malicious."[76]

Certworthiness   The hundred or so cases that are given plenary attention annually by the Court in the mid-1990s have exhibited, in the jurisdictional petition to the Court, a number of qualities that make them certworthy. Doris Provine's research suggests that, during the Vinson and Warren Court eras, four types of issues led to unanimous grants of certiorari: (1) ones in which the solicitor general is a petitioner, (2) labor relations cases, (3) civil rights and civil liberties issues, and (4) federalism cases.[77]

Chief Justice Rehnquist once observed, quite candidly, that "the most common reason members of our Court vote to grant certiorari is that they doubt the correctness of the decision of the lower court."[78] His comment reflects a reality that researchers have uncovered: "Most justices vote to grant certiorari, in part, because they want to reverse the decision of the lower court."[79] This is not accidental and not surprising, since the Court reverses approximately two-thirds of the cases it reviews on the merits. For example, the 1991 term produced 108 full opinions; 67 (62 percent) were reversals of lower-court decisions.[80]

In a subsequent television interview, the chief dramatically softened his earlier strategic perception when he said that "the Court should be reserved only for important, disputed questions of law, not for individual injustices that should be corrected in other courts."[81] His colleague, Justice Sandra Day O'Connor, said that "we generally don't take easy cases around here. We take cases, generally speaking, because other courts around the country have reached conflicting results on that issue."[82] For them, and for others on the bench, real, serious conflict over important issues in the lower courts is an important factor that may lead to a grant of certiorari.

Rule 10, the certiorari rule, provides substantive guidance for identifying certworthiness in a petition. It lists, initially, conflict between the courts, and second, the importance of the issues raised, especially as they impact the federal system. In general, the following factors account, though not wholly, for the Court's decision to grant certiorari: (1) conflict in the federal circuits;[83] (2) the importance of the issues raised in the petition, for example, the breadth of the effect of the issue's resolution by the Court or the effect on the federal government; (3) the justices' interest in the legal question; and (4) the plain egregiousness of the matter as defined in the petition.[84]

Additionally, the presence of certain actors is a factor. The identity of the lower-court judge who wrote the opinion—or who dissented—can affect the judgment of the Court to grant or deny certiorari. If the jurist is held in high esteem by the justices; an *amicus curiae* brief filed with the petition for certiorari;[85] or, very significant, a brief from the U.S. solicitor general, whose office has already screened out about 80 percent of the filings from governmental agencies or U.S. attorneys before submitting its set of petitions.[86]

Chief Justice Rehnquist, on another occasion, wrote that granting or denying the certiorari petition "strikes me as a rather subjective decision, made up in part of intuition and in part of legal judgment."[87] For the Court, evidently an important factor in granting a cert petition is real conflict in the lower courts. Another is the general importance of the issue. Even if conflict is real, the Court may deny certiorari if there is not general importance.[88] As Rehnquist and Warren have suggested, the decision to grant certiorari is a subjective one, one "not susceptible of scientific verification."

In the Court's 1992 term there was a grant of certiorari in the *Jason Daubert v. Merrell Dow Pharmaceutical Co.* case.[89] It was a product liability tort case involving a youngster whose mother had taken a drug, Bendectin, for morning sickness. She then gave birth to Jason Daubert, who was born with two fingers on his right hand and without a lower bone in his right arm.

The family sued the corporation in federal court, and the trial judge, following the *Frye* rule, created in 1923 by a federal appellate judge who refused to allow as evidence in a criminal trial the results of an early lie detector, did not allow scientific testimony linking Benectin to the deformity because it "relied on an unconventional method of interpreting medical data."[90] His judgment was upheld in the federal circuit. Only evidence produced as a result of using generally recognized scientific methodology could be admitted at trial.

The *Frye* rule, as the Court was informed in the *Daubert* brief, clashed with the congressionally authored Federal Rules of Evidence (FRE), written in 1975. That document "broadened the admissibility of scientific testimony to include theories not widely embraced."[91] As a consequence, in the many product liability cases heard in the federal and state courts since 1975, judges have selected one of the two standards, *Frye* or FRE, and then, on that basis, determined what witnesses will be allowed to testify before juries.

In granting certiorari, the Supreme Court was reaching an issue of national importance, one that went beyond the immediate case and the injury Jason

Daubert allegedly received because of the prescription his mother took during her pregnancy. The Court took the case because there was conflict in both state and federal judicial systems and because the conflict seemed ripe in the eyes of the justices. It was reported that "legal authorities hope the Supreme Court will clear up the confusion and inconsistency" in this area of law.[92] The Court was prepared to "tackle an issue with vast legal and ethical implications," not simply a single though sad product liability case.

This fact and law scenario, for the justices of the Court who voted to grant certiorari in *Daubert*, is a classic paradigm of a certworthy petition. First of all, the technical guidelines of jurisdiction, standing, and justiciability were met. There was injury, and the proper party brought suit in federal court. The Court had jurisdiction to hear the appeal from the court of appeals. There was real conflict in both the federal and state court systems. The conflict had raged since 1975, almost two decades, without any resolution. The kind of scientific evidence a jury should hear and evaluate in these civil cases is an important national question. The Court, the justices implied, could resolve the dilemma and in so acting would have a dramatic and immediate impact on product liability litigation. Finally, if the Court did not grant cert, there would be no resolution of an important conflict that involved many thousands of petitioners across the nation.

The Denial of Certiorari: Meaning?

The denial of certiorari means that the lower-court judgment "remains undisturbed."[93] Denial does not mean that the result reached in the lower court was the correct one. It means only that the Court did not think that the petition was significant enough to be granted plenary review by the justices.[94] Research indicates that all justices, whether labeled liberal or conservative, are convinced that certain cases should not be heard. They generally agree about what cases to review and not to review "largely because they share a concept of the Court as resolver of only the most significant class-action type conflicts."[95]

The vote to deny certiorari is not the same as a vote on the merits, although the vast majority of petitions are granted or denied on the basis of five or more votes in conference.[96] A justice who disagreed with the majority on the certworthiness of the petition participates in the substantive examination and discussion of the case on its merits. Justice Black wrote: "I have frequently voted to reverse cases where I voted against bringing them before our Court for review. This is because that for many reasons a vote to grant certiorari is not the equivalent of a final vote on the merits."[97]

However, repeated denials of certiorari "inevitably send signals as to which and what kind of cases [are significant]."[98] The denial does suggest that the Court is transmitting a substantive message to the legal community.

Dissent from a Denial of Certiorari

In recent years, a formerly rare by some justices has expanded, the dissent from the denial of certiorari. H. W. Perry argues that a dissent from a denial of certiorari is a strategic action on the part of a minority of justices.[99] If the case is on the discuss list and picks up two votes to grant, the justice who listed it or who voted to grant may state, to try to convince one or two more justices to switch their votes, that she will write a dissent from the denial.

For Justice John P. Stevens, writing in a dissent from a denial, such a

> written statement of reasons for granting certiorari is more persuasive than the Justice's oral contribution to the Conference. For that reason the written document sometimes persuades other Justices to change their votes, and a case is granted that otherwise would have been denied. That effect, however, merely justifies the writing and circulating of these memoranda within the Court; it does not explain why a dissent which has not accomplished its primary mission should be published.[100]

As a matter of course, Justices William Brennan and Thurgood Marshall wrote short, "stock" dissents from denial of certiorari in death penalty cases. "Adhering to our views that the death penalty is in all circumstances cruel and unusual punishment prohibited by the Eighth and Fourteenth Amendments, *Grigg v. Georgia*, 428 U.S. 153, 227, 231 (1976), we would grant certiorari and vacate the death sentences in these cases." In 1987–88, these two dissenters accounted for 78 percent of all the dissents from denial—and these 394 dissents were all issued in death penalty denials of the Court.[101]

More justices have begun to dissent from a denial of certiorari. Early in the 1992 term, in the abortion case from Guam, *Joseph Ada, Governor of Guam v. Guam Society for Obstetricians and Gynecologists, et al.*, No 92-104, three justices dissented from the Court's denial of certiorari, which meant leaving "undisturbed" the court of appeals decision declaring the Guam abortion statute unconstitutional. Justice Scalia wrote the dissent, with Rehnquist and White joining, from the Court's denial of the certiorari petition. A ninth circuit court of appeals panel had ruled that a Guam law broadly restricting abortions was "clearly unconstitutional"[102] under *Roe v. Wade*, as modified, in 1992, by the five-person majority's addition of the "undue burden" test in the *Planned Parenthood of Southeastern Pennsylvania v. Casey* decision.[103]

One of the four dissenters in *Casey*, Justice Clarence Thomas, did not join his three fellow dissenters (Rehnquist, Scalia, and White) in their dissent from the denial. His absence from the trio's dissent in the Guam case, which meant that the cert petition was not granted, "was an unexplained surprise. . . . It takes five votes [however] to vacate a lower court opinion as the three dissenters urged. Had Thomas voted with the other three in an effort to force the Court to hear the case, the remaining five could have countered by voting simply to affirm the Ninth Circuit's decision."[104] This case illustrates the rule of five exception. Had Thomas switched his vote, there would be a vote of four—but the five-person *Casey* majority, on the merits, would have upheld the court of appeals judgment.

THE SUPREME COURT'S WORKLOAD: A QUANTITATIVE VIEW AND ANALYSIS

The Supreme Court's docket has grown dramatically in the last seventy years. In 1920, the Court received 560 petitions for review. By 1950, there were 1,300 cases on the docket. A decade later, in 1960, the Court had almost doubled its docket listings to 2,300 cases. By the 1970 term, the Court's docket of petitions received had almost doubled again to over 4,200 cases. By 1980, the docket had gone over

5,000 cases (about 5,300) and, in the 1990 term, the Court had received over 6,300 petitions. At the end of the 1991–92 term, the number of cases docketed reached 6,770, of which 5,825 were actually denied by the justices by the end of the term.[105]

In recent years, however, the justices have been reducing the number of grants of certiorari. In the 1991 term, the brethren handed down 108 full opinions, down from the 1990 term figure of 116. These two terms are substantially different and down from the 1988 and 1989 figures, 170 and 146 full opinions, respectively. By the end of the Court's 1993 term, only 100 full opinions were announced.

Another measure of the quantitative growth of the caseload is the increase in the number of IFP petitions received by the Court. In 1935, the year the Court created the IFP mechanism, 59 IFPs were received. In 1960, the early years of the Warren Court, the number had increased to 1,000. By the 1970 term, over 2,000 IFPs were received by the Court. And by the 1990 term, the Court received almost 4,000 IFP petitions.

Through Earl Warren's tenure as chief, these indigent petitions, mostly from prisoners (80 percent), were managed in the chief's chambers by his law clerks. Given the huge increase, Warren began to distribute the IFPs to all the chambers. Since then, law clerks have received, reviewed, and prepared recommendations to their justice about these petitions. Of the 4,207 IFP petitions docketed during the 1991 term of the Court (62 percent of the total number of petitions received that term), 3,755 were disposed of by the clerks and justices, with 39 of them decided on the merits (or just 1 percent of the petitions).[106] (See Figure 5.3.) The rest were sent certiorari denied letters from the clerk of the Court.

The increased caseload burden falls on staff as well as the justices of the Court. Since the 1960s there has been a doubling of the law clerks in each chamber. The increased load has made it almost impossible for the Court to act as a collegial organization with full discussion on each of the petitions. The clerk of the Court's office has three staff members dedicated to the management of the IFP petition. Since the indigent petitioner is not bound by the dictates of Rule 15 (and does not have to pay the three-hundred-dollar filing fee), the Court has to properly prepare the materials received for distribution to the respondents and then to all the chambers.

Sources and Types of Petitions to the Court

Since the 1988 legislation, 99 percent of the petitions received by the Court are requests for the grant of certiorari. They come to the Court from two basic sources: after judgment by the highest state court (about 30 percent of the total) and from the federal judicial system (about 70 percent).[107]

Fifty years ago, the cases heard were predominantly commercial filings. Since the 1960s, civil rights and liberties and criminal cases have appeared with regularity and, in the 1990s, constitute more than one half of the Court's docket. A comparative analysis of the subject matter disposition with full opinions of the 1945 and 1991 terms of the Court clearly depicts the pronounced shift away from commercial issues toward civil rights and liberties issues. As Lawrence Baum has written, "Constitutional cases dominate the Court's docket and the largest portion of these cases raise civil liberties issues."[108]

As seen in Table 5.1, the contemporary Supreme Court clearly had fewer tax, commerce clause, and international law suits in 1991 than in 1945. Conversely,

No..5025.....*Miscellaneous*
SCHNEBLE v. FLA.
3/13/69 - Cert.

No..5026.....*Miscellaneous*
WILLIAMS v. LA.
3/15/69 - Cert.

4/16/71 - Grant
4/2/71 Relist for WJB circulate Memo
3/26/71 Relist for WJB & hold at

	GRANT	REFUSE	RULE
	✓	✓	
Blackmun, J.		✓	
Marshall, J.	✓		
White, J.	✓		
Stewart, J.		✓	
Brennan, J.	✓		
Harlan, J.		✓	
Douglas, J.	✓		
Black, J.		✓	
Burger, Ch. J.		✓	

	GRANT	REFUSE	RULE
		✓	
Blackmun, J.		✓	
Marshall, J.	✓		
White, J.		✓	
Stewart, J.		✓	
Brennan, J.	✓		
Harlan, J.	✓		
Douglas, J.	✓		
Black, J.		✓	
Burger, Ch. J.		✓	

No...5027....*Miscellaneous*
SEGURA v. PATTERSON.
3/19/69 - Cert.

No.5028.....*Miscellaneous*
HUBBARD v. ALA.
3/24/69 - Cert.

Together with No. 5172.
Same H...

	GRANT	REFUSE	RULE
Blackmun, J.		✓	
Marshall, J.			
White, J.			
Stewart, J.			
Brennan, J.		✓	
Harlan, J.		✓	
Douglas, J.			
Black, J.		✓	
Burger, Ch. J.		✓	

5172	GRANT	REFUSE	RULE
Blackmun, J.		✓	
Marshall, J.		✓	
White, J.		✓	
Stewart, J.		✓	
Brennan, J.		✓	
Harlan, J.		✓	
Douglas, J.	✓		
Black, J.		✓	
Burger, Ch. J.		✓	

FIGURE 5.3   A typical page from the miscellaneous docket of the Supreme Court.

TABLE 5.1   **U.S. Supreme Court Plenary Opinions by Subject Matter, 1945 and 1991**

Subject of Court Opinion	1945 Term	1991 Term
Admiralty	3 (2%)	0
Antitrust	2	2
Bankruptcy	7 (5%)	9 (5%)
Bill of Rights	9 (6%)	11 (9%)
Commerce Clause:		
Federal statutes, regs	28 (20%)	5 (4%)
State regulations	4 (3%)	5 (4%)
Common Law	3	0
Due Process:		
Economic	1	1
Rights of Accused	7 (5%)	18 (15%)
Impairment of Contract	1	1
International Law	12 (9%)	2
Jurisdiction, Procedure	27 (20%)	17 (14%)
Miscellaneous Statutory Interpretation	9 (6%)	20 (16%)
Native American	2	2
Patents	2	1
Suits Against Government	2	15 (12%)
Suits by States	0	4
Taxation	19 (14%)	7 (6%)
Total Number of Plenary Opinions	138	122

the contemporary Court hears more Bill of Rights, due process, and suits against government (alleging violations of rights by public officials) petitions than were heard in 1945.

Factors Affecting Docket Pressure

After reviewing the caseload information, a justice has to wonder why the dramatic increase in the number of petitions filed. What has accounted for that phenomenal rise in the amount of petitions brought to the Supreme Court? It was not until after the Civil War ended, the frontier closed, population exploded with waves of immigrants to America,[109] Reconstruction and the Gilded Age of raw capitalist industrialization emerged, and Congress and state legislatures "began to enact regulatory legislation," all of which created new kinds of lawsuits that could be brought in the federal courts,[110] that the litigation explosion occurred in the Supreme Court. These filings raised questions about civil rights, labor–management issues, and the capacity of legislators and executives, both state and national, to intervene, through the creation of regulatory statutes and agencies, in the economic affairs of the nation.

Because of the increase in the number of cases and because of the Court's circuit responsibilities, which created a three-year backlog of petitions for the justices, in 1891, the Congress passed legislation that created the circuit courts of appeal. The 1891 statute was a reflection of the growing caseload and of the need to provide a mandatory appeal of federal district court decisions in a court other than the Supreme Court.

Then, too, as Mr. Sidram's petition suggests, America is a litigious society. Americans like to sue other Americans and to claim that they will take their appeal all the way to the Supreme Court—and many do just that! We have more lawyers per one hundred thousand persons than any other nation in the world.

There has also come into being, beginning in the late 1930s and full-blown in the Warren Court era,[111] a view held by many groups in America, especially those who have traditionally been viewed as powerless, that the Court is receptive to certain cases and controversies coming to it from these groups. Starting slowly in the late 1930s,[112] there grew the perception that the courts, especially the Supreme Court, "stand against any winds that blow as havens of refuge for those who otherwise might suffer because they are helpless, weak, outnumbered, or because they are non-conforming victims of prejudice and public excitement."[113]

The high tide of the revolution in constitutional adjudication was the fourteen years, the 1956–69 terms, of the Warren Court. In that period, beginning with the arrival of William Brennan and ending with the retirement of the chief justice, the Court majority wrought significant changes in the society's constitutional landscape, including the "incorporation" or absorption of significant protections in the Bill of Rights into the language of the Fourteenth Amendment, thereby making the Bill of Rights protection applicable to persons in the various states. For Earl Warren, the central themes were equality and fairness for all persons. His view of what the Court could do, reminiscent of Black's dicta in *Chambers*, was presented in an opinion he wrote in 1963, *N.A.A.C.P. v. Button*: "Under the conditions of modern government, litigation may well be the sole practicable avenue open to a minority to petition for redress of grievances."[114]

Paralleling the emergence of this new and quite different perception of the Court applying a heightened judicial scrutiny test when reviewing civil rights and liberties cases was the dramatic increase in the number of IFPs received by the Court, beginning in the late 1930s and increasing substantially during the Warren Court years. The jailhouse lawyers' view of legal events was that the Supreme Court majority wished to review criminal justice issues and therefore encouraged appeals. They all heard about IFP petitions such as the one filed by Clarence Earle Gideon that led to watershed changes in the constitutional law of procedural due process.[115] Eighty percent of the IFP petitions come from persons who are incarcerated, and the prisoners were happy to oblige the justices—especially since they had little else to do with their time.

Again, the Warren Court's procedural cases involving standing to sue encouraged parties to bring suit challenging issues previously thought to be non-justiciable. Clearly, this perceived attitude about the Court opening wide the gates to its docket has changed somewhat in recent years, with a more conservative Court modifying the Warren Court's liberalizing of the Court's technical guidelines. If the Warren Court had thrown open the gates of the Court to certain kinds of cases and controversies, the Burger and Rehnquist courts began the process of closing the judicial gates.[116]

Another major reason for the enlargement of the Court's docket is the expanded jurisdiction of the federal courts created by the variety of congressional statutes that provide for judicial review by the federal courts. The Congress has developed the habit of passing substantive legislation and giving, in the legislation itself, the federal courts, including the Supreme Court, the authority to re-view actions flowing out of the legislation. Consequently, lower federal courts will interpret these statutes in different ways, occasionally leading to Supreme Court review in order to end these differences.

Whatever the legislative focus, whether the statute involved civil rights,[117] health,[118] consumer safety,[119] environment,[120] truth in lending,[121] working condi-tions,[122] freedom of information,[123] or social security,[124] persons affected adversely by the legislation could go into federal district court to challenge the enactment. If rebuffed in the federal court, the losing party could appeal to the court of ap-peals and then, on certiorari, to the Supreme Court. Because the national legis-lature has passed controversial legislation in these areas, litigants challenging these statutes have appeared in all the circuits, creating conflict between the federal courts of appeal. These conflicts, the result of congressional action, have also led to the increased number of filings in the Supreme Court.

Is the Court Overworked? The National Court of Appeals Argument

Given the phenomenal growth of the Court's caseload, is the Court over-worked to the point where the justices are not doing the job that they must do? The justices themselves have been divided on this issue ever since the question was raised in the early 1970s. Two chief justices, Burger and Rehnquist, along with other justices including Byron White, Harry Blackmun, and John P. Stevens, have supported the creation of a national court of appeals to assist the Supreme Court in managing the caseload. They have been met with vigorous opposition by other justices, including William O. Douglas and William Brennan. The justices have shown, in cases and controversies examined during that decade, their concern about the consequences of the increased caseload.

In one 1978 term case, actually a denial of certiorari, *Brown Transport v. Atcon*,[125] a number of justices added statements and a dissent from the denial, to vent their frustrations about the workload. Chief Justice Burger noted that the Court "was accepting more cases for plenary review than [we] can cope with in the manner they deserve." The chief called, in his statement, for a reexamination and adoption of the National Court of Appeals proposal.

Justice White penned a dissent from the denial, joined by Justice Blackmun. White wrote: "Although I dissent from the denial of certiorari, it must be ac-knowledged that this case is no more deserving of plenary consideration than many other cases in which certiorari has been denied this term. . . . There is grave doubt [given the workload of the Court] that the appellate system has the capac-ity to function in the manner contemplated by the Constitution." His dissent from the denial ended with the call for the immediate adoption of the National Court of Appeals proposal.

Justice Brennan also appended a statement to the denial of certiorari. Brennan's statement in the case disagreed with the Burger and White comments. Brennan was "completely unpersuaded . . . that there was any need for a new National Court." Brennan did not believe that the Court's caseload reality was a problem that needed major surgery.

The surgery, however, that was being proposed by Burger and supported by White was the change in Court jurisdiction and the creation of a national court of appeals to help the Supreme Court better manage its workload. There have been, especially in the 1970s, suggestions and formal reports that have addressed the Court's caseload problem.

All the reports called for the creation of a national court of appeals that would either screen cases for passage to the Supreme Court or have cases referred to it by the Supreme Court.[126] The criticism was immediate and strong, and it came from some of the justices and the legal community, including many law reviews and law professors. There were practical as well as conceptual concerns about the constitutionality of a second Supreme Court.

While the idea of a new intermediate court of appeals located between the thirteen courts of appeals and the Supreme Court was attractive to some because they felt it would enable the Court to fully and collegially concentrate only on nationally important cases, others were concerned about the loss of authority if the Supreme Court took cases that had been screened by the new appellate tribunal. Even case referral by the Supreme Court to the judges of the new court would mean either a surrender of jurisdiction or micromanagement by the justices of the Supreme Court. Either path concerned many persons, and none of the proposals was seriously considered by Congress.

Shortly before he stepped down from the Court, Chief Justice Burger put forth a new idea: Create a national court of appeals as a pilot project, with a five-year experimental term. The experimental court, a rotating panel of judges from the court of appeals, federal circuit, would hear only cases involving intercircuit conflicts. Burger believed that this idea, if implemented, would reduce the Court's plenary docket by forty to fifty cases annually.[127]

Although the Senate Judiciary Committee, in June 1986, approved legislation creating, for a five-year test period, a thirteen-person intermediate court of appeals to ease the load of the Supreme Court, limiting its jurisdiction to cases involving contradictory rulings in two or more of the existing circuits, the legislation never left the Congress. And so, for the time being, the creation of another federal court has been put off. If, however, the caseload problem continues and the justices find themselves incapable of functioning "in the manner contemplated by the Constitution," then the question will be revisited. After all, the history of the federal judicial system's growth reflects, sooner or later, the felt necessity of changing the federal judiciary's jurisdiction and structure to provide Americans with a viable federal judiciary.

SUMMARY

As you have seen to this point in examining the Supreme Court's work processes, there is a mountain of work that has to be processed by the Supreme Court. However, the Court has managed to process the almost seven thousand petitions received annually. Given almost total discretion over its docket, asked for by the Court and granted by the Congress, the justices, with the critical assistance of their law clerks, have been able to sort through the petitions and select for plenary review the 100 or so cases they feel warrant judicial review. Case management has come at a cost, however—

the loss of personal communication between the brethren and fuller discussion of the plenary cases.

The consequence of the increased caseload has been obvious. As you have seen, there has developed an increased isolation of the justices, each working in his or her own little law firm as well as an increase in the number of concurring, dissenting, and separate opinions written by the justices. As Justice David Souter noted recently: "We are being forced [because of the huge caseload] to forego the kinds of efforts and opportunities [to discuss cases fully]. . . . We should spend more time with very close cases. [Unfortunately] it is quicker and easier to write a concurring or dissenting opinion than to sit down and try to work out common ground."[128]

The probability of jurisdictional or organizational change in the federal judicial system exists; action will occur when the petitions received annually by the Court continue to increase until a point is reached where the justices' plight is noted by Congress and changes are made in Court jurisdiction or in federal court structure. You know that different justices react differently to the increase in the number of cases filed. When a majority of them feel too stressed over the number of petitions, then, you know, things will change. But change occurs very incrementally in the Supreme Court.

NOTES

[1]Justice Harry Blackmun told Bill Moyers that his workday begins at 7:00 A.M. in his office, and includes a one-hour "uninterrupted" breakfast with his law clerks. The formal day ends twelve hours later when, at 7:00 P.M., he heads home for dinner with his wife. After dinner he reads the cert pool memos and other work until midnight. Only then does Blackmun retire for the evening. Another justice, Hugo L. Black, would stay up until four in the morning writing opinions and doing other court work (*Bill Moyers: In Search of the Constitution,* Public Broadcasting System, 1989).

[2]U.S. Congress, Senate Committee on the Judiciary, *A Bill to Reorganize the Judicial Branch of Government: Hearings Before the Committee on the Judiciary on Senate Bill 1392,* 75th Cong., 1st sess., Mar. 10, 1937, p. 78.

[3]H. W. Perry, Jr., "Indices and Signals in the Certiorari Process" (Paper presented at the annual meeting of the Midwest Political Science Association, Chicago, Ill., Apr. 9–11, 1986), p. 5.

[4]William H. Rehnquist, *The Supreme Court: How It Was, How It Is* (New York: Morrow, 1987), p. 253.

[5]David M. O'Brien, *Storm Center* (New York: Norton, 1991), pp. 219–220.

[6]Rule 33, "Form of the Jurisdictional Statements," includes instructions regarding type size (eleven point or larger), text (pica type, ten characters per inch), paper (opaque, unglazed, 6 1/8 × 9 1/4 inches), cover page, cover (cert petitions, white; responses, light orange; amicus curiae, green; solicitor general, gray; others, tan), and so on. (Title 28 USCA, *Rules of the Supreme Court of the United States,* pp. 415–16).

[7]Justice William O. Douglas, in particular, was critical of Frankfurter's efforts to develop procedures for screening petitions. He wrote Frankfurter: "If we unanimously adopted rules on such matters we would be plagued by them, bogged down, and interminably delayed. If we were not unanimous, the rules would be ineffective. I, for one, could not agree to give anyone any more control over when I vote than over how I vote" (Douglas to Frankfurter, Oct. 13, 1960, William O. Douglas Papers (hereinafter cited as WODP). Washington, DC).

[8]In the first three terms of the Supreme Court, a total of five cases were heard by the brethren.

[9]Speech to the American Bar Association, 1976 (quoted in Richard L. Williams, "Supreme Court of the United States," *Smithsonian,* Feb. 1977, p. 89). Justice David Souter came to the Court expecting much more discussion in conference than exists and, because substantive discussion is so im-

portant for him, he has called for a reduction in the number of grants of certiorari to a maximum of one hundred plenary discussions per term (interview with author, Washington, DC, Dec. 9, 1992).

[10]H. W. Perry, Jr., *Deciding to Decide: Agenda Setting in the U.S. Supreme Court* (Cambridge, MA: Harvard University Press, 1992), p. 144.

[11]Quoted in Perry, *Deciding to Decide*, p. 143.

[12]Laura Ingraham, clerk for Justice Clarence Thomas, interview with author, Washington, DC, Dec. 9, 1992. Ms. Ingraham was editor of the *Dartmouth Review* and, afterward, a speech writer for the Reagan White House, prior to clerking in the federal court system.

[13]Quoted in Perry, *Deciding to Decide*, p. 78.

[14]This does not include the many concurring and dissenting opinions that the justices write each term.

[15]Rehnquist, *Supreme Court*, p. 263.

[16]O'Brien, *Storm Center*, p. 223.

[17]Quoted on "This Honorable Court," Paul Duke, narrator, Public Broadcasting System, 1988.

[18]Perry, *Deciding to Decide*, p. 91.

[19]Quoted on "This Honorable Court." PBS.

[20]Justice Harry A. Blackmun to Howard Ball, Nov. 26, 1986.

[21]See, for example, Lawrence Baum, *The Supreme Court*, 2d ed. (Washington, DC: CQ Press, 1985,) pp. 95ff.

[22]Article III lists both the original and appellate jurisdiction of the Supreme Court. Article III, Section 2, also states that the Supreme Court has appellate jurisdiction, "both as to Law and Fact, with such Exceptions, and under such Regulations as the Congress shall make."

[23]Included in a listing of federal legislation that has affected Supreme Court activity are the following congressional enactments: the 1789 Judiciary Act, which, in part, established the three-tiered federal judicial system: district courts, circuit courts of appeals, and the Supreme Court; the 1875 Act, which expanded the jurisdiction of the Court over civil matters as well as granting the Court full federal questions review from the state courts; Circuit Court of Appeals Act, 1891, which established and staffed nine circuit courts of appeals and provided the Court with limited discretionary appellate review through the writ of certiorari; the Act of 1892, which provided for indigent, in forma pauperis review by the Court; the Judiciary Act of 1925, which extended the Court's discretionary appellate jurisdiction by replacing mandatory appeals with discretionary petitions for certiorari; the Voting Rights Act, 1965, which provided the Court with the power to hear direct appeals from three-judge courts in the area of voting rights; the Federal Courts Improvement Act of 1982, created the court of appeals for the federal circuit; the 1988 Act to Improve the Administration of Justice, which eliminated almost all nondiscretionary appellate jurisdiction, except for appeals from three-judge decisions in the areas of apportionment, voting rights, antitrust, and the Presidential Election Campaign Fund Act.

[24]Chief Justice Rehnquist said that the 1988 legislation abolishing most obligatory appeals to the Court "has been for many years the primary legislative goal of the Court" (Stuart Taylor, Jr., "High Court Expected to Gain Freedom in Selecting Its Cases" *New York Times*, June 9, 1988), p. A-18.

[25]PL 100-352. Bob Kastenmeier, the chairman of the subcommittee that produced the first draft of the legislation, said of its passage and signing that it was the "most significant jurisdictional reform affecting the High Court in over 60 years. [The Act would be of] substantial assistance to the Court in managing its caseload" (Taylor, "High Court Expected to Gain").

[26]*Ex parte McCardle*, 74 U.S. 506 (1869). In this case, the Court dismissed the suit because it lacked jurisdiction. The lack of jurisdiction came about because of an 1868 repeal of a habeas corpus act by the Reconstruction Congress.

[27]See the angry congressional response to the Court's decision in *Watkins v. U.S.*, 354 U.S. 178 (1957), restricting legislative investigations, and in other cases that limited legislative powers or protected the rights of persons who had to confront allegations of Communist affiliation. Court-curbing bills were introduced by the dozen in Congress to restrict the Court's appellate jurisdiction. The Court, aware of the anger in the national legislature, clearly modified its views on legislative investigations (see, for example, *Barenblatt v. U.S.*, 360 U.S. 109 (1959)).

[28]"This Honorable Court."

[29]*Luther v. Borden*, 48 U.S. 1 (1849); *Colegrove v. Green*, 328 U.S. 549 (1946); *Baker v. Carr*, 369 U.S. 186 (1962); *Goldwater v. Carter*, 444 U.S. 996 (1979); and *Renne v. Geary*, 111 S Ct 2331 (1991).

[30]See Frankfurter's opinions in *Colegrove v. Green* (majority) and *Baker v. Carr* (dissenting).

[31]Alexander M. Bickel, *The Least Dangerous Branch* (Indianapolis: Bobbs-Merrill, 1962), p. 7.

[32]392 U.S. 83 (1968), at 94–95.

[33]John M. Harlan, II, "A Glimpse of the Supreme Court at Work," *University of Chicago Law Review* 11, (1963): 4.

[34]Jack Peltason, *Federal Courts in the Political Process* (New York: Random House, 1965), p. 29.

[35]O'Brien, *Storm Center*, p. 194.

[36]There are four other avenues, all based on statutory grants (except for constitutionally based original jurisdiction), for parties seeking Court review: through petitions under (1) original jurisdiction; (2) appeal as of right; (3) certification, where an appellate court asks the Supreme Court to clarify a question or interpretation of federal law; and (4) extraordinary writs such as prohibition, habeas corpus, or mandamus. Since 1988, these produce a total of approximately 1 percent of the petitions to the Court.

[37]Article III, Section 2, states that "in all other Cases before mentioned, the supreme Court shall have appellate Jurisdiction." The cases before mentioned, in Article III, Section 1, include "all cases, in Law and Equity, arising under this Constitution, the Laws of the United States, and Treaties made; or which shall be made, under their Authority;—. . . to all cases of admiralty and maritime Jurisdiction;—to controversies to which the United States shall be a Party;—. . . between citizens of different States."

[38]Article III, Section 2: "In all cases affecting Ambassadors, other public Ministers and Consuls, and those in which a State shall be Party, the Supreme Court shall have original Jurisdiction."

[39]A petitioner could ask the Court to hear her case under appeal as of right if the following conditions were present in the legal record: (1) a federal court invalidated an act of Congress; (2) a federal court of appeals invalidated a state statute; (3) a decision from a special federal three-judge court was appealed; (4) a state court invalidated a federal treaty or statute; or (5) a state statute was upheld as valid when challenged as being repugnant to the U.S. Constitution, or a federal law or treaty.

[40]*U.S. v. Nixon*, 418 U.S. 683, the 1974 case heard by the Court, was one of a few rare instances of the Court taking a case on certiorari before the judgment or decree of the court of appeals was announced. Indeed, it was taken before the court of appeals heard arguments. Justice William Brennan argued long and hard in conference session for the Court to take the case before judgment (see Howard Ball, *"We Have a Duty": The Supreme Court and the Watergate Tapes Litigation* [Westport, CT: Greenwood Press, 1992]).

[41]Quoted in Perry, *Deciding to Decide*, p. 36.

[42]William J. Brennan, Jr., "Inside View of the High Court," *New York Times Sunday Magazine*, Oct. 6, 1963, p. 24.

[43]*Rules of the Supreme Court*, pp. 404–5.

[44] Perry, *Deciding to Decide*, p. 16.

[45]Perry has noted that Brennan, referred to as the "Wizard of Cert," who did not participate in the cert pool, would read all the cert petitions once the term began and could, by simply reviewing the "questions presented" segment of the petition, determine which of the petitions were certworthy (Perry, *Deciding to Decide*, p. 67).

[46]See Ball, *"We Have a Duty."*

[47]O'Brien, *Storm Center*, p. 213.

[48]325 U.S. 161 (1945).

[49]See Ball and Cooper, *Of Power and Right*, pp. 95–97.

[50]The Court's own rules lay out the appropriate technical characteristics of the jurisdictional briefs that are sent to the Court.

[51]Perry, *Deciding to Decide*, p. 56.

[52]Quoted in Tom C. Clark, "Internal Operations of the U.S. Supreme Court," *Judicature* 43, pp. 45, 48 (1959).

[53]Some justices are very interested in particular issues and have their clerks flag petitions that raise these matters.

[54]Perry, *Deciding to Decide*, p. 85.

[55]Comments made at George Washington National Law Center, Feb. 16, 1988 (quoted in *The New York Times*, Feb. 22, 1988), p. A-1.

[56]A justice of the Supreme Court (quoted in Perry, *Deciding to Decide*, p. 47).

[57]"This Honorable Court."

[58]On fluidity in the Court, see J. W. Howard, "On the Fluidity of Judicial Choice," *American Political Science Review* 62, (Mar. 1968), p. 48.

[59]Quoted in Perry, *Deciding to Decide*, p. 47.

[60]Albert P. Melone, "Revisiting the Freshmen Effect Hypothesis: The First Two Terms of Justice Arthur Kennedy," *Judicature* 74, no. 1 (June–July 1990): 6.

[61]Ibid., 12–13.

[62]Ibid., 13.

[63]Toni House, "Q&A," *Docket Sheet of the Supreme Court of the United States* 28, no. 1, (Spring 1991).

[64]Justice David Souter, interview with author, Washington, DC, Dec. 9, 1992.

[65]"This Honorable Court."

[66]See Perry, *Deciding to Decide*, p. 92ff.

[67]"This Honorable Court."

[68]Perry, *Deciding to Decide*, p. 222ff. passim.

[69]Quoted in *Time*, Dec. 11, 1972, p. 77.

[70]William J. Brennan, Jr., "National Court of Appeals: Another Dissent," *Chicago Law Review* 40, 473 (1973): 477.

[71]Quoted in *U.S. News and World Report*, Feb. 14, 1983, pp. 38, 40.

[72]Rehnquist, *Supreme Court*, p. 264. Chief Justice Rehnquist, in a talk in 1985, said that "a lot of the filings are junk" (remarks to the Jefferson Literary and Debating Society, Charlottesville, VA, Sept. 20, 1985).

[73]Quoted in George Middleton, "High Court's Case Load Too Heavy: Three Justices," *American Bar Association Journal* 68, (1986): 1201.

[74]*In re Sindram*, 111 S Ct 596 (1991). Justices Brennan, Marshall, and Stevens dissented.

[75]See *In re Jesse McDonald*, 489 U.S. 180 (1989); and *In re John Robert Demos*, 111 S Ct 1579 (1991).

[76]See *In re Amendment to Rule 39.8*, 111 S Ct 1572 (1991).

[77]See Doris M. Provine, "Deciding What to Decide: How the Supreme Court Sets Its Agenda," *Judicature* 64, no. 7 (Feb. 1981): 320.

[78]Quoted in Baum, *Supreme Court*, p. 105.

[79]John F. Krol and Saul Brenner, "Strategies in Certiorari Voting on the U.S. Supreme Court: A Re-evaluation," *Western Political Quarterly* 43, no. 2 (June 1990): 335–42. Justices who voted to reverse at the final vote (as expressed in joins on the written opinions) were more likely to have voted to grant certiorari than justices who voted to affirm at the final vote.

[80]Note, "Supreme Court Statistics," *Harvard Law Review.* 382.

[81]"This Honorable Court."

[82]Ibid.

[83]Assuming *real* conflict, a fact that the clerks have to address when preparing the cert pool memo, it is a strong but not categorical reason for granting cert. There are at least three types of lower-court conflict: (1) a disagreement between a lower court and an appellate court; (2) a conflict alleged by the petitioner's attorney between two state courts, or between two federal circuits, or with Supreme Court precedent, or a conflict between a state court and a federal court; and (3) an actual conflict. The law clerks have to determine whether there *really is* the conflict alleged in the petition (see Gregory Caldiera and John R. Wright, "Organized Interests and Agenda Setting in the U.S. Supreme Court," *American Political Science Review* 82 [1988]; 1109–27). Annually, dozens of conflicts in the lower courts are not heard on appeal to the Court. Justice John M. Harlan II, in response to questions raised regarding the Court not hearing all cases involving conflicts in the lower courts, said that "the conflict may be resolved as a result of future cases in the Court of Appeals, or where the impact of the conflict is narrowly confined and is not apt to have continuing future consequences" (quoted in O'Brien, *Storm Center*, p. 215).

[84]Perry, *Deciding to Decide*, p. 246ff., passim. O'Brien argues that the most important factor in granting cert is "simply the majority's agreement on the importance of the issue presented" (*Storm Center*, p. 215).

[85]Pressure groups, especially economic interest groups, who file amicus curiae briefs with the certiorari petition, do have some impact on the Court's decision to grant certiorari (see Gregory Caldiera and John R. Wright, "Amici Curiae Before the Supreme Court: Who Participates, When and How Much," *Journal of Politics* 52 [1990]: 803).

[86]Provine notes the special role of the solicitor general in the granting of petitions. Between 70 and 80 percent of the petitions filed by the SG are granted by the Court, whereas the overall grant rate is 5 percent (see Doris M. Provine, *Case Selection in the United States Supreme Court* [Chicago: University of Chicago Press, 1980]). Another chapter will examine in greater detail the role of the solicitor general.

[87]Rehnquist, *Supreme Court*, p. 265.

[88]Ibid. The Court, he wrote, should pick only "those cases involving unsettled questions of federal constitutional or statutory law of general interest" (p. 269).

[89]Docket no. 92-1786 (1992).

[90]Natalie Angier, "Supreme Court Set to Decide What Science Juries Can Hear," *New York Times*, Jan. 2, 1993, sec. A.

[91]Ibid.

[92]Ibid. In January 1995, the lawsuit was dismissed by a federal court of appeals. See "Birth-Defect Lawsuit That Set Science Standard Is Dismissed," *The New York Times*, Jan. 8, 1995, p.26.

[93]William J. Brennan, quoted on "This Honorable Court."

[94]Alan F. Westin, ed., *The Supreme Court: Views from Inside* (New York: Norton, 1961), p. 48.

[95]Provine, "Deciding What to Decide," 322.

[96]See Provine, *Case Selection*, where she discovered unanimity is more common than imagined in agenda setting on the Court—even across time and ideological lines. Between 1947 and 1957, at least 82 percent of the petitions were unanimously disposed of by the justices (79 percent unanimous denial of certiorari; 3 percent unanimous grants of certiorari). A review of Brennan's docket notes indicates that this was the case during the 1970s where, in 1973, for example, after the Nixon appointees were on the Court for more than one full term, 79 percent of the petitions were disposed of by unanimous votes (see also O'Brien, *Storm Center*, p. 231).

[97]Justice Hugo L. Black to Howard Ball, Jan. 31, 1969. Justice Frankfurter, in *Maryland v. Baltimore Radio Show*, 338 U.S. 912 (1950), wrote that "this Court has rigorously insisted that . . . denial carries with it no implications whatever regarding the Court's views on the merits of a case which it has declined to review."

[98]O'Brien, *Storm Center*, p. 237.

[99]See Perry, *Deciding to Decide*, p. 170ff. In 1980, Rehnquist wrote 32 percent of all the dissents from denials; in 1987, Brennan, then in the minority, wrote 44 percent of all the Court's dissents from denial (see O'Brien, *Storm Center*, p. 238).

[100]*Singleton v. Commissioner of Internal Revenue*, cert denied, docket no. 78–78, in *Law Week* 47 (1977). For Stevens, "the *primary* mission of a dissent [from a denial] is to pick up votes" (Perry, *Deciding to Decide*, p. 171), p. 3299.

[101]O'Brien, *Storm Center*, p, 239.

[102]The Guam legislation prohibited all abortions except those found by any two doctors to be necessary to save the woman's life or to prevent a grave threat to her health (see slip opinion, 92-104; and Linda Greenhouse, "High Court Spurns Guam Bid to Revive Curbs on Abortion," *New York Times*, Nov. 30, 1992).

[103]505 U.S. 672 (1992).

[104]Greenhouse, "High Court Spurns Guam Bid."

[105]See Note, "Supreme Court Statistics," *Harvard Law Review* 106, no. 1. (Nov. 1992): 376, 384.

[106]Ibid.

[107]See Howard Ball, *Courts and Politics: The Federal Judicial System*, 2d ed. (Englewood Cliffs, NJ: Prentice Hall, 1987).

[108]Baum, *Supreme Court*, p. 101. Criminal cases, since the 1940s, have risen dramatically and presently constitute about 50 percent of the "constitutional question" docket.

[109]And it is still exploding with a doubling of the population in America in the last fifty years, accompanied by urbanization. By 1920, the Census Bureau indicated that, for the first time, more Americans lived in cities than in rural America. Certainly, this event has led to litigation in the federal courts because of the efforts by national and state legislatures to deal with the consequences of such a population explosion. Crime, drugs, poverty, homelessness, and lack of educational benefits are but a few of the problems that have emerged due to the growth of population in urban areas (see Andrew Hacker, *Two Nations, Black and White, Separate, Hostile, Unequal* [New York: Scribner's, 1992]).

[110]See, for example, Rehnquist, *Supreme Court*, pp. 268–69.

[111]See Ball and Cooper, *Of Power and Right*, for an analysis of the Warren Court.

[112]See *U.S. v. Carolene Products*, 304 U.S. 144 (1938). In a famous footnote, n. 4, Justice Harlan F. Stone suggested that the Court review with greater scrutiny legislation that was challenged as being in violation of fundamental constitutional rights and liberties. He inquired:

[Should legislation] be subjected to more exacting judicial scrutiny under the general prohibitions of the Fourteenth Amendment than are most other types of legislation? [Should] similar considerations enter into the review of statutes directed at particular religions, . . . or national, . . . or racial minorities? . . . ; whether prejudice against discrete and insular minorities may be a special condition, which tends seriously to curtail the operation of those political processes ordinarily to be relied upon to protect minorities, and which may call for a correspondingly more searching judicial inquiry (at 152–53).

[113]*Chambers v. Florida*, 309 U.S. 227 (1939), at 241. Justice Hugo Black wrote the majority opinion in a case that involved coerced confessions of young black men accused of murder. The confessions were elicited from the youths after eight days and nights of police questioning. The Supreme Court set aside the convictions because of the gross violation of the due process clause of the Fourteenth Amendment.

[114]371 U.S. 415 (1963), at 429–30.

[115]See *Gideon v. Wainright*, 372 U.S. 335 (1963).

[116]See, for example, Rehnquist Court opinions limiting the habeas corpus appeals from state courts (*Coleman v. Thompson*, 111 S Ct 2546, [1991]); restricting standing to sue (*Lujan v. Defenders of Wildlife*, 112 S Ct 2130, [1992]; and *Renne v. Geary*, 111 SCt 2331 [1991]).

[117]See, for example, the Civil Rights Act (1964), PL 88–352.

[118]See, for example, the Narcotic Addict Rehabilitation Act (1966), PL 89–733.

[119]See, for example, the Consumer Product Safety Act (1972), PL 92–573.

[120]See, for example, the National Environmental Protection Act (1970), PL 91–190.

[121]See, for example, the Truth in Lending Act (1970), PL 91–508.

[122]See, for example, the Occupational Safety and Health Act (1970), PL 91–596.

[123]See, for example, the Freedom of Information Act, 1966, PL 89–487.

[124]See, for example, the Social Securities Amendments of 1972, PL 92–603.

[125]Certiorari denied, 58 L Ed 2d 687 (1978).

[126]A number of committees were formed, by the Court and Congress, to examine the workload problem. The major ones were (1) the Federal Judicial Center Report of the Study Group on the Case Load of the Supreme Court (1972), chaired by Professor Paul Freund; (2) the Haynsworth Report (1973); (3) the Kurland Report (1973); (4) the American Bar Association Special Committee on Coordination of Judicial Improvements (Hufstedler) Report (1973); and (5) the congressional (Hruska) Commission of Revision of the Federal Court Appellate System (1976) (see Ball, *Courts and Politics*, pp. 67–70, for analysis of these proposals).

[127]See David M. O'Brien, "Managing the Business of the Supreme Court," *Public Administration Review*, 45 (Nov. 1985): 670. See also Warren E. Burger, "Reducing the Load on 'Nine Mortal Justices,' " *New York Times*, Aug. 14, 1975, p. A-28.

[128]Justice David H. Souter, conversation with author, Washington, DC, Dec. 9, 1992.

The Office of Chief Justice: Primus Inter Pares

6

Returning from your first conference session, you find yourself thinking about the chief justice. When you first came to the Court, the chief, as he (there has not yet been a female chief justice) is generally called, welcomed you and helped you to get settled into your office and into the Court routine. But it was at the Court's oral arguments and in conference that you first began to see some of the special functions performed by the chief justice. There is a certain irony in the fact that while the chief has no supervisory authority over you and has no more of a vote than you in Court decisions and Court operations, he is nevertheless in a special position.

The chief is indeed *primus inter pares*, "first among equals." The attributes of the office that make it special are both functional and symbolic, internal to the Court and also of wider national significance beyond the doors of the Marble Temple. To understand the Court on which you serve, it is important to understand these special roles and responsibilities of the chief justice. That challenge can be aided by an examination of the work of one chief who is often regarded as among the greatest occupants of the office.

CHARLES EVANS HUGHES: THE CHIEF FROM CENTRAL CASTING

If the president had called central casting in Hollywood and asked them to send over a chief justice, Charles Evans Hughes would have been an obvious choice. And when he took the center chair at the Court, he did so, as so critical an ob-

132

Chief Justice Charles Evans Hughes speaking at the cornerstone laying ceremony for the Supreme Court building, October 1932. President Herbert Hoover is seated at extreme left of photo.

server as Justice Felix Frankfurter put it, "with a mastery, I suspect, unparalleled in the history of the Court, a mastery that derived from his experience as diversified, as intense, as extensive, as any man ever brought to a seat on the Court, combined with a very powerful and acute mind that could mobilize these vast resources in the conduct of the business of the Court."[1] His colleagues regarded him with a respect that was based on their experience with lesser leaders, and, following Hughes's departure from Court, more than one justice looked back fondly on the days when Hughes presided. Their admiration came from their view of his suitability to occupy the center chair, his understanding of the job, his habits as presiding officer in the courtroom and in the conference room, his workways, and his ability to perform his institutional tasks as chief justice of the United States.

Fitting the Center Chair

For many Americans, Hughes was perfect for the job at least in some measure because he looked the part. From his white beard to his patrician bearing, Hughes seemed every inch the chief justice. Justice William O. Douglas told a tale that summarized the powerful presence that Hughes projected. It seems that the chief justice and his wife were waiting for dinner on the porch of their cottage at Jasper National Park in Canada, one of their favorite vacation retreats, when a bear ambled toward them. Douglas recalled:

> The bear came closer, reached the steps of the porch and started up. Mrs. Hughes screamed.

"Don't be nervous," he admonished. Then he walked to the edge of the porch where the bear was climbing the steps.

"I summoned," he said, "all the dignity that I could command, and raising my hands, I shouted at the bear, 'Stop!' "

"What did the bear do?" I asked.

"What did he do?" he replied with a note in his voice that indicated disgust that anyone should wonder what happened. "What did the bear do? He stopped, of course."[2]

Other observers presented different reasons that made Hughes a solid choice. Born in 1862, Hughes attended Brown University, where he attained Phi Beta Kappa honors and graduated fourth in his class. After completing his legal training at Columbia Law School, Hughes embarked on a distinguished career. In his early years he taught law and entered private practice.

Hughes's public career began in 1905 as counsel to a New York State legislative committee investigating public utilities. After that, he was off and running. He was elected governor of New York and served in that capacity from 1907 to 1910. Though his politics were very different, Hughes, like later Chief Justice Earl Warren, brought his experiences from the state house to Washington.

President William Howard Taft named Hughes to the Supreme Court in 1910. Though he was appointed associate justice, the president had considered naming him to the center seat. In fact, he intimated that he might very well elevate him to that post later if the opportunity arose.

Don't misunderstand me as to the Chief Justiceship, I mean that if the office were now open I should offer it to you and it is probable that if it were to become vacant during my term, I should promote you to it; but of course conditions change, so that it would not be right for me to say by way of promise what I would do in the future. Nor, on the other hand, would I have you think that your declination now would prevent my offering you the higher place, should conditions remain as they are.[3]

Hughes took the associate justice position and served until 1916, when he left the Court to run as the Republican nominee for president against Woodrow Wilson. Following his unsuccessful bid for the White House, Hughes returned to what became a very successful private legal practice. He remained in private life only until 1921, when he was appointed secretary of state by President Warren Harding. Although Hughes returned to private practice in 1925, his life was far from private. He spoke out on public matters and accepted appointment to the World Court. President Herbert Hoover returned Hughes permanently to public life by naming him chief justice in 1930 to replace Taft, as had been Taft's hope. Taft had been fearful that Justice Harlan F. Stone would be named and that Stone would be unable to lead the Court.[4]

Hughes knew exactly what he was getting into and had very mixed emotions about taking the job. He told Hoover: "There are various reasons why you should not nominate me, one of them being that I'm too old."[5] He was nearly sixty-eight, and he was well aware that the burdens of the chief justiceship would be heavy. He told Hoover, "I think I've earned the right to finish life in peace."[6] Hughes ultimately served until he was seventy-nine. There was also the fact that his son was then solicitor general. Hughes's elevation to the Court would necessitate the son's resignation.

There was one other matter. Hughes had had an active political career, and he had made enemies. He had seen what could happen during confirmation fights when a nominee's past became a target, and he wanted none of it. He told the president: "I don't want a fight over the nomination. I want you to ascertain whether my nomination will have support. . . . If you are convinced that the nomination will be confirmed by the Senate without a scrap, I will accept it. But I don't

By "J. N. Ding" in the New York *Herald Tribune*, February, 1930.

CONCEDED TO BE ONE OF THE OUTSTANDING JURISTS
OF THE WORLD

want any trouble about it."[7] Hoover immediately assured Hughes that the confirmation would be no problem. He was quite wrong. Although Hughes was ultimately confirmed, it was not without a fight that resulted in a divided fifty-six to twenty-nine vote in the Senate.

Understanding of the Job

When he came to the center chair, Hughes brought his wide array of experiences with him, but there was more. He had reflected carefully on the task he was about to face. Just two years prior to his return to the bench as chief justice, Hughes had quite literally written the book on the subject, *The Supreme Court of the United States*,[8] in which he demonstrated not merely his understanding of the Court as a legal body but also the Court's position as a political institution and the complex role of the chief justice within it.

It was in this book that Hughes wrote that the Constitution may be the law, but, in some sense at least, the Constitution means what a Supreme Court majority says it means. He observed that the sources of authority and strength for the Court in the performance of this role include the law, but more than that. "The Court has found its fortress in public opinion. . . . With Congress responsive to the will of the nation, it is apparent that it is that will which has sustained and has made effective the extraordinary authority of the Supreme Court."[9]

With respect to what was about to become his own office, Hughes observed:

> The chief justice as the head of the Court has an outstanding position, but in a small body of able men with equal authority in the making of decisions, it is evident that his actual influence will depend upon the strength of his character and the demonstration of his ability in the intimate relations of the judges. It is safe to say that no member of the Supreme Court is under any illusion as to the mental equipment of his brethren. Constant and close association discloses the strength and exposes the weaknesses of each. Courage of conviction, sound learning, familiarity with precedents, exact knowledge due to painstaking study of the cases under consideration cannot fail to command that profound respect which is always yielded to intellectual power conscientiously applied. That influence can be exerted by any member of the Court, whatever his rank in the order of precedence.[10]

Although he recognized the limitations and problems of leadership in the Supreme Court, he was very much aware that "while the Chief Justice has only one vote, the way in which the Court does its work gives him a special opportunity for leadership."[11]

Handling the Court and the Conference: Workways and Leadership

Various chiefs, including Hughes, have left enduring reputations for their ability or ineptitude as presiding officer of the Court because of the manner in which they led the oral arguments or by virtue of their management of the Court's conferences. Taking over the Court in 1930 was a particular challenge for the new chief justice. His ability to preside effectively over its activities would be critical to ensuring that it could accomplish its growing number of tasks and to the Court's prestige as a political institution. The Court's docket was growing, in spite of its recent acquisition of certiorari discretion, which helped to weed out cases. Moreover, the Great Depression meant that the Court could expect more and a wider variety of litigation in both public law and business-oriented cases.

Hughes was more than equal to the task. So effective was he as a presiding officer that Felix Frankfurter referred to him as " 'Toscanini Hughes,' the maestro, the man with the remarkable gift of bringing things out of people."[12] The public saw the "maestro" in action in the Court's oral arguments, and his brethren saw an equally impressive performance in the conferences.

It was clearly understood that Hughes would not allow a waste of the Court's time or suffer precious moments to pass without careful presentation of cases. With his eye on his gold watch, Hughes was always ready to stop an attorney who droned on beyond his allotted time or talked without apparent purpose. He was legendary for the story, told by the famous lawyer John W. Davis, that he "would cut off counsel in the middle of the word 'if' . . . when the hour allotted for oral arguments came to an end."[13] He was known to pass a note to his colleagues and, on receiving assent from them, say to the counsel before the Court, "The Court does not wish to hear any further argument in this case."[14]

Still, his handling of argument was not generally thought to be harsh. Rather, it was his style and presence that dominated the courtroom. As Justice Robert H. Jackson explained it: "The majestic presence of Chief Justice Hughes as a presiding officer shed a native and simple dignity upon all of the Court's proceedings. A keen and experienced advocate of the bar, he knew the problems and arts of the working lawyer. No one ran away with his Court."[15]

Most observers of the Court, however, regard his orchestration of the conference sessions as the demonstration of Hughes's true virtuosity. Highly respected scholar David Danelski has observed that Hughes was truly both a task leader and a social leader in his management of the conference. He made certain to get the Court's work done but was also careful to do it in a manner that reinforced the Court's collegial tradition. In managing the conference, Hughes's watchwords were "preparation" and "decisiveness." He had learned those principles the hard way. He said:

> Whatever little success I may have achieved when I became Chief Justice, I think was largely due to the lessons I learning [*sic*] in watching [Chief Justice] White during the years when I was an Associate Justice and seeing how it ought not to be done. I am fond of saying that perhaps parents help their children most through their faults, because children hate the faults and failings of their parents and are helped thereby. And so if I had any virtues as Chief Justice they were due to my determination to avoid White's faults. . . . White did not take hold the way a Chief Justice should in guiding the discussion and taking a position in expounding the matters before the Court.[16]

Hughes used a variety of tools to streamline the work of the conference. First, he exploited the possibilities of certiorari jurisdiction. Not only would the Court refuse to hear cases that lacked merit, the justices would not even discuss the certiorari petitions in conference unless someone forced the issue. Hughes launched a system under which his law clerks would review the petitions and prepare summaries. This screening process eliminated virtually 60 percent of the cases. The chief justice would then circulate the so-called dead list of certs that would not be considered further unless one of the justices wanted one of them added to the conference discuss list.

Once in the conference, Hughes had an uncanny ability to keep the discussion focused and fast-paced. His law clerks helped the chief prepare for the conference with memoranda on each case, to which Hughes added his own notes and carefully marked materials from the case record. As he began discussion of a case, Hughes would provide an extremely thorough and accurate summary of the case. Justice Owen Roberts observed, "I do not remember an instance when he was found to have erred in his original statement."[17] Justice William O. Douglas challenged the characterization of Hughes as "being as undramatic as an adding machine." Douglas observed: "He was indeed like a terrier after a rat—intent on cornering every fact. Hughes believed in God but believed equally that God was on the side of the facts."[18] Frankfurter later responded to the accusation that Hughes was merely attempting to dominate discussion of the conference: "There was less wasteful talk. There was less repetitive talk. There was less foolish talk. You just didn't like to talk unless you were dead sure of your ground, because that gimlet mind was there ahead of you."[19]

Every justice had the opportunity to talk about the case, and only Justice, later Chief Justice, Harlan F. Stone complained about Hughes's leadership of the conference. Justice Roberts summarized the view of most of the justices:

> Strong views were often expressed around the conference table, but never in eleven years did I see the Chief Justice lose his temper. Never did I hear him pass a personal remark. Never did I know him to raise his voice. Never did I witness his interrupting a Justice or getting into a controversy with him, and practically never did any one of his associates overstep the bounds of courtesy and propriety in opposing the views advanced by the Chief.[20]

Once the conference began, Hughes pressed the other justices through all of that day's business. The object was to avoid carryover work. The sessions were long and taxing, but the justices appreciated the fact that at least along with the feelings of fatigue they could feel a sense of accomplishment on Saturday evening. While the others headed home, however, Hughes stayed behind to complete the list of assignments for opinion writing in the cases on which a preliminary decision had been reached at that day's conference. Referring to this process as the "deployment of his army," Hughes was aware that the making of assignments was "my most delicate task. . . . I endeavored to do this with due regard to the feelings of the senior Justices and to give to each Justice the same proportion of important cases while at the same time equalizing so far as possible the burdens of work. Of course, in making assignments I often had in mind the special fitness of a Justice for writing in the particular case."[21]

Hughes had a number of rules of thumb for making assignments. Although he was aware that some of the justices had a particular interest in or knowledge of one area of the law or another, he tried to avoid excessive specialization. He thought that "every judge should have a chance to demonstrate through the writing of opinions the wide range of his reasoning powers and not be kept before the public as an extremist or specialist working in one particular groove."[22] He looked for situations in which a normally conservative justice took what might be regarded as a liberal position and vice versa, assigning the writing of the opinion to that justice. In sharply divided cases, he would select a justice who appeared to be adopting a moderate position in the hope that he could pull some of the more extreme justices to a more centrist conclusion.

As for his positions, Hughes was not hesitant to assign the writing of important decisions to himself, usually on the expectation that such opinions would gain force if they were issued under the authorship of the chief justice. Beyond that, however, he was careful to avoid two sorts of behavior that might have been divisive. First, he did not indicate his position on a case until he actually came to the conference. Second, and related to that, was his habit of avoiding lobbying his colleagues. Some of the justices regarded this as a mark of respect for their judgment.

Hughes was indeed both a social and a task leader. In pressing for the efficient disposition of the Court's business, he never forgot that he was dealing with a group of independent and sometimes difficult men. He worked to maintain a positive and cooperative atmosphere amidst this tension. He was well aware that the Court consisted of what was often called "the four horsemen," made up of Justices James McReynolds, Pierce Butler, Willis Van Devanter, and George Sutherland, and the so-called three musketeers, Louis Brandeis, Oliver Wendell Holmes, and Harlan Stone, but he never let himself become identified with either group. He was aware that each group went so far as to hold rump sessions of the conference, at which its members would contemplate their positions on upcoming cases. Nevertheless, Hughes remembered that his task was to preside, not to foster voting blocs.

For that matter, he did not want the blocs or the tough debates in conference to carry over into the interpersonal interactions of the brethren any more than necessary. Justice Frankfurter noted that Hughes "had no lingering afterthoughts born of a feeling of defeat, and thereby avoided the fostering of cleavages."[23] He was known to leave a vigorous argument on the bench only to sit next to the justice with whom he had just been locked in debate and immediately strike up a lighthearted conversation. Despite the fact that some people regarded him as solemn, several justices recalled a surprising sense of humor from this incredibly dignified personality. They tell the story of how a woman in a New York hotel walked out of an elevator and, seeing the chief justice, said in hushed tones, " 'Oh, I thought you were dead.' Hughes smiled and bowed, saying, 'Sorry to disappoint you, madam.' "[24] His colleagues report flashes of that humor, seemingly at just the right time.

But in addition to his concerns with collegiality, Hughes also remembered that each of the justices was a man who needed attention to his personal problems if he was to be able to function effectively in the Court. Hughes's biographer, Merlo Pusey, tells one of the most revealing stories.

> Most of the assignment slips were delivered [Saturday] evening in deference to the eagerness of the brethren to know promptly what opinions they would write. But there were two exceptions. Justice Cardozo had suffered a heart attack before his appointment to the Supreme Court. Knowing that Cardozo went to work on his opinions immediately after getting his assignment on Saturday night, the Chief made a practice of withholding Cardozo's assignment slip until Sunday. To keep Cardozo from suspecting that his health was being shielded, Hughes also held back the assignments of Justice Van Devanter, who was a neighbor of Cardozo in a Connecticut Avenue apartment house.[25]

As Van Devanter and Holmes reaches ages at which they had difficulty completing their writing assignments, Hughes carefully reduced their assignments, but he did so in manner that he characterized as respect for their age and a desire to ease their excessive burdens, thus avoiding demeaning criticism.

He knew of the difficult and sad parts of the job. Hughes recounted the story he had been told by Justice John M. Harlan, who had the task of seeking Justice Stephen J. Field's resignation because of his failing health. Harlan recalled to Field the fact that Field himself had once had a similar duty with respect to Justice Grier. He answered, "Yes! And a dirtier day's work I never did in my life!"[26]

Addressing Outside Audiences

Although Hughes was intensely concerned about life within the Court, he was also acutely aware that he was the chief justice of the United States, with responsibilities not only for the external interactions of the Supreme Court with other political institutions but also for leadership in the administration of the entire federal judiciary. He knew that public opinion was a critically important aspect of judicial power. Indeed, one of the reasons that he was adamant about the improvement of judicial efficiency was that "the spectacle of a weak and incompetent judge in action, or in inaction does more to undermine public confidence than abuse of the institution by hostile critics."[27]

His efforts paid off when in 1937 President Franklin D. Roosevelt presented his "Court packing" plan for adding additional justices to the Court to help the aging justices keep up with their work. In truth, of course, the president was merely trying to find a way to pack the Court with justices more favorably disposed toward New Deal programs. Hughes was able to point out in his famous letter to Congress that the Court was already doing a very good job of keeping up with its docket. Most critics of FDR's Court-packing plan wondered if the president could say as much for the efficiency of the executive branch. That fact, plus Hughes's dignified response that reinforced the Court's public image, helped to defeat the president's efforts.

Beyond the Supreme Court, Hughes made good use of his long experience as a trial lawyer to consider the need for judicial reform across the range of federal courts. He headed the work on the development of federal rules of criminal procedure, which were produced in 1934. As soon as those rules were enacted, he presided over the efforts that eventually produced the federal rules of civil procedure in 1938.

He encouraged the use of senior judges, those who had reached retirement age but who decided to remain on the bench, in jurisdictions that needed extra assistance to deal with caseload backlogs. He also sought to involve the senior judges in leadership of federal judicial administration through a conference of senior circuit judges as well as the development of circuit councils in each judicial circuit. He supported the creation and development of the Administrative Office of United States Courts (known as the AO) as a staff body to support the Conference of Senior Circuit Judges. Later, the Judicial Conference of the United States took over as the central committee of judges to administer the judicial branch, supported by the AO.

In sum, Hughes explored most of the dimensions of the role of chief justice of the United States. He understood many of the keys to the leadership of the

Court as a political institution and as a small collegial body of strong-willed and independent people. Despite the fact that he is often criticized for his votes on important cases before the Court, few challenge his claim to a place in the history of the Court as a great chief.

SAME ROBE, DIFFERENT HATS

New members of the Court notice very quickly the irony in the chief justice's role. First, she dons a robe at the same time and in the same way as other members of the Court do just before each session of Court. Her vote counts the same as every other justice, neither more nor less. She cannot prevail unless she obtains enough of her colleagues' votes to command a majority in any given matter before the Court. The chief can do nothing to force another justice to take the course of action or decision he prefers. The story is often told of how Chief Justice Hughes, the man who never permitted a sitting of the Court to begin even one minute late, was worried one morning when Justice McReynolds did not appear as the noon Court session approached. He dispatched a messenger to remind the justice that the others were waiting. McReynolds told the messenger to "tell the Chief Justice that I do not work for him."[28] Despite all of these problems, the chief is expected to lead the Court.

The second problem is that while she may wear the same robe as everyone else, she must wear several additional hats. In addition to her tasks as a judge, she is also chief justice and must manage the operation of the Court, and also shoulder the responsibility for leadership of and representation of the federal judiciary to the other branches and the public.

The Judge

Whatever else the chief justice may be, he is first of all a judge. For some chiefs, like Hughes, Stone, and Rehnquist, for example, it was the case that they were associate justices before their elevation to the center chair, and their performance as justices was to one degree or another a factor in their elevation. But since one cannot really anticipate moving up to the position of chief, it would be a mistake to assume that associate justices worry about their performance in terms of possible elevation.

On the other hand, it is true that the perception of the chief's performance as chief justice and external representative of the Court and other federal courts will be affected by the view of his performance as a judge. There is no question that Chief Justice Earl Warren's inability to obtain resources from Congress was affected by the public perception of him as a liberal activist who was not likely to be a particularly responsible judicial manager, given his ideological proclivities. The fact that he had been one of the most successful chief executive officers of one of the nation's largest states for years did not reduce those adverse congressional assumptions a bit. It was often said that Congressman Rooney, the chair of the House Appropriations Committee, "would not give Earl Warren a pencil if he didn't have to." In slightly longer-term historical perspective, there is no doubt that Chief Justice Roger Taney's opinion in the infamous *Dred Scott* case eclipsed everything else in his career on the Court. More recently, there is little question

that some of the impressions of the Burger Court had some basis in the professional assessment of the chief justice himself.

The point is that, as a justice, the chief must wrestle with the same difficult
cases, the same caseload of opinions to be written, and the same difficulties of
managing his chambers as any other member of the Court. The fact that one is
chief does not eliminate any of those challenges. Indeed, it adds some, since the
chief is expected to be fair and balanced in the handling of cases and opinion assignments and, for many reasons, lacks the luxury of, like Justice Douglas, accepting the role of loner on the Court and consequently fashioning raging dissents
and biting concurrences without concern for a wider institutional role.

The Chief

Those special expectations of the chief justice emerged the moment her
nomination was made and the press began to describe the Court as the Warren
Court, the Burger Court, the Rehnquist Court, and so on. The chief's role has two
dimensions that can be described as the internal and external chief justice.

The internal chief is the presiding officer of the Court and is the Court's
chief executive officer. As presiding officer, in addition to chairing the oral arguments before the Court and the conferences, the chief performs a number of
other functions. She may call special sessions if the need arises and preside over
them. A classic example here is the time that Justice Douglas issued a stay of execution in the case of Julius and Ethel Rosenberg, convicted of betraying U.S. nuclear secrets to the Soviets in the early postwar years. The nation was clamoring
for their electrocution. So important was the culmination of this case for FBI director J. Edgar Hoover that he posted agents inside the Court with the covert cooperation of the marshal of the Court.[29] Douglas issued the stay on grounds that
a serious question had been raised about whether the Rosenbergs had been convicted under the proper statute and, therefore, whether the electrocutions were
authorized. The Court, however, convened in special session called by the chief,
rejected Douglas's concerns, and permitted the executions to take place.[30]

As presiding officer at regular Court sessions, the chief has a number of responsibilities. She works with the clerk to manage the actual hearings, including
such matters as requests for VIP seating. The capacity of the courtroom is extremely limited, and some of the most controversial cases generate large numbers
of requests from the press and dignitaries for special arrangements. The chief also
works with the marshal to ensure that the proper sense of decorum is maintained
in the courtroom by means ranging from the management of the seating of observers to the assurance of security for the Court.

Then there are the attorneys to be managed as well. That process starts with
the admission to the bar of the Supreme Court of a would-be advocate. Some
chiefs, most notably Earl Warren, regarded the brief ceremony that takes place at
the opening of the Court's session as particularly important.[31] Although many of
those admitted may never actually practice before the Court, the ceremony is a
fleeting opportunity to develop good will and a positive image among the members of the bar for the Court.

On a day-to-day basis there is the much more particular task of disposing of
special requests for oral argument time or participation by *amicus curiae* parties.

These matters require coordination by the chief with both the members of the Court and the Office of the Clerk. In cases like the *Regents v. Bakke* litigation, involving a challenge to the University of California at Davis affirmative action program for admission to medical school, where there were nearly four dozen *amici*, the management of these participants can be no small undertaking.[32]

In these and other matters, like protocol concerns for visitors to the Court, the chief is both a presiding officer and administrator. She must also manage the various support offices within the Court, ensure the maintenance of the Court buildings and grounds, prepare the budget, and prepare for the unexpected, whether it is the announcement by a member of the Court of retirement and all of the media focus that it brings, to the arrival at the Court of a new justice, to the death of a justice and the associated arrangements for a lying-in-state in the great hall of the Court and the participation of the justices in the funeral.

While the chief has the assistance of the administrative assistant to the chief justice, the clerk, the marshal, and others, she is ultimately responsible for the management of the Court. And since many of the tasks require discussions with the members of the Court, the chief takes a more direct and active role in their accomplishment than do many high-ranking executives in other organizations who can essentially delegate their functions to staff members.

The Statesman

At the same time that the chief accomplishes these many and varied internal responsibilities, he must also attend to duties as the external chief, taking quite literally the title "Chief Justice of the United States." Although the significance of the title is lost to most Americans, and even to many observers of the Court, chiefs as far back as Salmon P. Chase have taken these words, which impose responsibility beyond the narrow confines of the Court, seriously. Here the chief justice is necessarily cast in the role of statesman.

Once again combining ceremonial and substantive obligations, the chief justice inherits a number of titles and responsibilities on assuming office. The Constitution makes the chief the presiding officer over the trial in the Senate if an impeachment is brought by the House of Representatives. Custom confers on the chief the obligation of administering the oath of office to each new president. In addition, the chief is likely to receive prestigious appointments to boards of directors such as that of the Smithsonian Institution.

Beyond these more or less symbolic positions, however, the chief inherits other titles with important ongoing responsibilities. The chief is chair of the Judicial Conference of the United States, the governing body for the federal judiciary; chair of the Administrative Conference of the United States, the body that provides research support and legislative recommendations on administrative-law matters; chair of the board of the Federal Judicial Center, the research unit that provides judicial-administration studies; and supervisor of the Administrative Office of United States Courts (AO). These bodies deal with the day-to-day problems of operating courts, including the Supreme Court, by making decisions about everything from housekeeping problems, like the purchase of computers, to the much more complicated problem of formulating the judicial branch budget.

In addition to these obligations, which are essentially internal to the judiciary, there are tasks that fall to the chief justice as head of the third branch, sometimes called the "court defender" and "third-branch chieftain" roles,[33] such as representing the interests of the courts to the other branches and to the public. To those, like Chief Justice Hughes, who believe that the federal courts in general, and the Supreme Court in particular, can be effective only if they retain a large reservoir of support and goodwill in the body politic, the task of representing the courts is crucial. To others, like Warren Burger, who believe that the courts can be effective only if they make known their needs and problems in the halls of Congress and in other professional forums, like the American Bar Association, the chief-as-spokesperson obligation is an ongoing, delicate problem. While the judge, chief, and statesman labels help us to understand what the chief justice does, more is needed to understand how he does it.

THE POWERS OF THE CHIEF

As students of the Court think about the chief's behavior, they find themselves asking just why there seems to be power in the position even though every other justice is the chief's equal in most respects. To chiefs like Hughes and Warren, men who previously occupied the top executive position in the nation's largest states, that question was important and occasionally vexing. Their response to it was an awareness that there are two sets of realities, the Supreme Court facts of life, as it were, and the real areas of specific attention.

The first fact of a chief's life is that the position holds little formal power. In truth, the only formal powers that matter are the ability to manage the conference and the ability to make assignments for the writing of opinions. Even here, there are limits. The chief can be an effective manager of the conferences if and only if she has the leadership skills necessary to guide a group of diverse, strong-minded people through a large body of difficult work. The title of presiding officer is of little real consequence. The other justices are not about to be controlled by the chief like law students by a professor or young associates in a law firm by the senior partner. And the chief can make assignments only if she is in the Court's majority. Beyond that are numerous practical and political constraints on the assignment power if the chief really wants to be effective over the entire docket.

There are a number of facts of life that, in truth, govern both the formal and informal reality in the Court. All justices hold an equal vote. That vote is subject to virtually no real control by any other member of the Court. All members of the Court were appointed by a president and confirmed by the Senate. They have no obligation to one another or to the chief.

It takes a number of votes, often a majority, to accomplish anything of consequence. The vote can be changed at any time up to the moment when a decision is rendered. Even an agreement by another justice can be couched in extremely limited terms in concurring or separate opinions. Moreover, justices can change their minds in later years. Thus, Justices William O. Douglas, Hugo Black, and Frank Murphy repudiated their own votes in the first flag salute case, *Minersville v. Gobitis*,[34] a case in which the Court majority validated a state regulation that required all students, regardless of religious beliefs, to salute the flag and recite the Pledge of Allegiance. Along with a new appointee to the Court, these three were able to reverse that earlier ruling in *West Virginia Board of Education v. Barnette.*[35] That occurred in a relatively short three years and was not inhibited by the fact that the earlier decision had had only one justice who had dissented, which frustrated Felix Frankfurter, author of the earlier ruling, to no end! Justice Douglas repudiated his critical vote in a major establishment of religion case. He wrote that "the Everson decision was five to four and, though one of the five, I have since had grave doubts about it, because I have become convinced that grants to institutions teaching a sectarian creed violate the Establishment Clause."[36]

In attempting to persuade one's colleagues today, one must always remember tomorrow. The Court is a small group of people who generally serve together for many years. The way a dispute or a problem is resolved in one setting today may very well affect one's options in the future. Thus, someone who wanted Justice Black's vote in a new case had to be concerned about Black's informal rule that he never knowingly joined an opinion that cited a precedent in which he had dissented.[37] More recently, in what Justice Sandra Day O'Connor has termed "the battle of the footnotes," the level of vituperative rhetoric expressed by one justice for the opinion issued by another threatens the likelihood that the critic will later be able to attract the target's vote in a difficult case. The point is not that justices who disagree in one setting will not agree in another, but that how one disagrees today may matter tomorrow.

The second reality emerges from the first. The chief can exercise leadership, indeed several types of leadership, but not power in the Court. The distinction may seem subtle, but it is nevertheless significant. In political science, power is generally defined as the ability to cause another person to behave predictably,[38] and also involves an ability to cause that behavior whether the other person wants what he or she is compelled to do or not.[39] The point is that the person wielding power is able to compel action because he desires it.

James MacGregor Burns has considered the differences between that approach to power and the concept of leadership.[40] For Burns, leadership requires the leader to engage someone else's interests. One leads not by wielding power, an imposition of will, but by convincing someone that cooperation is a matter of mutual interest.

Within the Supreme Court, the art of leadership is always necessary if one seeks to mobilize the Court. The larger the goals and the longer term the effort, as when a justice seeks to significantly alter a particular area of legal doctrine or the institutional character of the Court, the more a careful, sustained, and sensitive leadership effort is required. On an individual basis, and in the short term, one might be able to maneuver one or two colleagues into positions where they are more or less compelled to accept one's view, but that is the exception and not the rule.

Leadership in the Supreme Court

Most observers of the Court have identified three types of leadership: task, social, and intellectual leadership.[41] And, although any justice may become a leader within the Court, chiefs are usually evaluated in part on the basis of the quality and effectiveness of their leadership skills.

Task leadership is the ability to get the work done. In this Charles Evans Hughes Hughes was virtually without peer. Many factors work against the timely accomplishment of the Court's business. The docket is heavy, the cases are generally complex, the schedule is taxing, and the volatility of the cases could lead to a tendency to avoid the toughest cases until they absolutely have to be resolved. Some justices have been virtually paralyzed by the decision. Some of his former colleagues on the Court said of Justice Charles Whittaker that he was never able to make a decision until he left the Court.

Other justices have argued that the Court should not give in to docket pressure but should remain above the fray, giving intensive and lengthy consideration to serious issues brought for decision. Justice Frankfurter advocated this position. Each term for several years, Frankfurter would begin the term with a lengthy memorandum to his colleagues setting forth his criticisms of the Court's performance and presenting his recommendations for change. One of his thoughts was that cases should normally be expected to go over from one term to the next to permit reflection and debate. In the interim, instead of preparing a draft opinion and then moving to refine it, those on various positions in the case would produce the equivalent of law review articles, articulating their views, debating alternative positions, and providing commentary on the doctrinal implications of various decisions. This would provide for a more thorough and scholarly set of opinions. To most of his colleagues, though, the last thing they wanted was a flurry of academic debates and drawn-out arguments with Felix (which most thought were already far too long) over cases. In these matters, the chief's abilities to manage the docket, the conference, and opinion assignment are crucial.

Social leadership, the ability to lead through force of personality and interpersonal skills, has been critical to many of the Court's leaders. In a group as small as the Court, and that operates under the facts of life described previously, cold and impersonal management capability is inadequate or at least limited. Thus, Hughes was an able taskmaster in part because he was an able interpersonal player. On the other hand, a lack of task leadership skills can intensify interpersonal difficulties, as in the case of Chief Justice Stone, who presided over "one of the bitterest, most schismatic periods in judicial history."[42]

Warren also exploited social leadership skills. No intellectual giant, Warren understood his limitations and his strengths. He realized that different justices require different kinds of treatment; each responds to different sorts of arguments and interpersonal style. Beyond that, he, like other chiefs, came to realize very quickly that the organizational culture of the Court is as much a function of informal relationships among members of the Court as formal organizational structure and practice. Such a culture can be reshaped only if its social dimension is clearly appreciated. Thus, Warren found that such apparently simple changes as introducing microphones and an amplifier to the bench and moving away from a fixed decision day, the so-called Decision Monday, to the announcement of opinions whenever they were ready was not to be done without resistance. The informal culture based on tradition was at least as difficult to bend as the more formal processes of the Court.

Finally, some chiefs have also been able to exercise intellectual leadership as well, to influence their colleagues by the force of their arguments. Chief Justice John Marshall is one of the leading examples. Plainly, the fact that a chief had an intellectual career before elevation to the Court does not guarantee the ability to lead on the bench. Chief Justice Stone had difficulty leading in part because he interacted with his colleagues more like a faculty member engaged in an academic debate than a justice of firm principles, independent judgment, and clarity of logic. Few doubt that Felix Frankfurter was an intellectual powerhouse by most definitions of the term, yet, at least by the late 1940s, it could hardly be said that he was successful in exercising intellectual leadership over his colleagues.

In the routine operation of the Court, these forms of leadership are manifest in two contexts in particular, the management of the conference, and the assignment of the writing of opinions.

Controlling the Conference

Experienced chief justices are aware that the management of tasks is not merely a problem of presiding over a meeting but requires continuous effort. The chief must operate both the "sitting" and the continuing conference. Much is accomplished at the regular meetings of the conference, including final decisions on certiorari petitions, review of oral argument, and initial votes on cases. Perhaps most important, the initial arguments and priorities of the individual justices are revealed in discussion. However, the shaping of opinions is really only begun at the meetings. It continues through the process of the development of draft majority opinions, concurring opinions, and dissents.

Various justices have summarized their view of their chief's performances as leader of the conference sessions. From them it is clear that the problem is to maintain the traditional and inevitable rules, given the nature of the Court, of respect for one's colleagues, acceptance of the need to allow full discussion, and avoidance of interruptions among the justices, while simultaneously maintaining control of the flow of work. The business must be done. New cases are constantly reaching the Court. State governments and individual citizens await the outcome of crucial cases for the resolution of important matters in their day-to-day activities. The calendar places dramatic restrictions on the Court's ability to carry too many cases over for too long.

Chiefs like Marshall and Hughes, who were powerful figures within the Court and who were decisive and clearly in control of conference sessions, were the most respected. Chiefs like Stone and White, who let both discussion and interpersonal disputes run unchecked within the meetings, were not appreciated.

Some chiefs, like Warren, although strong leaders in their own right, have called on their colleagues for assistance in the management of conferences. When he first came to the Court, Warren called on his much more experienced colleague, Hugo Black, to preside over a number of sessions until he became accustomed to the Court's operation. Later, Warren often relied on Justice William Brennan's advice on the management of upcoming meetings.

The task of leading the conference can be complicated by factions such as those that existed within the Hughes Court. Chiefs have often been aware that groups of justices have sometimes held rump conference sessions. The situation is exacerbated if the chief is perceived by the Court to be heading a bloc or behaving in a manner that is less than evenhanded. The latter problem usually manifests itself more in the assignment by the chief of opinions than in the operation of the conference session.

Opinion Assignment

The power to assign the drafting of the opinion for the Court is usually regarded as the chief's most important power. While there is no guarantee that the person assigned to write the opinion will prepare something with which the Chief agrees or that, in the pull and haul of debates among the justices, the person who prepared the initial draft of the Court's opinion will ultimately be able to attract a majority of votes, by knowing his or her colleagues and selecting carefully from among them, the chief can indirectly shape the momentum of the ultimate opinion.

The rules of thumb followed by Chief Justice Hughes when making assignments provide a good description of the considerations employed by most chiefs. The first problem is to assure a fair distribution of work. Regardless of the differences within the Court, there must be some contribution by virtually everyone to the majority opinions for the Court if the workload is to be manageable. Thus, it is interesting to examine the opinion writing for the Burger Court during its later years, when the Court was quite fragmented. Although there were large numbers of concurrences and dissents, the actual distribution of majority opinions among the justices was amazingly even, as shown in Table 6.1.

The workload distribution issue can be a problem if there are justices who are too old, ill, or unskilled to carry a fair share of the drafting chores. A number of chiefs have faced this dilemma. Chief Justice William Howard Taft had a major difficulty in this respect, given the fact that he had a number of aging and infirm colleagues.

The same difficulty arises if there is a vacancy on the Court for an extended period. Chief Justice Stone faced that problem while Justice Robert Jackson was

Chief Justice William Howard Taft.

TABLE 6.1   **Opinion Production, October Term, 1983**

	Opinions of Court	Concurrences	Dissents	Total
Blackmun	16	6	9	31
Brennan	16	10	29	55
Burger	16	2	0	18
Marshall	15	2	16	33
O'Connor	17	10	9	36
Powell	18	11	7	36
Rehnquist	∿19	3	14	36
Stevens	16	18	34	68
White	18	6	9	33
Per Curiam	12	—	—	12
Total	163	68	127	358

Source:"The Supreme Court, 1983 Term," *Harvard Law Review* 98 (1984), p. 307.
Copyright © 1984 by the Harvard Law Review Association.

in Europe after World War II as the American prosecutor at the Nuremburg war trials. More recently, the fact that the Bork battle was so protracted meant that the Court was short a justice for virtually an entire term.

On the other hand, the tendency to assign an opinion to someone on the Court who is a recognized expert in a particular field argues against equal distribution of work and in favor of more targeted assignment practices. Justice Lewis Powell said of Justice William O. Douglas that "he knew more corporate law than everyone else on the Court put together."[43] Powell included securities law as a part of that comment. If a justice came to the Court from the D.C. circuit and therefore had substantial experience in administrative law cases coming from major federal agencies, he should not be surprised to find an assignment involving those types of opinions in the early going.

The chief might play to a justice's perceived strength for another reason. He might, as the expression goes, throw the new colleague a slow pitch with the hope that he or she will "knock it out of the park." It is not uncommon for a chief to assign a new person opinions with which the new justice is expected to do a great job and thereby start a career with a positive image and good feedback. It can also be done to mitigate a problem. After Hugo Black was confirmed, the news broke that he had at one time been a member of the Ku Klux Klan. Although Black gave a radio address in which he explained his membership and made clear that he had long since resigned from that organization, it came as no surprise that civil rights activists were angry and suspicious as Black took his seat on the Court. However, the chief justice intentionally assigned him civil rights cases early on, and the opinions that Black produced changed the critics' charges to congratulations with suprising speed.[44]

Some justices have become the resident expert on a subject by virtue of experience. Thus, Justice Brennan came to be regarded as an obscenity expert because he wrote most of the Court's rulings on that subject from the late 1950s until 1972. In that year Brennan more or less resigned as obscenity expert when he announced that he had become frustrated by his inability to find an acceptably clear standard for judging the boundaries of First Amendment–protected expression in sexual matters. Having spent months developing a thorough survey of the history of obscenity law, Brennan served notice on his colleagues that, unless the allegedly obscene material was distributed to minors or foisted off on unwilling adult recipients, he would not support convictions.[45] Chief Justice Burger accepted Brennan's implied resignation when he wrote a countermemorandum to Brennan's and called for "a division of the house" among his colleagues. He told them plainly that they must indicate whether they were with him in favor of tougher obscenity standards that would allow greater flexibility to local communities to prohibit what they regarded as pornographic materials or with Brennan's far more permissive view.[46] Burger ultimately got enough votes to prevail, and the Court announced a tougher standard in the 1973 *Miller v. California* ruling.[47]

Some chiefs, including Hughes, thought the system of assignment by expertise was not a particularly good idea. For one thing, it saddled some members of the Court with relatively boring tasks in fields in which they did not particularly enjoy repeated writing. Pushed far enough, it also limits a chief's options in assignment, and, after all, there are many things to consider apart from expertise.

The chief's first problem is to find someone who can draft an opinion that will command a majority of votes. Just because a justice voted with the chief in conference is no guarantee that the vote will not change once draft opinions begin to circulate. A justice may have understood colleagues to be moving in one legal direction to reach the conclusion on which a majority agreed, only to find from the draft opinion that the author saw the consensus in a different way or based on a different principle. If so, that justice may very well conclude that he or she will wish to write separately in a concurring vote or may join others in an opinion that they hope will attract enough votes to displace the one from the person originally assigned to write for the Court. In either case, the chief hopes that all nine justices will ultimately vote in support of one clear majority opinion.

If the chief saw a strong, clear majority or even unanimity (something chiefs these days more often see in their dreams than in the Court), he has a great deal more latitude. If the person assigned does not carry one or two other justices, it is not a major problem so long as there are sufficient numbers of other justices on the same side of the case to make a strong majority. Therefore, the chief can pick someone whose views may be relatively extreme and thereby shape the opinion in a particular direction. Even if that opinion must undergo changes before it emerges from the Court, the fact that it starts out further to the Left or the Right on the political spectrum affects the locus of debate.

The assignment to "get a Court" as the justices often put it, involves a number of considerations and can be a very difficult task. That is particularly true when the Court was sharply divided in conference. The story of Justice Brennan's attempt to navigate through a rocky Court in search of a majority in *Baker v. Carr*[48] is an example. *Baker* was a watershed decision for the Court. It enabled the federal courts to hear cases involving the constitutionality of apportionment plans in the states. As Brennan came closer to a majority, it became more and more difficult to make the changes needed to attract the critical votes without losing the justices who had already indicated a willingness to join an earlier draft of the opinion.[49] But as one of the most politically astute and sensitive justices in modern history, Brennan was precisely the right choice for the job at hand.

The judgment about just who is the right person in a sharply divided Court involves a number of considerations. In the *Baker v. Carr* case, the choice of the master Court builder, William Brennan, is illustrative. A practical, careful, affable, and alert justice, Brennan could forge the kind of compromises needed to fashion a majority in a difficult situation. In a very different case, however, Chief Justice Warren selected a very different draftsman. Former attorney general Tom C. Clark has never been regarded as excessively liberal in a broad political sense or soft on crime. His selection as the author of the opinion in *Mapp v. Ohio*, in which the Court announced the exclusionary rule barring the use of illegally obtained evidence in a criminal trial, was appropriate precisely because he was more likely to be able to hold the votes of the moderates and conservatives than could his more liberal colleagues. Even assuming that the chief cannot find someone who is usually seen as conservative among the liberal majority, or vice versa, he might be able to select from among the conference majority a person whose arguments and position seem more moderate and centrist than others. That moderate justice may be precisely the person to attract and hold votes. This use of assignment to build consensus is a technique of which Charles Evans Hughes spoke more than once.

There is also the issue of just how the chief decides which cases he or she should write. Ever since the days when Chief Justice John Marshall issued tremendously important interpretations of constitutional powers, it has been traditional for the chief justice to write opinions in cases for which the opinion should have a kind of extra stamp of authority. Thus, it was no accident that Warren assigned *Brown v. Board of Education*[50] to himself. As a unanimous opinion written by the chief justice, that decision carried virtually all of the symbols that the Court can attach to a ruling to indicate its importance and the Court's commitment to it.

Precisely because of the interpersonal dynamics that accompany the discussion of the merits of the cases, the assignment power can be a point of considerable contention within the Court. Justices have occasionally been known to desire the prestige associated with writing an opinion in a good case and to regard others as "dogs," drudge work that must be done but not providing particular intellectual stimulation or personal commitment. That implies, of course, that chiefs can use assignments as rewards or punishments for individual justices.

Some justices have objected to what they saw as attempts to manipulate assignments for other than appropriate reasons. That includes objections by some members of the Court to what they regard as unfair self-assignments by the chief. There have even been cases in which the chief was charged with manipulating vote counts in conference to control the assignment in a case.

One of the classic confrontations of this sort took place as a running battle between Chief Justice Warren Burger and Justice William O. Douglas in the early 1970s. At that time Douglas was the senior liberal justice, meaning that Douglas was generally the person who would assign opinions when the chief justice was not in the majority. On several occasions Douglas took the position that Burger simply miscounted conference votes to control the assignment.[51] Douglas was not the only justice who had difficulties with Burger's assignments. Potter Stewart wrote Burger on December 29, 1970, citing four assignment errors in a single assignment list.[52] In one of these, *Rosenbloom v. Metromedia*, Stewart found that he was assigned an opinion in which he was one of three justices on the losing side with five justices in the majority.

The clash over the assignment in *Lloyd v. Tanner*, a major free speech in private shopping centers case, caused Douglas to vent some of his frustration with the chief. After noting that he just found out that, in spite of an April 21 assignment by Douglas of the opinion to Thurgood Marshall, Burger had made a new assignment three days later, the outraged Douglas prepared a reply to Burger. After reading Burger the "riot act," Douglas concluded by insisting that the case "stays assigned to Thurgood."[53]

One of the most dramatic of these clashes came over the 1973 abortion cases, *Roe v. Wade*[54] and *Doe v. Bolton*.[55] Douglas took issue with Burger's assignment in *Doe*, the Georgia case, on grounds that the alignment was Brennan, Stewart, Marshall, and Douglas to strike elements of the law and Burger, White, and Blackmun to uphold it.[56] Burger disagreed, claiming that "there were, literally, not enough columns [in the docket sheet] to mark up an accurate reflection of the voting in either the Georgia or the Texas cases."[57] The stakes were raised considerably when Blackmun produced his memorandum calling for reargument in both abortion cases,[58] and issued his memorandum in *Roe v. Wade*, suggesting that the Court could avoid the direct constitutional question on abortion and strike the state bar on grounds of vagueness.[59] Douglas and Brennan tried to persuade Blackmun to take on the issue directly and disputed the need for reargument. When, on June 1, the recently appointed justices Lewis Powell and William Rehnquist decided to vote for reargument in the case, Douglas was outraged. He warned Burger that he would "file a statement telling what is happening to us and the tragedy it entails" if the Court held the cases over to the next term.[60] He immediately set to work on a memorandum, which he had printed and sent to Brennan.[61]

The Douglas memorandum charged that Burger improperly assigned the cases in the face of a request from Douglas not to do so. Douglas insisted that "the matter of assignment is not merely a matter of protocol." He recalled the tradition of assignment by senior associates in cases where the chief was not in the majority and warned that "when a Chief Justice tries to bend the Court to his will by manipulating assignments, the integrity of the institution is imperilled."[62] He wondered in print if "perhaps the purpose of the Chief Justice . . . was to try to keep control of the merits. If that was the aim, he was unsuccessful."[63]

In sum, Chief Justice Hughes was quite correct when he observed that assignment discretion was one of the most important powers he possessed. He was also right when he observed that it involved the marshaling of his troops, as was Frankfurter when, speaking of Toscanni Hughes, he observed that the chief had to have the qualities of the maestro of a world-class orchestra. The qualities are critical within the Court, but they are also important as the chief plays his or her role outside the Court.

THE CHIEF JUSTICE OUTSIDE THE COURT: JUDICIAL BRANCH ADVOCATE

Among other duties, justices will find themselves traveling to the circuit conference for the judicial circuit in which they serve as circuit justice. When they get there they are likely to get an earful from their colleagues on the lower courts.

The federal judges will express their views on opinions, the quality of legal practice they encounter, the problems engendered by recently enacted statutes, and the lack of resources they must accept as they attempt to handle their dockets. Returning from the conference one may reflect a bit on the tasks of the chief justice outside of the day-to-day operation of the Supreme Court as she wears the statesman's hat. In that capacity, the chief is both federal judicial administrator and judicial branch advocate. The previous discussion of the chief's responsibilities with the Administrative Office of United States Courts (AO), the Federal Judicial Center, and the Judicial Conference of the United States indicates some of those administrative tasks and their various nuances. So consider for a moment the chief as representative of the Supreme Court and the third branch to others in the political arena.

As the Court's representative, the chief at some points takes the offensive and seeks to be an agent of change, while on other occasions she plays the role of defender. Hence, Chief Justice Hughes managed the defense in the political trial of the nine old men facing prosecution by President Franklin D. Roosevelt. While there were many potentially hostile congressional judges, the Court was ultimately acquitted thanks in large part to Hughes's brilliant performance. Other chiefs have played a more aggressive offensive role, seeking to move the political process in the interest of the Supreme Court, the lower courts, or the law in general. Here, Chief Justice William Howard Taft continues to win honors as the leading judicial lobbyist. Taft numbers among his accomplishments the construction of the Marble Temple itself and the passage of the Judiciary Act of 1925, which gave the Court control over its docket by authorizing certiorari jurisdiction.

Like Hughes and Taft, all chiefs realize that, whether they are on offense or defense, they are in an unusual position for a political player with numerous institutional and traditional constraints. Defensively, the chief's ability to do very much to obtain external support for the Court's rulings is very limited. Probably no chief was more frustrated by that than Earl Warren, who was convinced that the aftermath of *Brown v. Board of Education* would have been very different had President Eisenhower supported the ruling. Nor can the chief even publicly defend the Court's rulings in any particular case, even when they are attacked by the president, Congress, or other officials.

The chief on offense can be more active and public but must still remain sensitive to the institutional constraints of the job. The chief is, after all, the head of a branch of government and must be ever mindful of issues of separation of powers. She cannot go hat in hand to the other branches seeking assistance, and she must maintain the dignity and independence of the judiciary. On the other hand, the chief is fully aware that the judiciary depends on the legislature for resources and the executive for enforcement of judicial decisions. The chief cannot play the kind of power politics with the other branches that are standard practice for the White House and the Congress.

There are a number of goals for which the chief lobbies. There is, of course, the budget. Here the chief works with the AO and the Judicial Conference in an effort to convince the legislature to fund judicial needs. Chief Justice Burger tried to move beyond the normal presentations to Congress with a series of meetings referred to as the Brookings Conferences, at which key legislators were invited to appropriate meeting locations outside Washington for a kind of sensitivity training session on the judiciary. The idea was not to lobby for particular needs but to make the legislators aware of what the judiciary was doing and the problems it faced in attempting to accomplish those tasks. Appearances before congressional appropriations committees is limited, and few judges are comfortable presenting the case for additional funds for judges and new courts in that forum. It is not a pleasant assignment for a justice to go to the Congress and ask for money or additional judges.

The chief also lobbies on jurisdictional issues. Chief Justice Taft wanted the Judiciary Act of 1925 in large part because it would give the Court discretion over a significant portion of its docket. Obviously, the more discretion any organization has with respect to its work, the more flexibility it has in setting not only its overall agenda but in determining what priority different issues will have on that agenda. He won his battle, but there were blocks of cases that, according to the statutes, the Supreme Court was still obligated to hear. A number of these cases came from federal district courts directly to the Supreme Court without facing a court of appeals. Chief Justice Burger made the elimination of that mandatory jurisdiction a major priority in his lobbying efforts, and he enjoyed some degree of success.

Another category of lobbying efforts can be called issues of judicial impact. These concern efforts to make known judicial fears about the implications of pending or recently enacted legislation. When Congress enacted a substantial revision of the federal criminal law in the 1980s, the judiciary was obviously mightily interested. Discussions about revising the procedures for death penalty appeals to the federal courts brought a major lobbying effort involving the chief justice. Chief Justice Rehnquist had been in discussions with the judges who make up the Judicial Conference of the United States regarding recommendations on how to handle death penalty appeals brought into federal court after condemned prisoners had exhausted all of the state court appeals. Rehnquist and some others favored dramatic constraints on federal court participation and review of state decisions, while others were extremely uncomfortable with the idea of federal judicial abandonment of the most critical kinds of issues of life and death. The conference instructed Rehnquist that it would not be prepared to recommend legislative changes until the evaluation of a pending study on the administration of the death penalty. Rehnquist nevertheless notified the Senate that it should proceed on the matter. Only later did the other judges find out that their instructions to the chief had been ignored. Liberal or conservative, no self-respecting judge could abide being ignored like that. His move cost Rehnquist mightily within the judiciary but also in Congress, where the standing rule is that it is unethical to finalize a deal when one does not have the support or agreement of the other parties.

The question that is often asked is just how the chiefs, and the courts, are in their lobbying efforts. The answer to that question depends upon where one sits. Certainly, many judges think the judiciary has become much more effective because it is more involved in such matters than it used to be and because the chief justices are becoming more alert to the need to become players in the political game. A good example is Chief Justice Burger, whose State of the Judiciary addresses announced in strong terms the intention of the Courts to make known their concern and draw attention to problems that seemed destined to affect the operation of the courts and the law.

One the other hand, if one asks judges who have served in the Congress, like Judge Abner Mikva of the U.S. Court of Appeals for the D.C. Circuit, the answer is very different.[64] Such seasoned observers make two points. The first is that the judiciary consists largely of a group of people who are at best novices in the well-developed arts of legislative influence, newcomers who lack not only expertise and experience but also resources needed to move the legislature. The idea that the chief justice can make annual pronouncements on judicial needs, hold a conference or two, and create an administrative assistant position with interbranch responsibilities, is simply not adequate to the task of competing with well-organized and -financed interests who vie for the same resources the courts seek from the legislature. Second, by contemporary terms, what the judiciary often seeks in the legislature is simply not of the magnitude that legislators consider important. Given the huge problems before the legislature, a request for a small number of people or dollars simply does not capture attention or imagination.

In the end, the last several chiefs can claim some victories on issues associated with jurisdiction. There are now more judges and more jurisdictional controls that permit workload discretion. However, with respect to the issues of budgets and matters with significant judicial impact, the courts can claim at best only limited success.

THE NAMING OF THE CHIEF

Despite all of the problems associated with the job, it is still a highly prized and respected assignment. The naming of a new chief is one of the most historically important actions a president can take. Not surprisingly, therefore, the politics of the selection and confirmation of a new chief are complex and intense.

The Abe Fortas nomination brought Senate foes out not only to get a man they disliked but also to attack the Warren Court record as a whole. And since Fortas was so close to President Lyndon B. Johnson, there was little question that an attack on Fortas was also a way for partisan opponents to make points against Johnson. The fact that Senate Judiciary chair Strom Thurmond and others attacked Fortas for decisions made by the Supreme Court years before he came to the bench seemed to make no difference whatever.

Warren Burger was clearly a symbolically important selection for President Richard Nixon, who had run against the Warren Court in favor of a "get tough" attitude toward criminal defendants. Burger had been a judge on the U.S. Court of Appeals for the D.C. Circuit and was a former assistant attorney general. He was well known as a judge with little sympathy for the claims of criminal defendants, having, for example, written against the exclusionary rule that would bar use of illegally obtained evidence from criminal trials. He would be a tough, conservative chief and, perhaps as important, would be viewed that way by the public.

When President Ronald Reagan named William Rehnquist as chief justice, there was no question that Rehnquist would be a symbolically important conservative. More than any other member of the Court, Rehnquist, originally appointed to the Court by Nixon, was understood to be the Court's most extreme conservative. Unlike a number of other justices, he was about as predictable in his voting as any member of the Court in modern history.

SUMMARY

However the chief came to be in the center chair, he or she is first among equals in a number of important respects. You will look to the chief as judge, chief, and statesman, and as a person who helps make it possible for you to carry out your own responsibilities. Despite the importance of the role, the chief is in many crucial respects dependent on your vote to accomplish the tasks of the chief justiceship.

As chief and as statesman, the chief has the duty of boundary spanning, often of being the point of contact between the members of the Court and those in the political and legal communities. Symbolically and practically, the Chief is important to those within the Court and those who must come before it. It is to those customers of the Court, as it were, to which we turn in the next chapter.

NOTES

[1]Quoted in Leon Friedman and Fred L. Israel, *The Justices of the United States Supreme Court 1789–1978*, vol. 3 (New York: Chelsea House, 1980), p. 1903.

[2]William O. Douglas, *The Court Years* (New York: Random House, 1980), p. 220.

[3]Steamer, Robert J. *Chief Justice: Leadership and the Supreme Court* (Columbia: University of South Carolina Press, 1986), p. 168, quoting Taft from David J. Danelski and Joseph S. Tulchin, *The Autobiographical Notes of Charles Evans Hughes* (Cambridge, MA: Harvard University Press, 1973), pp. 159–60.

[4]Merlo J. Pusey, *Charles Evans Hughes*, vol. 2 (New York: Macmillan, 1951), p. 650.

[5]Quoted in ibid., p. 651.

[6]Quoted in ibid., p. 652.

[7]Ibid.

[8]Charles Evans Hughes, *The Supreme Court of the United States* (New York: Columbia University Press, 1928).

[9]Ibid., pp. 24–25.

[10]Ibid., p. 57.

[11]Ibid., p. 58.

[12]Quoted in Steamer, *Chief Justice*, p. 55.

[13]Peter Fish, *The Office of Chief Justice* (Charlottesville: University of Virginia Press, 1984), p. 22, quoting Paul Freund, "Charles Evans Hughes as Chief Justice," *Harvard Law Review* 81 (1967), p. 35.

[14]Quoted in Pusey, *Charles Evans Hughes*, p. 665.

[15]Justice Robert H. Jackson, "The Judicial Career of Chief Justice Charles Evans Hughes," in Jesse H. Choper, ed., *The Supreme Court and Its Justices* (Chicago: American Bar Association, 1987), p. 103.

[16]Quoted in Joseph P. Lash, *From the Diaries of Felix Frankfurter* (New York: Norton, 1975), pp. 313–14.

[17]Quoted in Pusey, *Charles Evans Hughes*, pp. 672–73.

[18]Douglas, *Court Years*, p. 215.

[19]Felix Frankfurter, "Chief Justices I Have Known," *Virginia Law Review* 39 (1953), pp. 833, 903.

[20]Quoted in Pusey, *Charles Evans Hughes*, p. 676.

[21]Quoted in ibid., p. 678.

²²Quoted in ibid., pp. 678–79.

²³Quoted in ibid., pp. 676–77.

²⁴Douglas, *Court Years*, p. 220.

²⁵Pusey, *Charles Evans Hughes*, p. 678.

²⁶Hughes, *Supreme Court*, p. 76.

²⁷Quoted in Pusey, *Charles Evans Hughes*, p. 684.

²⁸Douglas, *Court Years*, p. 219.

²⁹Federal Bureau of Investigation File, United States Supreme Court, FBI Headquarters, Washington, DC.

³⁰*Rosenberg v. United States*, 346 U.S. 273 (1953).

³¹Bernard Schwartz, *Super Chief* (New York: New York University Press, 1983), p. 131.

³²*Board of Regents v. Bakke*, 438 U.S. 265 (1978).

³³Fish, *Office of Chief Justice*, chap. 5. See also Stephen L. Wasby, *The Supreme Court in the Federal Judicial System* (Chicago: Nelson-Hall, 1988), p. 241.

³⁴310 U.S. 586 (1940).

³⁵319 U.S. 624 (1943).

³⁶*Walz v. Tax Commission*, 397 U.S. 664, 703 (1970).

³⁷Justice Harry Blackmun, interview with authors, Washington, DC, Nov. 19, 1986.

³⁸David Easton, *The Political System, Second Edition* (New York: Alfred A. Knopf, 1971), p. 144.

³⁹Robert A. Dahl, *Modern Political Analysis* (Englewood Cliffs, NJ: Prentice-Hall, 1963), p. 40.

⁴⁰Ibid., pp. 18–23.

⁴¹See David Danelski, "The Influence of the Chief Justice in the Decisional Process," in Walter F. Murphy and C. Herman Pritchett, eds., *Courts, Judges, and Politics* (New York: Random House, 1979). Wasby, *Supreme Court*, p., uses the terms "task or intellectual leadership; social leadership . . . ; and policy leadership" (*Supreme Court*, p. 241; see also Steamer, *Chief Justice*, chaps. 2–4).

⁴²J. Woodford Howard, *Mr. Justice Murphy* (Princeton, NJ: Princeton University Press, 1968), p. 398.

⁴³Justice Lewis F. Powell, interview with author, Washington, DC, Nov. 18, 1987.

⁴⁴See, for example, *Chambers v. Florida*, 309 U.S. 227 (1940).

⁴⁵William J. Brennan, Jr., MTTC, May 22, 1972, box 283, William J. Brennan Papers, Library of Congress (hereafter cited as WJBP). The file also contains Brennan's lengthy memorandum that resulted from his study of the history and problems associated with crafting an obscenity standard.

⁴⁶Warren E. Burger, MTTC, Nov. 13, 1972, box 283, WJBP. See also Burger, MTTC, Nov. 20, 1972, box 283, WJBP.

⁴⁷413 U.S. 15 (1973). See also *Paris Adult Theatre v. Slaton*, 413 U.S. 49 (1973).

⁴⁸369 U.S. 186 (1962).

⁴⁹See Schwartz, *Super Chief*, pp. 410–28.

⁵⁰*Brown v. Board of Education of Topeka, Kansas*, I, 347 U.S. 483 (1954).

⁵¹In *Gooding v. Wilson*, Burger indicated that the conference vote had been inconclusive and he intended to put the case down for another conference. Douglas, who had decided to assign the opinion to Brennan, wrote Burger, objecting that the vote had been a clear five to two to affirm (William O. Douglas to Warren Burger, Dec. 17, 1971, box 1524, WODP). Burger's purpose became more clear when he replied: "Here again there is no harm in writing, but if your position is now firmed up, I see no point in reviewing a Conference discussion. Indeed, I think it very likely this case will be reargued. I, for one, will not take part in overruling *Chaplinsky*, directly or indirectly, with a seven-member Court" (Warren Burger to William O. Douglas, Dec. 20, 1971, box 1524, WODP). Brennan also wrote a memorandum indicating his disagreement with Burger's handling of assignments.

Douglas had a similar problem with Burger in *United States v. United States District Court*, in which Burger assigned the opinion to White even though Douglas was convinced that there were five votes in support of a more expansive ruling on constitutional grounds. He assigned the opinion to Lewis Powell, though Burger continued to support the idea that White should write (William O. Douglas to Warren Burger, Mar. 6, 1972, box 1523, WODP; Warren Burger to William O. Douglas, Mar. 7, 1972, box 1523, WODP; and William O. Douglas to Lewis Powell, Mar. 8, 1972, box 1523, WODP).

[52]Potter Stewart to Warren Burger, Dec. 29, 1970, box 1485, WODP.

[53]William O. Douglas to Warren Burger, May 1, 1972, box 1523, WODP.

[54]410 U.S. 113 (1973).

[55]410 U.S. 179 (1973).

[56]William O. Douglas to Warren Burger, Dec. 18, 1971, box 1523, WODP.

[57]Warren Burger to William O. Douglas, Dec. 20, 1971, box 281, WJBP.

[58]Harry A. Blackmun to Warren Burger, Jan. 18, 1972, box 1523, WODP.

[59]Memorandum to the Conference, May 18, 1972, box 282, WJBP.

[60]William O. Douglas to Warren Burger, June 1, 1972, box 281, WJPB.

[61]Memorandum from Mr. Justice Douglas, June 2, 1972, box 1588, WODP.

[62]Ibid., p. 2.

[63]Ibid., p. 3.

[64]Judge Abner Mikva, United States Court of Appeals for the D.C. Circuit, interview with author, March 1990, Washington, DC.

Getting to Know
the Customers: Litigants
Before the Court

7

You now have a sense of the historic processes of Supreme Court governance. The petitions for certiorari initiate the process. Receipt of the cert pets triggers a rapid review process that leads, in more than 95 percent of the filings, to a denial of the petition by the justices.

But who files the thousands of petitions received by the Clerk of the Court annually? In the twentieth century, especially the last half of the century, interest groups in America came to realize that lobbying the federal and state courts, especially the U.S. Supreme Court, could lead to the achievement of their policy goals.

Initially, after World War I, it was interest groups that had not been successful in lobbying the more traditional political agencies of government—the legislative and executive branches—that discovered and successfully employed litigation as a form of pressure group lobbying. The National Association for the Advancement of Colored People, civil liberties groups such as the American Civil Liberties Union, religious groups such as the Jehovah's Witnesses, and labor organizations achieved some degree of success when they took their petitions into the federal courts. As of the 1990s, almost all pressure groups go to Court to try to achieve their goals through litigation.

LOBBYING THE COURT: TYPES OF INTEREST GROUPS

Supreme Court justice Robert Jackson once wrote that American government "is government by lawsuit. These constitutional lawsuits are the stuff of power politics in America."[1] Given an understanding of the Court's work, one has to agree

159

with Jackson's observation. Clearly, as seen when examining the manner in which the Court's annual docket is created by the Court, a great deal of the litigation heard by the Court can have major policy implications for the society. The Court's clients, to a large extent, are society's "organized groups" who seek, in the Court, "to produce—or retard—social change."[2]

Most of the public-policy cases heard by the Court illustrate pressure group activities of one kind or another. In addition to participating in the judicial selection process, both the nomination and the confirmation phases, as observed in the Robert Bork hearings, interest groups also participate in the litigation process itself.

Litigation before both the federal and state courts has become a staple strategy of interest groups—liberal or conservative, public or private interest—seeking to achieve their goals through political participation. More than half of the noncommercial litigation cases decided by the justices had at least one brief filed by an interest group. Some groups use the litigation strategy so often that they are called "repeat players." Other groups use litigation as a group strategy for the remediation of a single issue and are called "single-shot" players.[3] Decades ago, a leading political scientist, Samuel Krislov, citing the limited financial resources available to most private persons compared with the funding available for groups to litigate, wrote about the increased presence of interest groups in the Court. He acknowledged the reality of "representational [rather than individual] litigation" that came before the justices in the form of test cases, class action suits, and through the *amicus curiae* briefs filed by a variety of interest groups.[4]

All kinds of interest groups have argued cases before or filed amicus curiae briefs with the justices of the U.S. Supreme Court. Businesses and corporations challenged New Deal economic policies in the Court in the 1930s. Civil rights and liberties groups such as the American Civil Liberties Union (ACLU), the National Association for the Advancement of Colored People (NAACP), the Jehovah's Witnesses, and other disadvantaged groups brought cases and filed briefs in the Court beginning in the early decades of the twentieth century, especially from the 1940s through the 1960s.

Social organizations such as the National Organization for Women (NOW), Common Cause, the Sierra Club, and the Environmental Defense Fund have sought to persuade the Court to adopt, through the litigation process, social policies that are on the groups' agendas. Likewise, given the personnel changes and subsequent legal outcomes of the Rehnquist Court, in recent years many conservative economic, social, and public-interest groups such as the Pacific Legal Foundation, Citizens for Decency Through Law, the Equal Employment Advisory Council, Americans for Effective Law Enforcement, and the National Right to Work Legal Defense Fund, have brought their policy views into the Court.

Any interest group can participate in Supreme Court decision making either directly or indirectly. The group can participate as a litigating party, that is, as a principal actor in a case. As a major actor in the case, the pressure group is assuming the role of a "political" litigant. The group behaves as someone who comes into the Court seeking to persuade the justices to accept the group's policy views when making a substantive determination on the merits of the case.[5]

Interest groups *directly* participate before the Court by filing a test case or by initiating a class action suit. These types of action enable the interest group to control the litigation strategy, "to frame the issues before the Court,"[6] as the case moves through the federal courts. A test case is one brought by an individual or a group to challenge the constitutionality of a statute—as written, as interpreted, or as implemented by the state. The interest group's litigators locate persons who agree to serve as plaintiffs to challenge the legislation or the regulation in court. As it moves through the judicial system, the group has the ability to control the direction of the arguments before the appellate judges.

The group can also seek, in the test case, a declaratory judgment from a federal judge, under the terms of the 1934 Federal Declaratory Judgment Act. Such a case, if heard by a federal court, leads to a determination by a federal judge of the person's rights before she is actually charged with violation of the challenged statute.

A class action suit brought to the Court is the mechanism a group employs to manage a very complex case involving hundreds or more persons who share the same legal or social situation.[7] The interest group, representing its membership, seeks an action—monetary damages, injunction—or declaratory-judgment relief from the Court. It has become common practice for a variety of groups, including civil rights, consumer protection, and other public-interest groups, to bring a class action suit on behalf of all persons who are or have been similarly adversely impacted by the actions or inactions of defendants.

Alternatively, but without the control of the case the group would have as a primary, or direct, party to the legal dispute, an interest group can indirectly participate in litigation by filing a "friend of the court," or *amicus curiae*, brief with the Court (see Figure 7.1). This form of *indirect* participation in the litigation process by the group is a much less expensive and time-consuming strategy. With the permission of both primary parties to the litigation or the approval of the Supreme Court, an interest group can file an *amicus curiae* brief that focuses on the jurisdiction or justiciability of the suit or that addresses the merits of the case. While interest groups participate in litigation in these two ways, the most frequent form is as *amicus curiae*.[8] A recent study of *amicus curiae* repeat players during the Warren and Burger Court years, 1953–86, indicates that there was a clear pattern of repeaters. For the most part, as Tables 7.1 and 7.2 indicate, liberal and public-service groups filed amicus briefs before the Court.[9]

Most interest groups can have some but not a great deal of impact on the Court's decision making. If the group does its work well, if the Court grants certiorari (which it does in only about 5 percent of the petitions it receives annually), and if the group's argument in the petition adequately challenges a lower court's ruling, the Supreme Court outcome may support the group's goals and policy agenda. A small handful of interest groups, especially the U.S. Solicitor General's Office, have a much greater impact on the Court than others.

The reality is that most interest groups have little impact on the Supreme Court's decision-making process, except for providing cues to the justices and their law clerks, during the agenda-setting or docket control phase of decision making, regarding the breadth of the public interest in the issue.[10] Indeed, to understand the litigation process's value to interest groups, one has to acknowledge the diversity of group goals. In addition to seeing their policy goals translated into legal doctrine by the justices, a group may litigate to gain publicity for its cause or even to maintain the group's membership roster.[11]

The more successful interest groups that work before the Court are those that (1) have the respect of the Court's personnel because they are proven, quality repeat players; (2) have good attorneys, whose arguments are well presented

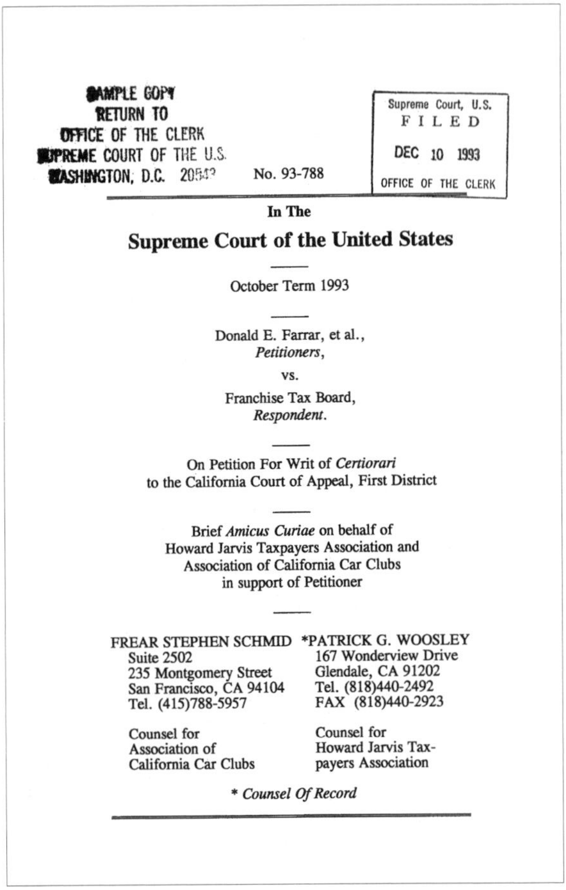

SAMPLE COPY
RETURN TO
OFFICE OF THE CLERK
SUPREME COURT OF THE U.S.
WASHINGTON, D.C. 20543   No. 93-788

Supreme Court, U.S.
F I L E D

DEC 10 1993

OFFICE OF THE CLERK

In The

Supreme Court of the United States

October Term 1993

Donald E. Farrar, et al.,
Petitioners,

vs.

Franchise Tax Board,
Respondent.

On Petition For Writ of *Certiorari*
to the California Court of Appeal, First District

Brief *Amicus Curiae* on behalf of
Howard Jarvis Taxpayers Association and
Association of California Car Clubs
in support of Petitioner

FREAR STEPHEN SCHMID   *PATRICK G. WOOSLEY
Suite 2502   167 Wonderview Drive
235 Montgomery Street   Glendale, CA 91202
San Francisco, CA 94104   Tel. (818)440-2492
Tel. (415)788-5957   FAX (818)440-2923

Counsel for   Counsel for
Association of   Howard Jarvis Tax-
California Car Clubs   payers Association

* *Counsel Of Record*

FIGURE 7.1

Typical *Amicus Curiae* brief filed
with the U.S. Supreme Court.

TABLE 7.1   **Amicus Participation During the Warren Court**

Group	Number of Amici Briefs
American Civil Liberties Union*	9
American Jewish Congress	5
American Jewish Committee	4
NAACP/NAACP Legal Defense Fund	4
American Federation of Teachers	3
American Veterans Committee, Inc.	3
Anti-Defamation League, B'nai B'rith	3
National Committee Against Discrimination	3
Japanese American Citizens League	2

*The ACLU was most successful when filing a liberal brief in support of the petitioner
rather than the respondent; no conservative briefs were filed.

Source: From Sherral Brown-Guinard, "Effect of Ideology on the Success of Repeat
Players," SPSA paper, November 1993.

TABLE 7.2   **Repeat Players, Burger Court Era**

Group	Number of Briefs Filed
American Civil Liberties Union*	78*
NAACP/NAACP Legal Defense Fund	58
AFL–CIO	35
Lawyers Committee for Civil Rights Under Law	32
Mexican American Legal Defense Fund	27
American Jewish Committee	22
Anti-Defamation League, B'nai B'rith	19
National Education Association	18
Chamber of Commerce	16
Women's Legal Defense Fund	16
American Jewish Congress	11
National Organization for Women, Legal Defense Fund	10

*The national level of the ACLU filed 59 briefs *amici.*

Source: From Sherral Brown-Guinard, "Effect of Ideology on the Success of Repeat Players," SPSA paper, November 1993.

in briefs and in oral arguments; (3) have the financial resources to do a good litigation job; and (4) work well with other groups.[12]

Some, but by no means all, pressure group litigation strategy does lead to changes in public policy in the form of Supreme Court opinions that break new ground in an area of law. Change in the law and in public policy as determined by the Court occurs because of personnel changes in the Court, changes in the political environment, and the impact of pressure groups on the judicial decision-making process.

"Legal change," note two scholars, "is the product of the motive force of evolving doctrine, the climate of the times in which cases are decided, the issues thrust upon the Court, and the configuration of actors [e.g., interest groups] pressing claims on the Court."[13] While interest groups have been increasingly involved in developing and implementing a litigation strategy, the critical question is whether that enhanced energy—with the corresponding increased financial expenditures—has led to the changes in public policy that they desired.

Arguments by highly skilled attorneys for a very respected group will not always lead to success. A Court majority may be unwilling to accept their arguments and effect change through its decisions. Even the most highly respected litigation organization, and the nation's most successful one, the U.S. Solicitor General's Office, does not win all the cases it argues before the Court. Changes in the Court's personnel lead to changes in constitutional and statutory interpretation. In reality, the impact of the interest group is minimalized and relative "to the predisposition of the Court at different points in time."[14]

INTEREST GROUPS BEFORE THE COURT: A CASE STUDY

In *NAACP v. Button* (1963), Justice William Brennan, writing for the Court majority, noted that "under conditions of modern government, litigation may well be the sole practicable avenue open to a minority to petition for a redress of grievances."[15] Many scholars, as well as the Court, believe that "disadvantaged groups are wise to pursue their goals through judicial lobbying."[16] The NAACP is the major mainstream civil rights interest group in America. Since 1915 it has brought many dozens of test cases and class actions into the federal courts on behalf of African Americans across the nation.

For many participants in the legal process, litigation is a social process. The process, conceptually, begins when "people start to see that they might understand what has happened to them as something for which the legal system may provide a remedy."[17] The interest group's leadership concludes that the problem can be redressed by taking legal action against the group's wrongdoers in the hope that the Court will make things right for the group's membership. The members of the interest group look to their leaders to formulate legal grievances to attack the wrong, and then to pursue remediation in the courts (because the group most probably does not have power and therefore access to the more overt channels of formal political power such as Congress or the executive branch).[18]

Central to this social and legal process is the interest group's need for persons with both legal and political skills, who can develop and implement the group's strategy in the courts. Understandably, restraints, both anticipated and unanticipated,[19] that call for quality legal, political, and management skills are placed on any group's litigation actions. Not only is there the problem of limited financial resources but there are the ulcer-producing dilemmas of internal clashes over the group's directions, legal uncertainty due to weak cases, missing petitioners, hostile appellate judges, and a changing social environment.[20]

For the disadvantaged groups working in the courts, there is the additional burden of trying to persuade judges of the constitutional necessity for reforming basic social and political institutions and the customary patterns and practices of a community that have the effect of discriminating against one group. Examining the problem of racial discrimination in America, "America's dilemma," as Gunnar Myrdal called it in his seminal work,[21] by focusing on the legal and political activities of the NAACP in ending *de jure* racial-discriminatory policies and practices, gives a clear picture of how litigation as a social process can work to effect social changes.

The NAACP's actions since 1915 have led to systemic reform of governmental and social actions that discriminated against persons solely on the basis of skin color. The NAACP litigation effort illuminates how the courts, both state and federal, and especially the U.S. Supreme Court, can be used to modify and then formally eradicate legal precedents and local customs that fostered an oppressive racial subordination that had existed in America for hundreds of years.

The NAACP Lobbies the Court

Racism in America has its roots in colonial America. Long before the 1787 Constitution's legal portrayal of African Americans as chattel property,[22] slave law in English America was extremely prohibitive for slave owners who wanted to free their slaves. Compared with slave owners in Spanish, French, Portuguese, and Dutch America, who could free their slaves with relative ease, slave owners in English America were under more confining laws, and therefore far fewer slaves were freed. As one scholar noted, if there "had been fewer restrictions on masters freeing slaves, [then] there would have been more slaves freed; there would have been more blacks with access to money and property; and freed blacks would have been accepted as citizens."[23]

That, unfortunately, was not the case, and, from the beginning of the English colonialization of America, "slaves had no legal personality and were firmly classed as things. [They were] . . . chattel."[24] By the early 1800s, then, more than a century later, most southern state constitutions contained clauses "for the perpetuation of slavery by forbidding the legislature to emancipate slaves without the consent of their owners. . . . [Clearly, there was a very high degree of] Southern consensus on the indefeasibility of the institution. . . . There was little real need to employ [the state constitution] for the protection of slavery in most [southern] states."[25]

The lengthy, bloody Civil War was an effort to end the pattern of slavery. The Civil War amendments were efforts by a victorious Union to formally codify, in the U.S. Constitution, essential legal and civil rights all American citizens possessed, especially the recently freed slaves. These rights included the right to vote, the right of citizenship for all slaves, and the entitlement of all persons to all the privileges and immunities of citizenship, to due process and the equal protection of the law. After the Reconstruction era ended in the late 1880s, however, there was a return to the use of many "badges of slavery" in the form of racial segregation and a wide variety of racially discriminatory practices against the recently freed blacks.

America continued to remain racially divided. *Plessy v. Ferguson,*[26] the 1896 opinion of the U.S. Supreme Court, ushered in the era of formal Jim Crowism, that is, race discrimination, in the South. In that decision, a seven to one Court majority held that the Equal Protection Clause of the Fourteenth Amendment did not prohibit a public instrumentality from providing facilities for its citizens that were "equal but separate." With that opinion, in which the Supreme Court gave its imprimatur to *de jure* racial segregation in America, the status of African Americans in America plummeted to the pre–Civil War level.[27]

In 1909, in response to the violence of the times committed by whites against blacks, including lynchings, beatings, and mob violence against blacks in cities such as Springfield, Illinois (the birthplace of Abraham Lincoln), William E. Walling, a white Kentuckian "voiced alarm that such violence was spreading from the South to the North. He saw an urgent need for a nation-wide effort to combat the evil."[28] As a consequence, an organization was formed to try to end the society's continual discriminatory practices against black citizens in America. It was created primarily by whites concerned about the violence against blacks and was called the NAACP. Its main focus, initially, was to push for what was then a radical idea: "achieve absolute political and social equality for African-Americans."[29]

The NAACP was the first and the largest of America's civil rights groups. By 1919, there were over 310 local chapters of the NAACP in America, with over one hundred thousand members (half residing in the South). In 1939, there were over 1,600 chapters with over three hundred thousand members. In 1993, there were over 2,200 chapters with over five hundred thousand members across the nation. The organization's central focus was the achievement of racial equality in America. Its early focus was on ending the practice of peonage in the South, introducing antilynching legislation in Congress, and ending the disenfranchisement of African Americans in the South.[30]

In 1915 the NAACP began to view litigation as the social process for achieving these goals. The judgment by the NAACP to use the courts to achieve racial equality "was almost a mandatory one. No other [political] avenue lay open" to the NAACP and to African Americans at that time that would enable government to respond in some positive way to the evil of racial inequality.[31]

Under Arthur Spingarn's leadership, the NAACP began to challenge the constitutional validity of Jim Crow segregation in the South as well as *de jure* denial of equal justice and due process for African Americans. Between 1915 and 1936, without the existence of a formal, strategic litigation plan, the NAACP brought ten cases before the Court (on the merits) on behalf of African-American petitioners in four general areas: African-American suffrage, residential racial-zoning ordinances, restrictive covenants, and due process and equal protection for African Americans accused of crimes.[32]

The NAACP won nine of these cases.[33] None of them, however, in this early period of legal activity, challenged what was for many African Americans the most critical characteristic of racial segregation: the separate and unequal public school system in America's South, as well as the segregated graduate and professional-school patterns that proliferated across America during this time. As Thurgood Marshall, the legal director of the fund, noted, for African Americans "the only solution to our problem is that of breaking down segregation in the public schools."[34]

In 1930, the NAACP received a grant of one hundred thousand dollars from the Garland Fund. The organization used the funding to bring on board a person to develop a litigation strategy for the group. Nathan Margold, a Harvard-trained attorney and protégé of Felix Frankfurter, and at that time one of the NAACP's legal counselors, was appointed and immediately began working on a plan. He believed that the NAACP should rely, to a great extent, "on the orderly process of litigation" and to use the courts, especially the Supreme Court, to bring about full legal and political equality for African Americans in America.[35] In the course of the following two years, he did develop a litigation strategy for the organization that would enable it to attack Jim Crowism and racial segregation in a fairly orderly, tactical fashion.

For Margold and the NAACP litigators that followed him in the mid 1930s (Margold left the organization in 1933), eradicating segregation in education was the major but not the only task. For Margold, and for Charles Hamilton Houston, former dean of Howard Law School, who was appointed as the first special counsel for the NAACP in May 1934, two strategies were developed that could be followed by the NAACP in the courts. These strategies were sketched out but, because Houston "felt more comfortable as a lawyer attacking targets of opportunity than as a long-range planner of litigation,"[36] there was no strategic, organizational decision making until the late 1930s.

At that time, Thurgood Marshall and his small staff of lawyers committed themselves to implementing the organization's litigation strategy. Marshall was one of Houston's law school students at Howard University. He graduated first in his class in 1933 and briefly practiced law in Baltimore before being called to the national NAACP in 1936 by his mentor. He was brought on as assistant special counsel in 1936 and replaced Houston as special counsel in 1937. In 1939, the dynamic lawyer was appointed director–counsel of the newly created corporation that would henceforth act as the legal arm of the NAACP, the Legal Defense and Educational Fund, Inc., known simply as "the Fund." It was created to take advantage of New York's favorable environment for nonprofit corporations, and its central purpose, noted in its charter of incorporation, was to provide free legal aid to African Americans who suffered legal injustice and who could not afford an attorney to plead their case in court. Marshall was to remain as the leader of the Fund for over two decades, years that were crucial ones for the NAACP and for American society.[37]

If Houston was the NAACP's outside-the-office legal representative, then Marshall was its "inside man,"[38] a man who understood the value of the Margold strategy, someone who "really believed in a coordinated litigation strategy,"[39] and someone who aggressively challenged racial discrimination in the areas of housing, education, transportation, electoral politics, and criminal justice.

For these two central NAACP strategic planners and litigators, the organization had to force the South to equalize expenditures by petitioning the Supreme Court for review of class action suits challenging racial segregation. Their hope: to convince the Court to issue orders that the Jim Crow separation of the public schools *as practiced* was unconstitutional and that there had to occur either the equalization of expenditures for public school education or desegregation of the schools themselves. The 1935 University of Maryland Law School case[40] was the first victory for the NAACP in this area of litigation. It was a particularly pleasant case for Marshall to argue and to win because, a few years earlier, that institution would not admit Marshall because of his race. That case "began the battle in which the NAACP directly challenged the practice of segregation."[41]

For Houston and Marshall, it was also legally and politically possible,[42] at the appropriate time, for the NAACP to attack, frontally, the concept of separate but equal itself by bringing appropriate cases to the Court. Their hope was that the NAACP could convince the Court, in oral argument and in briefs presenting social, economic, and psychological data,[43] that the *Plessy* concept injured African Americans by denying them the equal protection of the laws and should be overturned in favor of the concept of racial equality.[44]

Houston and Marshall also had to contend with internal criticism of the organization's primary commitment to a litigation strategy to achieve its goals. In 1934, for example, W.E.B. DuBois, editor of the organization's journal *Crisis* since 1909, attacked the emergent strategy, arguing that there was more discrimination in 1934 than there was in 1915 when the organization first went into the courts. While Du Bois left the NAACP because of this clash, other critics of the litigation strategy continued their attacks for another decade.[45]

Bringing class actions or test cases challenging racial segregation meant that the NAACP had to convince federal judges, most especially the justices of the U.S. Supreme Court, to overturn or to narrow a precedent such as *Plessy*. For Houston and Marshall, this was a legal challenge of immense proportions. In addition to everything else involved in developing and implementing a litigation strategy, they had to deal with the Court's personnel, the nine black-robed justices. Sitting on the bench listening to oral arguments, reading the NAACP briefs, discussing the case in conference session, and circulating memos in the course of reaching consensus on a case, these nine white men ultimately determined the success or failure of the group's legal arguments.

For the NAACP to achieve its goals, the justices of the Court had to react positively to its message. The NAACP's two-decades-long campaign to eradicate Jim Crowism in America was the consequence of a deliberate design of its legal leadership after 1934. It was a plan designed in large part based on the perceived attitudes of the men on the Court and on the NAACP's perceptions of how the justices would respond to the legal issues raised by the organization.

For Houston and Marshall, there were "broadly defined evils" such as lynch mobs, Jim Crowism, economic and political suppression, and cruel poverty, that had to be ended through strikes and picketing, but most important for the NAACP, through court orders.[46] However, the Court majority not only had to acknowledge the reality of these broadly defined evils, it also had to conclude that the case was properly before them and that they could provide a remedy that dealt with the legal issue identified in the briefs. These judgments, procedural and substantive, were made by men who had to be persuaded, using legal arguments, to act in a certain way.

Sitting on the Court during this period of NAACP litigation were dozens of justices, some from the South, who held different views about a number of issues such as the role of the Court and of its justices, the sacredness of precedent, and whether or not *Plessy* and the formal outgrowth of *Plessy*, Jim Crowism, were constitutional.[47] Houston and Marshall, and their legal staff, had to implement the litigation strategy in a manner that took into account southerner Tom Clark's views of *Plessy*; capitalized on former NAACP legal counselor Felix Frankfurter's presence on the high bench; and responded tactically to the pleasantly surprising behavior of an Alabamian and former Klansman on the Court, Hugo Black.

Justice Frankfurter, appointed in 1939, whether asked or not, continually offered his colleagues on the Court his views on all issues, including the problem of race in America. For example, he told Justice Wiley Rutledge that

> before coming down here, when I was of counsel for the Association for the Advancement of the Colored People [*sic*], considerable practical experience with problems of race relations led me to the conclusion that the ugly practice of racial discrimination should be dealt with not by the eloquence of action, but with austerity of speech. . . . It does not help toward harmonious race relations to stir our colored fellow citizens to resentment by even pertinent rhetoric or by a needless recital of details of mistreatment which are irrelevant to a legal issue before us. Nor do we thereby wean whites, both North and South, from what so often is merely the momentum of the past in them.[48]

Frankfurter's comments reflect the justice's views of the black and Caucasian races as well as a sense of how America's racial conflict could be resolved. The NAACP lawyers had to understand Frankfurter's perceptions and then had to implement a litigation strategy that enabled the group to take advantage of such judicial perceptions.

When Hugo Black was confirmed as justice in August 1937, African Americans were "greatly horrified, sad, disappointed, and sickened."[49] This was because of the fact that, when he arrived at the Court at the beginning of the 1937 term, it was publicly revealed that, in the early 1920s, he had been a member of the Ku Klux Klan in Alabama. Walter White, then the executive director of the NAACP, wrote a friend that Black would be "on the spot" whenever a civil rights case came before the Court. Black told White, "frankly and soberly that he realized this and that he hoped that he would be able to measure up to what I [White] and others of his friends expected of him."[50]

Chief Justice Charles Evans Hughes made the "conscious effort to assign Hugo Black opinions that would rehabilitate him in the view of the liberal community."[51] Voting with the majority in *Missouri ex rel Gaines v. Canada*,[52] led an African-American newspaper to editorialize about Black:

To our great surprise and infinite relief, our good friend Justice Hugo L. Black, was found with the majority. . . . Not a Negro in America would have been surprised if Justice Black had been found in the minority mumbling nothings with Justices Butler and McReynolds, two old men still actuated by the tenets of slavery days. Along with thousands of other Negroes, we fought confirmation of Justice Hugo Black, and were loud in our wailing after he was confirmed. . . . To say truth, the action of the Justice is too good to believe, and we are still waiting for another occasion to see if our ears and eyes are deceiving us.[53]

Hughes's efforts to "rehabilitate" Black led to the Alabamian writing the opinion for the majority in a case brought to the Court by the NAACP, *Chambers v. Florida* (1940).[54] While it was a difficult opinion for Black to write,[55] he did write for a unanimous Court. Said the justice: "Under our constitutional system, courts stand against any winds that blow as havens of refuge for those who might otherwise suffer because they are helpless, weak, outnumbered, or because they are non-conforming victims of prejudice and public excitement." The chief justice had Black announce the opinion on February 12, 1940: Lincoln's birthday. And his words, as Hughes had hoped, electrified the African-American community. Mary McLeod Bethune, a leading figure in the civil rights movement, wrote Black: "God bless you. Our prayers are that you may live long to render just such decisions. The Negro race has been waiting for men like you on the bench for many years. May He give you courage, vision, and a growing spirit of justice. We need you in a day like this."[56]

After 1939, strategically taking into account the presence of new justices like Frankfurter, Black, William O. Douglas, and others appointed by Franklin D. Roosevelt, the legal staff of the NAACP, led by Thurgood Marshall, began to implement the first of the two Margold strategies. Marshall was also successful, in 1948, in involving the Department of Justice in the effort to overturn *Plessy*. In *Shelly v. Kraemer*, a 1948 restrictive covenant case, the U.S. Solicitor General's Office filed, for the very first time, an *amicus curiae* brief on behalf of the NAACP. Four more *amicus curiae* briefs were filed by the solicitor general in civil rights suits brought to the Court by the NAACP between 1948 and 1952. In 1950, again for the first time, the solicitor general argued, in the *amicus* brief filed in *Henderson v. U.S.*, an Interstate Commerce Commission suit, that *Plessy* should be overturned.[57]

Marshall, who had carefully built a legal staff of six black attorneys, most graduates of Howard Law School, went about the work of implementing the equalization plan. Marshall's discussions with his staff "were more like open forums where various strategies were bandied about and different arguments and tactics were discussed and debated."[58] Selecting cases strategically, that is, good equal-educational-facilities cases that would be appealed "to the courts and the Supreme Court in those areas where the likelihood of success was the greatest,"[59] Marshall and his troops continually hammered away, indirectly, at *Plessy*, while arguing and winning in the Court cases that focused on police brutality against African Americans[60] and on other forms of violent racial discrimination.[61]

During this time, in addition to filing suits challenging gross violation of due process of law for African Americans, the NAACP and the Fund instituted three different types of school desegregation suits: desegregation of public graduate and professional schools,[62] equalization of the salaries of black and white public school teachers,[63] and inequities in the physical facilities of black public schools in the segregated separate-but-equal environment.[64] Marshall and the NAACP brought almost three dozen cases to the Court, winning all but four.[65] For the NAACP, it was an attrition strategy that set the stage for the overturn of *Plessy*.

Through 1947, Marshall "seldom mentioned plans for launching a [direct] legal assault on segregated education [*Plessy*]." However, he knew that the solution to the problems African Americans faced in America lay in the overturn of *Plessy*. "You cannot accomplish this," he said, "by giving lip service to opposition to Jim Crow education and then continuing to build monuments to this segregation in the form of Jim Crow schools in order to establish 'Jim Crow DeLuxe.' . . . The only sane approach is a direct attack on segregation [*Plessy*] per se."[66]

He was, with his small Fund staff, employing the tactic of successfully challenging the "equality" end of the *Plessy* concept, thereby weakening the foundation of the 1896 precedent. But, strategically and tactically, the Fund had not yet "launched a broader assault on all segregated public education."[67] This was to come about in 1947, when, in an essay in an African American newspaper published in Baltimore, the *Afro-American*, Marshall announced the change in the NAACP's litigation strategy, stating that it would now

> attack the separate but equal doctrine by establishing in court—by a preponderance of evidence (scientific, sociological, biological)—that there was no rational basis for race based distinctions. . . . The NAACP lawyers in order to get the campaign under way accepted the doctrine that the state could segregate . . . provided equal accommodations were afforded. . . . Now the NAACP is making a direct, open, all-out fight against segregation. There is no such thing as "separate but equal." Segregation itself imports inequality.[68]

Starting with cases involving graduate and professional schools, and finally targeting segregated public elementary and high schools, the Fund, led by Marshall, brought class action suits in eight cases involving segregated public-educational facilities. Ultimately, in 1954, came the decision that overturned *Plessy*: *Brown v. Board of Education*. *Brown*, however, created a new agenda for Marshall and the Fund: dismantling the consequences of over one half a century of adherence to the precedent in accordance with the Court's implementation framework of "with all deliberate speed."[69]

This has proven to be more difficult than Marshall and the Court thought in 1954. After the overturn of *Plessy*, the task for the NAACP became much more complex. From the 1960s to the present, the fund attorneys have had to deal with *de facto* segregation, institutional racism, and the creation of new remedies to end dual school systems in the North.[70]

Reviewing the NAACP's activities between 1915 and 1955, it is clear that the organization's litigation actions "were shaped by a combination of personal preferences and organizational concerns."[71] The NAACP was blessed, during this time, with the vigorous, skillful legal and political leadership of Charles Hamilton Houston and Thurgood Marshall. Both were very talented attorneys who also acknowledged the importance of the general organization. They were aware of the political, legal, and social environment in which the civil rights interest group had to operate to achieve its goal of racial equality. Indeed, one scholar suggests that the "immense dedication of Houston and Marshall to their work may have done more to foster success than any strategic decisions they made."[72]

Thurgood Marshall, head of the NAACP's Legal Defense
Fund, with fellow NAACP attorneys George E.C. Hayes (left)
and James Nabrit (right), on the steps of the Supreme Court
after the Court's historic decision, *Brown v. Board of
Education*, was announced, May 1954.

For some of the time, the NAACP legal leaders were able to control events.
However, even they had to deal with a "tremendous amount of matter extraneous
to policy which determined whether a case was brought in one place rather than
another; [their policy was made primarily] around Thurgood Marshall's desk with
a lot of improvisation."[73] The NAACP had to weigh the societal context and mood,
the values of the personnel sitting on the court, and the climate for change in
America when planning and implementing litigation strategy. Changes in any one
of these important extraneous issues had an important impact on the NAACP.
Marshall could never operate in a political and legal vacuum!

Generalizations About Litigation as Interest Group Strategy

What does account for change in legal precedent in American law? How
does one account for the overturn of the 1896 *Plessy* precedent by the Supreme
Court in 1954? One knows that the Court reverses a majority of the opinions it reviews under certiorari. One explanation for this focuses on the Court's person-

nel. Many justices do undergo change; they evolve intellectually and jurisprudentially over the years. There is also doctrinal evolution. Justices perceive, through the case/controversy process, that a precedent like *Plessy* loses vitality or utility. Justice Tom Clark, in 1950, said to his colleagues that while he supported the retention of *Plessy*, it was not immutable: "If some say that this [the Court's decision in *McLaurin*, a 1950 segregation case] undermines *Plessy* then let it fall, as have many Nineteenth Century oracles."[74]

In addition, justices die, resign, or retire, and new ones with different positions on critical legal issues are appointed.[75] According to Philip Elman, a law clerk of Frankfurter's and on the staff of the U.S. solicitor general, the NAACP's leadership did not do a good job of assessing the dynamics of Court change at the time of *Brown*. Elman, a former law clerk and confidant of Felix Frankfurter and an assistant solicitor general in the U.S. Solicitor General's Office at the time of *Brown v. Board of Education*, maintained that all the strategic moves of Thurgood Marshall and his staff were really of little value in accounting for the Court's unanimous overturn of *Plessy*. Rather, according to Elman, it was the dramatic change in Court personnel that accounted for the overturn.

In September 1953, Chief Justice Fred Vinson died suddenly, and President Eisenhower's appointment of Governor Earl Warren of California as chief led to the unanimous opinion of the Court. Marshall, said Elman, "just didn't know how to count votes on the Court; they were lacking a sense of subtlety about the Justices' concerns [about overturning *Plessy*]. It had been a mistake to push for the overruling of segregation per se so long as Vinson was Chief—it was too early."[76]

An examination of the activities of the NAACP suggests a second explanation for legal change. Change can occur because of the impact of interest group litigation on the law. Without the NAACP's litigation strategy, implemented by Marshall and his colleagues for over two decades, the Court would not have been sensitized to the legal and political issues inherent in the organization's agenda.[77]

The NAACP systematically brought cases to the Court that forced the justices to examine the issue of racial equality over and over again and from different angles of law. The organization is a model for planned litigation in the Court. Most interest groups have not developed the kind of litigation campaign implemented by the NAACP. It is extremely difficult for a group to develop a long-term strategy, to select an area or areas of law in which to litigate the group's agenda, or to select good cases that, over a period of time, will "turn" the Court and lead to victory.

Reviewing the NAACP's activities and those of other interest groups, there emerge a number of factors that account for interest group success before the Court. Control of the litigation by the group is important. For the group to impact the justices of the Court, there has to be a sharp focus and clear direction in the litigation. While it is true that all successful groups have to "quickly take advantage of a favorable judicial climate,"[78] without a continuing focus on the goal (for the NAACP the goal is racial equality) by the group's litigators, then the advantage may be missed.

A second factor is the climate on the Court and in the society. As noted, the Court underwent significant personnel changes beginning in 1937, a development that came close to the NAACP's decision to begin the frontal attack on *Plessy*. Had the Court not experienced these personnel changes or had another president been nominating justices, the outcome could have been different and the end of Jim Crowism might have been delayed accordingly.

An additional factor that can account for success in the Court is the support a group receives from other interest groups through the filing of *amicus curiae* briefs and the weakness of other interest groups in opposing the litigation. For example, the NAACP found critically important support for its efforts to overcome *Plessy* when the U.S. Solicitor General's Office filed *amicus curiae* briefs with the Court in support for overturning the 1896 precedent. The Solicitor General's Office also participated in oral arguments in the *Brown* litigation, and some of the office's staff were in close personal communication with members of the Court. Obviously, the intervention of this important group did have a significant impact on the Supreme Court.[79]

TYPES OF MECHANISMS OF PRESSURE GROUP PARTICIPATION

Legal action of an interest group, for the most part, is "responsive and reflexive" rather than fixed and frozen.[80] Litigation strategy is appropriate for long-term planning purposes. Interest group litigators are always looking for the "good" case through which to try to influence the justices. A good one for a pressure group is one in which the fact and law situation is clear and favorable to the group's goals and for which there is the "good" plaintiff, that is, someone who has clear "standing" and who raises a legal question that the Court is ready to examine on the merits. For example, in an establishment-of-religion case, the ACLU will look for an orthodox Jew who wants to bring suit as opposed to an aggressive, militant atheist such as Madeline Murray O'Haire,[81] to serve as the plaintiff—although there are times when such a militant atheist is the only available plaintiff.

The group's influence, direct or indirect, is in the form of the written briefs, both jurisdictional and on the merits, as well as the quality of the oral argument before the justices. The perfect case for an interest group to litigate does not exist, however, and a group's litigation strategy cannot wait for that which is nonexistent. With this noted, how do groups participate in litigation and how does the Court respond to their participation?

Interest Groups as Primary Participants in the Litigation Process: Direct Participation

In both the test case and the class action suit brought to the Court by interest groups, the major goal is to have the Court respond favorably to the arguments, written and oral, of the group's counsel. These types of direct involvement try to elicit a ruling from the Court on a policy issue that is of great interest to the group. The NAACP is the model for direct, primary participation by a pressure group; the ACLU is another example.

The impact of direct participation on the Court is much greater than a group's indirect participation through the *amicus curiae* brief. For one thing, "the briefs and arguments of counsel for the direct parties [are] . . . significantly higher" in quality than are the *amicus curiae* briefs filed by other groups.[82] For another reason, it seems clear, given the nature of Supreme Court personnel and decision making, that the Court is "much less responsive at the merits phase" to the information in the *amicus curiae* briefs filed by the groups.[83]

Indirect Group Participation Through the *Amicus Curiae* Brief

The major goal of an *amicus curiae* brief filed by an interest group is to alert the Supreme Court to a case's importance and to "persuade the Court to rule on behalf of a particular litigant."[84] Such a brief provides the Court with political, social, and philosophical cues about the issue or issues in the litigation before the Court for judgment. And some of the justices, including Hugo Black, William Brennan, Thurgood Marshall, and William O. Douglas, appreciated such inputs for that reason. The *amicus* brief kept them in touch with the many communities, and their interests, beyond the Court's chambers and ornate courtroom.

The interest group participating indirectly through the filing of the *amicus* brief is not a party to the dispute. Occasionally, a group uses the *amicus curiae* process to its "show the flag" in an inexpensive way.[85] Most groups, however, file *amicus curiae* in cases that they believe can further their organizational goals. They file, as the 1989 *Webster* abortion case suggests, three types of *amicus* briefs on the merits: (1) a general repetition of the major party's arguments, (2) technical, nonlegal briefs that provide the justices with "specialized [historical, medical, scientific] knowledge," and (3) risk-taking *amicus* briefs, that is, those that are unconventional and/or emotive.[86]

Rule 37 of the Supreme Court Rules establishes the guidelines for the filing of *amicus curiae* briefs in the Court. It stipulates that a brief should be submitted to the Court only when it adds relevant material not already brought to the Court's attention by the parties in the dispute before the Court.

A question often raised is whether the *amicus curiae* brief filed by an interest group is repetitious at best and "emotional explosions at worst."[87] How important is the brief for the Court? What is its impact on Court decision making? Does it provide the justices and their law clerks with helpful and relevant data? Does it make a difference in Supreme Court decision making?

Justice Hugo Black, for one, answered some of these questions. He understood the value of the *amicus curiae* brief quite well. In a memo to the conference (MTTC), written October 16, 1957, he stated that

> most of the cases before this Court involve matters that affect far more people than the immediate record parties. I think the public interest and judicial administration would be better served [by allowing for greater amicus participation by groups] rather than tightening the rule against *amicus curiae* briefs.[88]

However, Black's colleague Felix Frankfurter had another perspective on the *amicus curiae* brief. Although at one time Frankfurter "started out with an easygoing hospitality toward all briefs that might be submitted for our enlightenment, such a latitudinarian view now seems to be undesirable."[89] For him, the amicus brief could "embarrass" the principal arguing the case because the brief "may give a different shape or twist to the argument called for by the litigation as the parties molded it." Also, Frankfurter, unlike Black, objected to having the Court "exploited as a soapbox or as an advertising medium, or as the target, not of [legal] arguments but of mere assertion that this or that group has this or that interest in a question that ought to be decided 'irregardless' [sic] of such pressures. . . . We ought not to countenance belief in others that we are amenable, or the assumption that such pressure is legitimate."[90]

Harry Blackmun's MTTC during the 1978 Court deliberation of the medical school quota case *Bakke*[91] sheds some additional light on how the justices respond to *amicus curiae* briefs filed by interest groups. He wrote to his colleagues that *amicus curiae* briefs from Jewish organizations take

> the "accepted" Jewish approach. . . . Nearly all the responsible Jewish organizations who have filed *amicus curiae* are on one side of the case. They understandably want "pure" equality and are willing to take their chances with it, knowing that they have the inherent ability to excel and to live with it successfully. Centuries of persecution and adversity and discrimination have given the Jewish population this great attribute to compete successfully and this remarkable fortitude.[92]

At bottom, the answer to questions about the impact of the *amicus curiae* brief depends on the group that files one with the Court. "Briefs filed by state and local governments appear to have little effect on the outcome of cases heard by the Supreme Court. Briefs filed by other amicus parties have the potential for a moderate impact on the changes for litigant success as long as they are not opposed by the United States as either a direct party or as *amicus curiae*. In contrast, briefs filed for the United States by the Solicitor General were shown to have a major impact on Court decisions."[93]

Webster and the Impact of *Amicus Curiae* Briefs on the Justices

Webster v. Reproductive Health Services[94] was an important 1989 term decision involving the issue of abortion. Many dozens of *amici* filed briefs with the Court. Indeed, an unprecedented number was filed: seventy-eight, with forty-six on behalf of the appellants (the state of Missouri) and thirty-two on behalf of the appellees (Reproductive Health Services), and another four hundred groups signing on as co-sponsors.[95] Given the possibility of the Court overturning the watershed *Roe v. Wade* decision, there was great national interest in this case involving the constitutionality of a set of very restrictive state abortion guidelines.[96] *Roe* was the watershed 1973 seven to two decision of the Court in which the majority, in an opinion written by Harry Blackmun, concluded that the constitutional right to privacy[97] is "broad enough to encompass a woman's decision whether or not to terminate her pregnancy."

Since *Roe*, there were three new Reagan nominees on the Court: Sandra Day O'Connor, Antonin Scalia, and Anthony M. Kennedy. The three were chosen by Reagan because it was felt that they believed in the "sanctity of life" value that had been enunciated by Ronald Reagan at the Republican national presidential conventions in 1980 and 1984 and throughout his tenure as chief executive. At the time of *Webster*, therefore, the feeling was that the Court was ready to overturn the controversial 1973 decision: the two dissenters in *Roe*, William Rehnquist and Byron White, had now been joined by three conservative jurists. This overturn-of-*Roe* "anticipation" led to the "unprecedented number of *amici* briefs."[98]

Did these many dozens of amicus briefs have an impact on the Court's decision in *Webster*? From a review of Thurgood Marshall's papers, they did not, in the end, carry much weight in the Court's decision-making process. Missouri's *amici* filed, at the "expense of repetition," a larger number than did the pro-choice groups. The latter worked together to try to avoid unnecessary duplication of the major party's argument.[99] Both sides focused sharply on Justice O'Connor and her concerns about the validity of *Roe*, as voiced in abortion cases decided earlier in the decade in which she was very critical of *Roe*'s place as valid precedent.[100]

In the end, O'Connor did not join Rehnquist's decision, which upheld most of the segments of the Missouri statute and contained language that seemed to end *Roe* as precedent without actually overturning it. Instead, she wrote a concurring opinion (one of five written in *Webster* by the justices) in which she noted that Missouri's statute did not place an undue burden on a woman's right to an abortion, but all she indicated about *Roe* was that it still remained "problematic."[101]

While some attribute O'Connor's change of heart to the fact that she accepted some *amici* arguments,[102] a review of Marshall's *Webster* files in the Library of Congress suggests something else at work: the intellectual interaction of justices when hammering out a decision on a controversial question such as abortion. A review of *Webster* memos indicates that Rehnquist believed he had O'Connor as one of his quintet that supported the validation of the state statute and the less-than-gracious death of the *Roe* precedent. (At one point in the circulation of draft opinions, May 30, 1989, one of the dissenters, John P. Stevens, shot back an angry note to Rehnquist about the chief's majority draft: "As you know, I am not in favor of overturning *Roe v. Wade*, but if the deed is to be done, I would rather see the Court give the case a decent burial instead of tossing it out the window of a fast-moving caboose.")[103]

Until the very last moment, Rehnquist thought he was writing the majority opinion of the Court for himself and Justices Scalia, White, O'Connor, and Kennedy. And the justices all saw his opinion as one that, for all practical purposes, overturned *Roe*. Blackmun, the author of *Roe* in 1973, drafted a dissent and circulated it on June 21, 1989, reflecting his feeling that *Roe* was overturned:

> Today a bare majority of this Court disserves the people of this Nation, and especially the millions of women who have lived and come of age in the 16 years since the decision in *Roe v. Wade*. . . . Let there be no misunderstanding: the two isolated dissenters in *Roe*, after all these years, now have prevailed, with the assent of the Court's newest members, in rolling back that case to the severe limitations that generally prevailed before January 22, 1973. I rue this day. I rue the violence that has been done to the liberty and equality of women. . . . I dissent.[104]

Chief Justice Rehnquist set June 29, 1989, as the decision day for *Webster*. On the day he set that date, however, Justice O'Connor circulated a draft opinion that concurred with the results announced in Rehnquist's opinion but not with the chief's reasoning. In the draft, she stated that she continued to think that *Roe* was "outmoded" but not deserving of overturn. In her next draft, circulated the following day, O'Connor thought that *Roe* was "problematic," not "outmoded."[105]

Rehnquist then penned two additional draft opinions in an effort to hold O'Connor and pushed the announcement of *Webster* off for four days, for July 3, 1989. In a new draft, however, while still concurring with his opinion, she referred to Rehnquist's opinion as a "plurality" one.[106] Seeing the change, Blackmun rewrote the ending of his dissent, changing "I rue this day" to "I fear for the future."[107]

By this time, June 29, 1989, Rehnquist himself in his fifth and final version of his opinion, referred to it as a "plurality" opinion of the Court and used the conditional in his last paragraph: "We would modify and narrow *Roe* and succeeding cases."

By the time of the next abortion case,[108] O'Connor had moved strongly away from Rehnquist, so much so that Marshall wrote to Brennan, on June 13, 1990, that "I think it is important for John [Stevens] to get as much support as possible, now that Sandra has for the first time joined us in holding invalid a law regulating abortion."[109] Because of her change, *Roe* was not overturned. According to the Marshall files, O'Connor attributed her change of view to Stevens's comments and his MTTC about the abortion issue.[110]

By June 1992, O'Connor, with Justices David Souter and Kennedy, jointly penned a highly unusual tri-authored opinion in *Planned Parenthood of Southeastern Pennsylvania v. Casey*[111] that upheld, once again, the *Roe* precedent while weakening it somewhat. They stated, in part, that "the essential holding of *Roe* should be retained and once again reaffirmed" while concluding that the Pennsylvania statute did not "unduly burden" women seeking an abortion in Pennsylvania.

In the case, Rehnquist, Scalia, White, and Clarence Thomas (who replaced Marshall on the Court) joined in a plurality opinion that upheld the state restrictions on abortion and would have expressly overturned *Roe*. Blackmun's partial dissent stated in part: "I remain steadfast in my belief that the right to reproductive choice is entitled to the full protection afforded by this Court before *Webster*. I fear for the darkness as four Justices anxiously await the single vote necessary to extinguish the light."[112]

Associate Justice John P. Stevens.

Looking at a very controversial issue, abortion, it seems as though the reason for change is the changed perceptions of the justices—changed primarily due to the interactions they had with each other through the MTTCs, the draft opinions, and the conversations in conference sessions. In this light, the impact of *amicus curiae* briefs seems to be marginal, except when the solicitor general files one or is asked by the justices to do so.

Indirect Participation: Achieving Policy Goals
Through Involvement in the Judicial Selection Process

A noted legal scholar, Herman Schwartz, has written that a pressure group will become involved in the selection process only when an "egregious candidate" is nominated by the president.[113] One significant reason is the cost of mounting a challenge to the president's candidate for the Court. In recent years, however, especially since the Court itself has been seen by interest groups and the American public as playing a significant role in the maintenance or modification of public policy,[114] groups have become more involved in the screening of Court nominees.

Pressure groups do have a major impact on the selection process. Clint Bolick, the litigation director for a conservative public-interest pressure group, the Institute for Justice, said, aggressively, when Lani Guinier was nominated for the position of assistant attorney general, Civil Rights Division, by President Bill Clinton in the spring of 1993: "It's payback time. . . . There will be a judicial Armageddon. We will force Clinton to expend enormous political capital by mobilizing activists at the grass-roots level. This is the issue [nomination of judges and civil rights administrators] that energizes conservatives more than any other."[115]

Groups become involved in both the nomination phase and the confirmation phase of the selection process. Labor and civil rights groups have been keenly interested in appointments to the Supreme Court. In 1930, both the American Federation of Labor and the NAACP vigorously, and successfully, opposed the nomination of federal appeals court judge John Parker to fill a vacancy on the Supreme Court. Labor, civil rights, and many other public-service and professional groups opposed, successfully, two of Nixon's nominees to replace Abe Fortas: Clement Haynsworth and G. Harrold Carswell.[116] When in 1987, Ronald Reagan selected Robert Bork to replace the retired Lewis Powell, the liberal opposition to the nomination was shrill and successful. Led by Ralph Neas, the executive director of the Leadership Conference on Civil Rights, the hundreds of groups in opposition to Bork coalesced and were able to mount a successful challenge that led to Bork's defeat in the Senate.

Given the centrality of the Supreme Court in the affairs of the nation, interest groups will involve themselves in the selection process. Also, as the 1993 Lani Guinier transaction suggests, interest groups have also become a basic part of the judicial-legal-selection process generally. By far the most successful and most active of the interest groups that work in the judicial environment is the U.S. Department of Justice (DOJ), in particular, the Solicitor General's Office in the DOJ.

THE FEDERAL GOVERNMENT AS LITIGATOR

One must acknowledge the central role of the federal government as an interest group litigator. The government lawyers in the federal courts are representing their clientele: personnel in various offices, bureaus, and agencies of the national government as well as, in criminal and civil cases, the American people. Federal appellate judges regularly hear cases from administrative-agency litigators as well as cases brought into court by a local U.S. attorney on behalf of the people.

Given the structure of the national government's executive branch, with its hundreds of agencies responsible for implementing congressional statutes and drawing up federal regulations—then enforcing them—there is a great deal of litigation involving the national government. In this litigation activity, two major units stand out: the Department of Justice (DOJ), led by the attorney general (AG) and the Office of the Solicitor General (SG).

The Attorney General and the Department of Justice

An enormous amount of activity is generated within the executive branch by the millions of civil servants employed by the federal government. Added to this bureaucratic output is the work and output of the several major independent regulatory commissions that have been created by Congress since 1877.

There is also the output generated by many thousands of cases brought into federal courts by the ninety-four U.S. attorneys' offices, ninety located in each of the fifty states and another four in the U.S. territories. These U.S. attorneys' offices are responsible for enforcing the federal civil and criminal codes. Clearly, there is the need to centralize the litigation that flows from the tremendous volume of work generated by the federal executive branch and its attorneys.

The management of litigation has been the responsibility of the U.S. attorney general since the 1789 Judiciary Act. That act, in one of its many sections, called for:

> a meet person, learned in the law, to act as attorney-general for the United States, . . . whose duty it shall be to prosecute and conduct all suits in the Supreme Court in which the United States shall be concerned, and to give his advice and opinion upon questions of law when required by the President of the United States, or when requested by the heads of any departments.[117]

President George Washington asked his Virginia friend and personal lawyer Edmund Randolph to serve as the first attorney general. (Washington set the pattern for future presidents when he selected his close friend to serve as his legal advisor and AG.) At the beginning of the republic, it was a part-time position. The AG lived in the national capital when the Court was in session, representing the government in the Court, advising the president on legal matters, and, until 1817, giving legal counsel to the Congress as it wrote legislation.[118] Most often, however, given the nature of the workload, the AG practiced law at home.[119]

From the beginning, the heads of the executive departments brought their own litigation in the federal district courts. There was no fixed relation between the U.S. attorneys in the districts, a national agency, and the AG. Because of this reality, there were legal coordination and control problems in the national government.[120] Fearful of centralized executive power, Congress created solicitors in a number of executive-department agencies to litigate suits in the federal courts. There was no coordination between these legal officers and the AG. Treasury, the Land Office, War, Navy, State, and Internal Revenue Service were some of the federal units who had their own litigators. There was, intentionally, a congressional "separation of law powers" concept implemented in the national government until 1870.[121]

Since the first Congress, AG's "have struggled to centralize government litigation authority."[122] The Department of Justice was created by the Congress in 1870, in the Department of Justice Act,[123] to try to provide some unity of legal decision making and jurisprudence in the executive. And the AG was made the administrative head of the national government's legal administration.[124]

Under the authority of the AG in the Department of Justice were all the U.S. attorneys, as well as the newly created solicitor general and two assistant attorneys general, sixteen clerks, and three messengers. After creating the DOJ, however, the Congress then went about the task of creating independent regulatory agencies such as the Interstate Commerce Commission (ICC), the Securities Exchange Commission (SEC), and the National Labor Relations Board (NLRB) and gave these agencies the power to represent themselves in litigation in federal court.[125]

As America grew, so too did the DOJ. By the time of the First World War, eight major divisions existed within the DOJ, each with its own assistant attorney general to manage them. In 1928, however, AG John Sargeant reported to Congress that of 900 attorneys in the federal government, only 115 were under his department's jurisdiction.[126]

By the time of the Roosevelt New Deal things had changed. President Franklin Roosevelt signed, in June 1933, Executive Order 6166. It required that all claims or suits brought by or against the United States be litigated by the DOJ, except as otherwise authorized by law. A few months later, Congress codified this order as 28 USC Section 516. With these actions, independent litigation powers and authority were taken away from the executive-department heads and placed in the hands of the attorney general and the DOJ.[127]

By 1993, the "institutionalized attorney general" had a seven-billion-dollar budget and employed over eighty thousand persons, including over five thousand attorneys.[128] The U.S. attorney general has become (1) a Supreme Court "barrister"; (2) a cabinet-level political advisor with very close ties to the president; (3) the administrator of the DOJ, supervising the more than three dozen divisions, bureaus, agencies, offices, and boards in it; as well as (4) the chief law enforcement officer in America.[129]

The U.S. attorneys are the government's trial lawyers in the federal district courts. The office of U.S. attorney was created in the 1789 Judiciary Act, along with the position of AG. All the litigation decisions that lead to trial are made, using prosecutorial discretion, by the U.S. attorney and her staff of assistant U.S. attorneys. They are "directly responsible for the enforcement of federal criminal law via prosecution."[130]

The office is considered a "piece of patronage" by observers of the judicial process in America.[131] The U.S. attorneys are political appointees of the administration in the White House, and studies indicate significant policy differences between Democratic and Republican U.S. attorneys.[132] (It was reported that a

Kennedy administration person in the DOJ told a disgruntled Republican U.S. attorney: "Look, pal, your party lost the election.")[133]

Appointed for four-year terms, the attorneys can be removed at the discretion of the president (with the advice of his AG). When a new administration enters the White House, however, "the lights [go] out in U.S. Attorney's Offices everywhere," commented Jimmy Carter's attorney general, Griffin Bell.[134]

The U.S. attorney, as a member of the Department of Justice organization, on occasion has discretion restricted by legal policy judgments from the office of the AG. Frequently, the president and the AG instruct the U.S. Attorney's Office to initiate prosecutions against a particular group of persons, for example, antiwar demonstrators, antitrust violators, or savings and loan executives. Sometimes the AG will send a DOJ attorney into the jurisdiction to argue a case before the federal trial judge. In the toxic tort radioactivity cases tried in federal district courts in Utah and Nevada in the early 1980s, for example, the DOJ had lawyers from the Department of Energy handle the government's defense.[135] Furthermore, "under no circumstances will a U.S. Attorney take the case on appeal to the federal circuit court, . . . the decision to appeal and to argue the case on appeal rests with the decision makers in Washington, D.C.," that is, the president and the AG.[136]

Centralization of legal activities in the national government leads to control of legal and political policy by the White House. It "strengthens the President's ability to dictate policy orientation through government litigation. The DOJ acts to control regulatory agencies that might otherwise advocate parochial positions regardless of the administration's political agenda."[137]

Given this growth, the AG has had to balance the office's commitment to the administration of justice with managing a political/legal system replete with discretionary authority held by U.S. attorneys, the AG, and the SG.[138]

The Tenth Justice: The U.S. Solicitor General

The Office of Solicitor General is critical to the operations of the U.S. Supreme Court. Indeed, the SG is the "most prolific [and the most successful] participant before the Court, both as direct party and as *amicus curiae.*"[139] Created in 1870 by the Congress, the solicitor general was to be, according to the statute, an "officer learned in the law, to assist the Attorney General in the performance of his duties, to be called the Solicitor General." While the office represents the executive branch of government before the justices, the SG generally has tried to avoid pushing the administration's political agenda too aggressively.[140]

There is no doubt, however, that the SG will take cues from the president and the attorney general on major, sensitive policy issues. When the Republicans left office in 1993, the new Democratic administration of President Clinton came into power with different views on a number of key legal and political issues including abortion and affirmative action. It is equally clear that the government's new SG, Drew Days III, a veteran Justice Department litigator who served as assistant attorney general, Civil Rights Division, during the Carter administration has different views about litigation than his Republican predecessor, Kenneth Starr, especially on controversial issues such as abortion.

Since 1981, Republican SG's have been telling the justices of the Court that *Roe v. Wade* was wrongly decided and should be overturned. It is clear that new

Solicitor General Wade McCree (Carter Administration).

amicus curiae briefs filed by Days will urge that *Roe* remain as a viable precedent. Moreover, the *amicus* briefs filed by the Clinton administration will argue that state statutes restricting abortions should be overturned. On such very divisive issues as abortion and school prayer, "points of view can change," said Starr, and the justices understand.[141]

This shift in legal-policy positions must be handled tactfully, because the justices have come to rely on stability and continuity—and excellent legal analysis—coming from the SG's office. Rex Lee, President Reagan's first SG, has said that "we [SG's] pay a price if the Court gets the impression that we are nothing more than an extension of ideology."[142]

There are occasions when the SG will disagree with the president and the attorney general on legal-policy directions. While one option is resignation, more often the SG will transmit to the Court his disagreement with the formal policy position of the administration. This often takes the form of a "Thatcher-type" notation in the brief filed by the SG in accord with the policy position of the president and the AG. Thomas Thatcher was SG from 1930 to 1933, and when he disagreed with a legal-policy position of the administration, he would sign the brief but disassociate himself from it by adding a footnote stating that the "SG does not fully subscribe to the position of the IRS," or whatever department was involved.[143]

There is, therefore, some degree of independence in the SG's office. The SG can distance the office from the policy position of the AG and the president.

Solicitor General Rex Lee (Reagan Administration).

Solicitor General Kenneth Starr (Reagan-Bush Administrations).

Solicitor General Charles Fried (Bush Administration).

Solicitor General Drew Days III (Clinton Administration).

The SG can "confess error" and ask the Court to rectify an error that occurred in the lower federal courts. Generally, the SG has freedom to make critical determinations regarding legal decisions—unless the law is not clear. "Then the SG should seek guidance on the policy question" from the AG.[144]

The SG clearly has a "dual responsibility," to the president and to the Court. The SG has an undeniable influence on the justices and is seen and referred to as the "tenth Justice" because of the special relationship that exists between the office and the justices. The SG pays office visits to the justices and has tea with them. In addition, the assistants to the SG work with the justices and their clerks throughout the year. The SG acts as tenth justice also because of the functions performed by the government's lawyers in the Court. The prime function, implicit in the 1870 congressional legislation is to control the flow of cases to the Court by screening all prospective federal cases, where the United States is a direct party to the dispute. Erwin Griswold, a former SG, has written that "the SG does most of the screening which is done in other cases by the Supreme Court, for he tries to take to the Court only cases which he thinks the Court will accept."[145]

Working with two dozen attorneys, the SG screens all cases involving the United States as a party and determines which will be brought to the Supreme Court under certiorari. Fewer than one in six such cases is petitioned to the Court. For example, in the 1985 term of the Court, the SG filed certiorari petitions in 48 of 655 government cases the office reviewed.[146] A case is appealed to the Court if there are good facts, if it can make good law, and if it presents issues the Court is willing to discuss.[147]

Because of this filtering function, the SG's "grant of certiorari" success rate is phenomenal. On average, regardless of the political party in the White House,[148] between 70 and 80 percent of the petitions for certiorari are granted. In addition, the office will submit *amicus curiae* briefs in cases where the government, though not a party, has an interest in the outcome of the litigation. The practice of *amicus curiae* participation by the SG is a relatively recent phenomenon. In 1950, the SG filed a single amicus brief with the Court. By the 1988 term, the SG had filed amicus briefs in 25 percent of the cases before the Court, 41 of the 170 cases heard by the justices that year.[149]

Given the very close, indeed intimate, relationship between the SG and the Court, the justices will occasionally ask the SG to submit briefs in cases in which the government is not a party. Additionally, the SG can argue cases before the Supreme Court when not a major party in the legal dispute. During the 1983 term of the Court, there were 262 oral arguments; the SG appeared in 150 of them and "won" in 85 percent of them.[150]

There is, however, the very real political side to the SG's behavior. Recent research (see Tables 7.3 and 7.4) clearly indicates that SG's "clearly pursue agendas concurrent with the ideological orientation of the administration in office at the time of oral arguments."[151] The staff attorneys in the SG's office, although not political appointees, do follow a somewhat similar path, "yet to a lesser degree."[152] This holds true whether the SG or his staff is filing *amicus curiae* briefs for certiorari to the Court.

The data suggest the reason for this reality: the SG staff are more successful than the SG because, "as a general rule, Solicitors reserve for themselves the 'hard and unpleasant' cases, those cases which are the most important to the administration and which might be politically volatile."[153] When given the choice, "both

TABLE 7.3   Ideological Position of U.S. Lawyer by President's Party

| | *PRESIDENT'S PARTY* | | | |
	Democrat	*Republican*	*Difference*	*Significance**
Solicitor General				
Liberal as Appellant	57.4%	36.8%	+20.6%	.02
	(54)	(87)		
Liberal as Respondent	15.6%	23.3%	–7.7%	.17
	(135)	(73)		
Liberal** Total	30.6%	27.5%	+3.1%	.52
	(189)	(160)		
Deputy/Assistant Solicitor General				
Liberal as Appellant	48.9%	35.3%	+13.6%	.01
	(131)	(258)		
Liberal as Respondent	26.0%	33.7%	–7.7%	.14
	(127)	(190)		
Liberal Total	37.6%	34.6%	+3.0%	.42
	(258)	(448)		

**The conservative position taken by the solicitor general, whether Democrat or Republican, constitutes the balance or the percentages in all categories in this table.
*Significance based on chi-square test of liberal/conservative by Democrat/Republican matrix.
From Michael Link, "The Solicitor General or His Staff," SPSA Paper, Nov. 1993.

the Solicitor General and the Solicitor's staff act politically,"[154] although the SG is a more overtly political actor.

To sum up, more than half the time the SG prepares briefs as a direct party to litigation heard before the Court. Almost one-quarter of the Court's caseload will have the SG's involvement in the form of the *amicus curiae* brief. About 30 percent of the cases heard on the merits have no SG involvement. On average, then, the federal government, in the form of the SG, is involved in about three-quarters of the 100 or fewer cases[155] heard on the merits during a term of the Court in the 1990s.

TABLE 7.4   Success Rates by U.S. Lawyer

	Overall Success Rate	*Success Rate as Appellant*	*Success Rate as Respondent*	*Advantage over Opposition**
Solicitor General	50.4%	81.7%	29.6%	+11.3%
	(355)	(142)	(213)	
Deputy/Assistant Solicitor General	66.5%	77.2%	53.5%	+30.7%
	(708)	(391)	(317)	

*Advantage is calculated by subtracting the success rate of the United States as respondent from the opponent's success rate when the United States is appellant.
From Michael Link, "The Solicitor General or His Staff," SPSA Paper, Nov. 1993.

The success rate of the SG, both as direct party and as *amicus curiae*, is extremely high.[156] As the major repeat player before the Court, the SG and staff are known and relied on by the justices. Given the continual high regard and respect the Court has for the SG, when that office "supports a litigant they will have a significantly higher chance of winning." For example, a state as litigant before the Court has a 17 percent estimated probability of success, but when the SG supports the state with an *amicus curiae* brief, the success rate shoots up to 85 percent.[157] Between 1925 and 1988, the SG had, on average, 70 percent of the petitions for certiorari granted by the Court; the SG, on average, "won" in the Court about 70 percent of the time. No other interest group comes close to these percentages.

SUMMARY

As you can see, a number of central factors impact a group's decision to litigate in the federal courts. First, there is the matter of resources, both human and financial, within an interest group. Because of the fact that many interest groups do not have the financial resources or legal talent to make a strong case in the federal courts, they must work with others in a common cause.

As the NAACP case study indicated, even a highly focused civil rights organization, with the best legal counsel and a well-developed strategic plan, can have significant organizational problems that often blur the movement and direction of the legal strategy. While that civil rights group ultimately won its legal battles in the Court, it took a generation of litigation—and other group activities outside the courtroom—before some of its goals were achieved. In addition, as you have seen, the intervention of Divine Providence, that is, the sudden death of Fred Vinson and the equally surprising appointment of Earl Warren as new chief justice of the United States, can move public policy in new directions!

Ultimately, interest groups come to understand that there are inherent constraints built into the litigation strategy. There is no perfect case, nor does the group maintain total control of the litigation as it moves through the judicial system. Furthermore, and very important, the interest group's success is based on the reception its arguments receive from the Court.

If the justices are not amenable to change, then change will not come about, regardless of the competence of the interest group's legal advocates. Most important for any interest group litigating in the federal courts is the reaction of the solicitor general's office to the arguments of legal counsel. If anything is clear, it is the potency of that office. If the interest group is supported by the SG, even as an *amicus curiae*, the chances of victory increase dramatically. If the SG opposes the group, then there is little hope for that group, regardless of the quality of its briefs and its oral arguments before the Court.

It is equally clear to you by now, however, that interest groups will continue to litigate in the courts and that litigation before the justices of the U.S. Supreme Court will continue to be one of a number of mechanisms through which the interest group in America can achieve its policy goals.

NOTES

[1]Robert Jackson, *The Struggle for Judicial Supremacy* (New York: Knopf, 1951), p. 287.

[2]Stephen L. Wasby, "Civil Rights Litigation by Organizations: Constraints and Choices," *Judicature* 68, no. 9 (Apr. 1985): 337.

[3]See Phillip J. Cooper, *Public Law and Public Administration* (Palo Alto, CA: Mayfield, 1983), p. 10.

[4]Samuel Krislov, *The Supreme Court in the American Political Process* (New York: Macmillan, 1965), p. 42.

[5]See Lawrence Baum, *The U.S. Supreme Court* (Washington, DC: CQ Press, 1985), pp. 68–69.

[6]Lee Epstein, *Conservatives in Court* (Knoxville: University of Tennessee Press, 1985), p. 10. She argues that some believe that such pressure group activity is "little more than a propaganda tool by which an organization can show support for its membership goals" (p. 11).

[7]See, for example, Howard Ball, *Justice Downwind: America's Atomic Testing Program of the 1950's* (New York: Oxford University Press, 1988), for an examination of a class action, nontraditional toxic tort suit brought by over one thousand plaintiffs against the U.S. government.

[8]Donald R. Songer and Reginald S. Sheehan, "The Impact of Amicus Briefs on Decisions on the Merits" (Paper presented at the annual meeting of the American Political Science Association, San Francisco, Sept. 1990).

[9]See Sherral Brown-Guinyard, "The Effect of Ideology on the Success of Repeat Players: Amicus Curiae and the U.S. Supreme Court" (Paper presented at the annual meeting of the Southern Political Science Association, Nov. 1993, Savannah, GA).

[10]Ibid., pp. 4, 14. They note that, except for the solicitor general's briefs, amicus curiae briefs filed by most interest groups "have very modest impacts" (p. 14).

[11]See Lee Epstein and C. K. Rowland, "Debunking the Myth of Interest Group Invincibility in the Courts," *American Political Science Review* 85, no. 1 (Mar. 1991): 206–7.

[12]Lee Epstein and Joseph F. Kobylka, "Exploring Legal Change on the U.S. Supreme Court: A Preliminary Report on Winners and Losers" (Paper presented at the annual meeting of the American Political Science Association, Sept. 1990, San Francisco).

[13]Ibid.

[14]Songer and Sheehan, "Impact of Amicus Briefs," 14.

[15]*NAACP v. Button*, 371 U.S. 415 (1963), at 429–30.

[16]Richard C. Cortner, "Strategy and Tactics of Litigation in Constitutional Cases," *Journal of Public Law* 17 (1968), p. 287.

[17]Mark V. Tushnet, *The NAACP Legal Strategy Against Segregated Education, 1925–1950* (Chapel Hill: University of North Carolina Press, 1987), p. xiv.

[18]Ibid., pp. xi, 143.

[19]Ibid., p. xiv.

[20]Wasby, "Civil Rights Litigation," 340.

[21]Gunnar Myrdal, *An American Dilemma* (New York: Random House, 1941).

[22]Article I, Section 3, discussing representation, notes that Indians nontaxed, and "three fifths of all other Persons" are excluded from determinations of state representation in the new Congress. In Article I, Section 9, states were allowed to continue the practice of slave trading because the section stated, in part, that such migration or importation "shall not be prohibited by the Congress prior to the Year 1808."

[23]Alan Watson, *Slave Law in the Americas* (Athens: University of Georgia Press, 1989), p. xii.

[24]Ibid., p. 72.

[25]Don E. Fehrenbacher, *Constitutions and Constitutionalism in the Slaveholding South* (Athens: University of Georgia Press, 1989), pp. 27, 28.

[26]163 U.S. 537 (1896).

[27]See C. Van Woodard, *The Strange Career of Jim Crow* (New York: Oxford University Press, 1957).

[28]Quoted in Denton L. Watson, "Assessing the Role of the NAACP in the Civil Rights Movement," *Historian* 55, no. 3 (Spring 1993): 453.

[29]Ibid., 454.

[30]Ibid. Under the leadership of James W. Johnson, the NAACP tried to arouse the Congress to address these issues. Although the House of Representatives passed an antilynching bill in 1922, due to Senate filibusters, antilynching legislation did not pass until 1968.

[31]Roger Goldman, with David Galen, *Thurgood Marshall: Justice for All* (New York: Carroll and Graf, 1992), p. 40.

[32]Ibid., p. 33, passim.

[33]These victories included *Guinn v. U.S.* (1915); *Harmon v. Tyler* (1923); *City of Richmond v. Deans* (1930); *Nixon v. Herndon* (1927); *Buchanan v. Warley* (1917); *Corrigan v. Buckley* (1926); *Moore v. Dempsey* (1923); *Hollins v. Oklahoma* (1935); and *Brown v. Mississippi* (1936). The sole NAACP defeat during this time was *Grovey v. Townsend* (1932).

[34]Quoted in Carl T. Rowen, *Dream Makers, Dream Breakers: The World of Justice Thurgood Marshall* (Boston: Little, Brown, 1993), p. 152.

[35]See Goldman, *Thurgood Marshall*, p. 39.

[36]Tushnet, *NAACP Legal Strategy*, p. 45. Given the *extremely* limited resources of the NAACP at the time, Houston took cases "that would increase the internal strength of the NAACP and thereby enable it to fight for leadership more successfully" (p. 45).

[37]In 1993, the Fund made history when the directorship of the organization passed, for the very first time, to a woman, Elaine Jones. After graduating from the University of Virginia Law School in 1970 (she was the first person of color to attend the school), she took a job in the Fund and worked her way up to the directorship. In 1993, the Fund employed thirty attorneys, had a nine-million-dollar budget, and a docket of over three hundred cases and controversies (see James Harney, "Defense Fund Chief Marks 26 Years Breaking Barriers," *USA Today*, Mar. 13, 1993), p. A-2.

[38]Tushnet, *NAACP Legal Strategy*, p. 47.

[39]Ibid., p. 48. However, once Marshall assumed the position of director of the LDF in 1939, he traveled fifty thousand miles a year throughout the South challenging Jim Crow statutes in state and federal courts.

[40]*Donald G. Murray v. University of Maryland*, 182 A. 2d 590 (1936).

[41]Watson, "Role of the NAACP," 455.

[42]Tushnet, *NAACP Legal Strategy*, pp. 29–35, passim.

[43]Watson, "Role of the NAACP," 455.

[44]Clearly, as Marshall knew, this was a major challenge, for the Court does not easily overturn precedent. Furthermore, close to a majority of the justices during Marshall's tenure as leader of the Fund came from the South and knew too well the deeply rooted prejudices of their fellow southerners. During discussions about the 1950 Oklahoma Graduate College of Education litigation, *G. W. McLaurin v. Oklahoma State Regents for Higher Education*, Justice Tom Clark, from Texas, wrote a memo to his brethren in which he said that "the issue of *Plessy v. Ferguson's* application to these cases must be met" but that he was "opposed to overrul[ing] *Plessy*. . . . It is entirely possible that Negroes in segregated grammar schools being taught arithmetic, spelling, geography, etc., would receive skills in these elementary subjects equivalent to those of segregated white students, assuming equality in the texts, teachers, and facilities" Tom C. Clark, (MTTC, Apr. 7, 1950, box 160, RHJP, LC, Washington, DC).

[45]See Goldman *Thurgood Marshall*, pp. 38–39.

[46]Tushnet, *NAACP Legal Strategy*, p. 144.

[47]See Ball and Cooper, *Of Power and Right*, for an examination of these views.

[48]Felix Frankfurter to Wiley Rutledge, Jan. 2, 1948, box 157, Wiley Rutledge Papers, Library of Congress (hereafter cited as WRP), LC, Washington, DC.

[49]George Flemings, president of the Fort Worth, Tx, NAACP, to Hugo Black, Mar. 23, 1940, box 258, Hugo L. Black Papers, Library of Congress (hereafter cited as HLBP), LC, Washington, DC.

[50]Walter White to Max Lowenthal, Aug. 20, 1937, box 79, FFP, LC, Washington, DC.

[51]Mark Silverstein, *Justices Black and Frankfurter: Constitutional Faiths* (Ithaca: Cornell University Press, 1984), p. 136.

[52]305 U.S. 337 (1938).

[53]Houston, Tx, *Informer*, "Mr. Justice Black," Dec. 24, 1938, box 255, HLBP, LC, Washington, DC.

[54]309 U.S. 207 (1940).

[55]For two reasons Black felt uncomfortable about siding with the NAACP argument. The case raised questions about federal judicial intervention in the activities of the states, and the NAACP called for the overturn of a jury verdict. Because of his prosecutorial background in Alabama and the great value he placed in democratic institutions such as a jury of one's peers, he raised some concerns, but ultimately he wrote a very powerful opinion. His wife recalled, three decades later, how Black would read passages from *Chambers* "with tears streaming down his face" (see Gerald Dunne, *Hugo Black and the Judicial Revolution*, p. 301; and Hugo L. Black and Elizabeth Black, *Mr. Justice and Mrs. Black* [New York: Random House, 1985], p. 73).

[56]Mary McLeod Bethune to Hugo Black, Feb. 24, 1940, box 258, HLBP, LC, Washington, DC.

[57]Cornell W. Clayton, *The Politics of Justice: The Attorney General and the Making of Legal Policy* (New York: M. E. Sharpe, 1992), pp. 128–29.

[58]Epstein and Kobylka, "Exploring Legal Change," p. 36, n 27.

[59]Davis and Clark, *Thurgood Marshall*, p. 110.

[60]*Brown v. Mississippi*, 297 U.S. 278 (1936).

[61]*Pierre v. Louisiana*, 306 U.S. 354 (1939).

[62]*McLaurin v. Oklahoma State Regents*, 339 U.S. 637 (1950).

[63]*Mills v. Lowndes*, 26 F Supp 792 (1939).

[64]*Carr v. Corning*, 182 F 2nd 14 (1950).

[65]Goldman, *Thurgood Marshall*, pp. 40–45, passim.

[66]Quoted in Rowen, *Dream Makers*, p. 152.

[67]Michael D. Davis and Hunter R. Clark, *Thurgood Marshall* (New York: Birch Lane Press, 1993), p. 118.

[68]Quoted in Davis and Clark, *Thurgood Marshall*, pp. 138, 141–42.

[69]The solicitor general, again in *Brown*, argued for the overturn of *Plessy*. However, the brief disagreed with the NAACP legal arguments and the NAACP's proposed remedy for dismantling the segregated dual school system: immediate integration. Instead, the solicitor general recommended that the affected school districts be given a "reasonable period of time" to end the dual public-school system (see James Hutchinson, "Unanimity and Desegregation: Decision-Making in the Supreme Court," *Georgetown Law Review* 68 [1979]: 1).

[70]The Reverend Benjamin F. Chavis, the recently fired executive director of the NAACP, was concerned about a development in the urban black communities that was not addressed by the NAACP in preceding generations. Environmental racism, for Chavis, is the practice of white community leaders selecting areas in the poor section of town to establish dump sites for hazardous, toxic wastes. "The highest concentration of dump sites was always in the black areas," he has said. Chavis has deep roots in the civil rights movement and was arrested, in 1971, for his alleged criminal actions as one of the Wilmington (Delaware) Ten. The conviction was thrown out by a federal court in 1980. As executive director through 1994, his task was to get younger persons interested in working with the NAACP to address the problems that emerged after *Brown* was decided in 1954 (see Neil A. Lewis, "Deep Civil Rights Roots," *The New York Times*, Apr. 9, 1993, p. 20).

[71]Tushnet, *NAACP Legal Strategy*, p. 45.

[72]Ibid., p. 157.

[73]Wasby, "Civil Rights Litigation," 339.

[74]Robert H. Jackson, Memorandum to the Conference, Apr. 7, 1950, box 160, RHJP, LC, Washington, DC.

[75]Epstein and Kobylka, "Exploring Legal Change," 4.

[76]Quoted in Richard Kluger, *Simple Justice* (New York: Vintage Books, 1975), p. 560.

[77]Epstein and Kobylka, "Exploring Legal Change," 9.

[78]Karen O'Connor and Lee Epstein, "Beyond Legislative Lobbying: Women's Rights Groups and the Supreme Court," *Judicature* 67, no. 3 (Sept. 1983): 134.

[79]See Herbert Brownell, with John Burke, *Advising Ike: The Memoirs of Attorney General Herbert Brownell* (Lawrence: University of Kansas Press, 1993), pp. 188–98, for an attorney general's perspective of the *Brown* litigation.

[80]See Wasby, "Civil Rights Litigation," 338.

[81]*Murray v. Curlett*, 374 U.S. 203 (1963).

[82]See Songer and Sheehan, "Impact of Amicus Briefs," 13.

[83]Ibid., 14.

[84]Susan Behuniak-Long, "Friendly Fire: Amicus Curiae and *Webster v. Reproductive Health Services*," *Judicature* 74 (Feb.–Mar. 1991): 261.

[85]The average cost for filing an amicus curiae brief with the Court is ten thousand dollars (see Caldiera and Wright, "Why Organizational Interests," p. 11).

[86]Behuniak-Long, "Friendly Fire," 266.

[87]Ibid., 262.

[88]Hugo L. Black, MTTC, Oct. 16, 1957, box 331, HLBP, LC, Washington, DC.

[89]Felix Frankfurter, Memorandum to the Conference, Oct. 28, 1949, box 331, HLBP, LC, Washington, DC.

[90]Ibid.

[91]*University of California Regents v. Bakke*, 438 U.S. 265 (1978).

[92]MTTC, May 1, 1978, Thurgood Marshall Papers, Library of Congress (hereafter cited as TMP), LC, Washington, DC.

[93]Songer and Sheehan, "Impact of Amicus Briefs," 12.

[94]492 U.S. 490 (1989).

[95]See Behuniak-Long, "Friendly Fire." Some portions of the Missouri statute defined when life began (at conception) and allowed abortion, and funding for abortions, only to save the life of the mother.

[96]*Webster v. Reproductive Health Services*, 410 U.S. 113 (1973).

[97]See the contraceptive case, *Griswold v. Connecticut* 381 U.S. 479 (1965).

[98]Behuniak-Long, "Friendly Fire," 261.

[99]Ibid., 267.

[100]See, for example, her dissent in *Akron v. Akron Center for Reproductive Health*, 462 U.S. 416 (1983), in which she said that "*Roe* was on a collision course with itself," and her dissent in *Thornburgh v. American College of Obstetricians and Gynecologists*, 476 U.S. 747 (1986).

[101]*Webster*, at 519.

[102]Behuniak-Long, "Friendly Fire," 269. See also Barbara Craig and David O'Brien, *Abortion and American Politics* (Chatham, NJ: Chatham House, 1993), pp. 226–27.

[103]John P. Stevens, MTTC, May 30, 1989, box 480, TMP, LC, Washington, DC.

[104]Harry Blackmun, MTTC, June 21, 1989, box 480, TMP, LC, Washington, DC.

[105]William Rehnquist, MTTC, June 22, 23, 1989, box 480, TMP, LC, Washington, DC.

[106]Sandra D. O'Connor, MTTC, June 28, 1989, box 480, TMP, LC, Washington, DC.

[107]Harry Blackmun, MTTC, June 28, 1989, box 480, TMP, LC, Washington, DC.

[108]*Hodgson v. Minnesota* (1989).

[109]Memorandum, Thurgood Marshall to William J. Brennan, Jr., June 13, box 463, TMP, LC, Washington, DC.

[110]Thurgood Marshall, MTTC, Dec. 8, 1989, box 492, TMP, LC, Washington, DC.

[111]*Planned Parenthood of Southeastern Pennsylvania v. Casey*, 112 SCt 2791 (1992).

[112]Blackmun was relieved somewhat when, in March 1993, Justice Byron White announced his retirement from the Supreme Court. President Bill Clinton, a moderate Democrat elected in 1992, nominated a moderate federal appeals court judge, Ruth Bader Ginsburg, to replace White. With this personnel change, the four justices who would overturn *Roe* lost one of the quartet.

[113]Herman Schwartz, *Packing the Courts* (New York: Scribner's, 1988), p. 78.

[114]For Schwartz and other scholars, the Court's overturn of *Plessy* in the 1954 *Brown* decision was the watershed, for it clearly cast the Court in an activist role. After *Brown*, critics begin to attack the legitimacy of such judicial activity in specific cases and controversies and through critical assessment of nominees to serve on the Court (ibid., p. xii).

[115]Quoted in *The New York Times*, April 18, 1993, p. A-1.

[116]See Joseph Harris, *Decision* (New York: Random House, 1975).

[117]1 U.S. Stat, 73, Section 35.

[118]See R. M. McReynolds, "The Department of Justice," in Donald R. Whitnah, ed., *Government Agencies* (Westport, CT: Greenwood Press, 1983), pp. 132–36, passim.

[119]Clayton, *Politics of Justice*, p. 16, passim.

[120]Ibid., pp. 22, 23.

[121]Ibid., p. 25.

[122]Ibid., p. 73.

[123]McReynolds, "Department of Justice," p. 133.

[124]Clayton, *Politics of Justice*, p. 25.

[125]See Phillip Cooper, *Public Law and Public Administration* (Palo Alto: Mayfield Publishing Co., 1986), p. 68.

[126]Clayton, *Politics of Justice*, p. 74.

[127]Ibid., p. 76.

[128]Ibid., p. 22.

[129]Ibid., pp. 25–26.

[130]Gregory Rathjen and Thomas D. Ungs, "United States Attorneys and the Lower Federal Courts: Some Effects on Law and Order" (Paper presented at the annual meeting of the Midwest Political Science Association, Chicago, Apr. 1977, pp. 2–3).

[131]A Kennedy staffer to a Republican U.S. attorney, quoted in Fred Schrum, "Fired: The Hiring and Firing of U.S. Attorneys," *New Times*, Feb. 20, 1978, p. 34.

[132]Schrum, "Fired," 9.

[133]Ibid., 35.

[134]John Saar, "The Philadelphia Story," *New Times*, Feb. 20, 1978, p. 31.

[135]See Ball, *Justice Downwind*.

[136]Howard Ball, *Courts and Politics: The Federal Judicial System*, 2d ed., (Englewood Cliffs, NJ: Prentice Hall, 1987), p. 221.

[137]Ibid., p. 77.

[138]See Nancy V. Baker, *Conflicting Loyalties: Law and Politics in the Attorney General's Office, 1789–1990* (Lawrence: University Press of Kansas), 1992.

[139]Songer and Sheehan, "Impact of Amicus Briefs," 5.

[140]Lincoln Caplan, *The Tenth Justice: The Solicitor General and the Rule of Law* (New York: Vintage Books, 1988), p. 256.

[141]Quoted in Tony Mauro, "Election Could Shift Solicitor's Positions," *USA Today*, Oct. 27, 1992, p. 5.

[142]Ibid.

[143]Clayton, *Politics of Justice*, pp. 54–55. Other devices for disassociating include removal of the SG from the case or language to the effect that the "SG fully subscribes to the position set forth on question number two, only" (p. 55).

[144]Office of Legal Counsel, *Memorandum Opinion for the Attorney General, Re: Role of the Solicitor General*, 1977, p. 229. At another point in the memo, the OLC stated, to Griffin Bell, that the SG is "permitted to exercise independent, expert judgment essentially free from extensive involvement in policy matters that might, on occasion, cloud a clear vision of what the law requires" (p. 223).

[145]See Caplan, *Tenth Justice*. Justice Potter Stewart referred to the SG as a traffic cop (p. 3, and Erwin Griswold, "Rationing Justice: The Supreme Court's Caseload and What the Court Does Not Do," *Cornell Law Quarterly* 60 [Mar. 1975]: 344).

[146]Office of the U.S. Attorney General, *Annual Report, 1986* (Washington, DC: U.S. Government Printing Office, 1986), p. 3.

[147]See Karen O'Connor, "The Amicus Curiae Role of the U.S. Solicitor General in Supreme Court Litigation," *Judicature* 66, no. 6, December–January 1983, 256.

[148]However, as Caplan points out in his book, during the Reagan/Bush administrations, the

Office of Solicitor General was politicized. As Burton Neuborne, the executive director of the ACLU, noted, politics in the Department of Justice can "demote the Solicitor General's office to our level, the level of an ideological interest group, a salesman for a partisan line just like the ACLU is" (quoted in Caplan, *Tenth Justice*, p. 209).

[149]Clayton, *Politics of Justice*, p. 66ff.

[150]See Caplan, *Tenth Justice*, p. 213.

[151]Link, "The Solicitor General or the Staff," 1.

[152]Ibid.

[153]Ibid., p. 5.

[154]Ibid., p. 12.

[155]Caplan, *Tenth Justice*, passim.

[156]Songer and Sheehan, "Impact of Amicus Briefs," 5.

[157]Ibid., 11.

The Business of the Court: The Organization in Action

8

You've already met the chief justice, and, over the past few weeks, met the rest of your colleagues. Two of the justices have known you for some time because they were colleagues of yours on the federal appellate bench prior to being called to serve on the Court. You are familiar with another duo, having read a great deal of their jurisprudential thoughts in the law reviews. A sixth justice, formerly a U.S. senator, is someone you know about from your congressional days when you were on the staff of the Senate Judiciary Committee. The rest of the justices, two men in their late seventies and early eighties, were appointed at least two decades ago, and you know about them only through their opinions, many of which you read while a student in law school, and from comments and gossip you have picked up from others over the past few years.

For you, as you met your colleagues, the immediate questions are two very basic ones: (1) Just what *do* these men and women do? Exactly what is the business of the U.S. Supreme Court? (2) How is the Court's business conducted; that is, how do you do your job?

FEDERAL APPELLATE JUDGES

Appellate court judges, as a federal appellate court judge once noted, "exist in a special limbo."[1] The appellate judge is unlike the trial judge, who, working in isolation, is the local technician of the law and is frequently in the midst of heated debates between legal adversaries over relevant facts and applicable law, presented before juries and an audience of court watchers.

Functioning as an officer of the national government, the U.S. district court judge, the trial judge in the federal judicial system, oversees the trial adversary process and "umpires the factual determination of legal culpability."[2] The district court judge is a trier of facts and "operates at the point where the political and legal systems meet. . . . [He] does not enjoy the rarified and cloistered atmosphere of appellate courts."[3] The federal trial judge's task, at bottom, is to encourage the legal advocates to present the facts and the law in an interactive manner "that helps bring about the result [the lawyers] want."[4] The district court judge, according to U.S. District Court Chief Judge Bruce Jenkins, hopes that the trial lawyers shape the facts and the law in such a way that they can then "justifiably ask a court to help [her] reach a particular result. One seeks a particular result from the court. One shapes the case to achieve that particular end. . . . It is [her] careful selection and presentation of the relevant law and facts in juxtaposition that helps bring about the result [she] wants, that makes your case. . . . In my opinion, thoughtful, on-going and careful consideration of the fact-law relationship is the most important function of the attorney in shaping the case."[5]

While the district court judge tries cases, federal courts of appeals exist in order to respond to appeals from the decisions in the trial court. Rather than listen to witnesses, as is the case in the trial court, federal appeals court judges read petitions that, in effect, claim that a fundamental right was denied the petitioner during the course of the trial. The briefs to the federal appeals judges examine whether a person's rights, statutory or constitutional, were tampered with (by police, prosecutors, or judges) before and during the trial.

"The heavy artillery of appellate practice," wrote a veteran U.S. court of appeals judge, "*is* the brief."[6] The brief to the appeals court outlines the application of law and the errors of law that occurred at the trial. Appellate judges, whether state or federal, and including the justices of the Supreme Court, "sit and all we [do]," wrote former U.S. appeals court Judge Thurman Arnold, "[is] to listen to argument and write opinions."[7] After the justices "sift" among the thousands of certiorari petitions to determine which of the petitions are worthy of review on the merits, after they read the briefs, after they listen to oral argument, and after they disappear behind the velvet curtains, they produce, months or years later, an opinion.

What, then, *is* the essence of appellate work on the Court? Justice Felix Frankfurter, ever the Harvard professor even on the Court, offered one answer:

> First and foremost, humility and an understanding of the range of problems and [one's] own inadequacy in dealing with them; disinterestedness . . . and allegiance to nothing except the effort to find [that] path through precedent, through policy, through history, through [one's] own gifts of insights to the best judgment that a poor fallible creature can arrive at in that most difficult of tasks, the adjudication between man and man, between man and the state, through reason called law.[8]

Does this description of the appellate "business" of adjudication, written by a justice of the Supreme Court, fit all appellate work? How is the work of the court of appeals and other appellate courts different from the U.S. Supreme Court's appellate business?

The Business of the Highest Appellate Court: The U.S. Supreme Court

Essentially, at one level, the business of the Supreme Court is like that of any appellate court in the American judicial system: to make sure that the trial judge correctly applied the appropriate rules of law to the facts. Should that initial decision, from the trial judge or the administrative law judge (when hearing cases from federal executive agencies), be upheld, or were there mistakes in the ruling that warrant reversal by the appellate court? Associate Justice John P. Stevens, who served on the U.S. Court of Appeals for the Seventh Circuit for five years before moving to the Supreme Court, said that he "was much more conscious of the similarities between the two courts than of their differences."[9]

There are, however, two important differences that serve to distinguish the federal courts of appeals and the Supreme Court: The courts of appeals must hear all cases that are properly in the court (although they usually reserve oral argument for the most important of the cases). The Supreme Court has total discretion with regard to the cases it hears on the merits. Also, the Supreme Court, as the nation's highest appellate tribunal, has the authority to redirect policy for the nation's legal and political communities. While federal circuit courts establish circuit guidelines for implementing Supreme Court policy, the Supreme Court sets—and resets—a national public policy through its opinions.

In the appellate business, the judge must adjudicate in the manner suggested by Frankfurter. The appellate judge must "apply the appropriate principles in accord with legal discipline to the facts that have been properly determined in accord with that discipline."[10] The appellate judge or justice clarifies and declares what the law is in the written opinion.[11]

Appellate judges are limited in their behavior, however, by the conventions that impact decisions.[12] These conventions, or normal expectations of behavior, are found in the Federal Rules of Civil and Criminal Procedure, created by legislators and interpreted by the courts, as well as rules created by the appellate courts themselves, especially the Supreme Court (in individual cases before the justices). They help guide trial judges regarding the consideration and admissibility of facts in their courts as well as the applicability of rules of law when charging juries. The trial judge must follow these rules about facts and must also make sure to apply the correct legal principles and precedent in all cases.

When reviewing an appeal from the lower federal trial court, the appellate judge's freedom is limited by these rules of evidence and by the rule of law, as determined over time by the appellate judges in the highest court of a jurisdiction, whether state or federal. The appellate judge must also decide what rule of law controls the kind of dispute that was argued in court and whether the law was correctly applied.[13]

Obviously, the justices of the U.S. Supreme Court are superior to all other judges, whether state or federal. As federal appeals Judge Frank Coffin once noted, "The higher courts are right because they are superior, not superior because they are right."[14] At this level, the business of the Supreme Court is to hear cases and controversies to ensure that the proper rule of law is applied as a matter of national public policy and if it is not to make sure that the correct rule of law is applied to the facts—even if it means that the Supreme Court has to create a new rule based on its power of statutory or constitutional interpretation.

Doing the Job

An elemental set of features characterizes the business of appellate decision making in America. All appellate courts have a reliance on structured advocacy; that is, in appellate courts there is the submission of the written briefs[15] and there is also oral argument.[16] Then there are the "rules" that must be applied by the appellate judge to determine the outcome of the appeal.

Early in America's legal history, Supreme Court justices delivered independent statements seriatim as opposed to delivering one collegial opinion for the Court. By the time Chief Justice John Marshall began to preside over the Court in 1801, the pattern of a single opinion for the Court, even though some might disagree with its conclusion, had taken hold and has remained a tradition. Today, all opinions of appellate courts are written by a judge or a justice; however, they are prepared *for* the three-judge panel (in the federal court of appeals) or for the majority of the Supreme Court. The Court opinion provides the parties to the dispute with the rationale for the decision of the Court.

Yet, paradoxically, individualism is dominant on the Supreme Court and has been for most of the twentieth century. Justice Frankfurter once wrote that the Supreme Court "is an institution far more dominated by centrifugal forces, pushing towards individuality and independence, than it is by centripetal forces pulling for hierarchial ordering and institutional unity."[17] Each justice, he noted, has "extraordinary independence . . . from every other Justice. . . . When one puts on the robe, one enters a world of public scrutiny and professional criticism which sets great store by individual performance, and much less store upon the virtue of being a 'team player.'"[18]

For Frankfurter, both in theory and in practice, a justice's individuality and independence was primary. A classic example of this characteristic was exhibited by Frankfurter in a critically important civil rights case, *Cooper v. Aaron.*[19] In this case, the justices agreed to have each justice's name affixed to the opinion to indicate to the South that the Court unanimously supported the principles enunciated in *Brown v. Board of Education.* William Brennan was the one who made the suggestion in conference. After agreeing to the suggestion, Frankfurter then dropped a bombshell on his brethren when he informed them that he was going to write a separate concurring opinion. Chief Justice Earl Warren, along with Justices Brennan, Hugo Black, and William O. Douglas, was furious with the little professor. "We almost cut his throat," recalled Brennan.[20] However, Frankfurter, the independent individualist, remained unpersuaded. Douglas recalled that Frankfurter "blew up in conference saying it was none of the Court's business and he wrote."[21]

In spite of the behavior of a jurist such as Frankfurter, the justices of the Supreme Court *must* try to do their decision making in a collegial manner. The decision itself should be a collegial one, arrived at by the judges after discussion and negotiation of the case, initially in the conference session and then, critically important, in the writing and circulation of the MTTC and drafts—majority, concurring, and dissenting—of the opinion.

Although there is a perpetual centrifugal force on the Court, the institutional pull is in the direction of group decision making a great deal of the time. "What is significant about opinions for the Court is that they are not statements of a particular justice's jurisprudence. Rather, they are negotiated documents forged from ideological differences within the Court."[22]

Can the Supreme Court, as the highest appellate court in the nation, function primarily as an "organic unit" with few dissenting factions to better provide coherent constitutional leadership for the nation? Is it possible for the Court to avoid the centrifugal pushes of judicial individualism and independence? Must institutional unity be sacrificed on behalf of the freedom of the justice to vote on a case "as conscience merits"?[23]

These kinds of questions point to the central and unique characteristic of Supreme Court appellate judicial decision making: collegiality within a Court workway context that has been described by some justices as nine small and independent law firms. Collegiality among the justices of the Supreme Court, although in the small-law-firm context and with conflict among the brethren an important subset of that concept, is as important a decisional characteristic as it is on the federal courts of appeals. Collegiality, however, is difficult to achieve in practice. Given the growth of the docket, the controversial nature of issues that have been coming to the Court for the past sixty years, and the ideological divisions on the Court, there are more concurring and dissenting opinions, as well as "judgments" of the Court in lieu of the majority "opinion" of the Court. In response to this lack of consensus and collegiality on the resolution of constitutional questions, Chief Justice William Rehnquist wrote: "It may well be that the nature of constitutional adjudication invites, at least, if it does not require, more separate opinions than does adjudication of issues of law in other areas."[24]

The Court, clearly, is a quasi-collegial appellate court.[25] Initially, the formal decisions are made largely individually (with the assistance of a justice's law clerks), but collegiality comes into play in the final product, the institution's decision, which is formulated by the Court majority. If the justices, at least five of them, are unable to agree on the wording and rationale for an institutional opinion, then the Court, and the legal community, is left with a much less satisfactory plurality "judgment." The plurality opinion is not generated most of the time; however, in critical, controversial cases, where there is deep division, such an opinion is unavoidable.

Creating an opinion for the Court, therefore, involves hard, continuous negotiations among the justices. In the end, this decisional paradox—collegiality and individualism—is overcome by the justices themselves as they arrive at some kind of consensus on a great many of the cases argued on the merits. "Though we endeavor to harmonize our views to reach a Court judgment," commented Justice Lewis Powell, "the members of this Court vote independently."[26]

There are, however, some very important cases for which the Court cannot arrive at an institutional opinion; the justices' independent opinions are a reflection of disharmony on the bench. Especially since the election of Ronald Reagan as president in 1981, the Supreme Court has been accused of being overly individualistic and fragmented, leading to confusing, muddled, plurality judgments.[27] Recently retired Justice Harry Blackmun has openly criticized some of his brethren for their "extremist" behavior and, generally, a "lack of accommodation."[28] This lack of accommodation means that the justices are less willing to negotiate to reach a workable consensus. For Blackmun, this has come about because of the increased ideological fragmentation on the Court. As a result of conservative Republican presidents nominating ideologues to the Court (Antonin Scalia and Clarence Thomas, for example), Blackmun has, in his own words, become "a flaming liberal" on the high bench.[29]

Clearly then, the writing of decisions in an appellate court is very demanding and unlike that of a trial judge's work in the federal system. The trial judge, as Chief Justice Warren Burger once wrote, is the local legal technician.[30] She rules on admissibility of facts, consistent with the Federal Rules of Criminal or Civil Procedure. She reaches judgment about the applicable precedents and the appropriate principles of law to apply, mechanically, to the task at hand.

The appellate judge, whether on the Court of Appeals or on the Supreme Court, does not "write on a clean slate."[31] The judge must write a judgment in the case before the court by referring to prior decisions. To do this, one must find and expose the basic reasons and principles of law for a court's earlier decision and show how they apply to the case before the appellate judges. This part of the business of appellate decision writing is called "establishing the principle of the case," or the "*ratio decidendi*," that is, the grounds (principle) on which a case is decided.

Acting in this fashion, the Supreme Court accomplishes two goals when deciding the outcome of a petition heard on the merits by the justices: (1) It provides the parties to the dispute with a definitive judgment that resolves their dispute. (2) It issues a jurisprudential statement of general principles of law on which the Court majority based its treatment of the principal parties in the dispute.[32]

Reaching the decision is done in an environment that is intimate, dynamic, with continuous, often conflict-laden, interactions over years and, on most federal courts of appeals as well as the Supreme Court, over decades. When concluded, the majority opinion of the Court sets forth the facts, the law, the logic, and the policy inherent in the case.[33]

Yet another characteristic of the business of appellate decision making is one that Coffin refers to as "ripening time." The appellate court's movement toward the decision takes time, and the process offers the appellate judges distance from the heat of the trial.

Appellate judges can take their time to reach decision. The Supreme Court justices, in the *Brown* case (and in other difficult, controversial cases before them), scheduled reargument, thereby delaying the final appellate judgment of the Court for another two years. Consequently, as Judge Coffin noted, the "genius of appellate decision-making" is that it is prolonged, graduated, and incremental.[34]

Felix Frankfurter: The Professor to His Colleagues and the Lessons Learned

Prior to his elevation to the Court, Felix Frankfurter, in addition to being a respected liberal legal advocate, was one of the nation's leading scholars on the business of the Court. Before and after his elevation to the Court, he wrote a number of significant essays, published in law reviews or as scholarly monographs, that addressed the business of the Court.[35]

As a preeminent professor of constitutional law at Harvard University, Frankfurter's erudition was widely recognized and highly regarded. While still at Harvard, Frankfurter tried to discuss the workings of the Court, as it existed and as he thought it should operate, with newly appointed justices such as Black and

Associate Justice Felix
Frankfurter.

Douglas.[36] Indeed, Chief Justice Harlan F. Stone was so concerned about Black's
capacity to function as justice that he asked then professor Frankfurter to assist
the Alabamian in learning the Court's processes and its business: "Do you know
Black well? You might be able to render him great assistance. He needs guidance
from someone who is more familiar with the workings of the judicial process than
he is. With guidance, and a disposition to follow it until he is surer of himself, he
might do great things."[37]

After his appointment to the Court in 1939, Frankfurter continued to
try to educate the justices. "I have an incorrigibly academic mind," he once told
Justice Charles Whittaker.[38] However, he tried to accomplish this while acting as
a colleague of the justices, and this did not sit well with his colleagues. For them,
it was quite different to receive criticism from someone external to the Court
than to be lectured by one of their own kind about the group's alleged
deficiencies.

When he came to the Court, Frankfurter really did not change his style. He
basically came across to his colleagues as a Harvard lecturer. Many were annoyed
at his pontificatory lectures to them, complete with notes, law review articles, and
records on a portable book rest, about the case before them. Justice Potter Stewart
recalled, "Felix, if he was really interested in a case, would speak for fifty minutes,
no more or less, because that was the length of the lecture at Harvard Law School."[39]
Douglas, for one, would be so angry at the professor from Harvard (Douglas was
a Yale Law School professor at one time in his career) that he would leave the
table and open his mail while sitting on a couch. On one occasion, according to

Stewart's notes, Douglas said to Frankfurter after a lengthy lecture by the little professor: "When I came into this conference, I agreed with the conclusion that Felix had just announced, but he's just talked me out of it."[40]

Annually, at the beginning of every new term of the Court, there would appear the lengthy memo from Frankfurter about the Court's business and how the Court could improve its workways by taking his advice. They were long, scholarly essays. However, they rarely elicited any response other than anger from the brethren, although the Court did have docket problems.[41]

He also wrote very irritating and condescending notes to his colleagues, critiquing their writings. One such letter to Douglas contained the following words: "I am bound to say that it is bad for both of us that we are no longer professors. Because if you were still a professor, you would have written a different elaboration and if I were still a professor, I would get several lectures out of what you have written."[42]

A few justices, including at one time or another Douglas, Black, Frank Murphy, and Chief Justices Fred Vinson and Earl Warren, on occasion found themselves in conflict with Frankfurter because of his demeanor. Some responded dramatically to his comments and attitude. Douglas drafted a letter to Warren in 1960 in which he indicated that he would no longer attend conference sessions because of the animosity between himself and Frankfurter:

> The continuous violent outbursts against me in Conference by my brother Frankfurter give me great concern. They do not bother me for I have been on the hustings too long. But he's an ill man; and these violent outbursts create a fear in my heart that one of them may be his end. . . . His outbursts against me are increasing in intensity. In the interest of his health and long life I reluctantly concluded to participate in no more conferences while he is on the Court. For the cert lists, I will leave my vote. On argued cases, I will leave a short summary of my views.[43]

Black, who never lost his temper, once commented after a conference session, "I thought Felix was going to hit me today, he got so mad."[44]

The irony of the Frankfurter experience with his brethren is quite clear. In a quasi-collegial environment, it is one's capacity to successfully interact with one's colleagues that is critical. It is as important to communicate well with the brethren as it is to be intellectually independent. For all his knowledge of the workings of the Court and his intellectual prowess regarding constitutional and statutory interpretation, Felix Frankfurter did not relate well to most of his brethren.

He did not have the capacity to comfortably interact with his colleagues, some of whom he ridiculed for their apparant lack of intellectual and legal acumen. As a consequence, Frankfurter never had the substantive impact on the Court's collegial decision-making process that his one-time student and lifelong jurisprudential nemesis, Hugo Black, did.

In conference sessions and in MTTC's, Frankfurter would proclaim while Black would try to persuade. Not without cause did Frankfurter criticize Black's "politics" and the Alabamian's ability to develop the "Axis," a group of justices (Black, Douglas, Murphy, and Wiley Rutledge) who agreed on some fundamental constitutional issues and who disagreed with Frankfurter's positions on most of them.

INSTITUTIONAL AND NONINSTITUTIONAL DECISION MAKING

Because of the dominance of politics and ideology in the selection of persons to serve on the Court, there are few chapters in the Court's history that evidence collegial, institutional decision making. And there are numerous situations in which the justices failed miserably and the Court wound up issuing individual opinions and plurality judgments. Three examples of the Court's operations, both good and bad, in the area of racial discrimination, are (1) the discussions, in 1953–54, surrounding the overturn of *Plessy*; (2) the conflicts in the Court regarding the sit-in cases in the early 1960s; and (3) the lengthy deliberations in a medical-school affirmative-action admissions case, *University of California, Davis v. Bakke.* Two of the three illustrate the justices of the Court struggling and failing to respond, institutionally, to a series of very hard constitutional questions that had, at their core, the scope of the Fourteenth Amendment's equal-protection clause. The third, the overturn of *Plessy*, illustrates the Court functioning in an institutionalist way.

Earl Warren and the *Brown* Decisions

On September 8, 1953, Chief Justice Fred Vinson suffered a massive heart attack and died. At that time, the Court had been embroiled, for more than a year, in intense and heated discussions regarding the vitality of *Plessy v. Ferguson,* the 1896 decision of the Court that established the principle of separate but equal. The National Association for the Advancement of Colored People (NAACP), under the leadership of the Fund's director, Thurgood Marshall, had been vigorously attacking *Plessy's* constitutional validity.

In 1950, seventeen states, mostly southern and border, and the District of Columbia had *de jure* segregated public schools, while four other states permitted separate-but-equal public schools. By 1950, for Marshall and the NAACP, the question was whether "the Supreme Court was now ready to meet the NAACP's direct challenge of segregation per se as unconstitutional."[45]

In June 1952, the Court agreed to hear arguments in a number of school segregation cases consolidated in *Brown v. Board of Education of Topeka.*[46] This case was chosen by the Court to be the lead case "so that the whole question," commented Justice Tom C. Clark, "would not smack of being a purely Southern one."[47] Given the rancor on the Court over the validity of *Plessy*, by the time of Vinson's death, there seemed to be very little collegiality left in a Court known for its continual conflicts among a number of the justices.

Two justices, Hugo Black and William O. Douglas, wanted the Court to issue an order overturning *Plessy* immediately—even though, according to Black, such an order would mean an end to southern liberalism and the introduction of a new era of violence and bloodshed in the South. The immediate overturn of *Plessy* was the position taken by the NAACP in its briefs and in oral argument. However, all the other justices, including Frankfurter (who was once on the board of the NAACP), wanted to procrastinate, to put off the case as long as possible.

Vinson, a conservative Democrat from Kentucky, refused to accept the view that *Plessy* was no longer a viable precedent. "*Plessy* had been the law of the land for over a half-century, and he was not ready to change it. . . . He was not going to overrule *Plessy*."[48] Two other southern justices, Tom Clark of Texas and Stanley Reed of Kentucky, also refused, initially, to even think of overturning the 1896 precedent. Justice Robert Jackson was troubled over the historic meaning of the Fourteenth Amendment: Did that amendment address the constitutionality of separate-but-equal schools?

> [Justice Frankfurter warned his brethren that] it is not our duty to give a Constitutional stamp to our merely personal attitudes toward these issues, however deep individual convictions may be. . . . However passionately any of us may feel, however fiercely any one of us may believe that such a policy of segregation . . . is both unjust and shortsighted, he travels outside his judicial authority if on the basis of his private feelings he declares unconstitutional the policy of segregation.[49]

Evidently, Frankfurter feared the consequences of a divided Court opinion that narrowly invalidated *Plessy*.[50]

After oral arguments that ran three days in December 1952, the Court, because it was so divided and lacking in collegiality, became immobilized. The NAACP's bold frontal attack on *Plessy* in *Brown* had frozen the justices into inaction. The NAACP's legal strategy in *Brown* was that group's "most militant position . . . ever taken in its forty two year history."[51] However, the majority of the justices did agree that an immediate overturn of *Plessy* would be catastrophic. Furthermore, *all* the associates, including Black and Douglas, believed that Vinson lacked the competence and the capacity to lead the fragmented Court to some kind of consensus on the issue of the continued constitutional viability of segregated public facilities.

Because the Court was deeply split, no vote was taken in December 1952. At a conference session at the end of May 1953, the Court majority, buying more time to find a way to some kind of consensus, scheduled reargument in *Brown*, asking the lawyers, among other questions, to examine the congressional intent when the Fourteenth Amendment was written, especially with respect to public-school education at that time.

The rearguments were scheduled for December 1953. Fate intervened at this time with the death of Vinson, the archenemy of racial integration and the champion of *Plessy*.[52]

Earl Warren came to the Court in October of 1953, facing a divided and noncollegial group of justices. In the course of the next seven months, under Warren's astute leadership, the Court went from a four to four split to a unanimous opinion in *Brown*, May 1954, that formally overturned the dreaded *Plessy* precedent. The return of collegiality in this critically important public-policy area was "attributable directly to Warren's leadership."[53]

***Brown v. Board of Education* I: 1954**   Avoiding any "public votes" in conference, Warren, after the December 1953 oral arguments were concluded (which were inconclusive with respect to any historical evidence of the intentions of the men who drafted the Fourteenth Amendment), moved very skillfully among the brethren to discuss the litigation with each of them, individually and privately. He did this after stating, in the initial conference session after the oral arguments, that the segregation brought on by *Plessy* was wrong. "Personally, I can't see how today we can justify segregation based solely on race."[54]

Warren's strategy for pulling the Court together, for developing a collegial, institutional opinion, was based on that observation. For a justice to defend *Plessy*, he would have to acknowledge the "inherent inferiority of the colored race."[55] In the end, none of the other justices was willing to publicly admit to that conclusion.

During the spring of 1954, Warren continued to have these informal meetings with the justices. He also began to write a short overturn opinion that was soft, nontechnical in its language, and nonaccusatorial. At last successful with the last two holdouts, Justices Reed (who had threatened to write a dissent until the very last moment) and Jackson (who planned on writing a concurrence until he was felled with a heart attack), Warren had miraculously brought the fragmented Court together on a very critical issue. By May 1954, Warren's private breakfasts, coffees, and dinners with the other eight justices produced a collegial consensus that led to a unanimous opinion to overturn *Plessy*.

Finally, Chief Justice Warren, on May 17, 1954, announced the opinion for a unanimous Court. He concluded the announcement by stating "that in the field of public education the doctrine of 'separate but equal' has no place. Separate educational facilities are inherently unequal." The *Plessy* era formally ended; however, the Court still needed to provide some guidance to the lower federal courts regarding implementation of the *Brown* opinion. *Plessy*'s consequences, institutionalization of an absolute Jim Crow segregation of the races in the South, now had to be dismantled. The justices faced the task of determining the speed and the scope of that relief, and who would be primarily responsible for overseeing the demise of *Plessy*.

Brown v. Board of Education II: 1955

While the 1954 opinion invalidated *Plessy*, it did not address the remedial issue. Warren scheduled reargument during the 1954 term, asking the parties to present further argument on the question of remedies and implementation, with submission of briefs into the Court by October 1, 1954.

Warren received significant input from Frankfurter and the U.S. Solicitor General's Office regarding the implementation phase of the *Brown* opinion. The little professor was opposed to a remedial decision that "set forth with detailed particularity" how a Jim Crow school system had to desegregate its facilities.[56] Frankfurter successfully encouraged Warren to develop an opinion that would have the U.S. district courts, rather than the Supreme Court, shoulder the burden of dismantling *Plessy* and that would provide for flexible deadlines for ending the dual school system.[57]

Oral arguments were held in April 1955. At the conference session afterward, Warren recommended that the Court issue instructions to have the federal trial courts manage the process with a flexible timetable, to have the school districts end segregation "at the earliest practical date." A Frankfurter MTTC made another suggestion that Warren adopted. Frankfurter wrote: "I have only one further and minor remark to make. I still think that 'with all deliberate speed' is preferable to 'at the earliest practical date.'"[58]

While Justice Black was concerned about the proposed "with all deliberate speed" language and the glaring weakness of the remedial opinion, he went along to show collegiality and unanimity in this critically important area of law and politics. Black's son noted that, while the justice was deeply concerned about the impact of that concept, "Daddy was not about to do anything to fragment the Court in that landmark opinion."[59]

In May 1955, the unanimous but weak and ambivalent remedial opinion was delivered by Warren. It did not offer much in the way of guidance to the federal district court judges, to the local school boards, and to the African American plaintiffs and the NAACP who had to develop desegregation plans in suits that they would have to file in the federal district courts.[60] It was, as Black feared, to be a less-than-successful strategy for ending segregated schools in the South. Stiff, creative resistance was thrown up by southern state leaders to avoid and delay the end of Jim Crowism in the South. As a result, a decade later, only a little more than 1 percent of black schoolchildren were attending public school with white youngsters in the eleven southern states. In 1969, the Court reluctantly concluded that the *Brown* policy of integrating schools with "all deliberate speed" did not work and, in *Alexander v. Holmes County, Mississippi* replaced that policy with the policy of "integration now."[61]

What is important to remember, however, is the manner in which one person, Chief Justice Earl Warren, the "Super Chief" as William Brennan referred to him, was able to get a fragmented Court to coalesce and, in a show of collegiality and consensus that was to last until the early 1970s, to act to try to redress a political/legal dilemma of national and international importance. When Warren arrived on the Court, it "had become the most severely fractured Supreme Court in history."[62] Given his very personable style, within seven months he was able to restore a degree of collegiality to the High Bench.

The Sit-in Cases Turn the Court Upside Down

Beginning in 1960 in South Carolina, civil rights protestors in the South, attempting to overcome the consequences of centuries of slavery and Jim Crowism in places of public accommodation, implemented a controversial, extralegal, action-oriented strategy. Under the leadership of the Student Nonviolent Coordinating Committee (SNCC), an activist civil rights organization working to achieve integration in the Deep South, the protestors, mostly high-school and college students, would enter a privately owned facility such as a restaurant that conducted its business with the general public, but on a segregated basis. They would sit down at the lunch counter, which was private property, and request service from the establishment's employees. They would "sit-in" until served or, more frequently, until they were arrested, often after a vicious beating from racist onlookers.

These arrests led to convictions for violating various kinds of local ordinances, from trespass and breach of the peace to loitering and vagrancy. Naturally, and somewhat to the annoyance of the more conservatively oriented NAACP Legal Defense Fund leaders, who were pursuing another strategy for ending Jim Crowism, these students were represented in the state courts by NAACP lawyers. Naturally, the students would be convicted in state courts and would, after exhausting state remedies to no avail, appeal to the U.S. Supreme Court, seeking reversal of their convictions.[63] Their legal argument: Officers of the state or locality were "suppressing free speech and enforcing racial discrimination in violation of the First and Fourteenth Amendments."[64]

For the justices of the Court, then, the question posed by these ardent civil rights students was this: Were the racially discriminatory actions of these private persons and organizations of the kind that would enable the Court to perceive sufficient "state action" that was prohibited by the Constitution's Fourteenth Amendment equal-protection clause? The critical linkage was the use of the local police to remove protesting students from restaurants and lunch counters. Could these police officers from the local community, state actors under the Fourteenth Amendment, act to help a private property owner discriminate against African Americans by arresting and charging them with trespass or breach of the peace?

Since the 1883 *Civil Rights Cases,*[65] justices of the Supreme Court have employed the state action concept that emerged in that opinion as precedent. In that opinion, the Court concluded that the Fourteenth Amendment's reach extended only to the actions of state and local officials and that it did not control or constrain private persons who were not otherwise violating state or local civil or criminal statutes or ordinances. The Court noted that "individual invasion of individual rights is not the subject matter of this amendment."

The justices in 1883 took the opening words of the Fourteenth Amendment, "'No State shall,' literally, to mean that only official acts of the state were barred by the Fourteenth Amendment."[66] Transposing that precedent to the 1960s, the question for the Warren Court was whether the private racial discrimination that lay at the heart of these sit-in cases could be, somehow, converted into state-assisted discrimination that was prohibited by the Fourteenth Amendment.

Needless to say, at least three different perspectives were held by the justices, and it became extremely difficult to develop a collegial, institutional opinion for the Court because of these irreconcilable jurisprudential differences. One group of justices, led by Brennan and joined by Clark and Stewart, declined to address the constitutional issue. Instead, they were able to set aside the convictions without relying on the state action concept. A second trio of justices, including Douglas, Arthur Goldberg, and Chief Justice Warren, would have extended the state action concept to reach segregated lunch counters. The third trio, led by Black, and including Byron White and John Harlan, were opposed to any change in the 1883 precedent and, further, defended the primacy of the concept of private property.

By the 1963 term of the Court, the justices were stressed over the issue. The strain worsened when the Court heard the *Bell v. Maryland* case during that term. In 1960, twelve African Americans sat-in at a lunch counter in Hooper's department store in Baltimore, Maryland, and had been convicted of unlawful trespass. The Court heard oral argument in mid October 1963.

At the October 23, 1963, conference session, Black noted in his conference notes, that Chief Justice Warren "had hoped we could take the cases step by step not reaching our final question until the states had worked out matters better." Warren's (and Douglas's and Goldberg's) view of the issue was caught by Black when he wrote that the "CJ says in the field of public accommodations owners abandoned their right of privacy by engaging in a public business."[67]

Goldberg argued that the "sit-downers'" constitutional rights had been violated and "impugned the basic premise of the Civil Rights Cases." Douglas argued that to uphold the convictions of the black protestors "fastens apartheid onto our society—a result incomprehensible in light of the purposes of the Fourteenth Amendment and the realities of our modern society." He strenuously argued that the states could not "constitutionally put a racial cordon around businesses serving the public."

Clark, agreeing with Black and Harlan, expressed the view that a property owner has a right to choose his customers as he pleases. Black chimed in with the observation that "I deny that people have a constitutional right to trespass or stay on property over the owner's protest." For Black, an "indicia of slavery," a term Goldberg used in his presentation, is "to make me associate with people I do not want to associate with." For White, there was no need to change the accepted view that there is a "right of a man who owns a business to run the business in his own way so long as some valid regulatory statute does not tell him to do otherwise."[68]

By the end of the conference, one that focused, in Black's words, on a "highly emotional field," Black had a narrow five-person majority to uphold the trespass convictions. The four who joined Black in his views were Clark, Harlan, Stewart, and White. So stressful was the environment in the Court that Black sent the first draft of the opinion only to the four others on his team. By the spring of 1964, all the opinions were circulating to the Court, but there was no consensus on the constitutional issue.

Both Douglas and Brennan were circulating dissents to the justices. In late April, Goldberg circulated a dissent in which he argued that the Fourteenth Amendment, of itself, prevents the enforcement of trespass laws against sit-in demonstrators. Warren, Douglas, and Brennan joined Goldberg after reading his draft opinion. Then Brennan dropped from the Goldberg group and circulated his own dissenting opinion to the justices. By the end of April, then, no less than four opinions were being reviewed by the justices, reflecting the three distinct views on the issue of state action.

The Court crumbled further, because in early May, the chief circulated a dissent from the Black majority opinion. By mid May, five opinions were circulating, and there was a great deal of discussion about whether or not the Court should address the constitutional question.

On May 27, 1964, Justice Clark dropped a bombshell with his announcement that he was "joining the opinion of Brother Brennan in these cases." This judgment meant that Black's opinion was now a minority dissenting one. The switch "upset HLB very much as HLB had hoped the Court would act promptly. There was considerable speculation as to why TC switched, but it now appears that he has concluded that these cases all represent 'state action.'"[69]

When Douglas heard about Clark's vote switch, in a memo from Brennan who "considered that *Bell* . . . [is] now all reversed on narrow grounds," he exclaimed to his clerk "Oh, shit!" and then wrote an MTTC. Because Brennan took the procedural rather than the substantive, constitutional, route to reverse the convictions (abatement of convictions due to passage of a Maryland antidiscrimination statute after the arrests), Douglas informed the brethren that he found it "impossible to join Brennan."

The brethren then fought over whether the convictions were *reversed* by the Court or whether the Court *vacated* the case back to the Maryland state court. Finally, Brennan, in an MTTC on May 28, 1964, tried to clear the air. He wrote that "the reality remains that whether the term used is 'reversed' or 'vacated,' the state judgment is nullified and the case sent back to the state court for further proceedings. There would thus be five votes in *Bell* to nullify the state judgment and send the case back, although Brother Douglas would go further than four of us and rest this disposition upon his view of the constitutional merits."

Meanwhile, Justice Black's response to the other draft opinions was evidently too strong for his colleague Harlan, who wrote to Black on June 2, 1964, that "the tone of your draft seems to me unnecessarily harsh on our three Brothers who would remand—something which should be avoided as far as possible." Harlan, in the effort to dampen the conflict, circulated his draft opinion to Black "for consideration by you and our other two Brothers."

This action brought the total of individual circulations in the sit-in cases to six! On June 11, 1964, Justice Clark circulated his own opinion, "headed simply, 'Mr. Justice Clark,'" because of the extent of the confusion among the justices regarding exactly what the Court was ordering! In his opinion, the seventh written by the justices, Clark simply noted that he would reverse the *Bell* convictions based on the Fourteenth Amendment, *Shelley v. Kraemer*, and the "totality of circumstances."

Even though some noted that it was "impossible to know what Clark's opinion rests on," at the June 11, 1964, conference, Clark was assigned the task of trying to write an opinion for the Court's new five-person majority to set aside the trespass convictions.

This did not work, and five days later, Brennan took over the task of writing an opinion for the majority, that is, Warren, Clark, Goldberg, and, another flip-flop, Potter Stewart, who had left Black's dissenting group of "scant and scared soldiers."[70] Douglas and Goldberg wrote separate concurring opinions, with Douglas hoping that some on the Brennan wing would move over and stand with Douglas and his constitutional views about private discrimination.

On the day Brennan sent his MTTC, however, White told Black that he was going to write separately on the matter, thus increasing the number of justices who would write in *Bell* to eight! Every justice but Potter Stewart wrote in *Bell*. Clearly, there was no institutional opinion for a collegial court.

The Brennan opinion was the one that spoke for the narrow majority on the matter. Douglas wrote to Brennan immediately afterward, noting that he "suffered a real shock when I realized you were in dead earnest in vacating *Bell* and remanding it to the state court and thus avoiding the basic constitutional question. I guess I underwent a real trauma when I realized that the spirit of Felix still was the dominant force here."[71] Many years later, Brennan revealed that he moved in that direction because he was "aware that Congress under Johnson's leadership was after the Civil Rights Act of 1964. I was so concerned that if we came down with *Bell v. Maryland* on constitutional grounds, it would kill the civil rights act. Hugo was just beside himself with me on that. He came storming in saying, 'You can't do that [reach the constitutional merits]!'"[72] The Court majority did not address the substantive constitutional questions, although in dissent Black addressed the value of private property and Douglas argued that the "store owner was a public utility."[73]

Clearly, in the *Bell* deliberations, there was no way the chief, who was an active participant in the discussions, was able to push the brethren to an institutional opinion. When there is serious constitutional disagreement among the justices, there is not much a chief can do to overcome the push toward individualism.

Warren's successor as chief, Warren E. Burger, found this to be the case when, in 1977–78, the Court was faced with an equally contentious constitutional

Associate Justice Thurgood Marshall.

issue: the constitutionality of affirmative action programs that attempted to overcome the consequence of centuries of slavery and second-class citizenship.

The Separate Opinion Leads to a Ruling: Justice Powell's Judgment in *Bakke*, 1978

In the *Bell* controversy, most of the justices were sympathetic toward the goals if not the tactics of the African-American petitioners; the majority did not reach the constitutional question, evidently for political reasons. In the 1978 affirmative action case *Regents of the University of California v. Bakke*,[74] five of the justices, including the liberal quartet led by Brennan and Thurgood Marshall, the first African American selected to serve on the Court, addressed the constitutionality of special treatment of minorities. Another, conservative, quartet rested its negative judgment on an interpretation of Title VII of the 1964 Civil Rights Act. In *Bakke*, a majority of the justices disagreed with the university's argument that special treatment for minority students in the form of "set-asides" for sixteen of one hundred incoming medical students was an appropriate state strategy and not in violation of the Fourteenth Amendment's equal-protection clause.

David O'Brien has written that a justice writing singly, in dissent or concurring, generally "does not carry the burden of massing other justices. But in extraordinary circumstances a separate opinion may be necessary, the only practical way of obtaining a ruling for the Court."[75] Clearly, this was the case in *Bakke*, a very controversial affirmative action case the Court heard during its 1978 term. Chief

Justice Burger, in a confidential MTTC written shortly after the initial conference session held after the *Bakke* oral argument, warned his colleagues that they should not "rush to judgment" on the difficult case. "The notion of putting this sensitive, difficult question to rest in one 'hard' case is about as sound a[s] trying to put all First Amendment issues to rest in one case. . . . If it is to take years to work out a rational solution of the current problem, so be it. That is what we are paid for."[76] It did not take years to resolve *Bakke*; given the hard and fast political/ideological positions of all the justices, the "solution" came quickly. But the result was not the cohesive, collegial majority decision of a unified Court.

Beginning in the late 1960s, institutions of higher learning began to adopt admissions policies that enabled them to increase the number of minorities enrolling as undergraduates and as students in graduate and professional schools. In 1974, the Court could have addressed the constitutional questions when it granted certiorari in *DeFunis v. Odegaard*. This case from Washington State involved the constitutionality of a preferential-admissions program for minority applicants to the University of Washington School of Law. The Court majority did not decide the case on the merits, declaring it moot because DeFunis had been admitted to the law school pending final determination and, given the length of time to get to the Court, was just about to receive his law degree.

However, Justice Douglas dissented and, in a substantive statement, maintained that all university applicants should be "considered in a racially neutral way":[77]

> The Equal Protection Clause commands the elimination of racial barriers, not their creation in order to satisfy our theory as to how society ought to be organized. . . . A segregated admissions process creates suggestions of stigma and caste no less than a segregated classroom, and in the end it may produce that result despite its contrary intentions. One other assumption must be clearly disproved; that blacks or browns cannot make it on their individual merit. That is a stamp of inferiority that a State is not permitted to place on any lawyer.

Brennan also dissented, joined by Douglas, Marshall, and White. He argued that the Court had to address the issue and if not in *DeFunis*, then in another case.

Three years later, in February 1977, the other case, *Bakke*, came to the justices and, again, the Court granted certiorari in an affirmative action, or reverse discrimination, case from California. The University of California, Davis, Medical School, in an effort to diversify its medical-school student population, provided for a separate review of minority applicants for admission to the medical school. Sixteen of the hundred first-year seats were set aside for the minority students selected by the admissions committee.

Allan Bakke, a white, male applicant who had been twice denied admission to the school while minority students with lower quantitative statistics were admitted, challenged the admissions policy. He argued that both the Fourteenth Amendment's equal-protection clause and Title VI of the 1964 Civil Rights Act prohibited discrimination against whites in the effort to remediate the consequences of past racial discrimination. The California Supreme Court concluded that the university's plan violated the equal-protection clause and was therefore unconstitutional. It also concluded that Bakke was entitled to admission to the medical school and that the university could not take race into account in any admissions program.

Affirmative Action Divides the Court   Because of the controversial nature of the issue, as soon as the oral argument ended the fur began to fly. Very quickly the forces coalesced. One group maintained, with William Rehnquist paralleling Douglas's warnings in *DeFunis*, that while an affirmative action admission program to overcome the consequences of past discrimination against African Americans and other minorities is "not an unappealing rationale," it was nonetheless one that was barred by Title VI of the 1964 Civil Rights Act.[78]

Brennan's group argued, however, that, in light of past grievous discrimination of African Americans and other minorities for hundreds of years, the Constitution was not "colorblind," and that it was constitutionally reasonable for special admissions programs to be implemented to enable "qualified minority students" to enter institutions of higher education.

The central question for the justices was whether university admissions policies that provided for preferential treatment for minorities were constitutional or whether the Fourteenth Amendment's equality language as well as Title VI of the 1964 Civil Rights Act invalidated such actions.

In a very unusual decision, in which six justices wrote opinions on the issue, the ruling of the Court was announced more than one year later by Justice Lewis Powell. It was not until May 2, 1978, less than two months before the announcement of the Court's action in the case, that Burger informed the justices about the possible disposition of the case. "Bill Brennan and I conferred with a view to considering what may fairly be called a 'joint' assignment. There being four de-

Associate Justice Lewis Powell.

finitive decisions tending one way, four another, Lewis's position can be joined in part by some or all of each 'four group.' Accordingly, the case is assigned to Lewis, who assures a first circulation within one week from today."[79]

Powell's reaction to his predicament was not without humor. In an MTTC asking input from his colleagues on the draft he circulated, he noted that "as I am a 'chief' with no 'indians,' I should be in the rear rank, not up front!"[80] The strategy did, however, succeed after a fashion. He delivered the opinion because the other eight justices were split four to four, and neither side was willing to compromise their respective, and mutually exclusive, positions in this matter.

Powell's lonely judgment upheld the validity of affirmative action admissions programs in general. It also concluded that a set-aside program such as the one the University of California, Davis, implemented ran afoul of the Fourteenth Amendment's equal-protection language.

Justice John P. Stevens, joined by Burger, Rehnquist, and Stewart, the "gang of four" as Brennan called them,[81] refused to raise the constitutional question because, for them, the set-aside admissions policy was an impermissible racial classification under Title VI of the Civil Rights Act. Congress, they argued, meant to prohibit all types of race-conscious remediation programs.

Four other justices, joined in an opinion written by Justice Brennan, reached the constitutional issue and concluded that the University of California, Davis, set-aside program and *all* other affirmative action programs, even ones with clearly earmarked quotas for minorities, were constitutionally permitted remedies to overcome the badges of slavery.

Brennan and his "gang" were successful in having the Court, in the final judgment, address the question of "whether race can ever be a permissible consideration in making admissions decisions. . . . The Court is duty bound to decide whether race can ever be a permissible consideration."[82] At the very end of the process, on May 10, 1978, Brennan told Powell that there would be an opinion from Brennan and his cohort because their views "differed so substantially from your own that no common ground seems possible."[83]

Powell had no problem with that decision, nor did he, at the end, find it difficult to incorporate in his opinion a passage that mildly supported the Brennan group's view that, under certain circumstances, race could be used as a factor in admissions decisions. On June 23, 1978, Powell told Brennan that, while the Court's (Powell's) judgment was "limited to the holding that a state university validly may consider race to achieve diversity," he did not object to Brennan's language that the "central meaning of this Court's judgment [is that] Government may take race into account when it acts not to demean or insult any racial group, but to remedy disadvantages cast on minorities by past racial prejudice." Powell accepted Brennan's "gloss" and noted that "one who reads my opinion carefully will conclude that your gloss goes somewhat beyond what I have written and what I think."[84] *Bakke*'s conclusion, in part, in Powell's opinion, was that race could be used as a factor in admitting students to a university or college. Justice Harry Blackmun's concurring opinion declared that "it is the unconstitutional use of race that is prohibited, not the constitutional use." Thurgood Marshall, angry, at times livid, at his colleague's attitude about past discrimination and that which is still heaped continually on African Americans in America, and especially angry at Powell (whom Marshall called a racist),[85] argued that it was payback time, that quotas were very appropriate, and that the

Davis program was "not a quota to keep someone out, it's a quota to get someone in."[86]

The Powell Judgment for the Court Justice Powell announced the "bifurcated" judgment of the Court in the "intrinsically difficult" *Bakke* case. He noted that "there is no opinion joined in its entirety by five members of the Court" and that he spoke "today with a notable lack of unanimity."[87]

It affirmed in part and reversed in part the California Supreme Court judgment. As such, it attracted both sets of justices' votes, but neither set fully "joined" him in his opinion. Powell affirmed the California court's ruling that a minority quota or set-aside program "discriminated unlawfully against Bakke, either under the Constitution or Title VI of the Civil Rights Act of 1964."[88] He also affirmed the California court's admission of Bakke into the medical school. His opinion was the Court's decision because the Stevens group concurred in part with him on these questions.

Because Powell supported, in one passage, the notion that school admission programs could consider race as a factor relevant to the admission of applicants to a university, thereby reversing in part the California court, the Brennan quartet concurred in very small part with Powell's opinion. Powell based this conclusion on the fact that universities need diversity to have academic freedom on campus. However, he disavowed the justification offered by Brennan and his group, that is, that affirmative action admission programs are permissible to begin to overcome past discrimination against minorities by universities in America.

In the end, *Bakke* was resolved through the employment of Powell's plurality judgment, supported only in part by each of the two four-person blocs. Understandably, "coherence and 'principled decisionmaking' are difficult virtues to achieve for a multimember Court that necessarily operates as a committee, attempting to stitch together a decision that can attract a majority. Compromises are needed."[89]

Frequently, or so it seems, compromise and collegiality are difficult to achieve in the Court. This is certainly the case in a controversial area such as racial discrimination. *Bakke* clearly is evidence of last-minute efforts at stitching together a result that is unsatisfactory to all parties—except for Lewis Powell. It was, indeed, as someone wrote, a "fractured judgment," yet one that probably captured the ambivalence of the society on the issue of affirmative action.[90]

ON THE MATTER OF SUPREME COURT COLLEGIALITY

The business of the Supreme Court, the nation's highest appellate court, is to resolve society's conflicts through the appropriate closure-producing opinions that settle the instant dispute and clarify the legal and political public policy that was the foundation of the dispute. This means that the justices must be able to work together to craft that opinion.

The Court, as an important quasi-collegial political and legal institution, has to craft *something* to announce to the public by the end of the term. To complete the work on the Court's annual docket, the justices *must* act collegially, even though there are ideological and personal differences that always produce stress and that occasionally lead to conflict that can become so dysfunctional as to lead the Court to a situation where the docket is not cleared by term's end.

What, then, is Court collegiality and what is the natural conflict that develops in the Court as a consequence of professional and ideological differences of opinion antithetical to the collegiality norm? Federal appeals court judge Frank Coffin has enumerated a judicial collegiality typology. It included two characteristics the judge labeled (1) anticipatory collegiality and (2) responsive collegiality.[91] These characteristics are useful for discussing the business of the Supreme Court.

Anticipatory Collegiality

Anticipatory collegiality is the kind of relationship that develops over time, when men and women work together and grow to know each other quite well, even intimately. "It is the instinctive and unself-conscious sensitivity to one's colleagues' sensibilities exhibited by a judge as he talks with or writes to his fellow judges."[92] It is a collegiality that is based on the judge's understanding of her colleagues' prejudices, jurisprudence, and legal biases. Such an understanding can, optimally, lead to MTTC's, written responses on the slip opinions, and conversations in the conference session that show respect for the brethren and, consequently, further the resolution of the legal problems that need closure by the Court.

Felix Frankfurter's behavior as justice on the Court is an example of a self-centered, individualistic jurist who did not believe in or practice anticipatory collegiality. Consequently, conflicts emerged because of the little professor's arrogant behavior in conferences, in written responses to his colleagues' ideas, and in MTTC's. Hugo Black, too, was a hard bargainer who could forget collegiality when he responded to his brethren on critical issues. In *Bell*, for example, Justice John Harlan had to request Black to tone down his written criticism of three of the brethren who disagreed with Black on the merits of the sit-in dispute.

William Brennan and Lewis Powell, on the other hand, were Supreme Court justices who practiced this type of anticipatory collegiality. Although the two disagreed with any number of their brethren on constitutional and jurisprudential matters of the first order, clearly evidenced by the discussions in *Bakke*, they went out of their way to respect the views of their brethren.

Responsive Collegiality

This is the collegiality associated with an awareness of a judge's range of responses when responding to the circulated, written work of a colleague. It is the written acknowledgment by a justice of the feelings of another colleague. Through the slip opinion or an MTTC, another colleague can respond to a colleague's ideas in a collegial manner, for example, by expressing criticism in a way that does not hurt feelings. She should feel comfortable about providing inputs to the writer; she should "not hesitate to proffer suggestions concerning wording, organization, footnotes, the use of authorities, and so on," unless she "cannot come up with anything really better."[93]

Justice Brennan once explained that one had to be able to work with different justices in different ways depending on the purpose at hand. When he wanted Black's vote, Brennan noted, "he would come to my chambers and we'd yell at each other and dictate some language. Then I'd go to his place and we'd yell some more and dictate more."[94] With other justices, Brennan took a different tack, fully cognizant of the extent to which he could go with each of his colleagues. This type of collegiality extends to situations in which a justice in the majority will suggest an improvement that will strengthen a dissenting opinion, and vice versa. The interactions between Powell and Brennan in the *Bakke* discussions and writings is an illustration of this type of responsive collegiality. Frequently, however, another kind of judicial response occurs that illustrates the lack of this type of collegiality. Court history is replete with examples of justices who were unwilling to do anything but attack other's efforts to draft concurring or dissenting opinions.

There are, additionally, other dimensions of collegiality that seem to be essentially commonsense characteristics appropriate in any small-group setting. Clearly, there should be mutual support and respect among the justices, each viewing the others as integral participants in a critically important institutional entity. This should exist whether the justice sitting next to one is a longstanding member of the loyal opposition, or, like William O. Douglas, a loner on the Court who marches to his own drum. But what about conflict within the Court? Is it of such a character that it makes collegiality an impossible goal?

CONFLICT WITHIN THE COURT: A CLASH WITH THE COLLEGIALITY NORM?

The justices themselves differentiate between conflicts that are principally *personal* and those that are *professional.* Disagreement is normal, but even serious disagreement is not considered problematic so long as it draws up short of personal attacks. The more personal the conflict, the less comfortable we are with it; hence, the recent concern with the strident exchanges among justices by name presented in harsh rhetoric. It is one thing when a majority and dissenting opinion focuses on arguments and rebuttals, but the more the debate shifts to sharp exchanges between specific justices by name in footnotes, the more the tension increases.

Justices *always* are in disagreement with *some* of their colleagues, but most of the time there is no personalization of their professional disagreements. Some justices, however, with Felix Frankfurter again a classic example, "took the refusal of the brethren to follow his lead as a personal affront, and unfortunately allowed full play to his considerable talent for invective."[95] When conflicts reach a stage where justices cannot communicate comfortably or are too ready to assume that some of their colleagues are more than eager to do battle on an issue, both the justices and observers begin to worry about the capacity of the institution to take care of its business.

Conflict kept largely within the Court has not been historically perceived as nearly as serious as that which goes public. A number of justices have used the ability to go public as a threat with which to convince their colleagues to yield or to moderate their views.[96] In theory at least, a Court that is seen to be conflict-laden encourages noncompliance because it suggests that a ruling is no more than a temporary victory in a particular case and does not announce any carefully considered principle that the Court is likely to apply uniformly in the future. Another assumption is that public battle undermines respect for the institution because it gives the impression that the Court operates on rules too much like that of other political bodies rather than an institution above the fray.

Categories of Court Conflict: The Artful Fighter, William O. Douglas

There are four categories of Supreme Court conflict: (1) internal personal clashes; (2) internal professional conflicts; (3) external personal disputes; and (4) external professional challenges. For many justices, the categories overlap. Conflict with Felix Frankfurter was, for Justice William O. Douglas, both personal and professional. This bitter relationship was the most continuous—and contentious—one during Douglas's long tenure on the Court.[97] It began in 1941 and persisted until Frankfurter's retirement in 1962. (It went beyond, for Douglas, alone among his colleagues, did not attend Frankfurter's funeral in 1965.) Frankfurter continually opposed Douglas's expansive views on the role of the judiciary and on the nature of constitutional rights and liberties, especially his views of due process, "incorporation," and the primacy of the First Amendment.

These professional disagreements, begun in the early 1940s, shortly after the *Gobitis* decision of the Court (written by Frankfurter), lasted for two decades and were seen as "wars" by the two men. These battles involved the justices, their law clerks, and their former clerks and others off the bench who stood in for Douglas and Frankfurter in surrogate battles.[98] Frankfurter would remind his clerks of the war he was fighting with Black and Douglas; Douglas would speak in confidence only to those he trusted. Walking with a Black law clerk, Douglas said:

Associate Justice William O. Douglas and his fourth wife, Cathleen, in front of Supreme Court building.

Associate Justice William O. Douglas,
taken at Goose Prairie, Washington.

"You're OK. You're one of Hugo's boys. You're loyal; I can trust you."[99] Certainly, for both justices, the conflict was deep and ugly and led to difficult and at times almost impossible professional relationships.

Frankfurter and Douglas sincerely disliked each other. According to Douglas, Frankfurter "personalized every dispute, no matter what its cause."[100] Frankfurter disliked Douglas for jurisprudential as well as personal reasons. For Frankfurter, Douglas was a political hustler who was using the Court position to further his own personal political ends. In an angry mood on this matter, Frankfurter in 1943 asked a perplexed Frank Murphy: "Doesn't it shock you to have this Court made a jumping off place for politics?"[101]

After the Court decided *Barnette*,[102] and for the rest of his tenure on the Court, Frankfurter viewed Douglas as a member of the enemy camp, one of the "Axis" who was continually at odds with Frankfurter. Privately, Frankfurter spoke viciously about Douglas.[103] He vilified Douglas in diary notes and in letters to friends on and off the Court. Douglas was "one of the two completely evil men I have ever met"; "malignant"; "narrow minded"; "the most cynical, shamelessly amoral character I've ever known"; and a "*mommser*" (a Yiddish epithet meaning "bastard").[104]

Douglas, whether due to shyness or impatience with colleagues, was generally a loner. "[He] enjoyed company but seldom sought it out."[105] Regarding Frankfurter, Douglas was none too kind. Over the two decades, Douglas referred to him as "Der Fuehrer"; "a little bastard"; "the little giant"; "Machiavellian"; "divisive"; and a "prevaricator."[106] Douglas saw Frankfurter as a cynical jurist, one who has "no sacred principle. . . . Every principle is made for manipulation. . . . I would say that Frankfurter's influence has been toward the disappearance of the ethical principle from the law."[107]

Some of Douglas's harshest battles, beyond his life-long clash with Felix and after Frankfurter's retirement, were over internal practices within the Court, and he was more than willing to threaten his colleagues that he would use opinions to expose abuses if he saw them. In particular, Douglas had little use for the new chief justice, Warren Burger, during their first few years on the bench together. Among the factors that engendered the clash, beyond their obvious philosophical differences, was the fact that Douglas was the senior liberal justice during most of the time he served with Burger. That generally meant that Douglas was the person who would assign opinions when the chief justice was not in the majority in a particular case.

On several occasions, Douglas took the position that Burger miscounted conference votes to control the assignment.[108] Douglas was not the only person who had difficulties with Burger's assignments. Potter Stewart wrote Burger on December 29, 1970, citing four assignment errors in a single assignment list.[109] Douglas also clashed with his colleagues in later years over access to the Court. For Douglas, philosophically, the matter of access was critical: The Supreme Court's doors must always remain open for the oppressed minorities and individuals to bring their cases for judicial review by the Court. Like the assignment question, Douglas plainly saw the significance of the standing cases and other access litigation as much broader and politically significant than any debate over technical rules of procedure. The fact that one of Douglas's last major opinions was in *Warth v. Seldin*,[110] a standing case, was as symbolically interesting as the fact that Black's valedictory was the *Pentagon Papers* case.[111] Douglas wrote:

> Standing has become a barrier to access to the federal courts, just as "the political question" was in earlier decades. The mounting caseload of federal courts is well known. But cases such as this one reflect festering sores in our society; and the American dream teaches that if one reaches high enough and persists there is a forum where justice is dispensed. I would lower the technical barriers and let the courts serve that ancient need.[112]

Most of the battles over legal points were, however, increasingly fought in the formal way in opinions, and the conflict between Douglas and his colleagues, while never resolved, did not adversely impact the business of the Court.

Conflict as Chronic Condition on the Court?

Skirmishes between strong-willed persons on the Court seem to be chronic and unavoidable. Given the contemporary role of the Supreme Court in American society, there will always be conflict among the brethren. Add to that mixture the varying temperaments of the justices as individuals, and we have the potential for explosiveness. When conflict does break out, it is often very painful for the parties. Some, like Justices Owen Roberts and Robert Jackson, sought release by leaving the Court permanently or for a time.

It takes powerful and persuasive social and task leadership on the Court, from the chief or other strong leaders, to bring the warring factions into line so as to be able to get on with the business of the Court. Chief Justice Harlan F. Stone, not a very good social or task leader, recalled, in a letter to a friend, "I have had much difficulty in herding my collection of fleas" and that he had to assign himself additional opinions to write because his colleagues were "so busy disagreeing with each other."[113]

Under these circumstances, then, and without good leadership by the chief to constrain and channel conflict, these clashes, especially those that have moved from professional disagreement to personal attacks, not only slow the business of the Court but make it more difficult for the brethren to write opinions that are well received in the community.

SUMMARY

As is evident to you, the U.S. Supreme Court is an often noisy "storm center,"[114] one of the most powerful and tumultuous locales of conflict and discord in American politics. The battles are not quiet and are not simply waged by litigants but also occur regularly within the Court among the justices. "Behind the marble facade, the justices compete for influence; the Court itself is locked in a larger struggle for power in society."[115] In this internal competition for policy control, the justices often engage in heated debate and occasionally clash.

There is, however, the reality that the Court is a quasi-collegial group of brief-reading justices and that the brethren have to work collegially to overcome the adverse consequences of conflict run amok. For the most part, the workways of the Court are adhered to in a way that enables the justices to reach closure on many controversial cases, even if it means divining a *Bakke*-type remedy.

How do you and your colleagues reach closure on these controversial cases? The next chapter focuses on the processes of decision making on the Court.

NOTES

[1]Frank M. Coffin, *The Ways of a Judge: Reflections from the Federal Appellate Bench* (Boston: Houghton Mifflin, 1980), p. 4.

[2]Mark W. Cannon and David M. O'Brien, eds., *Views from the Bench: The Judiciary and Constitutional Politics* (Chatham, NJ: Chatham House, 1985), p. 28.

[3]Phillip J. Cooper, *Hard Judicial Choices: Federal District Court Judges and State and Local Officials* (New York: Oxford University Press, 1988), p. 3.

[4]Bruce S. Jenkins, "Remarks," given by the chief judge, U.S. District Court, District of Utah, at the midyear meeting of the Utah State Bar Association, St. George, Utah, Mar. 6, 1987, p. 1.

[5]Ibid, pp. 1, 3.

[6]Frank M. Coffin, *On Appeal: Courts, Lawyering, and Judging* (New York: W.W. Norton, 1994), p. 107.

[7]Quoted in Cannon and O'Brien, *Views from the Bench*, p. 28.

[8]Ibid., p. 27.

[9]John P. Stevens, "Some Thoughts on Judicial Restraint," *Judicature* 66, no. 5 (Nov. 1982): 177.

[10]Coffin, *Ways of a Judge*, p. 52.

[11]See Chief Justice John Marshall's comments on this function in *Marbury v. Madison* (1803).

[12]Coffin, *Ways of a Judge*, p. 56.

[13]Walter F. Murphy and C. Herman Pritchett, *Courts, Judges, and Politics* (New York: Random House, 1986), p. 389.

[14]Coffin, *Ways of a Judge*, p. 53.

[15]As noted earlier, there is the *jurisdictional* brief and, if certiorari is granted by the Supreme Court, the filing of the brief *on the merits.*

[16]Coffin, *Ways of a Judge*, p. 52ff.

[17]Felix Frankfurter, "The Supreme Court in the Mirror of Justices," *University of Pennsylvania Law Review* 105, 781 (1957): 786.

[18]Ibid., 789.

[19]*Cooper v. Aaron*, 358 U.S. 1 (1958).

[20]Justice William J. Brennan, interview with authors, Washington, DC, Oct. 1986.

[21]William O. Douglas, Memo to the File, n.d., box 1198, William O. Douglas Papers (hereafter cited as WODP), LC, Washington, DC.

[22]David O'Brien, *Storm Center* (New York: Norton, 1992), p. 276.

[23]John R. Schmidhauser, *Judges and Justices: The Federal Appellate Judiciary* (Boston: Little, Brown, 1979), p. 174ff.

[24]William H. Rehnquist, "The Supreme Court: Past and Present," *American Bar Association Journal* 59 (1973): 361, 363.

[25]Baum, *Supreme Court*, p. 134.

[26]Quoted in Cannon and O'Brien, *Views from the Bench*, p. 73.

[27]See Note, "Plurality Decisions and Judicial Decisionmaking," *Harvard Law Review* 94 (1981): p. 1127.

[28]Quoted in Fred Barbash and Al Kamen, "Supreme Court: 'A Rotten Way to Earn A Living,'" *Washington Post National Edition*, Oct. 1, 1984, p. 33.

[29]Quoted in Ibid.

[30]Warren E. Burger to Howard Ball, Aug. 20, 1970.

[31]Coffin, *Ways of a Judge*, pp. 57–58.

[32]Baum, *Supreme Court*, pp. 103–4.

[33]Coffin, *Ways of a Judge*, p. 57.

[34]Ibid., p. 61.

[35]See, for example, Felix Frankfurter and James L. Landis, *The Business of the Supreme Court* (New York: Macmillan, 1938); and idem, "Some Reflections on the Reading of Statutes," *Record of the Association of the Bar of the City of New York* 2 (1947), p. 213.

[36]See Ball and Cooper, *Of Power and Right*, Chaps. 2–5, passim.

[37]Quoted in ibid., p. 88.

[38]Frankfurter to Whittaker, April 9, 1959, box 111, Felix Frankfurter Papers, (hereafter cited as FFP), LC, Washington, DC.

[39]Quoted in Schwartz, *Super Chief*, p. 39.

[40]Quoted in ibid., p. 53.

[41]Justice Robert Jackson, no friend of Black's, wrote a note to the Alabamian about the Court's docket problem: "You and I often disagree but rarely as to the way in which business should be expedited. We must agree that this log jam at the end of the term is bad for many reasons. I would like to make a suggestion as to how it might be *helped some* but hesitate to do so alone. I should like to talk with you about it and see if we could handle some idea along the line of cleaning up faster" (Jackson to Black, n.d., HLBP, LC, Washington, DC).

[42]Frankfurter to Douglas, Dec. 2, 1941, box 52, FFP, LC, Washington, DC.

[43]Douglas to Warren, MTTC, Nov. 12, 1960, WODP, LC, Washington, DC.

[44]Hugo Black, Jr., *My Father* (New York: Random House, 1980), p. 234.

[45]Quoted in Richard Kluger, *Simple Justice* (New York: Random House, 1975), p. 290.

[46]Five separate cases were consolidated by the Court. Three petitions were filed in three-judge U.S. district courts (South Carolina, Virginia, and Kansas); one came from the Delaware state court;

and the fifth, *Bolling v. Sharpe,* came to the Court from the U.S. district court for the District of Columbia.

⁴⁷Kluger, *Simple Justice,* p. 540.

⁴⁸Philip Elman, "The Solicitor General's Office, Justice Frankfurter, and Civil Rights Litigation 1946–1990: An Oral History," 100 *Harvard Law Review* 817 (1987).

⁴⁹Frankfurter to Jackson, Sept. 26, 1952, box 7, RHJP, LC, Washington, DC.

⁵⁰See Ball and Cooper, *Of Power and Right,* p. 174.

⁵¹Kluger, *Simple Justice,* p. 294.

⁵²Bernard Schwartz, *Unpublished Opinions of the Warren Court* (New York: Oxford University Press, 1983), p. 446.

⁵³Ibid.

⁵⁴Ibid.

⁵⁵Ibid.

⁵⁶Frankfurter to Warren, July 5, 1954, box 574, EWP, LC, Washington, DC.

⁵⁷Frankfurter was an influence on Warren's decision-making activities for about two terms. By the time William Brennan joined the Court, in 1956, Frankfurter's influence on Warren had ended.

⁵⁸Frankfurter to Warren, May 24, 1955, box 574, EWP, LC, Washington, DC.

⁵⁹Black, *My Father,* p. 209.

⁶⁰See Jack Peltason, *Fifty Eight Lonely Men: Southern Federal Judges and School Segregation* (New York: Harcourt, Brace and World, 1961), for an excellent account of the dilemmas federal district court judges faced when trying to implement *Brown.*

⁶¹*Alexander v. Holmes County, Mississippi* 396 *US* 1218 (1969).

⁶²Bernard Schwartz, *Super Chief* (New York: Random House, 1985), p. 72.

⁶³The leading sit-in cases were *Garner v. Louisiana,* 368 U.S. 157 (1961); *Peterson v. Greenville, S.C.,* 1963; *Lombard v. Louisiana,* 1963; *Bouie v. Columbia, S.C.,* 378 U.S. 342 (1964); *Hamm v. City of Rock Hill,* 1964; and *Bell v. Maryland,* 378 U.S. 226 (1964).

⁶⁴Jack Greenberg, "The Supreme Court, Civil Rights, and Civil Dissonance," *Yale Law Journal* 77 (1968), 1520, 1521.

⁶⁵109 U.S. 3 (1883).

⁶⁶Donald W. Jackson, *Even the Children of Strangers: Equality Under the U.S. Constitution* (Lawrence: University Press of Kansas, 1992), p. 52.

⁶⁷Compilation of conference notes by A. E. Dick Howard and John G. Kester, law clerks, Hugo L. Black, HLBP, June 22, 1964, box 377, LC, Washington, DC. Subsequent quotes in this chapter are from this file.

⁶⁸William O. Douglas, MTTC, Oct. 21, 1963, box 1299, WODP, LC, Washington, DC.

⁶⁹William O. Douglas, Memorandum to the File, May 19, 1964, box 1311, WODP, LC, Washington, DC.

⁷⁰Black and Black, *Mr. Justice and Mrs. Black,* p. 92.

⁷¹Douglas to Brennan, June 3, 1964, box 1312, WODP, LC, Washington, DC.

⁷²William J. Brennan, Jr., interview with authors, Washington, DC, Oct. 29, 1986.

⁷³WODP, Box 1289, LC, Washington, DC.

⁷⁴438 U.S. 265 (1978).

⁷⁵O'Brien, *Storm Center,* p. 335.

⁷⁶William J. Brennan, MTTC, Oct. 21, 1977, WJBP, LC, Washington, DC.

⁷⁷416 U.S. 312 (1974).

⁷⁸Title VI provides: "No person in the United States shall, on the grounds of race, color, or national origin, be excluded from participation in, be denied the benefits of, or be subjected to discrimination under any program or activity receiving Federal financial assistance."

⁷⁹Warren Burger, MTTC, May 2, 1978, box 426, WJBP, LC, Washington, DC.

⁸⁰Lewis Powell, MTTC, June 27, 1978, box 426, WJBP, LC, Washington, DC.

⁸¹Brennan to White, May 30, 1978, in which Brennan refers to the Stevens quartet as the "gang of four," box 426, WJBP, LC, Washington, DC.

[82]William J. Brennan, Jr., MTTC, Dec. 13, 1977, box 426, WJBP, LC, Washington, DC.

[83]William J. Brennan, Jr., MTTC, May 10, 1978, box 426, WJBP, LC, Washington, DC.

[84]Powell to Brennan, June 23, 1978, box 426, WJBP, LC, Washington, DC.

[85]See William J. Brennan, Jr., Memo to the File, *Bakke*, July 1978, WJBP, LC, Washington, DC.

[86]In an MTTC dated April 13, 1978, Marshall wrote that there was a "vast gulf between White and Black America. That gulf was brought about by centuries of slavery and then by another century in which, with the approval of this Court, states were permitted to treat Negroes 'specially.' This case is here now because of that sordid history. . . . We are stuck with this case. We are not yet all equals, in large part because of the refusal of the *Plessy* Court to adopt the principle of color-blindness. It would be the cruelest irony for this Court to adopt the dissent in *Plessy* now and hold that the University must use color-blind admissions." MTTC, April 13, 1978, WJBP, LC, Washington, DC.

[87]Powell, proposed statement from bench, June 26, 1978, WJBP, LC, Washington, DC.

[88]Ibid., p. 2.

[89]Louis Fisher, *Constitutional Dialogues* (Princeton, NJ: Princeton University Press, 1988), p. 182.

[90]David G. Barnum, *The Supreme Court and American Democracy* (New York: St. Martin's Press, 1992), p. 189.

[91]See Coffin, *Ways of a Judge*, pp. 181–92.

[92]Ibid., p. 181.

[93]Ibid., p. 185.

[94]Justice William J. Brennan, interview with authors, Washington, DC, Oct. 29, 1986.

[95]Melvin I. Urofsky, "Conflict Among the Brethren: Felix Frankfurter, William O. Douglas and the Clash of Personalities on the United States Supreme Court," *Duke Law Journal* (1988): 71, 78.

[96]Examples include Justice Jackson's threat directed at Justice Murphy to publish an opinion exposing Murphy's involvement as U.S. attorney general in approving wiretaps when Murphy was later preparing vehement dissents on the evils of wiretapping (*Goldman v. United States*, 316 U.S. 129 [1942]) and Black's threat to his brethren that he would dissent from any order of the Court that did not call for an end to the "with all deliberate Speed" standard and replacing it with the "integrate now" standard in school integration cases. He succeeded in convincing his colleagues to issue the per curiam opinion (*Alexander v. Holmes County, Mississippi*, 396 U.S. 19 [1969]).

[97]For a bitter Frankfurter, it was an anger directed at Douglas and, to a lesser extent, at Black and Earl Warren. In a 1957 letter to his friend Learned Hand, Frankfurter wrote that the three were men "whose 'common denominator is a self-willed self-righteous power-lust, . . . undisciplined by adequate professional learning and cultivated understanding' who make decisions on the basis of their prejudices and their respective pasts and self-conscious desires to join Thomas Paine and T. Jefferson in the Valhalla of 'liberty' and in the meantime to have the avant-garde of the Yale Law School . . . praise them." Quoted in Urofsky, "Conflict Among the Brethren," 105.

[98]Frankfurter's surrogates included former law clerks who became law school professors. Alexander Bickel, who clerked for Frankfurter during the *Brown* litigation, was an especially harsh critic of Douglas's as a Yale Law School professor. According to one student of Bickel's, later to clerk for Hugo Black, Bickel talked about Douglas as if the justice were "practically a criminal, as a dishonest, scheming, evil man" (Charles Reich to Melvin Urofsky, quoted in Melvin I. Urofsky, "Getting the Job Done: William O. Douglas and Collegiality in the Supreme Court" [paper presented at the William O. Douglas Symposium, Seattle, Washington, April 1989], p. 30).

[99]William O. Douglas to Charles Reich, n.d., quoted in Urofsky, "Getting the Job Done," p. 24.

[100]Urofsky, "Getting the Job Done," p. 27.

[101]Quoted in Ball and Cooper, *Of Power and Right*, p. 92.

[102]Ibid., p. 56.

[103]Frankfurter spoke contemptuously about Murphy, another of the Axis members of the Court. And directly to Murphy at times. For example, he passed a note to him in the 1944 term, listing Murphy's clients: "Reds, Whores, Crooks, Indians and all other colored people, Longshoremen, M[ortgagors], and other Debtors, R.R. Employees, Pacifists, Traitors, Japs, Women, Children, and Most Men. Must I become a Negro Rapist before you give me Due Process?" (quoted in Urofsky, "Conflict Among the Brethren," p. 80).

[104]See Simon, *Independent Journey*, pp. 243, 247; FFP, LC; FFP, Harvard; and Lash, *From the Diaries of Felix Frankfurter*, 343.

[105]William O. Douglas, *Go East, Young Man* (New York: Random House, 1974), p. 35.

[106]Quoted in Sidney Fine, *Frank Murphy: The Washington Years* (Ann Arbor: University of Michigan Press, 1975), p. 254; Simon, *Independent Journey*, p. 9; and Douglas, *Go East, Young Man*, p. 327.

[107]Douglas to Fred Rodell, Oct. 27, 1949, Rodell Papers, LC (quoted in Urofsky, "Getting the Job Done," p. 30).

[108]In *Gooding v. Wilson*, Burger indicated that the conference vote had been inconclusive and he intended to put the case down for another conference. Douglas, who had decided to assign the opinion to Brennan, wrote Burger objecting that the vote had been a clear five to two to affirm (William O. Douglas to Warren Burger, Dec. 17, 1971, box 1524, WODP). Burger's purpose became more clear when he replied: "Here again there is no harm in writing, but if your position is now firmed up, I see no point in reviewing a Conference discussion. Indeed, I think it very likely this case will be reargued. I, for one, will not take part in overruling *Chaplinsky*, directly or indirectly, with a seven-member Court" (Warren Burger to William O. Douglas, Dec. 20, 1971, box 1524, WODP). Brennan also wrote a memorandum indicating his disagreement with Burger's handling of assignments.

[109]Potter Stewart to Warren Burger, Dec. 29, 1970, box 1485, WODP.

[110]422 U.S. 490 (1975).

[111]*The New York Times v. United States*, 403 U.S. 713 (1971).

[112]*Warth v. Selden*, 422 U.S., at 519, Douglas dissenting.

[113]Quoted in Urofsky, "Conflict Among the Brethren," 89.

[114]"We are very quiet here, but it is the quiet of a storm center," wrote Justice Oliver Wendell Holmes (quoted in Howard Ball, *No Pledge of Privacy* [New York: Kennikat Press, 1976], p. xi).

[115]O'Brien, *Storm Center*, p. 13.

Supreme Court Decision Making: The Heart of the Job

9

After being on the Court barely two months, you are aware of many of the practices and most of the facets of jurisprudential life on the Court. Norms of behavior and a structured advocacy process are carefully followed by the justices, if they have a chief who is a capable social and task leader—and the chief does seem to be a good leader. There is, at the heart of the Court's business, the pushing and pulling of judicial individualism versus group collegiality.

Essentially, the Court is a paradox: a quasi-collegial group of nine small law firms doing intimate business with each other largely through indirect personal communications. However Justice William Brennan, for one, generally discounted the value of collegiality on the Court. There may have been collegiality on the Court at some earlier time in history, he said, but not during his tenure on the Court.[1] "The way you attract votes is through circulations," not through personal conversations with colleagues.[2]

The written memos to the conference (MTTC's); the circulation of draft, or slip, opinions; and the substantive comments written on these draft opinions by the justices are the basic communications through which the business of the Court is conducted. The conference session is the biweekly opportunity for the justice to voice her opinion on the particular case after oral arguments have been concluded earlier in that week. Brennan noted that "we do have one to one conferences on occasion, but," he added quickly, "rarely."

Another justice, Lewis Powell, reflected on the quietness of Court life. "It's really very quiet. I could sit here for a week without a phone call."

"There's very little visitation [between the justices]," he noted, adding that was "a shock to me. The only jurisdiction I have over anyone is within these chambers."[3]

Recalling Justice David Souter's rueful remarks about the ideal conference, you know that the conference session simply does not provide the time for full, substantive discussion of the issues in the case, including the justices' perceptions of the constitutional values the litigation addresses. You discover that the conference session is unlike the quite substantive conferences among the three federal appeals judges that you have experienced.[4]

The most difficult part of the job of the Supreme Court justice is writing the opinion for the Court majority. Clearly, you have to artistically craft an opinion that is tolerable to one segment of the majority while, at the same time, bearable to another segment, those who wanted a stronger, more vigorous statement coming from the Court. Writing an opinion that mollifies all individuals composing the majority will take all your skill, and intellect, and artistry!

THE CONTEMPORARY FUNCTION OF THE CONFERENCE SESSION

The reality is that the conference session, in the last three decades of the twentieth century, has become a place where the individual justices' initial position, the "vote," on the case on hand is announced and recorded on the docket sheets kept by the others. In part because a majority of the cases the Court decides to hear in contemporary times are fraught with very difficult constitutional questions, there is greater fragmentation in the Court, with many more dissenting and concurring opinions today than there were at the turn of the century.

Some of the justices do not seem to mind the existence of fragmentation on the Court. The recently retired Justice Byron White, for one, said that while there is "some value in the clarity" that comes with a strong majority opinion, he nevertheless strongly defended the view that diverse opinions were acceptable and perhaps even useful. Such fragmentation, for example, the multi-opinion situation in *Bakke*, "left it up to the lawyers to interpret the opinions. . . . I always thought that wasn't a bad way to do things. So I've never been upset about plurality opinions." Also, for Justice White, Court fragmentation leads to another positive outcome: legal change from a fragmented Court comes "in small increments rather than in big steps."[5]

Furthermore, the justices' reliance on the law clerk for the drafting of initial opinions, which are then edited by the justices, has, to some extent, turned the Court from writers into editors. The enhanced use and changed role of the law clerk in the initial drafting of opinions has led to the production of extremely lengthy, heavily footnoted opinions, most written in the turgid style of the law review article. Although some justices, such as David Souter and Harry Blackmun, complain loudly about this new reality, for them to do the opinion-writing work means laboring with their law clerks to frame the draft opinion, then editing the work of the clerks before circulating the slip opinion to the other justices.

Given the additional reality of the dramatically increased number of certiorari petitions filed with the contemporary Court, there really is no time in conference to fully explore the subtleties of cases. By the time of the conference session, many justices have barely reviewed the cert pool memos and the markups of the cases heard in oral argument that week. Justice Lewis Powell recalled Justice Potter Stewart's advice to him about preparing for the conference session: "You'd better know as much about a case before you hear it [in oral argument] as you will [not review it again] until you write the opinion." There simply was "no time to study a case between the time it was heard and the conference," concluded Powell.[6]

Clearly, the conference session "now serves only to discover consensus."[7] As Chief Justice William Rehnquist recently wrote about the conference, rarely does persuasion take place in the room. Instead,

> the justices sitting in conference . . . have presumably read the briefs, they have heard the oral arguments of the lawyers, who generally know far more about the particular case than the justices do, and they have the opportunity to discuss the case with one or more of their law clerks. The party who wishes to have the decision of the lower court reversed has attempted to show the Court, by citation of relevant case law and statutes, how and why this should be done; the party who wishes to sustain the judgment of the lower court has made a similar effort on behalf of his point of view. . . . The conference [moves] the Court to a final decision of a case by means of a written opinion.[8]

Moving to a final decision after the tentative conference vote highlights the shifting biases exhibited by some of the justices as they move forward. Richard Wasserstrom in his book *The Judicial Decision*[9] distinguishes between two processes of Supreme Court decision making. By the time of the conference session, the justice, with the aid of briefs about the case prepared by the law clerk, has probably gone through the "process of discovery." The jurist has, on the basis of a quick reading of the briefs as well as attendance at oral argument, preliminarily at least, come to a conclusion and presents these views in conference, although very briefly and without a great deal of substance.

After the votes/comments of all the justices in conference are tallied, then the serious, difficult "process of justification" begins. There is the assignment of the opinion to one of the justices for her to craft the rationale for the particular judgment in that case. Within the next few days, on the basis of the Court's views in each case in conference, opinions are strategically assigned, based on a variety of factors, to particular justices by the chief or, if he is not in the majority in a particular case, by the senior associate justice in the majority. Geography, ideology, religion, and party affiliation are a few of the characteristics possessed by justices that on occasion warrant the assignment of an opinion—or the taking away of an assignment.[10]

Negotiations after the conference session and the opinion assignment process take place in a very fluid setting, and some form of conflict between the jurists is always present. The justice assigned the task of writing the opinion for the majority then gets to work, with her clerks, in the effort to get a first draft circulated within a month or so. "Writing opinions is the justice's most difficult and time consuming task," writes David O'Brien.[11]

WRITING THE OPINION FOR THE MAJORITY

The comments of the justices in the conference session, often very sketchy and certainly preliminary views subject to change under the right circumstances, are used as jurisprudential markers by the justice assigned to write the majority opinion. The person assigned the task of writing an opinion for the majority has the difficult, occasionally onerous, task of drafting an opinion for the Court majority that all can join with no great deal of discomfort. Simultaneously, other justices are at work drafting dissenting and concurring opinions, and these are circulated to the brethren in addition to the majority-opinion draft.

Writing forces the clerk and the justice to think about basic values and the relationship of values to facts in the case. The exercise enables the participant to discover weaknesses in the initial decision. The opinion is rewritten time and again, especially in controversial cases. After the opinion writer has framed the document with the aid of his law clerks, it is circulated as a slip opinion to all the members of the Court.

Successive draft versions are circulated to all the members until those who joined in conference feel comfortable enough with both the style and the substance of the opinion to join it. Justice Oliver Wendell Holmes once remarked about the circulation process that "the boys generally cut one of the genitals"[12] out of his opinion, but, for him to keep his majority from disappearing, he had to tolerate their comments and suggestions for changing the *majority* opinion of the Court.

The Fluidity of Judicial Choice

There is enough fluidity in the decision-making process that the dissenting opinion occasionally becomes the majority opinion, and vice versa.[13] "The books on voting are never closed until the decision actually comes down," observed Justice John M. Harlan II. "Until then any member of the Court is perfectly free to change his vote, and it is not an unheard of occurrence for a persuasive minority opinion to eventuate as the prevailing opinion."[14]

Finally, some months after the conference session vote, but not in all cases argued before them, and based in great part on the capacity of the chief or an outstanding broker on the Court such as Justices William Brennan or Lewis Powell, the brethren coalesce on the case, come to some kind of agreement, and collegially produce the Court's final product: the majority opinion of the Court. Optimally, the Court's opinion is a clearly written document that explains and justifies the decision in the present case involving competing parties. Done well, the Court's opinion will be applicable to other cases as well as binding on the federal district court and court of appeals judges.[15]

However, a great deal of the time the Court does *not* do the job well. Justice Harry Blackmun once noted that, because of the increased workload and fragmentation of the Court, second-rate writing was being produced in abundance by the justices of the Supreme Court. The 107th justice appointed to the Supreme Court, Ruth Bader Ginsburg, recently noted that there were many occasions when she, as a member of the federal court of appeals in the District of Columbia, was "impelled," "constrained," "required" to "strictly" follow weak Court precedents.[16] "Despite misgivings," as a court of appeals jurist, Ginsburg decided cases in light of these guidelines, however weak. As she noted, a lower-court federal appellate judge had to follow "if not marching instructions, then at least some pathmarkers" from the Supreme Court.[17]

Justice Harlan was an exemplary Supreme Court jurist. His opinions were always well-reasoned, and lawyers who wanted to get a clear perspective on a case decided by the Court would turn to a Harlan opinion, whether majority, concurring, or dissenting, to get the salient facts and legal issues raised in the litigation. Indeed, Justice Ginsburg once wrote of Harlan that "of the judges in my time, there's no one, whether you agree with him or disagree with him, who was more honest in telling you the grounds of his decision—the competing interests and why he came out the way he did."[18] Harlan once said about Court opinions: "A Court opinion should honestly explain the judgment." He also expressed his view that "if a [Court] result was inexplicable, the judgment was probably wrong."[19] As another Supreme Court justice, William Brennan, recently commented: Some opinions "just don't write,"[20] that is, the justices cannot generate a rational justification for their view of a case's outcome.

For Justice Harlan, the essential task of the writer of the decision was to get to the nub of the case both clearly and correctly. This takes intelligence and the capacity to dispassionately hunt out the core of the legal conundrum facing the Court's justices. Said one of Harlan's clerks, Harlan's "great love was the craft of lawyering—breaking down a problem by research and analysis to uncover the essential questions which called for his [and the Court's] judgment."[21] Since the conference session gives the writer at best only some murky clues about her colleagues' thinking on the legal principles raised in the litigation, the writer must use her judgment as well as her knowledge of her brethren's views on jurisprudential matters in drafting the opinion.

But this discussion of Court decision making has been merely a description of the tactics and strategy, the mechanics and the politics of the Court's decision-making process.[22] What lies beneath the structure and mechanics of decision making, and at the heart of the process, are the very tough questions raised in the cert petitions, questions that get to a discussion of core values and legal principles enunciated in the opinion of the Court.

Each certiorari petition asks the justices of the Court to answer some very controversial questions about the meaning of statutes, administrative regulations and actions, or about the breadth of the Constitution's contours regarding governmental power and limits on that power. Does the Congress have the power to curtail the travel of U.S. citizens who are members of the Communist party?[23] Can a Connecticut statute constitutionally prohibit couples, including married couples, from receiving birth-control information?[24] Does a state have the right to prohibit women from seeking abortions?[25] Does the president have the power to unilaterally terminate a treaty with another sovereign nation?[26]

These are examples of the tough questions the Court has to answer. It does so through the Court's substantive decision-making processes. The writer for the Court's majority has to answer these kinds of questions in a way that meets with the approval of the cohort in the majority, with the legal community, and, ultimately with the larger society beyond the courtroom.

The Sources for the Court's Answers to the Questions Raised

There are three sources for the "law" in America a justice of the Court must choose from when writing an opinion for the Court with her clerks, whether it is a majority, a concurring, or a dissenting one. Some cases call for the Court to (1) interpret the Constitution's language to reach judgment in the case. Others call for the Court to (2) define the contours of a statute to decide the controversy. Still others draw on (3) the common law in America, as found in prior judicial decisions of the Court.

The problem, as Justices Harlan and Black knew so well, was that the rules and guidelines "contained in [Constitution, statutes, and legal precedent] are often vague, ambiguous, or not self-evident."[27] Consequently, as Harlan has said, the Court's justices must rely on their intelligence, their judgment, and their ability to uncover and then to answer the essential questions in the case before the Court.

Understanding Supreme Court decision making, then, is understanding the manner in which a justice (1) breaks down the legal and societal problem, (2) constructs a principled and well-reasoned decision for the Court and, finally, (3) gets colleagues to agree on both the values expressed and on the adequacy of the reasoning in the opinion. Doing this means, at some point, that the justice will select one of the three sources to rest her judgment.

At the heart of *Brown*, for example, were the very controversial questions concerning the continued validity of racial segregation in America as seen in the *Plessy* doctrine of "separate but equal," and the resolution of the conceptual and ethical conflict between *Plessy* and the Court majority's categorical commitment to the core value of equality as well as the arguments, legal and otherwise, against the continuation of the value of separate-but-equal educational facilities.

At the very heart of a decision, then, is a set of core values expressed by the majority of the Court in response to the hard questions raised in the case. The values are the foundation of the judgment, as expressed using sound legal reasoning. The person who has the greatest challenge at this point in the justification process is the justice asked to write the opinion for the Court majority.

The Opinion Writer

Writing an opinion for the Court is indeed challenging. One has to have core values to draw on when framing the justification for the Court. A "great" justice, for example, a Hugo Black or a William Brennan, is a person who is unafraid to answer tough societal questions in the legal context. A great jurist is one who has a well-developed set of core values and who, over his entire career, is able to communicate them consistently in the MTTC's, in the slip opinions, and in the opinions for the Court, as well as in dissents and in concurrences. A great justice is one, ultimately, whose legal values are consistent with those of the national community and that have an effect on the national community.[28]

Obviously not many justices who have sat are considered "great" by contemporary scholars. Of the 108 who sit or have sat on the Court from 1789 to 1995, perhaps two dozen or so can be classed as great or near-great.[29] There have been a number of Court appointees who were by no means intellectual giants who contributed to the development of American constitutional law. Indeed, many were political allies of the president and were appointed for reasons other than their jurisprudence and sense of constitutional values. Many of them had no judicial philosophy to speak of when nominated and never did develop one, nor did they even care to think along those lines.

Abe Fortas comes to mind as one such Court jurist. While no doubt a very bright lawyer, administrator, and presidential confidant, he had no developed jurisprudence when appointed to the Court. Fortas was, instead, a very pragmatic, result-oriented person. He was, as were most of the 108 persons who have been selected to sit on the Court, a "politician," and like so many of his brethren, he never completely transcended this pragmatic reality. While on the Court, he remained a valued advisor to the president who appointed him, Lyndon B. Johnson. As a justice, Fortas "would listen to the clerks' principled arguments for a particular decision and say, 'Well, yes, in theory, that is where we should come out. But we just can't do that in this case.' . . . Fortas was seen as too much the wheeler-dealer. In time, [his] clerks came to see Fortas as totally unprincipled and intellectually dishonest."[30]

But the opinion for the Court has to be written, and the work of writing it has to be evenly shared among the justices, whether they are great writer–philosophers or mediocre political hacks who had a close friend in the White House. Consequently, as Antonin Scalia, Harry Blackmun, Ruth Ginsburg, Stephen Breyer, and other former federal court of appeals judges know only so well, many if not most of the Court's majority opinions are not candidates for legal anthologies because of their literary or jurisprudential merit.

Just how difficult is it to tackle tough problems and to then engage in principled decision making? Lower federal appellate judges do not have much choice in tackling the tough ones, but that is because they are obligated to hear all cases and then, when addressing the questions raised in the litigation, to follow the guidelines, the "markers," principled or otherwise, of the Supreme Court decisionmakers.

A justice of the U.S. Supreme Court has a much more difficult task sitting on the nation's highest appellate tribunal. As Harvard Law professor Laurence Tribe has noted: "The rules of the game for an appeals court judge and for a Supreme Court justice are quite different."[31] Not only must the Court answer the questions the two parties in the legal dispute have raised in their briefs and in oral argument, the Court has to produce an opinion that contains a "statement of general principles of law on which the Court bases its treatment of the parties."[32] Of necessity, this means revisiting the essential characteristics of legal reasoning that should be implemented by appellate judges.

THOUGHTWAYS OF THE WRITER FOR THE MAJORITY

For reasons already presented, writing for the majority is not an easy task. Indeed, most of the time, writing and then negotiating with the brethren can become downright stressful. Hugo Black, after hearing his friend and colleague William Brennan turn cross during a phone conversation, immediately walked over to Brennan and said to him: "This place can be a pressure cooker and it can beat the strongest of men. You should get out of here and forget it for a few days."[33] Brennan did take some time off, but not a great deal of time off is taken by the justices, given the pressure they all have to write and circulate the draft opinions, whether majority, concurring, or dissenting.

There is a fairly even distribution among the justices of this jurisprudential work. Each of the justices on the Court, on average, write between ten and fifteen majority opinions each term. This average is only for the *majority opinions* written for the Court by a justice, however; it does not take into account the concurring and dissenting opinions he may write.

A review of the statistics for the 1992 term of the Court, reprinted in Table 9.1, indicates that the justices wrote from nine (Clarence Thomas) to sixteen (Byron White) majority opinions for the Court. When one adds to this number the additional concurring and dissenting opinions, the subsequent total number of signed opinions ranged from a low of twenty-one (David Souter) to a high of forty-five written opinions (John P. Stevens).

TABLE 9.1　Actions of Individual Justices

	OPINIONS WRITTEN [a]				*DISSENTING VOTES* [b], *IN DISPOSITION BY*		
	Opinions of Court [c]	*Concur-rences*	*Dissents* [d]	*Total*	*Opinion*	*Memo-randum*	*Total*
Rehnquist	11	2	9	22	21	1	22
White	16	2	7	25	15	1	16
Blackmun	10	12	10	32	34	3	37
Stevens	12	11	22	45	34	4	38
O'Connor	15	11	11	37	19	0	19
Scalia	12	16	15	43	25	1	26
Kennedy	11	10	5	26	11	1	12
Souter	13	5	3	21	8	0	8
Thomas	9	6	7	22	23	1	24
Per curiam	7	—	—	7	—	—	—
Total	116	75	89	280	190	12	202

Note: A complete explanation of how the tables are compiled my be found in "The Supreme Court, 1967 Term," *Harvard Law Review* 82 (1968): 93, 301–2; and "The Supreme Court, 1969 Term," *Harvard Law Review* 84 (1970): 30, 254–55.

　Table 9.1, with the exception of the dissenting votes portion of section (A) and the memorandum tabulations in section (C), concerns only full-opinion decisions disposing of cases on their merits. Seven per curiam opinions were long enough to be considered full opinions. The memorandum tabulations include memorandum orders disposing of cases on the merits by affirming, reversing, vacating, or remanding. They exclude orders disposing of petitions for certiorari, dismissing writs of certiorari as improvidently granted, dismissing appeals for lack of jurisdiction or for lack of a substantial federal question, and disposing of miscellaneous applications. Certified questions are not included.

[a] A concurrence or dissent is recorded as a written opinion whenever its author provides a reason, however brief, for his or her vote.

[b] A justice is considered to have dissented when he or she voted to dispose of the case in any manner different from that of the majority of the Court. Votes to reverse in a decision affirming by an equally divided Court are not, however, considered as dissenting votes because there is no majority of the Court.

[c] Plurality opinions that announce the judgment of the Court are counted as opinions of the Court. There were 107 signed opinions during the Term, but the joint opinion of Justices O'Connor, Kennedy, and Souter in *Planned Parenthood v. Casey*, S. Ct. 112 2791 (1992), has been credited to each of the three Justices.

[d] Opinions concurring in part and dissenting in part are counted as dissents.

Fragmentation on the contemporary Court of the 1990s is not as great as it was a decade ago. In the 1992 term there were 164 concurring (75) and dissenting (89) opinions written by the justices. In addition, there were over 200 dissenting votes cast by all nine justices in the 107 signed opinions of the Court during the 1992 term. However, in the 1986 term of the Court, there were 230 concurrences (76) and dissents (154). In 1986, 368 dissents were written by justices of the Court.

Clearly, given the Reagan and Bush appointments to the Court, as well as the agenda created by the majority, the Court's fragmentation has decreased since the 1980s. With Blackmun, Brennan, and Marshall no longer on the Court, the clashes between ideological cohorts has diminished. This homeostasis, however, typically does not last for very long. With changes in the White House, inevitably there will be changes in the Court.

Once the Supreme Court's term begins in October, the justices, with their clerks, are intensely engaged in the art and craft of opinion writing. Beyond the process of holding the majority together through to the formal announcement of the Court's judgment in open court, there is the actual structure and the craftsmanship that has to be addressed by each writer—every time one writes an opinion. In the end the opinion is seen as a public document that explains the opinion to the national, and international, community.

Even though very difficult value judgments must be made by the writer and then by colleagues on the Court, these conceptual conflicts and the accompanying intellectual pain should not be a part of the final statement. "Harry," Justice Hugo Black once said to freshman justice Blackmun, "never display agony in public in an opinion. Never display agony. Never say that this is an agonizing, difficult decision. Always write it as though it's clear as crystal."[34] For Blackmun, however, and for most of the people who have served on the Court, there is constant pain associated with crafting a satisfactory, workmanlike opinion for the Court. Very few justices who have served on the Court have the capacity that Justice William O. Douglas displayed. The brilliant westerner wrote drafts of opinions while sitting on the bench hearing oral argument!

Black, like his friend and colleague John Harlan II, was an unusual jurist because he relished the task of opinion writing and was excellent at that difficult task. For the steely Alabamian, as for the gentle Harlan, the job of writing called for the employment of all the positive skills of lawyering. Exemplary jurists like Black and Harlan had the "genuine instinct for the heart of the matter, 'what is really involved.' "[35] Using his law clerks as "research assistants, critics, sounding board, and tenderers of suggestions," Black would "dive into reading the record and all briefs" to get to the essence of the case. In this activity, Black would "absolutely master the facts and the arguments."[36] After mastering them, Black then

> moves into the relevant literature—cases, statutes, treatises, and law reviews. The clerks often read along with him or dig out additional material and feed it to him. The issues will be discussed intermittently. After a while Black will feel that he is ready to do a first draft of an opinion, assuming he has not changed his mind and decided to vote the other way, and that occasionally happens. . . . When the Judge has an opinion in the mill he does not drop it for anything else.[37]

In a short time, Black, often working until four in the morning, would circulate the draft and await the responses from his brethren. Like Oliver Wendell Holmes,

Black would grimly modify opinions in the effort to keep his majority. Said Justice Brennan of Black, "I rarely had situations with [Hugo] where he didn't adjust."[38]

Justices of the Supreme Court cannot all be Blacks, Harlans, Cardozos, and Hugheses when writing opinions for the Court majority. However, whether a hack plodder or a creative genius, the writer has to tap into a framework of concepts, tools, doctrines, and techniques as well as draw on her moral values and views of social policy when drafting a majority opinion for the Court.[39]

The Essentials

Any well-written opinion of the Court contains an essential set of elements. A solidly done piece of legal craftsmanship will contain a statement of the facts, an analysis of the legal claims and counterclaims made by the parties to the dispute, information about the case's track record in the lower courts, an enumeration of the legal questions the Supreme Court has been asked to deal with, the Court's judgment in the case, and finally, the justifications for the judgment reached by the brethren.[40]

In determining the justification strategy, that is, "the general approach the opinion takes to the task of justifying the judgment of the Court,"[41] the opinion writer must make choices about facts and values, and these selections must, in the end, reflect the views of at least four other justices.

Whether engaged in statutory or constitutional interpretation, the writer and the Court must make decisions that reflect their views of the state of the law as well as their views of public policy and society's norms and trends. Given the open endedness of the language of the law, whether constitutional, statutory, or common-law precedent, the opinion writer and the majority have wide latitude when choosing and defending the opinion in the written justification for the Court's decision.[42]

Understanding Constitutional and Statutory Interpretation

A case comes to the Supreme Court because at least four of the justices believe it raises an important set of questions about the use of governmental power and the limits on power. "Most cases [that] come before the Court require the justices either to construe the U.S. Constitution or to interpret a legislative statute or an administrative regulation."[43] These, the Constitution's words, the general principles of governing in the Constitution and its amendments, the intent of the men who wrote the document, and prior decisions of the Court are, as van Geel noted, the "building materials," the persuasive tools, of the opinion.[44]

Answering the legal question in the case calls for some form of legal explanation by the Court majority. The opinion writer for the majority, whether employing constitutional interpretation or statutory construction as the justification, answers the question for the Court by implementing one of the traditional building materials.

In constitutional interpretation, Court writers justify the Court's decision in a case by selecting one legal value from among a number of conceptual modes presented in the briefs, in oral argument, and in discussions with the justices, using precedent to buttress their basic value judgment. In developing the justification for the decision, the opinion writer generally employs one of the following major jurisprudential concepts as justification: (1) the original intent of the framers, (2) the adaption of the constitutional premises to contemporary problems, and (3) the meaning of the Constitution's words.

Original Intent of the Framers

An opinion writer can justify a decision by indicating that the judgment is in line with the intent of the framers. Inherent in this mode of legal reasoning is the notion that contemporary constitutional interpretation should faithfully reflect the original values and perceptions of the men who wrote the Constitution, or the Civil War amendments, and so on.

Former attorney general Edwin Meese called for such behavior by the justices. The Supreme Court's adjudicatory task, he said, is to "resurrect the original meaning of constitutional provisions . . . as the only reliable guide to judgment. . . . The Court must adopt a jurisprudence seriously aimed at the explication of original intention which would produce defensible principles of government that would not be tainted by ideological predilection."[45]

For the conservative Meese, a close friend and advisor to President Ronald Reagan, contemporary decisions of the Supreme Court were really, in his words, "policy choices" rather than "articulations of constitutional principle."[46] Federal judges, especially the justices of the U.S. Supreme Court, should "judge policies in light of principles, rather than remold principles in light of policy."[47]

This conservative approach to constitutional interpretation, when used as justification by an opinion writer on the Court, clearly calls for the Court majority to practice a narrow, ideological form of judicial self-restraint. Under "original intent," the majority's hands are figuratively tied in the decisional process because of the ongoing strength and continued vitality of the values of the men who wrote the Constitution and its amendments. The decision we reach today is premised on our understanding of how the 1789 writers viewed congressional power or executive privilege or due process of law.

Meese, of course, assumed that these values were indeed shared by the Founders and that they can be readily observed and drawn on for jurisprudential sustenance. It is clear, from his critical comments about the contemporary Court, that his call for a jurisprudence based on original intent is, at base, a criticism of federal judges interpreting the constitutional phrases in creative ways to address contemporary societal issues that were not foreseen in 1787.[48]

While some members of the contemporary Court, such as Justices Scalia and Rehnquist, have adopted the Meese conceptual framework when they engage in constitutional interpretation, others, such as Justice O'Connor, have adopted a narrower original-intent frame of reference. As O'Connor wrote in *Minneapolis Star and Tribune v. Minnesota Commissioner of Revenue,* "In general . . . we have only limited evidence of exactly how the Framers intended the First Amendment to apply. . . . Consequently, we ordinarily simply apply [that] general principle. . . . *But when we do have evidence that a particular law would have offended the Framers, we have not hesitated to invalidate it on that ground alone*" (emphasis added).[49] Her last sentence, summarizes precisely the essence of the original-intent value employed by some federal judges when justifying decisions reached by a Court majority.

The Constitution as Living Document

For many jurists and legal scholars, the intent-of-the-framers justification for a decision of the Court has been very dissatisfactory. A number of justices, especially Justices William Brennan and

Thurgood Marshall, have presented an alternative methodology when writing a decision in a constitutional case. They crafted and then implemented an evolutionary mode of constitutional interpretation. In Brennan's words, in direct response to Meese, the "genius of the Constitution rests not in any static meaning it might have had in a world that is dead and gone, but in the adaptability of its great principles to cope with current problems and current needs."[50]

For an opinion writer using this set of values, the Constitution must evolve and has evolved over the generations by judges interpreting its general guidelines. While admitting that some problems are always with a democratic political community, the opinion writer also argues that the society must cope with problems and dangers not acknowledged or reckoned with by eighteenth-century politicians. One way to deal with these new dangers is for the Court, through cases and controversies, to address and try to resolve them through constitutional interpretation for the national community.

"Judges," wrote another former federal court of appeals judge, Irving R. Kaufman, "are constantly required to resolve questions that 18th century statesmen, no matter how prescient, simply could not or did not forsee and resolve."[51] For these noninterpretivist jurists, "the Constitution's primary purpose was to restrain government from acting in ways that would violate individual and group freedoms. Restraint of freedom takes on many twentieth century guises that the 'founders' never understood."[52] Judges such as Brennan, Marshall, Kaufman, and others, including Justice Ruth Bader Ginsburg, while respecting the output of the men who attended the 1787 constitutional convention and drafted the document, do not, however, look on them as "oracular guides" and continuously examine and give meaning to the "majestic generalities"[53] of the Constitution. As Justice Brennan wrote, in dissent in a 1983 establishment case involving the constitutionality of prayers in a legislature,

> The Constitution is not a static document whose meaning on every detail is fixed for all time by the life experience of the Framers. . . . To be truly faithful to the Framers, our use of the history of their time must limit itself to broad purposes, not specific practices. . . . Indeed, a proper respect for the Framers themselves forbids us to give so static and lifeless a meaning to their work. To my mind, the Court's focus here on a narrow piece of history is, in a fundamental sense, a betrayal of the lessons of history.[54]

The "Plain Meaning" of the Words   A justice writing for the majority uses this form of jurisprudential explanation to link the decision to the original meaning of the constitutional *language* itself, rather than trying to find out just what the delegates meant when they coined a constitutional phrase. "Like original intent, this mode emphasizes that decisions are based on continuity with the past."[55] And, like the intent-of-the-framers argument, this mode suggests that the writer and the majority are constrained and restrained in their decision making by the language of the past.

Statutory Construction   Many cases heard by the Court call for the justices to decide the case by examining statutes or regulations written by legislators and executive-department bureaucrats and that have been challenged as being unconstitutional. If such a judgment is made by the Court majority in conference, then the opinion writer's task is to determine what the writers of the challenged legislation meant and whether or not the statute or regulation, as written or as implemented, is valid. That, of course, is the difficulty the Court faces in statutory construction. In addition to the general interpretational problems associated with defining the community's language, "lawmakers often find it difficult to convey their exact purpose in clear and plain language."[56] Legislation is very often vague, containing language that is unclear and very ambiguous due to compromises struck during the legislative process. Again and again, in such cases, the Court has to try to define *exactly* what the body who wrote the legislation or the regulation meant. This has to be done tactfully, for the Court is not the sole nor the initial interpreter of the language of the Constitution.

Another such case occurred when Congress, facing a civil rights crisis in the nation, passed the 1964 Civil Rights Act based on the Congress's power to regulate commerce as found in Article I, Section 8.[57] The central question that the Court then had to grapple with was whether Congress had exceeded its grant of power to regulate commerce by applying it to rectify segregation in public facilities.

For instance, Congress, in 1910, passed the Mann Act, to put a halt to the "white slave trade," making it a crime to transport women across state lines "for the purpose of prostitution, or debauchery, or for any other immoral purpose." But just what was Congress's intent regarding the meaning and scope of "debauchery"? The Court, as in a number of cases, was asked, in effect, to clarify the language used by Congress.[58]

The writer of the opinion can use a number of strategies to address statutory or regulatory matters. She can have the law clerks dig through the record to get to the congressional debates on the legislation or, alternatively, review committee reports prepared by legislative staff that provide background data for the legislation's rationale.

In addition to uncovering the legislative history of the statute or regulation, the opinion writer can try to define, through textual exegesis, the plain meaning of the words of the legislation. She must determine which of these modes best informs her and, through her, the Court majority,[59] and then use that device to justify the decision of the Court. Determining what the legislative intent was for a statute is often very difficult, but the Court must decide the controversy. Generally, the opinion writer has to go beyond the statutory language to glean the legislative intent, and that means trying to reconstruct the legislative history of the statute. However, searching for understanding through the discovery of legislative intent is fraught with uncertainty, given the nature of the legislative process.[60]

Chief Justice Warren Burger, writing for the Court in the case of *Tennessee Valley Authority v. Hill*,[61] underscored another point about the optimal quality of statutory construction by the Court.

> Our individual appraisal of the wisdom or unwisdom of a particular course consciously selected by Congress is to be put aside in the process of interpreting a statute. Once the meaning of an enactment is discerned and its constitutionality determined, the judicial process comes to an end. We do not sit as a committee of review, nor are we vested with the power of veto.

The Court majority's view is that if they misinterpret the congressional intent when they give meaning to the statutory language, there will be legislative rectification of judicial error. However, Congress often does not correct judicial misreading of legislation and of congressional intent.

Precedent as a Justification of the Decision of the Court
In both statutory-construction and constitutional-interpretation cases, the opinion writer will generally rely on precedent to buttress his justification for the decision of the Court majority. Precedent consists of a body of past written opinions of the Court that provide some form of guidance to a sitting justice when writing an opinion for the majority. Based on the Anglo-Saxon concept of *stare decisis*, "let the decision stand," an opinion writer will search the "black-letter law" to find an earlier case whose facts and law are similar to the facts and legal questions found in the case at hand.

In addition to examining the constitutional questions, the writer will reason by example by looking at past decisions of the Court to provide guidance to the contemporary Court. He will compare the fact-law situation in the present case with the fact-law situation in related constitutional conflicts decided earlier by the Court. When the similarities are noted and the "determination of similarity or difference is the function of each judge,"[62] then the earlier case will be used to justify the decision of the contemporary Court majority.

Of course, throughout American legal history, precedent has proven to be less than inviolate. While accepting the values of predictability and consistency inherent in the concept of precedent, Supreme Court majorities nevertheless regularly distinguish, modify, ignore, or overturn precedent.

THE NATURE OF AUTHORITY AND EVIDENCE IN LAW

As all first-year law students know, the law in America reflects both stability and change. It is, consequently, a dynamic entity because of this need to contain these two trends. The opinion writer of the Court is the fulcrum through which continuity and change occur at the highest level of judicial authority.

However, the reality of continuity and change in the same legal vessel means that there is, in America, the chronic problem of ambiguous authority. Statutes and regulations are not clearly written; a plethora of precedents enables judges to literally pick and choose their rationale. It is almost impossible to determine the original intent of the men who constitutionalized their values into the 1787 document, and, if that were not enough, the words of the Constitution are general ones, wide open to different judicial interpretations.

This problem is compounded by the presence on the highest Court of ideological fragmentation among the justices. The consequence for the legal community and for the society of this characteristic is clear: an increasing number of individualized opinions, concurring and dissenting, as well as an increase in the number of plurality opinions of the Court. Additionally, the consequences for society of these individualized opinions is greater uncertainty and ambiguous direction in the law.

Based on different perceptions of constitutional and statutory interpretation, the perception has developed that the fragmented Supreme Court is not nine small law firms but a smaller number of patterned voting blocs. Divided cases, plurality opinions, and *Bakke*-type decisions "tell us that judges are operating on different assumptions, that their inarticulate major premises are dissimilar, that their value systems are differently constructed and weighted, that their political, economic, and social views contrast in important respects."[63]

Voting blocs have emerged on the Court in recent decades because of this dissimilarity in values and in judicial role. The fundamental values a justice possesses, regardless of the state of their conceptual development, are "central to the explanation of judicial decision making."[64] The justices respond to the cert petitions because of their commitment to these values. And groups of justices share these values to the point that they act as a voting bloc on these issues.

Judicial blocs, that is, small subsets of justices who join together on decisions because of their shared outlook on particular values, do exist and function on the Court over a period of time. A bloc exists when there is *conscious* agreement as well as overt cooperation by the members of the group on at least one set of issues that confronts the Court, whether it is a social issue (abortion) or an economic one (plenary power of Congress in commercial regulation).[65]

AFTER CRAFTING THE OPINION: STRATEGIES AND TACTICS FOR HOLDING THE MAJORITY

It is clear that when writing opinions for the Court, the professional skills and work habits exhibited by justices such as Black and Harlan are critically important in the effort to mass and then to hold a Court majority. "If a Justice is able to mass legal precedents and history to bolster an intellectually and morally defensible policy and can present his arguments in a convincing manner," observed Walter Murphy, "he stands an excellent chance of picking up votes."[66] While all the justices are political appointees, nevertheless they are lawyers and respond to legalistic cues. "The real process of judicial policy-making is a very subtle business; . . . judges often think largely in traditional legal categories, though their behavior may actually be more accurately described under different concepts."[67]

Assuming there is the mastery of precedent and legal history, the task of the opinion writer is to employ certain tactics to marshal and to keep the Court majority. One consolation that assists the justice who has done her work well is the fact that, as Murphy suggests, "to a significant extent judges can and do weigh such factors as legal principles and precedents and well thought out ideas of proper public policy."[68] If there is intellectual honesty in the slip opinion, and if the opinion writer gracefully uses intellectual persuasion, then judges often do change their minds about specific cases. Reviewing the files of the Court's justices, invariably there is the note from one justice to another, indicating such change—and thanking the opinion writer for bringing it to the attention of the others. Tom Clark, for example, jotted a note to Hugo Black: "I'm sorry about the FHA case—I never studied the claim frankly—From what I've read of the brief since you called my attention to it, I believe you are right—I may change my vote tomorrow."[69]

Murphy has written that "all intra-Court bargaining takes place with the understanding that if the opinion writer ignores the suggestions that his colleagues scribble on slip opinions, he risks the disintegration of his majority."[70] The writer knows that receipt of the slip opinion is the initial occasion for the other justices to substantively examine the issues, the values, and the justification for the decision.

There are occasions when the readers of a slip opinion are very impressed with a unique premise put forward by the opinion writer. Commenting on Brennan's draft opinion concerning the constitutionality of a New York statute that prohibited the selling of pornographic magazines to minors while allowing the magazines to be sold to adults,[71] Justice White wrote Brennan:

> Perhaps you ride both horses in this case, that is, this junk is outside the First Amendment, but if it is not, it still may be kept from children because there is a sufficient reason to do so which overrides both the minor's right to read and the right of the publisher to disseminate. *This is admirable eclectisism if it gets four other guys.* In the end, I shall probably be one of them. . . . I am not moved to write separately, at least not for now. Good luck.[72]

What a rational, reasonable opinion writer tries to avoid is direct confrontation with colleagues. While conflict is ever present on the Court, it is generally limited to clashes that do not threaten the institution itself. When bright egoists come together there is the capacity for personalities to clash unless the jurists make efforts, continually, to minimize these negative interactions.

Given different ways of resolving cases and controversies, as expressed in the majority, concurring, and dissenting slip opinions that circulate, the opinion writer for the Court majority employs a number of short-term tactics to hold the majority and minimize conflict between the majority and the minority who dissent. The writer, in the slip opinion, in notes to particular brethren, and in MTTC's, tries to communicate reasons for his colleagues to join her.

In certain cases, the loyalty and patriotism of a justice will be targeted in the hope that there will be a change in the vote. During the Second World War, for example, Felix Frankfurter and Harlan Stone called on the patriotism of Frank Murphy and William O. Douglas to persuade them not to dissent in the Jananese exclusion cases.[73]

In this process of marshaling the Court majority, "bargaining is a simple fact of life."[74] As the *Bakke* case illustrated so well, the Court, even a very fragmented one, knows that it must come down with a decision, that it cannot walk away from the conflict. Given the reality that five justices must agree for there to be an "opinion" of the Supreme Court, "despite conflicting views on literary style, relevant precedents," and so on, the general "pattern is still one of negotiation and accommodation to secure consensus."[75] And in a closely divided, highly fragmented Court such as the one Lewis Powell was on from 1971 to 1987, a noncommitted jurist such as Powell can become a critically important fifth vote. In his last term on the Court, for example, Powell was the fifth, decisive vote in 71 percent (thirty-two of forty-five) of the Court's five to four opinions.

FLUIDITY OF CHOICE REVISITED: THE CASE OF THE 1963 EASTER SUNDAY MARCH BY THE SCLC

In the complex process of reaching closure, there is always some fluidity of choice on the part of the Court.[76] There are numerous occasions when a justice informs others that, after review and deliberation, he has changed his mind. Every justice has had occasion to move from one side of the case to the other, including

Justices Black and Harlan. A 1967 civil rights case, *Walker v. Birmingham*, is illustrative.

In this case, civil rights workers, including Martin Luther King, Jr., and other leaders of the Southern Christian Leadership Conference (SCLC), had been arrested for violating a local ordinance prohibiting them from marching without a permit in a 1963 Easter Sunday protest march in Birmingham, Alabama. A Birmingham ordinance stated that it was unlawful to hold or organize a parade or public demonstration unless a permit had been secured from the city commission. A written application had to be submitted by the organizers, after which the permit would be issued unless the commission determined that the public welfare, peace, safety, health, decency, good order, morals or convenience require that the permit be refused.

"Bull" Connor, the police commissioner, flatly rejected the request for a march permit. The civil rights protesters marched anyway and were arrested for parading without a permit, and the state court issued a temporary ex parte restraining order enjoining the protesters from all types of protest activities in Birmingham. After failing to set aside the temporary restraining order, the protesters marched again and were arrested for violating the temporary injunction. They were sentenced to five days in jail and a fifty-dollar fine for contempt of the court.

On appeal to the Supreme Court, the petitioners argued that the restraining order was overly broad and vague, denying them their First Amendment right to protest against segregation. They argued that, because the issuance of the injunction was invalid, they could not be punished for disobeying it.

The Court heard oral argument during the week of March 13, 1967, and, at the Friday, March 17, conference session, voted five to four to reverse the convictions. The five who voted for reversal (or to vacate) were Justices Fortas, Brennan, Douglas, Chief Justice Warren, and, surprisingly, Justice Harlan. Warren told the group that he felt that the ordinance was "void on its face since it gives unfettered discretion to control First Amendment rights without standards. The injunction was simply a copy of the ordinance and [he] didn't think [the city] can bootstrap it by putting it in the form of an injunction."[77] Justice Harlan was more circumspect in the conference. He thought that the petititoners "should have had an opportunity to prove discriminatory application and [he] would vacate for a hearing on the merits."

Those who voted to affirm the convictions were Justices White, Black, Stewart, and Clark. Justice Clark summed up the position of the minority: "There was an outright violation of the injunction [by the black protesters]."

Over the weekend, however, Harlan, who had called for a vacating of the convictions, had second thoughts. On Monday morning, March 20, he sent the following brief MTTC (see Figure 9.1):

> I should like to ask that this case be listed for further discussion at next Friday's conference. I am not at rest with my vote and wish to give the matter more study before the case is assigned on the basis of the present vote, five to four to reverse or vacate, my vote being in the majority.[78]

At the March 24, 1967, conference session, Harlan did indeed switch his vote, and the convictions were *upheld* by the five to four vote. As Black once said, votes at conference "are never final. They are tentative and I am always ready to

Supreme Court of the United States
Washington, D. C. 20543

March 20, 1967

Re: No. 249 – Walker v. City of Birmingham

Dear Chief:
    I should like to ask that this case be listed for further discussion at next Friday's Conference. I am not at rest on my vote and wish to give the matter more study before the case is assigned on the basis of the present vote, five to four to reverse or vacate, my vote being in the majority.

                                                    Sincerely,

                                                    J. M. H.

cc: The Conference

FIGURE 9.1
Associate Justice John M. Harlan II's
MTTC to Chief Justice Earl Warren,

change the vote if I reach the conclusion that my vote was wrong."[79] The decision, written by Potter Stewart that Harlan joined, upheld a rule that "a court order must be obeyed until it is set aside, and that persons subject to the order who disobey it may not defend against the ensuing charge of criminal contempt on the ground that the order was erroneous or even unconstitutional." Because Walker, King, and others did not make an effort to dissolve the injunction or to comply with the local permit ordinance, their claim was not considered by the five-person majority. "Respect for judicial process is a small price to pay for the civilizing hand of law, which alone can give abiding meaning to constitutional freedom."[80]

    The majority turned into four dissenters, who produced three separate dissents in *Walker*. Fortas wrote a memo to two of the dissenting opinion writers, Douglas and Brennan (Chief Justice Warren wrote the third dissent), indicating that "it is seldom in this life that a person gets two for the price of one. Here I have the opportunity, which I hereby seize, to join each of you in his magnificent dissent."[81] Douglas's dissent stated that the "right to defy an unconstitutional statute is basic in our scheme. Even when an ordinance requires a permit to make a speech, to deliver a sermon, to parade or to assemble, it need not be honored when it is invalid on its face."

SUMMARY

An opinion of the Court announces the decision of the Court in the particular case or controversy. The decision of the Court is a policy choice made in a very legalistic context.[82] While your colleagues are political actors and interact in predictable ways in their highly unusual small-group setting, they rationally cannot avoid the language and the logic of legal analysis as they go about their business of adjudication. However political they may be, you and your colleagues are bound by canons of constitutional and statutory interpretation and by the principle of *stare decisis*. However ideological the majority might be, they cannot abuse the legal and legislative facts in a dispute they decide to resolve. However partisan your colleagues might be, the Court majority cannot, without adverse responses from society, treat the explanation/justification for their decision lightly.

In resolving societal conflicts, individually and collectively, you, and your decisions, are affected by the dominant values of the Court's majority; the level of conflict on the Court that, if too high, creates an intolerable work environment; the development of the law applicable in the argued cases; and the nature of the social, political, economic, ethical, and legal environment external to the Court.

Pulling a court majority together by you, as opinion writer, means that you accommodate the others and bring them together to agree on the justification for the decision. As noted, opinion writing is a craft in which, optimally, the justice writing "marshals facts and precedents, . . . and the broad policy implications of the decision in contemporary society so that the result is seen as fair, expectable, and perhaps even inevitable."[83] Although there are differences in interpreting the Constitution, statutes, and precedent, and although there is a great deal of fragmentation on the Court, there is the constant effort to reach consensus on cases and controversies heard by the Court. You have an understanding of how complex and difficult it is for an appellate judge to craft an opinion for the majority. The next chapter addresses the ways in which you *evaluate* the output of the appellate process.

NOTES

[1]Justice William J. Brennan, Jr., interview with authors, Washington, DC, Oct. 29, 1986.

[2]Ibid.

[3]Justice Lewis Powell, interview with authors, Washington, DC, Nov. 18, 1987.

[4]See Coffin, *Ways of a Judge.*

[5]Justice Byron White, interview with authors, Washington, DC, Nov. 18, 1986.

[6]Justice Lewis Powell, interview with authors, Washington, DC, Nov. 18, 1987.

[7]O'Brien, *Storm Center*, p. 294.

[8]William H. Rehnquist, *The Supreme Court: How It Was, How It Is* (New York: Morrow, 1987), p. 295.

[9]Richard A. Wasserstrom, *The Judicial Decision* (Stanford, CA: Stanford University Press), 1961.

[10]For example, in the 1944 white primary case, *Smith v. Allright*, 321 U.S. 649, Frankfurter was given the assignment to write for the majority by Stone, but within days it was reassigned to Stanley Reed. Stone took the advice of Justice Jackson, who argued that, given Frankfurter's background (a Jewish immigrant from Massachusetts), the opinion would not be tolerable to many who would be adversely affected by the judgment of the Court. Reed, a Protestant from Kentucky, wrote the opinion for the majority.

[11]O'Brien, *Storm Center*, p. 314.

[12]Quoted in Walter F. Murphy, James Fleming, and William F. Harris, *American Constitutional Interpretation* (Mineola, NY: Foundation Press, 1986), p. 60.

[13]See J. W. Howard, "On the Fluidity of Judicial Choice."

[14]John M. Harlan, II, "A Glimpse of the Supreme Court at Work," *University of Chicago Law School Record* 11 (1963): 1, 7.

[15]Baum, *Supreme Court*, pp. 104ff.

[16]Joan Biskupic, "A Human Touch, a Judicial Restraint," *Washington Post National Edition*, Aug. 2–8, 1993, p. 8.

[17]Quoted in Ibid.

[18]Quoted in Ibid., p. 10.

[19]Harlan, "Glimpse of the Supreme Court," 8.

[20]Justice William J. Brennan, Jr., interview with author, Washington, DC, Oct. 1986.

[21]Harlan's clerk, quoted in Tinsley Yarbrough, *John M. Harlan* (New York: Oxford University Press, 1993) pp. 63ff.

[22]For a discussion of these facets of Court activity, see Baum, *Supreme Court*; and O'Brien, *Storm Center*.

[23]See *Herbert Aptheker v. Secretary of State* 378 U.S. 500 (1964).

[24]See *Griswold v. Connecticut* 381 U.S. 479 (1965).

[25]See *Roe v. Wade* 410 U.S. 113 (1973).

[26]See *Goldwater v. Carter* 444 U.S. 996 (1979).

[27]Ibid.

[28]See, for example, the impact of Justices Black, Douglas, and Brennan, and Chief Justice Warren on the national community's values as recounted in Ball and Cooper, *Of Power and Right*.

[29]See William D. Pederson and Norman W. Provizer, *Great Justices of the U.S. Supreme Court: Ratings and Case Studies* (New York: Lang, 1994).

[30]Bruce Allan Murphy, *Abe Fortas: The Rise and Ruin of a Supreme Court Justice* (New York: Morrow, 1988), p. 219.

[31]Quoted in Biskupic, "Human Touch," 8.

[32]Baum, *Supreme Court*, p. 104.

[33]Quoted in O'Brien, *Storm Center*, p. 319.

[34]Quoted in John Jenkins, "A Candid Talk with Justice Blackmun," *New York Times Sunday Magazine*, Feb. 20, 1983, p. 38.

[35]Daniel J. Meador, "Justice Black and His Law Clerks," *Alabama Law Review* 35 (1963): 60.

[36]Ibid., 59, 60.

[37]Ibid., 60.

[38]Justice William J. Brennan, Jr., interview with authors, Washington, DC, Oct. 29, 1986.

[39]Meador, "Justice Black and His Clerks," p. 23ff.

[40]See T. R. van Geel, *Understanding Supreme Court Opinions* (New York: Longman, 1991), p. 47ff.

[41]Ibid., p. 47.

[42]See, H.L.A. Hart, *The Concept of Law* (London: Clarendon Press), 1961.

[43]William C. Louthan, *The United States Supreme Court: Lawmaking in the Third Branch of Government* (Englewood Cliffs, NJ: Prentice Hall, 1991), p. 126.

[44]van Geel, *Understanding Supreme Court Opinions*, p. 9.

[45]Edwin Meese III, "The Attorney General's View of the Supreme Court: Toward a Jurisprudence of Original Intent," *Public Administration Review* 45 (1985): 701–4.

[46]Ibid., 704.

[47]Ibid.

[48]See Howard Ball, "The Convergence of Constitutional Law and Politics in the Reagan Administration: The Exhumation of the 'Jurisprudence of Original Intention' Doctrine," *Cumberland Law Review* 17, no. 3 (1986–87): 877–90.

[49]*Minnesota Star and Tribune v. Minnesota Commissioner of Internal Revenue*, 460 U.S. 575 (1983).

[50]William J. Brennan Jr., Address given at Georgetown University, Washington, DC, Oct. 12, 1985 (reprinted in *The New York Times*, Oct. 13, 1985, sec. A).

[51]Irving R. Kaufman, "What the Founding Fathers Intended," *New York Times Sunday Magazine*, Feb. 23, 1986, p. 59.

[52]Ball, "Constitutional Law and Politics," 884.

[53]David A. Shaman, "The Constitution, The Supreme Court, and Creativity," 9 *Hastings Constitutional Law Quarterly*, (1982), p. 261.

[54]Brennan, dissenting, *Marsh v. Chambers*, 463 U.S. 783 (1983).

[55]Louthan, *United States Supreme Court*, p. 128.

[56]Walter F. Murphy and C. Herman Pritchett, *Courts, Judges, and Politics: An Introduction to the Legal Process*, 4th ed., (New York: Random House, 1986), p. 433.

[57]See *Heart of Atlanta v. United States;* and *Katzenbach v. McClung*, 379 U.S. 294 (1964).

[58]*Mortensen v. United States*, 322 U.S. 369 (1944).

[59]Justice Potter Stewart, interview with author, Washington, DC, Mar. 2, 1976.

[60]See Kathanne W. Greene, *Affirmative Action and Principles of Justice* (Westport, CT: Greenwood Press, 1989), pp. 166–67.

[61]437 U.S. 153 (1978).

[62]Edward H. Levi, *An Introduction to Legal Reasoning* (Chicago: University of Chicago Press, 1960), p. 3.

[63]Sheldon Goldman and Charles M. Lamb, *Judicial Conflict and Consensus* (Lexington: University Press of Kentucky, 1986), p. 7.

[64]Walter F. Murphy, *Elements of Judicial Strategy* (Chicago: University of Chicago Press, 1960), p. 59.

[65]Ibid., p. 78.

[66]Ibid., p. 45.

[67]Ibid., p. 44.

[68]Ibid., pp. 43–44.

[69]Tom C. Clark to Hugo Black, box 58, HLBP, LC, Washington, DC.

[70]Murphy, *Elements of Judicial Stragegy*, p. 59.

[71]*Ginsberg v. New York*, 1968.

[72]Byron White to William J. Brennan, Mar. 4, 1968, box 169, WJBP, LC, Washington, DC.

[73]See Howard Ball, "Politics over Law in Wartime: The Japanese Exclusion Cases," *Harvard Civil Rights Civil Liberties Law Review* 19, no. 2 (Summer 1984), for an analysis of the Court's deliberations in *Hirabayashi, Korematsu,* and *Endo.*

[74]Murphy, *Elements of Judicial Strategy*, p. 57.

[75]Ibid.

[76]See H. Woodford Howard, "On the Fluidity of Judicial Choice," *American Political Science Review.*

[77]Conference Notes, William J. Brennan, Jr., box 229, WJBP, LC, Washington, DC.

[78]John M. Harlan II, MTTC, *Walker v. Birmingham*, Mar. 20, 1967, box 229, WJBP, LC, Washington, DC.

[79]Hugo Black to Howard Ball, Jan. 21, 1969.

[80]*Walker v. Birmingham*, 388 U.S. 307 (1967).

[81]Abe Fortas to William O. Douglas and William J. Brennan, June 7, 1967, WODP, LC, Washington, DC.

[82]Baum, *Supreme Court*, p. 111.

[83]Coffin, *Ways of a Judge*, p. 197.

To Judge a Justice: Statesmanship and Craftsmanship

It was a lovely party, though not as much of a surprise as some of your friends had hoped. Everyone had turned out for a celebration of your first ten years on the Court. Almost all of your clerks (past and present) and staff had come. There were friends from around Washington and even a few who flew in for the occasion. There were more bad jokes than anyone should have to endure, and the food was not fantastic. Still, it wasn't all bad to have an evening with friends and admirers who said so many wonderful things.

The tradition of celebrating anniversaries on the bench is an old one. There is the well-known story of the time that Justice William O. Douglas was feted at one of Washington's most exclusive clubs. President John F. Kennedy dropped by and had the temerity to order a beer. He was promptly informed that the club did not stock such pedestrian swill. Even so, a good time was had by all. It's sometimes difficult to know exactly how these traditions came about, but it might very well be partly because people who know what the job is like realize how helpful it is to receive some support and praise for one's effort.

Still, in the quiet after the party, the thought does arise, how will you be judged as a justice? When the surveys of scholars and lawyers are taken, will you be called great, near-great (whatever that means!), mediocre, or worse?[1] Oh, you have had your fair share—maybe even a little more—of criticism in the press. On the other hand, the law review articles analyzing your opinions have been, on the whole, positive. Of course, there has been the inevitable blizzard of nasty anonymous letters following some of the religion cases and a few of the sexually oriented material decisions. But how will history judge you? And what are the criteria to be used for that purpose?

In a sense, it seems embarrassing and foolish to think about such things. The score tallied from the historical scorecard for public figures changes over time, and the hero of one decade is often the goat of the next. Perhaps Voltaire was right; maybe history is a pack of tricks we play on the dead.[2]

Still, it is true that there is a common recognition that some justices were especially outstanding and that others were not particularly successful. Some, like Felix Frankfurter, who were celebrated at one time, fade as more is understood about their careers. Others, like Chief Justice John Marshall, Oliver Wendell Holmes, Jr., and Hugo Black, are generally regarded as great, notwithstanding their sometimes enigmatic characteristics. As John Frank, a former Black clerk, friend, and biographer, once put it:

> Probably every Supreme Court historian considers Hugo Black one of the ten great Justices in American history. There may be marginal differences as to the other nine. Marshall, Taney, Hughes, Miller, Field, should be, I suppose, on all lists, and from this century, Holmes and Brandeis, to name only those not sitting. After these archangels of the law, the lists begin to vary, and it is not important to argue about one as against another. The point is simply that Black belongs with the giants. The question is why? The answer is partly a matter of results and partly a matter of method.[3]

Why indeed? After all, it is relatively easy to speak of those who are generally regarded as among the worst of the justices, people like James C. McReynolds and Charles Whittaker or, in the competition for worst chief justice, Edward D. White or Fred Vinson. Then there are some who are regarded as near-great, like Douglas. But why is Black considered great, while his nemesis, Felix Frankfurter, counted as one of the greats in a 1970 survey, is currrently not, even though the feisty Felix still has many champions in the legal and academic communities? For most justices, as for Black, greatness seems to be a combination of the person and the professional legacy. To Frank, the legacy is evaluated in terms of the results and the method.

JUDGING JUSTICE WILLIAM J. BRENNAN

A figure to whom we have seen such judgments applied is Justice William J. Brennan, Jr. In some respects, Brennan is a more enigmatic figure than Hugo Black. His was not a name that was widely recognized by those beyond regular followers of the Court. Few people lined up to be Brennan people the way those who celebrated Black, Felix Frankfurter, William O. Douglas, and others promoted their justice's greatness. However, the more that serious students of the Court have studied the records, the more obvious it has become that Justice Brennan was a central force in the life of the Court during the years in which he served.

Associate Justice William J.
Brennan, Jr.

Despite the fact that few knowledgeable observers of politics can name a string of landmark opinions with his name attached, Brennan had a profound impact on the shaping of the law and American life as we know it today. Even a judge as completely opposite from Brennan as Robert Bork was willing to acknowledge Brennan as "the most powerful justice of this century."[4] Two commentators in the conservative *National Review* wrote:

> There is no individual in this country, on or off the Court, who has had a more profound and sustained impact upon public policy in the United States for the past 27 years. . . . Although Warren's influence on the Court can hardly be questioned, close analysis of Brennan's role indicates that he was the one responsible for making the Warren Court what it became.[5]

Mark Tushnet went so far as to say, "From his appointment on, he was the Court's central figure."[6] Tushnet joined several other legal scholars, like Paul Gewitz, who have said that "people call it the Warren Court, but in many ways it was the Brennan Court."[7] Professor Leon Friedman added, "Warren may have been the conscience and the spirit but Brennan was really the brains and the presence behind the Warren Court's initiatives."[8] Professor Gerald Gunther summarized Brennan's career by observing: "He simply is one of the most important figures of the latter half of the 20th century."[9] A *Congressional Quarterly* summary of his career observed, "For Congress, Brennan's mark was neither all positive nor all negative, just ringing and powerful."[10]

Was he all these things? If so, why? But even if he was "powerful," is that a measure of greatness? Should it be? Or, as conservative Supreme Court observer and Felix Frankfurter supporter Wallace Mendelson put it: "If a great man is one who leaves his mark upon the social order, Brennan . . . is a very great man indeed. But was he a great judge?"[11]

The answer to the inquiry about Brennan's stature is not manifest only, or even primarily, in his own opinions, though he wrote many very important opinions—some twelve hundred in his thirty-four years on the High Court, but in the way he enabled others charged with writing an opinion for the Court to bring a majority together or hold it together around critical judgments, and in the way he led so much of the discussion within the Court on the issues that served as the cornerstones of major Supreme Court pronouncements. It is also present in the way he affected the institution itself as well as the law it produced. Consider Justice Brennan, the man and the legacy.

State Courts and State Politics: Political Roots and Legal Development

Brennan is originally from New Jersey. His father, an Irish immigrant, started by stoking boilers at the Ballentine brewery in Newark but moved on to political involvement as a labor union activist. In that role, the elder Brennan and his colleagues came to understand the importance of political action in support of their goals. Justice Brennan told the following story:

> They were up against a company owned by a family that you might say had a monopoly on the whole state. It was like a company state. . . . When the transit workers struck, the Newark police were on the side of the employers. My father came up with the idea "My God, the only way we're going to be able to do anything about this is for labor to take over the city government." He sponsored a movement that resulted in the abolition of the mayor-and-alderman form of city government and replaced it with five commissioners, each of whom was assigned to supervise a department. In the 1917 election, my father ran as a labor candidate with the prospect that if he won he'd be named the Director of Public Safety. That way, he'd have control of the Police and Fire Departments, so there'd be no more strikebreaking.[12]

His father remained an honest and politically astute public servant for the rest of his life.

Watching the struggle for dignity and a decent standard of living in those early years helped to form the approach Brennan would later take on the bench. As he put it, "What got me interested in people's rights and liberties was the kind of family and the kind of neighborhood I was brought up in. I saw all kinds of suffering—people had to struggle."[13]

Brennan worked hard in high school and went on to complete an economics degree with honors at the prestigious Wharton School of the University of Pennsylvania. After that, he attended Harvard Law School, where he finished in the top 10 percent of his class. It is not surprising to learn that he was also president of the student legal aid society. An interesting anecdote about his education is that one of his professors in law school was none other than Felix Frankfurter, with whom he later served on the Court. Frankfurter has been quoted many times with respect to this relationship. "I always encouraged my students to think for themselves, but Brennan goes too far,"[14] a reference to the fact that when the discussion moved around the table from Frankfurter to Brennan, the student was often on the other side of the case from the professor.

As a labor lawyer, a partner in the firm of Pitney, Hardin, and Skinner, Brennan developed an interest in judicial administration and joined with other New Jersey lawyers urging reform of the state's trial court structure. The result was the creation of the New Jersey Superior Court. Governor Alfred Driscoll promptly appointed Brennan to a seat on that bench. Brennan developed his budding interest in judicial administration there and was elevated to the Appellate Division, where he continued the administrative activities that were so rapidly bringing him a reputation for innovation. Chief Justice Arthur Vanderbilt of the New Jersey Supreme Court was another advocate for reform of judicial administration. He was impressed by Brennan's efforts and in 1952 recommended him for elevation to the state's highest court.

In fact, it was Brennan's continuing efforts regarding judicial administration that took him to the U.S. Supreme Court five years later. Vanderbilt had been scheduled to deliver an address in May of 1956 at a conference convened by Attorney General Herbert Brownell on administration of justice. Vanderbilt fell ill, and Brennan agreed to deliver the speech for him. After perusing the Vanderbilt manuscript briefly, Brennan decided to deliver his own address, without a prepared text. His speech was warmly received. In particular, his comments impressed Attorney General Brownell—so much so that when Justice Sherman Minton retired five months later, Brownell quickly recommended Brennan for the position. When President Dwight Eisenhower agreed and Brennan was contacted, the president's press secretary was heard to say, "I never heard a man say yes so fast."[15]

There were other reasons why Brennan was an opportune choice for the time. It was an election year, and the Eisenhower forces were concerned about attempting to carry eastern Catholics, if possible, in the upcoming vote. Naming Brennan permitted Eisenhower to claim nonpartisanship and, unusual for a Republican in those days, boast an Irish Catholic from New Jersey among his key appointments. Besides, Eisenhower thought he had found a person who was all those things and also sufficiently conservative for his tastes. When Eisenhower was asked whether Brennan really had the right politics, he replied that the New Jersey justice's speech in May certainly suggested he was right. The president did not know, of course, that he was referring to the text written by Vanderbilt, not the speech that Brennan actually delivered.

Eisenhower's people might have known something more of their new justice had they considered his public speeches attacking Senator Joseph McCarthy and defending freedom of speech against "witch hunts." Although McCarthy, the "disgusting little tyrant" as Brennan called him, was permitted to sit with the Judiciary Committee and grill Brennan for a day during the confirmation hearings, only McCarthy voted against Brennan when the nomination reached the floor.

Still, the president thought he had an Irish, Catholic, Democrat, son of an immigrant who was really more like other Republicans. He later acknowledged his error in his now-famous answer to a reporter's question. Asked whether he had made any serious mistakes while president, Eisenhower answered, "Yes, two, and they are both sitting on the Supreme Court."[16] He was referring, of course, to Chief Justice Earl Warren and Associate Justice William Brennan.

Court Maker: At the Core of the Warren Court

While Eisenhower thought he erred because Brennan turned out to vote in ways that the president and other Republicans considered excessively liberal, most Supreme Court observers disagree with Ike's judgment of the quality of his appointment. It might have upset Eisenhower and friends even more had they known what a central role Brennan was to play in molding the Court as a group. Indeed, some regard Brennan's role as a Warren Court player, a majority builder, and, ultimately, as leader of the loyal opposition during his later years on the Court as his most important contributions.

The Matter of Influence   Bernard Schwartz and others have described the Warren Court as one grounded on the solid core of "BBD&W."[17] Black, Brennan, Douglas, and Warren were indeed in accord on a wide range of important cases that we now identify with the Warren Court. In such areas as school desegregation, the Court issued a surprising number of unanimous opinions over a prolonged period of time. However, it would be a mistake to think of the first decade or so of Brennan's tenure on the Court as a period of stable, predictable majorities, particularly if we look beyond the outcome of cases at the array of differing opinions expressed by members of the Court even when they agreed with the ultimate disposition of a case. From the unpublished opinions and memoranda exchanged among the members of the Court, the range and intensity of the differences and varying perspectives become clear.[18] Some of the justices, like Abe Fortas and Hugo Black, had sharp conflicts in a number of fields. Even Black and William O. Douglas, thought by many people to be the two closest members of that Court, had many differences, some of them quite serious.[19]

If it is true that there were significant legal and interpersonal differences, how did the Court manage to build so many important opinions and appear to many Americans to be a relatively cohesive body of men at the same time? It is increasingly clear to scholars studying the period that one of the answers is Justice William Brennan.

Carpentering Majorities   Justice Brennan demonstrated not merely an ability to build critical majorities in difficult cases during the Warren Court years but to play a major role during the Burger Court period as well, even though he was essentially the leader of the loyal opposition in his later years on the bench.

When asked how he worked with various members of the Court to achieve consensus, Brennan answered, "It depends on what I'm after."[20] He explained that each person had a preferred way of interacting with colleagues. In the case of Black, Brennan reported that the two would meet in his chambers, argue vigorously, and then dictate some language. Then they would go to Black's chambers and repeat the process, revising the material they had previously developed. On the other hand, Douglas adopted more of a "take it or leave" approach, asking what Brennan thought and then responding one way or the other, often without much give or take. That knowledge of just what approach worked best with each member of the Court, coupled with flexibility on doctrinal positions, though not on fundamental principles, and a highly developed sense of the long-term implications of the Court's actions, allowed Brennan to build a base for influence.

On the other hand, Brennan recognized that most of what the justices do is participate in direct and relatively formal exchanges of memoranda and draft opinions. The memoranda exchange was not some sophisticated political manipulation of colleagues but, instead, these notes reflected, for the most part, a justice's sensitivity to the concerns of others, an ability to craft opinions and offer suggestions in ways that would make accommodation possible without sacrificing core principles.

It would, however, be wrong to paint Brennan simply as a compromiser. He was adamant on many key principles, and he drafted any number of strong, forthright declarations in matters of constitutional rights and liberties. Brennan led the Court in some of the toughest fights against the Communist witch hunt, writing in ringing tones about the need to protect freedoms of speech and association and working to block efforts to purge public employees on bogus allegations of subversion.[21] He fought vigorously to protect freedom of the press, condemning the use of libel laws to frighten newspapers into silence.[22] It was Brennan who wrote the opinion, later signed by all of the justices, in the Little Rock school desegregation case, warning that the rights of the African-American children involved would not be sacrificed to the threats of state officials or be thwarted by political artifice.[23] And after another decade had passed without effective action to truly implement the *Brown v. Board of Education* decision requiring desegregation, it was Brennan who penned the opinion for a unanimous Court in *Green v. County School Board of New Kent County*, which admonished the states that "the burden on a school board today is to come forward with a plan that promises realistically to work, and promises realistically to work now."[24]

Because of his skill and alertness, Brennan was able to bring together majorities in critical cases like *Baker v. Carr*, which opened the door to federal judicial consideration of apportionment cases and paved the way for the one-person, one-vote standard that has reshaped the face of every state legislature as well as the Congress. Chief Justice Warren considered that ruling one of the two most important decisions handed down while he served on the Court.[25]

Brennan's importance was not limited to his craftsmanship of majority rulings, however. During the Warren years, he was the chief's closest advisor, often meeting with Warren before conferences. In the later years of his tenure on the Court, Brennan was even known to convene a rump conference session when negotiations bogged down over the historic Watergate tapes case.[26]

Another of Brennan's increasingly well known successes was his ability to assist others in constructing opinions that could command majorities but simultaneously move effectively in the direction of serving the principles Brennan thought most important. One of the best examples arose in connection with development of the *Griswold v. Connecticut* opinion, which, for the first time, announced a constitutionally protected right to privacy.[27] When Justice Douglas prepared his first draft of the *Griswold* opinion, it was a brief commentary based on the right to freedom of association, which the Court had concluded in 1958 was implied by the First Amendment.[28] He reasoned that any freedom of association must surely apply to the marital relationship, the most basic association of all. And, if it was necessary to protect privacy in associations, then surely the right of a married couple to determine whether to use contraceptives must be included in that protection. Brennan wrote Douglas and convinced him that his approach was too narrow and that a stronger statement of the right to privacy was necessary, along the lines that Douglas had advocated in some of his public speeches and writings. Douglas cut his original opinion and placed the suggestions made by Brennan in the middle; thus was born the broad statement of the right to privacy that has been so important ever since. A few years later, Justice Brennan would use that strong concept of a right to privacy, along with the equal-protection clause of the Fourteenth Amendment, to apply protections to unmarried persons wishing counsel regarding contraceptives.[29]

Leading the Loyal Opposition: The Burger and Rehnquist Courts

While it is true that Brennan's position on the Court changed during the Burger and Rehnquist Court years, as more justices were added by presidents bent on appointing people who seemed as nearly opposite to their Warren-era predecessors as possible, it would be a mistake to suppose that he lost the ability to influence his colleagues or build important decisions. Indeed, from 1980 to 1990, his last decade on the Court, he authored 174 opinions for the Court. In fact, in his last year on the Court, Brennan was able to "get a Court," as the expression goes, behind his opinions upholding federal minority preferences in the granting of broadcast licenses,[30] striking down patronage constraints on lower-level public employees,[31] and prohibiting efforts to block symbolic speech that involved the use or destruction of the American flag.[32]

Neither would it be correct to assume that he could carpenter a majority because these cases just happened to present matters on which there was strong consensus within the Court. He remained able during the Burger and Rehnquist years to pull majorities, or at least pluralities, together in some of the most hotly contested and divisive cases, such as a number of important decisions in the area of affirmative action.[33] In 1973, the Court announced its ruling in *San Antonio Independent School District v. Rodriguez*,[34] which marked a turning point toward deference to local control of schools and away from the *Brown v. Board* view that

Chief Justice Warren E. Burger.

Chief Justice William Rehnquist.

where the state has undertaken to provide education, it "is a right which must be made available to all on equal terms." *San Antonio* concluded that education is not a right.[35] Even so, in that same year, Brennan led the Court in the first opinion applying the *Brown* and subsequent desegregation rulings to northern school districts.[36] In fact, in 1982, Brennan was able to lead his colleagues to a decision that Texas could not deny educational opportunity to the children of illegal immigrants.[37] Despite the fact that he lost more often than he won in the areas of freedom of speech and press in the later years, he was able to garner a plurality, limiting efforts by political extremists to censor books in a high school library.[38] Though he could not get a majority of his colleagues to agree that gender, like race, should be treated as a suspect classification calling for the highest level of judicial scrutiny,[39] Brennan was able to convince his colleagues to adopt an intermediate level of scrutiny that at least would not be satisfied by the government's claim merely that it could find some rational basis for its action whether it was grossly discriminatory or not.[40] He rejected the idea that classifications based on gender were really different from those based on race, declaring that many government actions affecting women represented archaic and overbroad generalizations, "an attitude of 'romantic paternalism' which, in practical effect, put women, not on a pedestal, but in a cage."[41] Despite heavy criticism from many quarters, he was repeatedly able to marshal support among his colleagues for rulings holding that government officials and state and local governments would be held responsible in damages for injuries to the constitutional and statutory rights of citizens.[42]

His ability to remain an important force with significant influence among his colleagues is all the more impressive because Brennan willingly accepted the mantle of the Court's leading dissenter during the 1970s and 1980s. His opposition to the directions in which the Court was taken by Nixon, Reagan, and Bush appointees was open, direct, and powerful. Sometimes he was able to fight a rearguard action to defend the Warren Court legacy, while in other situations he simply found it necessary to take on his colleagues in powerful dissenting opinions. He had worked hard in earlier years to defend the poor and weak[43] and to ensure that they received their full measure of due process protections if government turned its power on one of them.[44] During the Burger and Rehnquist years, Brennan found it necessary to battle against rulings either directly overturning or dramatically weakening these earlier rulings, particularly in such matters as the availability of due process protections and the opportunity to get a defendant's concerns through the procedural barriers and into courts for judicial review.[45] He fought rulings on free speech and press that represented challenges to his many efforts in an earlier time to defend them.[46] He wrote dissent after dissent to the numerous rulings that he saw violating a woman's right to choose to have an abortion.[47] But there was probably no field in which he was a more ardent opponent of the changing Court than in the matter of the death penalty.

Brennan was absolutely convinced that the death penalty is cruel and unusual punishment, regardless of how it was determined or executed.[48] He would not reduce his opposition even after it became abundantly clear that a majority of his colleagues rejected his position and were regularly upholding state capital-punishment statutes and prosecutions brought under them. "In 1987–1988, for example Brennan and Marshall issued 197 dissents from the denial of applications for review of death sentences."[49] His dissents were vivid and powerful.[50] In one, Brennan wrote:

> Th[e] evidence suggests that death by electrical current is extremely violent and inflicts pain and indignities far beyond the 'mere extinguishment of life.' Witnesses routinely report that, when the switch is thrown, the condemned prisoner 'cringes,' 'leaps,' and 'fights the straps with amazing strength.' 'The hands turn red, then white, and the cords of the neck stand out like steel bands.' The prisoner's limbs, fingers, toes, and face are severely contorted, the force of the electrical current is so powerful that the prisoner's eyeballs sometimes pop out and 'rest on [his] cheeks.' The prisoner often defecates, urinates, and vomits blood and drool.
>
> 'The body turns red as its temperature rises,' and the prisoner's 'flesh swells and his skin stretches to the point of breaking.' Sometimes the prisoner catches on fire, particularly 'if [he] perspires excessively.' Witnesses hear a loud and sustained sound 'like bacon frying,' and 'the sickly sweet smell of burning flesh' permeates the chamber. This 'smell of frying human flesh' in the immediate neighbourhood of the chair is sometimes bad enough to nauseate even the Press representatives who are present. In the meantime, the prisoner almost literally boils: 'the temperature in the brain itself approaches the boiling point of water,' and when the post-electrocution autopsy is performed 'the liver is so hot that doctors have said that it cannot be touched by the human hand.' The body is frequently badly burned and disfigured.[51]

He listed a number of examples of botched executions and concluded that electrocution was "nothing less than the contemporary technological equivalent of burning people at the stake."[52] He was no more willing to accept lethal injection or any other means than he was to sanction electrocution. Neither was he willing to keep his opposition within the Court and his dissents. Brennan took his opposition public. In his Holmes lecture at Harvard, Brennan insisted: "The calculated killing of a human being by the state involves, by its very nature, an absolute denial of the executed person's humanity and thus violates the command of the Eighth Amendment."[53]

As Judge Abner Mikva put it, Brennan had "stepped on large toes" during his years on the Court.[54] He was the target of "a President whose Attorney General waged open warfare against [him]."[55] Brennan was the epitome of what Ronald Reagan had disliked about the Supreme Court since the 1960s, and Attorney General Edwin Meese was the spokesperson for the administration's ongoing campaign against the Court. Meese even went so far as to challenge Brennan and his colleagues in a speech in which Meese advocated his so-called jurisprudence of original intent and attacked Brennan and his colleagues for their failure to adhere to it.

Meese made three mistakes. First, he overestimated his own intellectual power in such a debate. Second, he dramatically underestimated both the intellectual force that Brennan could bring to bear and Brennan's political savvy in doing so. Finally, he failed to understand that the affable little Irishman who has been variously described as a leprechaun and as Yoda, the master teacher of Jeddi Knights in the *Star Wars* movies, has also been likened to the pugnacious Jimmy Cagney. When pressed to the wall on a matter of fundamental principle and faced with an attack on the institution to which he had dedicated his life, Brennan would ask no quarter and give none. His reply to the original-intent speech carved Meese up like a holiday turkey.

Brennan: Craftsman and Statesman

But how could a person so willing to face such conflict inside the Court and out, so ready to defend what were increasingly unpopular positions on matters of constitutional rights and liberties, and so committed to continually fighting the trend in the Court remain so capable of shaping critically important decisions long after the Warren Court era had passed? To these questions, both friend and foe alike have answered that it was Brennan's statesmanship and craftsmanship that account for his success and influence.

Most commentators immediately recognize that Brennan has been able to fight hard professional battles and yet remain friends with his colleagues. Both colleagues and Court watchers extol his personal virtues, including his warmth and genuine concern for others. He has been called "the supremely collegial Justice."[56] As Justice Harry Blackmun described him: "He is a friend to all, of whatever status. He likes people and is interested in listening to them. Although I know he has been hurt on occasion by unfair barbs directed at him, he has never retaliated in the same vein or been rude, arrogant, or ruthless."[57] Justice Byron White added, "Anyone who knows Bill Brennan would surely agree that he is as amiable as anyone can be. He is quiet and gentle, friendly and sociable, unfailingly polite, sensitive and sympathetic. He is interested in others, and those others realize it. Among other things, he is an excellent conversationalist, in large part because he is an acute observer of current events, but also because of his fine sense of human nature. Being with Bill Brennan is always a pleasant personal experience."[58] Such a comment by one who has often been on the opposite side of major decisions bespeaks far more than a polite expression of respect.

Still, even beyond his interpersonal skills, it is said that Brennan's "career had been a triumph of character."[59] His principles were clear and just as plainly grounded not only in the formal document that is the Constitution but also in his genuine and "deep empathy" for those affected by the Court's judgments.[60] He was not doctrinaire, dogmatic, or so in love with the sound of his own words that he was unwilling to bend to make it possible for colleagues to agree with him. "Brennan could be trusted to choose his words in a way that would minimize the disagreement among the justices, not only to avoid those silly squabbles that might interfere with the smooth functioning of a collegial institution, . . . but also to produce a majority opinion and strengthen the force of what the Court had to say."[61]

In working with his colleagues, his manner and character plainly facilitated his ability to exercise leadership and influence, but it would be a mistake to attribute his impact solely to his personality and obvious political skills. He is regarded as "a statesman: not a person who tempers principle with prudence, but rather someone who is capable of grasping a multiplicity of conflicting principles, some of which relate to the well-being of the institution."[62] His devotion to the Court as a critically important American constitutional institution is well known. His workways and efforts outside the Court sought to preserve the best in the institution and to foster respect for it in the larger political community.

On the other hand, much of that respect comes from the belief that members of the Court ought to have, as Brennan has demonstrated, "a consistent legal vision of how the Constitution should be interpreted . . . based on an unwavering commitment to certain core principles. . . . Justice Brennan's commitment to these interpretive principles was never in doubt. It did not depend on the peculiarly compelling facts of a case; it was never outweighed by the lesser values that sometimes compete for a judge's allegiance."[63] Brennan had the "ability to see issues, not just from the perspective of a white, male octogenarian, but also through the eyes of the black, the young, the alien, the handicapped, and the female."[64] He strove to make the promise of the Constitution and the values it embodies meaningful in the day-to-day life of a busy nation operating in the midst of a dangerous world. He knew that the courageous protection of fundamental American values in a way that would work in a changing society would reinforce the nation from within and garner it respect and support from around the world.[65]

On the other hand, it is also not enough to say that Brennan was a popular man with solid constitutional values. He was also a craftsman. As one former clerk put it, "Aside from a proper regard for institutional needs, a successful opinion requires mastery of legal craft, which Warren also found in Brennan. Justice Brennan was as much the lawyer as the statesman. . . . He was the lawyer's judge."[66] Marshall observed, "His canny ability to forge a majority was most apparent in the drafting process—as he pruned a paragraph here or recast a thought there to accommodate his colleagues' concerns."[67] Brennan was no manipulator who attempted to build support by empty flattery. He knew his colleagues and his own principles well enough that along with his skill in crafting a document, he was able to make the case on the merits in the opinions.

Bernard Schwartz explains the kind of problem Brennan routinely faced:

> The *Winship* drafting process illustrates once again the need to compromise. In order to hold his Court, Brennan had to write more narrowly than he might otherwise have wished. At one extreme, there was the need to appease Justice Harlan. . . . At the other extreme was Justice Douglas. It was necessary to avoid any statement that the due process to be accorded children may differ from that given adults. The *Winship* opinion carefully avoided such a declaration, though the unstated assumption of the opinion was that juvenile and adult due process are not necessarily identical in their content.[68]

That was true not only of the opinions Brennan wrote himself but also of the assistance he provided to others in the preparation of their work products.

In the end, then, there is relatively little surprise at the widespread and growing sense that this was a truly great justice.

EFFECTIVENESS AND GREATNESS

In a classic treatment on the effort by justices to accomplish their goals within the Court, Walter Murphy laid out a framework of power within which to understand what justices can and must do to reach the goals they believe appropriate in individual cases or, more strategically, for the long term in larger areas of the law. It was against the backdrop of the challenges faced by the justices that he suggested the evaluation of their accomplishments as statesmen and craftsmen. He began from the proposition that the strategies, tactics, opportunities, and constraints he described were viewed from the vantage point of a policy-oriented justice. This was a judge, Murphy said, who understood his or her power, the institutional forces shaping the discretion available to a member of the Court, and the opportunities to use that discretion in the service of appropriate ends.

Murphy explained that to know what justices can do, one must understand the sources of the Court's power, the instruments by which that power can be exercised by individual justices, and the constraints on that power constraints that stem from the nature of the Court as an institution and the political context in which it operates.

Sources of Power

Murphy recognized that the Court, and the justices within it, may exercise authority that is traditional, rational/legal, or charismatic. These categories were borrowed from the work of Max Weber, who described them as the sources of authority, that is, properly vested power, that can be exercised by any governmental institution. While we are used to hearing these referred to as the sources of authority that can be used by the court to get others to comply with its rulings, they are also the sources of authority that can be used by members of the Court in an attempt to influence their colleagues. The traditions of mutual respect, equality among members of the Court, deference to the decisions of "the conference" on matters of internal governance as well as the decision of cases, the regularity of procedure within the Court, and the norms of communication among colleagues all provide justices avenues of influence, ways to make their voices heard. Of course, the ability to make oneself heard and to have that message accorded some degree of importance has much to do with the ability of the speaker. There have indeed been members of the Court whose leadership skills have approximated the idea of charisma, though that term is somewhat strong for the kind of personal influence that is often acknowledged among colleagues. One of the most common mistakes that observers of the Court make is to underestimate the importance of rational/legal authority in the Court, the power that derives from the ability to marshal the law, the facts, and effectively reasoned written arguments in support of one's position.

It is also of importance, for Murphy, and for other Court watchers who have followed his lead, that the vehicles employed by the Court for action have something to do with the Court's power. Also important are the roles played by members of the Court toward one another. The justices do not simply decide cases, but take a host of actions with respect to each case. Will the Court accept a case for its docket? If so, how will oral argument be shaped by the questioning process? To what degree will the conference discussion be routine, or is this one of those cases that inspire some members of the Court to make particularly strong arguments around the table? Will the Court focus on procedural or jurisdictional issues, the so-called passive instruments, or will it reach the merits of the case? What will be the holding on the key issues in the case, if the Court decides to reach them? Which ones will the Court seek to answer, and which will remain unresolved, pending future cases? What will be the disposition of the case, that is, what is to happen next in light of the holding? How much instruction or guidance will be given to the lower courts if the case is remanded for further action? Who will prepare the draft opinion? What tone and framework will that opinion present? Will it mark a major change or tend to follow or elaborate earlier benchmarks? Will justices expend time and energy and conflict costs to challenge the proffered opinion for the Court? Can the justice preparing the opinion "get a Court," or will the group fragment into a plurality opinion and a multiplicity of concurrences? Will there be dissenters? Will the dissenters be more able to build consensus among themselves than the majority justices? How hard will the dissent be? Each decision, each answer to these questions, represents a vehicle for action within the Court and, potentially at least, for impact outside it.

Each answer to these questions presents a possible opportunity for influence and, just as clearly, poses potential problems that could undermine his or her effectiveness or importance with colleagues. Moreover, the setting is different for different kinds of cases and issues. Cases posing classic judicial-review arguments over the constitutionality of federal or state-and-local action set a somewhat different context for action than do cases that focus principally on issues of statutory interpretation or administrative procedure. Cases that present disputes over matters affecting foreign or national security policy often come with a different kind of personality than domestic cases do.

Limits on Power

There are, of course, other types of constraints on the choices made by the justices individually, and the Court as a group, many of which have been introduced in earlier chapters. Murphy groups them into technical legal limits, institutional checks, and political constraints. Regarding technical legal limits, the justices are subject to the cases brought to them, particular issues in unique factual settings shaped by attorneys with whatever peculiar skills and resources, or lack thereof, that they bring to a case. Despite the wide range of discretion generally available to judges, the cases arise within jurisdictional limits and can be addressed with a limited number of available remedies. And, notwithstanding the cynicism that members of the legal community and general public often express on the matter, the plain fact is that most judges, most of the time, consider themselves bound by canons of interpretation and the principle of *stare decisis*, at least the obligation to consider precedent or the need to change it, in their decision processes. The evidence indicates that justices are acutely aware of the institutional constraints, the importance of collegiality, the need for four votes plus their own in most instances, the significance of decision majorities versus opinion majorities, and the fact that they make neither the first nor the last decision in a case, but that the implementation of their ruling is subject to the actions of lower courts and other officials. They are also very much aware of the potential political limits on their action. While they know it is unlikely that they will be impeached, the configuration of the Court changed, their jurisdiction modified, or their resources restricted, these things are possible and have been considered at one time or another in the nation's history. More to the point, though, they are clearly aware that: their decisions may be reversed by statute or by constitutional amendment depending on the type of issue; that reaction to their rulings may affect public opinion, elections, and even the nature of future appointments; that there may be outright resistance or simply footdragging by federal or state officials in responding to rulings; or that politicians may use the Court as a rallying point to mount political attacks.

Given these realities, how are the justices to be evaluated? There seem to be two common means, and neither appears very helpful.

The Activism/Restraint Problem

The first mechanism of evaluation is by opinion poll, but this is a kind of broad-brush reputational measure rather than a more focused inquiry. Moreover, the categories on which respondents are asked to rate justices are arbitrary and vague. The classic example is the category of "near-great" justices.

The more common, and even more problematic, approach when evaluating justices, is the use of the shorthand terms "activism" or "restraint" to characterize the justices. Anyone who follows the activities of the Court at all has heard frequent condemnation of particular justices as judicial activists by critics and praise as the very model of judicial restraint by their supporters; but what do the terms mean and why do they seem to carry so much power? Despite years, even decades, of criticism of the concepts and their misuse, they persist as a kind of judicial bar sinister, with the word "activist" often followed by a facial expression roughly equivalent to that of a person who has taken a large bite of a lemon or inhaled sulfur fumes.

Consider first the uses and abuses of the concepts of judicial activism and restraint. The first problem is understanding in some nonarbitrary way what the terms mean. There are two sets of commonly used explanations: Professor Stephen Wasby's formulation, and the often-cited framework employed by Bradley Canon.

Wasby notes that among the most commonly used features of restraint (presumably the opposite of activism) are (1) "deference to other branches"; (2) "a lack of result-orientation, that is a concern with legal principles, not the social or economic effects of decisions"; (3) "reliance on precedent"; and (4) "avoidance of political questions."[69]

Of course, the ambiguities are obvious. How much deference should the Court show to the "elected" branches if those branches' actions are plainly unconstitutional or in violation of statute? How much deference can the Court grant before it ceases to exercise its responsibilities as a co-equal third branch of government charged with deciding "all cases in law and equity arising under this Constitution and the laws made pursuant thereto . . . , including those to which the United States shall be a party"?[70] Justice Arthur Goldberg once said, "We're all result-oriented," depending on what one means by that idea.[71] Should the justices never give any consideration to the likely impact and implications of their rulings? Should questions of justice never affect the application of specific legal interpretations in particular cases?

Justice Brennan told the story of how he decided to write the opinion in *Bell v. Maryland*, which concerned the use of state trespass laws to enforce segregation of amusement parks and recreational facilities.[72] He thought about whether the Court should attack the state action enforcing segregation directly or indirectly. If Brennan wrote substantively, with the debate in full progress across the street in Congress over the Civil Rights Act of 1964, how much pressure would be brought to bear on border-state congressmen? Would the furor created by the Court's ruling tip the balance, in what was sure to be a close vote, against the civil rights bill? On the other hand, if the Court could strike down state-sponsored enforcement of segregation by more technical interpretation would that serve to reach the same conclusion but manage to keep the Court out of the center of the legislative debate and allow the political process to work its way, unimpeded, through the difficult legislative debate? What should the restraint-oriented justice do, one wondered, listening to Brennan as he told the story?

Surely, reliance on precedent is a clearer criterion of restraint, but is it really? As Justice Hugo Black put it, he took an oath to uphold the Constitution, not his predecessors' interpretation of it. There have been differences in perspective regarding the meaning and requirements of the rule of precedent in the fields of statutory and constitutional interpretation.[73] Even more ambiguity exists with respect to the idea that justices should avoid "the political thicket," as Justice Felix Frankfurter said, by refusing to decide "political questions."[74] Of course, there is precious little agreement regarding precisely what constitutes a political question.

The Canon formulation seeks to form some kind of understandable synthesis of what scholars and professionals mean when they use the terms "activism" and "restraint."[75] Canon pulls the elements together into evaluations of majoritarianism, interpretive stability, interpretive fidelity, the making of substantive policy, specificity of policy, and the availability of alternative policy making. The majoritarianism criterion considers the degree to which the Court or individual justices reject policies adopted through the democratic political process. Interpretative stability is an assessment of the degree to which the justice maintains a reliance on precedent. On the other hand, interpretive fidelity is a measure of the degree to which the justice focuses on the language and intent of the framers of the Constitution. The substantive-policy assessment has to do with whether a justice makes substantive policy choices as compared with acting to protect the democratic process. The specificity criterion evaluates the degree to which justices provide general statements of principle as compared with the promulgation of detailed policy pronouncements. Finally, the availability of alternative policymaking measures evaluation considers whether the justice defers to others who might be able to solve the problem in an institution with elected officials as compared with the Court intervening in matters that could be left to others.

There are two sets of difficulties here. First, can we agree on precisely what these criteria mean and whether they indeed properly characterize activist- as compared with restraint-oriented behavior? Second, are the measures mutually consistent or compatible?

Regarding the ambiguity issue, it is difficult to know in the abstract why a Court should be considered activist if it strikes down congressional enactments that violate the Constitution or strikes down state legislation that breaches either federal law or the Constitution. Activist relative to what? While there are some who have qualms about the relationship between the Court and the Congress, the same kinds of constitutional arguments do not apply when the Court strikes down a state statute, and the Court strikes down far more of those than it does legislation adopted by the Congress. Moreover, if the sheer number of pieces of legislation struck down is the measure of activism, then the Burger Court must plainly rank as one of the most, if not the most, activist Supreme Court in history, a charge rarely made by those who most vigorously indicted the Warren Court for activism.[76]

There are numerous difficulties with the ambiguity involved in the concepts of interpretive stability and interpretive fidelity as well. The value of interpretive stability is that precedents are honored so that citizens may order their lives on the expectation that the ways in which a question was resolved in the past will govern how it is applied in the future. Otherwise, in Justice Owen Roberts' famous criticism, the rulings of the Court will be no better than a train schedule "good for this day and train only."[77] The first problem is that no two cases are ever exactly alike, and the greater the difference between the facts that gave rise to a later case, the less clear it is just how precedents apply. After all, the idea is that precedents are important because situations with comparable facts should be treated alike. When the circumstances are different, the precedent may either not apply at all or only with significant modifications. Moreover, why is it that the value of stability is the most important factor? Should the Court's ruling that searches and seizures by administrative officials are not covered by the Fourth Amendment continue to be applied in a time when it had become abundantly clear that most people are far more likely to feel the power of government from the hand of the bureaucracy than from the police?[78] Should the *Plessy v. Ferguson* ruling upholding legally mandated segregation continue to be honored a century later simply because it was a precedent?

Interpretive fidelity is the very different notion that the justices have an obligation to interpret the Constitution according to the precise language of the document and the intent of the framers. Yet only one member of the Court, Hugo Black, joined on some issues by William O. Douglas, has ever really advocated a literal interpretation, and even he was known on many occasions to depart from a verbatim application of the language of the Constitution. Certainly, some of those, like Felix Frankfurter, who have most often been celebrated as paragons of judicial restraint could not be accused of having applied the language of the

Constitution with great fidelity to its terms or the intent of its framers. His famous application of the "shocks-the-conscience" test to determine whether police behavior violated the due process rights of a suspect is the most often cited example.[79] There is even sometimes a problem in reconciling the language of the document with what was supposedly the intent of the framers. As Justice Brennan pointed out in his debate with Attorney General Meese, just how do we determine precisely what the framers meant when there were so often disagreements among those present at the Philadelphia convention; when there were pitched battles in the state ratifying conventions; and in light of the fact that the Bill of Rights, which is so often the focus of such debate, was not written until after the Constitution was ratified? Some points appear to be clear, but many do not.

The policymaking questions are equally unclear. On what ground can it be said that it is a restraint-oriented stance to take actions that support the political process but activist to issue rulings that amount to a substantive-policy statement?[80] The Constitution, particularly as amended over time, plainly provides both procedural and substantive protections. Considering the fact that some of the most heated debates about activism have arisen in cases presenting issues like apportionment, voting rights, and access to the ballot, it is difficult to determine how that type of ruling is more activist than, say, the recognition of a right to privacy. Similar problems arise with respect to specificity of policy. There is a serious question whether a Court's ruling is more principled and less result-oriented if it is reached according to a broad standard or by a balancing test as compared with a more carefully and precisely tailored standard. Is the Court more restrained when it defines such a standard with care or when it avoids careful articulation of the test by which it will act? The final policy test, the idea that justices ought simply to state the law and leave to other available policymakers the choice of what to do next, is equally problematic. It is unclear why restraint is demonstrated by automatic deferral to other branches when they have, sometimes repeatedly, failed to bring themselves into compliance with the law as it had been interpreted. This problem has been most obviously demonstrated by the school desegregation cases, but it is also true in disputes involving prison conditions, mental-health facilities, and voting rights.

Finally, the fact is that these principles, which Canon quite accurately and effectively synthesizes, are also not necessarily mutually consistent, even if we could agree on precisely what they mean and that they can be accurately classified as demonstrating activism or restraint. The classic battle here has been between those who, like Black, insist that their task is to be faithful to the document, not the interpretations of it provided by their predecessors, and those who insist that the Court undermines its own credibility if it is inconsistent and fragmented on important issues of interpretation. What should a justice do who concludes that a prior ruling was simply wrong as a matter of constitutional interpretation but finds a long line of cases that maintain that interpretation in the years before he reached the bench? Judge Robert Bork's conundrum during confirmation illustrates the point. He had repeatedly attacked the *Griswold* opinion announcing a right to privacy, and yet he simultaneously insisted, when pressed to the wall on the issue, that even though it was wrong, the right to privacy should continue to be protected because it is settled law. This situation presents a clear conflict between interpretive stability and interpretive fidelity.

Interestingly, this tension often has proven most difficult for those who consider themselves judicial conservatives. Writing for the Court in *Haig v. Agee*,[81] upholding the claim by the secretary of state of a power to revoke a passport even though two precedents plainly went the other way, Chief Justice Burger tried to reconcile the competing precedents, but the effort was doomed from the start. Justice Blackmun concurred on grounds that the secretary ought to have that power but chided Burger for not forthrightly overturning the two earlier cases,[82] at least to the degree that they were in conflict with the *Agee* ruling. The result of such rulings as *Agee* is to leave multiple inconsistent precedents standing.

A similar inconsistency often exists between majoritarianism and interpretive fidelity. Why should a justice defer to the Congress or the executive branch when the Constitution and statutes provide law to interpret in cases properly presenting those issues? If the justices' understanding is contrary to the action taken by the Congress or an administrative agency on an issue of interpretation, the choice must be made.

A similar conflict exists between the norm opposing the making of substantive policy and the principles of interpretive fidelity and interpretive stability. In any but the narrowest procedural ruling,[83] decisions on constitutional or statutory matters plainly amount to a making of policy.

Consider, for example, the cases testing retirement annuity programs under claims of sex discrimination based on Title VII of the Civil Rights Act of 1964.[84] Most employers, including public employers, offer a variety of annuity programs from which an employee may select a program that best suits his or her needs. However, nearly all of them calculate the amount to be paid into the plan during working years and the amount to be paid back in retirement based on life insurance actuarial tables that estimate the likely length of survival to determine the pay out. Women argue that making them choose between paying more than men do per month into an annuity while working or receiving less per month at retirement is discrimination based on gender. The Court agreed on grounds that Title VII prohibits discrimination against any person on the basis of sex. The judgment that some women may live longer than some men does not mean that any particular woman will be around to collect retirement benefits longer than any specific man. The Court recognized that these rulings could (and plainly would) have a very significant impact but that the Congress could change the statute if it wished. In the interim, said the Court, it would rule in accordance with the existing language of the legislation, as they interpreted it.[85]

The same is true with interpretive stability and the policymaking question. Plainly, once the Court has issued a ruling in an area, that opinion will both present a policy judgment and prompt the filing of more suits in the future based on the policy. Interpretive stability calls for the Court to continue to rule in general conformity with its own precedents, but each new step in doctrinal development plainly implicates new policy. The school desegregation cases provide an obvious example, with literally decades of policy making following from the *Brown v. Board of Education* rulings.

Plainly, then, even if one wishes to be regarded as the quintessential restraint-oriented justice, one has serious problems. As long as justices limit themselves to espousing the belief that Courts ought to be careful with the use of their power, should not needlessly interfere in the democratic process, should show proper respect for coordinate branches of the federal government, and regard, within limits, the actions of state and local governments, there is no difficulty. It becomes a problem only if a justice attempts to implement opposing beliefs in decisions.

Then the ambiguities and inconsistencies in the concepts of activism and restraint will haunt him or her endlessly.

The final, and perhaps most common, problem is that activism and restraint have for some years been used as ideological proxies. This is best seen in the failure of the critics of the Warren Court, who pressed the activism/restraint terminology to critique Warren but failed to apply the same critical standards to the Burger Court (which was every bit as activist as the Warren Court but in a conservative direction). The activism/restraint rhetoric was and is often little more than a respectable cover for polemics. Whatever utility those terms may once have had, taking into account their inherent conceptual difficulties, the fact is that they are not helpful or useful in the day-to-day work of the justices or in their effort to understand the actions of colleagues on the Supreme Court or in other courts around the nation. They have become heavily laden with ideology, baggage that has become so heavy that it is not particularly useful to try to salvage the concepts any longer.

IN SEARCH OF STANDARDS FOR JUDGING JUDGES

Well, if the reputational measures and the standard shibboleths of activism and restraint are not helpful, what basis is there for judgment? Are there characteristics evidenced by opinions of those justices considered to be great or near-great members of the Supreme Court that people of diverse views can use in evaluating greatness? Is it possible to read opinions of justices with whom one disagrees on the merits of the case and yet appreciate the quality of the opinion presented by that justice? Can we analyze opinions that present decisions with which one is in complete agreement and yet find those opinions of poor quality? The reasons that explain the positive answers to both of these questions may be found in assessments of craftsmanship and statesmanship.

An interesting tension is involved in evaluations of the performance of the justices individually and of the Court as a whole. On the one hand, the Court is a political institution that should presumably be as subject to examination and criticism as any other agency of government. On the other, the Court has a special place in the society and a tradition in which it is above the kind of criticism by ordinary mortals applied to other institutions. Justice Robert Jackson alluded to this situation in his oft-quoted observation that even assuming that one accepts the idea that judicial decisions are the ultimate authority, "We are not final because we are infallible, we are infallible only because we are final."[86]

One of the leading nonlawyer critics of the Court, Alexander Meiklejohn, put the matter in slightly different terms.

> The Supreme Court, like any other teacher, may be wrong as well as right, may do harm as well as good. . . . As they study their cases, the members of the Supreme Court are not merely trying to discover what they are going to say. They are trying to decide what, in that situation, it is right to say in fact and principle. And as they grapple with that problem, they are keenly aware of their difficulties, of their lack of success. The individual members recognize frankly their own frailties, as well as those of their brethren. . . . Granted, then, that on any specific occasion we must, as Mr. Hughes suggests, "abide by" the rulings of the court; it does not follow that we must "agree with" them. Our duty, as free men, to reflect upon judicial pronouncements

is quite as imperative as our duty to submit to their temporary legal authority. Not even our wisest interpreters, those whom we trust most, can give us final dogmas about self-government. They and we together must still be thinking about what freedom is and how it works.[87]

Walter Murphy focused that analysis not just on individual cases but on the performance of individuals over the variety of cases they address and conditions in which those decisions develop. Like Meiklejohn, he urged careful and deliberate evaluation.

The role of the scholar, insofar as it is critical, is to hold decisions and opinions of judges up to the highest criteria of craftsmanship and statesmanship—to determine not whether judges have exercised discretion but whether they have done so to an extent and in a manner permitted by relevant standards; to determine not whether judges have influenced policy but whether that influence is to the benefit, both in the long and the short run, of society.[88]

But how can a justice or an analyst think about these concepts of craftsmanship and statesmanship?

Judicial Craftsmanship

The reason one can agree strongly with the outcome of opinions and yet find them of poor quality is that there are some minimum requirements of craftsmanship. Judicial craftsmanship is evidenced when a judge, assuming a formal concept of jurisprudence as a base of analysis, decides cases on principle announced in a reasoned opinion that both resolves the case and reconciles the ruling with the entire corpus of the law, taking responsibility for any change or new directions.

Before considering just what the elements are that analysts look for in evaluating a justice's reasoning behind these opinions, a number of important caveats must be recognized. One need not assume that judges reproduce the story of how they arrived at a decision. The work of the justice is evaluated, not on the basis of what he or she presumably thought while moving through the process of decision, opinion preparation, and negotiation in the effort to marshal "a Court" in support of the opinion, but by the explanation of the ultimate decision. That is not a naive assumption but a judgment that the Court and its justices are responsible for what they did and what they advanced in support of it.

Second, one can accept the proposition that sometimes the reasoning is a rationalization to support a hunch, a feeling of a compelling right decision, and yet assess the quality with which the principled decision is stated and the argument on which it is based. It is possible to accept Judge Frank Coffin's idea that decision making is often a process of shifting biases.[89] As he explains it, when a judge first encounters a case, his or her "judicial nose" senses something about the case that suggests one or another conclusion. That judgment is by no means final, but it is a starting point. Coffin reminds us that this ability to smell something on the wind when a case comes to court is no more irrational than the use of smell and touch by a physician in the making of a diagnosis. The contemporary Italian lawyer Pierro Calamandrei put it differently. He spoke of the amazement with which some of his young associates reacted when they brought him a brief description of a case, only to have him provide something that seemed like an off-the-cuff response that turned out to be surprisingly accurate.[90] They wondered at how he could operate so effectively by what appears to be the use of a hunch. His reply was that it may be a hunch, but it is a hunch informed by decades of study and experience. For Coffin, that preliminary assessment becomes a kind of working hypothesis that is modified during the course of the reading of briefs, the oral argument, and the process of writing the opinion. Thus, in some crude sense, one might say that opinions are sometimes reasons supporting a hunch.

On the other hand, that observation is often put forth less as an attempt to understand than as a charge of prejudgment. While there are doubtless examples of this kind of behavior, there is much to indicate that such one-liners vastly oversimplify reality. The frequent finding by a justice that the opinion he or she had in mind at the outset "just won't write" suggests that the opinion preparation process plays an important role in decision making. For example, Felix Frankfurter once put it to his colleagues that "th[is] case would not write according to the vote of the Conference including my own. Full consideration has convinced me that the judgment should be affirmed. Accordingly I am circulating this view of the case as a memorandum."[91]

Since it is also true that opinions that began as dissents sometimes acquire a majority of votes; that a majority opinion often changes dramatically from the first draft through the exchange of comments, draft concurrences and dissents; and that so many justices feel the need to file concurrences, any analyst who really wishes to understand behavior within the Court would miss much of the most important action by taking the relatively cynical rationalization premise. Indeed, some of those commenting on the work of Justice Brennan point out precisely that he is not understood by those who begin from that sort of knee-jerk premise or who merely count votes or patterns of decisions.[92]

Regardless of how the opinion came about, however, standards of craftsmanship are still applied to assess a justice's work. These standards focus on the treatment of facts, the presentation of issues, the presence of a principled judgment, the effectiveness of the reasoning, the availability of guidance and explanation, and some indication of awareness of consequences.

A well-crafted opinion should treat the facts of a case with accuracy and sensitivity. That can be a more difficult task than seems apparent. By the time a case reaches a justice's desk, it has already been years in the making. Once in the system, there may have been numerous hearings and decisions before a final ruling was issued that began to move up through the appellate process. The appellate courts focus on matters of law rather than fact, so the summary of facts in their rulings is often relatively limited as compared with the information before the trial judge. By the time the Supreme Court receives the opinion, there is both time and distance between the events that gave rise to the suit. Moreover, the facts provided by counsel may be true, but they are presented in each side's best light. Each tries to tell her story, or the story as she sees it, rather than recounting the events as they actually unfolded.

It is not unusual for justices who came to the Court from legal practice rather than lower courts to bring the advocate's mode of recitation of the facts to their opinions. Among the most obvious examples of this behavior are Justices

Rehnquist and Powell, on the conservative end of the Court, and Justice Fortas on the liberal side. Another person who tended to present facts more as an advocate than as an impartial observer was Chief Justice Burger, though Burger came to the Court from the D.C. circuit rather than legal practice. For example, in a case involving a challenge brought by child advocacy organizations to Georgia's process for the commitment of minors by their parents to state mental-health facilities, it is difficult to read the detailed lower-court opinion and then the opinion for the Supreme Court and believe one is reading about the same case.[93]

In *Parham*, a three-judge federal district court found that the practice of permitting parents to admit children indefinitely to the state mental hospitals without a hearing at or after the time of commitment violated the due process clause of the Fourteenth Amendment. The head of the state's major mental hospital testified that large numbers of children who should not be in such institutions were forced to remain there under the state law simply because there was nowhere else to put them and parents refused to take them to a more appropriate place. Hospital staff had repeatedly warned that keeping children in such surroundings ensured that they would face the likelihood of deterioration in their mental health. Asked why hospital personnel did not refuse the parents' request on grounds that there was no significant diagnosable mental illness that would justify institutionalization, the supervising physician answered that they simply were trapped. When parents arrived at the facilities insisting that the children be admitted and refusing to accept further responsibility for them outside an institution, the admitting physician was left with an untenable choice. He or she could either admit the child, even if it was not an appropriate placement, or try to force the child back into the custody of parents who did not want her or felt they could not handle him. Given that choice, few clinicians would want to pressure the parents to take the children. At some point, the district court concluded, children, like adults, are entitled to some due process protection when state laws are used to commit them to a mental-health facility.

Burger, for a five to four majority, found that although it was clear that commitment to a mental facility was a deprivation of liberty to which the protections of the due process clause apply and agreed that children as well as adults were entitled to due process protections, the presumption that parents would care for the best interest of the child plus the check provided by the law's requirement of a diagnosis by the admitting clinician were adequate to protect the child's interest. Of course, the hospital personnel had testified without challenge that there were large numbers of children in the state system who should not have been there. Moreover, the chief physician at the largest state facility testified that clinicians were in no position to make truly independent diagnoses, given the conditions under which the children were brought to them. Furthermore, some of the children represented in the suit were admitted by the state and had no parents. Whatever one might think of the ruling on the issue of law, the Court's recitation of the facts was neither empirically valid nor an accurate summary of the lower-court record.

Justice Brennan, by contrast, was able to present extremely useful and accurate statements of fact in hotly contested, complex cases, which is one of the factors that has made it possible for him to build majorities or pluralities among justices whose views on many issues are very unlike his own. On the other end of the ideological spectrum, Justice Antonin Scalia has been able to make very strong arguments more palatable to some court commentators because he tends to be careful in his presentation of facts.

Another dimension of craftsmanship is the ability to present issues clearly and precisely. When properly crafted, an issue can be read almost by itself and be enough for an informed reader to understand the nature of the case. Thus, to take the example used above, the issue in *Parham* was: Does a state statute that permits commitment of a minor by parents to a mental-health facility without a hearing at or after commitment violate the due process clause of the Fourteenth Amendment? Even without any more information than the issue statement, a reader has a fairly good idea of what the case is about.

Presumably, the question of the statement of issues is not a significant problem, since the parties are required to present the issues precisely in their petitions for certiorari and, if the case is ultimately taken by the Court, in the briefs. However, in an opinion, justices will sometimes engage in a bit of strategic obfuscation, deliberately blurring an issue or even avoiding a precise statement of the issue. On other occasions, the Court will ultimately make a ruling turn on an issue different from those presented by the parties. In still other instances, the Court will claim that it has ruled on one issue when it has, in truth, used one issue to rule indirectly on another. This is, in part, Felix Frankfurter's old trick, what some of his devotees have referred to as the "passive virtues." Finding reasons to call an issue a political question or resolving a case on grounds of standing when the Court simply meant to uphold a lower-court ruling or a government policy on the merits allows justices to achieve the result they seek without actually engaging the difficult core issues in the case. The more common norm, however, is that justices should state the issues forthrightly and then decide the issues they state or explain why they are taking a different course.

Craftsmen are expected to render principled decisions; that is, they are to resolve the issues in a case on the basis of some principle that is stated with sufficient clarity that it can be understood by reasonable people and consequently may be criticized by them.

For example, Justice Brennan wrote in *New York Times v. Sullivan* that the First Amendment requires public officials to face a high burden of proof to win a libel judgment against a publisher, because they need to recognize that critics of public events are going to make erroneous statements given that events are developing even as stories are being written.[94] Therefore, he wrote, a public official cannot collect for libel unless he or she shows that the writer acted with actual malice, that is, with knowledge that what was said was false, or acted with reckless disregard for the truth or falsity of what was written. One can disagree with Brennan's premise, his logic, or his conclusion, but the principle on which the decision was based is plainly stated and can be applied to many factual settings.

Some scholars refer to this attempt to ensure that opinions are principled as the search for "neutral principles."[95] The idea is that the principle should be crafted and ultimately applied in such a way that it is not designed solely to achieve the outcome in the case that the justice would like to reach. However, the term "neutral principle" is, in a variety of respects, an oxymoron. Principles have content and do tend to steer a decision in some direction. Thus, the principle that supports the actual-malice standard plainly implies that it will, and indeed should, be very difficult for public officials to win libel suits. But whatever one thinks of that semantic debate, the term "neutral principles," there is general agreement that opinions ought to be principled.

Of course, more is involved in an opinion than merely stating a principle by which decisions will be made. The reasoning process by which the justice moves from the constitutional or statutory premise, to the principle that represents the justice's interpretation of the legal premise, to the formulation and application of the rule in a particular case is a critically important element of craftsmanship. Court evaluators expect opinions to be reasoned effectively and according to the principles of *stare decisis*, meaning that the opinion should develop the issue and principles and apply to them the facts with a sensitivity for the role of precedent in the Anglo-American legal tradition. It is perfectly possible, of course, to reason effectively from existing precedents and reach what many might regard as an unjust or incorrect decision, but from the standpoint of craftsmanship this is no problem. Neither is it necessary always to follow precedent to have a well-crafted opinion. Indeed, it is generally accepted that the Court is free to overturn prior rulings as long as it does so clearly and for sufficient reasons stated in the opinion.[96]

There is also the expectation that the opinion will provide some kind of guidance and explanations. This is a difficult dimension, because justices should not write what amount to advisory opinions, answering questions well beyond those presented in a case. On the other hand, justices are expected to provide guidance and explanations sufficient to make clear to the losers why they lost and enable the winners and others to conform their behavior to the Court's ruling. As Hugo Black used to say, he felt an obligation to write his opinions so that his uncle behind the plow back in Alabama could read and understand what he was doing. That is one, though not the only, reason why Black was such an ardent opponent of the use of judicial balancing tests to decide cases. Black considered that when the Court issued an opinion that in essence said, "We'll weigh each case individually," it was issuing no principled decision and providing no guidance. The only way citizens could know whether they had broken the law or obeyed it was to act and wait for a court to rule for or against them.[97]

Finally, court evaluators often search for some indication in an opinion of an awareness of the consequences of the Court's action. They desire some reassurance that the Court has thought through the implications of its rulings. This is often one of the points that dissenters raise when they think the majority has been insensitive or narrow-minded. Thus, in the *Parham* case, Brennan spoke for the dissenters, pointing out that the Court had not even considered the plight of the children who were wards of the state. To say that these children had no need for due process protections because the state, acting *in loco parentis* (in the place of the parent), could be assumed to be looking after the best interests of the child is tantamount to an assertion that criminal defendants do not require a trial because the state would, of course, never accuse an innocent person. The omission of the consideration of such a major dimension of the case was plainly a serious defect in the opinion.

A similar criticism has been made of Chief Justice Earl Warren's opinion for the Court in the *Reynolds v. Sims*[98] reapportionment case, which required that both houses of bicameral state legislatures be apportioned solely on the basis of population. The dissenters pointed out that the Court's relatively quick dismissal of the importance of such other interests as geographical differences and economic diversity within states suggested that the majority had not fully considered some of the implications of its ruling.[99]

Judicial Statesmanship

The criteria for evaluating craftsmanship, then, are relatively well understood and widely accepted. Statesmanship is a more complex concept and engenders considerably more disagreement. Even so, there are some touchstones of statesmanship against which justices are often assessed, though the labels that are attached to these measures often vary dramatically. Moreover, from a wider point of view, as Murphy puts it, we have expectations that people in high office who have a profound influence in the shaping of our lives will behave as statesmen and should be subject to criticism if they fail to do so. It should not be particularly surprising, therefore, that we have often in history found a justice complimenting a colleague on the craftsmanship displayed by his draft opinion while simultaneously explaining that she would not be able to join it because of its premises, conclusions, or implications. It also explains why many scholars can admire Earl Warren as a great judicial statesman, while criticizing some of his most important opinions on craftsmanship grounds. Alternatively, it explains why many relatively liberal admirers of the Warren Court's overall impact can be so complimentary about the craftsmanship of Justice John Harlan II while expressing considerable frustration that he joined or wrote so many opinions that, for example, rejected civil liberties claims. The task, then, is to consider what kind of a framework can be used to evaluate a justice's performance as a judicial statesman and what kind of evaluations can be given.

Statesmanship has to do with qualities of deciding cases and working with other significant actors to arrive at a judgment. One definition is the quality of leadership that assumes the preeminence of values superior to self-interest or temporary gain in pursuit of the public interest, where the public interest is defined in terms of the effort to serve the long-term best interests of the people. Thus, statesmanship has two dimensions: (1) the behavior in office exhibited by a particular official; and (2) the ends he seeks and attains. Thus, we ask whether a justice provided a good or bad decision in the sense of advancing or impeding movement toward those goals or values our polity considers fundamental, for example, liberty of thought or equality of opportunity and right. Statesmanship can only partly be a function of process. One is not a statesman merely because one plays by the rules or because one protects democratic processes. That is part of statesmanship, but only part. Indeed, the concept assumes that ends and means are related.

On the other hand, while ends are critically important, means matter as well. Therefore, statesmanship also has to do with how well or badly a justice works toward achieving support for a decision within the court. A policy-oriented judge must, if he is to be a statesperson, be concerned with more than eliciting votes in support of a draft opinion. It requires a sense of one's office and of the institution of which that office is a part. It requires as well a sense of the position of that office in the polity, defined in the modern era at least, as the nation. Furthermore, a number of justices in the history of the Court have been accorded praise precisely because their vision extended beyond the confines of the institution and the nation to a more universal, global, or timeless sense of value and appropriate ends of government, and others have been criticized for their failure to consider this wider set of concerns.

Given these elements, it is possible to contemplate the statesmanship performance of a justice along four dimensions: (1) statesmanship with respect to the internal operation and decision processes of the Court, (2) statesmanship with respect to other units of government, (3) statesmanship with respect to the national or public interest, and (4) statesmanship writ large (with respect to wider values and beyond parochial or narrowly nationalistic ends).

Statesmanship Within the Court It is on this dimension that Justice William Brennan is often rated highly because he so intimately understood the institutional character of the Court and the informal, as well as the formal, workways of its justices and staff. His tenure demonstrated the ability of a justice to be forthright regarding his own positions and yet sensitive to the art of persuasion in a small group of powerful equals, and the ability to retain an effective working relationship with colleagues across a wide range of dramatically different issues over a sustained period. He also demonstrated a selflessness that permitted him to provide extensive help to his colleagues, to draft important *per curiam* opinions that would not bear his name, and to help build majorities, as in the *United States v. Nixon* case, that were truly group products. This combination of knowledge and skills provides a kind of working definition of statesmanship within the Court.

Brennan also proved that it is possible to have convictions and yet be flexible enough to change, and to do so in a way that respects the opinions of others. One of the better examples is Brennan's change in view on issues of obscenity. The justice had become the Court's leading writer on the subject of obscenity from his earliest days on the Court until 1972, writing most of the majority opinions in that field, often upholding anti-obscenity laws. However, he became increasingly dissatisfied with his inability to define obscenity with sufficient clarity and precision so as to permit the society to protect itself against smut peddlers while simultaneously preventing prudes, hypocrites, and self-appointed guardians of the American way of life from using charges of obscenity to interfere with legitimate exercises of the freedoms of speech and press. To help him work through this dilemma, and knowing that the Court was about to hear a substantial number of obscenity cases, Brennan set to work on a lengthy memorandum examining the history of anti-obscenity law, which he ultimately made available to colleagues. At the beginning of the 1972 term, he wrote his colleagues informing them of his explorations and indicating that from that point forward, he would not vote to uphold an obscenity standard, statute, or prosecution against a First Amendment challenge unless it involved the distribution of obscene material to minors or the dissemination of the material to adults who did not wish to receive it.

Chief Justice Burger, who was ardently opposed to this view, prepared a brief memorandum of his own and called for "a division of the house."[100] The justices were to choose his approach or that of Justice Brennan. It is one thing for a justice to issue his or her own position and explain why, but quite another for the chief justice to demand that the members of the Court choose sides. The fact is, of course, that four members of the Court had been appointed by Richard

Nixon, who had run, in part, against the Supreme Court and who had called for the Court to play a major role in rolling back what was regarded as the permissiveness of the 1960s.

From that time on, Brennan often found himself in dissent on obscenity cases,[101] but on a clearly principled basis. His was a change that developed with care and careful reasoning shared with his colleagues. It was the kind of performance that wins respect even from those who disagree with the position.

Felix Frankfurter, by contrast, could behave like a statesman when he wanted to (as when he helped the Court fashion the strategy of calling for a carefully defined rehearing process in the *Brown v. Board of Education* case,[102] allowing the Court to buy time to build consensus and decide on a course of action), but he never seemed to understand that he could not get away with playing the statesman on the level of a particular case and yet disregard critically important institutional norms of collegiality and mutual respect in his overall performance. For example, Frankfurter had a regular routine that was so well known by his colleagues that it came to be something of an annoying standing joke. Whenever a new member was named to the Court, Frankfurter would greet him (in those days all members were men) with letters of congratulations and with a welcome that veritably dripped with honey. On the new member's arrival at Court, Frankfurter would appoint himself mentor and set about bringing the newcomer along into the fold. The recent arrival could expect memoranda with fulsome praise for draft opinions and promises that he would ultimately be one of the Court's greats. That happened even when everyone on the Court, including the object of the accolades, knew very well that the praise was not deserved. Frankfurter would share information about the other justices, a bit of inside gossip to convey the sense that one was truly connected. All of these things came, unless and until the new justice crossed Felix. Then things changed—the level of vituperation that could come from Frankfurter's pen to the apostate, and to other members of the Court about him, was legendary. Suddenly the person who only days before was the greatest person ever to hit the Court, next to Frankfurter himself, of course, was now unintelligent, dull-witted, incapable of writing anything above the level of prep-school essays, politically untutored, and a variety of other unflattering qualities. His obvious duplicity and personal abuse of his colleagues took its toll over the years, despite the fact that his colleagues still admired his brilliance.

Apart from these personal attacks, there was the annual memorandum from Felix at the beginning of each term lecturing his colleagues on the ways in which the Court should improve the overall quality of its opinions and other institutional matters. His sanctimonious messages hardly ingratiated him to his colleagues as a group. His willing use of surrogates outside the court to attack his adversaries on the bench was no more appealing. Whatever other accomplishments he may have had, Justice Frankfurter hardly rates high marks for institutional statesmanship.

Statesmanship with Respect to Other Units of Government   This includes the need to protect the independence and integrity of the judiciary and to meet, rather than avoid, its responsibilities. Thus, there is little doubt that one of the leading reasons that Chief Justice John Marshall is rated a great justice is because of the leadership he exercised in helping the Court to establish itself as the head

of an independent, coequal third branch of government with an important function, not only in striking down unconstitutional actions by the states or other branches of the federal government but also in legitimating appropriate exercises of constitutional authority.[103] More recently, the opinion for a unanimous Court citing John Marshall and holding against President Richard Nixon's claims in the Watergate case reaffirmed the Court's role.

On the other hand, Marshall and his colleagues have always been aware of the complex, and often delicate, relationships between the Court and the other branches of the national government as well as with states and localities and their attendant judiciaries. Whether Horace Greeley's famous observation that President Andrew Jackson had rejected the authority of the Court, stating, "John Marshall has made his decision, now let him enforce it" is accurate or apocryphal, the message has never been lost on the Court.

Members of the Court have watched states and localities evade or oppose school desegregation rulings for decades, and they have faced severe criticism when they have moved vigorously to compel action. At the same time, however, they have sometimes moved to protect states from being overwhelmed by the national government. Thus, at a time when it appeared that the federal government would be permitted to use the doctrine of preemption to remove state decision makers from important fields, the Court set warnings. The State of California enacted a moratorium on the licensing of new nuclear power plants until assurances could be provided that the problem of the handling and disposal of nuclear waste had been resolved. The federal government charged that the authority granted by Congress to the U.S. Nuclear Regulatory Commission preempted any attempt by the state to act in that field, but the Supreme Court held for the state.[104] The ground for the decision was that the federal government had preempted regulation of safety issues but left consideration of economic issues, like the impact on the state's economy, to the states. However, the case was also an indication of concern by members of the Court with the apparent jeopardy of traditional areas of state authority.

It is clear that one of the reasons that Justice Hugo Black is regarded as a great justice is because of his concern for "our federalism" and his insistence on respect by the Court for the Congress and presidency. It was not that Black was unwilling to rule against the Congress or the president; in fact, he had authored the majority opinion for the Court striking down President Harry Truman's seizure of the steel mills during the Korean War, one of the most celebrated examples of judicial challenges to executive power. Nor was Black willing to tolerate violations by the state or local governments of rights protected by the Bill of Rights. Indeed, it was Black who led the charge to "nationalize" or incorporate all the provisions of the Bill of Rights, making them applicable to the states through the due process clause of the Fourteenth Amendment. Rather, it was Black's concern that the Court never rule without carefully considering its actions in light of the proper role of the Court relative to other branches and levels of government.

Statesmanship with Respect to the National or Public Interest   In Walter Murphy's and Alexander Meiklejohn's discussions of judicial statesmanship, they had in mind something clearly quite normative in character. Murphy points out that the question is "not whether judges have influenced policy but whether that influence is to the benefit, both in the long and the short run, of society." The point that both Murphy and Meiklejohn make is that the Constitution and laws of the nation are not value neutral: Some actions serve the public interest and others do not. That is generally accepted notwithstanding the fact that there are many continuous debates over whether specific policies are or are not in the public interest. Moreover, it is still true even though some have argued that there is no such thing as the public interest.[105]

Clearly, when Justice Brennan, for example, is lauded as a judicial statesman, it is in part because he took strong positions in cases that were seen, either at the time of the decision or later in the cool reflection of history, as serving core values. His efforts to ensure due process for the poor and the weak touched a responsive chord in Americans, a spirit of fundamental fairness and equality. His forthright leadership in the attack on gender discrimination made the point in very clear terms that it is not in the public interest to deny equality to women.

Thus, notwithstanding all of the ambiguities and disagreements that may arise from time to time, it is often possible to come to substantial agreement that some actions taken by a justice served the public interest while others did not. Thus, there seems little debate that, despite the normal deference shown by the Court to the White House, the Court's rejection of Truman's seizure of the steel mills[106] and of Nixon's blanket claim of executive privilege in the Watergate case[107] reinforced the concept of the Rule of Law and supported the critically important, if sometimes troublesome, concept of separation of powers, as well as bolstered the efficacy of the Court as a significant political institution. There is surprisingly little challenge, pompous political rhetoric to the contrary from various quarters notwithstanding, to the Court's rulings in cases involving the American flag. Justice Robert Jackson's famous opinion in the *Barnette* case, striking down the mandatory flag salute, is recited regularly today as one of the best expositions of why Americans' willingness to see the flag challenged or to suffer some to refuse to be compelled to pledge allegiance to it in patriotic ceremonies supports the very concept of liberty for which the flag stands.[108] That opinion received warm praise when it was issued, in spite of the fact, or perhaps because of it, that the nation was in the middle of a world war at the time. Justice Brennan's opinions, which carried the day even in a Court dominated by conservative appointees, in the flag desecration cases,[109] still call forth Thomas Jefferson's admonition that a testimony to the strength of the republic is that it can permit the harshest critics to stand unchallenged.

On the other hand, it is possible to point to rulings that were plainly not in the public interest. Probably the best known of these were the *Dred Scott* case,[110] reinforcing slavery, and the *Korematsu v. United States*[111] case, upholding the exclusion of Japanese Americans from their homes on the West Coast and leading to their incarceration in concentration camps during World War II.

More recently, the Court rejected an attempt by a condemned prisoner to obtain a hearing at which to present new evidence that very strongly suggested his innocence. Eight years after his trial and original state appeals, Leonel Torres Herrera obtained affidavits from his dead brother's attorney, who swore that the brother had confessed to him that he had been guilty of the murders, and the brother's son testified that he had been a witness to the crimes when he was nine years old. Justice William Rehnquist, writing for the Court, could not understand why it had taken so long for this information to come forward or why the two potential witnesses had waited until the brother had died to talk. The Court concluded that the affidavits fell far short of what would be needed to justify an order for a new trial, but it did not specify how much or what kind of evidence would be adequate. Thus, in this case, the Court refused the condemned man an opportunity for a hearing to determine whether there should be a new trial, even though there was a very real chance that the man was actually innocent of the crime for which he was about to be executed. Justice Blackmun, writing for the dissenters warned: "Of one thing, however, I am certain. Just as an execution without adequate safeguards is unacceptable, so too is an execution when the condemned prisoner can prove that he is innocent. The execution of a person who can show that he is innocent comes perilously close to simple murder."[112] The issue here is not something that can be narrowly confined to technical issues of *habeas corpus* (the writ sought by the prisoner) but a much wider notion that it is fundamentally at odds with basic constitutional values and hence with the public interest to execute such a person without at least examining the new evidence in some kind of serious way.

Thus, justices will be judged for what they did from the standpoint of the public interest and the consistency of their actions with fundamental constitutional values.

Statesmanship Writ Large But there is an even larger sense in which statesmanship is evaluated, that is, statesmanship beyond the narrow ends or values of the United States and toward more universal ends. There are times when the justice may look to the world beyond the borders of the United States in contemplating action. Thus, it was clear to members of the Court at the time of the ruling in *Brown v. Board of Education* that the ruling would play on the world stage. For even as the United States was joining other nations to condemn racial segregation in other parts of the world, segregation was legally practiced within our own borders. Brennan's opinion for the Court in *Plyler v. Doe*, striking a denial of education for children of illegal immigrants, stands for another proposition that this country has championed abroad, namely, that whatever disposition is ultimately made in a matter of immigration, it is fundamentally wrong to punish the children of those immigrants by denying them an opportunity to learn while they are here.

On the other hand, such rulings as *United States v. Alvarez-Machain*,[113] upholding prosecution of suspects kidnapped from Mexico on the orders of U.S. officials, not only do not consider the wider implications of U.S. actions, but also ignore clear international condemnation. To underscore that point, Justice John P. Stevens quoted a South African opinion issued the year before rejecting the authority of the government to try a member of the African National Congress who had been kidnapped by South African authorities relying in part on U.S. precedent.[114] The ruling showed contempt for the Mexican government with whom we had an extradition treaty and a willingness to tolerate and even to encourage international lawlessness, since plainly any other country would be equally justified in taking similar actions against the United States.

It is true that over the course of justices' service on the Court, they may find actions that they take receiving differing evaluations on these measures of statesmanship. The overall assessment of their performance will include these varying evaluations.

SUMMARY

For good or ill, then, your performance will be evaluated and judgments will be passed on you as a member of the Court. While it is true that many of those judgments will be purely political or subject to the whims of passing public fancy, others will be more substantive and systematic. Among your evaluators are those who will contemplate your skills as a craftsman, and they may rate you highly even if they do not agree with the outcomes of many of the opinions in which you set forth your views. On the other hand, there are a number of dimensions of statesmanship against which your performance will also be measured. These evaluations will consider your sense of the institution and the way your performance affects it, your ability to consider and incorporate an understanding of the relationship of the Court to other institutions of government, your commitment to the public interest broadly understood as a reinforcement of basic constitutional values, and your vision and sensitivity to issues that extend beyond American shores into the international community.

In some respects, though, part of the evaluation of your service on the Court may be based on what you do off the bench. Criticisms of off-the-bench activity are frequently attacks on various dimensions of statesmanship, but they may even be the foundation for challenges to craftsmanship. It is to that portion of your life that we turn next.

NOTES

[1] See, for example, Albert P. Blaustein and Roy Mersky, "Rating Supreme Court Justices," *American Bar Association Journal* 58 (1972): 1183.

[2] See Robin W. Winks, ed., *The Historian as Detective* (New York: Harper and Row, 1968).

[3] John P. Frank, "Hugo Black: He Has Joined the Giants," in Jesse Choper, ed., *The Supreme Court and Its Justices* (Chicago: American Bar Association, 1987), p. 115.

[4] Quoted in Joan Biskupic, "Brennan's Unique Judicial Stamp," *Congressional Quarterly Weekly Report,* July 28, 1990, p. 2412.

[5] Stephen J. Markman and Alfred S. Regnery, "The Mind of Justice Brennan: A 25-Years Tribute," *National Review,* May 18, 1984, p. 30.

[6] Quoted in Linda Greenhouse, "An Activist's Legacy," *New York Times,* July 22, 1980, p. 1.

[7] Ibid.

[8] Quoted in ibid.

[9] Quoted in David A. Kaplan, "A Master Builder," *Newsweek,* July 30, 1990, p. 19.

[10] Ibid.

[11] Wallace Mendelson, "Brennan's Revolution," *Commentary,* Feb. 1991, p. 36.

[12] Nat Hentoff, "The Constitutionalist," *New Yorker,* Mar. 12, 1990, p. 46.

[13] Ibid.

[14] Quoted in Bernard Schwartz, *Super Chief* (New York: New York University Press, 1983), p. 205.

[15] Markman and Regenery, "Mind of Justice Brennan," 30.

[16] Quoted in Henry Abraham, *Justices and Presidents,* 2d ed. (New York: Oxford University Press, 1985), p. 263. There is some dispute about the comment. Abraham quotes Elmo Richardson, *The Presidency of Dwight David Eisenhower* (Lawrence: Regents Press of Kansas, 1979), p. 1008. However, a recent Brennan biographer observed: "According to Burton's handwritten diaries, a bewildered

Eisenhower expressed disappointment at the decisions of Warren and Brennan. . . . The President told Burton he just didn't understand how Vanderbilt could have been so 'off-base' as to recommend Brennan for the Supreme Court. It was those comments by Eisenhower that later translated through the rumor mill to a statement that Eisenhower said: 'I have made two mistakes and they are both sitting on the Court.' The truth was that Eisenhower didn't say it exactly that way to Burton. But the thought was there" (Kim Isaac Eisler, *A Justice for All* [New York: Simon and Schuster, 1993], p. 159).

[17]See, for example, Schwartz, *Super Chief*, chap. 6.

[18]Bernard Schwartz, *The Unpublished Opinions of the Warren Court* (New York: Oxford University Press, 1985).

[19]Howard Ball and Phillip Cooper, *Of Power and Right* (New York: Oxford University Press, 1992).

[20]Justice William J. Brennan, Jr., interview with authors, Washington, D.C., Oct. 29, 1986.

[21]*Keyishian v. Bd. of Regents*, 385 U.S. 589 (1967). See also *Speiser v. Randall*, 357 U.S. 513 (1958).

[22]*New York Times v. Sullivan*, 376 U.S. 254 (1964); and *Time v. Hill*, 385 U.S. 374 (1967).

[23]*Cooper v. Aaron*, 358 U.S. 1 (1958).

[24]*Green v. County School Bd.*, 391 U.S. 430, 438–39 (1968).

[25]The other was *Brown v. Board of Education of Topeka, Kansas, I*, 347 U.S. 483 (1954) (see Schwartz, *Super Chief*).

[26]*United States v. Nixon*, 418 U.S. 683 (1974).

[27]381 U.S. 479 (1965).

[28]*NAACP v. Alabama*, 357 U.S. 449 (1958).

[29]*Eisenstadt v. Baird*, 405 U.S. 438 (1972). See also *Carey v. Population Services*, 431 U.S. 678 (1977).

[30]*Metropolitan Broadcasting v. FCC*, 497 U.S. 547 (1990).

[31]*Rutan v. Republican Party*, 497 U.S. 62 (1990).

[32]*United States v. Eichman*, 496 U.S. 310 (1990); and *Texas v. Johnson*, 491 U.S. 397 (1989).

[33]*United Steelworkers v. Weber*, 443 U.S. 193 (1979); and *Johnson v. Transportation Agency of Santa Clara County*, 480 U.S. 616 (1987). This accomplishment would not go unnoticed by Court watchers with an interest in the efforts of the Reagan administration to move the court to the Right (David G. Savage, *Turning Right* [New York: Wiley, 1992], pp. 251–60, 326–27).

[34]411 U.S. 1 (1973).

[35]More specifically, Brennan wrote: "Education, of course, is not among the rights afforded explicit protection under our Federal Constitution. Nor do we find any basis for saying it is implicitly so protected" (ibid., p. 35).

[36]*Keyes v. School District No. 1*, 413 U.S. 189 (1973).

[37]*Plyler v. Doe*, 457 U.S. 202 (1982).

[38]*Board of Education, Island Trees Union Free School Dist. v. Pico*, 457 U.S. 853 (1982).

[39]*Frontiero v. Richardson*, 411 U.S. 677 (1973).

[40]*Craig v. Boren*, 429 U.S. 190 (1976).

[41]*Frontiero v. Richardson*, at p. 684. See also *Roberts v. United States Jaycees*, 468 U.S. 609 (1984).

[42]*Bivens v. Six Unknown Agents, Federal Bureau of Narcotics*, 403 U.S. 388 (1971); *Davis v. Passman*, 395 U.S. 228 (1979); *Maine v. Thiboutot*, 448 U.S. 1 (1980); and *Owen v. City of Independence*, 445 U.S. 622 (1980).

[43]*Lindsey v. Normet*, 405 U.S. 56 (1972), dissent; *Ortwein v. Schwab*, 410 U.S. 656 (1973), dissent; *San Antonio Ind. School Dist. v. Rodriguez*, 411 U.S. 1 (1973); *Shapiro v. Thompson*, 394 U.S. 618 (1969); and *U.S. Dept. of Agriculture v. Moreno*, 413 U.S. 528 (1973).

[44]See *Bell v. Burson*, 402 U.S. 535 (1971); *Goldberg v. Kelly*, 397 U.S. 254 (1970); and *Wheeler v. Montgomery*, 397 U.S. 280 (1970).

[45]See his dissents in *Board of Regents v. Roth*, 408 U.S. 564 (1972); *Mathews v. Eldridge*, 424 U.S. 319 (1976); *Cleveland Bd. of Education v. Loudermill*, 470 U.S. 532 (1985); *Weinberger v. Salfi*, 422 U.S. 749 (1975); *Bishop v. Wood*, 426 U.S. 341 (1976); *Paul v. Davis*, 424 U.S. 693 (1976); and *O'Bannon v. Town Court Nursing Center*, 447 U.S. 773 (1980). On Court access, see *Warth v. Seldin*, 422 U.S. 490 (1975), dissent.

[46]*Gertz v. Welch*, 418 U.S. 323 (1974), dissent; *Miller v. California*, 413 U.S. 15 (1973), dissent; *Paris Adult Theatre v. Slaton*, 413 U.S. 49 (1973), dissent; *Herbert v. Lando*, 441 U.S. 153 (1979), dissent; *Time v. Firestone*, 424 U.S. 448 (1976), dissent; *Hazelwood School Dist. v. Kuhlmeier*, dissent; *Perry v.*

Sindermann, 408 U.S. 593 (1972); *Connick v. Myers*, 461 U.S. 138 (1983), dissent; and *Perry Education Assoc. v. Perry Local Educators' Assoc.*, 460 U.S. 37 (1983), dissent.

⁴⁷See his dissents in *Beal v. Doe*, 432 U.S. 438 (1977); *Maher v. Roe*, 432 U.S. 464 (1977); *Poelker v. Doe*, 432 U.S. 519 (1977); *Harris v. McRae*, 448 U.S. 297 (1980); and *Webster v. Reproductive Health Services*, 492 U.S. 490 (1989).

⁴⁸See his dissents in *Profitt v. Florida*, 428 U.S. 242 (1976); and *Gregg v. Georgia*, 428 U.S. 153 (1976).

⁴⁹David O'Brien, *Storm Center*, 2d ed. (New York: Norton, 1990), p. 173.

⁵⁰Stanley H. Friedelbaum, "Justice William J. Brennan, Jr.: Policy Making in the Judicial Thicket," in Charles M. Lamb and Stephen C. Helpern, eds., *The Burger Court* (Champaign: University of Illinois, 1991), p. 115.

⁵¹*Glass v. Louisiana*, 85 L.Ed.2d 514, 520–21 (1985).

⁵²Ibid., 525.

⁵³William J. Brennan, Jr., "Constitutional Adjudication and the Death Penalty: A View from the Court," 100 *Harvard Law Review* (1986): 313, 330.

⁵⁴Abner J. Mikva, "Tribute to Justice William J. Brennan, Jr.," *Harvard Law Review* 104 (1990): 9, 10.

⁵⁵Richard A. Posner, "Tribute to Justice William J. Brennan, Jr.," *Harvard Law Review* 104 (1990): 13, 14.

⁵⁶Ibid., 14.

⁵⁷Harry A. Blackmun, "A Tribute to Mr. Justice Brennan," *Harvard Civil Rights/Civil Liberties Law Review* 26 (1991): 1.

⁵⁸Byron R. White, "Tribute to the Honorable William J. Brennan, Jr., *Yale Law Journal* 100 (1991): 113, 114.

⁵⁹Posner, "Tribute to Justice Brennan," 14.

⁶⁰Norman Dorsen, "Tribute to Justice William J. Brennan, Jr.," *Harvard Law Review* 104 (1990): 15, 24.

⁶¹Owen Fiss, "A Life Lived Twice," *Yale Law Journal* 100 (1991): 1117, 1120.

⁶²Ibid., 1120

⁶³Thurgood Marshall, "A Tribute to Justice William J. Brennan, Jr.," *Harvard Law Review* 104 (1990): 1, 2.

⁶⁴Nina Totenburg, "Tribute to Justice William J. Brennan, Jr.," *Harvard Law Review* 104 (1990): 33, 34.

⁶⁵William J. Brennan, Jr., "The Worldwide Influence of the United States Constitution as a Charter of Human Rights," *Nova Law Review* 15 (1991): 1; and idem, "Why Have a Bill of Rights?" *Oxford Journal of Legal Studies* 9 (1989): 425.

⁶⁶Fiss, "Life Lived Twice," 1120.

⁶⁷Marshall, "Tribute to Justice Brennan," 5.

⁶⁸Bernard Schwartz, *The Ascent of Pragmatism* (New York: Addison-Wesley, 1990), p. 343.

⁶⁹Stephen L. Wasby, *The Supreme Court in the Federal Judicial System*, 2d ed. (Chicago: Nelson-Hall, 1984), pp. 224–26.

⁷⁰Article III

⁷¹Justice Arthur Goldberg (retired), interview with authors, Washington, D.C., Aug. 27, 1987.

⁷²Justice William J. Brennan, Jr., interview with authors, Washington, DC, Oct. 29, 1986.

⁷³William O. Douglas, "Stare Decisis," in Alan F. Westin, ed., *The Supreme Court: Views from the Inside* (Westport, CT: Greenwood Press, 1983).

⁷⁴*Baker v. Carr*, 369 U.S. 186 (1962).

⁷⁵Bradley C. Canon, "A Framework for the Analysis of Judicial Activism," in Stephen C. Halpern and Charles M. Lamb, eds., *Supreme Court Activism and Restraint* (Lexington, MA: Lexington Press, 1982); and Bradley Canon, "Defining the Dimensions of Judicial Activism," *Judicature* 66 (1983): 236.

⁷⁶See O'Brien, *Storm Center*, p. 60.

⁷⁷Quoted in Alpheus T. Mason, *The Supreme Court from Taft to Warren* (New York: Norton, 1958), p. 194.

[78]*Frank v. Maryland*, 359 U.S. 360 (1959); *Camara v. Municipal Court*, 387 U.S. 523 (1967); and *See v. Seattle*, 387 U.S. 541 (1967).

[79]*Rochin v. California*, 342 U.S. 165 (1952).

[80]See John Hart Ely, *Democracy and Distrust* (New Haven, CT, Yale University Press, 1980).

[81]*Haig v. Agee*, 453 U.S. 280 (1981).

[82]*Zemel v. Rusk*, 381 U.S. 1 (1965); and *Kent v. Dulles*, 357 U.S. 116 (1958).

[83]Such a ruling is plainly a making of policy, though by indirect means (see *Poe v. Ulmann*, 367 U.S. 497 [1961]).

[84]See *Los Angeles Department of Water and Power v. Manhart*, 435 U.S. 702 (1978).

[85]See also *TVA v. Hill*, 437 U.S. 153 (1978).

[86]Brown v. Allen, 344 U.S. 443, 540 (1953), quoted in Wasby, *Supreme Court*, p. 2.

[87]Alexander Meiklejohn, *Political Freedom* (Chicago: University of Chicago Press, 1948), pp. 32–33.

[88]Walter Murphy, *Elements of Judicial Strategy* (Chicago: University of Chicago Press, 1964), p. 2.

[89]Frank Coffin, *The Ways of a Judge*. (Boston: Houghton Mifflin, 1980), p. 63.

[90]Pierro Calamandrei, *Procedure and Democracy* (New York: New York University Press, 1956).

[91]Felix Frankfurter, MTTC, re: *Merrill v. Fahs*, Jan. 25, 1945, box 106, WODP.

[92]Mikva, "Tribute to Justice Brennan."

[93]*J. L. v. Parham*, 412 F.Supp. 112 (MDGA 1976), rev'd sub. nom. *Parham v. J.R.*, 442 U.S. 584 (1979).

[94]*New York Times v. Sullivan*, 376 U.S. 255 (1964).

[95]See Herbert Wechsler, "Toward Neutral Principles of Constitutional Law," 73 *Harvard Law Review* 1 (1959).

[96]Howard Ball, *Judicial Craftsmanship or Fiat? Direct Overturn in the Supreme Court* (Westport, CT: Greenwood Press, 1978).

[97]See Black's dissents in *Barenblatt v. United States*, 360 U.S. 109 (1958); and *Konigsberg v. State Bar*, 366 U.S. 36 (1961).

[98]377 U.S. 533 (1964).

[99]See dissent in *Lucas v. Forty-Fourth General Assembly of Colorado*, 377 U.S. 713 (1964).

[100]Warren E. Burger, MTTC, Nov. 13, 1972, box 283, WJBP. See also Burger, MTTC, Nov. 20, 1972, box 283, Brennan Papers.

[101]See *Paris Adult Theatre v. Slaton*, 413 U.S. 49 (1973); and *Miller v. California*, 413 U.S. 15 (1973).

[102]Schwartz, *Super Chief*, chap. 2.

[103]See Charles Warren, *The Supreme Court in United States History* (Boston: Little, Brown, 1926); and Leonard Baker, *John Marshall: A Life in Law* (New York: Macmillan, 1974).

[104]*Pacific Gas and Electric v. State Energy Commission*, 461 U.S. 190 (1983).

[105]See Glendon Schubert, "The Public Interest: Theorem, Theosophy, or Theory?" *American Political Science Review* 51 (1957): 346.

[106]*Youngstown Sheet and Tube v. Sawyer*, 343 U.S. 579 (1952).

[107]*United States v. Nixon.*

[108]*West Virginia Board of Education v. Barnette*, 319 U.S. 624 (1943).

[109]*United States v. Eichman*, 496 U.S. 310 (1990); and *Texas v. Johnson*, 491 U.S. 397 (1989).

[110]*Dred Scott v. Sandford*, 19 Howard 393 (1857).

[111]323 U.S. 214 (1944).

[112]*Herrera v. Collins*, 122 L.Ed 2d 203, 246 (1993).

[113]119 L.Ed2d 441 (1992).

[114]*S. v. Ebrahim*, 1991 (2) S. Afr. L. Rep. 553 (Apr.–June 1991).

After Hours: The Justices off the Bench

It is a strange life, you think to yourself as you sit back in your office and muse on your years on the bench. You recall a story told to you by one of the retired justices.[1] He remembered how much his world had changed from the life he knew when he was in private practice. He had been extremely active, not only in practice but in various professional organizations as well. His phone rang incessantly. He had standing luncheon engagements with professional friends. Then he was appointed to the Supreme Court, and everything changed. He recalled many days when he found himself staring at his telephone, as he described it, "like a teenage girl waiting for someone to call for a date."[2] Finally, he got to the point where he could endure the isolation no longer. He picked up the phone and called that old friend, a partner in one of Washington's leading firms, with whom he had eaten lunch every week. But when he reached the friend, the justice found himself in a terribly awkward conversation. His friend reminded him that although he would love to have lunch with him, it was well known that his firm had cases before the Court and it just wouldn't do for the two of them to be seen together.

There are days when you feel about the same as your colleague. It is not that life in the Court is dull or that there are no interesting and stimulating people on the Court and among the staff with whom to share a meal or a brisk walk around the area at lunchtime. But you know you are not as free as you were prior to coming onto the Court. Your life is more limited, and not just your social life either.

Before you came to the bench, you had been politically aware and involved. Indeed, if you had not been, it is unlikely that you would have reached the Supreme Court, with or without intervening service on a lower court. Yet once on the Court, you remembered Justice Felix Frankfurter's admonition:

> When a priest enters a monastery, he must leave—or ought to leave—all sorts of worldly desires behind him. And this isn't idle, high-flown talk. We are all poor human creatures, and it's difficult enough to be wholly intellectually and morally disinterested when one has no other motive except that of being a judge according to one's full conscience.[3]

Indeed, many justices have taken a similar view, if not monastic vows, of their service on the Court. Justice Hugo Black's widow Elizabeth told the story of her husband's proposal. After discussing the marriage, Hugo added that she had to understand something at the outset. If she ever insisted on a divorce, he would cooperate, but he would have to leave the Court.[4] As she put it, the Court was so much a part of him that almost everything else had to be subordinated to the good of the institution. Similarly, Justice William Brennan's commitment to the institution was very strong, leading him to recuse himself in situations in which others might not have thought twice about participating.

On the other hand, the stories about justices who disregarded the monastery rule are legion, including the tales of the very same Felix Frankfurter who so adamantly proclaimed the rule. Sometimes the off-the-bench activities of members of the Court create considerable difficulty; in the case of Justice Abe Fortas they led to his resignation from the Court. Still, the history of the Court is rife with examples of justices who were actively, and often politically, involved outside the institution.

What are the factors that play a role in the off-the-bench activities of the justices, and why do they matter? One approach to that question is to consider the very full life led by one of the Court's legendary off-the-bench activists, Justice William O. Douglas.

WILLIAM O. DOUGLAS: CITIZEN AND JUSTICE

From his youth onward, William O. Douglas lived a life of action and involvement. Except for an early bout with infantile paralysis, which weakened him physically and caused him to focus his competitive energies on schoolwork rather than athletics, there was nothing in his formative years that would suggest a quiet, staid future. As he matured, he continually discovered more avenues for political involvement and personal discovery. It was therefore no surprise to anyone who considered his past that Douglas would be, indeed would be driven to be, active and involved outside the Court as well as within it. And whether by design or by accident, many of these activities had an impact on his own life on the Court, on his colleagues, and on the Court itself.

Justice William O. Douglas hiking the B&O Canal trail, Washington, D.C.

Building a Public Career

Even as a young man, growing up in Yakima, Washington, Douglas's pan-theon of political heroes was populated by Progressive-era activists like William Jennings Bryan, Hiram Johnson, William Borah, and Gifford Pinchot. He developed an early dislike and distrust for "the establishment," those scions of the social and economic community who seemed to espouse one set of values publicly and engage in quite a different brand of behavior in their day-to-day lives. He found that business leaders and even churchmen were often up to their ears in the seamy side of life. As a child in a poor family, most of whose meager inheritance had been squandered by an attorney who invested it in a scheme he was promoting, Douglas worked at all manner of odd jobs, including as a field hand. These experiences instilled in him an appreciation for the downtrodden, the outcasts, and the despised people of society. Even a brief examination of his early years makes it clear why Douglas saw himself "taking the side of the helpless, the suckers, the underdogs."[5]

When he moved East to begin his professional study at Columbia Law School, and later as a young academic at Columbia and Yale, he found himself in exactly the kind of environment that would mold his predisposition for action into a life of involvement. First Columbia and then Yale became the focus of the legal-realist school of jurisprudence. For many of his teachers, and later colleagues, the central point of that approach to the field was that law could not be abstracted from dynamic social, economic, and political life, that it was more than an exercise in logic and fact-finding. Law was a social tool, created by the community to accomplish its needs and goals, and judges, who play a central role in the life of the law, are important players in government and in the society it serves.

From his years as a student with Underhill Moore to his work as a scholar of business failures, Douglas had never been content to confine to the law library his quest for understanding or change. As a professor at Yale, Douglas sought to understand bankruptcy law by interviewing those involved in bankruptcies. He learned more about corporations by studying the failures that brought firms into reorganization and by perceiving them as organisms with a life cycle than by examining the case law that governed their operations. It was his expertise as a corporate coroner that brought Douglas to the attention of Washington insiders and led to his eventual position as chair of the Securities and Exchange Commission, his steppingstone to the Supreme Court.

Once in Washington, Douglas moved himself into Franklin Roosevelt's inner circle. He was a far more involved and active political player than his role at an independent regulatory commission would have suggested. On a personal level, his background with polio was shared by President Roosevelt, and his budding reputation as a legal tough guy and iconoclast in the midst of Washington society made him attractive to the leader of the New Deal. Douglas reveled in the whole spirit of New Deal reform. He wrote, "These were the heady days of the New Deal when Washington, D.C., teemed with brave dreams and bold experiments."[6]

One other factor is important in understanding Douglas's commitments and enthusiasm as he faced appointment to the Court. He was a young man. He had managed all of his accomplishments by the tender age of forty, becoming one of the youngest nominees in history for the High Court. His old mentor from Columbia, Harlan Fiske Stone, wrote Douglas, welcoming him to the Court and recognizing the importance of his youth. "You are fortunate in being able to begin at a good age, forty. How much I would have enjoyed the years between forty and fifty on the Court, and how much more it would have meant to the influence and success of my work."[7]

A Vote for Freedom

For all these reasons, William O. Douglas was not ready to take Felix Frankfurter's monastic oath on entering the Supreme Court. On the contrary, he was ready to plunge into the most important phase of his personal and professional life. He was not prepared to relinquish either and fully prepared to use his life on the Court to develop both.

As Douglas explained it, an event occurred early in his tenure on the Court that helped him to overcome once and for all any lingering concerns he might have had regarding constraints on him as a justice and a man. He cast a vote in a case that would permit taxation of judges. From that point on, he decided that, if he was to be a taxpayer, like everyone else, then there was no reason why he should not have the full rights of any citizen to participate in his own governance.

Still, his early years on the Court saw Douglas continuing to grow and develop, both personally and professionally, following more often than leading the Court in many important opinions, some of which he would later repudiate. Some of the forces that would plunge him into a life of controversy in pursuit of justice were historic in nature, while others had to do with his own expanding horizons.

Political Activist and Citizen of the World

For anyone who becomes involved in politics, there is a choice of arena, a decision about where to concentrate one's energies. One broad division is between foreign policy and domestic issues. For Douglas in his early years in Washington and on the Court, the political world was largely defined by the United States, but that was to change dramatically during the late 1940s and 1950s.

The Washington Wars   There was never any doubt in Douglas's mind that the Supreme Court was a political body. And if he had had any question, it would quickly have been resolved by the situation he found as he entered the Court. He joined a Court in 1938 that was split between laissez-faire, conservative jurists, some middle-of-the-road justices, and fellow New Dealer Hugo Black. Those realities were highlighted as well by his continuing personal participation in the life of the New Deal and his involvement long after FDR had passed from the scene.

Douglas was a dedicated New Dealer who brought those commitments to the Court. Contrary to his later protestations, Douglas was clearly involved in the 1930s Court-packing fight, working to line up supporters for the plan among members of the law school community.[8] He was also at the core of the group of New Dealers appointed to the Court with the intention of reversing the string of rulings that had constrained the ability of both the federal and state governments to battle the Great Depression and to create a regulatory process that would protect the marketplace. Of course, the entire political context changed considerably not long after Douglas came to the Court, as the United States entered World War II. As in other areas, particularly in the early years, Douglas was a solid vote in defense of the commander in chief, and voted to support the exclusion of Japanese Americans from the West Coast under Executive Order 9066.[9] Douglas was more than just a good New Deal soldier on the Court, though. He remained actively in touch with his New Deal colleagues, including FDR; so much so that he was a serious possibility for the vice-presidential nomination in 1944, which ultimately went to Harry Truman. Douglas even seriously entertained the idea of leaving the Court to take a position with the wartime administration, though there is a dispute among scholars about how actively his services were sought.

After the war, Douglas remained actively involved with events at the other end of Pennsylvania Avenue. Truman, who succeeded FDR as president after FDR's death, was a very different man from FDR, and a dramatically different president. He appointed several new members of the Court very unlike the sort sent there by his predecessor. It would have been difficult to find four men more different from the justices they replaced than Justices Fred Vinson, Sherman Minton, Harold Burton, and Tom Clark. Their presence did not calm the waters of the troubled Court; in some measure at least, they instead contributed to the stormy relationships that had already developed there.

The nation had been scandalized when Justice Robert Jackson, convinced that he had been denied elevation to the chief justiceship by a cabal managed by Hugo Black, wrote scathing attacks on Black to the congressional leadership and the newspapers.[10] Jackson, who was in Germany at the time prosecuting the

Nuremberg war trials, rejected Truman's denial of the charges and fervent requests to withhold his public blast. It was partly because the public conflicts on the Court were endangering confidence in the institution that Truman put the former Congressman, and apparently effective politician, Vinson in the center chair. The evidence is that, if anything, Vinson fueled rather than moderated the conflict.

Despite a host of rising tensions, Douglas remained close to Truman for a considerable period. The poker games at the White House, known as "command performances" during the FDR days, continued, though with a slightly different atmosphere. Truman asked Douglas to serve as his secretary of the interior and later as his running mate in 1948. He went so far as to state that the only thing Douglas lacked to be a viable presidential candidate was more visibility in an executive-branch position. Douglas refused, though he was sorely tempted to move toward the White House. His life was changing, and the changes led to profound differences in his relationship with the White House and his views on the Court. He was discovering the reality of the great, wide, politically explosive world outside the United States.

A New World   Ironically, the force that made Douglas a citizen of the world who traveled, thought, and wrote widely about global issues and their implications at home was not found in Washington, D.C., but in the influence of a boyhood friend, Douglas Corpron. Corpron was a medical missionary in China as World War II approached, and he returned to China again after the war, experiencing the turmoil of the revolution. Beginning in 1940, Corpron's letters about the turbulence in Asia and its human cost stimulated Douglas to recognize his own parochialism and see the need to expand his knowledge.[11] Starting in 1949, Douglas began traveling every year during the summer recesses of the Court, financing his activities by writing magazine articles or books for the popular press and giving speeches, like his Tagore Lectures in India, also published as a book.[12] His adventures found him visiting with nomadic tribes in the desert of Iran, hiking the Himalayas, and slogging through the jungles of Southeast Asia.[13] It is no small irony that on one of these trips, Douglas sent a paperweight made of French coins from the battlefield at Dien Bien Phu, Vietnam, to his lawyer and friend Clark Clifford, who would later become Lyndon Johnson's secretary of defense in charge of prosecuting the war in Southeast Asia. It was also interesting that he wrote twenty-five years before the events that Iran and its strategic place in the world, as well as its oil resources, would make it a central problem of U.S. foreign policy in the decades to come.[14] Much of the time Douglas met with the common people, but he also talked with political leaders, an option afforded him by his position as a Supreme Court justice. He was important enough to engage but not politically visible enough to be too dangerous to take part in conversations with key figures. Corpron had been worried about the fate his friend might meet wandering in such turbulent parts of the globe, but he recognized the unique situation from which Douglas operated and the possibility that it might lead to important opportunities for international communications and understanding.[15]

Indeed, Douglas tried to accomplish exactly that goal. He communicated what he learned to President Truman privately. He packed his articles and books that were ostensibly travelogues with important political information. His speeches took on an international flavor as he tried to make it clear that the world was watching America's behavior in such fields as free speech, particularly as the Red Scare moved from early postwar anxiety about the growing power of the Soviet Union to outright hysteria. The fact, for example, that he found himself actively questioned about the abuses of Senator Joseph McCarthy and company in, of all places, Hobart, Tasmania, drove home to Douglas just how obvious it was to people around the world that the United States was not living the ideals it espoused to everyone else.[16] It was precisely the need to recognize that acting on America's ideals was the country's most powerful tool in international affairs that Douglas continued to espouse.[17] He wrote: "The contest is on for the uncommitted people of the earth. These ideals express the one true advantage we have over communism in that contest."[18]

But many Americans, including Truman, were not prepared to hear the message, preferring instead to operate from a narrow, politically limited perspective. At a press conference in the fall of 1951 on the return from one of his trips, Douglas answered a reporter by saying that the United States should recognize the Peoples' Republic of China. As soon as news of his comment hit Washington, Douglas's enemies on the Hill mounted an attack that eventually, in combination with his actions in the Russian spy case of Julius and Ethel Rosenberg, led to the first attempt to impeach him. It also essentially brought an end to the relationship between Douglas and Truman.

Truman wrote to Douglas: "As long as I am president, if I can prevent it, that cutthroat organization will never be recognized by us as the Government of China and I am sorry that a justice of the Supreme Court has been willing to champion the interest of a bunch of murderers by a public statement." He added, "I am being very frank with you Bill because fundamentally I am very fond of you but you have missed the boat . . . if you really wanted to get into politics."[19]

Douglas was saddened by the president's reply, but he understood all too well the basis for it. First of all, he tried to get Truman to understand that he cared for the future of the nation more than any possible political career. "I have no ambition except to stay on the Court. That has indeed been my consistent course: I called off my friends in 1944 and denied them the opportunity to get the Vice Presidential nomination for me; and I declined your most gracious invitation for me to be Secretary of the Interior in 1946 and your running mate in 1948." He reminded Truman of the many things he had told the president a year earlier, including the assertion that crossing the thirty-eighth parallel in Korea would have disastrous results. On the more fundamental challenge leveled by the president, Douglas answered, "Your view is an understandable one. It is today perhaps the popular view. But my travels in Asia during the last three summers have convinced me that there is only tragedy to our country if it is maintained." He concluded:

These are times that try the souls of all of us. I have returned from Asia full of fear. The world you and I love is shrinking each year, Mr. President. I have been to Asia three summers now and each year I have found that the influence of the West has grown smaller and smaller. The trend against us is alarming. I have returned this time with fear in my heart for the country I love. The red tide rolls on and on in Asia; the bulk of the people of the world are slowly lining up against us; we rather than Russia are tragically coming to be the symbol of their enemy. The day may not be far distant when we are left in all our loneliness with our atomic bombs.[20]

Years later, a similar disagreement, this time about Vietnam, would bring an end to a longstanding relationship between Douglas and President Johnson.

In the years following the break with Truman, Douglas's stock at the White House varied in value, and that despite the fact he had a longstanding friendship with the Kennedy family and with LBJ. His ability to have an impact shifted over time—more significant than some of his detractors claimed but less dramatic than Douglas himself might have thought. It is no small irony that in matters of world affairs Douglas was more often right than wrong and usually well ahead of many of his adversaries in the State Department.

Throughout the 1950s and into the 1960s, Douglas traveled and wrote extensively in an effort to develop his own ideas about how to address global change, from the clashes among superpowers to the struggles of newly formed nations emerging from colonial rule. His consistent theme was that the United States could influence the global community only if it respected the fact that the needs of people of other lands are very much like those of people in the United States and that the failure to honor freedom and equality in the United States speaks louder than any military action abroad. He took American people to task for failure to be true to the Bill of Rights and singled out the Supreme Court itself as a central part of the problem for failing to exercise the authority and independence necessary to protect freedom and equality during turbulent times.[21]

However, Douglas was not content simply to write books and give speeches. One of his lectures inspired the creation of the Parvin Foundation, with which Douglas became associated. At the same time, he was actively involved with the

Justice William O. Douglas and President Lyndon Baines Johnson in the President's Oval Office, discussing the war in Vietnam.

Center for the Study of Democratic Institutions. These organizations focused on development of literacy and education programs in Third World countries, and Douglas was actively engaged in their programs. It was one of their events, the *Pacem in Terris* convocation in 1967, that was a central factor in the break with President Johnson over Vietnam policy.

Some of the center leaders had interviewed Ho Chi Minh and were certain he would attend the *Pacem in Terris* conference and would be willing to engage in private talks with U.S. representatives. The State Department cleared the invitation, and Douglas met with the president on June 8, 1966, to ensure support. Douglas reported, "I asked him if he had any objections to our getting together with Ho Chi Minh and others from Asia, including, hopefully, the Peking regime. He said without hesitation he had no objection and that he hoped we could do it."[22] In May 1967, Douglas wrote Senator Charles Percy (R–Ill.), "I might note, in confidence, that what appeared to be an effort in the State Department to undercut the convocation has now been reversed in the White House, and we are now proceeding with full (if still reluctant in some quarters) approval."[23] However, Douglas learned that the president later moved to disrupt the conference and block any chance for participation by Hanoi, undercutting his own efforts and those of the center to bring an end to the developing conflict in Vietnam.[24]

Douglas tried again to help with the situation in Vietnam when his services were sought as an intermediary to get messages through to Johnson past the State Department. The second and most crucial of these communications took place in February of 1968. P. K. Banerjee, one of Douglas's old friends, was then serving as Indian Ambassador to the Soviet Union. Banerjee passed a message from Hanoi to Douglas for delivery to Johnson. Johnson had given a speech on a possible end to the bombing in Vietnam, and Defense Secretary Clifford had elaborated on the theme in testimony he gave in Congress in January 1968. Douglas wrote to Clifford:

> The attached message from Hanoi has just reached me through the good offices of a noncommunist country. It has not apparently been presented as yet to the Department of State, the desire of the intermediary nation being to get the message directly to the President. The message read:
>
> Q. If the bombing ceases, when will talks start?
> A. 7 to 15 days.
> Q. What will be the subject matter of the discussion?
> A. Anything within the frame of reference of the Geneva Conference.
> Q. Who will be parties to the talks?
> A. North Viet Nam and the United States. Either can bring in another party.
> Q. Will any advantage of the United States be taken in case of cessation of the bombing?
> A. Hanoi accepts Clark Clifford's statement of January 25, 1968.[25]

Douglas later concluded that Johnson had ignored this opportunity as he had others. The clash over the war broke another important friendship for Douglas.[26]

Domestic Activities   His active and controversial international activities did not stop Douglas from adopting a frenetic and controversial domestic agenda as well. His writing and speaking schedule would rival that of any figure in public life. The stories of Douglas's whistle-stop tours of college campuses are legion. He would deliberately provoke and challenge audiences. He had no patience with Americans who seemed willing to intellectualize about everything from environmental degradation, to abuses of civil rights and liberties, to the implications of the end of colonialism in Africa and Asia and yet not be moved to do anything about any of these causes. In one of his more famous forays, his Madison Lecture at New York University in 1962, Douglas managed in one evening to criticize his own Court about timidity in the maintenance of rights and liberties, challenge the American people's commitment to the values at the core of the Bill of Rights, warn the national leadership about inevitable failures in foreign policy, and call for enlightened global cooperation that would move nations beyond the irrationality of the Cold War.[27]

Neither was Douglas willing to limit his challenges to American life to the pages of law reviews or the confines of college lecture halls. In one celebrated case, Douglas championed the effort to save the Chesapeake and Ohio Canal by challenging the editors of the *Washington Post* to hike the route with him. At the end of the day, Douglas won that fight, and tourists now ride river barges along the canal into Georgetown as Park Service guides explain life for those who built the canal and the freight handlers who plied the waterway.

Personal Life, Public Impact   One of the reasons Douglas was so controversial was his manner. His early life led him to a complex double life. On the one hand, he very much needed to be successful within what many contemporary observers would call the power structure or the establishment. Douglas thoroughly enjoyed his Ivy League educational pedigree and the instant entrée afforded him by his status as justice of the U.S. Supreme Court. He could drop names and tell fanciful stories with the energy of a new college graduate recently arrived in Washington to build a power career. And Douglas genuinely had the knowledge, accomplishments, and glittering circle of acquaintances needed to back a good deal of his bragging with fact.

On the other hand, Douglas loved to thumb his nose at polite society and assert his western loner image, particularly when it drove the scions of the establishment into apoplectic rage. He could be enormously charming in a Washington drawing room one moment and incredibly acerbic and downright uncouth the next. At least one member of the Supreme Court bemoaned Douglas's departure from the Court because it meant the loss of one his best sources of ribald humor.

Douglas's visibility and controversial behavior meant that his private life was extremely visible. Divorced three times, Douglas remarried quickly and in each case to a very young woman. What is generally ignored is that his first marriage lasted nearly thirty years and his last from 1967 until his death in 1980. Neither was it any secret that his relationships with his children were difficult at best. The issue was not whether his behavior was more worthy of condemnation than anyone else's, but that it provided a lightning rod for his critics and, to some at least, of the Warren Court of which he was a prominent member.

A Large Target

Douglas was indeed a large target, and his life off the bench was something critics within the Court and outside it could attack without seemingly challenging the Court itself or the merits of the specific and significant opinions delivered by

Warren and his colleagues. External criticism of Douglas reached a high point in the efforts made to impeach him in 1970.

Douglas was threatened with impeachment three times, only one of which was truly serious. The first came in 1953. It was part of the anti-Communist hysteria of the 1950s and, not incidentally, the desire of some Senate Republicans to bring down a former leading New Deal Democrat. The argument was that Douglas had said in 1951 that the United States should recognize the People's Republic of China, that he had written a scathing dissent from the Supreme Court's ruling upholding the convictions of the leaders of the Communist Party,[28] and that he had issued a stay of execution in the notorious Russian espionage case involving Julius and Ethel Rosenberg. There were also rumblings of an impeachment attempt when Douglas married his third wife.

The most serious attempt to impeach Douglas, in 1970, was ostensibly based on allegations about Douglas's off-the-bench activities, but the real reason involved the politics of the Nixon administration and the desire by FBI director J. Edgar Hoover to help Nixon get as many of the Warren Court justices as possible. At the time Nixon took office, Hoover told him that he would be able to appoint four new members of the Court and replace Douglas, Black, and other key Warren Court justices.[29] Then there was the Fortas affair. When Abe Fortas resigned from the Court under a cloud because of allegations concerning delays in terminating a relationship with a former client, it encouraged other Nixon administration officials to push an end to the Warren Court.

After all, Earl Warren had resigned, and President Johnson's effort to put Fortas in his placed failed. Then Fortas left, providing Nixon with an appointment to the center seat and one associate justice. Although he got his chief justice quickly, Nixon's nominees for the other seat faced defeat. After the nomination of Clement Haynsworth failed, and before Nixon's choice of G. Harrold Carswell met the same fate, then House minority leader Gerald Ford issued thinly veiled threats in a speech on the floor that rejection of the next nominee would result in reprisals.[30] Nixon publicly attacked the Senate Judiciary Committee in April 1970, when the Carswell nomination went down to defeat. Ford launched the assault on Justice Douglas the next week.[31] Hoover supplied Ford with support from FBI files.

Ford's case against Douglas, to the degree that one can make out any serious allegations in the midst of such an obvious act of crude political reprisal, had to do with his off-the-bench activities. And while J. Edgar Hoover would have been just as pleased to have been rid of William Brennan as William Douglas, Douglas's off-the-bench activities had made him a particular target of FBI interest over the years.

Douglas had been speaking and writing throughout the 1950s about the need to defend essential liberties and resist the pressures for conformity that threatened to stifle the American spirit as well as to injure U.S. standing abroad. His Walter E. Edge Lectures at Princeton in 1960 were particularly hard-hitting. The book that emerged from the lectures, *America Challenged*,[32] inspired Albert Parvin to create a foundation to support Douglas's aims,[33] and Douglas accepted a post as director of the foundation.[34] Since Douglas was also a director of the Fund for the Republic and its Center for the Study of Democratic Institutions,[35] he and his friends from both organizations worked together on a variety of projects including exchange programs at UCLA and Princeton, literacy programs in Central and South America, and the *Pacem in Terris* convocations.

When the Internal Revenue Service took an interest in Parvin's finances, three kinds of difficulties emerged. First, there were allegations, subsequently leaked to the press, that the foundation was obtaining funds from the operation of gambling casinos in Las Vegas. In fact, the foundation was not involved in casinos, but Parvin, through the Parvin–Dohrman Corporation, was. Second, because Parvin remained an officer of the foundation in control of finances, the investigation included the foundation as well as his personal finances.

Douglas had the foundation retain none other than Abe Fortas's wife, Carolyn Agger, to represent the organization. She recommended that the foundation move to an arm's-length relationship with Parvin, which produced an angry response from the benefactor. At that point, one of Douglas's friends and colleagues at the foundation warned Douglas that trouble was brewing and that it could make the justice vulnerable to attacks from congressional foes.[36] It also became clear that Parvin was willing to use the names of foundation officers in an attempt to protect himself from various charges. As if all that were not enough, Parvin had a connection with a man named Louis Wolfson, who was the central figure in the debacle that ultimately brought down Abe Fortas.[37] Douglas's lifelong friendship with Fortas, along with the Parvin connection, made it relatively easy for Douglas's enemies to establish a seemingly sinister connection.[38] Douglas ultimately resigned from the foundation.

The third problem was even stickier. Douglas had refused to accept a salary as a director of the foundation. However, since he traveled a great deal in connection with foundation activities, he did accept an open-ended expense account. He ultimately wrote a letter to Chief Justice Warren and the brethren explaining his connection with the Parvin Foundation.[39] The Parvin business, plus the fact that Douglas had a longstanding practice of earning income from books and honoraria, made his finances a tempting target. There had also been allegations that he had used the typing pool at the Court to support these extracurricular activities. Douglas not only wrote to Justices Black and Clark explaining the fact that some of his staff had erroneously sent materials to the pool but announced that, henceforth, he would not use the typing pool for anything, period![40]

Three other major factors rendered Douglas vulnerable, two of which had something to do with his off-the-bench activities. His books and speeches challenged the anti-Communist hysteria of the 1950s and 1960s. J. Edgar Hoover had the justice's work analyzed and reports forwarded to him during the period.[41] Douglas also had the temerity to resist abuses of power at home and challenge the refusal of the United States to recognize the legitimate demands by former colonies for self-determination. He resisted vehemently what he regarded as a patently unconstitutional war in Vietnam, though most of his criticism of Vietnam came within the Court as he battled to get the Court to take a case that would bring a constitutional judgment on the war. He was viewed as acting in the wider political arena on the issue, though his method of highlighting the question and setting up a case for consideration was by granting orders blocking the movement of troops into active duty or their shipment overseas.[42] So frustrated were his critics that House Armed Services committee chair F. Edward Hebert wrote first Chief Justice Warren, and later Chief Justice Warren Burger seeking to have Douglas barred from involvement in any Vietnam-related cases.[43]

Then there was his family life. To say that there was more than a little hypocrisy in the challenges to his domestic life by those in Congress and the media would be a gross understatement. Clearly, Douglas went through a particularly turbulent period in his life in the 1950s and 1960s. He had developed a notorious reputation during the period for, among other things, his rapid divorces and remarriage to two very young women, and this after his first marriage of three decades had ended. His last marriage, to Cathleen Heffernan, lasted from 1967 to his death in 1980.

Finally, and at the core of it all, Douglas was a Warren Court stalwart who was adamant in his views on free speech and association, due process, and equal protection. He, like other members of the Court, was fighting to protect the underdog, and doing so made him many powerful enemies. One member of Congress, fresh from apparent victory in driving Fortas from the Court, proclaimed openly: "The confidence of the American people in the Federal judiciary cannot be restored until Abe Fortas's resignation is followed by a like departure of Earl Warren, William Douglas and William Brennan."[44] And just as the primary thrust of attack on the nomination of Fortas to be chief justice had been the decisions of the Warren Court, some made even before Fortas was appointed to the bench, so too much of the force behind the attack on Douglas was a patently political challenge to a Warren Court stalwart.

Publicly, at least, Douglas was inclined to ignore the whole thing, assuming that Ford's ridiculous attack would be recognized for what it clearly was. Douglas's friends, however, convinced him to take the matter seriously. The case was assigned to the House Judiciary Committee, chaired by Emmanuel Celler, one of Douglas's friends of long standing. A defense team consisting of Simon Rifkind, Ramsey Clark, David Ginsburg, Charles A. Miller, J. Roger Wollenberg, and Sidney M. Davis was formed. Douglas opened his files to the investigation without demand or subpoena.

On a personal level, though, Douglas was anything but calm. He had seen the political attack coming.[45] He knew there was no substance to the charges, but he also knew there really was nothing he could do about them. He found it difficult to believe that anyone could take any of this seriously. On the other hand, he knew enough history to know that the real attack was based on ideology and the fact that he had the temerity to be a nonconformist who spoke out against the tide of political opinion. He vented his rage and frustration by writing two plays that were never produced. The first was the story of the trial of William Penn; the connection between that political trial and his own situation was obvious. The other play, entitled *The Couch*, which he wrote under the pen name William Frazier, a name he had used on some short stories in pulp magazines,[46] was more interesting. Ostensibly a comedy, it was a tale of the first man ever named to the post of secretary of mental health. It seems that the man began by suggesting that the place to start to improve America's mental health was with remedying some of the problems of motherhood. From there, he proceeded to criticize every popular icon in American life. He was brought down in the end, not because he was wrong in his criticisms or his prescriptions, but because he had been so bold as to attack the symbols of the social and political establishment.

Douglas's family and friends saw the impact of the attack on the justice and were both frustrated and angry.[47] Fred Rodell, a longtime friend, wrote Hugo Black, "I do hope you're helping Bill keep his chin up. He does need loyal friends these days, despite the absurdity of what Ford is trying to do."[48] Black replied: "You may rest assured that if there is anything I can do to help our friend Bill 'to keep his chin up,' I shall do it. In fact it seems to me that he is weathering the storm very well indeed. I cannot believe that it is possible that anyone would think that Bill Douglas has been guilty of a 'high crime or misdemeanor.' Unless I am mistaken, the present political hub-bub about him will get exactly nowhere. Only should he do something which is really bad (which he will not do) could he be in danger."[49] Concerned that perhaps Black might have misunderstood, Rodell wrote, "Of course, I knew that you would do anything possible to help Bill Douglas against that damn-fool ex-student of mine, Gerald Ford. But I'm delighted to know you agree with me that the hoopla is a lot of nonsense."[50] Black answered, "I still do not believe it is possible for anyone to succeed in stirring the Senate up to do anything serious about the suggested impeachment of Bill Douglas. There is nothing he has done to justify impeachment and I do not believe the Senate can be bamboozled into believing he has."[51]

It was not until after Black's death that Douglas learned the depth of Black's support, even though it had been a difficult period in their own relationship. Some months after his father's death, Hugo Black, Jr., explained to Douglas that when he had learned that a number of southerners had tried to get the younger Black to convey a message to Hugo about their desire to be rid of Douglas, the elder Black had replied: "I have known Bill Douglas for thirty years. He's never knowingly done any improper, unethical or corrupt thing. Tell his detractors that in spite of my age, I think I have one trial left in me. Tell them that if they move against Bill Douglas, I'll resign from the Court and represent him. It will be the biggest, most important case I ever tried."[52]

While Douglas was ultimately cleared, the experience came at a time when he was already becoming increasingly discouraged. In fact, he had been seriously contemplating retirement before the impeachment attempt. Naturally, he put aside his retirement plans in the face of the attack, vowing not to be driven from the Court. Still, as he saw changes on the Court, with the addition of four Nixon appointees, and in the nation, Douglas came to question whether all of his efforts had been worth it, doubting that anyone really cared how hard he tried to wrestle with difficult issues in his opinions.[53]

The later years were difficult for Douglas within the Court as well, even before his illness brought the personal struggle that ended with his retirement in 1975. There was the loss of his friend and colleague Hugo Black, the obvious movement of the Court away from principles he had championed for so long, and the tensions brought about by the Fortas resignation and his own impeachment battle. In some instances, Douglas's off-the-bench activities exacerbated tensions with some of his colleagues. Indeed, first Hugo Black, and later William Brennan, played a role as buffer between Douglas and some of his colleagues when nerves were frayed. Douglas's busy travel schedule caused him to miss a number of conferences. He was involved in so many things that his schedule drove him to be buried in his work when other justices gathered for lunch. His high visibility on some issues made him a target, and there is little question that by being a target, he provided an avenue of attack against the Court. His heavy writing commitments led to his felt need to respond to suggestions that he was using Court staff to support his outside activities. The involvement with the Parvin Foundation and the Center of the Study for Democratic Institutions made him a very visible target for charges by Warren Court adversaries, the spillover from which could potentially have injured the Court. His attempts to pressure the Court into accepting a case on the validity of the Vietnam War, by issuing stays and orders, long after it was apparent that he did not have the votes, brought criticism to both Warren and Burger.

On the other hand, a number of his colleagues reject the charge that his activities outside the Court actually caused any serious difficulty inside it.[54] He may have missed conferences, but he left memoranda with his positions on all the cases. He could hardly be accused of shirking his duties, since virtually no member of the Court wrote more, more often, or more promptly than Douglas. The fact that his speeches and some of his publications were prepared within the Court was certainly no departure from precedent. The charges made against him because of his ideology or his willingness to attack majoritarian political viewpoints hardly differentiated him from a number of his colleagues. It is also true that more than one president had called Douglas a close friend and had been willing to solicit his opinion and use his knowledge of the world to learn of important developments. In truth, Douglas had been more often right than wrong when, returning from travels abroad, he advised Truman and Johnson on the dangers of the policies in which the United States was engaged. When he saw the opportunity to help bring a halt to the tragedy in Vietnam, his efforts were facilitative rather than personal adventures, and he acted in direct consultation with the White House. He carried messages and provided an opportunity for conversations. The environmental activities that in earlier years got him branded as eccentric later were cause for his recognition as one of America's most important conservationists. Regarding his personal life, one is left with the continuing question of the degree to which the personal lives of officials are appropriate subjects for titillating public scandals when performance in office is not adversely affected.

The story of William O. Douglas's off-the-bench activities highlights a number of issues of continuing concern to the members and students of the Court. It is useful to look more generally at the types of off-the-bench activities in which the justices have been engaged as well as the debates over the implications of those activities.

OFF-THE-COURT OFFICIAL ASSIGNMENTS

One of the first things that a justice learns when she arrives at the Court is that it seems like everyone has something they want the justices to do. Some simply need a highly placed official to help with some money-raising event, or their university is in need of speeches and visits from dignitaries. A few invitations even set off red flags immediately, since it seems likely that those seeking the assistance of a justice had less-than-noble interests in mind. Indeed, some justices, like Clarence Thomas, have been criticized merely for publicly addressing some ideological political groups, the grounds being that the justice was attaching the prestige of the office to groups not considered "mainstream."

On the other hand, every justice engages in off-the-bench activities. Just how significant or controversial that is depends a great deal on how those terms are defined and what type of activity is considered to have a significant impact on the Court. As a starting point for contemplating their actions, though, justices can categorize the opportunities as either official requests to accept some kind of off-the-bench assignment or those that are unofficial.

There have been a number of times in the history of the Court when the strongest critics of off-the-bench activity were the justices themselves, while others outside the Court pushed for judicial involvement in the affairs of other branches. Among the more important of these off-bench roles were attempts to obtain advisory opinions, the use of justices in foreign-policy matters, and the search for appointments that would be "above politics."

The Advisory-Opinion Debate

There are times when presidents or their representatives have asked the Court to behave not as a Court but to provide assistance quite outside the normal process of deciding cases and controversies as provided by Article III of the Constitution. Of course in the early days, there was little to define the nature or role of the Court, including few lists of things the justices either individually or together should not do. Alexander Hamilton as secretary of the treasury and Thomas Jefferson as secretary of state both sought advisory opinions from the Court, in the form of requests to review and approve in advance plans of the Washington administration.

There were, however, two problems with the requests. The first was that the framers had rejected the notion of a council of revision, consisting of the president and members of the Supreme Court, to review the constitutionality of legislation. The reason, however, was that it was assumed the Court would eventually be called on to deal with the constitutional issue in the process of deciding an actual case brought before it. The other principle that has guided many justices over the years comes from a protective instinct for the Court and the integrity of its work. That is, the Court has mechanisms for responding to cases and controversies, but it is not a good institution for making policy judgments outside the adversarial process.

Thus, the Court rejected Hamilton's and Jefferson's requests.[55] That did not stop Chief Justice John Jay from advising President George Washington, though he claimed to do so individually and not on behalf of the Court. The same was later true of Justice Abe Fortas, who operated from the White House in support of President Johnson's administration, and, as Jay did, felt he could separate his advice from the legal issues he might be called on to face on the Court. In Fortas's case, the involvement was not one-time or even sporadic involvement but a continuing and active presence at the White House. As his biographer, Laura Kalman, put it: "During the Johnson years, Fortas was part of the judicial branch and, as well, an unofficial member of the executive branch."[56] The degree of his involvement and the amount of time he spent at the other end of the avenue caused some of his colleagues concern. "One clerk knew he could safely take naps in the justice's chambers because Fortas spent so much time [at the White House]."[57]

The Foreign-Policy Person

One of the most controversial areas of off-the-bench activity has concerned foreign affairs. On occasion, presidents have asked members of the Court to undertake assignments abroad or in time of war. Chief Justice John Jay served as ambassador to England and negotiated a very controversial treaty that put the chief justice and the Court in the midst of the political fray.[58] In fact, at one point Jay was both chief justice and secretary of state. In 1799, Oliver Ellsworth was sent to France as the chief U.S. negotiator in the effort to resolve the problems of seizure of American ships.[59] Ironically, years later, even something so simple as an agreement by Chief Justice Warren to undertake goodwill visits to Europe and India at the request of the State Department met with criticism.[60]

As the world grew more complex and wars became all-out national efforts for victory, justices seemed useful people to appoint to jobs in the war mobilization. However, some, like Chief Justice Harlan Fiske Stone, refused. President Roosevelt had asked him to investigate shortages of war materials. He wrote:

> I cannot rightly yield to my desire to render for you a service which as a private citizen I should not only feel bound to do but one which I should undertake with zeal and enthusiasm. . . . We must not forget that it is the judgment of history that two of my predecessors, Jay and Ellsworth, failed in the obligation of their office and impaired their legitimate influence by participation in executive action in the negotiation of treaties. . . . True, they repaired their mistake in part by resigning their commissions before resuming their judicial duties, but it is not by mere chance that every Chief Justice since has confined his activities directly to the performance of his judicial duties.[61]

Justice Douglas seriously contemplated leaving the Court to accept an appointment in war production. He wrote to Hugo Black and a longtime friend agonizing over whether to take the job and resign from the Court when he really wanted to remain on the bench.[62]

However, not everyone who decided to undertake war-related duties saw a need to resign from the Court. Justice Frank Murphy sat on the bench while also carrying the title "Lieutenant Colonel Murphy," causing considerable consternation in many quarters. The fact that Murphy's action came as a surprise to his colleagues added to the distress. Congressman Emanuel Celler wrote Chief Justice Stone, raising what appeared to be rather obvious questions about Murphy's commission.

> Is Supreme Court Justice Frank Murphy a member of the Supreme Court or is he a member of the Armed Forces of the Union?
>
> Can he be both? Can one, simultaneously, hold two offices of trust in distinct branches of the Government and take two distinct oaths in reference thereto?
>
> Some papers reported that he refrained from sitting on the bench during the hearing in the petition for a writ of *habeas corpus* filed on behalf of the eight Nazi saboteurs. Did he thus disqualify himself because he was a member of another duly constituted branch of the Government—the Executive? Did his fellow members request that he refrain from participating in the case?
>
> Is it meet and proper for one at will to shed his Army uniform and don his judicial robe?
>
> Did he consult his confreres on the Bench before he "joined" the Army?
>
> This entire matter is too important to ignore. I ask these questions as ranking member of the House Judiciary Committee.
>
> Furthermore, I ask them knowing Justice Murphy's patriotism and high record of achievement.[63]

Justice Frank Murphy in his wartime
colonel's uniform during World War II.

Chief Justice Stone answered, "I can only say that Mr. Justice Murphy did not bring
to my attention or to that of the Court, his intention to seek a commission in the
Army. My first information on the subject came from newspaper reports published
after the Court had adjourned for the summer."[64]

Probably no such service has been more controversial than Justice Robert
Jackson's role as the prosecutor at the Nuremberg war crimes trials. The fact that
a justice served as a prosecutor at all raised obvious concerns; all the more so in
light of the fact that many critics saw the war crimes trials as less legal and more
political. He also left the Court short a member during the period. However, more
than anything else, the circumstances of his presence in Europe when Chief Justice
Vinson was named to the center chair helped to precipitate the explosion in which
Jackson publicly accused Hugo Black of attempting to block his elevation to the
chief justiceship. The battle that ensued between Black and Jackson, and their allies Douglas and Frankfurter, respectively, played an important role in exacer-
bating already-difficult relationships within the Court.

The Appointment Above Politics

One reason why justices have been asked to undertake foreign and domestic roles is that they seem to be above politics and, since they are not really under
the control of the White House, may lend an air of credibility and impartiality to

the resolution of difficult problems. The classic example of this behavior was the arm twisting by Lyndon Johnson of Chief Justice Earl Warren to head up the investigation of the Kennedy assassination. Warren did not want to undertake the job, both because he had serious reservations about the propriety of that sort of off-the-bench behavior and because it would clearly have an impact on his ability to accomplish his work at the Court. After all, the chief has to carry out the management tasks associated with running the Court as well as his share of the decision chores like any other justice.

In fact, the chief justice has a number of off-the-bench tasks that are now more or less institutionalized; they simply go with the job. For example, the chief serves on boards of directors or trustees for the Smithsonian Institution and the National Gallery of Art. Indeed, these and other activities have caused some commentators to wonder just what constitutes off-the-bench activity and just what is official and what is purely voluntary and unofficial.

In the early years, the justices rode circuit and participated in the then common practice of giving to juries long-winded charges that sounded a great deal more like political speeches than definitions of the law. One of the things that got Justice Samuel Chase into trouble and played a part in the attempt to impeach him was criticism for giving politically loaded charges to juries.[65]

Of course, one difficulty is defining precisely what constitutes off-the-bench activity. Chief Justice Burger chaired the Commission on the Bicentennial, but some argued that this was a wholly appropriate activity for him to undertake as chief, since, after all, what institution should more clearly be involved in the celebration of the Constitution than the Court? Even in less ceremonial matters there are questions. The chief justice has duties beyond the internal operations of the Court. As chair of the Judicial Conference of the United States, the chief is involved in debates among judges and with other organizations, including the Congress, on a variety of important issues. Chief Justice Burger, working with his administrative assistant, initiated the Brookings Conferences, retreats to which key decisionmakers were invited to educate them regarding the resource needs of the federal courts. On one level, every other organization in government seeks to make its needs known, and Congress does provide the appropriations. On the other hand, the myth is that agencies cannot and do not engage in lobbying. The debate involves more than general discussions about budgets, however. Burger also pressed the Congress for a recognition of the potential impact on the judiciary of pending legislation. Chief Justice Rehnquist conducted a very controversial conversation with the Hill on changes in the process for handling death penalty appeals.

Indeed, one of the complex questions that has never been completely resolved is how best to structure judicial testimony before Congress on pending legislation, whether fiscal or substantive in nature. One technique has been to select a panel of judges, including, on occasion, a member of the Supreme Court. For some, this practice remains controversial, since it is equivalent, in terms of separation of powers, to a president going hat in hand to a congressional committee.

One of the mechanisms for avoiding some of the more obvious and public issues associated with off-the-bench activity is to invite retired justices to fill these roles. Thus, Justice Powell chaired a study for the Judicial Conference on death penalty appeals. In an earlier time, Justice Tom C. Clark was very active in reform of judicial administration both before and after his retirement from the bench, ultimately leading to the development of the Federal Judicial Center, a body that does research and training for the federal courts in cooperation with the Judicial Conference of the United States and the Administrative Office of U.S. Courts.

In other words, even though everyone recognizes the dangers associated with off-the-bench activities, occasionally justices will receive a call from the White House, seeking help. For some of the justices over the years, the response has been to "just say no," but that decision ultimately belongs to each individual justice. Of course, there may very well be consequences for the justice or for the Court if an invitation is accepted.

OFF-THE-COURT UNOFFICIAL POLICY INFLUENCE

Far more common than such White House calls, however, are the unofficial activities in which justices engage and that also raise issues of propriety. Among the more common of these are the direct involvement of justices in political contests, the relationships between members of the Court and their surrogates in debates over important issues, and the participation by judges in battles on or off the Court.

Justices in Politics

Some members of the Court have run for office, some have campaigned for announced candidates, and some have actively lobbied the White House on judicial appointments. Probably the best-known example of the justice as candidate is John Jay, who ran for governor of New York while he was a member of the Court. Justice David Davis (1862–77) was the nominee of the Labor Reform party for president in 1872, which led the famous political cartoonist Thomas Nast to produce a cartoon for *Harper's Weekly* entitled "The Presidential Fever on the Supreme Bench."[66]

Samuel P. Chase was active on behalf of John Adams in the 1800 campaign. Justice Bushrod Washington was also openly involved in the 1800 presidential campaign, supporting Charles C. Pinckney.[67] Indeed, no less an authority than Charles Warren said of the Court's early years: "It is clear, therefore, that mere activity had not been regarded as unfitting a Judge for his position."[68] On the other hand, some justices, like Charles Evans Hughes, disagreed, and resigned from the Court so they could run for the presidency. Still others attacked their colleagues on grounds that they were using the Court as a steppingstone to political office.

Felix Frankfurter consistently assailed William O. Douglas on grounds that his younger colleague was trying to get from the Court to the White House. In truth, a part of Douglas would have been pleased had he been drafted and elected to the presidency. On the other hand, despite the allegations, Douglas took a series of actions to stop any attempt to get him into the race. In 1944, when it was clear that there would be a new vice president and that President Franklin Roosevelt would be reelected, the choice for the second spot was obviously important. Roosevelt was ill, and there was every likelihood that the selection as vice president would mean, in reality, the choice of the person who would succeed to the presidency in the near future. Because of that, the politics of the vice-presidential nomination were intense. Roosevelt let it be known that he would be sat-

THE PRESIDENTIAL FEVER ON THE SUPREME BENCH

Chief Justice. "Mark but my fall, and that that ruin'd me.
Judge Davis, I charge thee, fling away ambition;
By that sin fell the angels; how can man, then,
The image of his Maker, hope to win by't?"—*Shakespeare*

FIGURE 11.1   Thomas Nast, "The Presidential Fever on the Supreme Bench." (*Harper's Weekly*, April 6, 1872. © 1995 Nawrocki Stock Photo, Inc. All rights reserved.)

isfied with either William O. Douglas or Harry Truman. Political boss Robert Hannegan led the fight for Truman and engineered the message from FDR to the convention to read that the president would be happy with either Truman or Douglas, recognizing that some would regard that order of names as a signal that Truman was the preferred choice. Douglas let it be known to his friends that he did not want the nomination and that he would not accept it if it were offered. He then left town. Douglas wrote Chief Justice Stone from his summer home in Lostine, Oregon:

> During the past week two items from eastern journals have come to my attention which indicate that I am being rather actively promoted as vice-presidential candidate on the Democratic ticket. There was some such effort made before I left Washington and I did all I possibly could to put an end to it. On the way to my summer place here in the mountains I was asked by certain delegates to the convention from the far western states if they could not be authorized to promote my candidacy at the Convention.
>
> I told them (1) that I was not a candidate, had not been a candidate, and would not be a candidate, (2) that no one was authorized to promote my nomination and that I would give no such authority, (3) that if nominated, I would not accept.
>
> I hope that puts an end to the matter. But I wanted you to know the facts. I think a person who desires to put in a political campaign should resign from the Court. I think political ambitions are incompatible with performance of our judicial frustrations. I do not think the Court should be used as a stepping stone to any public office.[69]

To ensure his distance, Douglas wrote to Stone "Just for extra protection I went with Jim Donald on a fishing trip to spots where not even the Lone Ranger could find me."[70]

Truman in 1948 considered Douglas as a possible running mate and offered him a cabinet post to increase his visibility for a possible run in 1952. Douglas rejected all offers, insisting that he simply wanted to remain on the Court. Indeed, the positions he was taking on the Communist witch hunt and U.S. foreign policy guaranteed that he could not have been a viable candidate in 1952.

Given contemporary politics, however, it would be beyond the pale for a justice to consider a run for office unless he or she left the Court, and any overt effort on his part in support of a political candidate would engender serious criticism. What has continued over time, and has tempted justices on occasion, is the history of efforts by members of the Court to influence decisionmakers, directly or indirectly.

Probably the best-known lobbyist in the history of the Court was Chief Justice William Howard Taft, whose chief accomplishments include passage of the Judiciary Act of 1925, giving the Court discretion over its docket, and the construction of the Supreme Court building itself. Taft was involved in many battles over legislation, and he was even alert to the possibility that other members of the Court might be lobbying on the other side. Thus, he wrote of Justice Louis Brandeis, who Taft thought was opposing him on reform of the bankruptcy law: "The truth is that when we make rules that interfere with the young Russian Jews [who composed the bulk of the bankruptcy petitioners] . . . we find him a real obstructionist."[71]

Some members of the Court were slightly more subtle in working with political players, but not much. Justice John Catron (1837–65) wrote to president-elect James Buchanan in 1857 telling him that the Court would be deciding a case concerning slavery and asked "Buchanan to drop [Justice] Grier a line, saying how necessary it is, and how good the opportunity is, to settle the agitation by an affirmative decision of the Supreme Court, the one way or another."[72] In a later exchange, Catron explained to Buchanan how the Court was going to treat the case.

Some members of the Court had ongoing relationships with the White House. Justice Stone was "a member of Hoover's 'Medicine Ball Cabinet.'"[73] Douglas continued to play poker with both Roosevelt and his successor, though he enjoyed the games with FDR more. He remained close both to Roosevelt and, for some time, to Truman. He provided Truman with a great deal of information on foreign-policy issues, and he did the same with Johnson in later years. Abe Fortas maintained an active, ongoing relationship with Johnson on everything from legislation to foreign policy.[74] Chief Justice Burger communicated with the Nixon administration as well.

Probably the most ardent advocate of abstinence for justices was Felix Frankfurter. Yet Frankfurter was known for his efforts to influence virtually anyone who would listen on any matter with which he was concerned. Frankfurter even went so far as to lobby his former colleagues after he had retired.[75]

As the chapter on appointments indicated, one of the things a justice may very well observe is attempts by colleagues on the Court to influence the selection of new appointees to the bench. Just how possible that is depends, of course, on the president in power and the connections of individual justices. The attempt to influence has been made both directly and by more subtle means, but it has been an ongoing fact of life in the history of the Court. Justices may assume that colleagues are engaged in those activities whether they are or not. Justice Douglas wrote Justice Black in 1941 complaining that he was sure Stone was named to the chief justiceship because of Frankfurter's effort. He said: "When we heard on the radio that Stone had been made C.J. I said to Mildred 'Felix has done it again' and there is no question in my mind that he was responsible. You will recall that I expressed my fear that Felix would make that move."[76]

The Justices and Their Surrogates

One way that some justices have managed to have an influence on ongoing debates while avoiding the appearance of impropriety has been through the use of surrogates. In some cases, this process has been overt, as was true of Felix Frankfurter. Not only is it clear that Frankfurter was willing to use surrogates, there is also a continuing debate over the degree to which Frankfurter acted as a surrogate for Justice Brandeis while Frankfurter was a law professor.[77] In other situations, surrogate advocacy has resulted simply from the fact that justices form relationships with their clerks, journalists, or scholars who tend to argue in support of "their justice's" position outside the Court and to attack "their justice's" critics.

One of the clearest examples of surrogate battles involved the conflict within and outside the Court between the forces of Hugo Black and Felix Frankfurter. Alexander Meiklejohn had written his book *Political Freedom*, criticizing, among others, a leading work on the First Amendment freedoms of speech and press published by Harvard Law professor Zachariah Chafee and insisting on absolute protection for political expression.[78] Meiklejohn attacked the efforts of the emerging anti-Communist crusade following World War II. When the Court upheld the convictions of the top Communist party officials under the Smith Act, Black and Douglas dissented.[79] Frankfurter, concurring with the Court, attacked Meiklejohn, and by extension the absolute theory that was advocated on the Court by Hugo Black. In particular, Frankfurter cited a critical review of Meiklejohn's work written by none other than Chafee. Meiklejohn took Frankfurter apart in an article published in the *University of Chicago Law Review* shortly thereafter. Black employed Meiklejohn's arguments in a number of opinions, often dissents, over the next several years.[80] Meiklejohn and Black struck up a friendship over that time and shared in correspondence their common struggle in an effort to obtain adequate protection for First Amendment freedoms.[81]

Frankfurter had a number of champions, and none more ardent than Alexander Bickel, his former clerk. For Black, much of the Constitution was written in plain words. Bickel, however, attacked Black in a piece subtitled "The Unobvious Meaning of Plain Words."[82] Black's supporters, including Meiklejohn, John Frank, William O. Douglas, and others were outraged and planned an immediate reply. Black would not call them off, but neither would he actively encourage them.[83] Finally, John Frank wrote a rejoinder to Bickel in the *New Republic* that could hardly be described as a polite exchange.[84]

At an earlier time, Frankfurter and Robert Jackson, Black's leading opponents on the Court, wrote Professor Charles Fairman congratulating him on his historical work on the Fourteenth Amendment, which Fairman had used to attack Black's interpretation of that amendment's due process clause.[85] Jackson went so far as to solicit Fairman's assistance as an advisor in *Sweatt v. Painter* and other civil rights cases then before the Court. In asking Fairman's help, Jackson saw himself as doing nothing unusual. He wrote:

> I know of no one who had made so thorough and disinterested a study of the origins and history of the Fourteenth Amendment as you have done. The work of the Court leaves no time to begin to approach your research. Yet we are probably faced with as important Fourteenth-Amendment decisions as any that have been rendered. Frankly, I should like to draw upon your store of knowledge. I suppose you have no interest in the litigations other than the intellectual interest which any legal scholar would have. It is considered quite permissible for a Justice to rely on the knowledge and opinion of a boy just out of law school to contribute to his judgment. I know of no reason why one should be foreclosed from consultation with more experienced and matured minds, if they are disinterested.[86]

Contemporary *Ex Cathedra* Battles

The participation in conflict by members of the Court has not been limited to surrogates on the outside and justices within the confines of the Court. In more recent times, the justices themselves have fought it out in what Justice Sandra Day O'Connor has termed the battle of the footnotes. Some have also fought other branches or interests as well.

Court watchers have been concerned for some time, but particularly since the appointment of Justice Antonin Scalia, about the intensity of the external conflicts among members of the Court, in which justices have attacked one another by name, first in the footnotes and then in the text of their opinions.[87] Two of the harsher examples of this kind of clash came in attacks by Justice Scalia on Justice O'Connor in a case involving an affirmative-action set-aside program operated by the City of Richmond, Virginia,[88] and another from Missouri in which anti-abor-

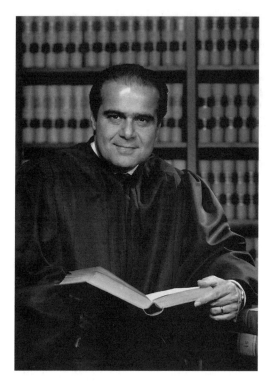

Associate Justice Antonin Scalia.

tion forces sought to push the Court to take the final step and overturn the *Roe v. Wade* ruling that recognized a woman's right to terminate a pregnancy.[89] A number of observers speculated that O'Connor seemed to be the potential swing vote to overturn *Roe* and Scalia appeared to be attempting to intimidate her. Sandra Day O'Connor, however, is not one to be intimidated by anyone.

These conflicts have not been limited to the opinions. Justice John P. Stevens, for example, gave a stinging speech at Northwestern University Law School in which he took his colleagues to task for issuing expansive rulings that went well beyond the issues presented in the cases before the Court. He indicated his concern with "my present colleagues' enthusiastic attempts to codify the law instead of merely performing the judicial task of deciding the cases that come before them."[90] Justice Thurgood Marshall, too, has taken on his colleagues from the rostrum.[91] Justice Harry Blackmun's comments on various occasions outside the Court have also raised eyebrows, even discounting the fact that he was significantly misquoted on at least one such occasion.[92]

Justices have also battled presidents and their surrogates. While some of the participants avoided using the names of their opponents, there was no question that Justice William Brennan was a point of attack by Attorney General Edwin Meese on behalf of President Ronald Reagan and his right-wing critics of the Court and that Brennan was taking on the president when he replied to Meese. Marshall did not even try to mask his contempt for presidents Reagan or George Bush in his speeches to the second circuit and broadcast interviews. Marshall had avoided interviews for years, but he finally reached the end of his rope and came out swing-

Associate Justice Sandra Day O'Connor.

ing. Most clashes in public, such as Brennan's battle against Meese or Hughes's fight against FDR's Court-packing plan, are direct but respectful of institutional independence. But where the clashes become more direct, personal, or partisan, tensions rise.

DEBATE OVER OUTSIDE ACTIVITY

As a justice is thinking about what to do, and just as important, what not to do, outside the Court, it is useful for her to consider the arguments that have been made on both sides of the question. Consider first the relatively obvious warnings about the dangers of off-the-bench activities.

Historian Bruce Murphy suggests that the grounds most often given for limiting off-the-bench activity include (1) the importance of protection of the separation of powers, since there is always a risk the justice will be called on to judge a policy that she participated in formulating during off-the-bench activity; (2) the need to guard the image of nonpartisanship, in order to preserve the concept of justice; and (3) the need to protect the image of the court as apolitical, reinforcing the principle that the justices focus on the merits of the cases and not the political forces associated with them.[93]

There are other complaints with evidence to support them. There is the problem that arises whenever off-the-bench activities involve money that goes directly to the justice. Abe Fortas survived most of the allegations against him, but there is no question that the assertions about the acceptance of money made him particularly vulnerable to attack and were ultimately what brought him down. In the case of Justice William O. Douglas, it is equally clear that of all the things he did off the bench, his involvement with the Parvin Foundation, and particularly the money that he accepted from it, was what came closest to causing him serious difficulties even though there is no allegation that he actually did anything inappropriate with the money or that he failed to use it for lawful purposes. Robert J. Donovan, Washington Bureau chief for the *Los Angeles Times*, wrote all members of the Court following the piece on Douglas's alleged involvement with Parvin and the money from gambling, demanding to know whether they thought some kind of rules on justices' outside activities were in order. Most members of the Court refused to respond, but Black, who was usually very circumspect in such matters, replied in plain terms. Rejecting the idea that such rules were appropriate or feasible, Black concluded: "Finally, I do not consider it to be a part of my responsibility or duty to sit in judgment upon the outside activities of my brethren on this Court."[94]

Douglas knew that the money issue could be used to present the image of impropriety even if none existed, which is one reason he had difficulty with the move to have members of the Court file disclosure statements. The issue of outside income arose in part because the Judicial Conference adopted an interim resolution in 1969, asking judges to "file comprehensive statements of all income, investments, debts, assets, etc., including much information concerning the financial affairs of the wife and children of each judge. The Interim Resolution calls on all Federal Judges to file a statement of earned income other than judicial salaries."[95] Douglas wrote Brennan to get his views on the matter. He answered that he had no particular difficulty with it and was willing to file.[96] Douglas was well aware that even if one had done nothing wrong, it was far too easy for the press to suggest the contrary. He knew that his enemies were after him long before the serious impeachment effort was launched. He wrote his attorney, former defense secretary Clark Clifford, in October 1969:

> Enclosed is a news item from yesterday's *Star*. It is, I think, a token that the campaign against me has started all over again. The grossly unfair and malicious character of this particular item is that it relates to episodes that happened before I ever met Mr. Parvin. He did, late in 1961 or early 1962, transfer a fractional interest in a mortgage on the hotel in question to the Parvin Foundation, an interest which the Foundation got rid of because it was on a Las Vegas property that had a gambling casino. But fractional interests in mortgages are always hard to liquidate. . . . There is nothing that this article pertains to with which I had any connection whatsoever.[97]

He also reported that he had learned from a newsman friend of his that "Clark Mollenhoff of the White House is planting a story that in 1963–64 I was in Santo Domingo trying to get out of Juan Bosch a gambling casino for certain Mafia interests. I was there at the time representing the Parvin Foundation, and preparing a TV adult literacy course." He closed the letter by asking Clifford, "Isn't it time I sued someone?"[98]

Another set of concerns expressed by critics has to do with the impact of off-the-bench activities on the operation of the Court. One such issue is the danger that justices who are excessively involved in outside activities may not carry their own load. It is true that justices sometimes missed conference votes because of other commitments. On more than one occasion, Douglas had to race across country or return from some far-flung corner of the world to make an important conference session. There is the danger that a justice may end up with a greater workload simply because he is present. That could conceivably develop antagonisms within the Court. In Douglas's case, for example, some of his colleagues concluded that Douglas was bored with the work of the Court. In the case of Fortas, some members of the Court felt that, although he was carrying his weight as an individual, the Court was deprived of his true energies and talents, which were being devoted to the Johnson administration.[99] Any of these results could breed increased criticism of the justices from the public and from members of Congress.

However, there have been arguments that the attacks on off-the-bench activities have been overblown. First, there is no way to eliminate all of what are sometimes called off-the-bench activities without also creating a bench of people so disconnected from the real world that they have no real understanding of the society in whose name they function. The plain fact is that no person is so pure that critics will not find avenues of attack. It has even been argued that the formal challenge to judicial participation in the wider problems of governance is not defensible from any but the most extreme positions. The Supreme Court upheld the creation of the U.S. Sentencing Commission, which uses Article III judges, though not members of the Supreme Court, to establish sentencing guidelines. In *Mistretta v. United States*, the Court held in part, that "the Constitution does not prohibit Article III judges from undertaking extrajudicial duties."[100] The statement in full reads as follows:

> Our inferential reading that the Constitution does not prohibit Article III judges from undertaking extrajudicial duties finds support in the historical practice of the Founders after ratification. Our early history indicates that the Framers themselves did not read the Constitution as forbidding extrajudicial service by federal judges. The first Chief Justice, John Jay, served simultaneously as Chief Justice and as Ambassador to England, where he negotiated the treaty that bears his name. Oliver Ellsworth served simultaneously as Chief Justice and as Minister to France. While he was Chief Justice, John Marshall served briefly as Secretary of State and was a member of the Sinking Fund Commission with responsibility for refunding the Revolutionary war debt.[101]

After reciting a litany of examples from the history of the Court, Justice Blackmun concluded, "Our 200-year tradition of extrajudicial service is additional evidence that the doctrine of separation of powers does not prohibit judicial participation in certain extrajudicial activity."[102]

There is also some reason to believe that not all off-the-bench activities are problematic. Indeed, there is substantial evidence that if the presidents Douglas advised had heeded his warnings, the United States might be in a far better posture in the world than it is today and freedoms at home may have been protected with far greater vigor. Douglas was right about Vietnam, right about the Soviet Union, right about much of what he said of Southeast Asia, and uncannily accurate about his observations in the Mideast. He was correct in his warnings about the importance of changing technology in this country and about the need to attend to critical issues of equality in ways far more sophisticated than most people contemplated in the 1960s and 1970s. He was equally correct in his observations about environmental policy. Besides, no one was more productive and few people have cast as many conference votes as he. It is said that he could have crafted far better opinions had he spent less time away from the bench. Perhaps, but Douglas's performance suggests that the opinions of the Court as a whole would benefit by more time spent in the real world and less in the splendid isolation of the Marble Temple.

SUMMARY

You do have a life off the bench. You do not cease to be a Supreme Court justice because you go to the supermarket, but neither do you cease to be a person with a full life because you sit behind a huge bench in front of marble columns under a frieze depicting the great lawgivers of history. The political instincts and experiences that had so much to do with the reason you are on the Court are not removed from you in a surgical procedure when you take the oath of office.

The plain fact is that, in one way or another, the justices of the Court have a rich, if controversial, heritage of off-the-bench activities. Some of these came in more or less formal terms, as the president or others turned to your predecessors and colleagues for special assistance. In other circumstances, individual justices made the decision that not all of their lives were constrained by the Court. Still others took an active role because of their perceived need to work in defense of a Court under attack from others in the political process.

The question for so many of your predecessors and colleagues has been, not whether, but how, how much, and when to participate in the life of the nation they serve. In so doing, however, they, like you, recognize that there are consequences for their own careers and for the Court as an institution.

NOTES

[1] This story is drawn from an interview with a member of the Court on condition of anonymity.

[2] Ibid.

[3] Bruce Murphy, *The Brandeis/Frankfurter Connection* (New York: Oxford University Press, 1982), p. 9.

[4] Elizabeth Black, interview with authors, Arlington, VA, Aug. 28, 1987.

[5] William O. Douglas, "Protecting the Investor," *Yale Review* 23 (1934): 521, 522; box 33b, WODP.

[6] William O. Douglas, "Jerome N. Frank," *Journal of Legal Education* 10 (1957): 1, 4.

[7] Harlan Fiske Stone to William O. Douglas, March 21, 1939, Box 74, Harlan Fiske Stone Papers, Library of Congress.

[8] In March 1937, in the midst of the fight, Douglas wrote Howard Meneely to explain the situation. "The President's court proposal has Wash DC (like the nation) stirred. Feelings run very high. I am for it. I am working behind the scenes long hours on it. It will pass—the only thing being 'when' and 'at what price.' I hope the price is not too heavy. I see Yale Law is for it 3 to 1; Harvard Law against it 9 to 1. I tell Jim Landis—Dean Elect—that that spells the difference between Yale and Harvard"

(William O. Douglas to Howard Meneeley, Mar. 13, 1937 box 10, WODP). His time was spent writing law school faculty members to arrange expressions of support and line up potential witnesses in favor of the plan (see, for example, William O. Douglas to Scott Rowley, Mar. 1, 1937, box 23, WODP). He corresponded with the president of the American Association of Law Schools about the usefulness of a poll of law professors, but the two agreed to drop that plan when they sensed that such a poll would produce overwhelmingly negative results (William O. Douglas to Lloyd K. Garrison, Mar. 1, 1937, box 23, WODP).

[9]*Korematsu v. United States*, 323 U.S. 214 (1944).

[10]Robert H. Jackson to Chairmen, House and Senate Judiciary Committees, June 7, 1946, box 26, RHJP.

[11]William O. Douglas to Dr. Douglas S. Corpron, June 3, 1940, WODP, Box 316.

[12]William O. Douglas, *We the Judges* (Garden City, NY: Doubleday, 1956).

[13]See William O. Douglas, *Strange Lands and Friendly People* (New York: Harper, 1951); *Beyond the High Himalayas* (Garden City, NY: Doubleday, 1952); *North from Malaya* (Garden City, NY: Doubleday, 1953); *Russian Journey* (Garden City, NY: Doubleday, 1956); *West of the Indus* (Garden City, NY: Doubleday, 1959); and *Exploring the Himalayas* (New York: Random House, 1963). He also wrote a host of articles, particularly in the early years of his travels, for *Look Magazine.*

[14]See "With Justice Douglas in Iran," *Life*, Aug. 15, 1949; "Justice Douglas on Iran," *Life*, June 18, 1951. See also Douglas, *Strange Lands and Friendly People.*

[15]Douglas S. Corpron to William O. Douglas, June 16, 1951, box 316, WODP.

[16]William O. Douglas to Hugo Black, Aug. 24, 1954, box 59, HLBP; and William O. Douglas to Earl Warren, Aug. 28, 1954, box 350, EWP.

[17]See his "Democracy Charts Its Course," *University of Florida Law Review* 1 (1948): 133; "Dialectical Materialism" *Vital Speeches* (Apr. 1949): 359–63; "America's Power of Ideals," *Social Research* 19 (1952): 269–76; "The Power of Righteousness," *New Republic*, Apr. 28, 1952, pp. 9–13; "Communists Here and Abroad," *U.S. News and World Report*, Dec. 4, 1953, pp. 110–12.

[18]William O. Douglas, *The Right of the People* (Garden City, NY: Doubleday, 1958), p. 12.

[19]Harry S Truman to William O. Douglas, Sept. 13, 1951, Harry S Truman Papers, Harry S Truman Library, Independence, MO, President's Secretary Files (hereafter cited as HSTP).

[20]William O. Douglas to Harry S Truman, Sept. 25, 1951, HSTP.

[21]William O. Douglas, "The Bill of Rights Is Not Enough," *New York University Law Review* 38 (1963): 207.

[22]William O. Douglas to Robert Hutchins, June 9, 1966, box 582, WODP, LC.

[23]William O. Douglas to Charles Percy, May 9, 1967, box 582, WODP, LC.

[24]Harry S. Ashmore, "Report on Pacem in Terris II," (Santa Barbara, CA: Center for the Study of Democratic Institutions, 1967), box 582, WODP.

[25]William O. Douglas to Clark Clifford, Feb. 29, 1968, box 315, WODP.

[26]William O. Douglas, *The Court Years*, (New York: Random House, 1980), pp., 329–30. This incident was confirmed by Cathleen Douglas-Stone (interview with authors, Boston, MA, Nov. 14, 1986).

[27]Douglas, "Bill of Rights."

[28]*Dennis v. United States*, 341 U.S. 494 (1951), Douglas dissenting.

[29]J. Edgar Hoover, Memorandum to Tolson, DeLoche, et al, April 23, 1969, describing his meeting with Richard Nixon, File 101-2983, FBI Files.

[30]See Milton Viorst, "Bill Douglas Has Never Stopped Fighting the Bullies of Yakima," *New York Times Magazine*, July 14, 1970, p. 8.

[31]*Congressional Record*, vol. 116, p. 11912, 91st Cong., 2d sess., 1970.

[32]William O. Douglas, *America Challenged* (Princeton, NJ: Princeton University Press, 1960).

[33]Most of the discussion concerning Douglas's activities with the Parvin Foundation and the Center for the Study of Democratic Institutions operated by the Fund for the Republic is taken from data found in U.S. Congress, House, *Final Report by the Special Subcommittee on H.Res. 920 of the Committee on the Judiciary; Associate Justice William O. Douglas*, 91st Cong., 2d sess., 1970 (hereafter cited as the *Final Report*).

[34]William O. Douglas to Albert Parvin, Aug. 7, 1960, (in *Final Report*).

³⁵Ibid., pp. 175–76.

³⁶Harry S. Ashmore to William O. Douglas, Dec. 8, 1966 (in *Final Report*, pp. 104–5).

³⁷See Laura Kalman, *Abe Fortas* (New Haven, CT: Yale University Press, 1990); Bruce Allen Murphy, *Fortas* (New York: Morrow, 1988); and Robert Shogan, *A Question of Judgment: The Fortas Case and the Struggle for the Supreme Court* (Indianapolis, IN: Bobbs-Merrill, 1972).

³⁸See *Congressional Record*, vol. 115, p. 11260, 91st Cong., 1st sess., 1969.

³⁹William O. Douglas, Memorandum to the Chief Justice, Oct. 31, 1966, box 352, EWP.

⁴⁰Memorandum from William O. Douglas to Justices Black and Clark, Feb. 23, 1961, box 59, HLBP.

⁴¹See Justice William O. Douglas file, FBI Files.

⁴²See, for example, *Johnson v. Powell*, 393 U.S. 920 (1968); *Scaggs v. Larsen*, 396 U.S. 1206 (1969); and *Jones v. Lemond*, 396 U.S. 1227 (1969).

⁴³F. Edward Hebert to Warren Burger, Aug. 9, 1969 (in *Final Report*, p. 61).

⁴⁴*Congressional Record*, vol. 115, p. 12949, 91st Cong., 1st sess., 1969.

⁴⁵See William O. Douglas to Clark Clifford, Oct. 23, 1969, box 315, WODP; William O. Douglas to Clark Clifford, Nov. 17, 1969, box 315, WODP.

⁴⁶William O. Douglas to Nancy Douglas, Dec. 5, 1970, box 1095, WODP.

⁴⁷Cathleen Douglas-Stone, interview with authors, Boston, MA, Nov. 14, 1986.

⁴⁸Fred Rodell to Hugo Black, May 6, 1970, box 47, HLBP.

⁴⁹Hugo Black to Fred Rodell, May 13, 1970, box 47, HLBP.

⁵⁰Fred Rodell to Hugo Black, June 1, 1970, box 47, HLBP.

⁵¹Hugo Black to Fred Rodell, June 5, 1970, box 47, HLBP.

⁵²Douglas, *Court Years*, p. 377.

⁵³Cathleen Douglas-Stone, interview with authors, Boston, MA, Nov. 14, 1986.

⁵⁴See William J. Brennan, Jr., interview with authors. This was confirmed by another member of the Court, who spoke on condition of anonymity.

⁵⁵Charles Warren, *The Supreme Court in United States History*, vol. 1 (Boston: Little, Brown, 1926), pp. 108–111.

⁵⁶Kalman, *Abe Fortas*, p. 310.

⁵⁷Ibid., p. 312.

⁵⁸A. O. Sarkissian, "Speeches and Statements of U.S. Supreme Court Judges on the Issues of the Day," Government Division, Library of Congress, Mar. 22, 1956, p. 1

⁵⁹Leon Friedman and Fred L. Israel, eds., *The Justices of the United States Supreme Court 1789–1969: Their Lives and Major Opinions* (New York: Bowker, 1969), pp. 233–34.

⁶⁰Bernard Schwartz, *Super Chief* (New York: New York University Press, 1983), pp. 202–3.

⁶¹Chief Justice Harlan Fiske Stone to President Franklin D. Roosevelt on July 20, 1942 (quoted in Elder Witt, *Guide to the U.S. Supreme Court*, 2d ed. [Washington, DC: Congressional Quarterly, 1990], p. 752).

⁶²William O. Douglas to Hugo L. Black, July 23, 1941, box 308, WODP; William O. Douglas to Hugo L. Black, Sept. 8, 1941, box 59, HLBP; William O. Douglas to Howard Meneely, Sept. 16, 1941, box 10, WODP; William O. Douglas to Howard Meneely, Oct. 31, 1941, box 10, WODP.

⁶³Emanuel Celler to Harlan Fiske Stone, August 13, 1942, box 357, WODP.

⁶⁴Harlan Fiske Stone to Emanuel Celler, August 15, 1942, box 357, WODP.

⁶⁵Sarkissian, "Speeches and Statements," pp. 2–3.

⁶⁶Ibid., p. 6.

⁶⁷Ibid., p. 1.

⁶⁸Warren, *Supreme Court*, p. 276.

⁶⁹William O. Douglas to Harlan Fiske Stone, July 12, 1944, box 74, HFSP.

⁷⁰William O. Douglas to Harlan Fiske Stone, Aug. 21, 1944, box 74, HFSP.

⁷¹Quoted in Alpheus T. Mason, *William Howard Taft: Chief Justice* (New York: Simon & Schuster, 1965), p. 219.

⁷²Sarkissian, "Speeches and Statements," p. 6.

73Susan E. Grogan, "The Extrajudicial Writings of William O. Douglas" (Paper presented at the annual meeting of the Law and Society Association, Washington, DC, 1987), p. 3, n. 6.

74See Kalman, *Abe Fortas*; and Murphy, *Fortas*.

75Frankfurter tried to lobby Black on the sit-in cases (Felix Frankfurter to Hugo L. Black, May 7, 1963, box 60, HLBP).

76William O. Douglas to Hugo L. Black, June 22, 1941, box 308, WODP.

77See, for example, Leonard Baker, *Brandeis and Frankfurter: A Dual Biography* (New York: New York University Press, 1986); Lewis J. Paper, *Brandeis* (Secaucus, NJ: Citadel Press, 1983); Philippa Strum, *Louis D. Brandeis: Justice for the People* (Cambridge, MA: Harvard, 1984); and Murphy, *Fortas*.

78Alexander Meiklejohn, *Political Freedom: The Constitutional Powers of the People* (New York: Oxford University Press, 1965). The piece he challenged was Zachariah Chafee, *Free Speech in the United States* (New York: Atheneum, 1969).

79*Dennis v. United States*, 341 U.S. 494 (1951).

80See, for example, *Yates v. United States*, 354 U.S. 298, 340 (1957), Black dissenting in part.

81This correspondence is found in box 42, HLBP.

82Alexander Bickel, "Mr. Justice Black: The Unobvious Meaning of Plain Words," *New Republic*, Mar. 14, 1960, pp. 13–15.

83Hugo L. Black to Alexander Meiklejohn, April 22, 1960, box 42, HLBP.

84John P. Frank, Letter to the Editor, *The New Republic*, Apr. 4, 1960, p. 30.

85Charles Fairman, "Does the Fourteenth Amendment Incorporate the Bill of Rights: The Original Understanding," *Stanford Law Review* 2 (1949): 5. Fairman had sent them advance copies of his forthcoming article. Jackson was very pleased with his work (Robert H. Jackson to Charles Fairman, Oct. 18, 1949, box 12, Robert H. Jackson Papers [hereafter cited as RHJP]).

86Robert H. Jackson to Charles Fairman, Feb. 28, 1950; Jackson to Fairman, Apr. 5, 1950; Fairman to Jackson Apr. 25, 1950, box 12, RHJP.

87Stephen Wermeil, "Low Roading on the High Court," *Wall Street Journal*, Sept. 13, 1982, p. A-13.

88*Richmond v. J. A. Croson*, 488 U.S. 469 (1989).

89*Webster v. Reproductive Health Services*, 492 U.S. 490 (1989).

90Stuart Taylor, "Justice Stevens Is Sharply Critical of Supreme Court Conservatives," *New York Times*, Aug. 5, 1984, p. A-1. See also idem, "Justice Stevens Assails Court Vote as Impugning the Role of Lawyers," *New York Times*, July 8, 1985, p. A-1.

91"Marshall Calls Justices Cavalier over Abuses," *New York Times*, Sept. 15, 1984.

92See, for example, "High Court Seen Moving to Right," *New York Times*, Sept. 21, 1984.

93Murphy, *Fortas*, p. 6.

94Hugo L. Black to Robert J. Donovan, Nov. 21, 1966, box 59, HLBP.

95Warren E. Burger, MTTC, July 21, 1970, box 1453, WODP.

96William J. Brennan to William O. Douglas, July 21, 1970, box 1453, WODP.

97William O. Douglas to Clark Clifford, Oct. 23, 1969, box 315, WODP.

98William O. Douglas to Clark Clifford, Nov. 17, 1969, box 315, WODP.

99Kalman, *Abe Fortas*, p. 312.

100102 L.Ed 2d 714, 747 (1989).

101Ibid.

102Ibid., at 748–49.

The Supreme Court
and the Coordinate Branches

12

How does your part of the federal system, the Supreme Court, relate, formally and informally, to the other political branches of the national government, the Congress, and the executive branch? Is the Supreme Court as well as the federal judiciary, as your new colleague Ruth Bader Ginsburg suggested during her confirmation hearings before the Senate Judiciary Committee, "third in line" behind the legislative and executive branches of government?

The justices of the Court, all 108 who have served on the high bench from 1789 through Stephen Breyer's appointment in 1994, were and are keenly aware of the Court's interrelatedness and yet separateness from the other coordinate branches of the central government. Justice Robert Jackson observed correctly that "while the Constitution diffuses power the better to secure liberty, it also contemplates that the practice will integrate the dispersed powers into a workable government. It enjoins upon its branches separateness but interdependence, autonomy but reciprosity."[1] The Supreme Court, Congress, and the presidency all share powers and interpret the U.S. Constitution in the course of carrying out their political and legal tasks.

THE RELATIONSHIPS BETWEEN THE COORDINATE
BRANCHES OF THE NATIONAL GOVERNMENT

Illustrative of Justice Jackson's observation about the interdependence of the three branches of the national government is the recent effort by Chief Justice William Rehnquist to enlist the Congress in his effort to restrict the use of fed-

312

eral *habeas corpus* petitions by prisoners on death row. While Congress did not fully cooperate with his efforts, Rehnquist was able to reach his objective through a decision of the Court in 1991 that modified earlier Court precedent.

In 1981, then Associate Justice Rehnquist began an effort to modify the Court's position regarding the number of opportunities a prisoner has for appealing a death sentence. In the effort to speed up the implementation of the death penalty, Rehnquist dissented from a denial of certiorari in the case of 1981 *Coleman v. Balkcom*, 451 U.S. 949 (1981). Attacking the Burger Court practice of certiorari denial in these cases, he argued that the consequence of such a denial left the prisoner free to challenge the constitutionality of the sentence in the federal court by filing *habeas corpus* petitions. Instead, Rehnquist suggested, the Court should grant each death penalty petition, decide it on the merits, thereby precluding additional appeals and speeding up the execution date. In 1981, he stood alone on this position.

However, a decade later, Rehnquist as chief justice had achieved his goal of curtailing prisoner use of the habeas corpus petition. His position became policy for the Court in the case of 1991 *McCleskey v. Zant*, 111 SCt 1454 (1991). However, before the victory, Rehnquist tried to enlist the Congress in the effort to bring a rapid closure to death penalty convictions. As the head of the Federal Judicial Conference, Rehnquist, in 1989, appointed a special committee, chaired by Justice Lewis Powell, who had recently retired, to make recommendations to the conference and to Congress regarding the issue.

In 1990, the Powell Committee recommended that Congress pass legislation to limit the number of *habeas corpus* petitions an inmate might file in federal courts. The Rehnquist effort to persuade Congress failed, however, "due to strong opposition from senior federal judges and Democratic leaders in Congress."[2] However, while he failed to convince one of the coordinate branches, he did have the support of the executive branch in this quest. Rehnquist ultimately succeeded in marshaling a six to three victory in *McCleskey*. The new standard: a second *habeas corpus* petition of a prisoner had to be dismissed by a federal court with one exception, when there was shown to be an "abuse of the writ."[3]

A basic tension does arise on occasion between the coordinate branches, one that affects the relationship between the Court and the others. The tension occurs when the federal judiciary is asked to determine whether the actions of one or both of the coordinate branches are consistent with the words of the Constitution. Policy making typically flows from the Congress and the executive; however, especially in the second half of the twentieth century, both Congress and the executive have generally deferred to the Court's role as interpreter of actions that are challenged in federal court.[4] Indeed, more often than not the Court places its seal of legitimacy on acts of Congress challenged in federal court. The justices are, however, very sensitive about this legal and politically charged issue and generally move carefully into these cases and controversies. But the Court does, from time to time, enter this arena and does tackle some very difficult and politically sensitive issues.

There has been a two-hundred-year discussion and oftentimes heated political and scholarly debates about the relationship between the federal judiciary and the popularly elected political branches of the national government: the Congress and the chief executive. In this process of constitutional decision making, termed by Louis Fisher "coordinate construction" of the Constitution, "courts are not the sole part in the process of shaping and declaring constitutional values." Nor are the federal courts and the Supreme Court, all the time, necessarily the final words on constitutional interpretation: "History shows that the Supreme Court is neither final nor infallible."[5] History, however, also shows that the Court is a major participant in the making of critically important public policy in America. These intellectual and political clashes have revolved around a number of concepts that resonate throughout American history: separation of powers; checks and balances; and the concept of judicial review, the notion that judges in America have the power to say what the law is when a case is properly before them.[6]

In America, the Constitution is fundamental law. It is the fount of legitimate, authoritative grants of power as well as the basis for restraints on the use of power. The Constitution ties all three branches of government together in that fundamental way. All public officers, whether local, state, or national, whether legislators, executives, or judicial officers, "shall be bound by Oath or Affirmation, to support this Constitution."[7] The essence of the tension between these three types of national political actors lies in the fact that these public officers have different roles and responsibilities in a constitutional system.

"Popular sovereignty suggests *will,*" wrote a political scientist some time ago; however, the Constitution also as "fundamental law [clearly] suggests *limit.*"[8] All public officers take actions based on their understanding of the constitutional powers granted to them in the 1787 document (with its amendments). Legislators and executives are elected to office because of ideas they espouse about the legitimate use of the constitutional powers to move the nation in a certain direction.

These actions, when finally written into law by the legislators and implemented by the federal executive, are frequently challenged in federal court as public-policy action that goes beyond the scope of legislative and executive authority. Though the *will* to act is there, litigation brought into federal courts by parties adversely affected by the action charge that these public officials have gone beyond their constitutional *limits.* The federal courts, essentially the U.S. Supreme Court, must then determine whether these constitutional limits have in fact been transgressed by the other political actors.

Ever since judicial review by the Court was justified in Hamilton's *Federalist* no. 78 and in John Marshall's *Marbury* opinion, however, questions concerning its validity have been continuously raised by critics of the Court. Critics have pondered the political, legal, and ethical legitimacy of the power of judges in America to interpose their view of the Constitution's meaning instead of the views held by other elected public officials.

For contemporary critics of judicial review such as the late Alexander Bickel, a student and law clerk of Justice Felix Frankfurter, the argument, plain and simple, is that "judicial review is a deviant institution in the American democracy."[9] For Bickel and others, "the central characteristic of American democracy is popular representation through election and that judicial review runs counter to this characteristic."[10]

On the other hand, there continue to be various defenders of the Court's power of judicial review. Noted legal scholar John Hart Ely, for one, has argued that, because the Constitution's major provisions, including both the due process and equal-protection clauses in the Fourteenth Amendment, exhibit what he has labeled an "open texture," there is a need for the federal courts, especially the Supreme Court, to dynamically, and finally, interpret the document.

Justice John P. Stevens reflected on Ely's view of the law's nature and judicial review when he said that "our common law heritage and the repeated need to add new stitches in the open fabric of our statutory and constitutional law foreclose the suggestion that judges never make law."[11] In so responding to the "open texture" of the law, Ely maintains, the Court is acting in a "representation reinforcing" manner, reinforcing the very concept of representation that Bickel—and Frankfurter—revered so much![12]

There is another position regarding judicial review, that of the noninterpretivists, who, like Justices William J. Brennan and Thurgood Marshall, and constitutional scholar Thomas Grey, maintain that the Court should in no way be restrained by the language of the Constitution in deciding cases and controversies. One cannot define the intent of the framers; therefore, the task for the judge is to make policy based on social reality.

Justice Brennan, in an impassioned 1985 response to Attorney General Edwin Meese's criticism of modern judicial review by the Supreme Court,[13] said, "It is the very purpose of a constitution and particularly the Bill of Rights to declare certain rights transcendent, beyond the reach of temporary majorities." The federal judge's function, for Brennan, is to "read the Constitution in the only way that we can: as Twentieth Century Americans. We look to the history of the time of framing and to the intervening history of interpretation. But the ultimate question must be, what do the words of the text mean in our time?"[14]

Judges do not sit and adjudicate in a vacuum. Even a noninterpretivist such as Brennan starts with the historic record. But history is not the end point; rather, for Brennan and others, it was the beginning of the Court's decision-making process. According to some legal scholars, the justices should determine outcomes on the basis of whether the challenged action is based on "basic national ideals." For Grey and others, "judicial review should not be encumbered by any theories of constitutional interpretation that depend on the meaning of original intent."[15]

THE COURT AS NATIONAL POLICYMAKER

Throughout history, although the debates surrounding judicial review have become heated at times, "the Supreme Court has always been largely invulnerable to political assault."[16] As political scientist Robert Dahl has written about the Court and judicial review, "The views of a majority of the justices of the Supreme Court are never out of line for very long with the views prevailing among the lawmaking authorities of the country."[17] Awareness of the Court's role in American history underscores the powers, and their constitutional limits, that the justices of the Court possess as well as their dynamic, almost symbiotic, relationship.

For some scholars, such as Dahl, the essential function of the Court, employing judicial review, "is to confer legitimacy on the fundamental policies" of these dominant national law-making majorities.[18] A careful review of the actions of the Court over the past two centuries validates Dahl's observation. Supreme Court judicial review of political actions, at the national level, often takes place *after* representatives elected by a majority have developed a public policy in light of *their* understanding of the meaning of the Constitution.

Most of the time the Court acts as validator of national actions. Very frequently, the justices place their imprimatur on the actions of Congress or the executive when those popularly elected branches are challenged in the federal courts. Historically, between 1789 and 1991, while the Supreme Court has struck down almost one thousand state laws (919) and over one hundred municipal ordinances (105), the justices declared unconstitutional only 142 congressional statutes (while overturning an earlier decision of the Court little more than two hundred times [206]).[19]

There are, as well, occasions when the Court is clearly asked by Congress and, indirectly, the administration, to clarify the law through the Court's interpretation of a statute. "The leaders of Congress during the debate over the Sherman Antitrust Act openly admitted that they had no idea what the law meant and called on the courts to turn its phrases into policy."[20] In 1984, Justice Harry Blackmun spoke bluntly about the relationship between the Court and the Congress. "Blackmun blamed Congress for leaving it to the Court to resolve controversial issues rather than handling them itself. He said one member of Congress once told him that legislators purposely insert 'unintelligible language' in statutes and let the Court 'tell us what we mean.' "[21]

Most of the time the Court tries to define the ambiguous language of the legislators. However, at times the majority shies away from such action. In the discussion of the Court's response to the sit-in petitions in the early 1960s, especially *Bell v. Maryland*, a Court majority, much to Justice William O. Douglas's anger and frustration, deferred to the other branches to resolve an important societal dilemma. Clearly, there is a dynamic, "complicated interplay" between the Court and the Congress and the presidency regarding policy making and the Constitution.[22]

It has become very clear, especially in recent years when Congress and the executive have had to create legislation in very complex and controversial areas that the national legislators intentionally leave out of statutes important segments because of questions that only the future will bring answers to and also "through haste, unintended ambiguity or vagueness that arises from compromise."[23] Congress has deferred more and more to the federal judiciary to flesh out the statutory language. While the Supreme Court wishes to have, in the words of Chief Judge Abner Mikva (U.S. Court of Appeals for the D.C. Circuit), the legislators "dot every 'i' and cross every 't.' But it's hard to get the prima donnas in the House and the super prima donnas in the Senate and the super-super prima donnas on Pennsylvania Avenue to agree on everything."[24]

Clearly, the justices of the Court have come to play an increasingly important role in the delineation of public policy for the nation. While the Congress and the president go about the politics of formulating policy, increasingly the justices have been asked to "fill in the blanks."[25] To do this task, the Court employs its powers in a prudent manner.

Sources and Instruments of the Court's Power in America

In America, all courts, including the U.S. Supreme Court, derive their powers, their legitimate authority, from both the Constitution and from statutes enacted by legislators to frame the powers of and limits on the judiciary. The jurisdiction of the Court, however, goes beyond Constitution and statute and gets to the values the justices have about (1) the role of the Court in America's constitutional democracy, (2) the ways in which separation of powers and checks and balances are interpreted by the Court, and (3) the force of history and tradition on the behavior of the Court majority.

If the Court, for example, engages in "supplemental lawmaking,"[26] that is, giving a statute a substantive interpretation to resolve the legal and political conflict surrounding the issue, some in Congress and elsewhere will maintain that such activity goes beyond the Court's jurisdiction. The Court, they will maintain, should not reinterpret a constitutional clause to determine whether Congress can legislate in a certain way, or decide whether the substantive action of Congress is or is not constitutional. There will also be those, in Congress and elsewhere, who will argue that the Court *must* engage in such an interpretive activity because of the character and content of legislative outputs.

Sources of Judicial Power   In America, as Tom Paine said in America's revolutionary days, the "Law is King." In *United States v. Lee*, the Supreme Court reflected this basic American concept when it said: "No man in this country is so high that he is above the law. No officer of the law may set that law at defiance with impunity. All the officers of government, from the highest to the lowest, are creatures of the law, and are bound to obey it."[27] For the men and women who sit on the Supreme Court and all other courts in America, there developed, reflected in these observations, the notion of the "cult of the robe" and the myth of judicial infallibility. By 1940, with the appointment of a number of New Deal justices, the myth died.

Even though today more Americans than ever understand and accept the political role of the federal courts, the Supreme Court has retained its credibility in the eyes of the public. Although the public hears more about the Court because of the nature of the litigation brought to it, there is still a high degree of respect for the Court as a political and legal actor in the American polity.

The forces of tradition in American law along with the general veneration of the concept of precedent have also provided the judges, who work with the traditional black letter law and the body of law created by judges and followed by them, with another source of power. The judge's task, whether a trial judge in a small town in Idaho or a justice of the U.S. Supreme Court, is to work with the language of the law in the continuing effort to balance continuity with change in American law.

Yet another source of judicial power, especially at the appellate level, is a result of the "open texture of the law." The reality is that judges, including justices of the Court, have the responsibility to provide meaning to what Justice Robert Jackson termed the "majestic generalities" of the law. The open texture of the law enables judges to use their discretion in cases before them.

Whether it is the interpretation of a statute or a regulation written by others and based on their perception of constitutional power and limits, or the interpretation of a clause in the Constitution itself, all judges in America have the weight of history as well as contemporary societal values on their shoulders. For the most part, what federal judges accomplish, in interpreting the law, is the legitimation of these initial interpretations of constitutional power and limits. Relatively few federal statutes or regulations have been invalidated by the Court; instead, the Court has played an instrumental role as agent for the political system. By validating statutes and regulations that are challenged in federal court, the Court buttresses the system. Clearly, the importance of legitimation by the Court is not underestimated by the nation's political actors.

Instruments of Judicial Power   The justices of the Court employ a number of power instruments in the course of deciding a case properly before them. Included in this arsenal are both active and passive tools. First is the constitutional as well as statutory power to hear and then to decide cases in a timely manner. Given the changes in processing petitions to the Court, the justices have total discretionary power to determine what cases will be decided by the Court—and when they will be heard.

There is, too, the issuing of opinions and orders of the Court, including the rarely employed extraordinary remedies and writs. This is a fundamental instrument of judicial power. Associated with the issuance of orders is the power to deal with those who do not respond to the order in an appropriate manner. Courts, including trial courts, have the contempt power. A judge can hold a person in contempt of court for failing to act as ordered by the court.

There are also less visible instruments of judicial power, including docket control of the Court's agenda and procedures used to delay and therefore avoid cases. Furthermore, as a part of the discretion the Court has to act freely as decision maker, it can decide cases narrowly or broadly, respond to all the questions raised in the briefs, or, alternatively, respond to only one question or, in some cases, respond to questions not raised at all by the parties to the dispute.

Limitations on Judicial Power

The flip side of judicial power contains the limitations on that power. While there are infrequent "broad-gauge congressional [and presidential] attacks on the Court,"[28] legislators do have the constitutional authority, in Article III itself, to control the appellate jurisdiction of the Supreme Court and any inferior federal courts created by the Congress.

Certainly, as all judges in the American political and legal system know only too well, the judiciary cannot be too much in front of public opinion and majoritarian attitudes for too long before their outputs, their opinions, are evaded or avoided. The Court must continuously acknowledge, in its actions, the view held by many that it is an antimajoritarian structure within a democratic polity.

Furthermore, there are technical checks on the Supreme Court. The Court cannot arbitrarily decide what legal issues to address; the justices must await cases that come to them from the states and from the lower federal courts. Given the jurisdictional parameters found in Article III and in the various judicial acts passed by Congress since 1789, the justices can hear cases only in which the parties have standing to bring suit in the federal courts and before the Supreme Court.

And if precedent is a flexible, powerful tool in the hands of the Court majority, it also serves, at the same time, as a restraint on them. Because the justices work in a particular political, social, and ethical context, because they are not wise persons sitting under a fig tree dispensing justice without concern for their place in the polity, Court majorities practice a basic judicial restraint in their decision making.

Institutional restraints are another category of limit placed on the justices of the Court with respect to how far they can go on a substantive issue. The very nature of opinion writing limits the scope of possible judicial action in resolving a case. The writer of the opinion of the Court works hard and is very flexible in marshaling the majority opinion. Writing an opinion for five or six other justices means formulating an argument with which all five or six in the majority can live.

Furthermore, there are the lower-court checks on the opinions of the Court. If a Court opinion is not well constructed or is too individualized a judgment of the Court, lower federal judges, whether intentionally or not, have the capacity to minimize its impact. Where there is no clarity from the Court, lower federal court judges must do the best they can to determine the policy direction the Court wants them to follow.

Finally, there are also political checks on the power of the Court. Both the Congress and the president, given the concept of checks and balances, can and do impact the decision making of the Court. Simply put, the justices of the Court do not reach their decisions in a political and social vacuum.

THE SUPREME COURT AND CONGRESS

Constitutionally and politically, the Congress has the power to dramatically affect the workings of the Supreme Court. The Court likewise has the capacity to influence congressional behavior through the interpretation of statutes, forcing Congress to respond to Court action or let the Court's interpretation of legislation stand. For a number of reasons, Congress cannot every time muster the votes to respond to the Court's interpretation of the legislation and pass remedial legislation.[29]

Congressional powers, in Articles I and III, include at least the following checks on the actions of the Court. Congress, through the House of Representatives, can institute impeachment proceedings against sitting justices who have incurred the wrath, for ideological, political, or personal reasons, of legislators. Justices Samuel Chase and William O. Douglas are two justices who were the subject of impeachment proceedings. The former's case actually went to the Senate, in 1805, for a vote on the impeachment charges. This effort to unseat Chase was clearly a political effort by the Jeffersonian Republicans to forcefully blunt the activities of the Federalists on the Court, led by Chief Justice John Marshall. Had the effort succeeded, Marshall too would have been impeached and the potency of the Court irrevocably impaired.

Congress also controls disbursement of budgetary funds for the judiciary, including remuneration of federal judges and justices. This control can be used to send a message to the Court about its decision-making outputs. Congress can and has prohibited the use of federal funds to pay for services that flowed from Court decisions that expanded constitutionally protected rights such as abortion and busing to achieve an end to segregated school districts.

Congress also has, in the "exceptions" clause of Article III, the power to modify the appellate jurisdiction of the Court as well as the jurisdiction of all federal courts.[30] This happened once in American history, the 1866 *McCardle* case,[31] but the Congress has often shown its displeasure with Court decisions by introducing dozens of bills that, if successful, would have replicated *McCardle*. These threats, for example, the Jenner bill, introduced in 1957 to restrict the appellate jurisdiction of the Court in the area of subversive activities and loyalty oaths, and conservative senator Jesse Helms's continuing efforts to restrict the jurisdiction of the Court in social areas, can send the brethren a clear, angry message from the Congress.

Congressional reversal of Court decisions by statute, after an opinion is rendered, is another check on the power of the Court. The Congress has the power to overturn Court opinions that involve statutory interpretation by the justices of congressional legislation. In 1990, for example, the Congress passed a civil rights act that invalidated a number of Court decisions regarding civil rights, including *Wards Cove Packing Company v. Antonio* 109 S Ct 2115(1989).

Congress can also overturn, under certain conditions, Supreme Court opinions that reflect the Court's interpretation of a clause in the U.S. Constitution itself. This has been accomplished by the ratification of constitutional amendments that diminished the power of the Court, or, at the very least, overturned an earlier opinion of the Court that interpreted the Constitution in a manner that gravely displeased others in the political process.

Clearly, the Eleventh, Thirteenth, Sixteenth, and Twenty-sixth Amendments all reflect successful congressional action to overturn opinions of the Court. There have been many other proposals for constitutional amendments that would invalidate Court decisions, involving "constitutional" matters such as school busing and prayer in the public schools, that have not yet gone beyond the legislative-anger stage.

Congress can also, consistent with its powers found in Article III, reorganize the federal judiciary, including the Supreme Court, through the addition of new justices or the refusal to fill vacancies that arise, or do away entirely with lower federal courts created by Congress. Also, congressional changes in federal judicial-retirement policy have led Supreme Court justices to depart the Court, enabling the president to appoint a new set of jurists. When the policy was changed in 1937, enabling justices to retire at full pay when they reached seventy years of age with ten years of Court service or sixty-five years of age with fifteen years of service, the impact was immediate. Very quickly, archconservative Justice Willis Van Devanter retired, thereby enabling President Franklin Roosevelt to nominate one of his own Senate New Dealers, Hugo Black, to serve on the Court. This congressional retirement policy change did for Roosevelt what his Court-packing plan failed to accomplish earlier in 1937. Between 1937 and 1945, the president was able to appoint eight new justices to the Court, turning it into the "Roosevelt" Court.[32]

Given these general checks on judicial behavior, the justices of the Court make every effort to generate a positive congressional reaction to the Court's outputs. But the Court must also deal with the reality of negative congressional action in response to unpopular Court decisions.

In addition to the instruments of legislative influence noted above, Congress can also affect future Supreme Court decision making by rejecting nominations to the Court. Since 1789, the U.S. Senate has defeated (12) or forced the withdrawal (16) of 28 of 147 persons nominated, by presidents, about 20 percent of the total.

The justices are not unmindful of these legislative efforts to curtail Court jurisdiction. In a push–pull manner, the Court, having received a harsh warning from the Congress in the form of an attempt to reduce the Court's appellate jurisdiction, will typically draw back from the precipice it was on due to one or more of its earlier opinions. Most of the time, the Court will try to prevent damage to itself because of negative or hostile congressional action by the avoidance of severe conflict through denying certiorari in politically sensitive cases.

Not only does the Court read the election returns as well as watch CBS's Dan Rather nightly, it notes very carefully the temper and evident anger of the other coordinate branches and acts accordingly. A classic example of this type of Court behavior was seen in the late 1950s, when the Court, under the leadership of Chief Justice Earl Warren, began to examine the scope of the congressional power to investigate.

The *Watkins* Case, 1957

An important power of the Congress, an adjunct to its fundamental responsibility to legislate for the public good, is the congressional investigatory power. To legislate effectively, legislators need information. Hearings are held to provide them with appropriate data so they can then create legislation that addresses problems in an appropriate manner. The investigatory power is a necessary and proper activity of the Congress. It can be misused, however. Legislators can bring witnesses before a committee not to seek information that will lead to legislation but to harass and publicly humiliate them.

During the period of America's second Red Scare (the first occurred during the period after World War I), the 1940s–60s, a number of committees, including the House Un-American Activities Committee (HUAC) and the Senate's Internal Security Committee, brought people to Washington, D.C., or to regional committee hearings across the country, with the purpose of exposing them for exposure's sake. A number of witnesses who refused to answer questions and were then held in contempt of Congress by the committee appealed to the Supreme Court.

Until 1957, the Court validated the broad use of the congressional investigative power—even when legislation was not the goal of the legislative investigaton. Indeed, one of the justices sitting at the time, Hugo Black, when he was U.S. Senator Black (D–Ala.), was a notorious chair of several important legislative committees investigating fraud in a number of areas, including air mail and maritime problems. (His committees did, however, produce legislation for congressional review and action.)

By 1957, many in the nation were growing somewhat weary of the "Communist menace" claims that had the consequence of negating the constitutional rights of American citizens. Included in this cohort were a majority of the justices sitting on the Court at that time. The Court heard a number of cases dealing with loyalty matters, the power of the congressional committee, and the status of the U.S. Communist party and, in what was immediately referred to as "Red Monday," on June 17, 1957, handed down a number of decisions that quickly led to angry denunciations from members of the legislature.

One of the three controversial decisions announced by the Court that Monday was *Watkins v. United States*.[33] In *Watkins*, the Court set aside the contempt citation received by Watkins because he refused to answer certain questions put to him by HUAC members about persons other than himself who may have been members of the Communist party decades earlier. In *Watkins*, Chief Justice Earl Warren noted the sad history of repression of ideas in America:

> [After World War II], there appeared a new kind of congressional inquiry unknown in prior periods of American history. . . . This new phase of legislative inquiry involved a broad scale intrusion into the lives and affairs of private citizens. It brought before the courts novel questions of the appropriate limits of congressional inquiry. . . . The central theme was the application of the Bill of Rights as a restraint upon the assertion of [this type] of governmental power.[34]

For the chief, *Watkins* raised two issues: the pertinence of the questions directed by the HUAC to Watkins and, second, the question of limits on the congressional investigatory power. All of the brethren acknowledged that the power to investigate is a necessary part of the Congress's rule-making function. Except for former Attorney General Tom Clark, who prosecuted Communists prior to his elevation to the Court in 1949 by President Harry Truman, the five other justices participating in the deliberations and vote favored reversal of the contempt of Congress citation. (Justice Harold Burton recused himself in *Watkins* because his nephew was one of the trial counsel representing the HUAC, Justice Reed had retired, and his replacement, Charles Whittaker, did not participate in the discussion of *Watkins*.)

Black, the former senator noted for his hard-hitting investigations into fraud and scandal, did not have any difficulty with Warren's observations in conference. Brennan and Douglas joined, as did the more conservative justices, Felix Frankfurter and John Harlan II.

While the *Watkins* opinion reversed the contempt conviction on a point of procedure, the issue of the pertinence of the questions, in dicta Warren criticized the Congress, stating that it does not have the

> general authority to expose the private affairs of individuals without justification in terms of the functions of Congress. . . . Clearly, an investigation is subject to the command that the Congress shall make no law abridging the freedom of speech or press or assembly. . . . We have no doubt that there is no congressional power to expose for the sake of exposure. . . . Fundamental fairness demands that no witness be compelled to [answer questions] with so little guidance.[35]

Very soon after the announcement of the opinion, the *New York Times* editorialized, positively, about the *Watkins* decision, stating that the "Supreme Court has shown itself by far the most courageous of our three branches of government in standing up for basic principles."[36] However, there was a "growing chorus of excoriation" from Congress.[37] State legislatures were introducing "impeach Warren" resolutions, and legislators in Congress were apoplectic with anger because of what the Court had said in *Watkins*.

The hue and cry from Congress after Red Monday was immediate and very threatening to the Court. Congress's response to these liberating decisions took the form of conservative legislative efforts, in dozens of bills introduced, to curtail the Court's appellate jurisdiction in the area of loyalty and subversive cases. This was seen in William Jenner's bill introduced in 1957, immediately after the *Watkins* decision was handed down. Although all these efforts failed, the message was received by the Court when, during the 1958 term, it heard *Barenblatt v. United States.*[38]

The *Barenblatt* Case, 1959

Barenblatt involved a psychology professor at Vassar College who refused to answer questions about his possible membership in the Communist party and who was subsequently found to be in contempt of Congress for failure to answer the questions. Justice Frankfurter, a judicial conservative who was extremely sensitive to the messages he received from Congress after *Watkins*, along with Harlan, argued for employment of the "balancing" test to resolve the question before the Court, that is, the validity of the contempt action. The Court divided, five to four, on the question, with the Frankfurter camp (Frankfurter, Harlan, Clark, Whittaker, and Stewart) winning over the Warren Quartet (Warren, Douglas, Black, and Brennan).

Frankfurter saw *Barenblatt* "in terms of the need for judicial restraint in the face of legislative action, and this led him to oppose Warren's approach in deciding the case."[39] Reflecting Frankfurter's concerns, Harlan wrote the opinion for the five-person Court majority. It backed away from the *Watkins* language about the primacy of free expression and, using the balancing test, argued that the government's interest in investigating Communist party activities outweighed Barenblatt's First Amendment associational rights.

> Where First Amendment rights are asserted to bar governmental interrogation, resolution of the issue always involves a balancing of the competing private and public interests at stake in the particular circumstances shown. . . . The balance between the individual and the governmental interests here at stake must be struck in favor of the latter, and that therefore the provisions of the First Amendment have not been offended.[40]

Hugo Black dissented, arguing that the First Amendment "says in no equivocal language that Congress shall pass no law abridging freedom of speech, press, assembly, or petition. The activities of this Committee, authorized by Congress, do precisely that, through exposure, obloquy and public scorn."[41]

Clearly, the cautious Court majority in *Barenblatt* reacted to the angry threats emanating from across the street. It was not until 1962, after Frankfurter left the Court, that the justices returned to the views expressed in *Watkins.*[42] Ironically, Frankfurter wrote Brennan, on January 7, 1959, a year after *Barenblatt,* the following message: "Need I add another word, namely, that there isn't a man on the Court who *personally* disapproves more than I do of the activities of all the Un-American Committees, of all the Smith Act prosecutions, of the attorney general's list [of subversive organizations], etc., etc."[43]

THE PRESIDENT AND THE COURT

The other major institutional "check and balance" on the activities of the Court is the chief executive and the federal executive agencies. Much like the Congress, the president and his executive minions have the capability of limiting, at times dramatically, the viability of Court decisions. The president, for example, can refuse to effectively enforce rulings of the Court. President Andrew Jackson, it is claimed, said of an opinion written by the great chief justice John Marshall, "Mr. Justice Marshall made his decision, now let him enforce it."[44]

Responding to significant changes in the White House after a presidential election is another challenge that the Court must confront from time to time, and one that has the potential to restrict the power of the Court. At a minimum such a change brings about new personnel in the Department of Justice, especially a new solicitor general,[45] the public official who has the significant responsibility for following the new president's views on legal policies. As a consequence, substantive changes of direction in public policy will occur in the Court because of the substantive change in leadership in the executive branch.

The president can have a strong influence regarding Supreme Court decision making. The "bully pulpit" of the president can also be used to restrict the impact of Court decisions, as President Dwight Eisenhower indicated when, at his regular press conference, he gave a very poor assessment of the correctness of the Court's watershed 1954 *Brown v. Board of Education* opinion. But, based on the occupant and his values, the presidential office can be used to support judicial pronouncements, as President John F. Kennedy did when, at various press conferences, he supported the Court's judgments in its reapportionment and its controversial establishment-of-religion cases in the early 1960s.

Clearly, the Court does not have the machinery and the personnel to force a reluctant party to implement an order of the brethren. It has to rely, in part, on the efforts of the Department of Justice, for example, to assist the Court in implementing its judgments in areas such as search and seizure, admissibility of evidence, and so forth.

Furthermore, the president can pardon persons after the Court has upheld their convictions. In addition, the president affects the composition of the Court, thereby limiting its potency in a particular area or areas of significant public policy. The president can also encourage, through his surrogates in the Congress, the introduction of impeachment proceedings against a justice. Clearly, in the 1970 Douglas impeachment effort, President Nixon and his attorney general, John Mitchell, along with the director of the FBI, J. Edgar Hoover, worked very closely with Gerald Ford to provide the Michigan Republican with information that became part of the accusations leveled against Douglas by Ford and other conservative Republicans. A year earlier, in 1969, Attorney General Mitchell gathered allegedly incriminating information about Justice Abe Fortas and presented it to Chief Justice Earl Warren (as well as giving it to a *Life* magazine reporter, who used it in a story critical of Fortas's behavior), which led to Fortas's resignation from the Court.[46]

The president can propose legislation to the Congress that would, if passed, overturn an opinion of the Court. Using his office as a bully pulpit, through speeches, media events, and press conferences, the president can arouse public opinion against the Court or particular justices. In 1968, Republican presidential candidate Nixon ran, in part, against the Warren Court's liberal opinions, especially in the criminal-justice arena. He repeatedly promised his listeners that, if elected, he would appoint different justices, ones who sided with the police and victims rather than with the criminals, to the federal courts and especially to the Supreme Court. In 1990, Republican presidential candidate Ronald Reagan also campaigned against the Court's position on abortion. He promised, and it became a part of the Republican party platform, to appoint judges to the federal courts who believed in the sanctity of life.

The Court has clashed with the president in a number of areas, including an issue central to the presidency itself: limiting the scope of presidential powers. Louis Fisher observed, correctly, that

> the general drift of authority and responsibility to the President over the past two centuries is unmistakable. This trend by itself should not be cause for alarm. More threatening is executive activity cut loose from legislative moorings and constitutional restrictions—presidential action no longer tethered by law. The record of recent decades is disturbing to those who fear executive power: Watergate during the Nixon administration, revelation of CIA abuses in the 1970s, and the Iran–Contra scandal during the Reagan administration.[47]

Court involvement in this arena has led to some significant opinions, and direct confrontations with the chief executive.

As with the legislative checks on judicial power, there are some standard judicial responses the Court can use when it faces conflict with the president. Typically, using the "political question" doctrine argument, clearly seen in the Court's response to petitions that touch the area of foreign affairs and war powers, it tries to avoid direct confrontation with the president by avoiding such cases.

During the Vietnam War era, Justice Douglas unsuccessfully sought to have the Court grant certiorari in cases that dealt with the constitutionality of American involvement in Southeast Asia.[48] In 1978, to cite another example, the Court chose not to hear, on the merits, a case involving the question of whether the president could unilaterally terminate a defense treaty with Formosa or whether the president, Jimmy Carter, had to seek the support of the Senate.[49]

On other occasions involving a flareup with the president, the Court will sometimes try to dampen the clash through informal conversations by a justice who is a friend of the president (and many have been close associates of the chief executive). Only very rarely have there been public efforts by the Court to challenge presidential actions, such as the Court's formal and informal responses to President Roosevelt's Court-packing plan, introduced—and defeated—in 1937. In large part, the defeat was credited to the information provided the Congress and the public by the highly respected chief justice, Charles Evans Hughes. More recently, in 1985, Justices William Brennan and John P. Stevens publicly criticized the Reagan administration's confrontational "original intent" arguments put forward by Edwin Meese and others regarding judicial review of constitutional questions.[50]

In 1974, the Court found itself confronting the question of executive privilege and power in a very controversial case, *United States v. Nixon*. This case is perhaps the most visible and controversial of the Court's direct confrontations with the chief executive during the twentieth century.

The President, the Supreme Court, and the Meaning of Executive Privilege: The Watergate Tapes Litigation, 1974

For almost two years, ever since the election of 1972, the country and the world had experienced both the spectacle and the spectre of the Watergate scandal. The five burglars were caught by police in the Democratic party national headquarters in April 1972 leading almost immediately and inexorably to allegations that top officials in the White House, possibly even the president, Richard Nixon, had been involved in the break-in and subsequent cover-up of White House involvement in the break-in.[51]

By the spring of 1974, a federal grand jury had indicted a number of key Nixon administration officials, including the former attorney general John Mitchell and key White House leaders H. R. Haldeman and John Ehrlichman, based in part on the discovery and use of some tapes of conversations made by the president and revealed to the public during the nationally televised hearings chaired by Senator Sam Ervin (D–N.C.). The indictments came after a tense period in American politics, a time in which the Watergate special prosecutor, Archibald Cox, was fired by the president because Cox insisted that Nixon turn over requested tapes so he could proceed with the grand jury deliberations; a period in which U.S. Attorney General Elliot Richardson and Deputy Attorney General William Ruckelshaus resigned rather than fire Cox (who was relieved of his duties, illegally,[52] by acting U.S. attorney general Robert Bork). Because of the national "firestorm" of criticism about the firing of Cox, Nixon did accept the court of appeals order and turned over the requested tapes to the newly appointed prosecutor, Leon Jaworski. The indictments came, too, after the House of Representatives, in March 1974, began impeachment proceedings against Nixon.

Jaworski and his staff began compiling the material to be presented to the trial jury, scheduled to hear the case against the White House officials, *United States v. Mitchell, et al.*, September 9, 1974, in federal district court. In April 1974, Jaworski went into federal district court to ask the judge, John Sirica, to order Nixon to turn over an additional sixty-four tapes needed by the prosecution in the preparation of their criminal case.

Nixon claimed, under the separation-of-powers concept, "executive privilege" and refused to turn the tapes over to the federal judge. In late May 1974, Sirica ordered the president to turn over the tapes to him for an in camera inspection and release of the relevant tapes to Jaworski. Nixon appealed the Sirica order to the federal court of appeals in the District of Columbia. On May 24, 1974, however, Jaworski took the extraordinary step of bypassing the court of appeals and asking the Supreme Court to grant certiorari under expedited review as permitted in Rule 20 of the Rules of the Supreme Court.

Only rarely does the Court grant expedited review; it had done so only five times in its history.[53] When the Court met in conference session, on May 31, 1974, it was to determine whether to hear the case on expedited appeal or to allow the court of appeals to hear the case and then respond to petitions from the parties after the court of appeals ruling was announced. Jaworski argued that it was important for the Court to hear the case under expedited review because otherwise the scheduled September 1974 trial would have to be delayed for many months and because "the issues involved were of grave national importance; and the Court of Appeals had essentially ruled on the relevant legal issues in *Nixon v. Sirica.* The President, in response, suggested that the expedited procedure would unnecessarily pressure the Court and the parties and inevitably lead to a hastily prepared decision."[54]

The chief justice, Warren Earl Burger, appointed by Nixon in 1969, called for the May 31 conference session to respond to the Jaworski petition. While concerned about the Court being "pressured or rushed by news media or anyone else; nevertheless, the case is one of obvious importance and time factors are important."[55] Interestingly, the fact that the Jaworski petition came at the end of the term meant the Court "was in the rare position of being able to give its undivided attention to this single case."[56]

Eight justices met to discuss the *Nixon* matter; William Rehnquist, who had come from the Nixon Justice Department and had been an associate of Mitchell, had recused himself. Surprisingly, in light of the final decisions of the Court in the case, the initial view of the men around the table, by a six to two margin, was *not* to grant expedited certiorari review and instead to have the court of appeals hear the appeal from the Sirica order. According to the docket sheets and notes taken by some justices, only Justices Brennan and Marshall were early supporters of expedited review. Justices Blackmun, White, Powell, Stewart, Burger, and liberal justice and mortal enemy of the president William O. Douglas did not seem inclined to take the case from the district court.

Brennan wrote (see Figure 12.1), that "initially, majority sentiment was not for bypass of the Court of Appeals. Two of the Justices were definitely against bypass and three others leaned that way. Only two of us felt strongly that the nation would think we had 'let the people down' if we didn't bypass."[57] Blackmun was one of the two brethren definitely against bypass. He argued that "a six month delay in a criminal case is no irreparable injury. . . . It may be an unpopular decision but I'd deny." White was the other adamant justice. He believed that Jaworski's application "doesn't really demonstrate immediate need. . . . [It was] just a transparent attempt to have an impact on the impeachment proceeding. I don't think we should let ourselves be used that way. . . . Prefer to deny," was White's final comment.[58]

Evidently, Brennan then lobbied the Court, according to Douglas, throwing in a veiled threat to write a lengthy dissent from a denial of certiorari should the Court so decide.[59] After a few hours of intense conversation and debate, Brennan convinced Powell, Stewart, Burger, and, finally, Douglas to vote to grant certiorari under Rule 20. Only Blackmun and White, at the conclusion of the conference session, voted to deny certiorari. The vote was totally reversed, from six to two against to six to two in favor of bypassing the court of appeals and bringing *Nixon* directly to the Supreme Court. For Justice Brennan, as he noted on his docket sheet, the Court had a "duty to our institution and to the public not to be one of them [other institutions not acting]" by hearing *Nixon* in an expedited fashion.[60] Had he not been insistent and persuasive, the history of the second Nixon administration might have had a different ending.

Later that day, the official Supreme Court journal noted that the petition for writ of certiorari to the court of appeals and motion for an expedited schedule was "granted," that briefs had to be filed by June 21, responses exchanged by July 1, 1974, with two hours of oral argument scheduled for July 8, 1974, and that Justice William Rehnquist would not participate in the proceedings.

On July 24, 1974, the Court voted unanimously that the president had to release the tapes to Sirica, ruling against Nixon's claim to an absolute right, under the separation-of-powers argument, to withhold materials. The Court ruled that, in this case, the federal prosecutors had need for relevant, material information for the criminal prosecution and that, under the circumstances, the president had to turn over the tapes.

𝔖𝔲𝔭𝔯𝔢𝔪𝔢 𝔔𝔬𝔲𝔯𝔱 𝔬𝔣 𝔱𝔥𝔢 𝔘𝔫𝔦𝔱𝔢𝔡 𝔖𝔱𝔞𝔱𝔢𝔰
𝔚𝔞𝔰𝔥𝔦𝔫𝔤𝔱𝔬𝔫, 𝔇. 𝔔. 20543

CHAMBERS OF
JUSTICE Wм. J. BRENNAN, JR.

January 4, 1988

Howard Ball, Dean
Professor of Political Science
The University of Utah
Office of the Dean
205 Orson Spencer Hall
Salt Lake City, Utah 84112

Dear Dean Ball:

Thank you so much for your letter of December 28. My notes
on the U.S. v. Nixon litigation disclose that (as you mention)
the Court held a conference session to decide whether certiorari
before judgment to the Court of Appeals should be granted.
Initially, majority sentiment was not for bypass of the Court of
Appeals. Two of the Justices were definitely against bypass and
three others leaned that way. Only two of us felt strongly that
the nation would think we had "let the people down" if we didn't
bypass. The Special Prosecutor, Mr. Jaworski, had petitioned the
Court on May 24 for certiorari before judgment. He had argued
that without bypass the trial scheduled for September 9, 1974
would have to be delayed months; the issues involved were of
grave national importance; and the Court of Appeals had
essentially ruled on the relevant legal issues in Nixon v.
Sirica. The President, in response, suggested that the expedited
procedure would unnecessarily pressure the Court and the parties
and inevitably lead to a hastily prepared decision.

I felt strongly that the Special Prosecutor's petition
should be granted. Based on some exhaustive research, I had
concluded that the President's claim of absolute executive
privilege was plainly without constitutional foundation, and that
we should say so at the earliest opportunity, lest the nation
lose all confidence in the criminal justice system. Moreover, I
urged that after two long and bitter years of Watergate it was
time the nation had access to the evidence that would reveal the
truth about Watergate. Finally, since most of the Court's cases
for the Term had already been decided, the Court was in the rare
position of being able to give its undivided attention to this
single case. After long and intensive discussion, the Special
Prosecutor's motion was unanimously granted.

I hope this may answer your question.

With warmest personal regards, I am

Sincerely,

Wm J Brennan Jr

FIGURE 12.1   Letter to the author from Justice William Brennan defending the Court's action in
U.S. v. Nixon.

In *Nixon*, the justices had to examine a number of issues that go to the very core of the relationship of the Court to the coordinate branches of the national government: separation of powers and more specifically with regard to the powers of the presidency, the scope of the implied presidential power of executive privilege. When the case came to the Court, the president was besieged with criticism in the press and was showing poorly in public-opinion polls of his presidency, congressional impeachment hearings were well under way under the leadership of Congressman Peter Rodino (D–N.J.), a fiercely liberal political critic of Nixon. Clearly, the presidency as an institution was under intense scrutiny, and Nixon was heavily criticized as America's "imperial president."[61]

For the president's lawyers, the separation-of-powers principle was a categorical one that meant no intrusion, by Congress or the Court, into the ways in which the president used the powers granted him in Article II of the Constitution. The concept extended to the conversations the president had with staff and others in the White House. These conversations were confidential, and neither the Congress nor the Court could overturn a judgment Nixon made about their continued confidentiality. The separation-of-powers concept, according to Nixon, meant that only the president could determine whether or not to release confidential data. If he felt release of confidential information was appropriate, he, the president, would make that judgment. Because of the separation of powers, no court, not even the Supreme Court, could order the president to release tapes. The Supreme Court did not have the jurisdiction to intervene in what was, for the executive, an intra-executive-branch matter and, consequently, a nonjusticiable issue. Bluntly, the lawyers for Nixon claimed, in their *Nixon* brief, "an absolute executive privilege against inquiry by the coordinate Judicial Branch." According to the separation doctrine, "The Judiciary is without jurisdiction to intervene in the intra-branch dispute between the President and the Special Prosecutor, . . . even at the request of a disputant."[62]

For Jaworski and the special prosecutor's staff, there was no constitutional basis for the president's categorical assertion of an immune executive privilege. For them, the Court had jurisdiction to examine the extremely political and legal question of release of information that was materially relevant to the proper administration of criminal justice in a federal courtroom.

The justices discussed these issues for almost two months and came to judgment after a period of circulating intense MTTC's that had the effect of substantially rewriting most of Burger's draft opinion for the unanimous Court. Essentially, the Court answered four major questions in *Nixon*: (1) Jaworski's ability to appeal, (2) the Court's capacity to hear an intra-branch dispute that, claimed Nixon, the Court could not examine because of the separation of powers, (3) the question as to whether the Jaworski request for the sixty-four tapes fell within the legal requirements for a judicial grant of a subpoena under Rule 17c of the Federal Rules of Criminal Procedure, and (4) the scope of the executive privilege, the power of the president to withhold evidence from other agencies.

On July 24, 1974, Burger read a shortened version of the Court's decision in *United States v. Nixon*.[63] The justices concluded that the Nixon concept of separation of powers was an unrealistic definition and that the Court did have jurisdiction to hear the appeal from the special prosecutor. Furthermore, it was a justiciable issue before the Court, that is, one in which the federal courts could provide a remedy.

Separation of powers did not bar the Court from looking "beyond names that symbolize the parties to determine whether a justiciable case or controversy is present." For the justices, the starting point was the criminal trial scheduled to start in September 1974, brought by the United States against John Mitchell and other defendants. The special prosecutor, the Court concluded, had been given authority by Congress and the attorney general to conduct the Watergate prosecution. There is "that concrete adverseness" that must be present for a case to be heard in the Court. Because of the presence of adverseness, the Court concluded that it could hear the case.

The Court then reasoned that the federal district court judge, Sirica, had correctly followed the subpoena procedures outlined in the Federal Rules of Criminal Procedure. Jaworski's request for the issuance of the subpoena to the president to produce the sixty-four tapes before the trial was a reasonable one by a prosecutor preparing a case for presentation to a trial jury. In his request for the subpoena, he cleared the three hurdles presented in the rules: Jaworski showed relevancy, admissibility, and specificity.

The segment of the opinion that dealt with the claim of executive privilege was the most controversial portion of the *Nixon* opinion.[64] Nowhere in the Constitution's Second Article is there mentioned a presidential executive privilege, that is, the right to maintain confidentiality of White House communications. The justices chose to answer the question of whether such a privilege is inherent in the Article II powers or whether it was a presidential prerogative that was not constitutionalized.

Over the shrill arguments of Douglas, Brennan, and White that the Court not constitutionalize the executive privilege concept, Burger successfully retained in the final version of *Nixon* his view that privilege was inherently a part of the presidential powers found in Article II. Accepting the value of confidentiality in presidential decision making, Burger wrote that there is a "presumptive privilege for presidential communications. The privilege is fundamental to the operation of government and inextricably rooted in the separation of powers under the Constitution . . . and to the extent this interest in confidentiality relates to the effective discharge of a president's powers, it is constitutionally based."[65]

After a day of reflection, the president obeyed the order of the Court to turn the tapes over to Sirica. This led to the discovery of a June 23, 1972, tape in which Nixon is heard agreeing to a cover-up of the break-in. This, in very quick turn, led to the resignation of Richard M. Nixon on August 8, 1974. The opinion of the Court in *United States v. Nixon* is a clear indication of the potency of a Court judgment, given the presence of an environment conducive to positively responding to that judgment. Nixon was in no position to ignore the order of the Court. While Burger had succeeded in protecting presidential privilege generally, in this specific case, Nixon had to turn materials over to the Court. Facing an imminent impeachment indictment by the House on a number of charges relating to his misuse of power, and without the votes to block adverse Senate action in the matter of his impeachment, Nixon had no choice but to obey and then resign.

There is a dynamic relationship between the Court and the presidency, and fairly regularly the Court affirms controversial presidential actions. Even in *Nixon*, the Court did define presidential privilege, for the first time, as having a constitutional basis. So, while Richard Nixon lost, the presidency was strengthened by virtue of Burger's insistence on incorporating his view of presidential privilege into the opinion of the Court.

SUMMARY

The justices of the Supreme Court are active participants in the political and social life of the American community. From the very beginning of the republic, the Court has determined that it is "emphatically the province of the Court to say what the law is."[66] Because of the clash of values America experienced in succeeding generations, society determined the types of cases and controversies petitioned to the Court for certiorari review.

Legislators and executives typically respond to those persistent and visible issues and legislate to remedy the particular dilemma that confronts the public, whether the issue is slavery or child labor or segregated schools or abortion. Invariably, as Tocqueville noted almost two centuries ago, these problems come before the Supreme Court. You and your brethren have attempted to resolve these conflicts, trying to avoid inflicting injury on the Court by announcing a poor judgment. There have been very few self-inflicted wounds. Through it all, the Court and its instruments of power have survived and, indeed, have played an increasingly important role in policy making in a democracy.

While there is a check-and-balance process in the American system of government, the Court has grown in stature, and its review of statutes has come to be respected and, in some instances, called for by the Congress. Likewise with the executive, there has developed a dynamic, complex relationship: The Court generally defers to presidential initiatives in the areas of foreign affairs and war powers but does not shy away from other issues involving presidential power, and for the most part, chief executives have managed to live with Court judgments regarding the scope of executive powers.

Carefully nurturing its powers, the Court, throughout American history, has been able to avoid countervailing negative action by presidents and legislators that would diminish judicial power in the American political system. As a consequence, the Court continues to play a significant role in the determination of the scope and direction of public policy in American society.

NOTES

[1] *Youngstown Sheet and Tube Co. v. Sawyer*, 343 U.S. 579 (1952), at 635.

[2] David M. O'Brien, *Supreme Court Watch: 1992* (New York: Norton, 1992), p. 189.

[3] Justice Kennedy, writing for the six-person majority, stated that a prisoner had to show "actual prejudice" from the constitutional error or show "cause" for not raising the habeas corpus claim earlier in the trial.

[4] See Melvin Urofsky, "John Marshall and All That," *New York Times Book Review*, Sept. 26, 1993, p. 33.

[5]Louis Fisher and Neal Devins, *Political Dynamics of Constitutional Law* (St. Paul, MN: West, 1992), pp. 2, 10.

[6]Stephen M. Griffin, "Judicial Review and Democracy Revisited" (Paper presented at the annual meeting of the American Political Science Association, Washington, DC, Aug. 1993), p. 12.

[7]U.S. Constitution, Article VI, Section 3.

[8]Quoted in William Lasser, *The Limits of Judicial Power: The Supreme Court in American Politics* (Chapel Hill: University of North Carolina Press, 1988), p. 250, n. 10.

[9]Alexander Bickel, *The Least Dangerous Branch* (New York: Bobbs-Merrill, 1962), p. 18. For Bickel, judicial review is a "counter-majoritarian force in our system. [When it declares an action unconstitutional] it thwarts the will of the representatives of the actual people of the here and now; it exercises control, not in behalf of the prevailing majority, but against it" (p. 16.) Jesse Choper also believes that judicial review works "sharply against the grain of majority rule." For him, and Bickel, "The effect of judicial review in ruling legislation unconstitutional is to nullify the finished product of the law-making process" (see Choper, "The Supreme Court and the Political Branches: Democratic Theory and Practice," *University of Pennsylvania Law Review* 122 [1974], pp. 810, 830, 832). Raul Berger is another critic of judicial review. For him, Courts have usurped legislative functions in several very important public-policy areas, including racial segregation and legislative reapportionment (see his *Government by Judiciary: The Transformation of the Fourteenth Amendment* [Cambridge: Harvard University Press, 1977]).

[10]Griffin, "Judicial Review and Democracy Revisited," p. 3.

[11]John Paul Stevens, "Some Thoughts on Judicial Restraint," *Judicature*, 66, no. 5 (Nov. 1982): 180.

[12]See H.L.A. Hart, *Democracy and Distrust: A Theory of Judicial Review* (Cambridge: Harvard University Press, 1980). Hart argues for a non-clause-bound concept of judicial review in which the Court's decisions are based on the "general themes of the entire constitutional document and not from some source entirely beyond its four corners." Because the Court went beyond the Constitution's four corners in the abortion litigation, Ely believes it acted in an "excessive" manner (see also Robert Clinton, *Marbury v. Madison and Judicial Review* [Lawrence: University Press of Kansas, 1989], p. 10).

[13]See Howard Ball, "The Convergence of Constitutional Law and Politics in the Reagan Administration: The Exhumation of the 'Jurisprudence of Original Intention' Doctrine," *Cumberland Law Review* 17, No. 3 (1986–87).

[14]William J. Brennan, Jr., Address given at Georgetown University, Washington, DC, Oct. 12, 1985 (Reprinted in *The New York Times*, Oct. 13, 1985, sec. A).

[15]Clinton, *Marbury v. Madison*, p. 9. See also Thomas C. Grey, "Do We Have an Unwritten Constitution?" *Stanford Law Review* 27, (1975): 703–18.

[16]Lasser, *Limits of Judicial Power*, p. 262.

[17]Robert A. Dahl, *Democracy and Its Critics* (New Haven, CT: Yale University Press, 1974), p. 190.

[18]Quoted in Lasser, *Limits of Judicial Power*, p. 248.

[19]O'Brien, *Storm Center*, p. 63.

[20]Urofsky, "John Marshall and All That," p. 33.

[21]Harry Blackmun, "Supreme Court: 'A Rotten Way to Earn a Living,' " *Washington Post Weekly Edition*, Oct. 1, 1984, p. 33.

[22]Ibid.

[23]Quoted in Joan Biskupic, "Asking the Court to Read Between the Lines," *Washington Post Weekly Edition*, May 9–15, 1994, p. 32.

[24]Ibid.

[25]Ibid.

[26]David Barnum, *Supreme Court and American Democracy* (New York: St. Martin's Press, 1985), p. 312.

[27]106 U.S. 196 (1882), at 220.

[28]Stephen Wasby, *The Supreme Court in the Federal Judicial System* (Chicago: Nelson Hall, 1987), p. 314.

[29]See Howard Ball, "The U.S. Supreme Court's Glossing of the Federal Tort Claims Act: Statutory Construction and Veterans' Tort Actions," *Western Political Quarterly* 41, no. 3, (Sept. 1988): 529.

[30]See Article III of the U.S. Constitution. The "exceptions" clause reads as follows: "In all other

cases before mentioned, the supreme Court shall have appellate jurisdiction, both as to Law and Fact, with such Exceptions, and under such Regulations as the Congress shall make."

[31]*McCardle, Ex Parte*, 74 U.S. 506 (1869).

[32]See Ball and Cooper, *Of Power and Right*, chap. 5.

[33]354 U.S. 178 (1957). Two other controversial cases announced that day were *Yates v. United States* and *Sweezey v. New Hampshire. Yates* essentially set aside the Smith Act convictions of a number of Communist party officials while *Sweezey* set aside the state legislative contempt citation for his refusal to answer questions posed to Sweezey by a New Hampshire legislative committee.

[34]*Watkins v. United States*, 354 U.S. 178 (1957), at 195.

[35]Ibid., at 187, 197, 200, 214.

[36]*New York Times,* June 17, 1957.

[37]See Bernard Schwartz, *Super Chief: Earl Warren and His Supreme Court—a Judicial Biography* (New York: New York University Press, 1983), p. 249.

[38]360 U.S. 109 (1959).

[39]Schwartz, *Super Chief*, p. 325.

[40]*Barenblatt v. United States*, 360 U.S. 109 (1958), at 126, 234.

[41]Ibid., at 140–46, passim.

[42]See *Russell v. United States*, 369 U.S. 749 (1962).

[43]Felix Frankfurter to William J. Brennan, January 7, 1959, box 30, FFP, LC, Washington, DC.

[44]Quoted in Wasby, *Supreme Court*, p. 325.

[45]See Lincoln Kaplan, *The Tenth Justice: The Solicitor General and the Rule of Law* (New York: Knopf, 1987), for an assessment of the impact on the Court of a change in presidents and solicitor generals.

[46]See Kalman, *Fortas*; and Bruce Murphy, *Fortas,*

[47]Louis Fisher, *Constitutional Conflicts Between Congress and the President*, 3d ed. (Lawrence: University Press of Kansas, 1992), p. 281.

[48]See Ball and Cooper, *Of Power and Right*, for an examination of this issue.

[49]*Goldwater v. Carter* 444 U.S. 996 (1979).

[50]See Ball, "Convergence of Constitutional Law," for an examination of this public clash between the federal judges and the executive-branch officials.

[51]See Howard Ball, "*We Have a Duty*": *The Supreme Court and the Watergate Tapes Litigation* (Westport, CT: Greenwood Press, 1992).

[52]See *Nader v. Bork*, 366 F. Supp 104 (1974).

[53]Ibid., p. 34.

[54]Philip Lacovera, assistant to the Watergate special prosecutor, interview with author, Hempstead, NY, Nov. 21, 1987.

[55]MTTC, May 25, 1974, William J. Brennan papers, Box 329, LC, Washington, DC (hereafter cited as WJBP).

[56]William J. Brennan to Howard Ball, Jan. 4, 1988.

[57]Ibid.

[58]All quotes from William J. Brennan Docket Book, 1973 term, box 423, LC, Washington, DC.

[59]William O. Douglas, *The Court Years* (New York: Random House, 1982), pp. 139-40.

[60]WJB Docket, Box 423, LC, Washington, D.C.

[61]See Arthur Schlessinger, Jr., *The Imperial Presidency* (Boston: Houghton Mifflin, 1976).

[62]Brief for Respondent, Cross Petitioner, Richard M. Nixon, President of the United States, in *United States v. Nixon* (reprinted in Alan Westin and Leon Friedman, eds., [New York: Chelsea House, 1975]).

[63]418 U.S. 683 (1974).

[64]Three justices were so concerned about the precedent being set that they threatened to write dissents. The three were Justices Douglas, White, and Brennan. None did write, because there was the collegial effort to arrive at a unanimous, institutional opinion for the Court.

[65]*United States v. Nixon*, 418 U.S. 683 (1974).

[66]Chief Justice John Marshall, in *Marbury v. Madison*, 1 Cranch 37 (1803).

Supreme Court Impact and Change

13

So what difference does it all make? Like many justices before you, you may get a perverse chuckle from the fact that you simultaneously get letters insisting that the Court is ineffectual and other letters chastising you for the horrendous impact that your opinions have had. Which is it? Do the Court's decisions matter or not?

The other ironic fact of life in the discussion of judicial impact is that one should have to ask about impact at all. Presumably, in a nation that operates under a constitution and the rule of law, and with the Supreme Court sitting at the pinnacle of the judiciary, one can assume that its rulings will be obeyed. History proves, however, that it is far from certain just how much and what kind of impact any given ruling will produce. It is clear from the continuing clashes over school desegregation cases, for example, that compliance is anything but certain and complete. On the other hand, sometimes decisions matter, and the impact is felt quickly. The Court's unanimous ruling upholding the demand for President Richard Nixon to turn over the Watergate tapes has been seen as the final push that forced him out of office.

Many social scientists have contemplated the question of whether, when, how, and why people respond to Supreme Court rulings.[1] They often view the issue as a question of outcomes on the ground where the people live. It is useful, though, to think of the subject from where you sit as well. A look at what Justice Thurgood Marshall saw as he watched the response to the Court's rulings provides an interesting perspective.

THURGOOD MARSHALL AND THE FRUSTRATION OF CIVIL RIGHTS IMPLEMENTATION

As much as any person who has ever sat on the Court, Justice Thurgood Marshall understood the relationship between what happens in the Supreme Court and what may or may not follow on Main Street. Before he came to the bench in 1967, Marshall had argued thirty-two cases before the Court, winning twenty-nine of them.[2] Still, the civil rights agenda on which Marshall had already labored for decades was far from accomplished. From the argument before the Court in the second *Brown v. Board of Education* case (to determine a remedy for the segregation the Court had found illegal the previous term), in which the attorney for the state and local education officials refused to tell Chief Justice Earl Warren that there would be a good-faith effort to implement the Court's order;[3] through the massive public resistance mounted by politicians like Arkansas governor Orville Faubus, who tried to block integration of Little Rock Central High School; through the obvious efforts at evading the Court's rulings through various means of subterfuge, like draining funds from public schools to support private segregated academies; to the increasingly vocal challenges that encouraged either intentionally or otherwise acts of open defiance and violence, Marshall had seen it all.

Even so, when he entered the Court, Marshall's views were aligned with those of the Warren Court majority. Marshall could both observe and participate as his colleagues fought to ensure implementation of the civil rights rulings that Marshall had worked so hard and long to achieve. But things were changing. The Court's rulings on desegregation, its persistent attempts to get local law enforcement officials to observe the constraints of the Bill of Rights, and its efforts to maintain a separation of church and state were targets of wide-ranging criticism from the Right and from certain key groups within the electorate. Congressman Mendel Rivers of South Carolina declared: "I know of nothing in my lifetime that could give more aid and comfort to Moscow than this bold, malicious, atheistic and sacrilegious [*sic*] twist of this unpredictable group of uncontrolled despots."[4] Leading southern legislators saw advantage to be gained in linking the opposition to these different kinds of rulings. Senator Sam Ervin of North Carolina, who later gained such notoriety in the Watergate investigation, warned on the Senate floor: "I should like to ask whether we would be far wrong in saying that in this decision the Supreme Court has held that God is unconstitutional and for that reason the public schools must be segregated against him?"[5] As *New York Times* columnist Anthony Lewis put it, "They did their best to suggest that the prayer ruling only showed how equally wrong the Court had been to outlaw segregation."[6]

As early as the 1964 campaign, Republican presidential candidate Barry Goldwater made attacks on the Court's rulings and a commitment to "law and order" centerpieces of his election bid. By the 1968 campaign, the Court had become an even more tempting target, and Richard Nixon used that to the hilt. He vowed to change the Court and get legislative reversal of some of its rulings.[7]

The Court was tired of waiting for compliance with its desegregation rulings—it had been doing so for a quarter century—and was preparing to take stronger positions. Marshall mused on the fears that he and his NAACP Fund colleagues had early on in the process:

We were sitting around the table up in my office, all of the lawyers—about 10 or 11 of us—trying to figure out what this word ["deliberate," in "all deliberate speed"] meant. And my secretary then, who was always a sharp tack, she went over to the Webster's dictionary. And she said, "Hey, why don't all of you shut your mouths and keep quiet. Look what the first definition of 'deliberate' is in the dictionary: 'slow.' "[8]

The Fortas affair, in which President Lyndon Johnson tried to replace the retiring chief justice Warren by elevating his confidant, Abe Fortas, to the center chair, blew up. The real attack was not on Fortas the justice, but on the Warren Court, with people like South Carolina senator Strom Thurmond assailing the hapless Fortas for rulings that had been handed down even before the justice had been appointed to the Court![9] Racial clashes in the spring and summer of 1968, following the assassinations of Dr. Martin Luther King, Jr., and Robert Kennedy, only increased the level of anger, fear, and backlash sentiments against the Court and the civil rights movement in general.

Following Nixon's election, Marshall began to see a transformation in the Court. It was not that the Court underwent some sort of instant dramatic reversal of prior rulings. Indeed, it was under Chief Justice Warren Burger's name that the Court issued *Swann v. Charlotte-Mecklenburg Board of Education*, which, for the first time, recognized the authority of district judges to impose remedies for segregation that included busing.[10] Even so, the change was coming, and Marshall could see that by 1973, with the addition of Justices William Rehnquist and Lewis Powell, it was clearly taking shape. He was watching as the Court moved, in his view, in ways that not only removed the pressure for implementation but actually encouraged evasion of civil rights mandates and erected barriers to those who sought to make the rights they possessed meaningful in their day-to-day lives. As he put it, "The only problem we've got now is everybody agrees to do it and the court moves in and says no."[11] A brief look at a few of his key battles demonstrates his changing role within the Court from supporting player to that of leading dissenter, fighting to preserve a lifelong civil rights effort and to make it real in the lives of Americans.

Manning the Barricades

The period from 1972 to 1974 was particularly difficult for Marshall, not only because he saw rulings that indicated a change in general attitude among the Court's dominant majority toward desegregation cases but also because of the symbolism of both the substance and the process of Supreme Court litigation. That Powell, a Nixon appointee formerly active in Virginia schoolboard politics, wrote the majority opinion in *San Antonio Independent School District v. Rodriguez*[12] was among the most important and most frustrating of these symbols for Marshall.

In the *Rodriguez* case, the Court rejected a challenge to the Texas property-tax-based school finance system that was alleged to enable discrimination on the basis of wealth and race. Despite what purported to be equalization programs, wealthy districts were able to obtain a great deal more funds per pupil than poorer, largely minority, districts, while taxing themselves at a far lower rate than those poor districts. More important for Marshall was that the Court took what he regarded as a giant step backward and away from meaningful implementation of the command of *Brown v. Board* that public education, "where a state has undertaken to provide it, is a right which must be made available to all on equal terms." In San

Antonio, Powell wrote that: "Education, of course, is not among the rights afforded explicit protection under our Federal Constitution. Nor do we find any basis for saying it is implicitly so protected."[13] In a powerful dissent, Marshall observed, "The majority's holding can only be seen as a retreat from our historic commitment to equality of educational opportunity and as unsupportable acquiescence in a system which deprives children in their earliest years of the chance to reach their full potential as citizens."[14] Denying that the political process alone would make the Brown mandate reality, Marshall recalled the language of Brown when he insisted, "In the meantime, countless children unjustifiably receive inferior educations that may affect their hearts and minds in a way unlikely ever to be undone."[15]

Beyond what appeared to be a frontal assault on the effort to make the promise of *Brown v. Board* meaningful was what Marshall saw as a complete failure to understand the true complexity of the civil rights challenge. The attempt by the Court to force all equal-protection analysis into a two-tier test announced by the majority frustrated Marshall in light of his knowledge of the sophistication and complex interrelationships of the elements of judgments about equality.[16] (The two-tier "test" created by the justices meant that a case would be strictly scrutinized by the justices if it involved racial or religious discrimination complaints. If those were not present, a different, less severe, type of judicial review would occur.)

Finally, and not surprisingly, Justice Powell ultimately rested his opinion for the Court on the primacy of local control of education. Marshall, who had faced too much racism and had fought too many battles against the abuses of local and state majorities, responded: "For the record, it is apparent that the State's purported concern with local control is offered primarily as an excuse rather than as a justification for interdistrict inequality."[17] The states dominated many key aspects of education and displaced local governments, such as in the design of systems of school finance, hardly leaving the matter to "local control." Besides, when local districts were challenged, their reaction was too often an argument that they had to accommodate state standards. Marshall had seen this "Catch-22" many times. As far as he was concerned, the Texas system under review amounted to little more than a "mere sham" version of equality.[18]

Still, Marshall's dissent in *Rodriguez*, while strong, did not amount to taking off the gloves. Unfortunately, Marshall could see that more was in the offing. He could also see that many recalcitrant communities and their leaders across the nation would read the Powell opinion, and the fact of his authorship, as signaling a significant shift in the Court's approach to desegregation.

Marshall's frustration and anxiety were exacerbated by what he saw happening in the Richmond, Virginia, and Detroit, Michigan, cases. In these cases, the ability of federal district judges who had found discrimination in the schools to require remedial plans that included more than one, and usually several, school districts was questioned. States had engaged in deliberate segregation in housing and education, creating community residence patterns that virtually assured continued segregation even after the formal legal bans on integration had been removed. In most instances, judges found themselves with largely black, often urban, districts surrounded by mostly white, suburban districts. Remedies that involved only the city district would mean little more than moving black children around and perhaps providing the remaining white families with an impetus to flee the cities. The result would be a continuation of the dual school systems that the Court had worked for so long to eliminate.

Judge Robert Mehrige had faced one such case in Richmond and had contemplated a remedy that would have involved three districts. The court of appeals rejected the proposal, and the case went to the Supreme Court. Justices Marshall, Byron White, William Brennan, and William O. Douglas voted to hear it.[19] The Court had discussed holding the Richmond matter to be decided with the Detroit case but decided that the Richmond case could not be delayed.[20] Justice Powell could not participate because of his Virginia schoolboard involvement, leaving the Court with eight voting members. Initially, it appeared that Justice White had produced a compromise that would command five votes. It recognized that the district courts could not simply ignore local jurisdictional lines but that they were free to look at the larger picture to determine whether plans for neighboring districts would be independently adequate. If not, the judge would be free to determine "whether the shortcomings of the individual county plans provided a sufficient federal foundation for merging the three districts or in any other way crossing district lines so as to eliminate, to the extent reasonable and practicable, racially identifiable schools and hence disestablishing what had been dual school systems in each of the three Counties."[21] Rehnquist took up the challenge and urged a more severe limit on district court remedial plans.[22] Marshall, who was very much concerned by the idea of serious limits on district courts in cases where there plainly had been legal segregation and massive resistance to desegregation after repeal of the legal bars, wrote White, "After worrying with the law, the precedents and my conscience, I now find myself willing to agree with your memorandum in the case."[23] The Court's deliberations ended with a four to four split that allowed the circuit court opinion to stand, with the result that Mehrige's efforts were rejected.

For Marshall, it rapidly became clear that with Powell, the author of the San Antonio ruling, free to participate in the *Milliken v. Bradley*[24] case concerning a multidistrict remedy in Detroit, there was a clear majority against metropolitan remedies, even where they seemed necessary to achieve any meaningful response to historic discrimination. The opinion striking down the multidistrict remedy in the Detroit case came the day after the announcement of the ruling in the Watergate tapes litigation. Marshall was frustrated on several counts. On the merits, *Milliken* meant that the Court would permit structural barriers to block the ultimate realization of the promise of *Brown*. The Court had not disturbed the findings of the lower Courts that it would be impossible to achieve any meaningful desegregation with a city-only remedy, but refused, nevertheless, to permit the district judge to go beyond the city district without evidence that the other districts were themselves guilty of purposeful discrimination that implicated the city. But there was more. Justices Marshall and White, in dissent, challenged the Court's opinion, which they believed obviously showed little concern for accuracy or careful analysis of the facts in the *Milliken* case.[25] It was clear that the press of the Watergate case and the fact that the real argument over the issues in *Milliken* had been fought within the Court during the debate over the Richmond case meant that the Detroit case did not receive the attention it deserved. To add insult to injury, Marshall was told that the opinion would be announced even though he had insisted that he needed more time to work on his dissent.

It was not surprising, then, that Marshall's dissent in the Detroit case was even stronger than his *San Antonio* rendering. He made it absolutely clear that he saw these rulings as "making a solemn mockery of *Brown*."[26]

The rights at issue in the case are too fundamental to be abridged on grounds as superficial as those relied on by the majority today. We deal here with the right of all of our children, whatever their race, to an equal start in life and to an equal opportunity to reach their full potential as citizens. Those children who have been denied that right in the past deserve better than to see fences thrown up to deny them that right in the future. Our Nation, I fear, will be ill served by the Court's refusal to remedy separate and unequal education, for unless our children begin to learn together, there is little hope that our people will ever learn to live together.[27]

The events of the preceding two years had caused both fear and anger to the man who had fought so long for equality. He saw, accurately as it turned out, an ominous trend at work in the nation.

Today's holding, I fear, is more a reflection of a perceived public mood that we have gone far enough in enforcing the Constitution's guarantee of equal justice than it is the product of neutral principles of law. In the short run, it may seem to be the easier course to allow our great metropolitan areas to be divided up each into two cities— one white, the other black—but it is a course, I predict, our people will ultimately regret.[28]

Not long after the *Milliken* ruling, Marshall saw another line of cases that added to his frustration. As long as the Court had been confronted with cases of discrimination in jurisdictions that had mandated segregation by law, the important questions had to do with whether segregation still existed and, if so, what to do about it. Once the Court found itself facing more cases from northern states, where the law may not have mandated discriminatory treatment by race, the problem was more complex. To find that there had been *de jure* discrimination, the Court said, it is necessary to prove not merely the effect of discrimination but the intent to discriminate as well.[29] The problem with that requirement is that unless someone or some jurisdiction was senseless enough to state an intention to discriminate, intent would be very difficult to prove.[30]

Marshall detected that the Court seemed to be tightening requirements for proof of intent to the point that some of its rulings "display[ed] a singularly myopic view of the facts."[31] None of these cases drew Marshall's ire more than *Memphis v. Greene.*[32] In that case, citizens of a white Memphis neighborhood petitioned the city to erect a barrier on a major access street between their neighborhood and an adjoining largely black residential area, purportedly to reduce "undesirable traffic." The Court did not find this a badge or incident of slavery within the meaning of the Thirteenth Amendment or a violation of the Civil Rights Act of 1866.

Justice Marshall issued a stinging dissent, joined by Brennan and Blackmun. He had no doubt what was meant by undesirable traffic, and neither did the black citizens of the adjoining neighborhood. Nor could he fathom how the Court could possibly have failed to see several different types of evidence demonstrating discriminatory intent. He could not understand how the Court could sanction the decision "by a group of white citizens . . . to keep Negro citizens from traveling through their urban 'utopia' " and the fact that "the city ha[d] placed its seal of approval on the scheme."[33]

It was one thing, according to Marshall, to fight about the nature of remedies that could be enforced against a state or local government to eliminate segregation, or the level of proof needed to establish the existence of discrimination, but it was quite another for the Court to block voluntary efforts by communities that had recognized their history of inequality and had moved to create affirmative action plans to respond to the problems. Two cases, in particular, drew Marshall's fire: The first was the *University of California Regents v. Bakke*[34] and the second was *Richmond v. Croson*.[35]

In *Bakke*, a badly fragmented Court ruled against the University of California, Davis, Medical School affirmative action admissions program that, in essence, set aside a number of seats for minority applicants, though the Court did not totally preclude consideration of racial diversity as one factor in admissions. In April 1978, Justice Marshall tried to explain to his colleagues that they needed to pay attention to the real impact and significance of the ruling in this case and not get lost in doctrinal debates. His memorandum to the conference is worth quoting at length. First, he addressed the principle of color blindness from a historical perspective.

> If only the principle of color-blindness had been accepted by the majority in *Plessy* in 1896, we would not be faced with this problem in 1978. We must remember, however, that this principle appeared only in the dissent. In the 60 years from *Plessy* to *Brown*, ours was a Nation where, by law, individuals could be given "special" treatment based on race. For us now to say that the principle of color-blindness prevents the University from giving "special" consideration to race when this Court, in 1896 licensed the states to continue to consider race, is to make a mockery of the principle of "equal justice under law."

Then Marshall turned to the reality of life in America and even within the Court.

> As a result of our last discussion on this case, I wish also to address the question of whether Negroes have "arrived." Just a few examples illustrate that Negroes most certainly have not. In our own Court, we have had only three Negro law clerks, and not so far have we had a Negro Officer of the Court. On a broader scale, this week's *U.S. News and World Report* has a story about "Who Runs America." They list 83 persons— not one Negro, even as a would-be runnerup. And the economic disparity between the races is increasing. . . .
>
> The dream of America as the melting pot has not been realized by Negroes—either the Negro did not get into the pot, or he did not get melted down. The statistics on unemployment and the other statistics quoted in the briefs of the Solicitor General and other *amici* document the vast gulf between White and Black America. That gulf was brought about by centuries of slavery and then by another century in which, with the approval of this Court, states were permitted to treat Negroes "specially."
>
> . . . We are not yet all equals, in large part because of the refusal of the *Plessy* Court to adopt the principle of color-blindness. It would be the cruelest irony for this Court to adopt the dissent in *Plessy* now and hold that the University must use color-blind admissions.[36]

Ultimately, of course, Marshall failed to convince his colleagues, and he turned his attention to a dissent.

Marshall attacked the narrow definition of remedy that barred a race-conscious affirmative action remedy in cases where no legally proven case of prior discrimination existed.

I do not agree that petitioner's admissions program violates the Constitution. For it must be remembered that, during most of the past 200 years, the Constitution as interpreted by this Court did not prohibit the most ingenious and pervasive forms of discrimination against the Negro. Now, when a State acts to remedy the effects of that legacy of discrimination, I cannot believe that this same Constitution stands as a barrier.[37]

His dissent was in three parts. First, he argued, there is a clear history of discrimination from before the Declaration of Independence to the mid twentieth century, during which virtually all levels and branches of government had participated, including the Supreme Court. Second, the current plight of blacks in America is directly traceable to that history. Third, there are and should be affirmative remedies available in light of the contemporary damage caused by that history; remedies that are not pinned to particular individuals but the larger class of persons disadvantaged by prior discrimination. Ironically, he said, the country had come full circle from the days of the Civil War.[38]

By the time of the *Richmond v. Croson* decision, Marshall was fed up with what he saw on the Court and in the larger society. In *Croson*, the Court struck down a contract set-aside program adopted by the City of Richmond, Virginia, because it had found that the history of discrimination in the area had curtailed minority business enterprises. The city relied in part on the information used by the federal government to create its own affirmative action contracting program that had been upheld by the Court in an earlier case.[39]

Few people alive knew better than Marshall the history of discrimination in Virginia in general, and in Richmond in particular. He wrote, "Richmond knows what racial discrimination is; a century of decisions by this and other federal courts has richly documented the city's disgraceful history of public and private racial discrimination."[40] How many years, he thought, does it take to remedy what should have been ended long ago? He warned that "today's decision marks a deliberate and giant step backwards,"[41] and that "the majority's unnecessary pronouncements will inevitably discourage or prevent governmental entities, particularly states and localities, from acting to rectify the scourge of past discrimination. This is the harsh reality of the majority's decision, but it is not the Constitution's command."[42] He concluded, "The majority today sounds a full-scale retreat. . . . The battle against pernicious racial discrimination or its effects is nowhere near won."[43]

Justices Harry Blackmun and William Brennan realized that, to Marshall, this was a bitter defeat, not only for himself, but for the cause for which he had fought for so long. Blackmun wrote:

I never thought that I would live to see the day when the City of Richmond, Virginia, the cradle of the Old Confederacy, sought on its own, within a narrow confine, to lessen the stark impact of persistent discrimination. But Richmond, to its great credit, acted. Yet this Court, the supposed bastion of equality, strikes down Richmond's efforts as though discrimination had never existed or was not demonstrated in this particular litigation. Justice Marshall convincingly discloses the fallacy and the shallowness of that approach. History is irrefutable, even though one might sympathize with those who—though possibly innocent in themselves—benefit from the wrongs of past decades.[44]

Coming Out Swinging

Marshall's attack on the Court, and in particular Justice Antonin Scalia, in *Croson* was only one of an increasing number of public battles that he was fighting. The decade of the 1980s was extremely hard for Marshall. For years he had refused to give interviews and kept his speeches relatively tame, but enough was enough. Not only was the Court making it harder to find remedies to turn the legal decisions of the 1950s and 1960s into economic and social realities, but the majority was even making it more difficult to get cases into the Court at all. Marshall began to give interviews and to take on his colleagues in his annual speeches as circuit justice to the second judicial circuit.[45] He also began a series of critical law review articles chiding the Court for its increasing use of summary dispositions (rulings without briefs or hearings on the merits of the case) and the nation for its willingness to undertake a celebration of the Bicentennial of the Constitution at a time when the promise of civil rights was not being kept.[46]

At the heart of much of what Marshall had to say in his last years on the bench was a concern about the need to maintain the tools needed to implement the rulings that had already been delivered by the Court over the years. The Court could do that only, he said, if it retained its independence from majoritarian pressures. "In our governmental scheme, there must be a detached independent judiciary that has the final legitimate authority to ensure that political majorities, caught up in the passions of the moment, do not trample the rights of minorities."[47] Speaking of the Court's unwillingness to support the penalties imposed by U.S. District Court Judge Leonard Sand for the flagrant contempt of court committed by officials of Yonkers, New York, in a housing discrimination case, Marshall observed:

> The Court ruled that sanctions against the councilmen would have been appropriate only if fining the city alone had failed to produce compliance. I find this reasoning particularly unfortunate not merely because the Court decided the case from a hindsight perspective far removed from the intricate, factual setting in which Judge Sand had to make his decision. What was at stake was the ability of a federal court to exercise delicate equitable judgment when faced with an impassioned majority whose prejudice spawned legislative defiance of the rule of law. The district court was called upon, in other words, to give effect to the judiciary's fundamental guiding principle of ensuring political respect for constitutional rights. In substituting its judgment—based only on legal briefs and oral argument—for that of a district judge intimately involved with the case for some eight years, the Court deprived a federal judge of a most effective tool for implementing his institutional missions.[48]

Among other things, Marshall was convinced that the Court was going out of its way to issue unnecessarily broad opinions striking down effective tools for remedying past discrimination.[49] Citing the *Patterson v. McClean Credit Union* and *Ward's Cove v. Antonio* cases, Marshall concluded: "Thus it is difficult to characterize last term's decisions as a product of anything other than a deliberate retrenching of the civil rights agenda. In the past 35 years or more we have truly come full circle. We are back where we started."[50]

Fearing the Future

While responding to all of these changes, Marshall also had to think about the future, a time when he would no longer be on the Court. He was constantly hounded by Reagan and Bush supporters to retire and give the Republican presidents another opportunity for an appointment. Marshall was just as determined to stay put: "For all those people who wish very dearly for me to give up and quit and what-have-you . . . I hope you will pardon me for saying it, but . . . 'Don't worry, I'm going to outlive those bastards.' "[51] He was not only worried about outliving them himself, but about the loss of colleagues like William Brennan. As Marshall put it: "There's nobody here that can persuade the way Brennan can persuade. Brennan can sit down and talk to you and show you where you are wrong. There's nobody with that power on the Court today. I say that Brennan cannot be replaced."[52]

Few justices have reacted as strongly to presidents as Marshall did to Reagan and Bush. Asked about the possibility that Reagan might have considered him for chief justice, Marshall replied, "I wouldn't do the job of dog-catcher for Ronald Reagan."[53] On the ABC TV show "Primetime Live," the following exchange took place:

Sam Donaldson:	What do you think of the president?
Justice Marshall:	No comment.
Donaldson:	Okay. I won't press you on that. The reason I ask you about President Bush—I know, just three or four years ago, you thought that Ronald Reagan was probably on the bottom . . .
Justice Marshall:	That's right.
Donaldson:	as civil rights—as a friend of civil rights. And I wondered where you put President Bush.
Justice Marshall:	Let me put it this way. It's said that if you can't say something good about a dead person, don't say it. Well, I consider him dead.
Donaldson:	Who?
Justice Marshall:	Bush!
Donaldson:	He's still alive, Mr. Justice.
Justice Marshall:	You're damn right he is. I just don't understand what he's doing. I don't understand it.[54]

In the end, Marshall felt that it was time to go, but before he left, he made it unmistakably clear that unless the Court was willing to do what was necessary to ensure that its rulings were indeed implemented, even when it meant offending temporary political majorities, it was not performing the task assigned to it under the Constitution.

A justice may view the question of the impact of the Court's decisions and the question of compliance in a manner quite unlike that of some students of the Court. First, a justice wants to know how to deal with the feedback that is being received following the issuance of important rulings. Second, she wants to know how to shape her actions in ways best calculated to achieve the highest level of compliance and the strongest impact. Finally, she wants to understand how to think about the relationship between important questions of principle and also matters of action in the real world far away from the nation's capital.

Interestingly, the impact of Supreme Court opinions is one of the more frequently studied aspects of the Court's business. From those studies, one can synthesize some basic premises for understanding impact.

DOES ANYBODY CARE? THE MATTER OF COMPLIANCE AND IMPACT

Some justices have wondered whether anyone out there really reads their opinions and whether those opinions have any real impact. They can put their minds to rest about that. The answer is yes. Although the cases in which officials or communities refuse to comply with Supreme Court rulings draw most of scholars' interest and cause justices the most serious headaches, most people do, in fact, comply most of the time, at least insofar as they understand what they are required to do.[55] That is true of administrative agencies of the federal government as well. And even where there is resistance to Supreme Court mandates, it can still usually be said that there is significant impact of one sort or another. The point, of course, is that there may be a considerable difference between impact and compliance. That is one reason why the field of impact analysis has generated a huge literature.[56] Plainly, Thurgood Marshall saw a dramatic impact from the Court's desegregation rulings, even though he remained convinced even as he left the Court that the nation was a very long way from realizing the promise of *Brown v. Board of Education.*

It does not take one long on the Court to realize that the potential impact of a particular kind of ruling is a frequent topic of conversation among colleagues as a case works its way from filing to published opinion. The first question, of course, is just how to picture the process that takes place once the chief justice announces from the bench as the Court begins its session in the morning that "we have for decision Number 93-247 which will be delivered by Justice . . ."

Picturing the Process

Just what kind of impact a particular justice's work will have and whether and how much compliance will be forthcoming from key players depend on an array of factors. At a minimum, impact is a result of the policy and the opinion that states it, as well as the nature and accuracy of the process by which that opinion is communicated and the action or inaction of key officials (Figure 13.1). Think about each portion of the process for a moment.

Policy and Opinions

Some policies will inevitably be controversial. They will be resisted by a significant number of groups and individuals even if the majority of people actually comply. It should come as no surprise that rulings in such areas as abortion,[57] the relation between church and state, desegregation, and the rights of criminal defendants are likely to draw intense opposition.[58] Justice Blackmun, author of the 1973 *Roe v. Wade* abortion rights opinion, was extremely concerned about how this obviously controversial decision would be received. He even went so far as to

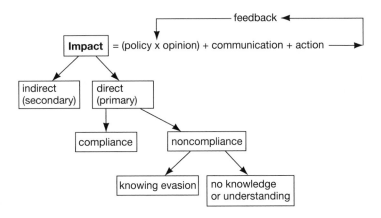

FIGURE 13.1　Tracing the impact of a Supreme Court opinion.

ask Justice Brennan, the Court's only Catholic, to review the opinion with an eye toward any language that might be unnecessarily offensive to people of that faith.[59] Of course, no language would have satisfied opponents of the ruling.

In other fields, there is relatively little awareness of the Court's rulings. Administrative law decisions may have a profound impact on environmental regulation, securities market operations, transportation, and health care. Yet they are not considered salient by most of the populace, even the informed public, and therefore do not necessarily arouse opposition except among interest groups with particular concern for that field. In fact, many of the rulings that may have the greatest impact in terms of financial burden, influence on the lives and education of children, and privacy of families may attract surprisingly little response.

All other things being equal, though, the assumption is that one can affect the impact of a particular policy ruling by the way in which the opinion is crafted to present the policy statement. Justice Black, who liked to picture himself as a "plain old country boy," as the expression goes, was anything but that. He strongly believed in the importance of strong, direct opinions that could be understood by the farmer behind a mule plowing the fields, as he used to put it. Many justices have believed, though the large volume of impact studies that we now have cannot actually prove the claim, that a well-crafted opinion (as defined in Chapter 10) is more likely to get compliance than a vague one. On the other hand, the stronger and more direct the opinion, the more difficult it may be to attract a clear majority of the justices' votes.

One of the claims that others have made is that a positive impact is more likely when the Court has spoken unanimously rather than in what Justice Marshall termed "the scourge of the contemporary Supreme Court—multiple opinions."[60] Plurality opinions leave everyone uncertain about the direction the Court may take on any given type of case in the future. Even so, the Court has been plagued since the late 1970s and into the 1990s by an inability to build strong majorities and thus avoid multiple concurring opinions.[61]

Communication

Whether and to what degree people react to opinions has a great deal to do with how those opinions are communicated. While the Court has a public information staff, albeit a very small one, the justices are primarily dependent on the media to carry their message to anyone outside the legal community. That is an unfortunate dependency, given the problems of covering the Supreme Court "beat."

Look at it from the reporters' point of view.[62] They sit in that relatively tiny room, in their respective cubicles, like graduate students closeted away in a university library, waiting for something to happen. It is hours and hours of sheer boredom, interrupted by moments of sheer panic. When they are informed that opinions are about to come down, they have relatively little time, perhaps as little as four hours, to digest from one to four opinions and prepare stories for deadline. The broadcast people have a particular problem, since they are aiming for the evening news, with its even earlier deadline.

Seasoned reporters prepare for these crash periods by attempting to do background work on major cases that they are expecting to "come down," as the expression goes. Still, several lengthy opinions, some over a hundred pages, may be announced on a given day. The complexity and nuances of those opinions may take law school professors months to unravel, but the reporter is expected to do it on the fly. As if that were not enough, the reporter normally has less than two minutes of air time within which to get the story of the day's announced opinions across, including whatever video clips might be available to add "production value" when the story airs on the network news. Besides, unlike stories from the Hill or the White House, there is no "talking head" from the Court, someone a reporter can interview on camera, who can explain what has happened. The best the Court reporter can do is, once an opinion has come down, try to catch the attorneys for the parties, who seek out the waiting cameras and microphones on the corner of the Court's plaza to give their sound bites about either their "victory" or the "great injustice" that has just been perpetrated by the Court. If time allows, they might even be able to get a crew out to interview the actual parties who launched a suit, assuming enough background work has been done ahead of time. Still, it is a difficult business at best.

From time to time in the Court's history, the news media representatives, both working reporters and the network heads, have tried to convince the Court to prepare what amount to press releases that would encapsulate an opinion and highlight the most important elements. On other occasions they have asked for more advanced warning regarding when opinions might come down. To facilitate the reporters' working relationship with the justices, they have even tried to develop some kind of ongoing discussion within the Court about the coverage. The Court has resisted. Ironically, some in the press admire the resistance of the justices to the temptations accepted by other officials to be stars of the evening news.

On the other hand, more justices have been willing over the past decade or so to participate in broadcast interviews than in earlier times on the Court. To that claim, some justices respond that history was not always so clear on the reticence of the predecessors. After all, consider how Chief Justice Harlan Fiske Stone used to take walks with Marquis Childs of the *St. Louis Post Dispatch,* during which Stone passed along derogatory comments about some of his colleagues, most notably Hugo Black.[63] Justice Douglas was accused of press leaks on more than one occasion, though he adamantly denied doing that sort of thing.[64] Ironically, some of those who have reported on the Court have themselves become celebrities. One of the better-known examples is Nina Totenburg of National Public Radio, who broke the story of Judge Douglas Ginsburg's marijuana experiences and the allegations of sexual harassment of then justice designate Clarence Thomas. A target of considerable congressional frustration during the Thomas hearings, Totenburg was the co-anchor of the PBS coverage of the confirmation hearings for Justice Ruth Bader Ginsburg.

The difficulties of covering the Court, and competing with more visually interesting stories for evening news time, is extremely important to the justices as well as to the reporter. A very small percentage of the public will ever read judicial opinions. Virtually everything the public knows about the Court and the justices comes from some kind of media report, and most of those from television. Few major national newspapers cover the Court's activities in any detail, and most newspapers and local radio and television stations rely on "rip-and-read" copy from the wire services to summarize the justices' work.

It is no wonder that so many Americans are absolutely wrong in their understanding of Supreme Court opinions. One of the more obvious examples of this sort of behavior came in the Bible reading and prayer in the schools cases. Studies of school officials indicated that, although the officials represented very disparate viewpoints, a substantial number of them read the news accounts of the opinions in such a way as to suggest that their own current practices were just fine.[65] Whether that was a result of selective perception on their part or the nature of the coverage is not clear. In other cases, decades after the prayer ruling, for example, officials continued to view the opinions as questions about the free exercise of religion rather than decisions on the establishment of religion. From that point of view, many thought they were on solid ground as long as they allowed students who did not wish to pray to remain silent or leave the room. Of course, those rulings were based not on a question of student coercion that would violate free exercise, but on establishment-of-religion grounds. The problem was not what the students did but the fact that teachers paid by tax dollars led the prayers and that public institutions authorized them, which constituted an establishment of religion. Even President Reagan made that obvious misinterpretation as late as the 1980s.

The other problem of communication is that the meaning and implications of opinions for current behavior within organizations are filtered from the top down. If the superintendent of schools was incorrect in his interpretation of an opinion dealing with, say, church and state, then the entire district has a problem. Moreover, since many people react to change in a homeostatic way, attempting to get their balance back with as little effort as possible, those officials may not be ready to interpret the news of an opinion as the Court intended it.

Action or Inaction

For all these reasons and more, there may be full compliance, limited reaction, no action, or serious resistance to Supreme Court rulings. Compliance is not a problem, but the other responses certainly are. After all, the Court has spoken, so why do people not comply? That is a complex question.

Given what has been said about the way rulings are conveyed to the public, it is clear that there are two possible explanations for the failure to comply. The first is that there are situations in which there is unintentional avoidance or failure to respond, while the second is intentional evasion of decisions.

There are ways to address the problem of unintentional noncompliance. Probably the most important of these is to provide clear opinions and to assist in educating the public about those decisions. That is no small undertaking in light of the historical tradition of the Court that the opinions should speak for themselves and should not be the subject of public commentaries by the justices.

Intentional evasion of the Court's mandates is a more difficult problem. It has been experienced at many times and in many ways, but few more obvious than the "massive resistance" undertaken by the southern states in the wake of *Brown v. Board of Education*.

In truth, the situation is far more complex than the simple dichotomy between compliance and noncompliance might suggest. Scholars Howard Ball, Thomas Lauth, and Dale Krane have suggested that the situation may more accurately be represented as a continuum, ranging on the one extreme from coercion to compliance through a middle ground of compromise for compliance to the other end of the spectrum represented by compliance by consensus.[66] Thus, those covered by particular rulings may refuse to respond at all, in which case they may be compelled by legal action to do so, at least in limited ways. They may simply agree to comply, which requires no further action at all. Or they may, as many officials choose to do, negotiate with the Justice Department or other officials to conform within limits to the rulings. In truth, whether they actually negotiate for such a position or simply understand an opinion to call for some kind

Alabama Governor George Wallace, flanked by Alabama state police, stands in the doorway of the University of Alabama, attempting to block its integration by black students accompanied by federal marshals, 1963.

of compromise between what they do now and what the Court really seeks, complete compliance may not be forthcoming unless the Court is prepared to go to the wall, which is a fairly dangerous place for an institution as vulnerable as the Court to be.

Put bluntly, most of the enforcement of rulings will be left to government attorneys and lower courts around the nation. The problem is that decisions of the Court are filtered through the final decisions of the district courts or state courts. Judicial scholar Jack Peltason paraphrased Chief Justice Charles Evans Hughes's famous line when he said that "the Constitution may mean what the Supreme Court says it means, but Supreme Court decisions mean what the district courts say they mean."[67]

Notwithstanding all of the alternative explanations, there are some situations in which the only accurate way to characterize the behavior of officials and citizens is outright evasion of the Court's rulings, ranging from open resistance to delaying tactics to simply ignoring the ruling. One of the more common tactics is what can be termed "conflict conversion," in which officials forget the party who sued them in the first place and create an image in which the officials are victims suffering at the hands of the justices, who are cast as the evildoers, with the plaintiffs pictured as pawns used to invoke judicial power.[68]

The other players in this particular game are the judges in the lower courts, who may themselves actively evade compliance. As Walter Murphy explains, there are simply too many lower courts to permit the Supreme Court to closely supervise everything that happens.[69] It is not unusual for the party that won in the Supreme Court to be unsuccessful in the lower courts when the case is sent back down for further proceedings.[70] Murphy explains that one of the things lower courts know very well is that the Supreme Court can review only a relatively small number of the opinions decided by lower courts. Besides, outright conflict is unnecessary, since the justices can rarely write an opinion so narrowly that it cannot be reinterpreted to mean something quite different from what was originally intended.

Feedback

Too often, the perspective held by many students of the judiciary is that the impact of judicial rulings is a kind of one-way action, with the Court handing down decisions and others complying or resisting. As Louis Fisher has often argued, however, the process is not unidirectional but a "constitutional dialogue" in which other institutions and stakeholders react to the Court.[71] On some occasions, the Congress, for example, may simply overturn rulings when they are based on statute. Both parties joined together to adopt what became the Civil Rights Act of 1991 to overturn a number of rulings announced by the Court interpreting existing civil rights statutes. At other times, the reaction may be more symbolic, as when the Congress reacted to the Court's ruling striking down the flag desecration statute by adopting a new one, realizing that it was highly likely that the Court would reject it as well. That is precisely what happened, but the legislature had made its point.

It is not only the Congress or the president that engages in this conversation with the Court. State and local governments have been in the discussion for years. Members of the Court have called on the states to take action in situations where the Supreme Court seems not to have provided the kinds of rulings some of the justices thought appropriate. Justice Brennan, a former state supreme court justice, called on civil rights and liberties groups to take their cases to the state courts, where they might find a more favorable forum. Justice Marshall came to the same position in 1989, after the Court's dramatic set of rulings during the October 1988 term that engendered the legislative response in 1991.[72]

SUMMARY

One of the things that you come to realize is that impact is measured on a very short term basis. Observers simply look to see if a ruling handed down last year seems to have had a significant impact or not. Some rulings take a long time to produce the kind of result that you, as the author, may have intended. It was clear to Justice Roger Taney and others during the Civil War that opinions issued contrary to the Union position were unlikely to be obeyed.[73] Nevertheless, those opinions provided a foundation on which to base later decisions, like Justice Black's opinion striking down the seizure of the steel mills by President Truman.[74] That ruling, in turn, was used to strike down Richard Nixon's actions in the Watergate case.[75]

While some justices become discouraged, the fact is that there are consequences of your opinions. Sometimes they are unanticipated and hard to tolerate, but often they produce some degree of, if not complete, compliance. However, the communication between the Court and other levels of government and between the Court and the public is much more dynamic than stacks of cold volumes on a library shelf could ever begin to convey. As Louis Fisher has repeatedly admonished, a Supreme Court ruling is rarely the end of anything. It is often but the next session of an ongoing conversation. That conversation may be difficult, and it may even break down, as has happened more than once in the history of civil rights case law. There will, however, very likely be another case coming to the Court, and another round of dialogue will be opened.

In the end, if you wish your opinions to have the maximum effect, you must take these dynamics into account as you draft them. Even so, you must take the long view and realize that there are limits to your ability to compel action. Sometimes you must content yourself with the belief that our culture is such that most people will comply most of the time. At the same time, you realize that there are times when you may not be around long enough to truly understand the impact of your own actions.

NOTES

[1]See, for example, Charles Johnson and Bradley C. Canon, *Judicial Policies: Implementation and Impact* (Washington, DC: Congressional Quarterly, 1984); Bradley C. Canon, "Courts and Policy: Compliance, Implementation, and Impact," in John B. Gates and Charles A. Johnson, eds., *The American Courts: A Critical Assessment* (Washington, DC: Congressional Quarterly, 1991); Theodore L. Becker and Malcolm M. Feeley, *The Impact of Supreme Court Decisions*, 2d ed. (New York: Oxford University Press, 1973); and Stephen L. Wasby, *The Impact of the United States Supreme Court: Some Perspectives*

(Homewood, IL: Dorsey Press, 1970). These works, done at very different periods, summarize the literature on impact and provide frameworks for understanding the lessons learned from the many studies done in this field.

[2]Juan Williams, "The Triumph of Thurgood Marshall," *Washington Post Magazine*, Feb. 7, 1990, p. 15.

[3]Bernard Schwartz, *Super Chief* (New York: New York University Press, 1983), p. 114.

[4]Quoted in Anthony Lewis, "Court Again Under Fire," *New York Times*, July 1, 1963, sec. E.

[5]Ibid.

[6]Ibid.

[7]*New York Times*, Mar. 11, 1968, p. 1.

[8]ABC News, "Primetime Live," July 26, 1990, transcript, p. 4.

[9]Bruce Allen Murphy, *Fortas* (New York: Morrow, 1988), p. 426.

[10]402 U.S. 1 (1970).

[11]Williams, "Triumph of Thurgood Marshall," p. 28.

[12]411 U.S. 1 (1973).

[13]Ibid., at 35.

[14]Ibid., at 71.

[15]Ibid., at 71–72.

[16]Ibid., at 98.

[17]Ibid., at 126.

[18]Ibid., at 130.

[19]Docket sheets in *Bradley v. State Board of Education of Virginia*, no. 72–550, and *School Bd. of the City of Richmond v. State Board of Education*, no. 72–549, box 419, WJBP.

[20]Warren Burger, MTTC, Apr. 26, 1973, box 301, WJBP.

[21]MTTC, Apr. 30, 1973, box 301, WJBP, p. 7.

[22]MTTC, May 3, 1973, box 301, WJBP.

[23]Thurgood Marshall to Byron White, May 10, 1973, box 301, WJBP.

[24]418 U.S. 717 (1974).

[25]Ibid., at 789.

[26]Ibid., at 808.

[27]Ibid., at 783.

[28]Ibid., at 814–15.

[29]*Washington v. Davis*, 426 U.S. 229 (1976).

[30]See *Arlington Heights v. Metropolitan Housing Development Corp.*, 429 U.S. 252 (1977).

[31]*Personnel Administrator v. Feeney*, 442 U.S. 256, 286 (1979), Marshall dissenting.

[32]451 U.S. 100 (1981).

[33]Ibid., at 155.

[34]438 U.S. 265 (1978).

[35]488 U.S. 469 (1989).

[36]MTTC, Apr. 13, 1978, box 465, WJBP.

[37]438 U.S., 265 at 388 (1978).

[38]Ibid., at 402.

[39]*Fullilove v. Klutznick*, 448 U.S. 448 (1980).

[40]488 U.S., at 529.

[41]Ibid., at 529.

[42]Ibid., at 529–30.

[43]Ibid., at 561.

[44]Ibid.

[45]Justice Thurgood Marshall, Remarks to the Annual Judicial Conference of the Second Judicial Circuit of the United States, July 1991, 136 F.R.D. 236; Justice Thurgood Marshall, Remarks to the

Annual Judicial Conference of the Second Judicial Circuit of the United States, Sept. 8, 1989, 130 F.R.D. 161; Justice Thurgood Marshall, Remarks to the Annual Judicial Conference of the Second Judicial Circuit of the United States, Oct. 17, 1987. 120 F.R.D. 141; Justice Thurgood Marshall, Remarks to the Annual Judicial Conference of the Second Judicial Circuit of the United States, Hartford, CT, Sept. 13, 1984. 106 F.R.D. 118; Justice Thurgood Marshall, Remarks to the Annual Judicial Conference of the Second Judicial Circuit of the United States, Sept. 30–Oct. 1, 1983, 101 F.R.D. 161.

⁴⁶See, for example, Thurgood Marshall, "Supreme Court Summary Dispositions: Either Change the Rules or Stop Giving Short Shrift to Important Rules," *Willamette Law Review* 19 313 (1983); and idem, *Thurgood Marshall*, "The Constitution: A Living Document," *Howard Law Journal* 30 915 (1987).

⁴⁷Justice Thurgood Marshall, Remarks to the Annual Judicial Conference of the Second Judicial Circuit of the United States, July 1991, 136 F.R.D., p. 236.

⁴⁸Ibid., pp. 237–38.

⁴⁹Justice Thurgood Marshall, Remarks to the Annual Judicial Conference of the Second Judicial Circuit of the United States, Sept. 8, 1989, 130 F.R.D. 161.

⁵⁰Ibid., pp. 166–68.

⁵¹Justice Thurgood Marshall, Remarks to the Annual Judicial Conference of the Second Judicial Circuit of the United States, Oct. 17, 1987, 120 F.R.D. 141, 204.

⁵²ABC News, "Primetime Live," p. 3.

⁵³Williams, "Triumph of Thurgood Marshall," p. 29.

⁵⁴ABC News, "Primetime Live," at p. 4.

⁵⁵"[N]oncompliance with court rulings gets more attention than compliance, even though the latter may be more frequent" (Wasby, *Impact of the Supreme Court*, p. 3.)

⁵⁶See ibid.

⁵⁷See Johnson and Canon, *Judicial Policies*, chap. 1.

⁵⁸Wasby, *Impact of the Supreme Court.*

⁵⁹Harry Blackmun to William Brennan, Nov. 21, 1972, box 282, WJBP.

⁶⁰Justice Thurgood Marshall, Remarks to the Annual Judicial Conference of the Second Judicial Circuit of the United States, Sept. 30–Oct. 1, 1983, 101 F.R.D. 161, 165.

⁶¹David O'Brien, *Storm Center* (New York: Norton, 1993), pp. 329–35.

⁶²Stephen Hess, *The Washington Reporters* (Washington, DC: Brookings Institute, 1981); David L. Gray, *The Supreme Court and the News Media* (Evanston, IL: Northwestern University Press, 1968); and Chester A. Newland, "Press Coverage of the U.S. Supreme Court," *Western Political Quarterly* 17 15 (1964).

⁶³Alpheus T. Mason, *Harlan Fiske Stone: Pillar of the Law* (New York: Viking, 1956), pp. 472–73.

⁶⁴See William O. Douglas to Harlan Fiske Stone, Jan. 5, 1994, box 74, HFSP; William O. Douglas, Memorandum to the Chief Justice, Jan. 6, 1994, box 98, WODP; William O. Douglas, Memorandum to the Chief Justice, May 21, 1945, box 106, WODP; and William O. Douglas to Warren Burger, July 4, 1972, box 1588, WODP.

⁶⁵See Kenneth H. Dolbeare and Phillip E. Hammond, *The School Prayer Decisions: From Court Policy to Legal Practice* (Chicago: University of Chicago Press, 1971).

⁶⁶Howard Ball, Thomas Lauth, and Dale Krane, *Compromised Compliance* (Westport, CT: Greenwood Press, 1982). Ball, Lauth, and Krane also relied on the important work by Harrell R. Rogers and Charles S. Bullock III, *Coercion to Compliance* (Lexington, MA: Heath, 1976).

⁶⁷Jack W. Peltason, idem, *Fifty-eight Lonely Men: Southern Judges and School Desegregation* (Urbana: University of Illinois Press, 1961), p. 21.

⁶⁸Phillip J. Cooper, *Hard Judicial Choices* (New York: Oxford University Press, 1988), p. 339.

⁶⁹Walter Murphy, *Elements of Judicial Strategy* (Chicago: University of Chicago Press, 1964), p. 46.

⁷⁰For evidence that this is not a new phenomenon, see D. Alan Tarr, "The Effectiveness of Supreme Court Mandates," in Stuart Nagel, Erika Fairchild, and Anthony Champagne, eds., *The Political Science of Criminal Justice* (Springfield, IL: Charles C. Thomas, 1983); Donald E. Wilkes, Jr., "The New Federalism in Criminal Procedure: State Court Evasion of the Burger Court," *Kentucky Law Journal* 62 421 (1974); Bradley C. Cannon, "Reactions of State Supreme Courts to a U.S. Supreme Court Civil Liberties Decision," *Law and Society Review* 8 109 (1973); Jerry K. Beatty, "State Court Evasion of United States Supreme Court Mandates During the Last Decade of the Warren Court," *Valparaiso Law Review* 6 260 (1972); Walter F. Murphy, "Lower Court Checks on Supreme Court Power," *American Political*

Science Review 53 1017 (1959); idem, "Evasions of Supreme Court Mandates in Cases Remanded to State Courts Since 1941," Note, *Harvard Law Review* 67 1251 (1951) and Note, "State Court Evasion of U.S. Supreme Court Mandates," *Yale Law Journal* 36 574 (1947).

[71]Louis Fisher, *Constitutional Dialogues* (Princeton, NJ: Princeton University Press, 1988).

[72]Justice Thurgood Marshall, Remarks to the Annual Judicial Conference of the Second Judicial Circuit of the United States, Sept. 8, 1989, 130 F.R.D. 161.

[73]*Ex Parte Merryman*, 17 Fed. Cas. 144, 153 (1861).

[74]*Youngstown Sheet and Tube v. Sawyer*, 343 U.S. 579 (1952).

[75]*United States v. Nixon*, 418 U.S. 683 (1974).

Leaving the Court

At some point, departure from the U.S. Supreme Court becomes a significant question for you. All the justices have a lifetime appointment, subject
only to the "shall hold their Office during good behavior" language in Article
III, Section 1. How do you know when it's time to leave? How does a justice
determine when his or her career as justice of the Supreme Court should
end?

The decision to end your tenure on the Court may be a painful one.
For one thing, you have worked in the small group setting for decades and
have developed a relationship with the personnel of the Court. For another
reason, the political one, there is a reluctance to step down when the president is not of your party. There have been times when justices tried to wait
out the presidential incumbent for this reason, only to succumb to the ravages of age and ill health. Finally, there is your effort to protect and defend
the positions you have taken—for decades—on critical constitutional issues
that are deeply important to you. However, the clock continues to move, and
fateful decisions have to be made by you and everyone who sits on the high
bench.

THE POLITICS OF LEAVING THE COURT

Justice Potter Stewart had one answer to the question of when to depart the Court.
"I've always been a firm believer in the principle that it's better to go too soon
than to stay too long."[1] However, looking at Stewart's Court colleagues' reasons

for leaving, one is struck with the fact that age and ill health are the primary reasons. Not many of Stewart's fellow brethren took his advice; rather, they remained on the Court until they could no longer function well due to age and its accompanying infirmities.

Of the sixteen justices who have retired since 1960 (see Table 14.1), from Charles Whittaker to Harry A. Blackmun, age and health problems are the primary reasons given for their decision to leave. For example, at age eighty-four, Justice William Brennan wrote his retirement letter to Republican President George Bush, indicating that he could no longer handle the "strenuous demands" of his work on the bench.[2] Justice Brennan's retirement from the Court was due to a series of strokes that weakened him and that, finally, forced him, reluctantly, to retire (see Figure 14.1). As he wrote, retirement "wasn't anything I wanted to do and, indeed, tried my best to avoid doing it, but the doctors persuaded me that unless I wanted to risk another stroke (I've had two), I should retire. I must say, it was a very difficult thing to do."[3]

For Thurgood Marshall, who retired in 1991, the appointment to the Court was, he constantly insisted, a " 'lifetime term' from which he would never retire."[4] However, answering the question, What's wrong with you? thrown at him by someone in the mob of the press people covering the announcement of his retirement, the justice said, frankly: "What's *wrong* with me? I'm old, and coming apart!"[5] In his letter to President Bush, Marshall said: "The strenuous demands of Court work and its related duties required or expected of a Justice appear at this time to be incompatible with my advancing age and medical condition."

As the factors accounting for the retirements suggest, even with an attractive retirement compensation package available, Supreme Court justices are loath to retire. This is, in great part, due to (1) the power a sitting justice has to mold constitutional jurisprudence, (2) the felt need to protect hard-earned jurispru-

TABLE 14.1 **Reasons for Leaving the Supreme Court, 1960–94**

Year	Justice	Age	Reason for Leaving	Death, After
1960	Charles Whittaker	61	Retirement; unhappiness	12 years
1962	Felix Frankfurter	79	Retirement; age/health	2 years
1965	Arthur Goldberg	56	Resignation; UN Ambassador	25 years
1967	Tom C. Clark	67	Retirement; son appointed AG	10 years
1969	Abe Fortas	58	Resignation	13 years
1969	Earl Warren	78	Retirement; age	5 years
1971	Hugo L. Black	85	Retirement; age/health	1 month
1971	John M. Harlan	72	Retirement; age/health	3 months
1975	William O. Douglas	77	Retirement; age/health	5 years
1981	Potter Stewart	66	Retirement	9 years
1986	Warren E. Burger	79	Retirement; age	—
1987	Lewis Powell	78	Retirement; age	—
1989	William J. Brennan, Jr.	84	Retirement; age/health	—
1991	Thurgood Marshall	82	Retirement; age/health	2 years
1993	Byron White	75	Retirement; age/politics	—
1994	Harry A. Blackmun	85	Retirement; age	—

Supreme Court of the United States
Washington, D. C. 20543

CHAMBERS OF
JUSTICE Wм. J. BRENNAN, JR.

August 3, 1990

Howard Ball, Dean
The University of Vermont
College of Arts and Sciences
Office of the Dean
Waterman Building
Burlington, Vermont 05405-0160

Dear Dean Ball:

Thank you for your warm and gracious letter
of July 30. It wasn't anything I wanted to do
and, indeed, tried my best to avoid doing it, but
the doctors persuaded me that unless I wanted to
risk another stroke (I've had two) I should
retire. I must say, it was a very difficult thing
to do.

I'm most appreciative of your invitation to
visit Vermont this fall. However, I've been
counseled to avoid any activities until at least
the first of the year. Consequently, much as I
regret it, I'll have to decline. Thank you very
much for thinking of us.

Sincerely,

[signature]

FIGURE 14.1   Letter to the author from Justice William
Brennan explaining his decision to retire from
the Court.

dential "victories" from attack by a shifting Court, and (3) the fact that the justice wishes to give her seat to an administration she supports and so stays on until
that presidency comes into office.

As political scientist John Schmidhauser wrote, "Ultimately, the partisan or
ideological inclination to remain on the Court, buttressed by a powerful sense of
professional and institutional achievement, have been of utmost significance
throughout the Court's history."[6] In reviewing Hugo Black's and William O.
Douglas's respective retirements from the Court, one is struck by the pathos associated with their extremely difficult decisions to part from an institution that
had been an intimate part of their lives for over three decades.

When Justice Byron White announced his retirement in the spring of 1993,
it was reported that, as the sole remaining sitting justice appointed by a Democratic
President, he "would like to retire if a Democrat was elected President."[7] The election of Democrat Bill Clinton in November 1992 therefore led directly to White's
decision to retire after thirty-one years of service on the Court. And the election
of 1992 also persuaded an aging, eighty-five-year-old Harry Blackmun, in January
1994 to retire at the end of that Court term. Said Blackmun, at the public an-

Associate Justice Thurgood Marshall at a press conference
announcing his retirement from the Supreme Court, June 1991.

nouncement of his retirement in April 1994, at a press conference held jointly
with President Clinton,

> It's been a privilege to be on the Federal bench for over 34 years, in 24 terms here,
> and to watch the country move along through those 24 years. *It hasn't been much fun
> on most occasions*, but it's a fantastic experience which few lawyers are privileged to
> [undergo]. And as Byron White put it, it's been a great ride and I'm indebted to the
> nation and, Mr. President, to you and your predecessors for putting up with the like
> of me. . . . *It's not easy to step aside, but I know what the numbers are, and it's time.*[8] [our
> emphasis]

One path off the Court is the infrequent and absolutely involuntary one of
a sitting justice dying while still actively serving on the Court. This happened regularly in the nineteenth century and has happened this century to a number of
justices, including Chief Justice Harlan Fiske Stone in 1945, Frank Murphy in 1949,
Chief Justice Fred Vinson in 1953, and Robert Jackson en route to the Court on
October 9, 1954. There are only two voluntary paths off the Court, resignation
and retirement.

When a justice resigns, for example, Justice Arthur Goldberg's resignation
from the Court in 1965 to become U.S. ambassador to the United Nations, he
absolutely relinquishes the title and the privileges of the position. A justice who

Associate Justice Harry Blackmun announcing his retirement
from the Supreme Court, with President Clinton behind the
justice, April 1994.

resigns can, if he has served for more than ten years at the time of his resignation, receive full pay, but there will be no increases in his remuneration during
the course of his life.

However, when a justice retires, as, for example, Tom C. Clark did in 1967
because his son Ramsey was nominated and confirmed as U.S. attorney general,
he retains the position, the salary, title, and office space (with law clerks and staff)
of a justice of the Supreme Court. Indeed, retired justices of the Court, for example, Clark and Lewis Powell, have been given temporary assignments to lower
federal courts that are in need of legal expertise to deal with the heavy caseload
problem.

From 1789 to the present day, over two hundred years, only 108 men and
women have ever sat as justices of the U.S. Supreme Court. This statistic is even
more illuminating when one considers that, in the Court's first decades, because
of a lack of power and prestige, many men either turned down the nomination
or moved from the Court to other positions of public power. In contemporary
times, "the position of justice of the Supreme Court is thought to be the highest
to be attained in the legal profession and is likely to be accepted readily when offered."[9]

"Tenure during good behavior" has meant, in reality, since the turn of the
twentieth century to the present time, men and women serving lengthy terms,
even though they may not be up to the work and in spite of the fact that they may
suffer from mental or physical disabilities that impair their effectiveness on the
Court. The change in reasons for departure from the Court between the nineteenth and twentieth centuries is very pronounced. Whereas in the nineteenth
century, almost 70 percent of the justices died while serving and only 17 percent
took retirement, in the twentieth century, 58 percent of the justices retired and

only 28 percent of the Court's occupants died while still sitting as an active justice. Since 1789, then, a little more than one half of all the sitting justices died in office, whereas 37 percent took retirement.

How does the system get justices off the Court "when they are old, ill, or not functioning effectively"?[10] What goes into the decision to leave, and what are some of its consequences? Earl Warren, concerned about the ravages of age and its health consequences, once suggested a change in the tenure policy, a time limit on the service of a justice. "For many years, I have been of the opinion that it would be a good thing to have a compulsory retirement date for all public officials."[11] To date, however, there has been no meaningful effort to modify, through the needed constitutional amendment, the "during good behavior" language of Article III, Section 1.

REMOVING JUSTICES

There have also been, on rare occasions, situations in which a form of *involuntary separation*—resignation—occurs. Threat of impeachment can induce a federal judge or justice to resign. Justice Abe Fortas, has been the only justice to resign under severe pressure from the White House—and from the Court's membership as well. Fortas's difficulties in 1969 led to his painful decision to resign from the Court rather than risk the possibility of being impeached—and convicted—for receiving twenty thousand dollars from the Wolfson Foundation, an organization run by the wealthy financier Louis E. Wolfson, who had been indicted for violating the Securities and Exchange Act. It was alleged, in a scurrilous story in *Life* magazine, written by Will Lambert, who had connections in the Department of Justice, that Fortas had tried to intervene on Wolfson's behalf after he was indicted, an allegation that led to the threat to impeach the liberal Fortas if he remained on the Court. In the end, because of "ill-conceived, downright stupid off-the-bench actions, [Fortas] found it necessary to resign."[12]

Only presidents Thomas Jefferson and Richard Nixon have tried to remove justices from the Court through threat of or actual introduction of impeachment charges. Impeachment of a Supreme Court justice has been introduced in Congress on a few occasions in the Court's history. Samuel Chase, a Federalist Supreme Court justice, was impeached in 1805 by the Democratic-Republicans in the House. The effort to replace the hated Federalist with a Jeffersonian Democrat through the impeachment route did not work.

Impeachment has rarely been used to involuntarily remove a justice from the Court, although Nixon did try to have Douglas impeached in 1970, in part because of Douglas's work with the Parvin Foundation,[13] and also because the Democrats and liberals had voted not to confirm two Nixon nominees for a seat on the Court, Clement Haynsworth and G. Harrold Carswell. Evidently, for President Nixon it was payback time, and how better to do it than to try to force liberals off the bench. Nixon did successfully induce Fortas to resign rather than face the burden of defending his actions in an impeachment process. In 1970, one week after Carswell was defeated, Douglas became the next target when Ford introduced the impeachment resolution in the House. And after Douglas was forced off the bench, Brennan, who also had associations with private foundations, would be the next target of the Nixon administration.[14]

In the unsuccessful effort to implement this strategy, Nixon asked the director of the FBI, J. Edgar Hoover, no friend of Douglas, to help gather information for Ford to use in Congress. As Hoover wrote, in a memo placed in his file, "The President asked if he had Gerry Ford call me, would I fill him in on Douglas; that he, Ford, is a good man. I told him I would."

Justice Douglas fought against the 1970 impeachment charges because he strongly believed that Nixon was planning a right-wing conservative effort to rid the Court, through the threat of impeachment, of liberal justices Fortas, Douglas, and, after forcing Douglas off the Court, Brennan. He also battled his nemesis Nixon because Douglas knew he had committed no impropriety that would trigger an impeachment move. For the embattled Douglas, Nixon, Ford, and Hoover, called "snapping hound dogs" by the justice, had to be prevented from this form of naked intimidation of justices of the Court whose views they disagreed with.

Douglas was planning to retire from the Court in 1969, at the end of thirty years on the Court. His retirement would have come at the same time Chief Justice Earl Warren was to step down, and the Super Chief had already selected office space for the two of them. His plans changed quickly, in the spring of 1969, when the impeachment talk began in Washington. Said Douglas: "I changed my mind about retiring and decided to stay on indefinitely until the last hound dog had stopped snapping at my heels—and that promised to be a long time, as Nixon naturally wanted to have my seat on the Court."[15]

DEATH IN OFFICE

For a majority of the brethren, over the Court's two-century history, termination from the Court comes with a visit from the angel of death. Whether because of financial difficulty or because of unwillingness to part with the powers of the position, or because of the need to stay to defend a record against the criticism from a shifting, changed Court majority, many brethren remain on the Court, although faced with illness, physical disability, or senility, until their death.

Only about 14 percent of the brethren have chosen to resign from the Court. The reasons vary for such action. Abe Fortas was faced with resignation or impeachment, with the chief justice and some of the other brethren encouraging him to resign rather than go through the impeachment process and possibly bring shame to the Court because of the ensuing publicity.

There are also political reasons for resigning. Charles Evans Hughes chose to resign in 1916 to run for the presidency as the Republican party standard bearer. Arthur Goldberg reluctantly resigned his seat, at the urging of the domineering president, Lyndon Johnson, to take over as U.S. ambassador to the UN in 1965.[16] President Franklin D. Roosevelt, in 1942, asked Associate Justice "Jimmy" Byrnes, a very close political and personal friend, to step down from the high bench to assume the critically important job of running the domestic economy as the wartime director of the Office of Economic Stabilization. (On the other hand, Justice William O. Douglas chose to turn down such job offers made to him by Presidents Roosevelt and Truman.)

Still other justices resigned because of frustration with the job and its attendant political and work-related stresses. John Clarke, 1922; Owen Roberts,

1945; and Charles Whittaker, who "eagerly withdrew"[17] from the Court in 1962, left the bench because of tension and personal clashes with others on the Court. Had not Justice Robert Jackson taken the war crimes prosecutor's job in 1945–46, he, too, might have resigned from the Court for similar reasons—especially his heated clashes with Hugo Black.

THE CONSEQUENCES OF STAYING ON: DISABILITY IN OFFICE

Given an understanding of the politics, power, and prestige of the institution, one can understand why a majority of the justices stay on the Court, even with infirmities and serious disabilities, including loss of mental acuity. "It is no secret that the Supreme Court has sometimes been concerned about senility on the part of some of its members."[18] At the turn of the twentieth century, William Howard Taft wrote to an old friend:

> The condition of the Supreme Court is pitiable, and yet these old fools hold on with a tenacity that is most discouraging. Really the Chief Justice is almost senile; Harlan does no work; Brewer is so deaf that he cannot hear and has got beyond the point of the commonest accuracy in writing his opinions; Brewer and Harlan sleep almost through all the arguments. I don't know what can be done. It is most discouraging to the active men on the bench.[19]

In the 1860s, Justice Robert C. Grier was so infirm that he asked the chief justice, Roger Taney, himself so feeble that his physician "remarked on his resemblance to a disembodied spirit,"[20] for permission to live in the Capitol, which at the time housed the Supreme Court's courtroom. "If I could have a room in the Capitol on the level of our Courtroom," requested Grier, "so as not to be compelled to 'get up stairs' I could attend to my duty in Washington as usual, if my health continues."[21] No room was made available for him.

Taft, as chief justice, had to try to convince Justice Joseph McKenna, infirm and in his early eighties, to retire from the Court. Because McKenna was extremely sensitive, it was a very difficult task. However, for Taft and the brethren, something had to be done because, as Taft wrote, "McKenna's vote may change the judgment of the Court on important issues, and it is too bad to have a man like that decide when he is not able to grasp the point, or give a wise and deliberate consideration of it. I don't know what to do."[22]

What the Court finally decided to do, through McKenna's 1926 retirement at age eighty-one, was avoid deciding cases in which McKenna's vote was a crucial one. Taft could not get older but healthy justices to assist him in removing McKenna because, as one of the more senior associate justices, Oliver Wendell Holmes implied, after McKenna the brethren might next try to get him to retire. Finally, working with McKenna's physician, Taft, who was delegated to go to the feeble justice, met with him and told him "how deeply regretful all the members of the Court were, how deeply they loved him, how chivalrous they found him, how tender of the feelings of others he always was, and how particularly trying it was, therefore, to act in the present instance from a personal standpoint."[23] McKenna finally retired, and the Court had a very dignified farewell ceremony honoring him.

In contemporary times, Justice John Harlan II was clinically blind toward the end of his tenure. He retired in late September 1971, within weeks of Hugo Black's retirement. The proximate medical reason was the discovery of cancer; Harlan died within months of his retirement from the Court. Justices Frankfurter, Douglas, Black, and Brennan suffered strokes that led to pain and disability and, finally, in all four cases, retirement from the Court. Frankfurter's retirement letter to President Kennedy, delivered on August 28, 1962, probably reflected the views of all four brethren: He told the president that he was forced, due to health, to retire from "the institution whose concerns have been the absorbing interest of my life."

A number of justices, including Powell, Brennan, and Blackmun, had operations for prostate cancer, while Justice Sandra Day O'Connor had a cancerous breast removed. For over a decade, Thurgood Marshall was in and out of the hospital with respiratory problems. Ultimately, for most of these justices who have left the Court, there was the fateful, fitful decision to retire rather than die while sitting.

Clearly, the problem of justices' personal health leads to a number of dilemmas for the Court. For one thing, an ailing justice typically is not able to carry his share of the Court's workload—nor would the Court majority, in disability situations involving senility, *want* the justice to participate. This dilemma, however, translates into additional work for the rest of the brethren, as the other justices must share in writing opinions that would have been assigned to the infirm colleague. Also, a disabled justice and his disability may be very visible from the bench and certainly visible because of her general absence from the Court's decision-making outcomes.

Finally, such disability can prove disastrous jurisprudentially when a number of justices have disabilities while serving together on the Court. Such negative visibility in the media, for example, comments about the "nine old men," cannot help but injure the reputation of the Court, and therefore the justices have to somehow persuade the ailing justice that it would be the appropriate thing for him to step down from the bench.

There have been occasions when delegations of justices would visit an ailing, infirm, senile justice and try to persuade him to resign from the Court. The aforementioned Grier was visited by a delegation of colleagues and presented with a unanimously agreed-to message from the Court that he step down due to his disability. The delegation visited him shortly after the Congress passed legislation, in 1869, allowing a judge to continue on full salary for life if the judge had reached seventy years of age and had served for at least a decade. Grier immediately submitted his resignation to the president.

By then, however, his infirmity had led the Court to commit one of its few self-inflicted wounds, the 1870 *Hepburn v. Griswold* legal tender decision. In the case, an enfeebled Grier changed his vote and the court went from four to four to five to three, striking down the controversial Legal Tender Act passed by Congress.[24] This Court decision, like that of the *Dred Scott* opinion in 1857,[25] was considered a self-inflicted wound because the four person Court majority handed down a decision overturning a congressional statute that was, by all accounts, erroneous and which led to immediate response by the other political agencies, Congress and President Ulysses S. Grant. One year later, an enlarged Supreme Court overturned *Hepburn* in the 1871 case of *Knox v. Lee*.[26]

Interestingly, almost three decades after the delegation visited Grier, one member of the delegation, Stephen J. Field, now himself infirm, was visited by John Harlan, who had been given the unenviable task of trying to induce Field to resign. Harlan reminded the feeble Field of his visit to Grier. "Do you remember what you said to Justice Grier on that occasion," Harlan asked. "Yes," answered Field, "and a dirtier day's work I never did in my life!"[27] Justice Field nevertheless resigned shortly after that conversation, in December 1897. He had served almost thirty-five years when he left, the longest tenure of any justice until Justice Douglas's time on the Court (36 years).

THE DECISION TO RETIRE

Naturally, then, the decision to retire from the Court is an easy one to understand in the abstract. Whether and why to retire are linked to the concepts of partisanship, ideology, and power, personal as well as institutional. Many of the justices try to retire at a time when a favorable wind is blowing from the White House. William O. Douglas would have greatly preferred to retire at another time if only because the president sitting in the White House, who would then nominate a person to replace Douglas, was none other than *President* Gerald Ford, the very person who, in 1970, as Republican minority leader in the House of Representatives, and as congressional surrogate for Nixon, tried to remove Douglas from the Court through the impeachment route!

Aside from forced resignation, from her brethren or from the Congress or the president, a justice will move to reflect on the efficacy of retirement with the passage of time and with the onset of disability or impairment, either physical or mental, or both. An examination of the decision to retire from the Court by two jurisprudential giants, Hugo Black and William O. Douglas, illustrates this reality that all justices must deal with at some time during their tenure.

Hugo Black's Retirement from the Court

In the summer of 1971, when Hugo Black was in his eighty-fifth year, the last thirty-four as justice of the Supreme Court, his health began to take a turn for the worse. A year earlier he had suffered a stroke and had slowly worked his way back to a semblance of good health—that is, good for a person of his age. On June 29, 1970, a year earlier, his wife wrote in her diary: "Last Day of Court. Will it be Hugo's last? He is pondering."[28]

With Black, as with so many major judicial leaders on the Court, this type of "pondering" was extremely painful. "He was not ready to leave the Court just yet. So much was happening, and there were so many things he wanted to do before it was time to go."[29] Surely Douglas said the same thing to himself and, indeed, tried valiantly to continue to serve after his major disability occurred—as did Brennan before he made the painful decision to retire from the Court. None of these men opted for the Stewart philosophy of retirement or probably saw it as a viable option.

Justice Black did sit for the 1970 term and selected his law clerks for the 1971 term. In mid July 1971, however, he was admitted to the Naval Hospital at Bethesda and seemed "joyless and apathetic."[30] In August, the doctors described Black's medical problem as that of temporal arteritis, an inflammation of the arteries in the left side of his head, and prescribed treatment for him.

In mid August, the Blacks visited John Harlan, also quite ill. These two men "were veritable giants of the law, . . . imbued with dedication, intelligence, and judicial excellence."[31] Hugo and Elizabeth Black found Harlan "in a depressed, defeated frame of mind. . . . [Harlan] worries about the Court. He thinks he, Bill Douglas, Hugo and possibly Thurgood Marshall may get off the Court, and what an impact on the country."[32] Black pondered these observations, noting his poor health and acknowledging that he did not want to be a burden or an embarrassment for the Court at a critical time in American history. Was it time for him to retire and give his seat to a Republican president, one Black did not like or respect?

By now, late August, according to his wife, Black was "deep in soul searching" about resigning from the Court before the 1971 term began in October. She wrote in her diary: "Hugo sits staring into space, his eyes looking like deep liquid pools. His face is thin. . . . He seems so weak in body but still so strong in spirit. His mind focuses fine and he argues with vigor. He knows exactly what he will say in his letter of resignation to the President. . . . He really is morose."[33] By the end of August 1971, after solemn conversations with a former law clerk of his, Louis Oberdorfer, then a U.S. district court judge in the District of Columbia, Black decided to write his letter stating that he would be stepping down from the Court. After many dozens of drafts, the letter was finally typed by his wife. Black's retirement letter to Nixon was finally written, and on September 17th, it was delivered to the president. Eight days later, on September 25, 1971, Hugo Black died in Bethesda's Naval Hospital.

William O. Douglas Departs

Justice William O. Douglas, after the 1970 impeachment effort, took on the role of major dissenter and senior Burger Court opponent. He continued to sit and participate in some very significant cases that came to the Court, but his age and a history of serious health problems eventually caught up with him. On December 31, 1974, New Year's Eve, Douglas was on vacation with his wife in Nassau, the Bahamas, when he suffered a massive stroke. It left his left arm and leg paralyzed and forced him to undergo major physical therapy. He was in constant pain throughout the ordeal to overcome, unsuccessfully as it turned out, his physical and mental disabilities.

During the summer of 1975, Douglas told a *New York Times* reporter that he would be back at work for the new term of the Court: "There's no chance I'll retire. . . . I'll be there in October, positively."[34] In his wheelchair and in great pain, Douglas did begin the 1975 term of the Court.

By mid November 1975, the strain, along with the terrible pain, proved to be too much for Douglas. On November 18, 1975, in one of the many ironies that surrounded his life, Douglas sent his retirement letter to President Gerald Ford, the man who had tried so hard to remove Douglas from the bench little more than five years earlier. It was clear that Douglas was trying to await the outcome of the 1976 presidential elections, ironically won by a Democrat, Jimmy Carter,

An ailing Justice William O. Douglas, with Chief Justice Warren Burger, 1975.

who did not have a single opportunity to appoint a person to the U.S. Supreme Court. It was also equally clear that, for Douglas, the pain was so unbearable that he could not remain on the Court awaiting the outcome of an election two years down the road.

Precisely to avoid these health problems, others have tried to structure safeguards. Justice Harry Blackmun, for example, set up an informal review of his behavior. Blackmun, formerly an attorney for the Mayo Clinic, constituted a committee of people to watch his health and mental condition and behavior to tell him when, in their "objective" judgment, it was time for him to leave the Court. In January 1994, Blackmun made that fateful decision and informed President Clinton.

One of the forces that causes justices who claimed for years that they would not wait too long to leave is the "Courtshift" tension. In their early years on the Court, justices have no legacy to defend, and the idea of leaving the Court means little more than retirement. As years pass, hard-won victories form a life's work and the record by which historians will assess one's career. Work with colleagues makes the legacy a matter of group pride as well as personal accomplishment. Now the justice has a body of opinions to defend and, given a changed Court, may very well feel the need to make that defense for as long as the justice has the strength to do so.

Finally, there is the traditional question, has the justice changed or did the Court shift? This is a question asked frequently of the late justice Hugo Black and, more recently, of Justice Harry Blackmun. If a new justice is added every two years or so, the likelihood is that the Court will have changed dramatically by the time a justice is ready to retire. Does the justice fight to protect the legacy until no longer physically able to do so (as with the William J. Brennan and Thurgood Marshall retirements) or does the justice more or less let go (as with the Byron White and Potter Stewart departures)? The answer varies with the justice, with the political context, and with the contributions the person has made to the law in America.

THE EFFECT OF RESIGNATION AND RETIREMENT

The loss of a justice can have a momentous effect on the Court, on lower federal courts who need decisions from the justice sitting in their circuit, on litigants before the Court, and on legal policy as well. It can create a political dilemma and political drama of the first order, especially if the justice who retired or resigned was a pivotal judicial player or an important "swing" justice on the Court. There is, too, the impact of the resignation or retirement on the Court's agenda of pending cases. This was the primary concern of John Harlan when he met with Hugo Black. He was very depressed because, when he reviewed the poor health of four of the justices, himself along with Black, Douglas, and Marshall, he and the others knew of the adverse impact on the caseload because Nixon would be the president to fill the vacancies created by their resignations and retirements.

Other justices contemplating retirement or resignation are concerned about the impact of their departure on the workings of the court of appeals the justice covered on circuit. Justice Lewis Powell announced his retirement from the Court in the spring of 1986, effective the end of the 1985 term of the Court. On July 1, 1986, President Ronald Reagan announced that he was presenting to Congress, for the Senate to confirm, Robert Bork, an extremely intelligent, and conservative, voice for a certain type of political jurisprudence: original intent.[35]

Because the nomination became a "bloody crossroads,"[36] there was no replacement for Powell for almost a year. Someone speaking to Powell in November or December 1986 would have met a jurist, retired, who was extremely perplexed because of the inordinate delay in selecting someone to fill his seat.

For Powell, what was unfair about the delay was the fact that his old circuit, the Fourth Circuit, did not have a Supreme Court justice who would respond, quickly, to petitions from that Court—especially the death penalty cases that go initially to the justice in the circuit. Powell was circuit justice for the fourth circuit court of appeals and, he recalled, "there were nights when I was here [in his Court chambers] until two" reviewing capital cases from the circuit. "Other times I've been awakened in the middle of the night" to respond to petitions from the circuit.[37]

In addition, another serious consequence of delay in replacing a justice who has left the Court is when the Court divides four to four on a particular case during the time of the empty seat on the bench. Justice Powell recalled that, during a time he was off the Court due to surgery, almost three months, eight such four to four cases were announced from the bench. This meant that the Court was not able to resolve the controversy and that the judgment of the lower court stood without any policy guidance from the Supreme Court. Such a consequence, for Powell, "was a disservice to all concerned."[38]

SUMMARY

As the Court documents and letters indicate, and as you are quickly finding out, "this Court grows on one." Continuing, Justice Powell observed that "the institution is so much greater than any one individual. The other justices, the sense of history in the place, and the rule of stare decisis all combine" to dramatically impact all 108 men and women who have sat on the Supreme Court. And for most of the justices, the decision to leave the Court and its environment is a very difficult one.

As you have reflected on your journey to the Court and the experience of being on it, you may be reminded of the view of your relationship to your colleagues over a lengthy period of time. No justice expressed a view of this judicial relationship more poignantly than Justice William O. Douglas. In a letter written and read to his brethren, at the time of his retirement in November 1975, this uniquely American justice said:

> I am reminded of many canoe trips I have taken in my lifetime. Those who start down a water course may be strangers at the beginning but almost invariably are close friends at the end. There were many strong headwinds to overcome and there were rainy as well as sun drenched days to travel. The portages were long and many and some were very strenuous. But there was always a pleasant camp in a stand of white bark birch and water concerts held at night to the music of the loons; and inevitably there came the last camp fire, the last breakfast cooked over last night's fire, and the parting was always sad. . . . The greatest such journey I've made with you, my brethren, who were strangers at the start but warm and fast friends at the end.[39]

NOTES

[1]Quoted by Fred Barbash in *The Washington Post,* June 20, 1981.

[2]See Linda Greenhouse, "Brennan, Key Liberal, Quits Supreme Court; Battle for Seat Likely," *New York Times,* July 21, 1990, sec. A.

[3]William J. Brennan to Howard Ball, Aug. 3, 1990.

[4]Andrew Rosenthal, "Marshall Retires from High Court; Blow to Liberals," *New York Times,* June 28, 1991, sec. A.

[5]Quoted in Carl T. Rowen, *Dream Makers, Dream Breakers: The World of Justice Thurgood Marshall* (Boston: Little, Brown, 1992), p. 3.

[6]Schmidhauser, quoted in Kermit Hall, ed., *The Oxford Companion to the Supreme Court* (New York: Oxford University Press, 1992), p. 730.

[7]Linda Greenhouse, "White Announces He'll Step Down from High Court," *New York Times,* Mar. 20, 1993, sec. A.

[8]Statement by Harry A. Blackmun on retiring, *New York Times,* Apr. 7, 1994, p. A24.

[9]Wasby, *The Supreme Court,* p. 87.

[10]Ibid., p. 91.

[11]Quoted in John D. Weaver, *Warren: The Man, the Court, the Era* (Boston: Little, Brown, 1967), p. 334.

[12]Henry J. Abraham, *Justices and Presidents* (New York: Oxford University Press, 1974), p. 261.

[13]See Douglas, *The Court Years*, pp. 357–77, for Douglas's description of the Nixon effort to remove him from the Supreme Court in 1970.

[14]See Douglas, *Court Years*, and Murphy, *Fortas*, for additional information regarding the Nixon administration's strategy regarding liberal justices on the Supreme Court.

[15]Douglas, *Court Years*, p. 377.

[16]"I shall not, Mr. President, conceal the pain with which I leave the Court after three years of service. It has been the richest and most satisfying period of my career" (Press conference, July 20, 1965, quoted in *The New York Times*, July 21, 1965).

[17]Abraham, *Justices and Presidents*, p. 253.

[18]Merlo J. Pusey, "Matter of Delicacy: The Court Copes with Disability," *Supreme Court Yearbook, 1979* (Washington, DC: Supreme Court Historical Society, 1979), p. 63.

[19]Quoted in Henry F. Pringle, *The Life and Times of William Howard Taft*, vol. 1, pp. 529–30.

[20]Pusey, "Matter of Delicacy," p. 64.

[21]Ibid.

[22]Quoted in Alpheus T. Mason, *William Howard Taft: Chief Justice* (New York: Simon and Schuster, 1965), p. 212.

[23]Quoted in ibid., pp. 214–15.

[24]Pusey, "Matter of Delicacy," p. 65.

[25]*Scott v Sanford*, 60 U.S. 393 (1857).

[26]Quoted in Charles Evans Hughes, *The Supreme Court of the United States*, p. 76.

[27]79 US 457 (1871).

[28]Hugo L. Black and Elizabeth Black, *Mr. Justice and Mrs. Black: The Memoirs of Hugo L. Black and Elizabeth Black* (New York: Random House, 1986), p. 244.

[29]Ball and Cooper, *Of Power and Right*, p. 297.

[30]Black and Black, *Mr. Justice and Mrs. Black*, p. 267.

[31]Abraham, *Justices and Presidents*, p. 9.

[32]Quoted in ibid., p. 269.

[33]Quoted in ibid., pp. 370–73.

[34]Warren Weaver, "Douglas Not Planning to Retire," *New York Times*, July 16, 1975, p. 47.

[35]See Howard Ball, "The Convergence of Constitutional Law and Politics in the Reagan Administration: The Exhumation of the 'Jurisprudence of Original Intention' Doctrine," *Cumberland Law Review* 17, no. 3 (1986–1987): 877–890.

[36]See Robert H. Bork, *The Tempting of America: The Political Seduction of the Law* (New York: Free Press, 1990).

[37]Justice Lewis Powell, interview with authors, Washington, DC, Nov. 18, 1987.

[38]Ibid.

[39]William O. Douglas, to Brethren, Nov. 14, 1975, box 1759, WODP, LC, Washington, DC.

Bibliography

ABRAHAM, HENRY J. *Justices and Presidents*, 2d ed. New York: Oxford University Press, 1985.
ABRAHAM, HENRY J., and BRUCE ALLEN MURPHY. "The Influence of Sitting and Retired Justices on Presidential Supreme Court Nominations." *Hastings Constitutional Law Quarterly* 3 (1976): 37.
ANGIER, NATALIE. "Supreme Court Set to Decide What Science Juries Can Hear." *New York Times*, Jan. 2, 1993, sec. A.
BAKER, NANCY V. *Conflicting Loyalties: Law and Politics in the Attorney General's Office, 1789–1990*. Lawrence: University Press of Kansas, 1992.
BALL, HOWARD. *Judicial Craftsmanship or Fiat? Direct Overturn in the Supreme Court*. Westport, CT: Greenwood Press, 1977.
———. "Politics over Law in Wartime: The Japanese Exclusion Cases." *Harvard Civil Rights Civil Liberties Law Review* 19, no. 2 (Summer 1984), 561.
———. "The Convergence of Constitutional Law and Politics in the Reagan Administration: The Exhumation of the 'Jurisprudence of Original Intention' Doctrine." *Cumberland Law Review* 17, no. 3 (1986–87), 887.
———. *Courts and Politics: The Federal Judicial System*, 2d ed. Englewood Cliffs, NJ: Prentice Hall, 1987.
———. *Justice Downwind: America's Atomic Testing Program of the 1950's*, New York: Oxford University Press, 1988.
———. "The U.S. Supreme Court's Glossing of the Federal Tort Claims Act: Statutory Construction and Veterans' Tort Actions." *Western Political Quarterly* 41, no. 3 (Sept. 1988).
———. *"We Have a Duty": The Supreme Court and the Watergate Tapes Litigation*. Westport, CT: Greenwood Press, 1992.
BALL, HOWARD, and PHILLIP COOPER. *Of Power and Right*. New York: Oxford University Press, 1992.
BALL, HOWARD, DALE KRANE, and THOMAS LAUTH. *Compromised Compliance*. Westport, CT: Greenwood Press, 1982.
BARNUM, DAVID G. *The Supreme Court and American Democracy*. New York: St. Martin's Press, 1992.
BAUM, LAURENCE. *The U.S. Supreme Court*. Washington, DC: CQ Press, 1985.

BEHUNIAK-LONG, SUSAN. "Friendly Fire: Amicus Curiae and *Webster v. Reproductive Health Services.*" *Judicature* 74 (Feb.–Mar. 1991).

BERGH, ALBERT ELLERY, ed., *The Writings of Thomas Jefferson.* Washington, DC: Thomas Jefferson Memorial Association, 1907.

BICKEL, ALEXANDER M. *The Least Dangerous Branch.* Indianapolis, IN: Bobbs-Merrill, 1962.

———. *Government by Judiciary: The Transformation of the Fourteenth Amendment.* Cambridge, MA: Harvard University Press, 1977.

BISKUPIC, JOAN. "A Human Touch, a Judicial Restraint." *Washington Post National Edition,* Aug. 2–8, 1993, p. 8.

———. "Asking the Court to Read Between the Lines." *Washington Post National Edition,* May 9–15, 1994, p. 25

BLACK, HUGO L. *A Constitutional Faith.* New York: Knopf, 1968.

BLACK, HUGO, JR. *My Father: A Remembrance.* New York: Random House, 1980.

BLACK, HUGO L., and ELIZABETH BLACK. *Mr. Justice and Mrs. Black.* New York: Random House, 1985.

BLACKMUN, HARRY. "Supreme Court: 'A Rotten Way to Earn a Living.' " *Washington Post Weekly Edition,* Oct. 1, 1984, p. 33.

———. "A Tribute to Mr. Justice Brennan." *Harvard Civil Rights/Civil Liberties Law Review* 26, no. 1 (1991).

BLASI, VINCENT, ed. *The Burger Court: The Counter-Revolution That Wasn't.* New Haven, CT: Yale University Press, 1982.

BLAUSTEIN, ALBERT P. "Rating Supreme Court Justices." *American Bar Association Journal* 58 (1972): 1183.

BLAUSTEIN, ALBERT P., and ROY M. MERSKY. *The First One Hundred Justices: Statistical Studies on the Supreme Court of the United States.* Hamden, CT: Shoe String Press, 1978.

BORK, ROBERT. "Neutral Principles and Some First Amendment Problems." *Indiana Law Journal* 47, no. 1 (1971).

———. *The Antitrust Paradox: A Policy at War with Itself.* New York: Basic Books, 1978.

———. *The Tempting of America: The Political Seduction of the Law.* New York: Free Press, 1990.

BRENNAN, WILLIAM J., JR. "Inside View of the High Court." *New York Times Sunday Magazine,* Oct. 6, 1963, p. 24.

———. "The National Court of Appeals: Another Dissent." *University of Chicago Law Review* 40 (1973): 473.

———. Address given at Georgetown University, Washington, DC, Oct. 12, 1985. Reprinted in *The New York Times,* Oct. 13, 1985, sec. A.

———. "Constitutional Adjudication and the Death Penalty: A View from the Court." *Harvard Law Review* 100 (1986): 313.

———. Remarks made on "This Honorable Court." PBS. 1988.

———. "Why Have a Bill of Rights?" *Oxford Journal of Legal Studies* 9, (1989), 425.

———. "The Worldwide Influence of the United States Constitution as a Charter of Human Rights." *Nova Law Review* 15, no. 1 (1991).

BRIGHAM, JOHN. *The Cult of the Robe.* Philadelphia, PA: Temple University Press, 1987.

BRONNER, ETHAN. *Battle for Justice: How the Bork Nomination Shook America.* New York: Norton, 1989.

BROWN-GUINYARD, SHERRAL. "The Effect of Ideology on the Success of Repeat Players: Amicus Curiae and the U.S. Supreme Court." Paper presented at the meeting of the Southern Political Science Association, Savannah, GA, Nov. 1993.

BROWNELL, HERBERT, with JOHN BURKE. *Advising Ike: The Memoirs of Attorney General Herbert Brownell.* Lawrence: University Press of Kansas, 1993.

BULLOCK, CHARLES S., III, and CHARLES M. LAMB, eds. *Implementation of Civil Rights Policy.* Monterey, CA: Brooks/Cole, 1984.

BURGER, WARREN E. "Reducing the Load on 'Nine Mortal Justices.' " *New York Times,* Aug. 14, 1975, p. A-27.

BURNS, JAMES MCGREGOR. *Leadership.* New York: Harper and Row, 1978.

CALAMANDREI, PIERRO. *Procedure and Democracy.* New York: New York University Press, 1956.

CALDIERA, GREGORY, and JOHN R. WRIGHT, "Organized Interests and Agenda Setting in the U.S. Supreme Court." *American Political Science Review* 82 (1988).

———. "Amici Curiae Before the Supreme Court: Who Participates, When and How Much." *Journal of Politics* 52 (1990).

CANNON, MARK W., and DAVID M. O'BRIEN. *The Judiciary and Constitutional Politics: Views from the Bench.* Chatham, NJ: Chatham House, 1985.

CANON, BRADLEY C. "Defining the Dimensions of Judicial Activism." *Judicature* 66 (1983): 236.

CAPLAN, LINCOLN. *The Tenth Justice: The Solicitor General and the Rule of Law.* New York: Vintage Books, 1988.

CASPER, GERHARD, and RICHARD A. POSNER. *The Workload of the Supreme Court.* Chicago: American Bar Foundation, 1976.

CASPER, JONATHAN D. *Lawyers Before the Warren Court: Civil Liberties and Civil Rights, 1957–66.* Urbana: University of Illinois, 1972.

———. "The Supreme Court and National Policy-Making." *American Political Science Review* 70 (Mar. 1976): 3.

CHOPER, JESSE, ed. *The Supreme Court and Its Justices.* Chicago: American Bar Association, 1987.

CLARK, TOM C. "Internal Operations of the U.S. Supreme Court." *Judicature* 43 (1959): 45.

CLAYTON, CORNELL W. *The Politics of Justice: The Attorney General and the Making of Legal Policy.* New York: M. E. Sharpe, 1992.

CLINTON, ROBERT. *Marbury v. Madison and Judicial Review.* Lawrence: University Press of Kansas, 1989.

COFFIN, FRANK M. *The Ways of a Judge: Reflections from the Federal Appellate Bench.* Boston: Houghton Mifflin, 1980.

———. *On Appeal: Courts, Lawyering, and Judging.* New York: Norton, 1993.

COOPER, PHILLIP J. *Public Law and Public Administration.* Palo Alto, CA: Mayfield, 1983.

———. *Hard Judicial Choices: Federal District Court Judges and State and Local Officials.* New York: Oxford University Press, 1988.

CORTNER, RICHARD C. "Strategy and Tactics of Litigation in Constitutional Cases." *Journal of Public Law* 17 (1968): 287.

COUNTRYMAN, VERN. *Douglas of the Supreme Court: A Selection of His Opinions.* Garden City, NY: Doubleday, 1959.

DAHL, ROBERT. "Decision-Making in a Democracy: The Supreme Court as a National Policy-Maker." *Journal of Public Law* 7, 279 (1957).

———. *Democracy and Its Critics.* New Haven, CT: Yale University Press, 1974.

DANELSKI, DAVID. *A Supreme Court Justice Is Appointed.* New York: Random House, 1964.

DAVIS, MICHAEL D., and HUNTER R. CLARK. *Thurgood Marshall.* New York: Birch Lane Press, 1993.

DEWEY, DONALD O. *Marshall Versus Jefferson: The Political Background of Marbury v. Madison.* New York: Knopf, 1970.

DOLBEARE, KENNETH M., and PHILIP E. HAMMOND. *The School Prayer Decisions: From Court Policy to Local Practice.* Chicago: University of Chicago Press, 1971.

DORSEN, NORMAN. "Tribute to Justice William J. Brennan, Jr." *Yale Law Journal* 100 (1991): 1113.

DOUGLAS, WILLIAM O. "Protecting the Investor." *Yale Law Review* 23 (1936).

———. *Strange Lands and Friendly People.* New York: Harper, 1951.

———. *Beyond the High Himalayas.* Garden City, NY: Doubleday, 1952.

———. *North from Malaya.* Garden City, NY: Doubleday, 1953.

———. *The Rights of the People.* Garden City, NY: Doubleday, 1954.

———. *Russian Journey.* Garden City, NY: Doubleday, 1956.

———. *We the Judges: Studies in American and Indian Constitutional Law.* Garden City, NY: Doubleday, 1956.

———. "Jerome N. Frank." *Journal of Legal Education* 10, no. 1 (1957).

———. *America Challenged.* Princeton, NJ: Princeton University Press, 1958.

———. *West of the Indus.* Garden City, NY: Doubleday, 1958.

———. "The Bill of Rights Is Not Enough." 38 *New York University Law Review* 207 (1963).

———. *Exploring the Himalayas.* New York: Random House, 1963.

———. *Go East, Young Man.* New York: Random House, 1974.

———. *The Court Years.* New York: Random House, 1980.

———. "In Defense of Dissent." In Alan Westin, ed., *The Supreme Court: Views from the Inside.* Westport, CT: Greenwood Press, 1983.

DUNHAM, ALLISON, and PHILIP B. KURLAND, eds. *Mr. Justice.* Chicago: University of Chicago Press, 1956.

DUNNE, GERALD T. *Justice Joseph Story and the Rise of the Supreme Court.* New York: Simon and Schuster, 1970.

———. *Hugo Black and the Judicial Revolution.* New York: Simon and Schuster, 1977.

EASTON, DAVID. *The Political System.* New York: Knopf, 1953.

EISLER, KIM ISSAC. *A Justice for All.* New York: Simon and Schuster, 1993.

ELLIS, RICHARD. "The Impeachment of Samuel Chase." In Michael R. Belknap, ed., *American Political Trials.* Westport, CT: Greenwood Press, 1981.

ELMAN, PHILIP. "The Solicitor General's Office, Justice Frankfurter, and Civil Rights Litigation." *Harvard Law Review* 100 (1987): 817.

ELY, JOHN HART. *Democracy and Distrust.* New Haven, CT: Yale University Press, 1980.

EPSTEIN, LEE. *Conservatives in Court.* Knoxville: University of Tennessee Press, 1985.

EPSTEIN, LEE, and JOSEPH F. KOBYLKA. "Exploring Legal Change on the U.S. Supreme Court: A Preliminary Report on Winners and Losers." Paper presented at the annual meeting of the American Political Science Association, San Francisco, September 1990.

EPSTEIN, LEE, and C. K. ROWLAND. "Debunking the Myth of Interest Group Invincibility in the Courts." *American Political Science Review* 85, no. 1 (Mar. 1991).

FAIRMAN, CHARLES. "Does the Fourteenth Amendment Incorporate the Bill of Rights? The Original Understanding." *Stanford Law Review* 2, no. 5 (1949).

FEHRENBACHER, DON E. *Constitutions and Constitutionalism in the Slaveholding South.* Athens: University of Georgia Press, 1988.

FINE, SIDNEY. *Frank Murphy: The Washington Years.* 1984.

FISH, PETER. *The Office of Chief Justice.* Charlotteville: University of Virginia Press, 1984.

———. "Spite Nominations to the U.S. Supreme Court." *Kentucky Law Journal* 77 (1988–89): 545.

FISHER, LOUIS. *Constitutional Conflicts Between Congress and the President,* 3d ed. Lawrence: University Press of Kansas, 1992.

FISHER, LOUIS. *Constitutional Dialogues.* Princeton, NJ: Princeton University Press, 1988.

———. "The Curious Belief in Judicial Supremacy." *Suffolk University Law Review* 25, no. 1, (Spring 1991).

FISHER, LOUIS, and NEAL DEVINS. *Political Dynamics of Constitutional Law.* St. Paul, MN: West, 1992.

FISS, OWEN. "A Life Lived Twice." *Yale Law Journal* 100 (1991): 117.

FRANKFURTER, FELIX. "Some Reflections on the Reading of Statutes." *Record of the Association of the Bar of the City of New York* 2 (1947): 213.

———. "Chief Justices I Have Known." *Virginia Law Review* 39 (1953): 833.

———. "The Supreme Court in the Mirror of Justices." *University of Pennsylvania Law Review* 105 (1957): 781.

FRANKFURTER, FELIX, and JAMES L. LANDIS. *The Business of the Supreme Court.* New York: Macmillan, 1938.

FREUND, PAUL. "Charles Evans Hughes as Chief Justice." *Harvard Law Review* 81 (1967): 35.

FRIEDMAN, LEON, and FRED L. ISRAEL, eds. *The Justices of the United States Supreme Court 1789–1969: Their Lives and Major Opinions.* New York: Bowker, 1969.

GINSBURG, RUTH BADER. "Confirming Supreme Court Justices: Thoughts on the Second Opinion Rendered by the Senate." *University of Illinois Law Review* 101 (1988).

GOEBEL, JULIUS, JR. *History of the Supreme Court of the United States.* New York: Macmillan, 1971.

GOODMAN, ROGER, with DAVID GALEN. *Thurgood Marshall: Justice for All.* New York: Carroll and Graf, 1992.

GOLDMAN, SHELDON. "Judicial Selection and the Qualities That Make a 'Good Judge.' " *Annals of the American Academy of Social and Political Science* 462 (July 1982): 112.

GOLDMAN, SHELDON, and CHARLES M. LAMB. *Judicial Conflict and Consensus.* Lexington: University Press of Kentucky, 1986.

GREENBERG, JACK. "The Supreme Court, Civil Rights, and Civil Dissonance." *Yale Law Journal* 77 (1968): 1520.

GREENE, KATHANNE W. *Affirmative Action and Principles of Justice.* Westport, CT: Greenwood Press, 1989.

GREENHOUSE, LINDA. "Brennan, Key Liberal, Quits Supreme Court: Battle for Seat Likely." *New York Times,* July 21, 1990, sec. A.

———. "High Court Spurns Guam Bid to Revive Curbs on Abortion." *New York Times,* Nov. 30, 1992, p. A-19.

———. "White Announces He'll Step Down from High Court." *New York Times,* Mar. 20, 1993, sec. A.

GREY, THOMAS C. "Do We Have an Unwritten Constitution?" *Stanford Law Review* 27 (1975): 703.

GRIFFIN, STEPHEN M. "Judicial Review and Democracy Revisited." Paper presented at the annual meeting of the American Political Science Association, Aug. 1993, Washington, DC.

GRISWOLD, ERWIN. "Rationing Justice: The Supreme Court's Caseload and What the Court Does Not Do." *Cornell Law Quarterly* 60 (Mar. 1975): 344.

GROSSMAN, JOEL B. "The Senate and Supreme Court Nominations: Some Reflections." *Duke Law Journal* (1972): 557.

GROSSMAN, JOEL B., and STEPHEN L. WASBY. "Haynsworth and Parker: History Does Live Again." *South Carolina Law Review* 23 (1971): 345.

HACKER, ANDREW. *Two Nations, Black and White, Separate, Hostile, Unequal.* New York: Scribner's, 1992.

HALL, KERMIT, ed. *The Oxford Companion to the Supreme Court.* New York: Oxford University Press, 1992.

HAMILTON, ALEXANDER, JAMES MADISON, and JOHN JAY. *The Federalist Papers.* New York: Mentor, 1961.

HARLAN, JOHN M., II. "A Glimpse of the Supreme Court at Work." *University of Chicago Law School Record* 11 (1963).

HARRIS, JOSEPH. *Decision.* New York: Dutton, 1975.

HART, H.L.A. *The Concept of Law.* London: Clarendon Press, 1961.

———. *Democracy and Distrust: A Theory of Judicial Review.* Cambridge, MA: Harvard University Press, 1980.

HELLMAN, ARTHUR. "Caseload, Conflicts, and Decisional Capacity: Does the Supreme Court Need Help?" *Judicature* 67 (1983): 41.

———. "Case Selection in the Burger Court: A Preliminary Inquiry." *Notre Dame Law Review* 60 (1985): 996.

HIRSCH, H. N. *The Enigma of Felix Frankfurter.* New York: Basic Books, 1981.

HOUSE, TONI. "Q&A." *Docket Sheet of the Supreme Court of the United States* 28, no. 1, (Spring 1991).

HOWARD, J. W. "On the Fluidity of Judicial Choice." *American Political Science Review* 63 (Mar. 1968): 43.

———. *Mr. Justice Murphy: A Political Biography.* Princeton, NJ: Princeton University Press, 1968.

HUGHES, CHARLES EVANS. *The Supreme Court of the United States.* New York: Columbia University Press, 1928.

HUTCHINSON, JAMES. "Unanimity and Desegregation: Decision-Making in the Supreme Court." *Georgetown Law Review* 68 (1979): 1.

JACKSON, DONALD W. *Even the Children of Strangers: Equality Under the U.S. Constitution.* Lawrence: University Press of Kansas, 1992.

JACKSON, ROBERT H. *The Struggle for Judicial Supremacy.* New York: Knopf, 1941.

———. *The Supreme Court in the American System of Government.* Cambridge, MA: Harvard University Press, 1955.

JEFFRIES, JOHN C., JR. *Justice Lewis F. Powell, Jr.* New York: Scribner's, 1994.

JENKINS, BRUCE S. "Remarks," given by the chief judge, U.S. District Court, District of Utah, at the midyear meeting of the Utah State Bar Association, St. George, Utah, Mar. 6, 1987.

JENKINS, JOHN. "A Candid Talk with Justice Blackmun." *New York Times Sunday Magazine*, Feb. 20, 1983, p. 38.

JOHNSON, CHARLES, and BRADLEY C. CANON. *Judicial Policies: Implementation and Impact.* Washington, DC: CQ Press, 1984.

KALMAN, LAURA. *Abe Fortas.* New Haven, CT: Yale University Press, 1991.

KAUFMAN, IRVING R. "What the Founding Fathers Intend." *New York Times Sunday Magazine*, Feb. 23, 1986, p. 29.

KETCHUM, RALPH, ed. *The Anti-Federalist Papers of the Constitutional Convention Debate.* New York: New American Library, 1986.

KING, WILLARD L. *Melvin Weston Fuller: Chief Justice of the United States.* New York: Macmillan, 1950.

KLUGER, RICHARD. *Simple Justice.* New York: Knopf, 1976.

KRAMNICK, ISAAC, ed. *The Federalist Papers.* New York: Penguin, 1987.

KRISLOV, SAMUEL. *The Supreme Court in the American Political Process.* New York: Macmillan, 1965.

KROL, JOHN F., and SAUL BRENNER. "Strategies in Certiorari Voting on the U.S. Supreme Court: A Re-evaluation." *Western Political Quarterly* 43, no. 2 (June 1990).

LAMB, CHARLES, and DAVID HALPERIN, eds. *The Burger Court.* Urbana, IL: University of Illinois, 1991.

LASH, JOSEPH P., editor. *From the Diaries of Felix Frankfurter.* New York: Norton, 1975.

LASSER, WILLIAM. *The Limits of Judicial Power: The Supreme Court in American Politics.* Chapel Hill: University of North Carolina Press, 1988.

LASSWELL, HAROLD. *Who Gets What, When, How?* New York: Meridian Books, 1958.

LEVI, EDWARD H. *An Introduction to Legal Reasoning.* Chicago: University of Chicago Press, 1960.

LIEBERMAN, JETHRO K. *Milestones.* St. Paul, MN: West, 1976.

LOUTHAN, WILLIAM C. *The United States Supreme Court: Lawmaking in the Third Branch of Government.* Englewood Cliffs, NJ: Prentice Hall, 1991.

LYTLE, CLIFFORD M. *The Warren Court and Its Critics.* Tucson: University of Arizona Press, 1968.

MASON, ALPHEUS T. *Brandeis: A Free Man's Life.* New York: Viking, 1946.

———. *Harlan Fiske Stone: Pillar of the Law.* New York: Viking, 1956.

———. *William Howard Taft: Chief Justice.* New York: Simon and Schuster, 1965.

———. *The Supreme Court from Taft to Burger*, 3d ed. Baton Rouge: Louisiana State University, 1979.

MAURO, TONY. "Election Could Shift Solicitor's Positions." *USA Today*, Oct. 27, 1992, p. A-15.

MCCLOSKEY, ROGER G. "Reflections on the Warren Court." *Virginia Law Review* 51 (1965): 1234.

———. *The Modern Supreme Court.* Cambridge, MA: Harvard University Press, 1972.

MCREYNOLDS, R. M. "The Department of Justice." In Donald R. Whitnah, ed., *Government Agencies.* Westport, CT: Greenwood Press, 1983.

MEADOR, DANIEL J. "Justice Black and His Law Clerks." 16 *Alabama Law Review* (1963): 57.
MEESE, EDWIN, III. "The Attorney General's View of the Supreme Court: Toward a Jurisprudence of Original Intent." *Public Administration Review* 45 (1985).
MEIKLEJOHN, ALEXANDER. *Political Freedom.* Chicago: University of Chicago Press, 1948.
MELONE, ALBERT P. "Revisiting the Freshmen Effect Hypothesis: The First Two Terms of Justice Arthur Kennedy." *Judicature* 74, no. 1, (June–July 1990): 6–13.
MIDDLETON, GEORGE. "High Court's Case Load Too Heavy: Three Justices." *American Bar Association Journal* 68 (1986).
MIKVA, ABNER J. "Tribute to William J. Brennan." *Harvard Law Review* 104 (1990):9.
MUIR, WILLIAM K., JR. *Prayer in the Public Schools: Law and Attitude Change.* Chicago: University of Chicago Press, 1967.
MURPHY, BRUCE ALLAN. *The Brandeis/Frankfurter Connection.* New York: Oxford University Press, 1982.
———. *Abe Fortas: The Rise and Ruin of a Supreme Court Justice.* New York: Morrow, 1988.
MURPHY, WALTER F. "In His Own Image: Mr. Chief Justice Taft and Supreme Court Appointments," *Supreme Court Review* 1961 (1961):159.
———. *Congress and the Court.* Chicago: University of Chicago Press, 1962.
———. *Elements of Judicial Strategy.* Chicago: University of Chicago Press, 1964.
MURPHY, WALTER F., JAMES FLEMING, and WILLIAM F. HARRIS. *American Constitutional Interpretation.* Mineola, NY: Foundation Press, 1986.
MURPHY, WALTER F., and C. HERMAN PRITCHETT. *Courts, Judges, and Politics: An Introduction to the Legal Process,* 4th ed. New York: Random House, 1986.
MURPHY, WALTER F., and JOSEPH TANENHAUS. *The Study of Public Law.* New York: Random House, 1971.
MYRDAL, GUNNAR. *An American Dilemma.* New York: Random House, 1941.
NOTE. "Plurality Decisions and Judicial Decisionmaking." *Harvard Law Review* 94, (1981): 1127.
———. "The Statistics." *Harvard Law Review* 106, no. 1 (Nov. 1992).
OAKLEY, JOHN BILEU, and ROBERT S. THOMPSON. *Law Clerks and the Judicial Process.* Berkeley: University of California Press, 1980.
O'BRIEN, DAVID M. "Managing the Business of the Supreme Court." *Public Administration Review* 45 (Nov. 1985): 670.
———. *Storm Center.* New York: Norton, 1991.
———. *Supreme Court Watch: 1992.* New York: Norton, 1992.
O'CONNOR, KAREN. *Women's Organizations' Use of the Courts.* Lexington, MA: Lexington, 1980.
———. "The Amicus Curiae Role of the U.S. Solicitor General in Supreme Court Litigation." *Judicature* 66, no. 6 (Dec.–Jan. 1983): 256.
———. "Amicus Curiae Participation in U.S. Supreme Court Litigation." *Law and Society Review* 16 (1981): 311–20.
O'CONNOR, KAREN, AND LEE EPSTEIN. "The Rise of Conservative Interest Group Litigation." *Journal of Politics* 45 (May 1983): 479–89.
———. "Beyond Legislative Lobbying: Women's Rights Groups and the Supreme Court." *Judicature* 67, no. 3, (Sept. 1983): 134.
OFFICE OF THE U.S. ATTORNEY GENERAL. *Annual Report, 1986.* Washington, DC: U.S. Government Printing Office, 1986.
OTT, J. STEVEN. *The Organizational Culture Perspective.* Chicago: Dorsey, 1989.
PADOVER, SAUL K. *To Secure These Blessings: The Great Debates of the Constitutional Convention of 1787.* New York: Ridge Press, 1962.
PASCHAL, J. FRANCIS. *Mr. Justice Sutherland.* Princeton, NJ: Princeton University Press, 1951.
PEDERSON, WILLIAM D., and NORMAN W. PROVIZER. *Great Justices of the U.S. Supreme Court: Ratings and Case Studies.* New York: Lang, 1994.
PELTASON, JACK W. *Federal Courts in the Political Process.* Garden City, NY: Doubleday, 1955.
———. *Fifty-eight Lonely Men.* New York: Harcourt, Brace, 1961.
PERRY, H. W., JR. *Deciding to Decide: Agenda Setting in the U.S. Supreme Court.* Cambridge, MA: Harvard University Press, 1992.
POSNER, RICHARD. "Tribute to Justice William J. Brennan, Jr." *Harvard Law Review* 104 (1990): 13.
POUND, ROSCOE. *An Introduction to the Philosophy of Law.* New Haven, CT: Yale University Press, 1922.
PRINGLE, HENRY F. *The Life and Times of William Howard Taft.* vol. 1.
PROVINE, DORIS M. *Case Selection in the United States Supreme Court.* Chicago: University of Chicago Press, 1980.
———. "Deciding What to Decide: How the Supreme Court Sets Its Agenda." *Judicature* 64, no. 7, (Feb. 1981).

PUSEY, MERLO J. *Charles Evans Hughes.* New York: Macmillan, 1951.

———. "Matter of Delicacy: The Court Copes with Disability." In *The Supreme Court Yearbook, 1979,* Washington, DC: Supreme Court Historical Society, 1979.

RATHJEN, GREGORY, and THOMAS D. UNGS. "United States Attorneys and the Lower Federal Courts: Some Effects on Law and Order." Paper presented at the annual meeting of the Midwest Political Science Association, Chicago, Apr. 1977.

REHNQUIST, WILLIAM H. "The Supreme Court: Past and Present." *American Bar Association Journal* 59 (1973): 361.

———. *The Supreme Court: How It Was, How It Is.* New York: Morrow, 1987.

RODELL, FRED. *Nine Men: A Political History of the Supreme Court of the United States from 1790 to 1955.* New York: Random House, 1955.

ROHDE, DAVID W., and HAROLD J. SPAETH. *Supreme Court Decision Making.* San Francisco: Freeman, 1976.

ROSENTHAL, ANDREW. "Marshall Retires from High Court: Blow to Liberals." *New York Times,* June 28, 1991, sec. A.

ROSS, DOUGLAS. "Safeguarding Our Federalism: Lessons for the States from the Supreme Court." *Public Administration Review* 45 (Nov. 1985).

ROWEN, CARL T. *Dream Makers, Dream Breakers: The World of Justice Thurgood Marshall.* Boston: Little, Brown, 1993.

RUMBLE, WILFRED E., JR. *American Legal Realism.* Ithaca, NY: Cornell University Press, 1968.

SAAR, JOHN. "The Philadelphia Story." *New Times,* Feb. 20, 1978.

SAVAGE, DAVID G. *Turning Right.* New York: Wiley, 1992.

SCHEIN, EDGAR. *Organizational Culture and Leadership.* San Francisco: Jossey-Bass, 1987.

SCHLESSINGER, ARTHUR, *The Imperial Presidency.* Boston: Houghton Mifflin, 1976.

SCHMIDHAUSER, JOHN R. "Stare Decisis, Dissent, and the Background of the Justices." *University of Toronto Law Review* 14 (1962): 194.

———. *Judges and Justices: The Federal Appellate Judiciary.* Boston: Little, Brown, 1979.

SCHRUM, FRED. "Fired: The Hiring and Firing of U.S. Attorneys." *New Times,* Feb. 20, 1978, p. 35.

SCHWARTZ, BERNARD. *The Unpublished Opinions of the Warren Court.* New York: Oxford University Press, 1978.

———. *Super Chief: Earl Warren and His Supreme Court—a Judicial Biography.* New York: New York University Press, 1983.

———. *The Unpublished Opinions of the Warren Court.* New York: Oxford University Press, 1985.

———. *The Ascent of Pragmatism.* New York: Addison-Wesley, 1990.

SCHWARTZ, HERMAN. *The Burger Years.* New York: Viking, 1987.

———. *Packing the Courts: The Conservative Campaign to Rewrite the Constitution.* New York: Scribner's, 1988.

SCIGLIANO, ROBERT. *The Supreme Court and the Presidency.* New York: Free Press, 1971.

SHAMAN. "The Constitution, the Supreme Court, and Creativity." *Hastings Constitutional Law Quarterly* 9 (1982).

SHAPIRO, MARTIN. *Law and Politics in the Supreme Court.* New York: Free Press, 1964.

SHOGAN, ROBERT. *A Question of Judgment: The Fortas Case and the Struggle for the Supreme Court.* Indianapolis, IN: Bobbs-Merrill, 1972.

SILVERSTEIN, MARK. *Justices Black and Frankfurter: Constitutional Faiths,* Ithaca: Cornell University Press, 1986.

SIMON, JAMES F. *Independent Journey: The Life of William O. Douglas.* New York: Harper & Row, 1980.

———. *In His Own Image: The Supreme Court in Richard Nixon's America.* New York: David McKay, 1973.

SOLBERG, WINTON U., ed. *The Federal Convention and the Formation of the Union of the American States.* Indianapolis, IN: Bobbs-Merrill, 1958.

SONGER, DONALD R. "The Relevance of Policy Values for the Confirmation of Supreme Court Nominees." *Law and Society Review* 13 (Summer 1979):927.

SONGER, DONALD R., and REGINALD S. SHEEHAN. "The Impact of Amicus Briefs on Decisions on the Merits." Paper presented at the annual meeting of the American Political Science Association, San Francisco, Sept. 1990.

STEAMER, ROBERT J. *Chief Justice: Leadership and the Supreme Court.* Columbia: University of South Carolina, 1986.

STEVENS, JOHN PAUL. "Some Thoughts on Judicial Restraint." *Judicature* 66, no. 5, (Nov. 1982).

STEWART, POTTER. "Reflections on the Supreme Court." *Litigation* 8 (1982).

STRUM, PHILIPPA. *Louis D. Brandeis: Justice for the People.* Cambridge, MA: Harvard University Press, 1984.

TARR, G. ALAN. *Judicial Impact and State Supreme Courts.* Lexington, MA: Lexington Books, 1977.

TAYLOR, STUART, JR. "High Court Expected to Gain Freedom in Selecting Its Cases." *New York Times*, June 9, 1988, p. A-18.

"This Honorable Court." Paul Duke, narrator. Public Broadcasting System, March, 1988.

TOTENBURG, NINA. "Tribute to Justice William J. Brennan, Jr." *Harvard Law Review* 104 (1990): 33.

TRIBE, LAURENCE. *God Save This Honorable Court.* New York: Random House, 1985.

TUSHNET, MARK V. *The NAACP Legal Strategy Against Segregated Education, 1925–1950.* Chapel Hill: University of North Carolina Press, 1987.

U.S. CONGRESS. HOUSE COMMITTEE ON THE JUDICIARY. *Final report by the Special Subcommittee on H.R. 920 of the Committee on the Judiciary: Associate Justice William O. Douglas.* 91st Cong., 2d sess., 1970.

U.S. CONGRESS. SENATE COMMITTEE ON THE JUDICIARY. *A Bill to Reorganize the Judicial Branch of Government: Hearings Before the Committee on the Judiciary, on Senate Bill 1392.* 75th Cong., 1st sess., Mar. 10, 1937.

———. *Hearings Before the Committee on the Judiciary: Nomination of William H. Rehnquist to Be Chief Justice of the United States.* 99th Cong., 2d sess., 1986.

———. *Report of the Committee on the Judiciary: Nomination of Robert H. Bork to Be an Associate Justice of the United States Supreme Court.* 100th Cong., 1st sess., 1987.

———. *Report of the Committee on the Judiciary: Nomination of Anthony M. Kennedy to Be an Associate Justice of the United States Supreme Court.* 100th Cong., 2d sess., 1988.

UROFSKY, MELVIN I. "Conflict Among the Brethren: Felix Frankfurter, William O. Douglas and the Clash of Personalities on the United States Supreme Court." *Duke Law Journal* 71 (1988).

———. "Getting the Job Done: William O. Douglas and Collegiality in the Supreme Court." Paper presented at the William O. Douglas Symposium, Seattle, WA, Apr. 1989.

———. "John Marshall and All That." *New York Times Book Review*, September 26, 1993, p. 31.

VAN ALSTYNE, JOHN. "A Critical Guide to *Marbury v. Madison*." *Duke Law Journal* (1969), no. 1: 15.

VAN GEEL, T. R. *Understanding Supreme Court Opinions.* New York: Longman, 1991.

VAN WOODARD, C. *The Strange Career of Jim Crow.* New York: Oxford University Press, 1957.

WARREN, CHARLES. *The Supreme Court in United States History.* Boston: Little, Brown, 1926.

WASBY, STEPHEN L. *The Impact of the United States Supreme Court: Some Perspectives.* Homewood, IL: Dorsey Press, 1970.

———. *Continuity and Change: From the Warren to the Burger Court.* Pacific Palisades, CA: Goodyear, 1976.

———. "Civil Rights Litigation by Organizations: Constraints and Choices." *Judicature* 68, no. 9, (Apr. 1985).

———. *The Supreme Court in the Federal Judicial System*, 3d ed. Chicago: Nelson-Hall, 1987.

WASBY, STEPHEN L., ANTHONY A. D'AMATO, and ROSEMARY METRAILER. "The Functions of Oral Argument in the U.S. Supreme Court." *Quarterly Journal of Speech* 62 (Dec. 1976): 410.

WASSERSTROM, RICHARD A. *The Judicial Decision.* Stanford, CA: Stanford University Press, 1961.

WATSON, ALAN. *Slave Law in the Americas.* Athens: University of Georgia Press, 1989.

WATSON, DENTON L. "Assessing the Role of the NAACP in the Civil Rights Movement." *Historian* 55, no. 3, (Spring 1993).

WEAVER, JOHN D. *Warren: The Man, the Court, the Era.* Boston: Little, Brown, 1967.

WESTIN, ALAN F., ed. *The Supreme Court: Views from Inside.* New York: Norton, 1961.

WESTIN, ALAN, and LEON FRIEDMAN, ed. *United States v. Nixon.* New York: Chelsea House, 1975.

WHITE, BYRON R. "Tribute to the Honorable William J. Brennan, Jr." *Yale Law Journal* 100 (1990): 1113.

WILKINSON, J. HARVIE, III. *Serving Justice: A Supreme Court Clerk's View.* New York: Charterhouse, 1974.

WITT, ELDER. *A Different Justice.* Washington, DC: Congressional Quarterly, 1986.

———. *Guide to the U.S. Supreme Court*, 2d ed. Washington, DC: Congressional Quarterly, 1990.

WRIGHT, S. KELLY. "Commentary: In Praise of State Courts—Confessions of a Federal Judge." *Hastings Constitutional Law Quarterly* 11 (1984).

Opinions Cited

About the Authors

PHILLIP J. COOPER is the Gund Family Endowed Chair in Political Science and Director of the Public Administration Program at the University of Vermont. His books include *Hard Judicial Choices: Federal District Court Judges and State and Local Officials; Public Law and Public Administration;* and *Of Power and Right: Hugo Black, William O. Douglas and America's Constitutional Revolution.* He is presently at work on a book examining the nature of conflict on the Supreme Court, entitled *Handshakes and Hard Times.*

HOWARD BALL is Dean of the College of Arts and Sciences and Professor of Political Science at the University of Vermont. He has written eighteen books including *Courts and Politics; Hugo Black: Cold Steel Warrior; Justice Downwind: America's Atomic Testing Program in the 1950's;* and *Constitutional Powers.* He is presently at work on a biography of Thurgood Marshall, entitled *A Life: Thurgood Marshall and the Persistence of Racism in America.*

Photo Credits

Chapter 1: Frantz Jantzen, Collection of the United States Supreme Court, 3; Collection of the United States Supreme Court, 6; **Chapter 3**: AP/Wide World Photos, 35; F. Lee Corkran/Sygma, 56; AP/Wide World Photos, 57; Ken Heinen, Collection of the United States Supreme Court, 67; Lois Long, Collection of the United States Supreme Court, 68; **Chapter 4**: Collection of the United States Supreme Court, 77; Frantz Jantzen, Collection of the United States Supreme Court, 96; **Chapter 5**: Peter Erenheft, Collection of the United States Supreme Court, 103; **Chapter 6**: Harris and Ewing, Collection of the United States Supreme Court, 133, 148; **Chapter 7**: AP/Wide World Photos, 171; copyright, The National Geographic Society/courtesy, The Supreme Court Historical Society, 177; Collection of the United States Supreme Court, 182, 183, 184; **Chapter 8**: Collection of the United States Supreme Court, 200; copyright, The National Geographic Society/courtesy, The Supreme Court Historical Society, 209, 211; Collection of the United States Supreme Court, 216, 217; **Chapter 10**: Ken Heinen, Collection of the United States Supreme Court, 247; copyright, The National Geographic Society/courtesy, The Supreme Court Historical Society, 252, 253; **Chapter 11**: Harris and Ewing, Collection of the United States Supreme Court, 282; Collection of the United States Supreme Court, 287, 297; copyright, The National Geographic Society/courtesy, The Supreme Court Historical Society, 304, 305; **Chapter 13**: AP/Wide World Photos, 348; **Chapter 14**: Lois Long, Collection of the United States Supreme Court, 357; AP/Wide World Photos, 358; Capitol and Clogan, Collection of the United States Supreme Court, 365.

Index